# CONTEMPORARY SCULPTORS

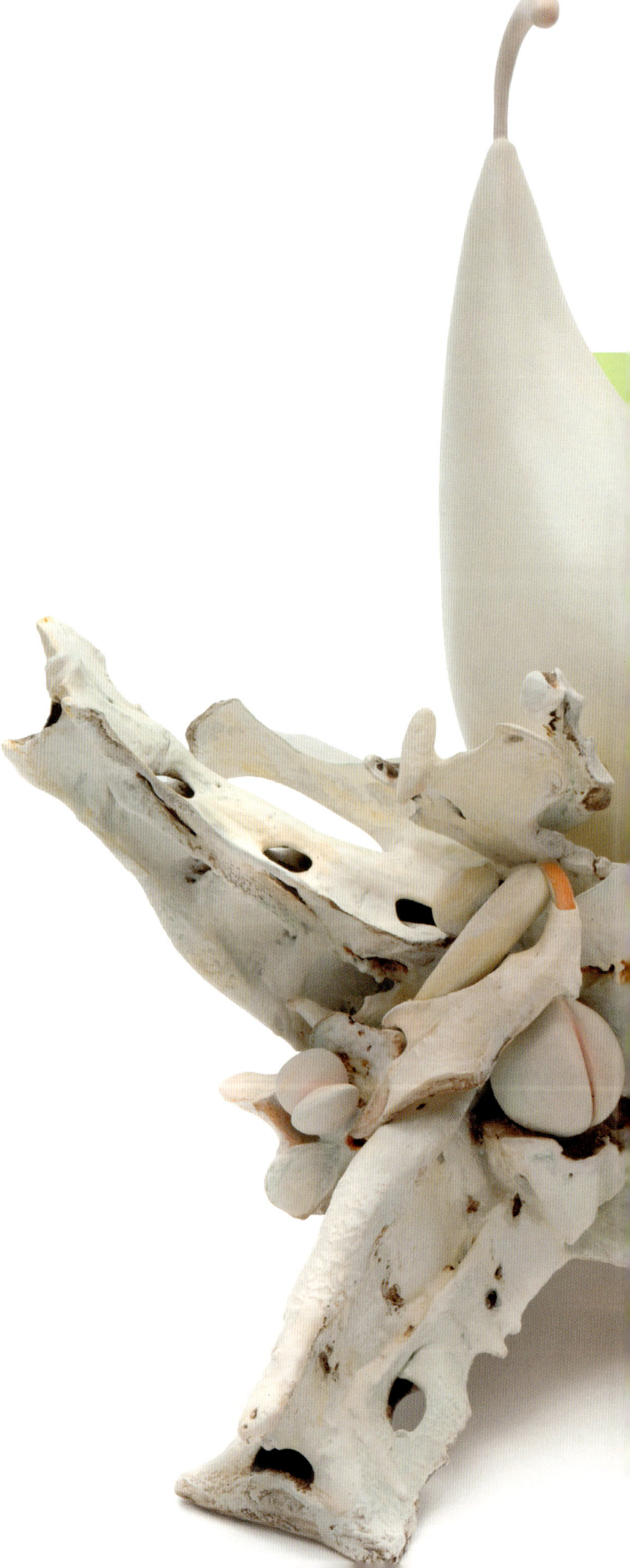

# Contemporary Sculptors

## 84 International Artists

Danijela Kracun
Charles McFadden

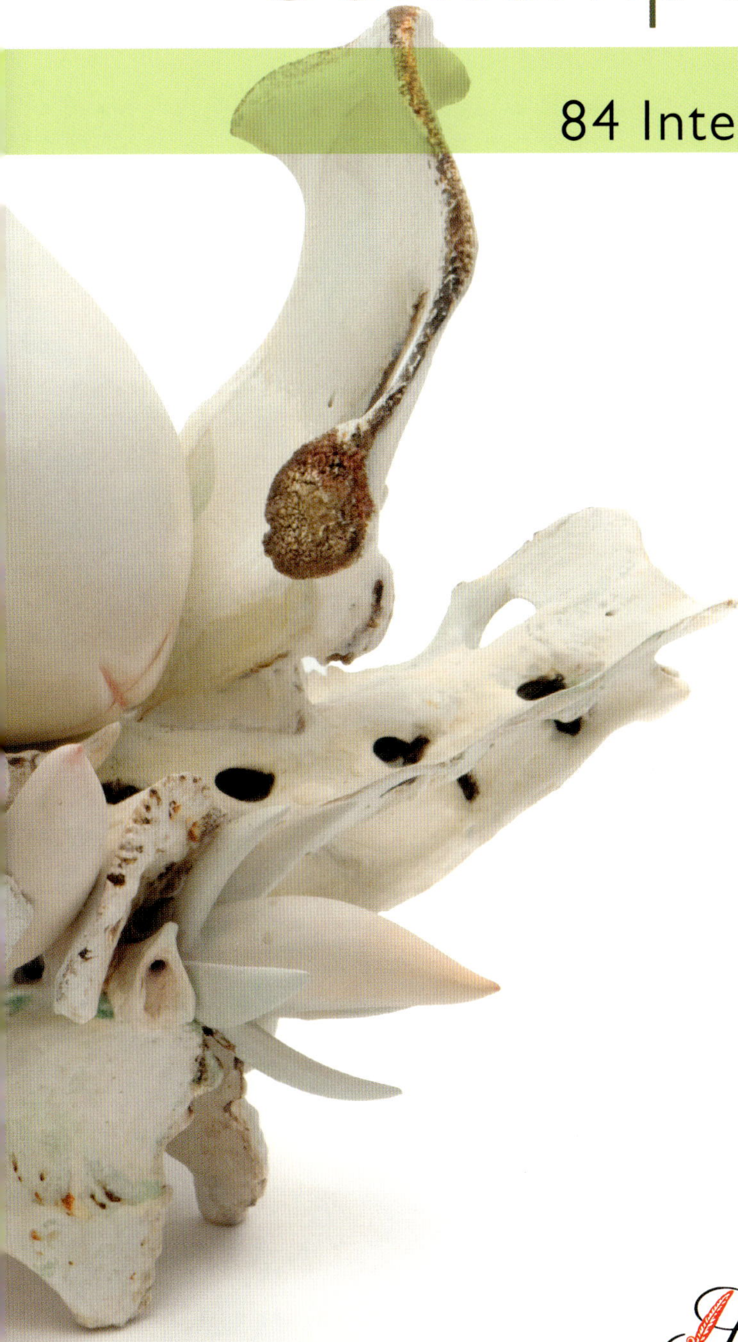

Schiffer Publishing Ltd
4880 Lower Valley Road • Atglen, PA 19310

Schiffer Books are available at special discounts for bulk purchases for sales promotions or premiums. Special editions, including personalized covers, corporate imprints, and excerpts can be created in large quantities for special needs. For more information contact the publisher:

Published by Schiffer Publishing, Ltd.
4880 Lower Valley Road
Atglen, PA 19310
Phone: (610) 593-1777; Fax: (610) 593-2002
E-mail: Info@schifferbooks.com

For the largest selection of fine reference books on this and related subjects, please visit our website at
**www.schifferbooks.com**
We are always looking for people to write books on new and related subjects. If you have an idea for a book, please contact us at
**proposals@schifferbooks.com**

This book may be purchased from the publisher.
Please try your bookstore first.
You may write for a free catalog.

In Europe, Schiffer books are distributed by
Bushwood Books
6 Marksbury Ave.
Kew Gardens
Surrey TW9 4JF England
Phone: 44 (0) 20 8392 8585; Fax: 44 (0) 20 8392 9876
E-mail: info@bushwoodbooks.co.uk
Website: www.bushwoodbooks.co.uk


Library of Congress Control Number: 2012935851



Designed by RoS
Type set in Gill Sans MT Pro/Times New Roman

ISBN: 978-0-7643-4103-8
Printed in China

# Acknowledgments

Much thanks to our editor Douglas Congdon-Martin, the entire Schiffer Team, and all of the artists in the book.

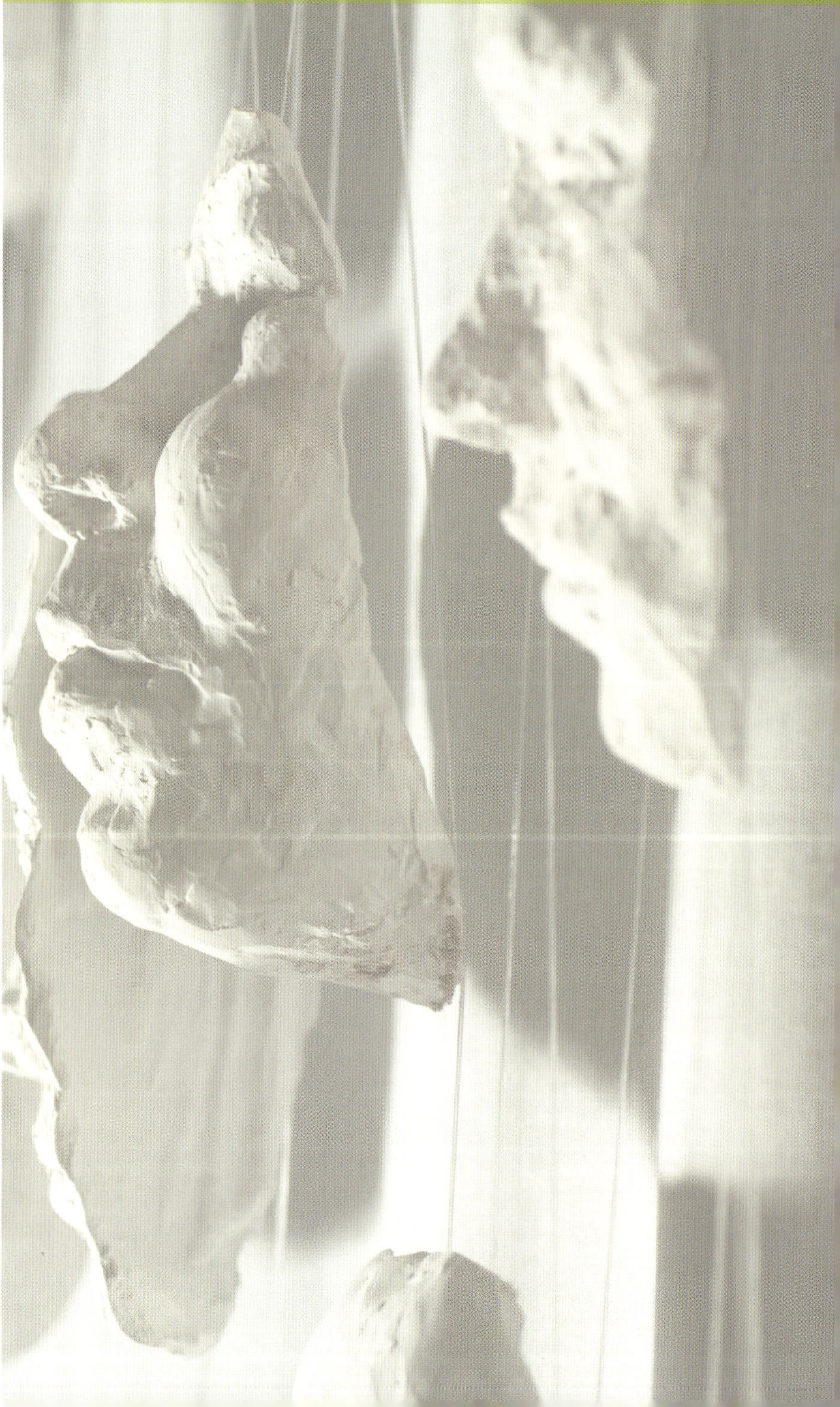

# Dedication

Dedicated and wishes of Peace and Love to Paisley, Sam, Tim, Kordy, Cameron, Lucia, Tristan and to all beings everywhere.

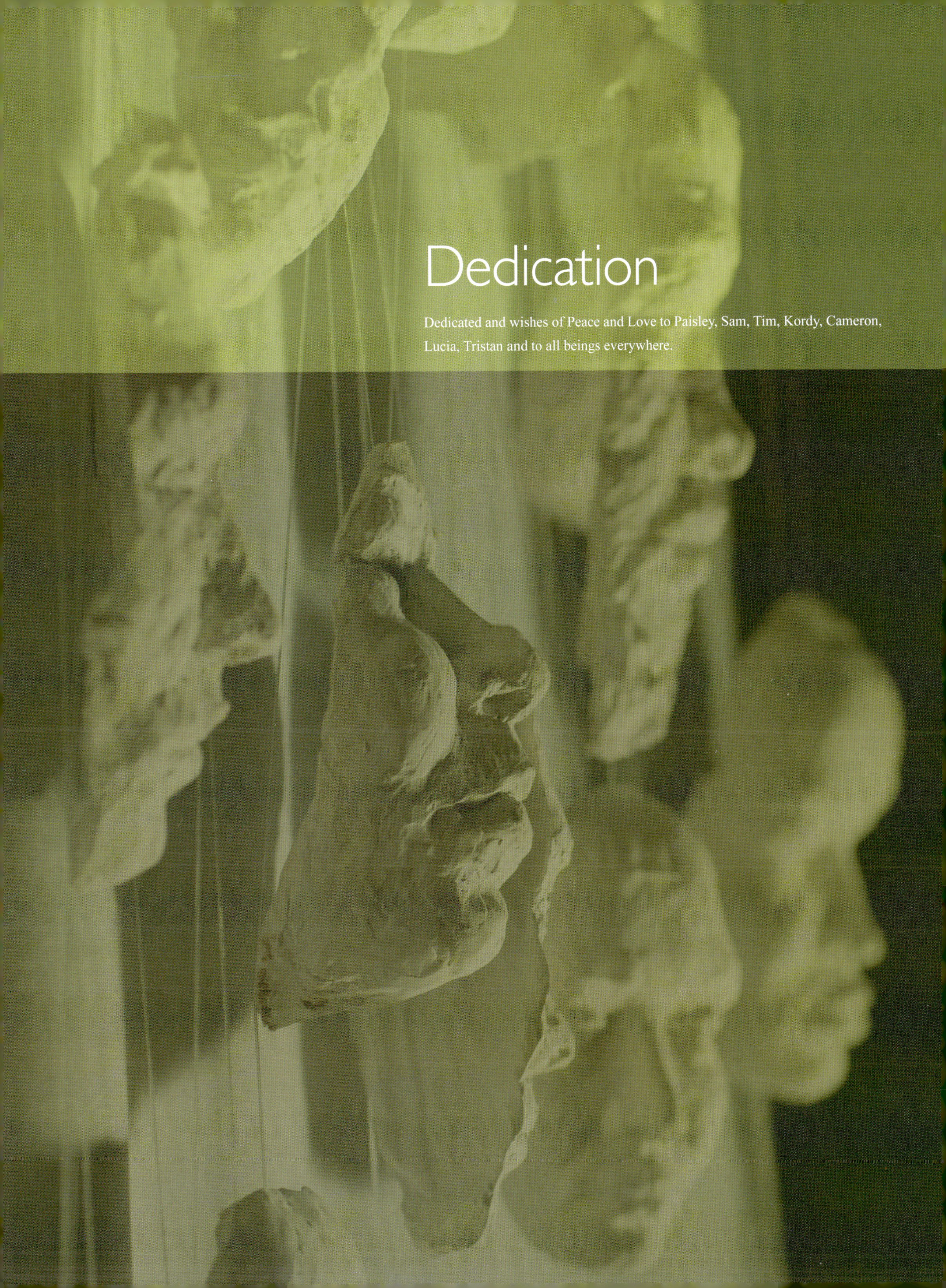

# Contents



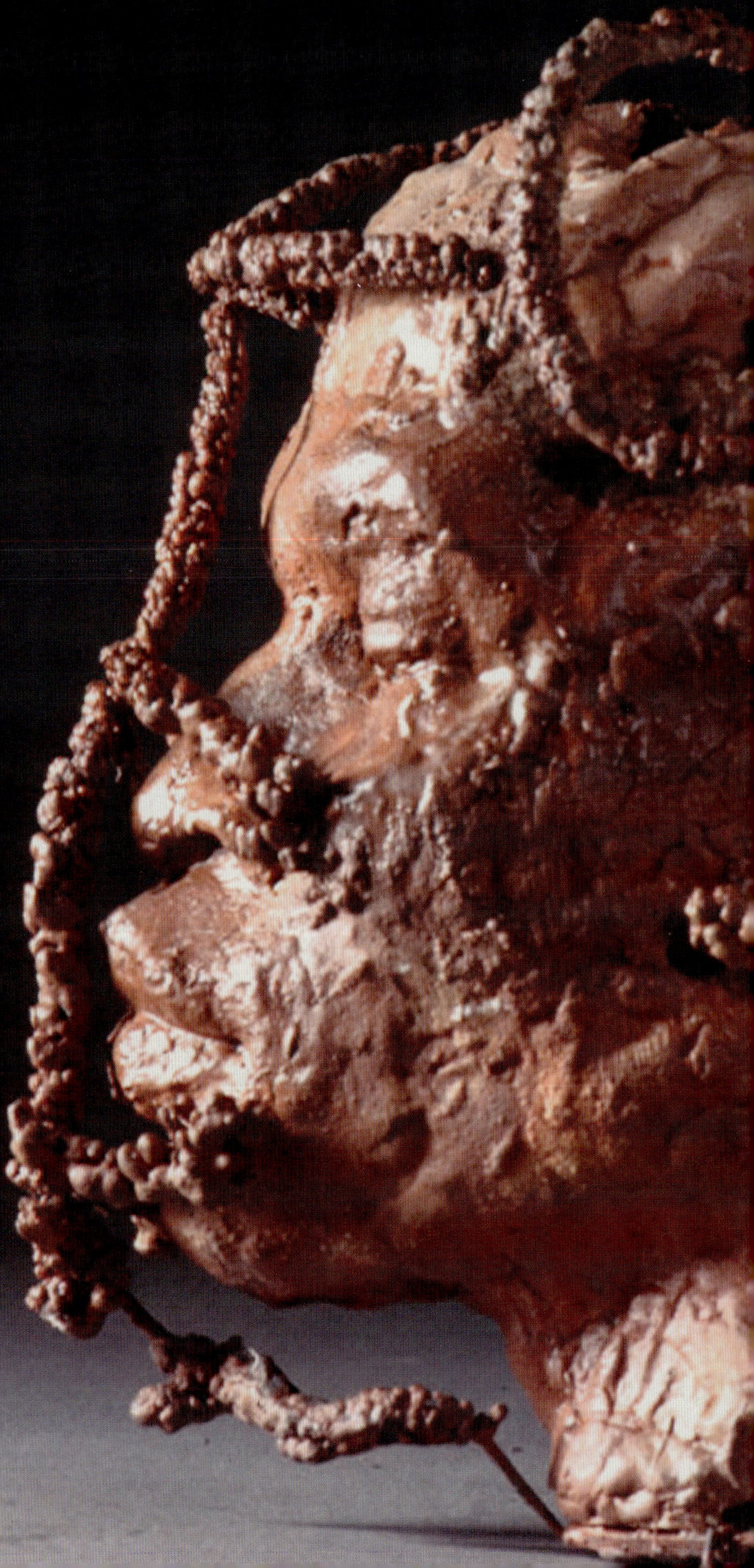

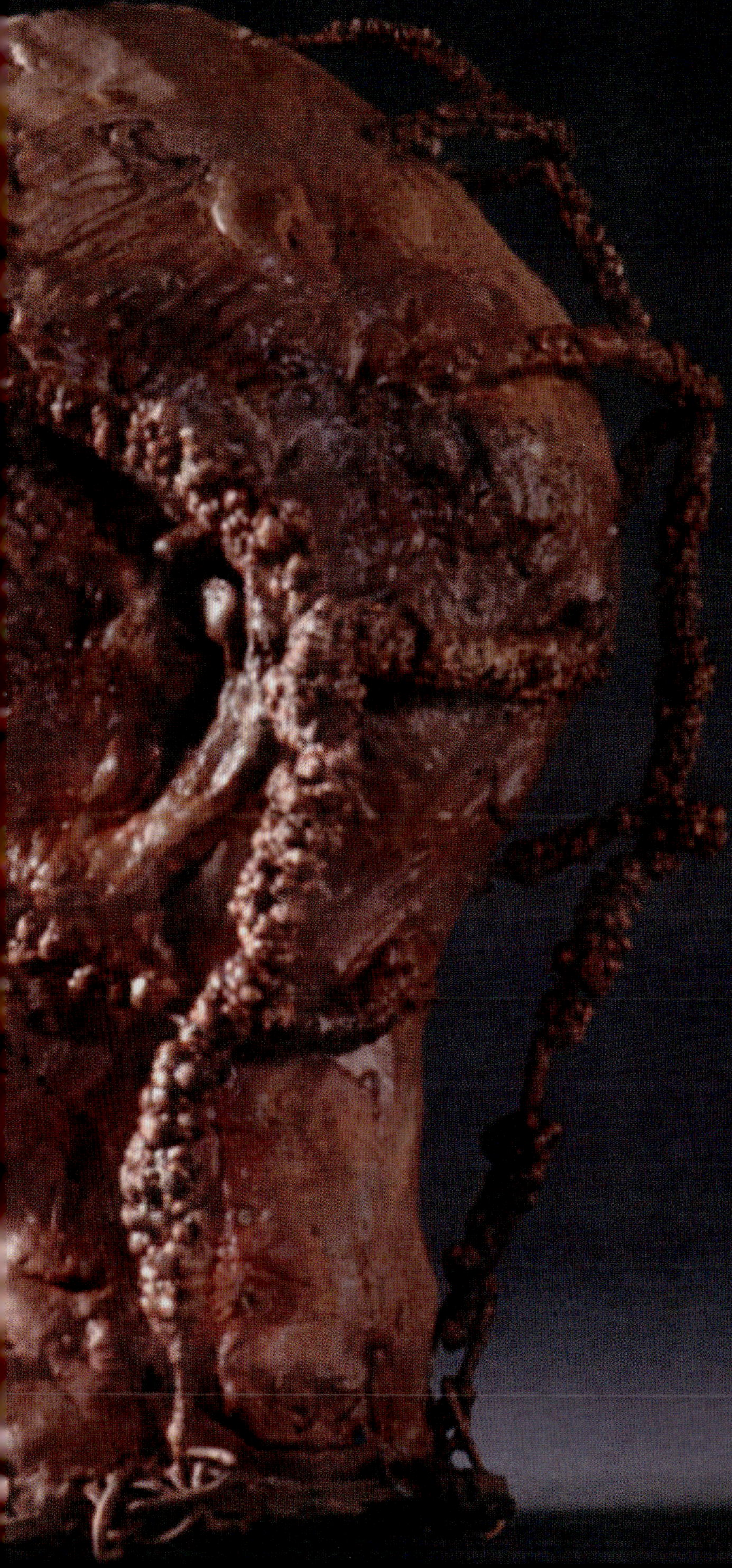

Jane Jaskevich
Gregory Johnson
Jeffrey Kennedy
Suprina Kenney
Linda Lewis
Jacob Linn
D. Dominick Lombardi
Angel Olegario Luna
Thomas Maes
Lauren Marems
Peter W. Michel
Milo Mirabelli
Brian Mock
Joe O'Connell and Blessing Hancock
James P. O'Neal
Judy Onofrio
Steven Panarelli
Arimathea Noel Pappas
Lane Patterson
Jolanta Izabela Pawlak
Joshua Pennings
Lauren Raine
Leisa Rich
Stefanie Rocknak
Ron Rodgers
Heath Satow
Leo Sewell
John E. Simms
Sandi Smith
Stan Smokler
Józef Sumichrast
Victor Tan Wee Tar
Dan Townsend
James Tyler
Derek Uhlman
David Vanorbeek
Jim Victor
Vivian Visser
Lynn Wartski
Dan Woodard
Joni Younkins-Herzog
Michael Zansky

# Introduction

THIS BOOK IS AN INVITATION FOR THE VIEWER TO EXPLORE AND INTERPRET sculpture, to engage it with his or her own story as opposed to being told the meaning behind the work. Although the artists gave descriptions of what their art is about, please take a look at the sculpture and explore your imagination first. We all get so lost in the meaning of things that often we forget to simply look and enjoy what is presented before us. Our own interpretation of the art work is just as factual as the artists, for it may trigger an emotion that validates the meaning of the art more than what the art was actually about.

While admiring the sculptures in this book it will become apparent that each work of art is exquisitely unique. Each artist is extremely talented and brings their inner sanctum to each piece of their sculpture. The hard work each artist put in their art work cannot be ignored as you view the beauty of each sculpture.

Narrowing down the piece selections was a challenging task. Each art work was as beautiful and striking as the next. Please enjoy the sculptures chosen and explore them well. If one captures your imagination, you can visit the artists' personal websites, which are provided beneath their names.

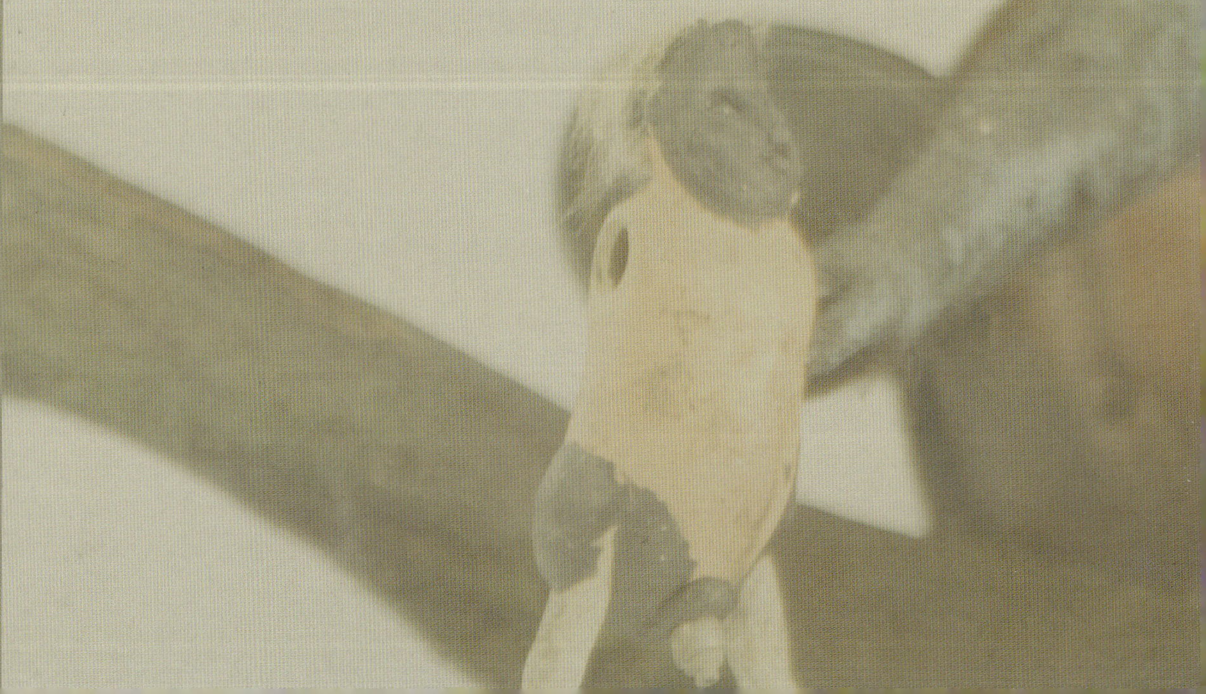

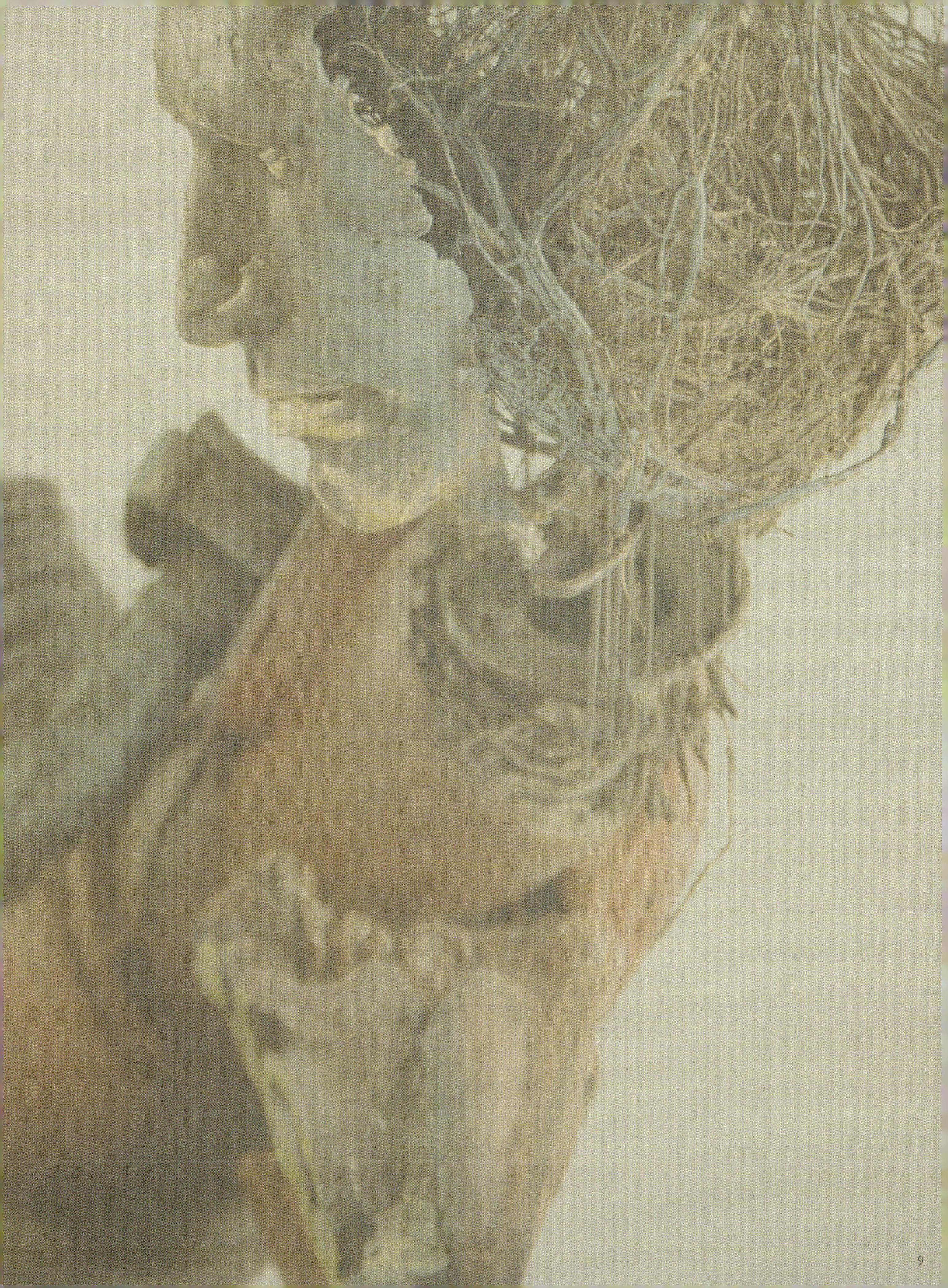

# Alabaster Masters
# Paul Hawkins and Susan Zalkind

Camp Verde, Arizona, USA
www.alabaster.net

*We have originated our art form 35 years ago and have professionally carved one-of-a-kind pieces of contemporary, abstract and functional sculpture from rare colored and translucent Alabaster-stone that we prospect ourselves throughout the Southwest deserts. We have trekked over seven states to unearth a full palate of color and figure.*

*Considering ourselves "stone carvers" rather than stone sculptors, our joy is to bring out the intrinsic beauty of each stone. Our creations reflect nature's simple elegance – its shapes and colors – and celebrate the materials of the Earth. We combine alabasters with other gemstones, rare fossils, mineral specimens, crystals, and fine woods.*

*Transforming raw stone into vessels of beauty is the creative process that engages us. There is a dialogue between the maker and the piece. The stone speaks. When we listen and respond, a harmony is created and we sing together. The resulting pieces speak for themselves – they have a life of their own.*

*Because we are the first generation of artists privileged to make a consistent living at art fairs; selling and promoting our work is part of and completes our process. Just as we have a dialogue with the stone, we also have one with our patrons, creating a trinity between the buyer, the maker, and the piece. The energy from that exchange is exhilarating and helps to initiate new beginnings.*

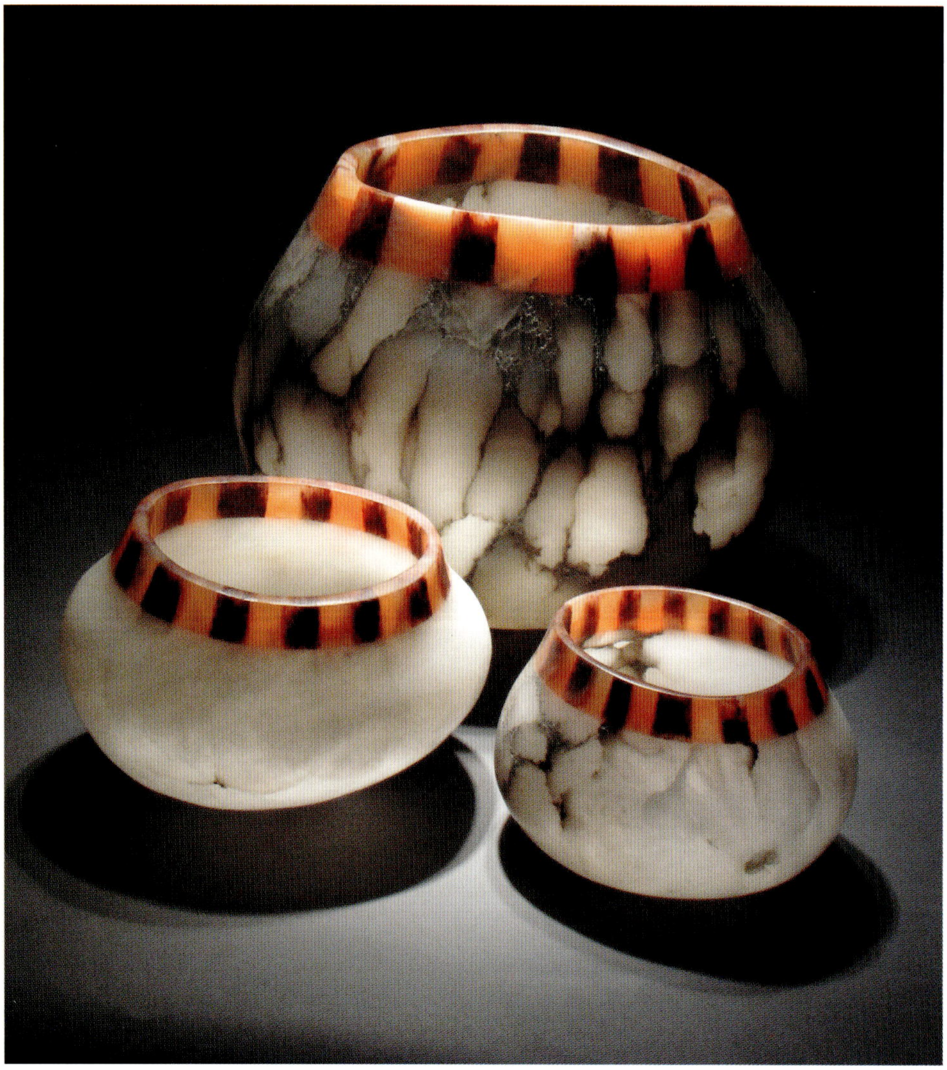

1

1 Paul Hawkins, *Sacred Tomb Bowls*. Orange, red, and white alabasters. Large: 12" h. x 14" w. x 11" d. Small: approx. 6" h. x 7" w. *Photograph by Paul Hawkins.*

2 Paul Hawkins, *Divine Illumination*. White alabaster. 16" h. x 20" diam. *Photograph by Paul Hawkins.*

3 Susan Zalkind, *Eternal Light*, 2005. Orange alabaster. 15" h. x 10" w. x 7" d. *Photograph by Paul Hawkins.*

4 Susan Zalkind, *Sacred Datura*. White, green, and black alabasters with Brazilian agate. 24" h. x 36" w. x 20" d. *Photograph by Paul Hawkins.*

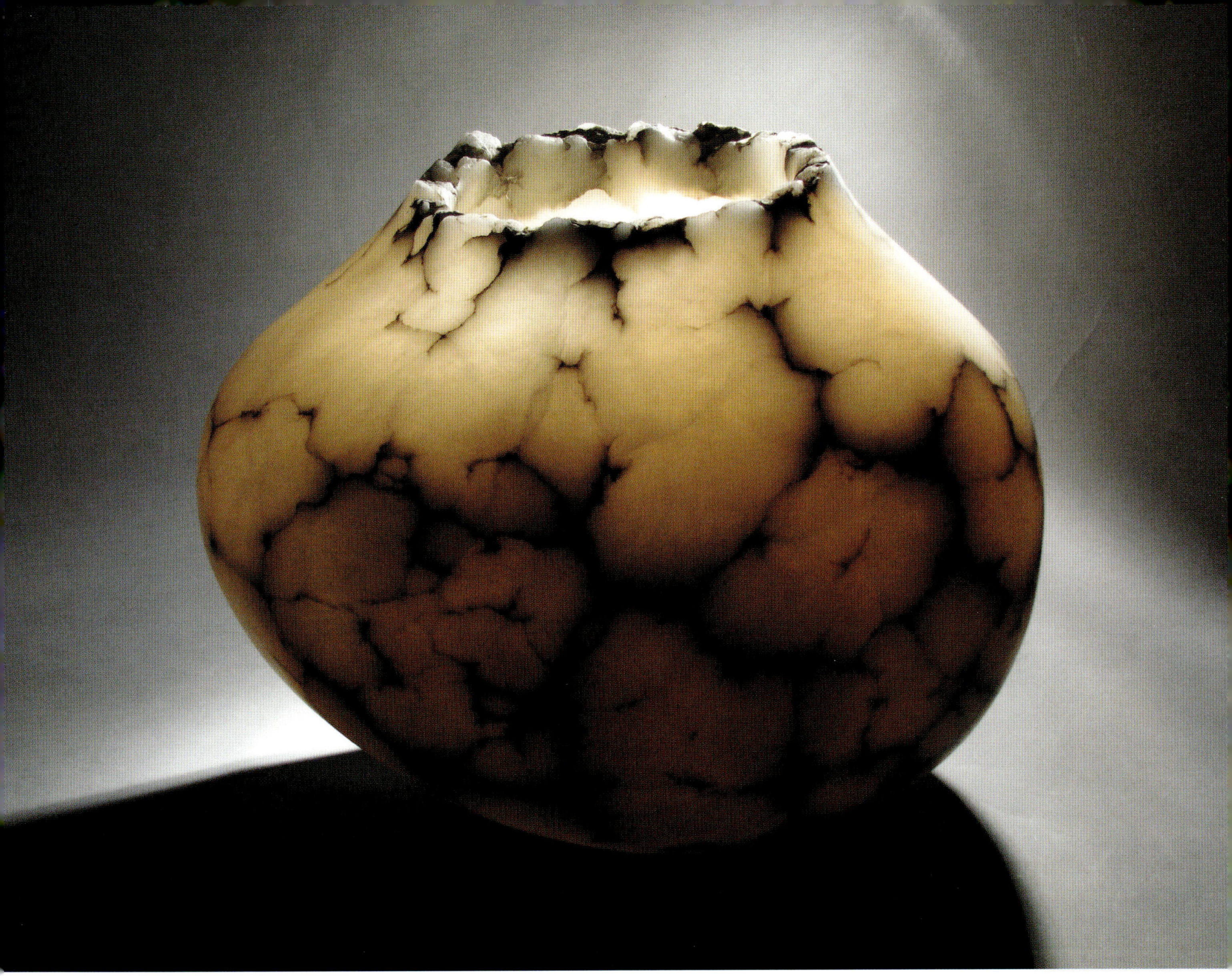

2

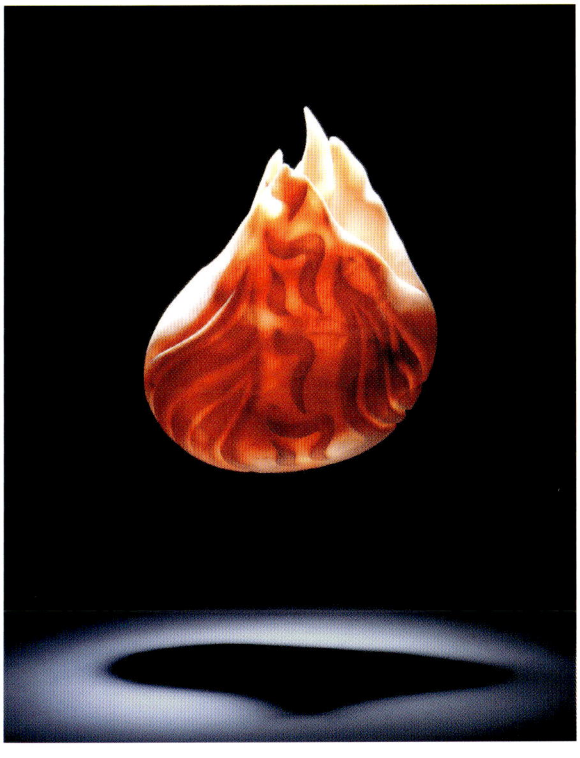

3

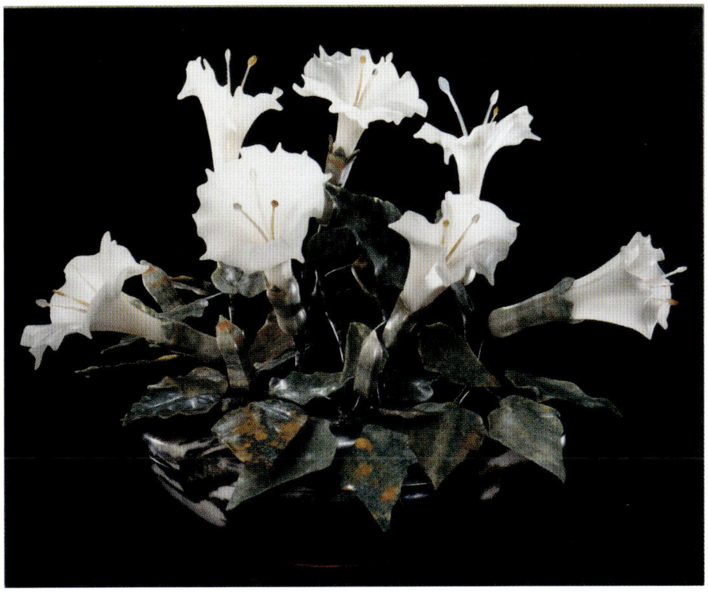

4

5 Paul Hawkins, *Dilemma the Doodleysquat,* 2009. Red and green alabasters, desert woods. 55" h. x 16" w. x 36" d. *Photograph by Paul Hawkins.*

6 *Dilemma the Doodleysquat* (detail), 2009. *Photograph by Paul Hawkins.*

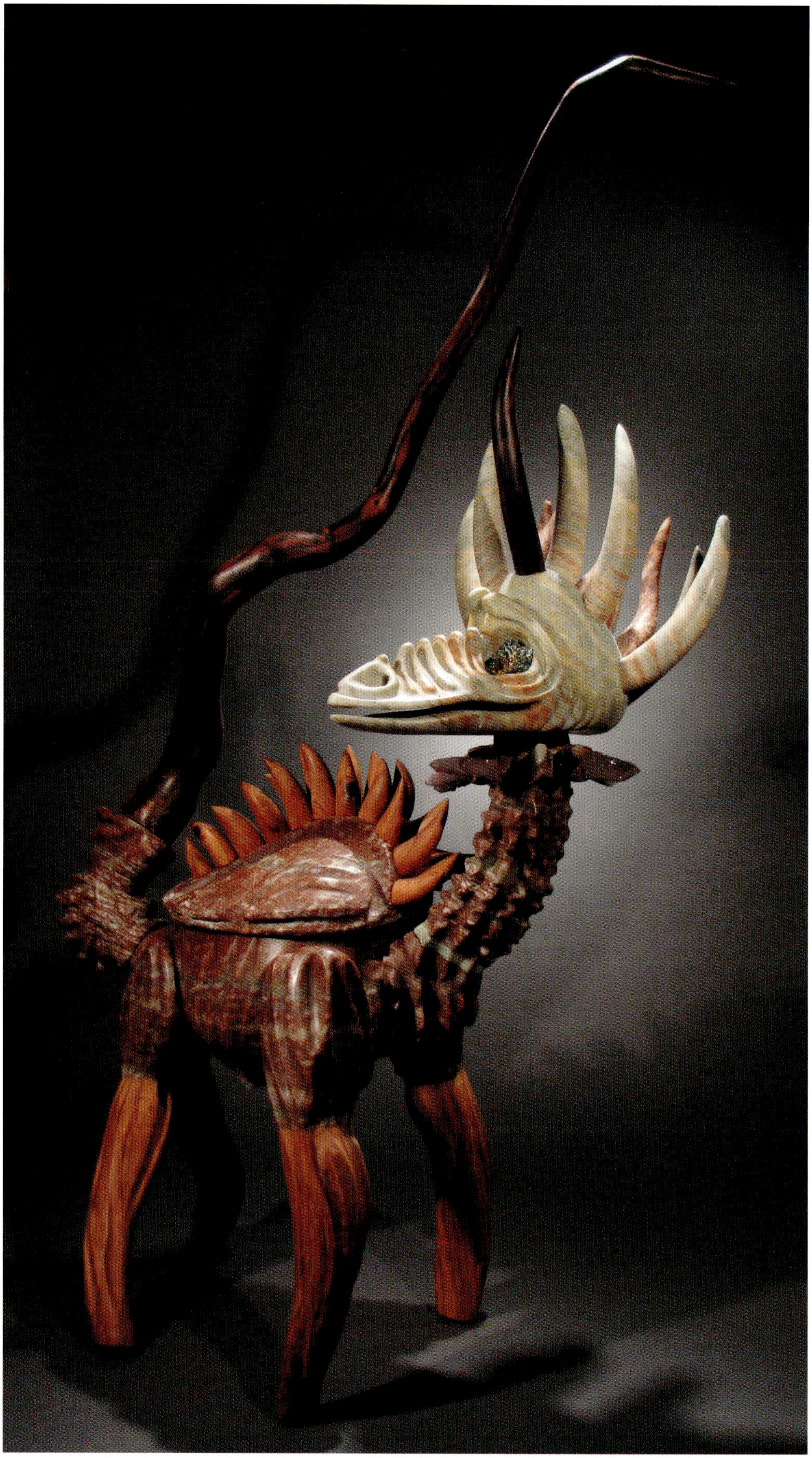

5

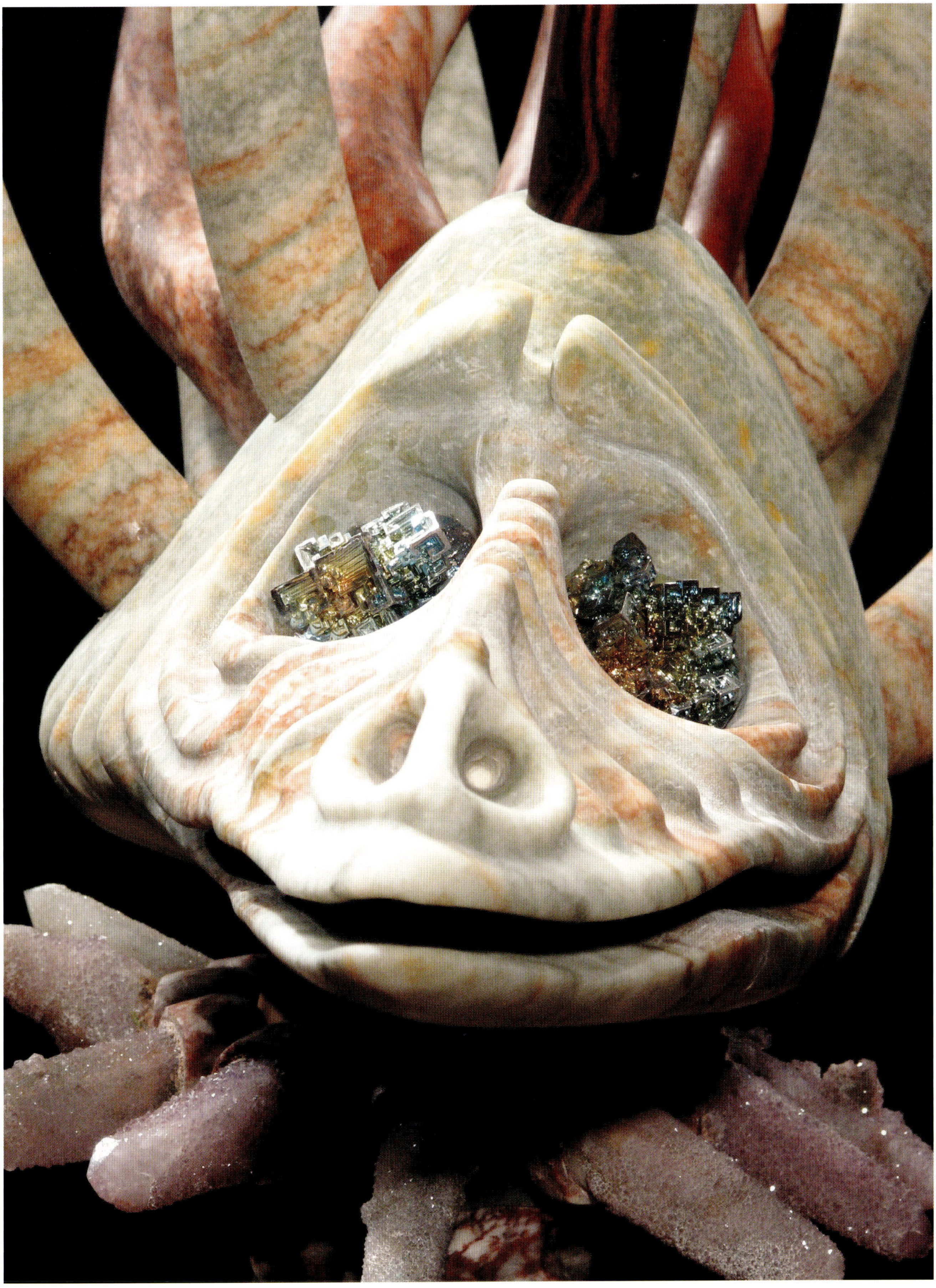

6

# Michael Alfano

Hopkinton, Massachusetts, USA
www.michaelalfano.com

*Over fifteen years ago, I left my stockbroker career and turned to sculpting so I could spend my days doing something I loved. I remained in my native New York to study at the Art Students League, sculpting the figure from the model. Since then, my art has garnered dozens of awards, including "Sculptor of the Year." I've also earned numerous commissions for monumental public art and portraits of world leaders. Most of my work is sculpted in clay to be cast in bronze, but I also create in wood, steel, resin, and other materials. Whatever the medium, it's gratifying to shape an image that conveys a personal idea to speak universally, and to know countless people are enjoying my art in parks, museums, and homes.*

*My sculpture starts with the human form, which I infuse with the surreal and philosophical, transforming classical imagery to resonate with our times. I begin a new piece with an idea that boils down our relationship with a specific experience to an essence. By combining symbols, figures, or other elements, I create an overarching image that initiates a dialog with viewers about the experience. Coming from a Buddhist perspective, my sculpture presents the distillation of that relationship neutrally and allows viewers to develop their own interpretations. This work is my passion: making art that speaks to the everyday yet compels viewers to experience, think, and understand life more fully.*

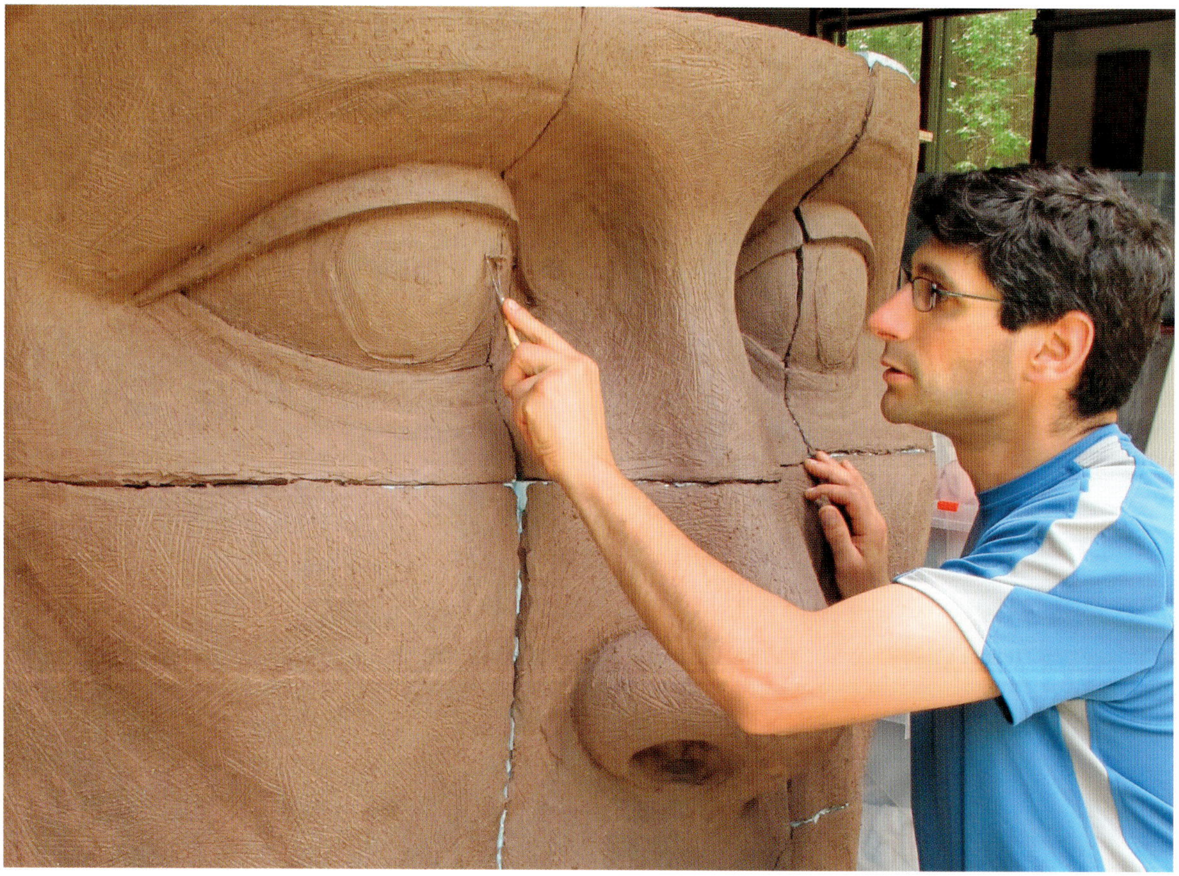

1

1 *Cubed*, 2011. Clay (to be cast), 48" x 48" x 60". *Photograph by Linda Chuss.*

2 *Gates of Transcendence*, 2005. Resin, 72" x 24" x 24". *Photograph by Michael Alfano.*

3 *Infinite Mind*, 2005. Bronze, 7" x 4" x 3". *Photograph by Michael Alfano.*

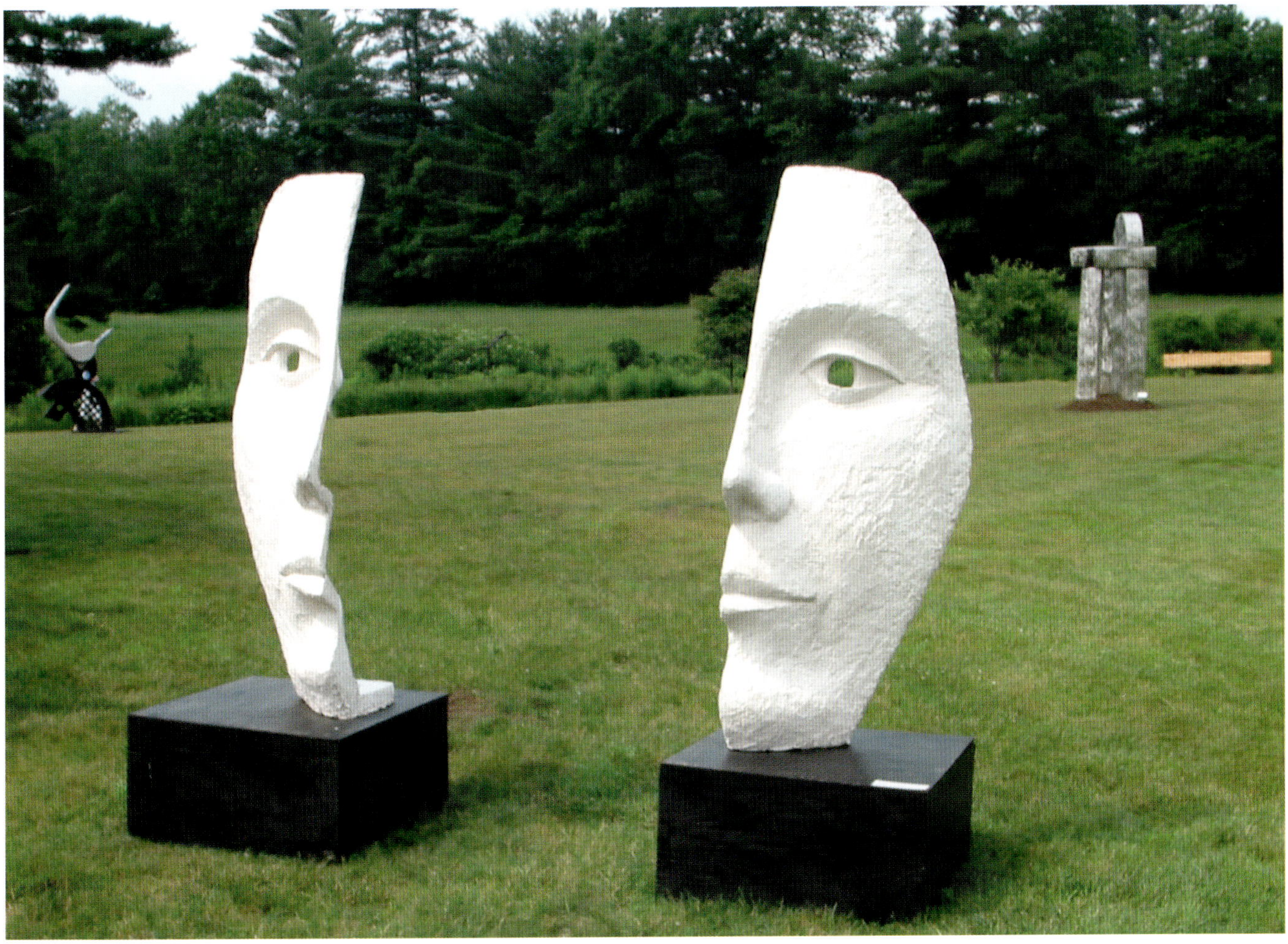

2

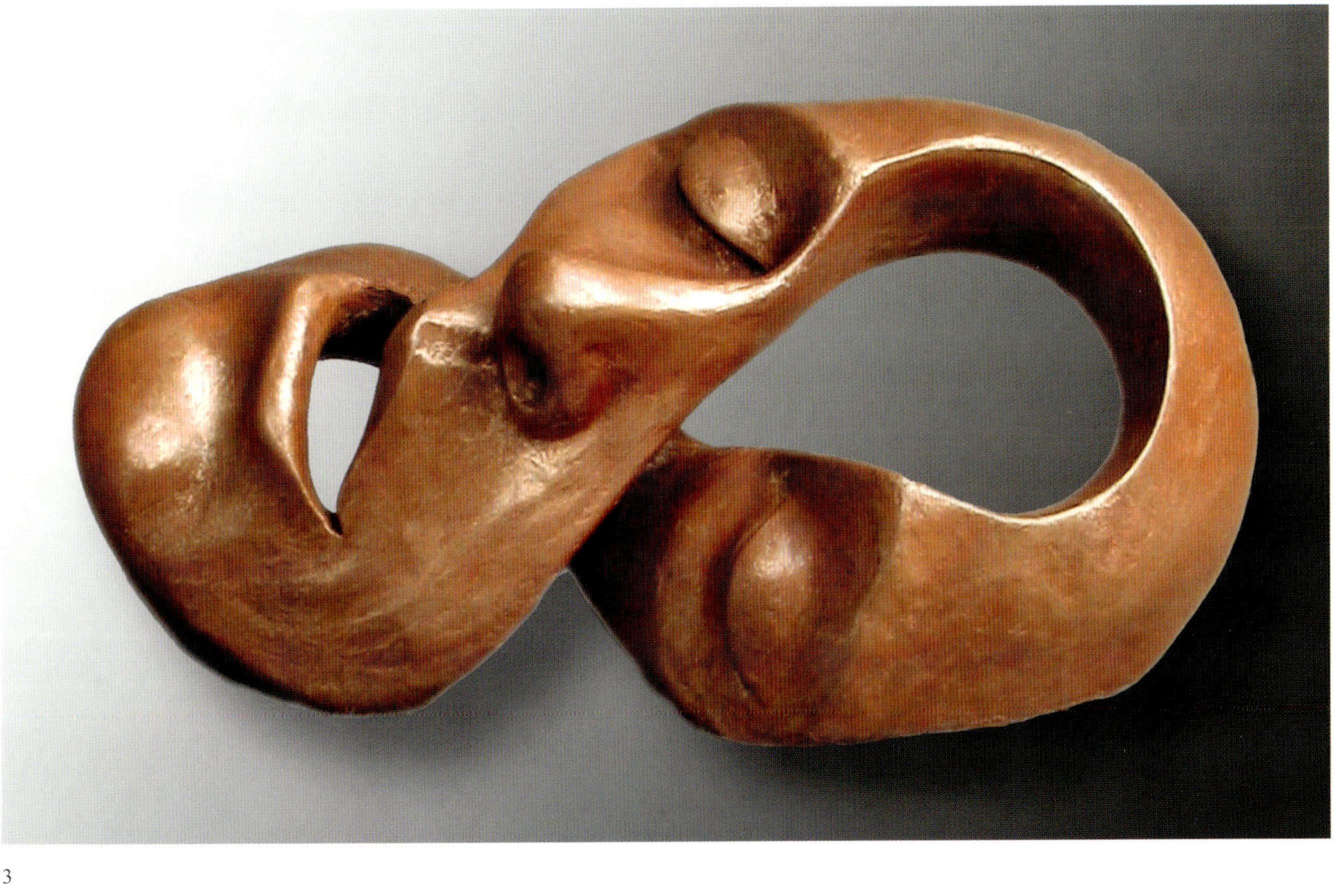

3

4 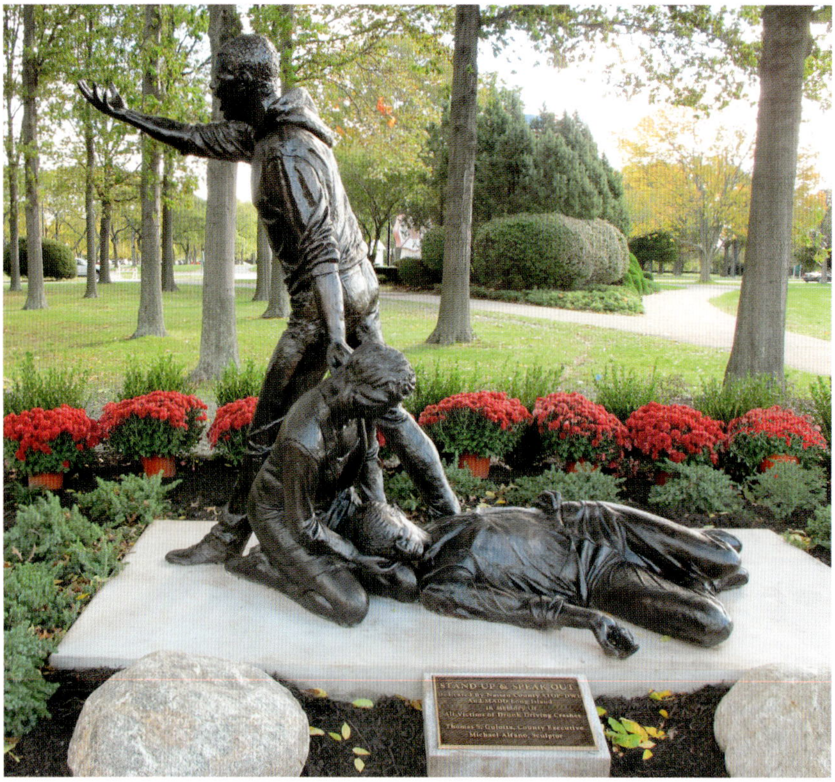


5 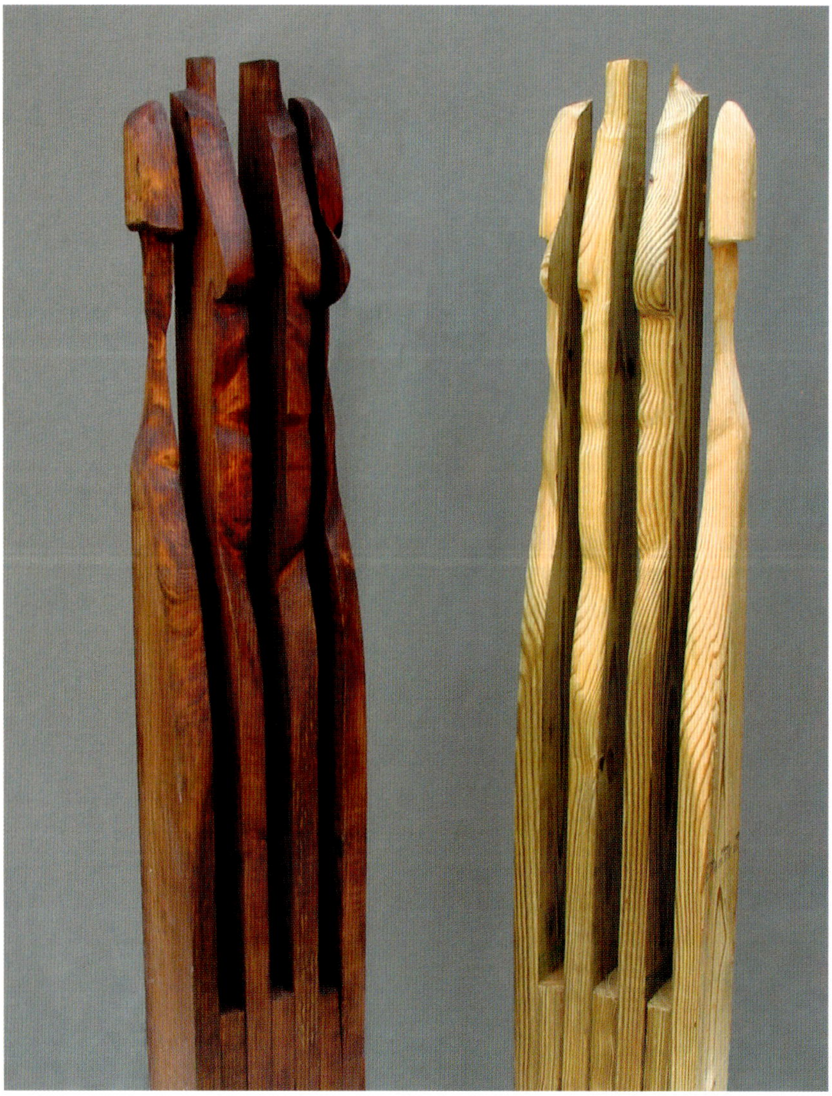

4 *Stand Up, Speak Out*, 1997. Bonded bronze, 120" x 84" x 60". *Photograph by Michael Alfano.*

5 *Torsos of Positive and Negative Space*, 2005. Wood, life size. *Photograph by Michael Alfano.*

6 *We Two Together,* 2001. Bronze, 10" x 10" x 9". *Photograph by Michael Alfano.*

7 *Yin Yang*, 2002. Bronze and granite, 14" x 14" x 5". *Photograph by Michael Alfano.*

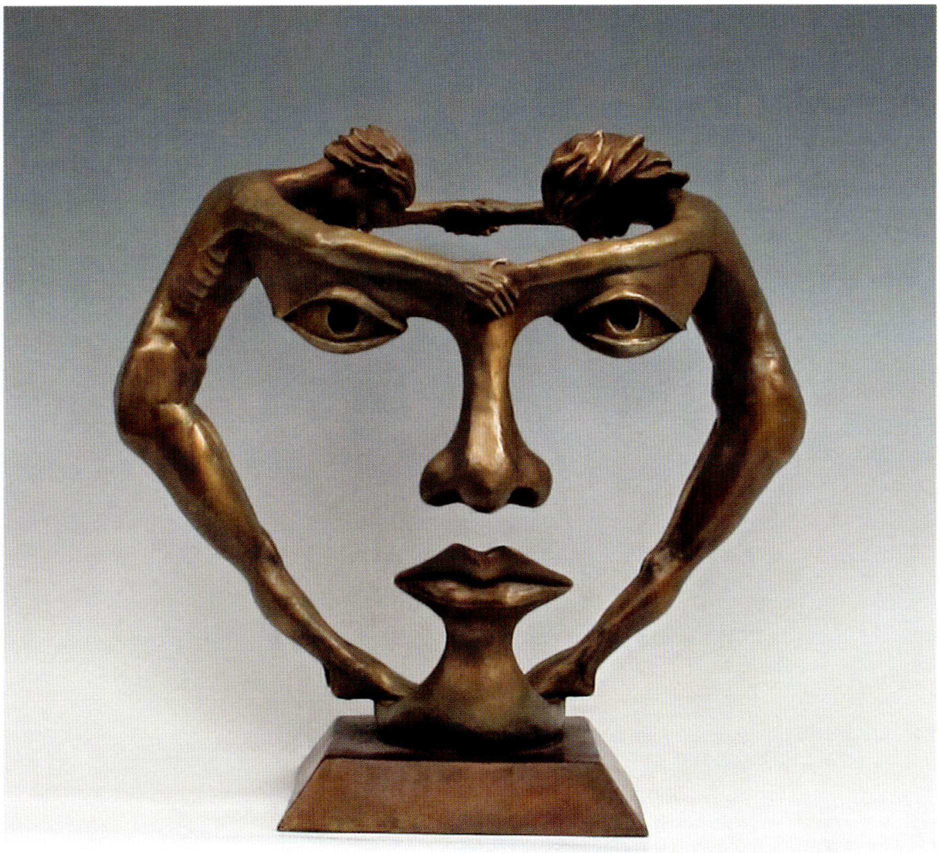

6

7

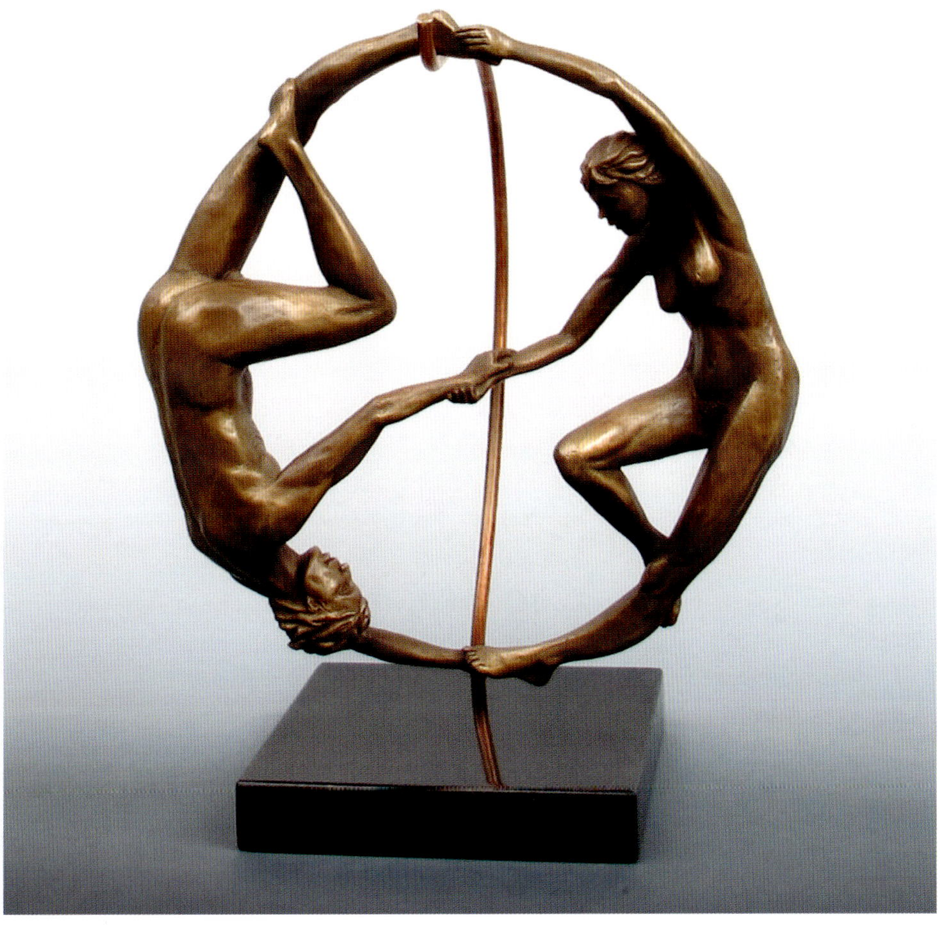

# Top of Form
# Emil Alzamora

Beacon, New York, USA
www.emilalzamora.com

Emil Alzamora was born in Lima, Peru 1975, and raised in Boca Grande, Florida. He later attended Florida State University where he graduated Magna Cum Laude in 1998 earning a Bachelor's Degree in Fine Arts. Alzamora started his sculpting career in the Hudson Valley working with Polich Art Works in the fall of 1998. Since his departure from P.A.W. in early 2001, he has produced his work full-time and shown regularly throughout the United States and Europe. He currently lives and works in Beacon, NY.

The human form is a constant in Alzamora's work. He often exaggerates or distorts it to reveal an emotional or physical situation, or to tell a story. Limitation and potential are as human as the flesh, yet hardly as tangible. In his works he strives to make visible this interaction.

1

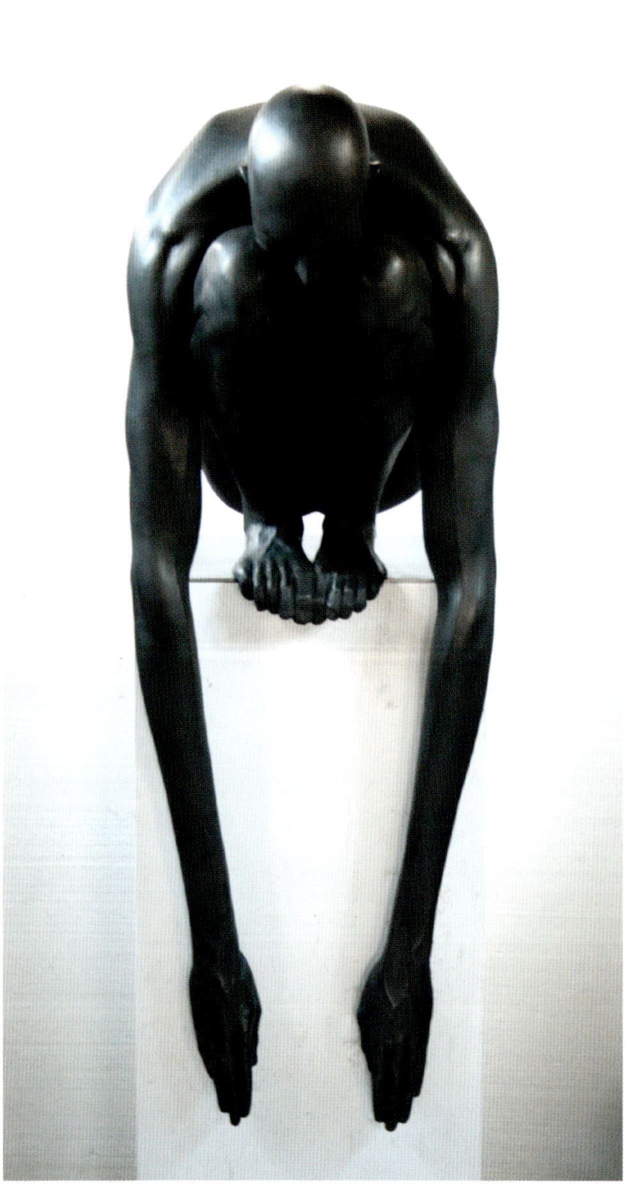

2

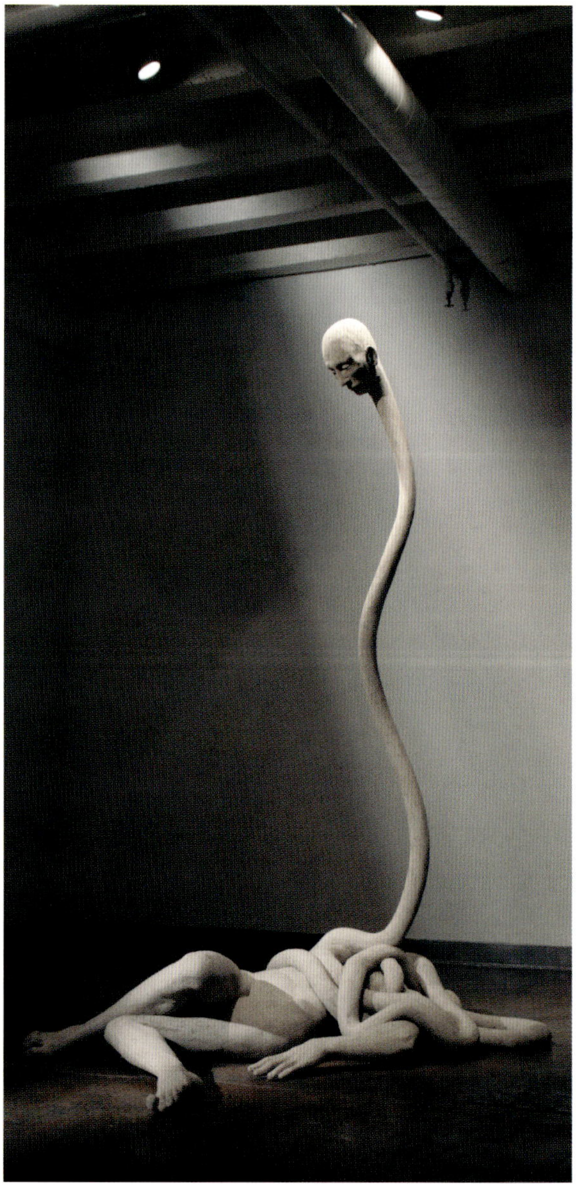

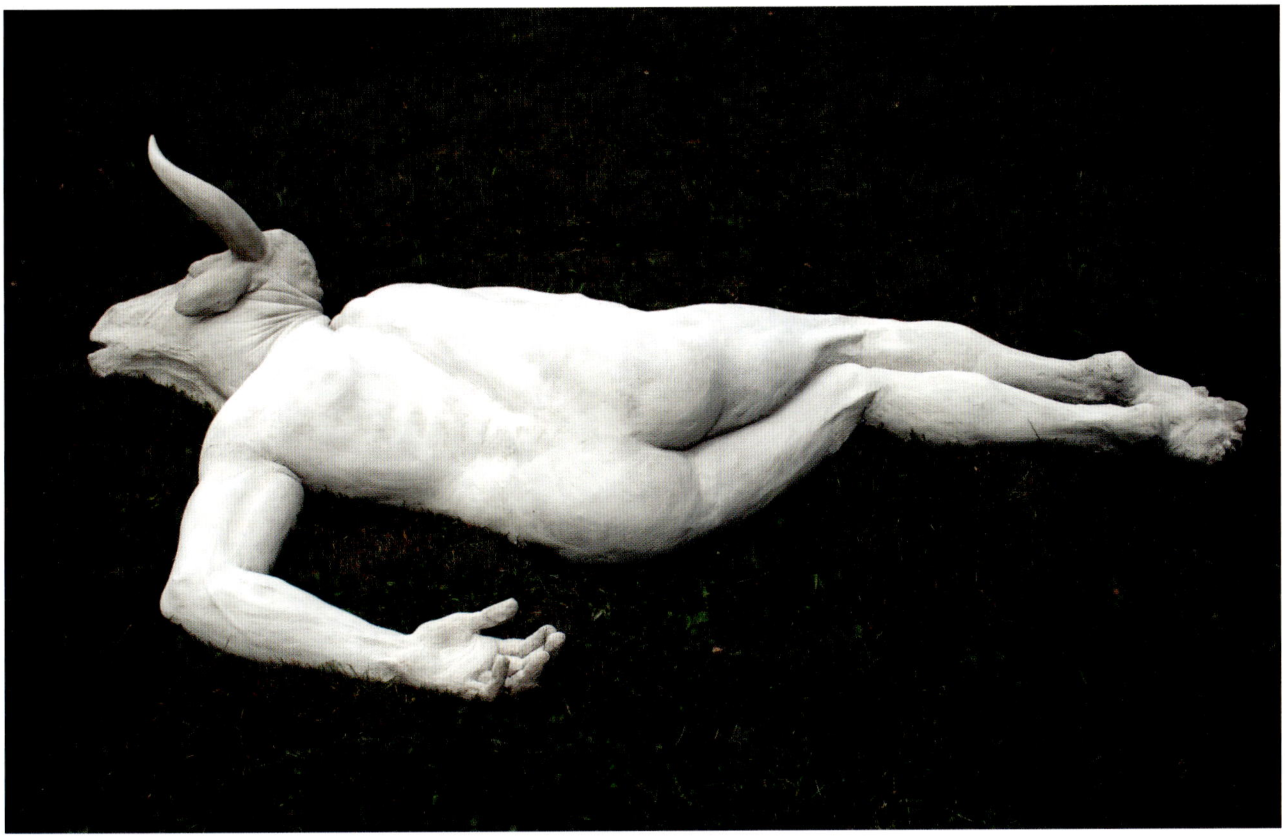

3

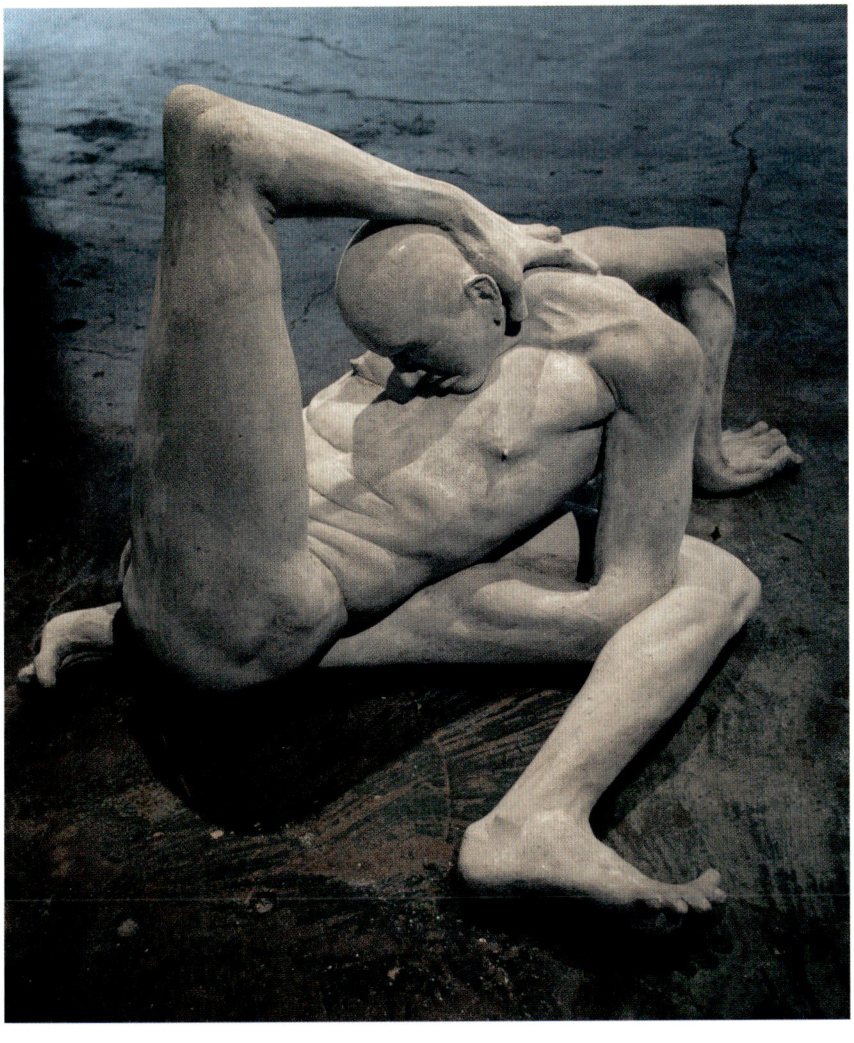

4

1 *Abyss*, 2008. Gypsum and graphite wax, 48" x 20" x 20". *Photograph by Emil Alzamora.*

2 *Afterlife Afterthought,* 2005. Gypsum, 90" x 48" x 60". *Photograph by Rudolf Van Dommele.*

3 *Minotaur,* 2005. Gypsum, 94" x 48" x 18". *Photograph by Emil Alzamora.*

4 *Masochist,* 2004. Gypsum, 40" x 32" x 24". *Photograph by Emil Alzamora.*

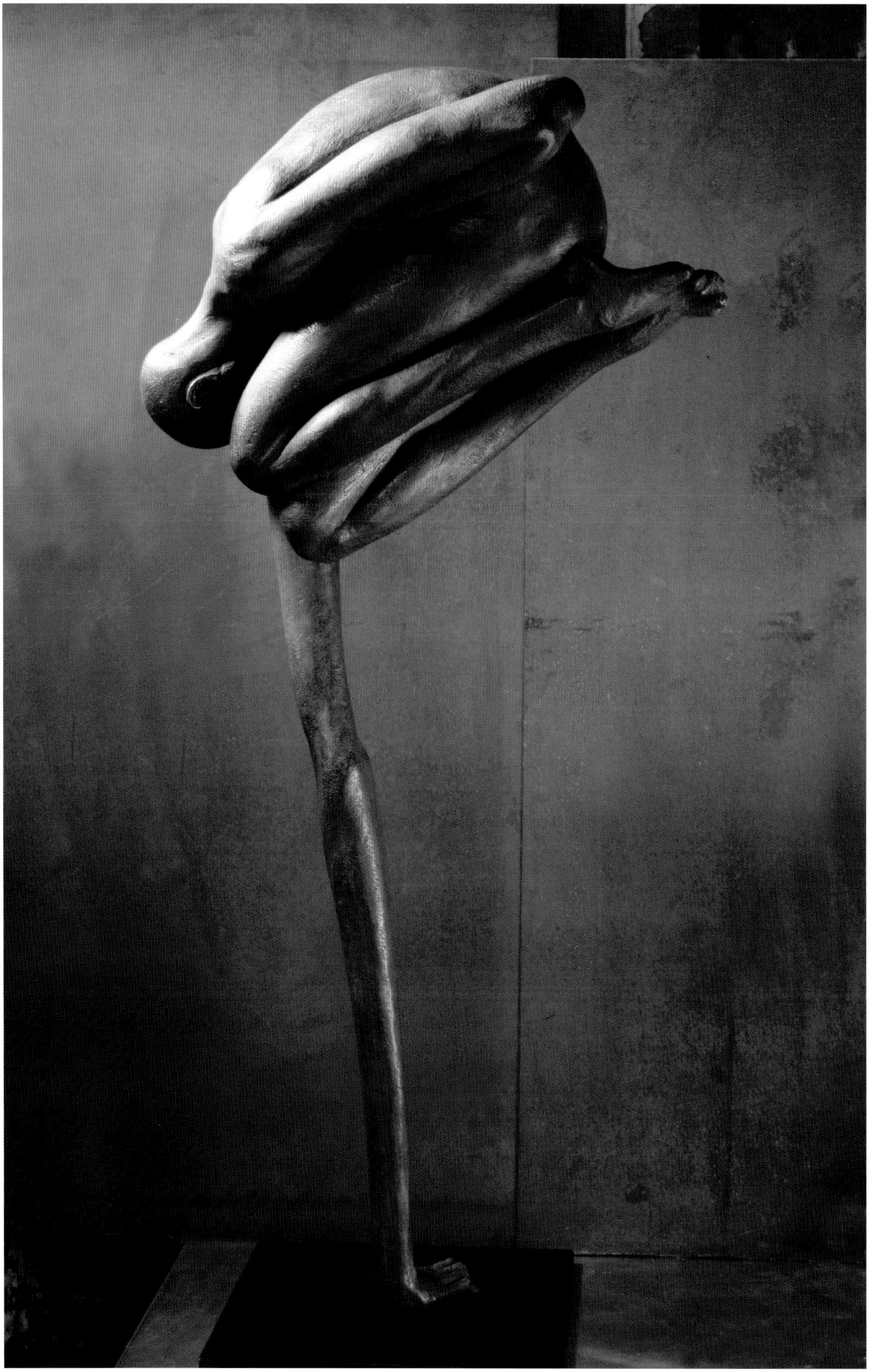

5

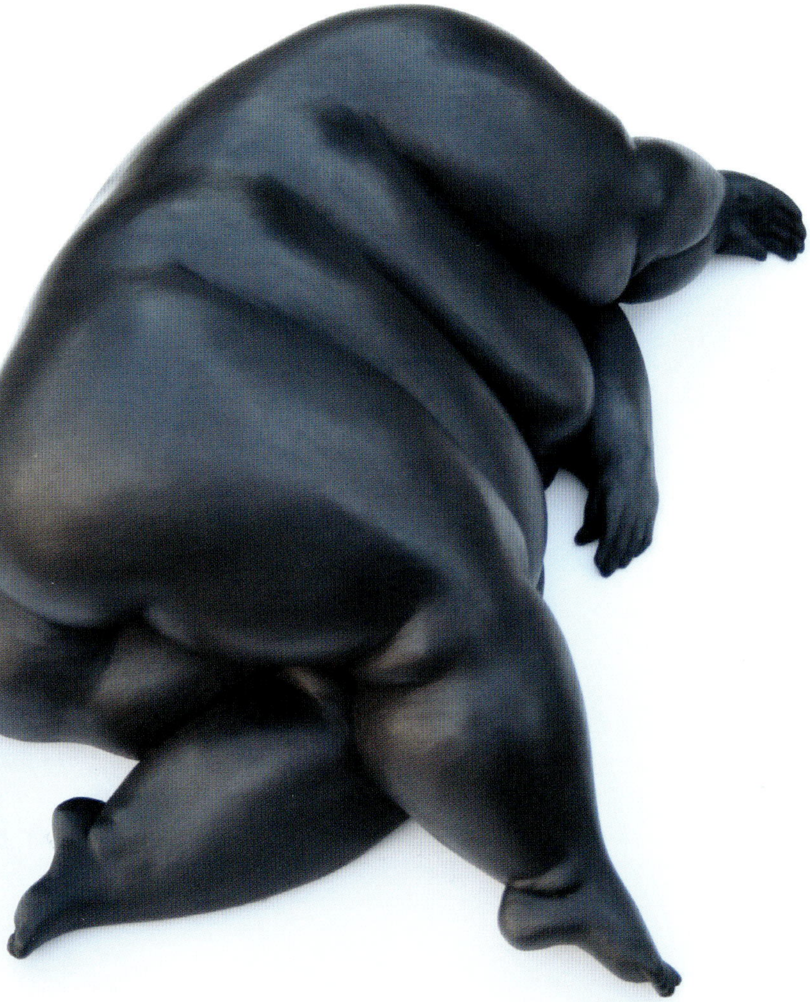

6

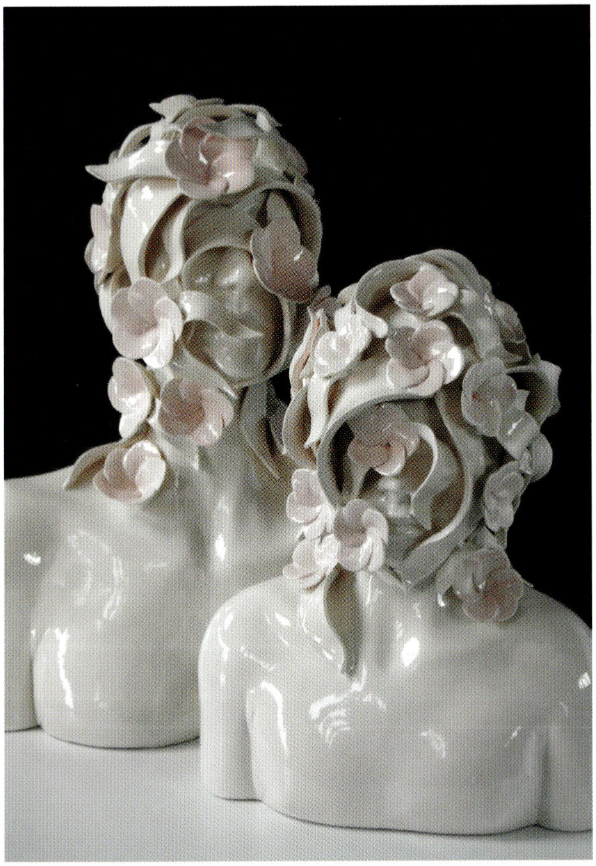

7

5 *Tether,* 2006. Bronze, 40" x 22" x 12". *Photograph by Emil Alzamora.*

6 *Mother and Child 10*, 2010. Slip cast and hand built ceramic, 18" x 20" x 12". *Photograph by Emil Alzamora.*

7 *Voluptuary,* 2008. Slip cast ceramic and graphite wax, 21" x 10" x 14". *Photograph by Emil Alzamora.*

# Mayumi Amada

Minneapolis, Minnesota, USA
www.mnartists.org/Mayumi_Amada

*I used to be a physical education teacher in Japan. To pursue my dream to become an artist, I quit my job and came to the U.S. I started with an ESL class and then studied art at the University of Minnesota. I graduated from the University in 2006 with an MFA degree in sculpture and have been very active in my professional career as an artist, including my recent solo exhibition at the Minneapolis Institute of Arts and a residency at the Bemis Center for Contemporary Art in Omaha.*

*My cultural heritage informs my work. Looking at my home country from a distance, I realize how much Buddhism has influenced the nation's mind: the way of thinking and the sense of value. The philosophy of Zen often gives direction to my creation. Thematically, my work explores women in a generational context using traditional techniques and their iconography. I use a doily in various settings and materials as a vehicle for this investigation. A doily is meaningful because the techniques for making them have been handed down through generations and the repeated stitches and patterns imply the repetition of generations. I often use recycled materials. The idea of "reuse" contains the meaning of "rebirth" and "giving new life." I'm exploring the connection between these materials and my thematic interests. My recent work is focused on mortality and meaning of life. Through my work, I'm hoping that the viewers have a moment to think about their own lives, and that they are motivated to consider what they want to or need to do to lead a fulfilling life.*

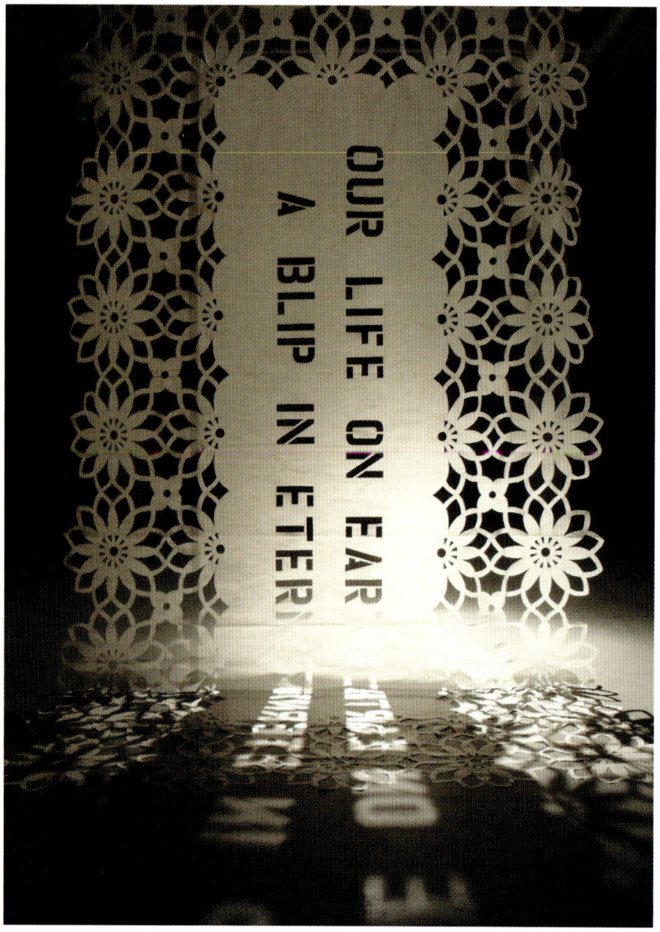


1

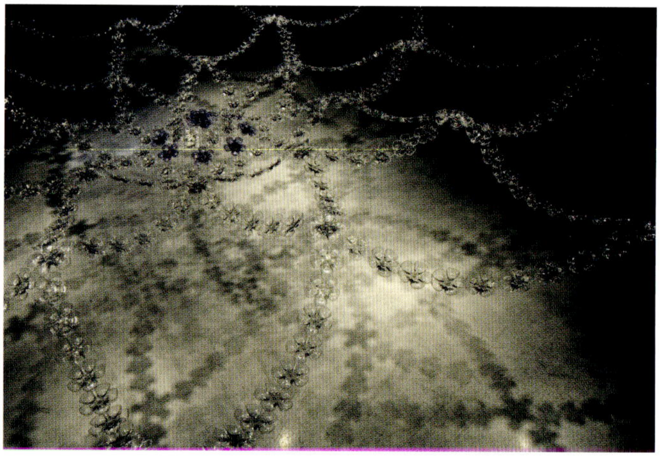

2

3

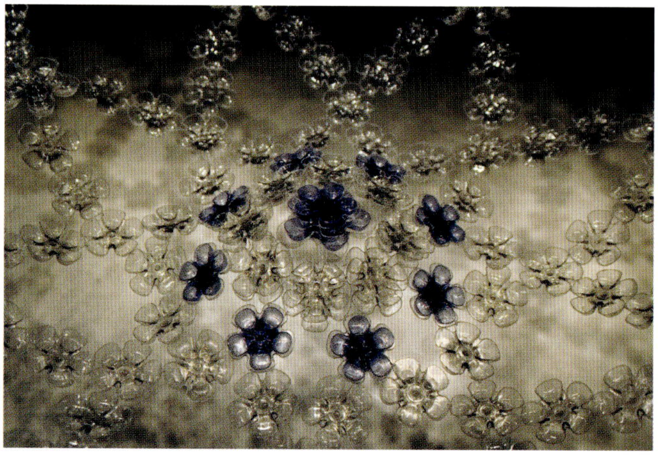

1 *A Blip In Eternity*, 2010. Cut out plastic tarp, 7.5' x 13.5'. *Photograph by Mayumi Amada.*

2 *Ripples of Regeneration* (part), 2006. Plastic bottles, fishing line, 15.5' diam. *Photograph by An Liu.*

3 *Ripples of Regeneration* (detail), 2006. *Photograph by An Liu.*

4 *Flower Field* (detail), 2008. Plastic bottles, acrylic tubing, blue LED lights, wire, 2.5' x 11' x 5.5'. *Photograph by Charles Walbridge/Minneapolis Institute of Arts.*

5 *Smithson's Grandma* (part), 2006. Mirror, skull, human bones, 3' x 2.5' x 4.5'. *Photograph by Mayumi Amada*

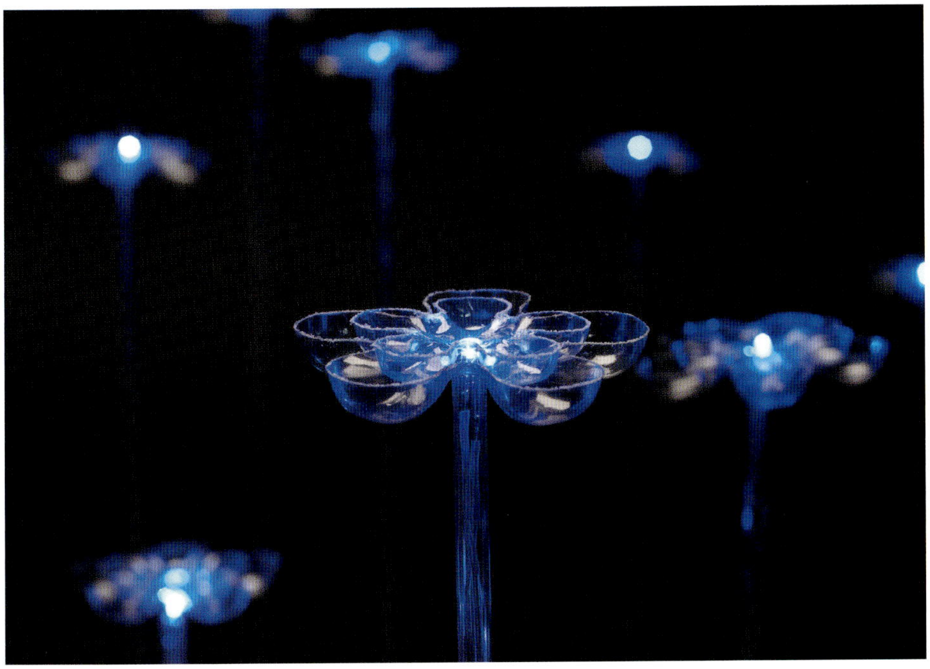

4

5

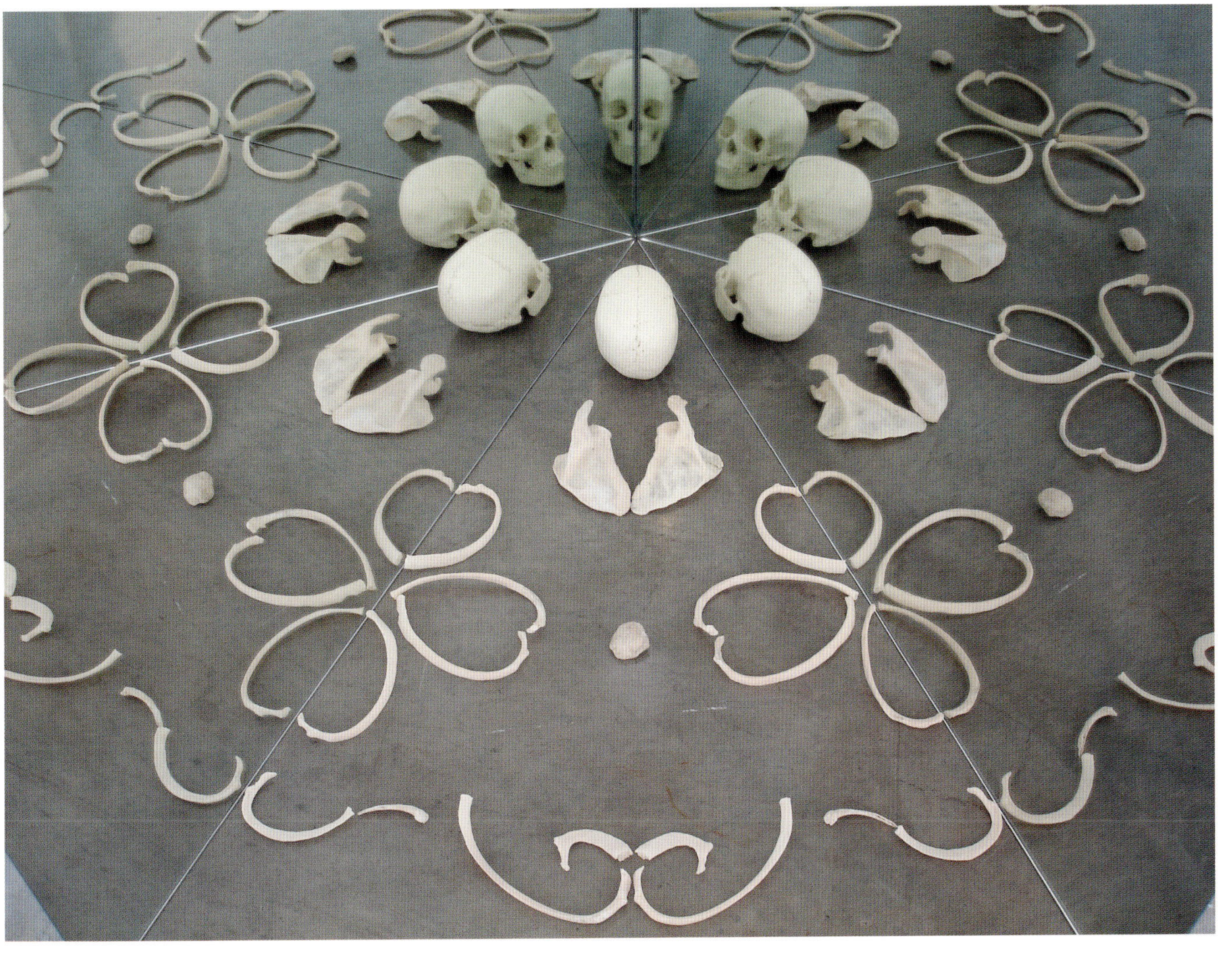

# Joan Baliker

Ormond Beach, Florida, USA
www.JoanBaliker.com

*After graduating from the American Academy of Art in Chicago where I studied design and illustration, I traveled to California and my first job as a color consultant in a decorating and design studio. Later I married a military man and while traveling the world, took art classes at each place the family called home — including portraits in Texas and wood carving in Florida, our last stop. In Florida, I assisted my husband for many years as he worked to become a nationally known sculptor. When we began clay, I knew I'd found my medium and then began putting my own passion, the Peace form.*

*Feeling an intense pull to explore the inner spiritual and psychological area and those of others, I began creating figurative sculptures of those people who walking the path of peace and inspiration from Mahatma Gandhi, who, after listing to his inner voice, led a nation down a different path, to the tribal men and men of Africa, who live peaceful lives of sharing and caring. I call them friends or Kir and we have become very close as I strove to enter into their thoughts and to experience their feelings. I hope that by being exhibited as a group, the sculptures reflect positively the common ground of humanity, the goal that gives my work its true meaning.*

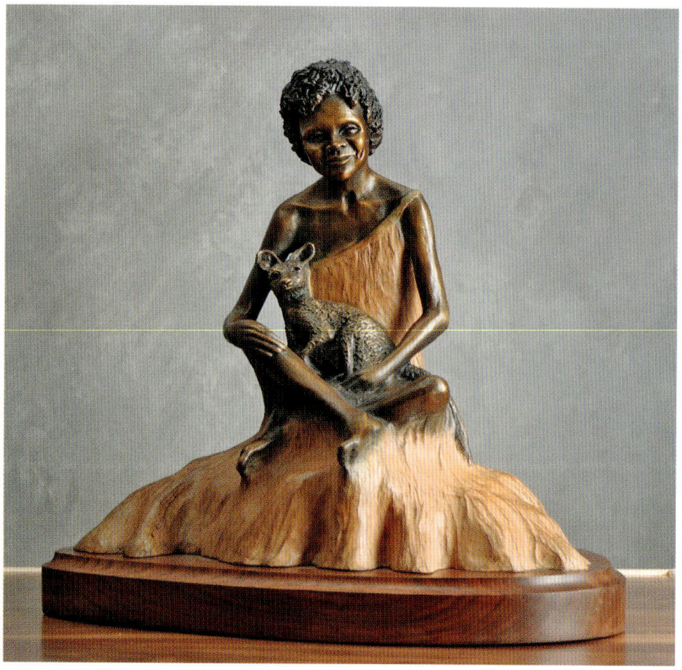

1

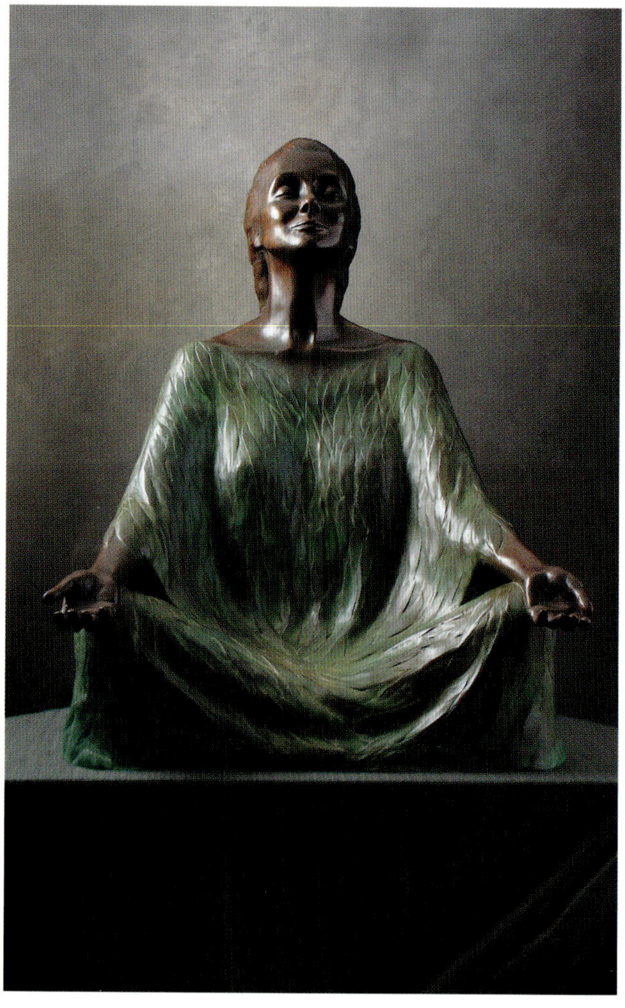

2

1 *Aborigine Tribute*, 2004. Bronze, 14". *Photograph by Patrick Ciatto.*

2 *Peace*, 2003. Bronze, 34". *Photograph by Patrick Ciatto.*

3 *Wodabe Ritual*, 2000. Bronze, 12.5". *Photograph by Patrick Ciatto.*

4 *Shanti*, 2007. Bronze, 15". *Photograph by Patrick Ciatto.*

5 *Vision Quest*, 2002. Bronze, 22". *Photograph by Patrick Ciatto.*

6 *Whirling Dervish*, 1999. Bronze, 14". *Photograph by Patrick Ciatto.*

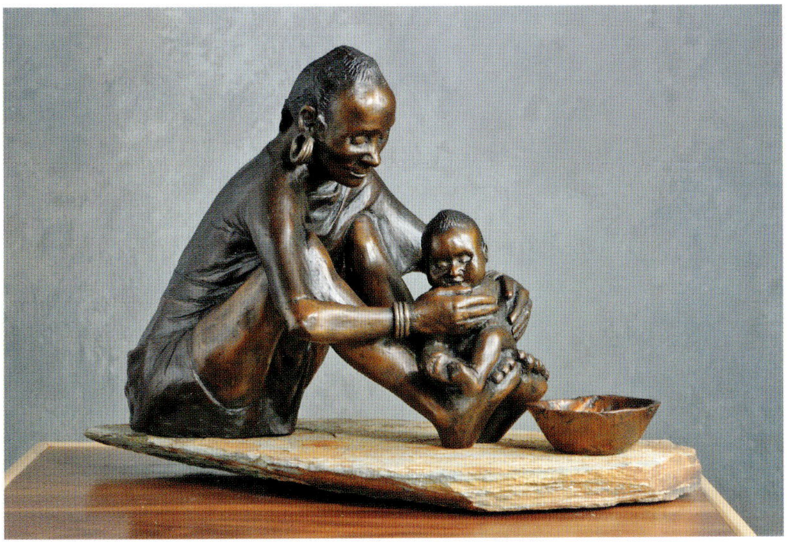

3

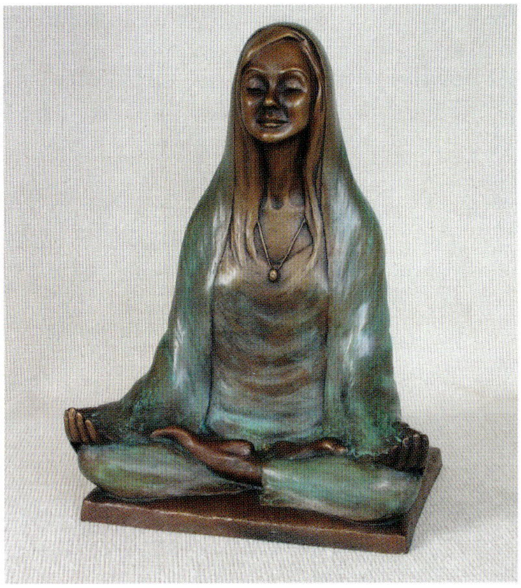

4

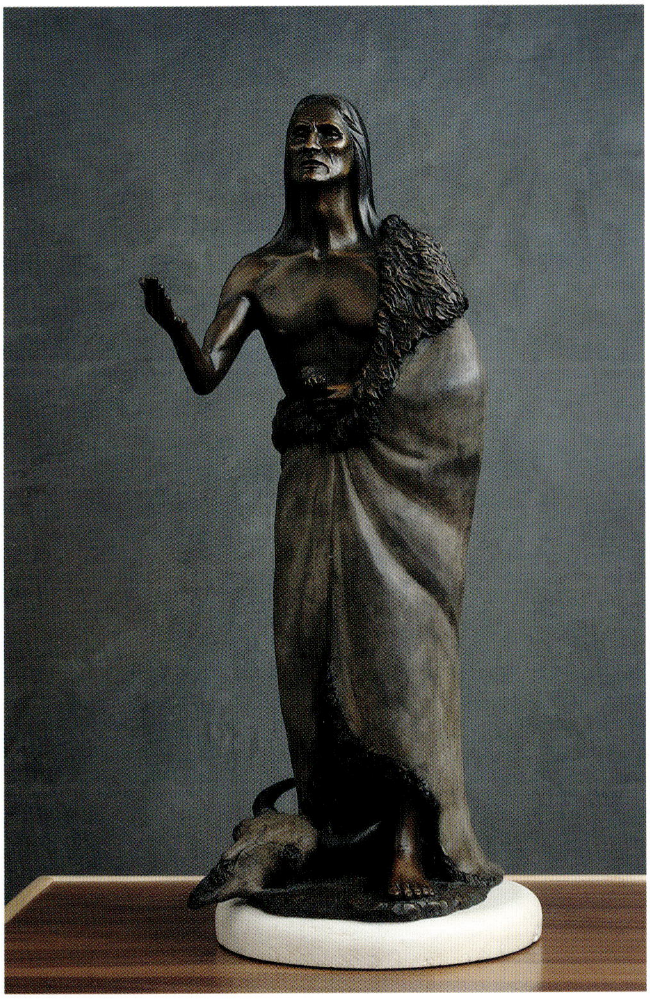

5

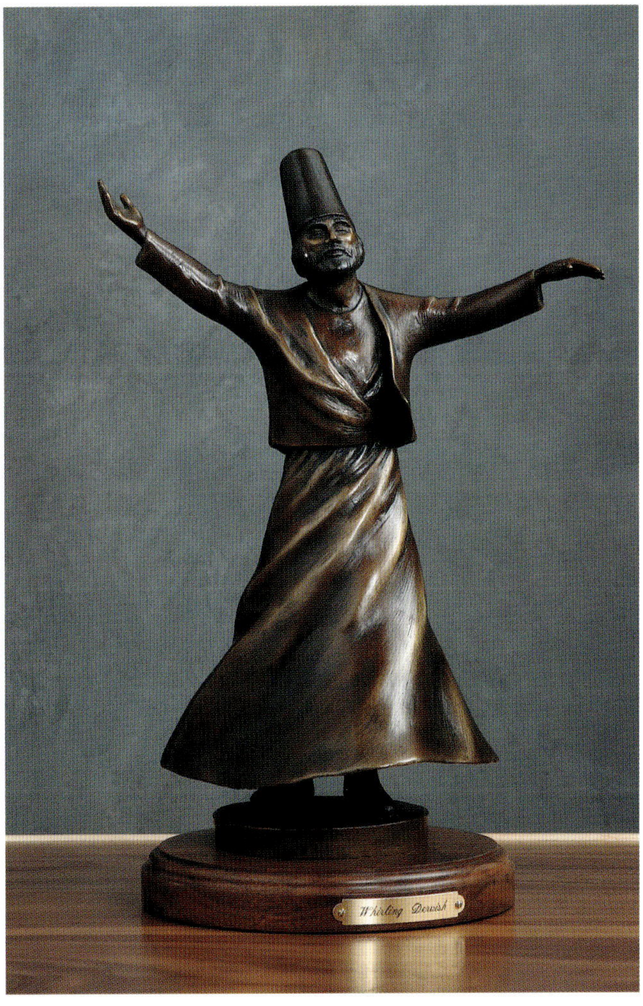


6

# Paul A. Baliker

Palm Coast, Florida, USA
www.paulbaliker.com

*A passion for nature has inspired me to create a body of work that is environmental in pith. I endeavor to capture a moment in wood or bronze that expresses potential for a symbolic relationship with nature.*

Paul's sculpture is included in "Art In Public Places" as well as corporate collections both nationally and internationally. In 2010, Paul placed a monumental sculpture in Mexico City, Mexico, and another in Toronto, Canada. He has been covered in numerous newspaper and magazine publications. He also had a PBS documentary, "For the Love of Manatees" filmed around his "Wellspring" sculpture.

1

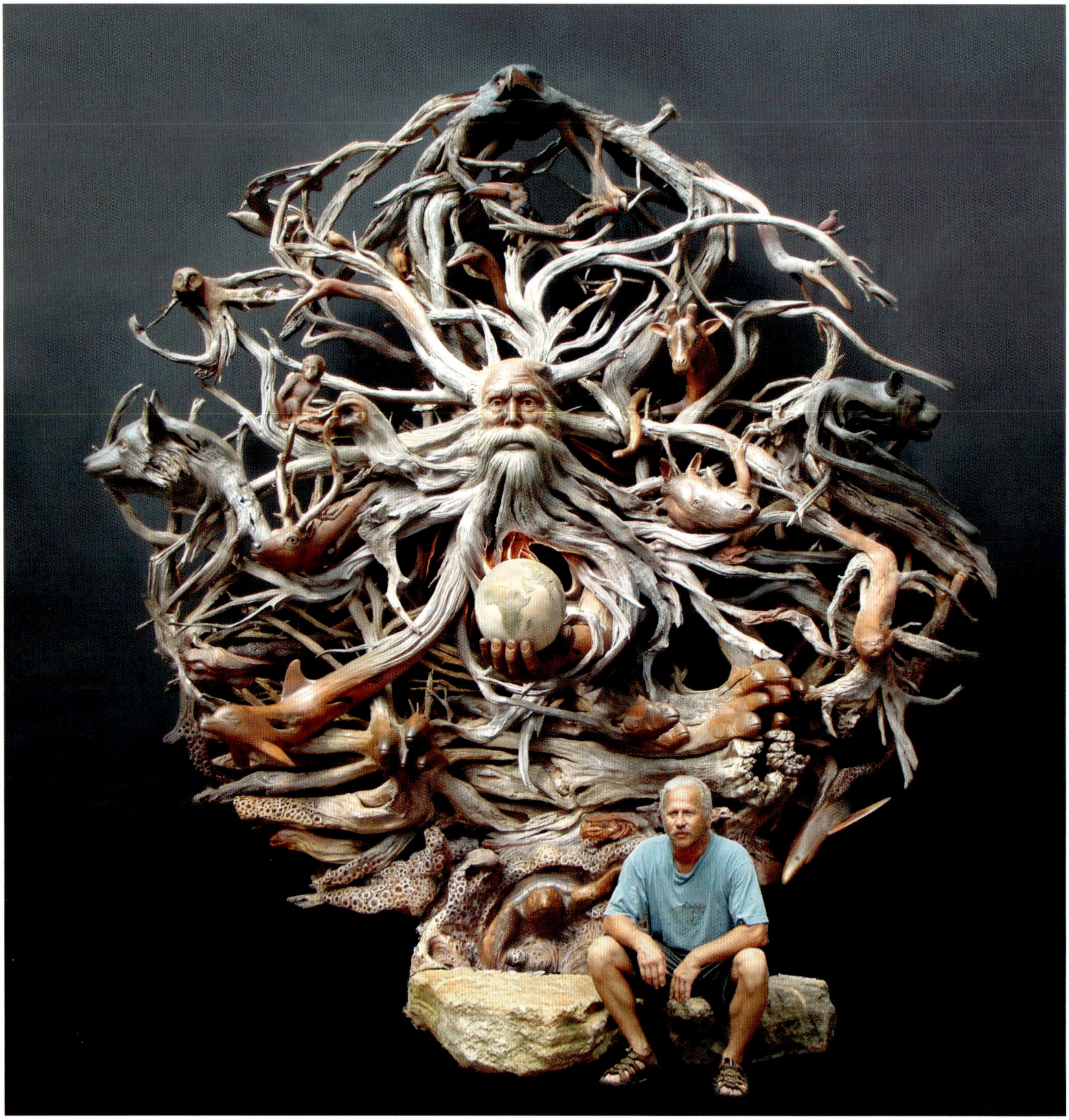

2

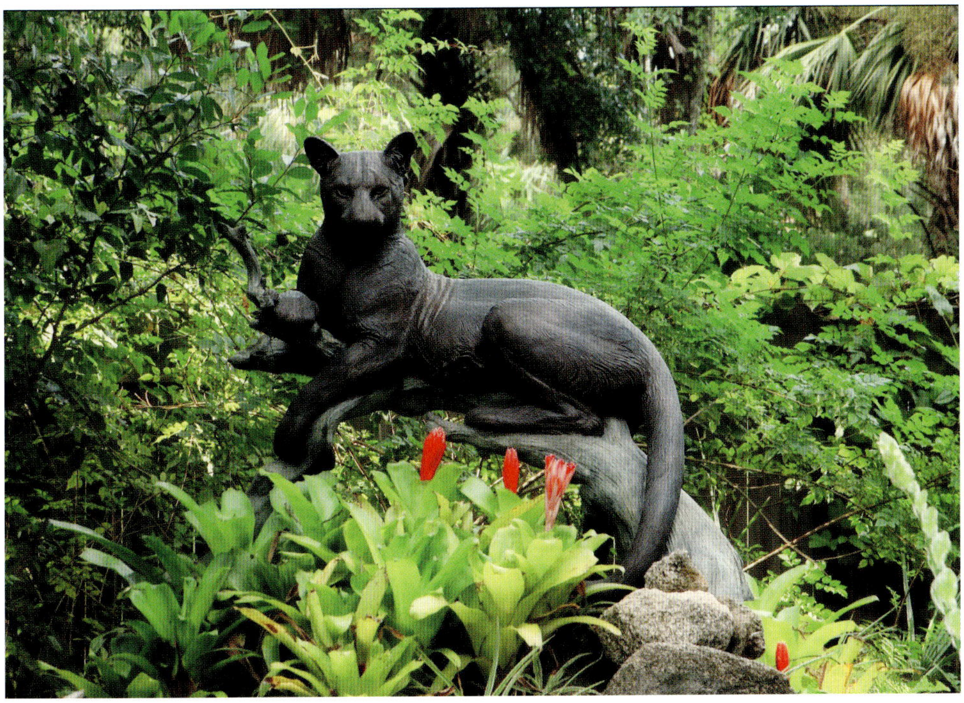

3

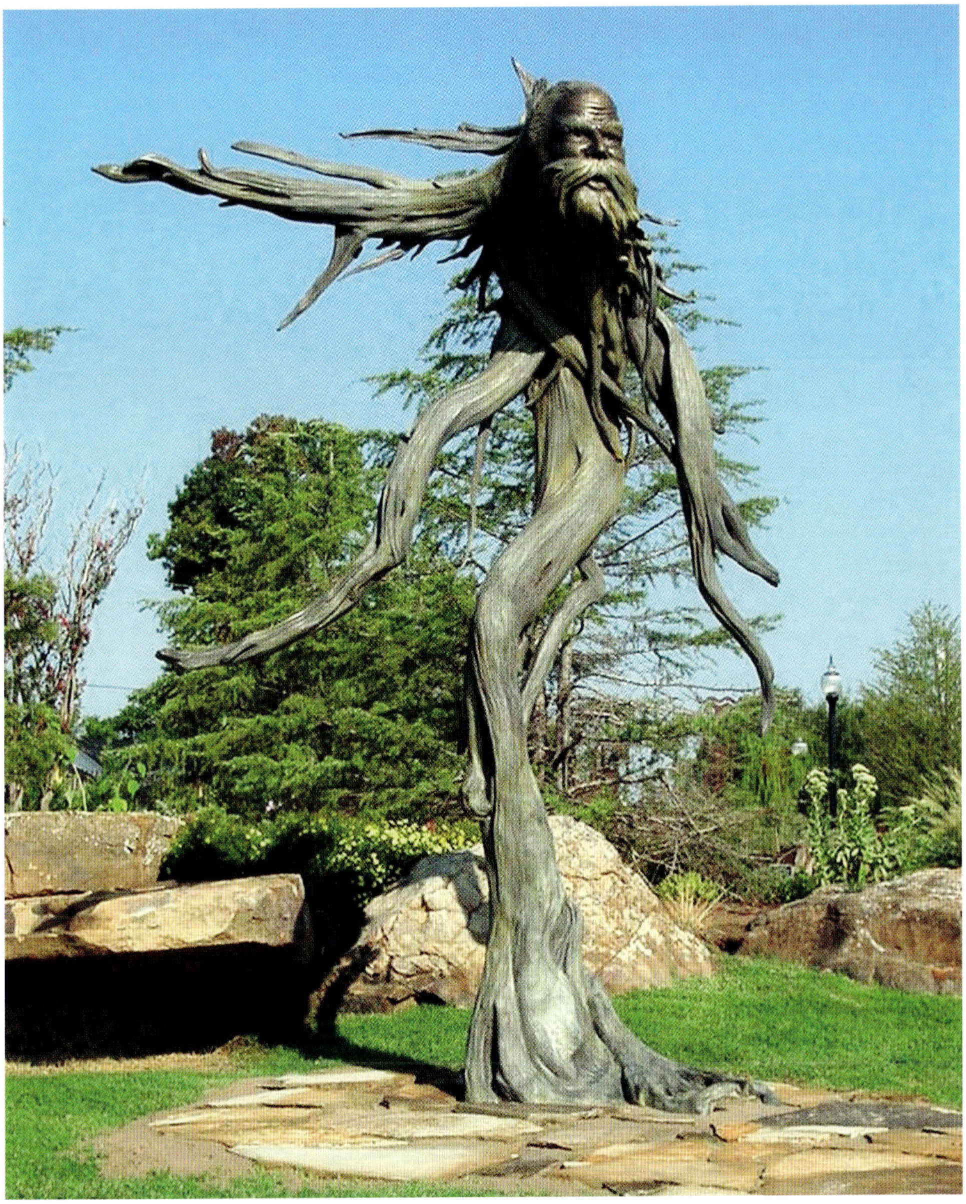

1 *A Matter of Time*, 2009. Cedar, 13' diam. *Photograph by Paull Baliker and Matt Beyer.*

2 *Lion Around*, 2000. Bronze, 52" x 40" x 29". *Photograph by Patrick Clatto.*

3 *The Wind*, 2004. Bronze, 13' x 6' x 6'. *Photograph by Paull Baliker.*

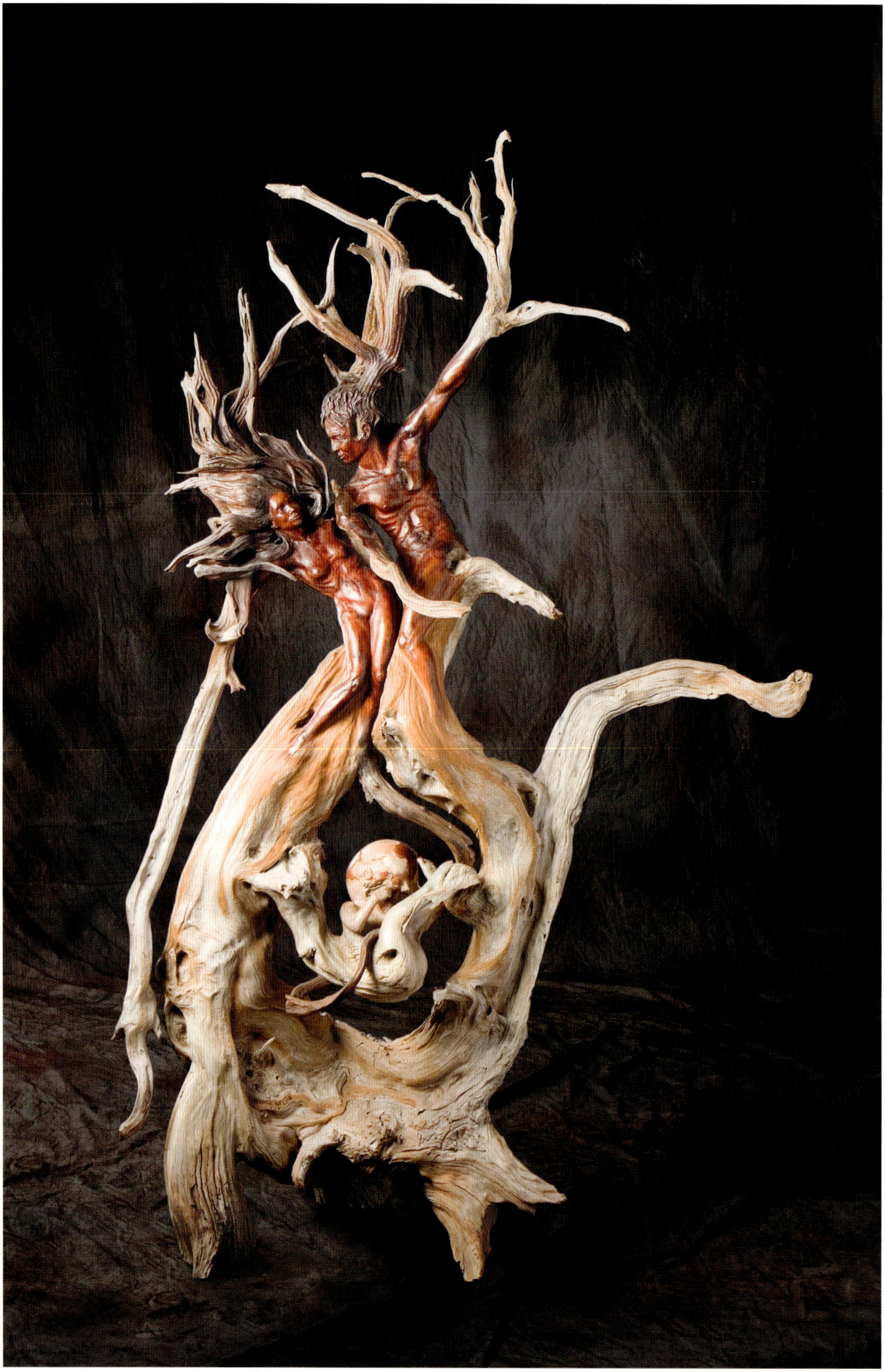

4

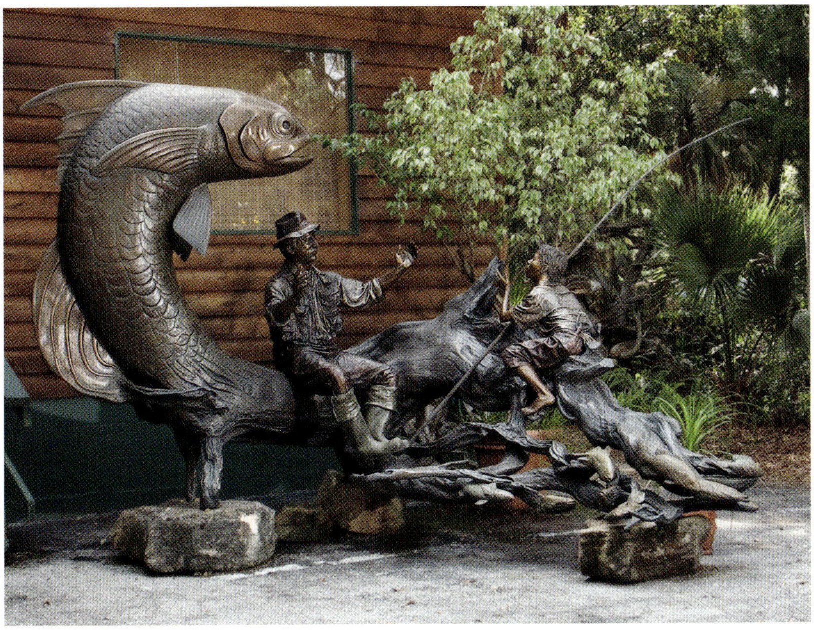

5

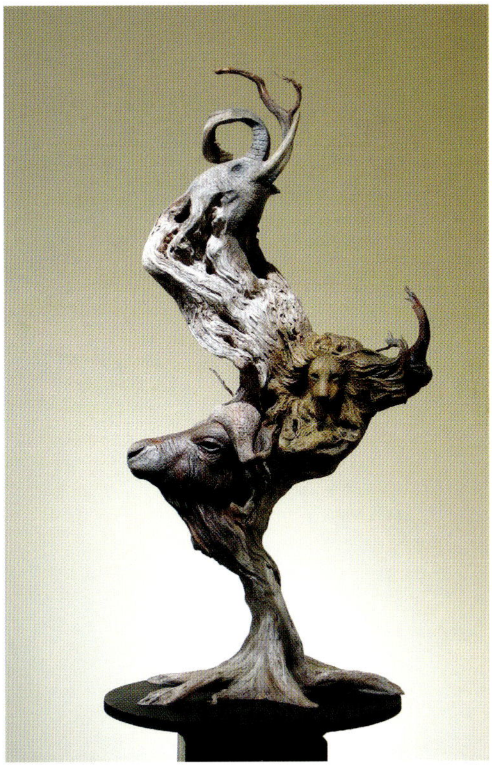

7

6

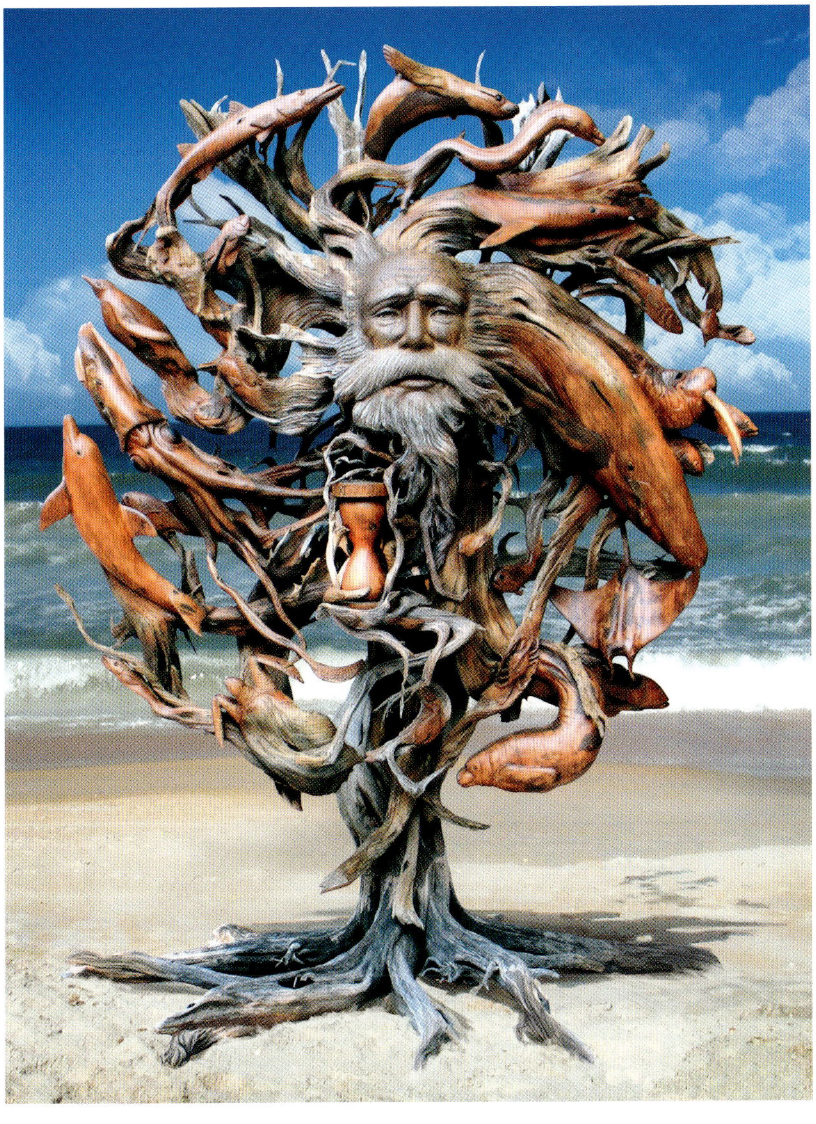

4 *Dance of Life*, 2000. Cedar, 54" x 36" x 24". *Photograph by Patrick Clatto.*

5 *Fish Story,* 1996. Bronze, 13' x 6' x 6'. *Photograph by Patrick Clatto.*

6 *Oceans 11th Hour*, 2009. Cedar, 10' x 8' x 3'. *Photograph by Paull Baliker and Matt Beyer.*

7 *African Dream*, 2006. Cedar, 48" x 22" x 22". *Photograph by Paull Baliker.*

# Chris Bathgate

Baltimore, Maryland, USA
www.chrisbathgate.com

Chris Bathgate is a self-taught machinist sculptor who was born in 1980 in Baltimore, Maryland. He still works and lives in Baltimore and has spent the last decade learning how to build and use a variety of metalworking tools and machinery. He has assembled an elaborate machine shop of repurposed and home made machine tools, along with a multitude of other equipment and inventions in the basement studio of his Baltimore home.

His body of work is a collection of intricately machined metal sculptures that represent the combination of his unique metalworking style with a traditional approach to sculpture. By combining the math and logistics used in performing the complex tasks of modern machine work with a more emotive and aesthetic problem-solving ethic, Bathgate's work shows that it is not creativity alone that drives human imagination, but also the need to solve and overcome problems that lead to inspiration. Be it through the necessity of his process or arbitrary guidelines set by the artist himself, each work becomes a creative response to a series of mathematical and subjective visual parameters. The result is a precise and other worldly art object that exudes a creative logic all its own.

Chris's work has been featured in numerous publications and belongs to private collections across the United States and abroad. In 2007, he was awarded grants from the prestigious Pollock-Krasner Foundation and the Creative Baltimore Grant for his work.

1

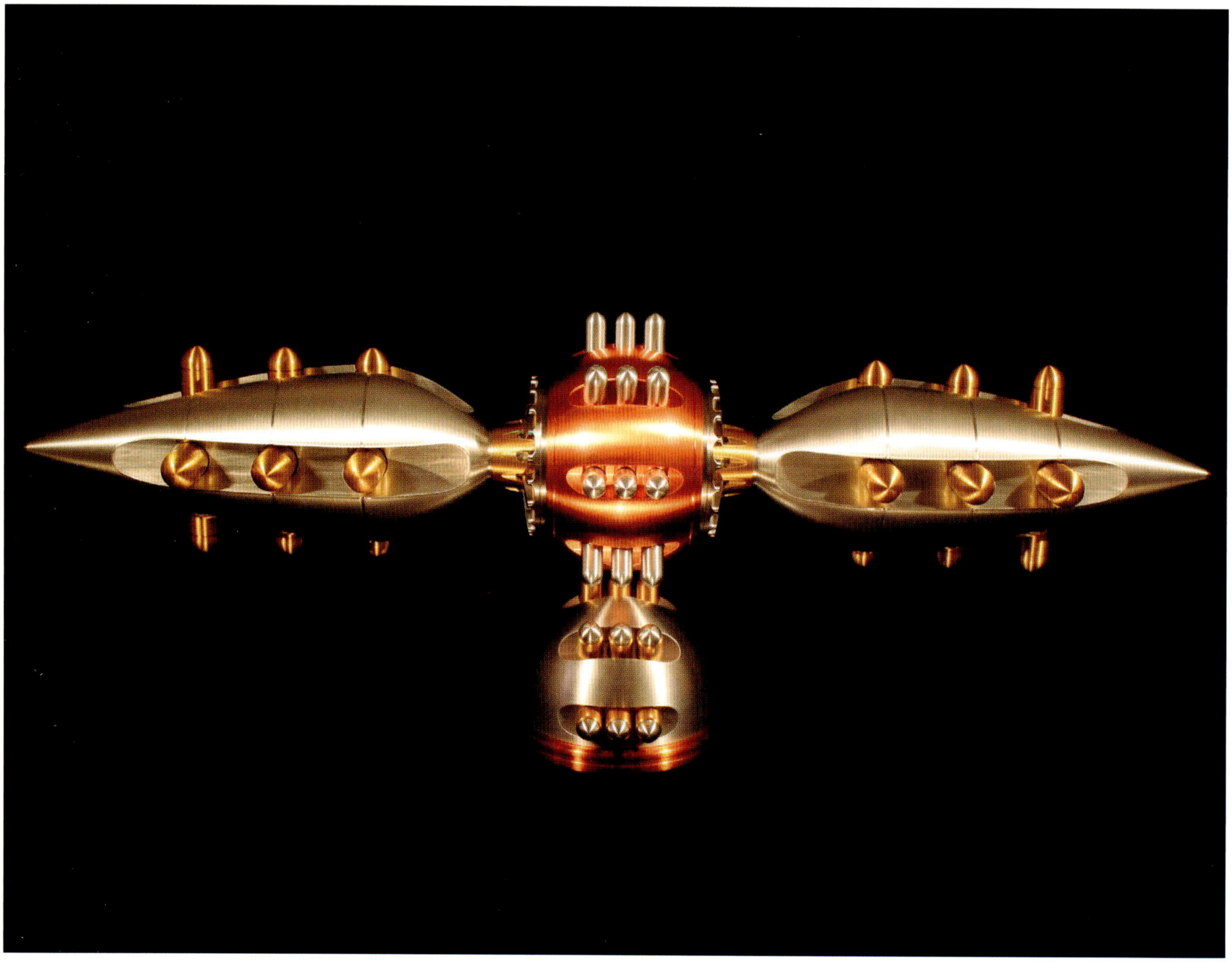

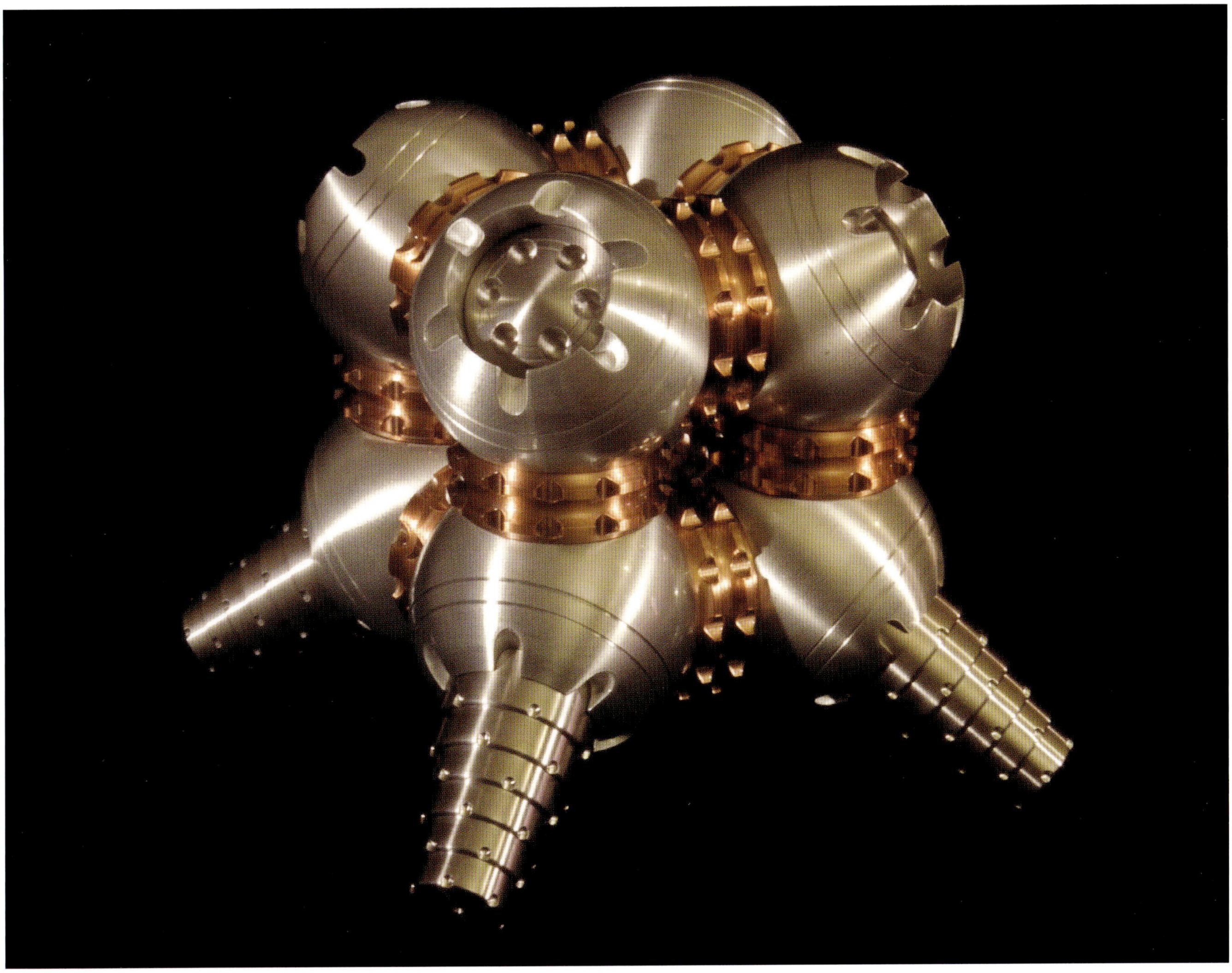

2

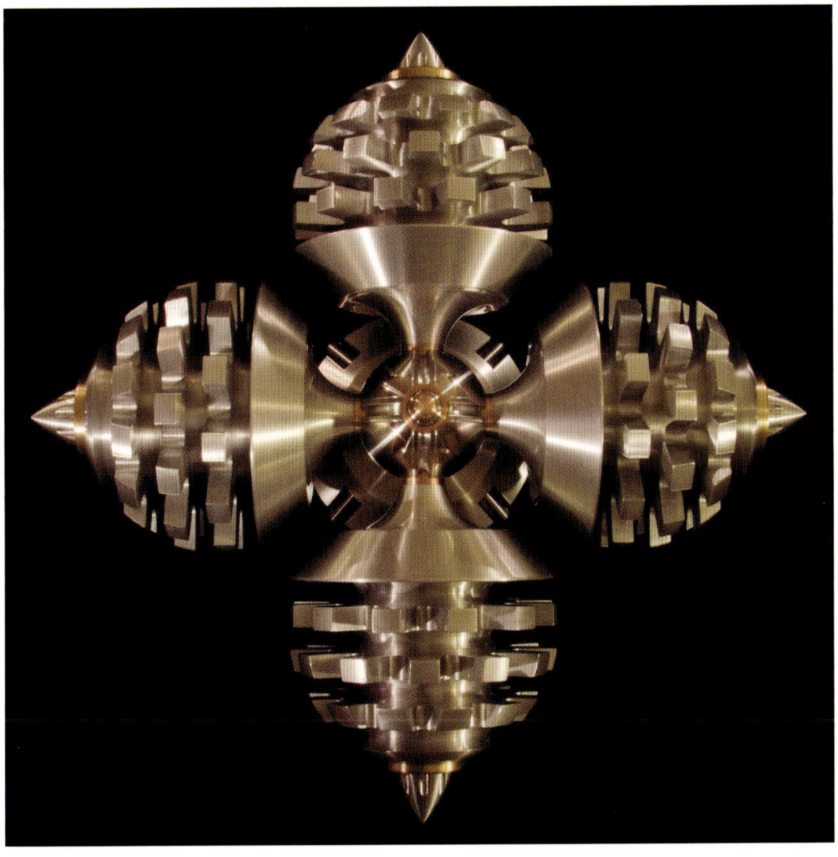

3

1 *BF 589489281*, 2009. Machined aluminum, copper, brass, stainless steel, 7" x 21" x 5". *Photograph by Chris Bathgate.*

2 *SH6333744515622293724.* Machined aluminum, bronze, stainless steel, 7" x 8" x 8". *Photograph by Chris Bathgate.*

3 *ST 7322328355636244 34.* Machined aluminum, brass, bronze, stainless steel, 18" x 18" x 7". *Photograph by Chris Bathgate.*

4

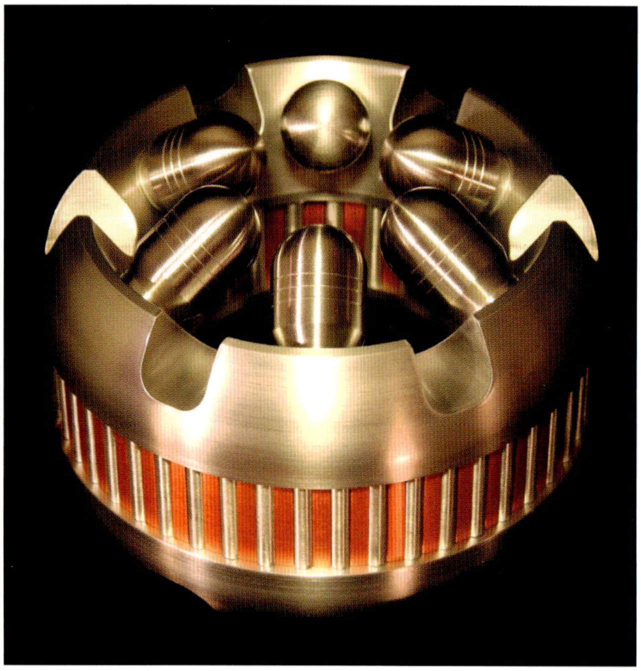

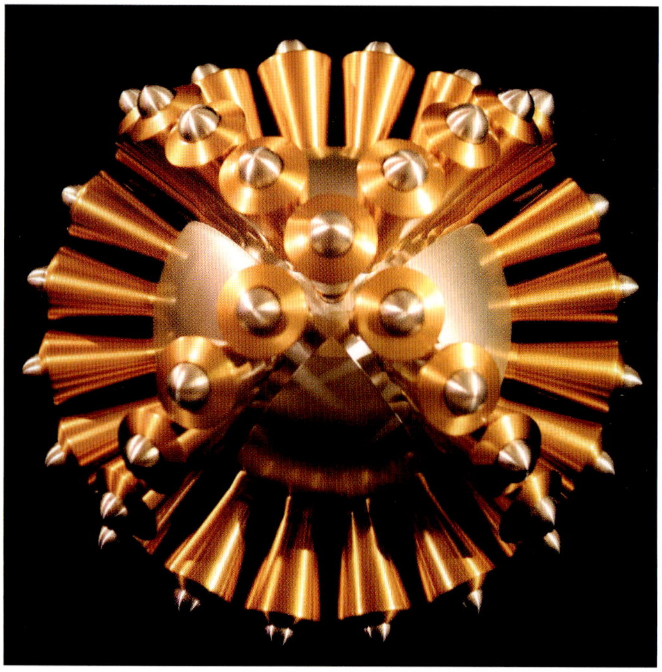

5

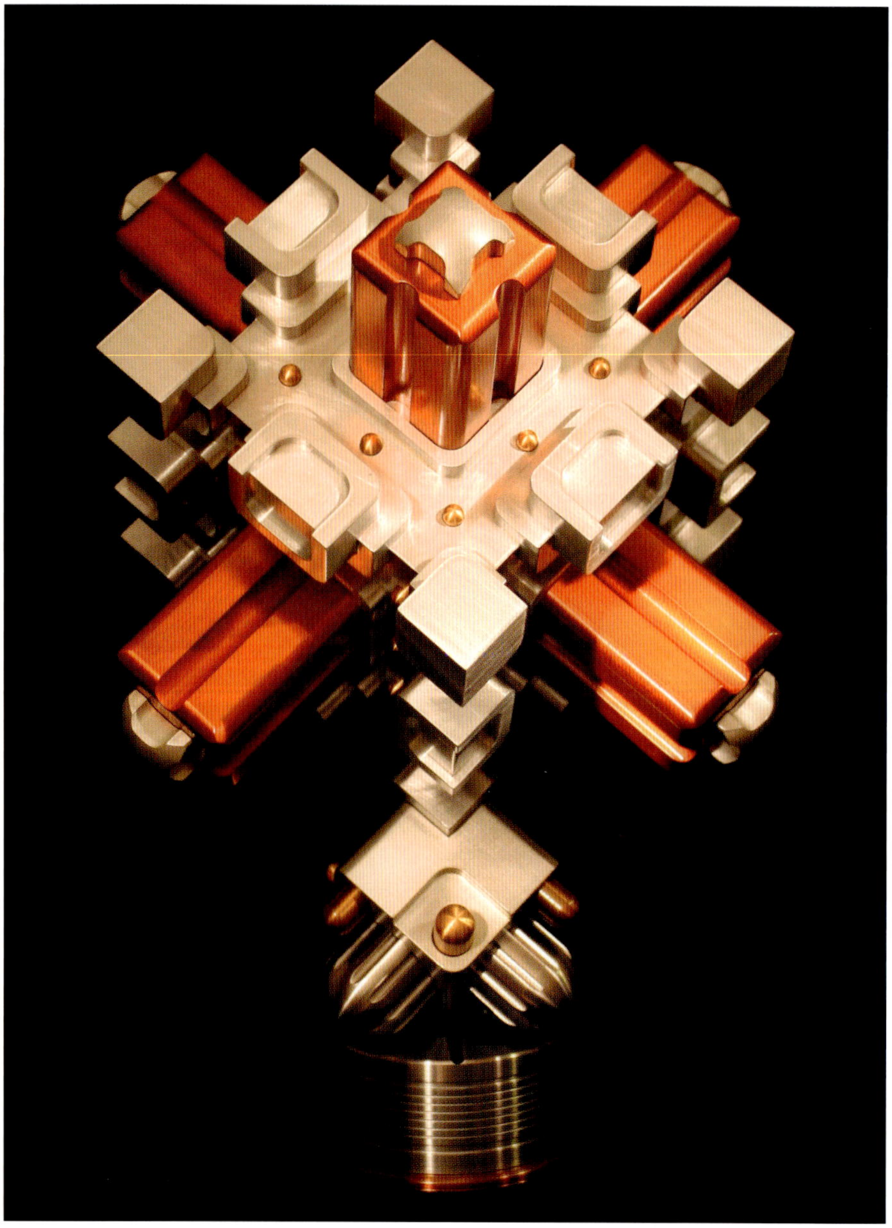

6

4 *RN 753362224531143*, 2010. Machined aluminum, stainless steel, 4.5" x 6" x 6". *Photograph by Chris Bathgate.*

5 *BC 443621141281783*, 2009. Machined aluminum, copper, brass, stainless steel, 13" x 9" x 9". *Photograph by Chris Bathgate.*

6 *Mn783485521265683*, 2009. Machined aluminum, brass, 5" x 5" x 5". *Photograph by Chris Bathgate.*

7 *RY555441253*, 2008. Machined aluminum, steel, brass, copper, 13" x 8" x 8". *Photograph by Chris Bathgate.*

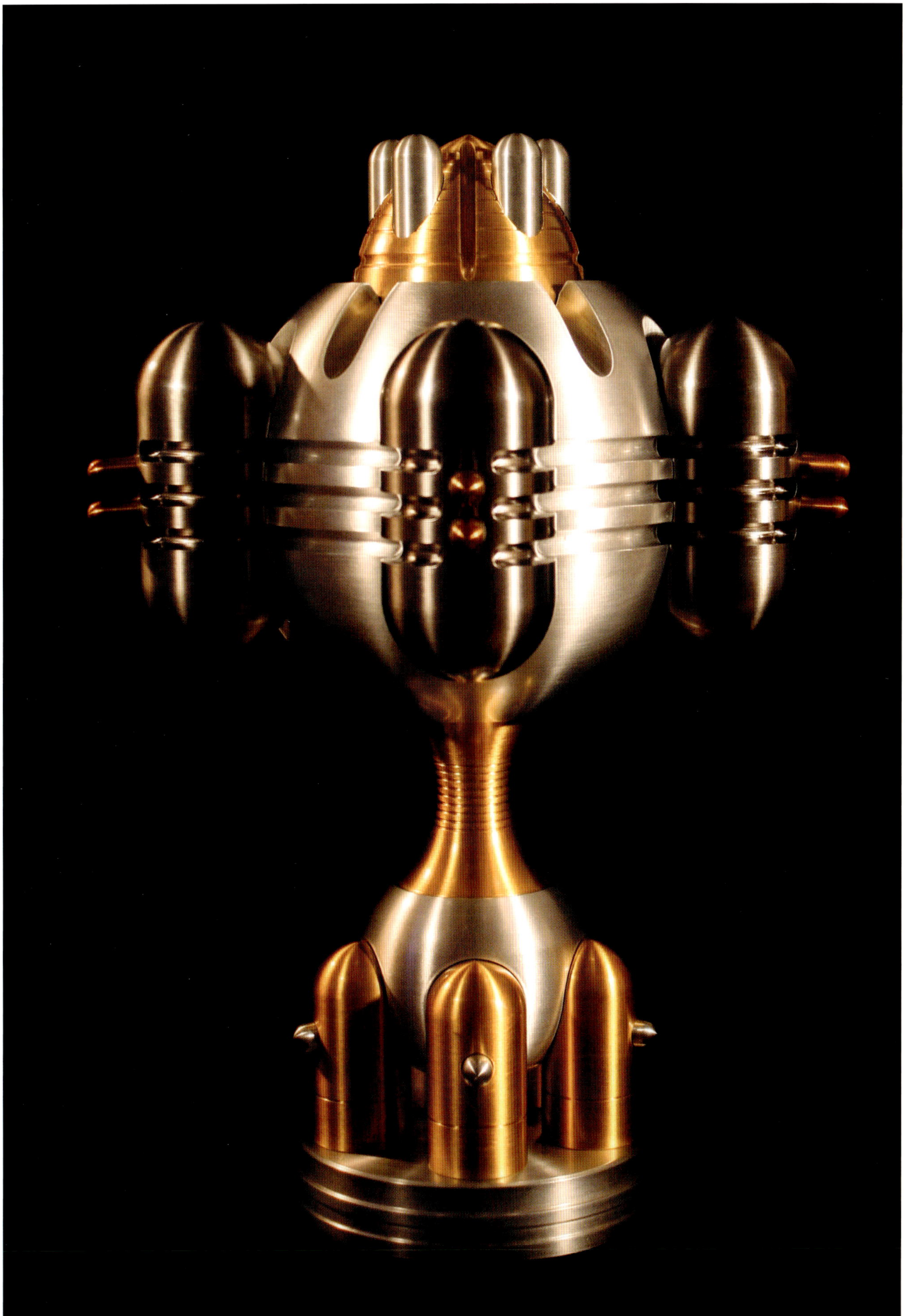

7

# Marie Bergstedt

San Francisco, California, USA
www.mariebergstedtartist.com

*Born in rural Michigan, I was the first in my family to attain a high school degree. After graduating from college, I first became a teacher, briefly an artist, and for more than 25 years, a fund development manager. In spite of my practical financial needs, the desire to become a full-time artist endured. In the 1970s and 1980s, I developed a body of hand-colored photographs. These large-scale images were selected for more than 30 solo and group juried exhibitions. However, it was not until 2006 that I was able to enter a full-time art profession.*

*Memories from my childhood establish a foundation for my current artwork. I build sculptures using deconstructed, torn, and degenerating antique pieces combined with new fiber, wire, and button work. The old and new unite to reconstruct and interpret the past in a contemporary art form. My pieces often convey a visual/mental dissonance that has been a fundamental element of my life experience. I believe my artwork is most successful when this discord evokes viewers to revisit their own history and prevailing impressions.*

*Recent sculptural work has been selected for exhibitions across the United States, receiving awards in national and international competitions. In addition to inclusion in news articles and exhibition catalogues, the sculptures have been selected for three book publications and a Collector's Edition web-book since 2010.*

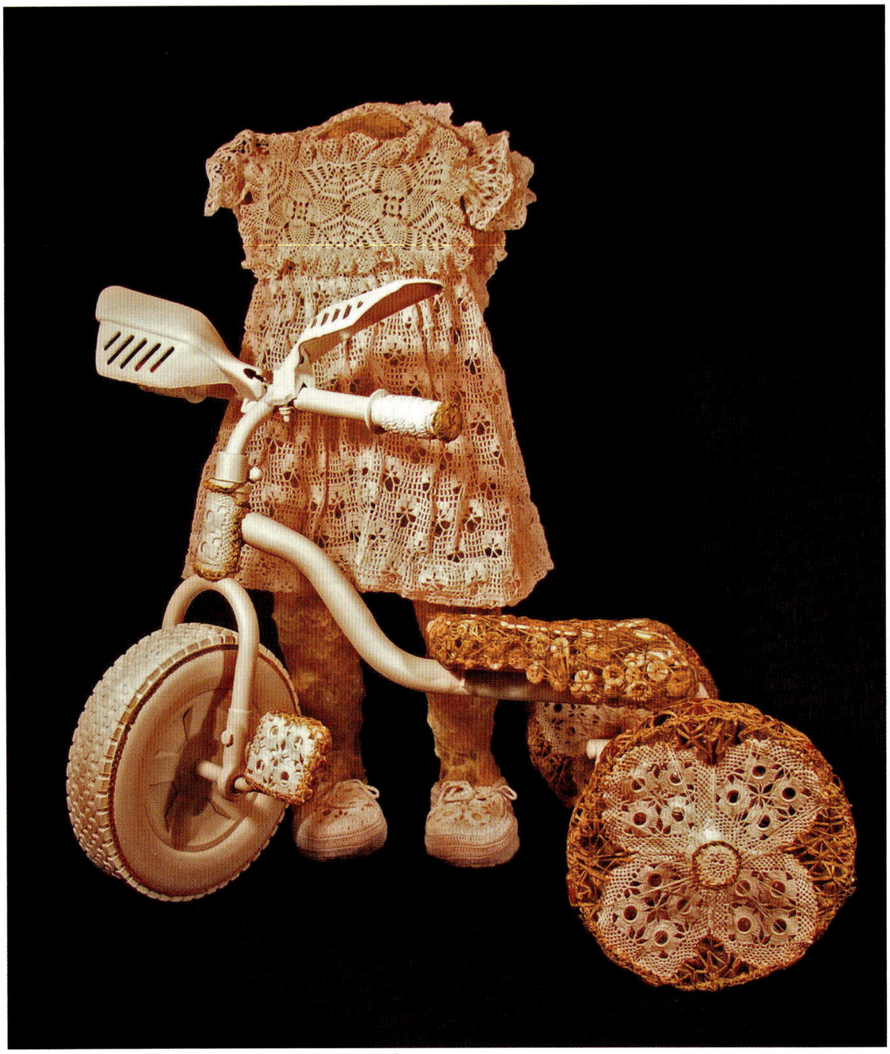

1

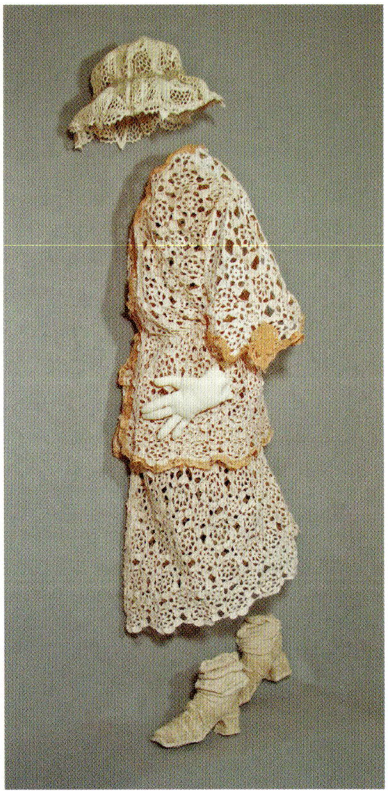

2

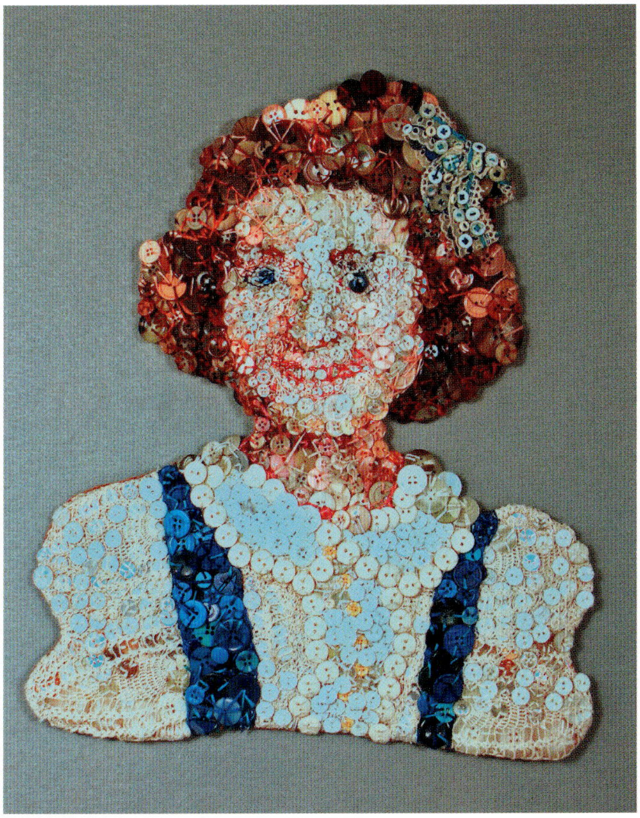

3

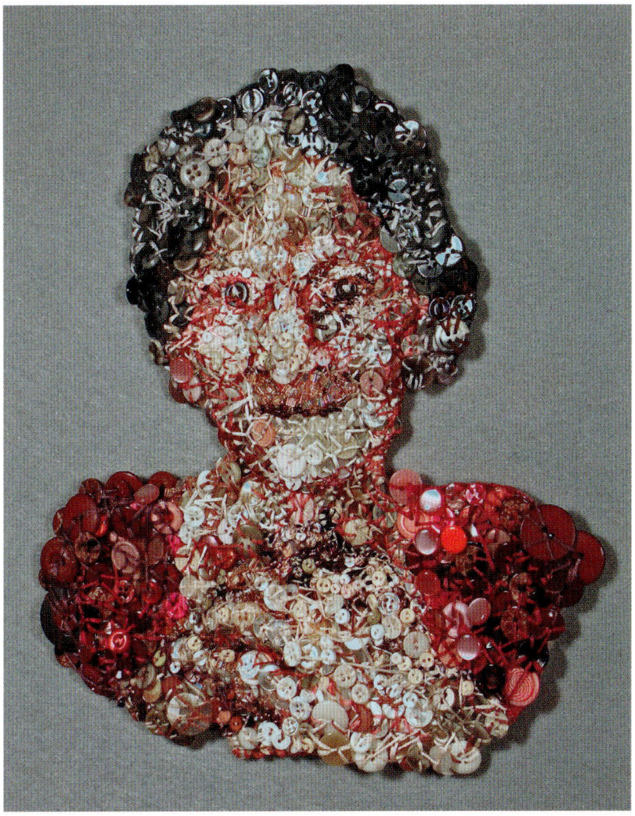

4

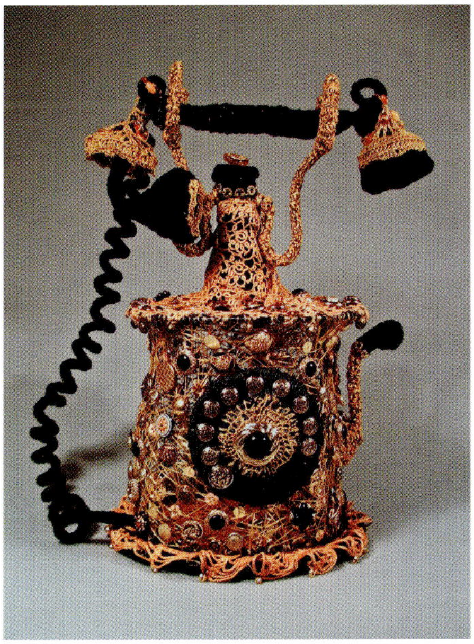

5

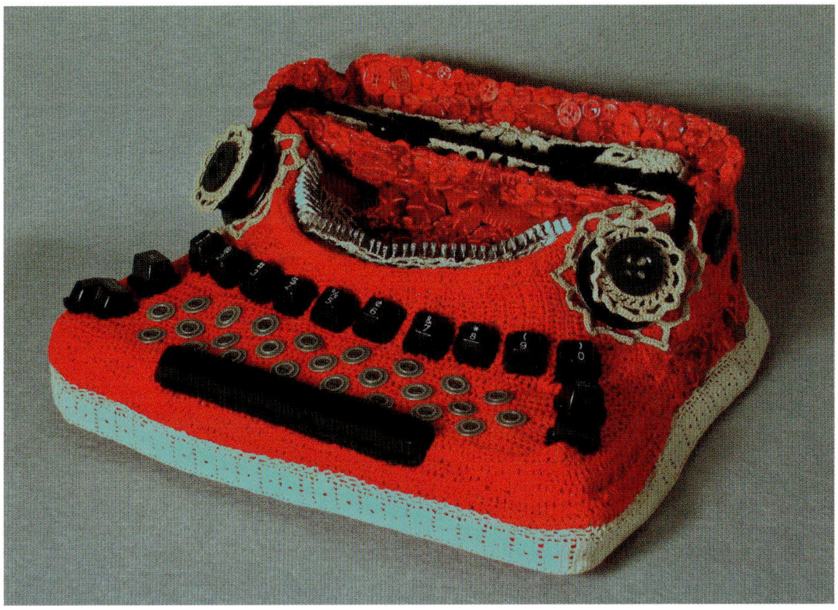

6

1 *Triker*, 2009. Mixed media, 32" x 28" x 28". *Photograph by Marie Bergstedt.*

2 *Getting On*, 2009. Mixed media, 59" x 24" x 15". *Photograph by Marie Bergstedt.*

3 *Self Portrait on the Happiest Christmas*, 2011. Mixed media, 16" x 14" x 1". *Photograph by Marie Bergstedt.*

4 *Clara,* 2010. Mixed media, 12" x 11" x 75". *Photograph by Marie Bergstedt.*

5 *French Connection*, 2010. Mixed media, 17" x 14" x 6.5". *Photograph by Marie Bergstedt.*

6 *The Happiest Christmas Typewriter,* 2011. Mixed media, 6" x 13.5" x 12". *Photograph by Marie Bergstedt.*

# Sarah Biondo

Kansas City, Missouri, USA
www.sarah-biondo.artistwebsites.com

Professionally trained as a sculptor at the Kansas City Art Institute during the 1960's, Sarah has become a full spectrum artist extending her expression to include various two-dimensional media. From realism to abstract, her sculpture is inspired by the human figure and the human condition. Her paintings include watercolor, oil, and mixed media, with imagery that includes figurative, landscape, floral and abstract color field. Sarah has won both international and national awards and was one of fifty international Artists to have her work shipped to Italy courtesy of the Cultural Ministry of the City of Piacenza for an International Women's Exhibit.

The second child in a family of six children, Sarah was raised in Louisiana by Italian-American parents. Her father was a furniture maker and her mother worked with her father while remaining a devoted homemaker. Sarah paid her own way to college and graduate school. Professionally, she was hired at two different colleges to establish a three-dimensional area of study where none previously existed. Both positions included initiating a program, developing curriculum, purchasing requisitions, inventory and equipment maintenance, and studio logistics for sculpture, ceramics, and three-dimensional design. Sarah has accomplished these things while raising a son as a single parent. She is very proud of her son, Damian, who is now an Intellectual Property Attorney in Philadelphia.

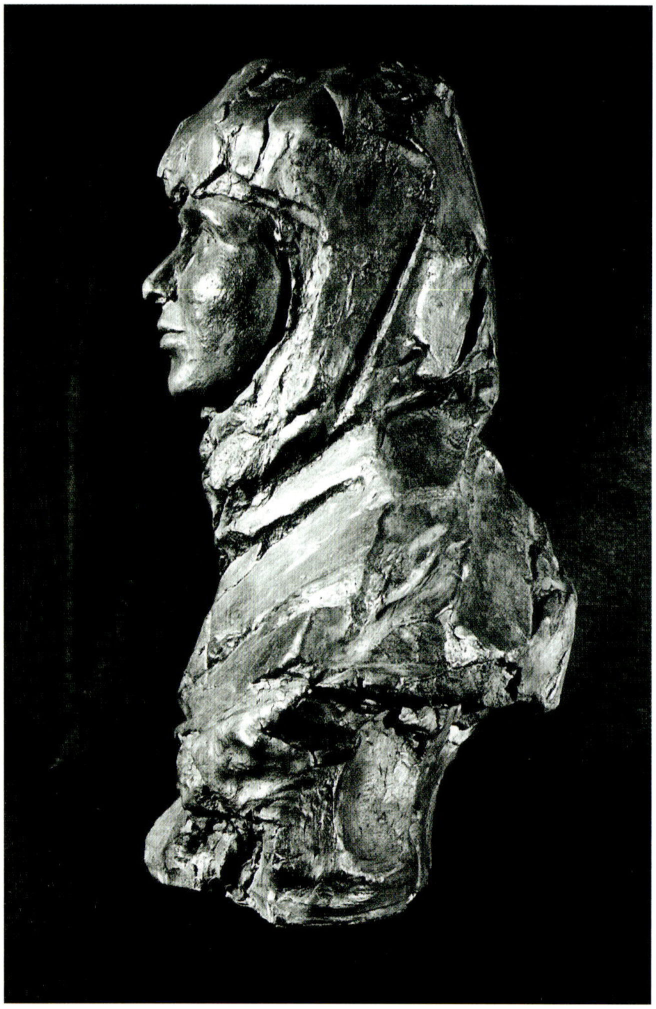

1

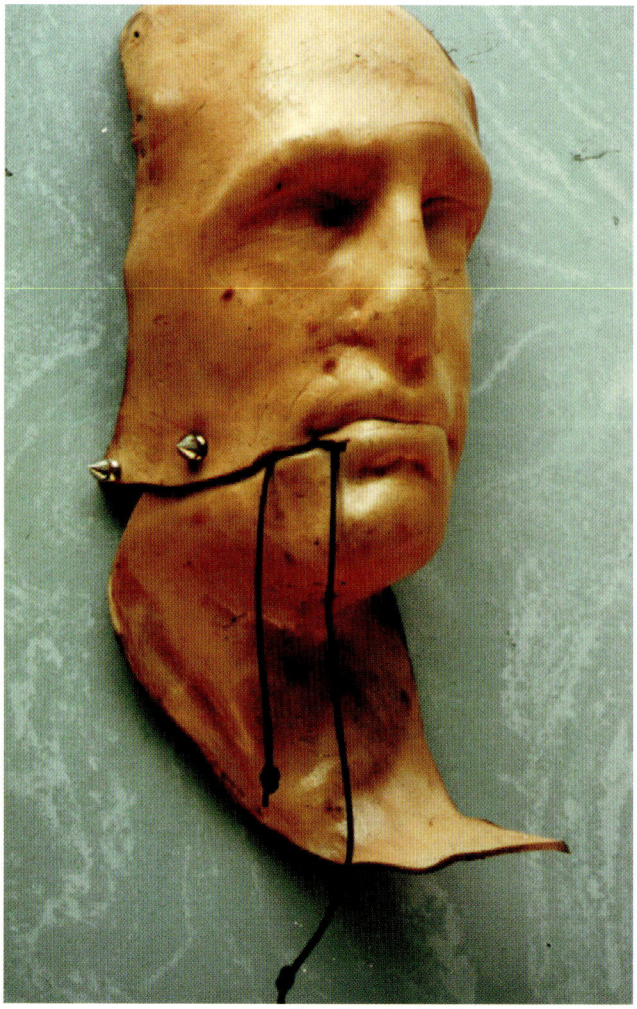

2

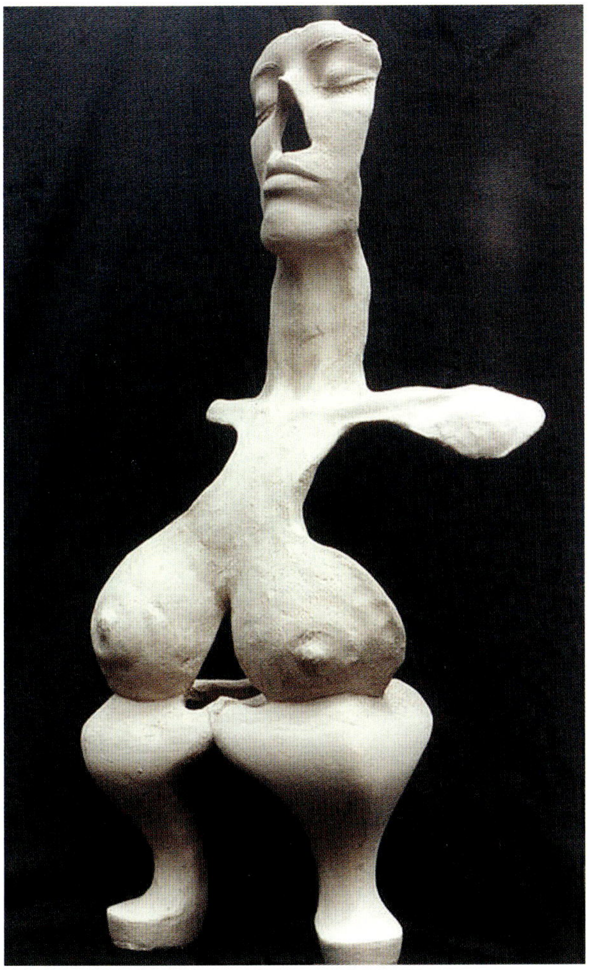

3

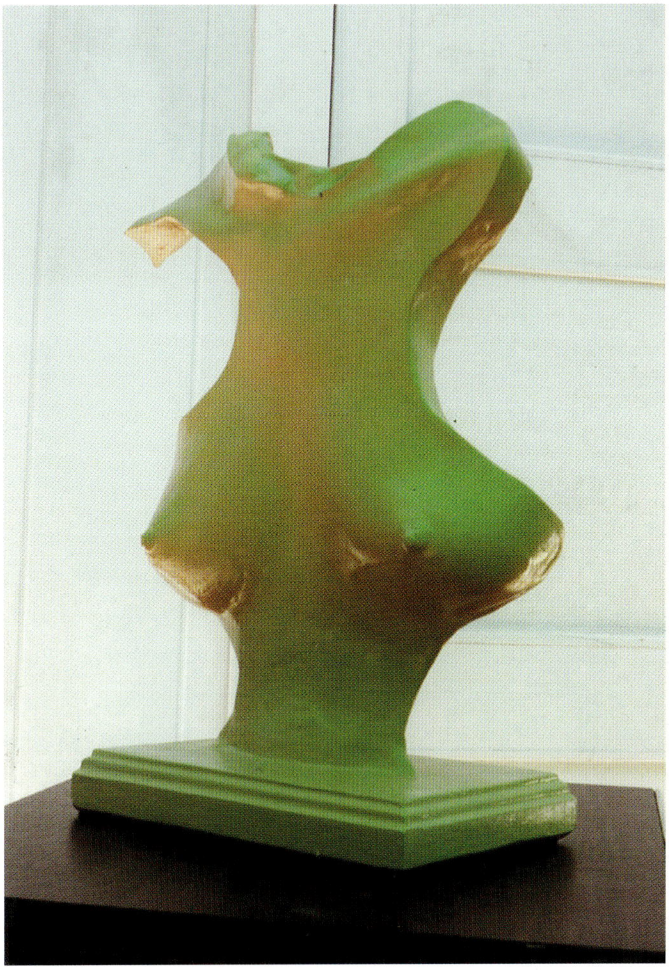

4

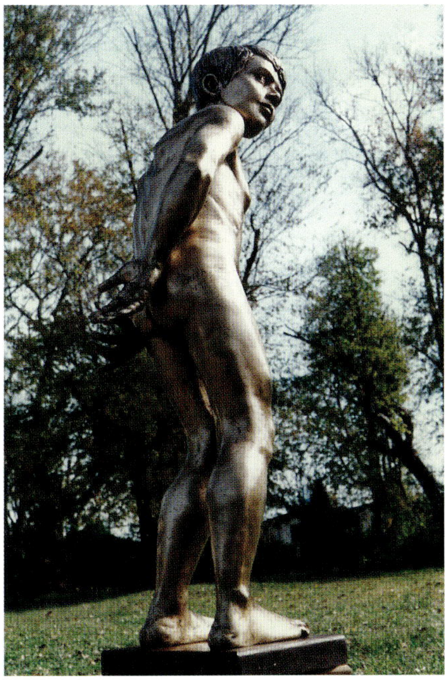

5

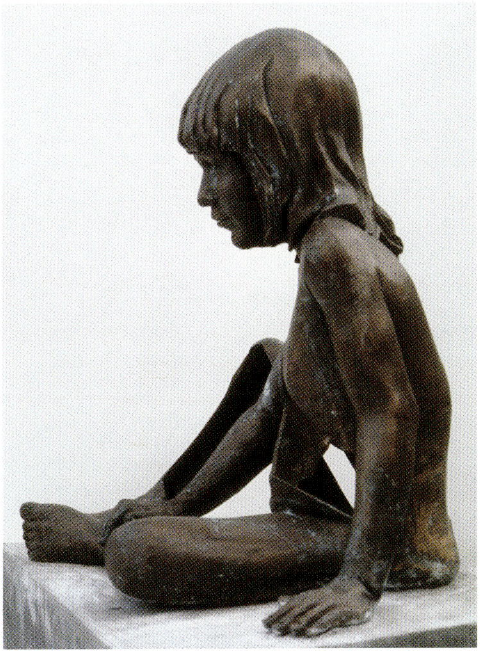

6

1 *Sharrinni*, 1969. Ceramic, 28" x 12" x 11". *Photograph by Sarah Biondo.*

2 *Man's Inhumanity,* 2001. Leather, 12" x 16" x 5". *Photograph by Sarah Biondo.*

3 *Memories of Queen Ann*, 1998. Ceramic, 19" x 15" x 8". *Photograph by Sarah Biondo.*

4 *Spirit of Youth*, 1993. Ceramic, 18" x 14" x 8". *Photograph by Sarah Biondo.*

5 *First Expectations,* 1986. Cast bronze, 42" x 26" x 25". *Photograph by Sarah Biondo.*

6 *Damian,* 1972. Life size bronze casting, 20" x 18" x 13". *Photograph by Larry Kohn.*

# Nancy L. Briggs

Des Moines, Iowa, USA
www.nancybriggspottery.com

*I first became an artist because I loved the clay. I loved throwing on the wheel, striving for control, and perfecting a form. Like music, it has rhythm, structure, and endless variation, and takes practice, practice, practice.*

*With the figure study, I look into human frailties and strengths. How do we react when facing a surprise or uncertainty? What are our emotions beneath the polite surface?*

*I have been on the faculty of the Des Moines Art Center since 1986 and currently teach ceramics to adults and children. I produce Raku fired pottery, which I market through art fairs and galleries in the Midwest. I also do life drawing in charcoal, and draw with pastels. I also garden, I guess I just like dirt!*

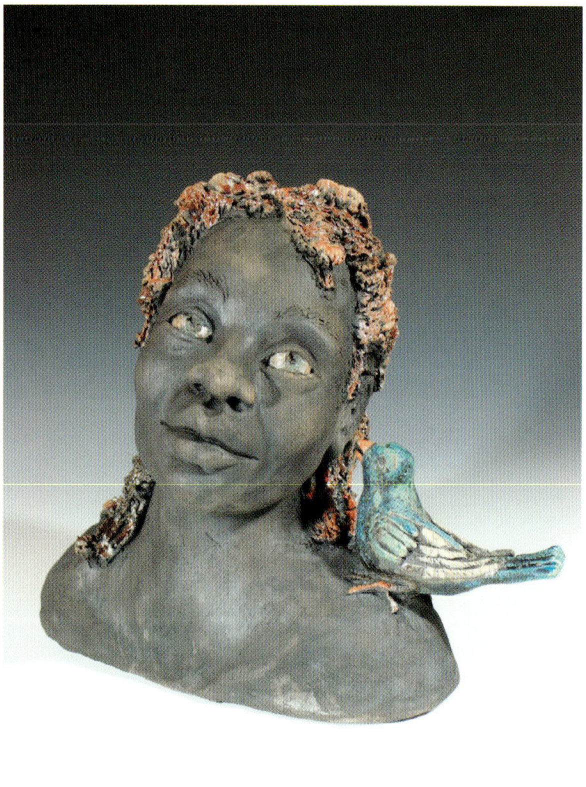

1

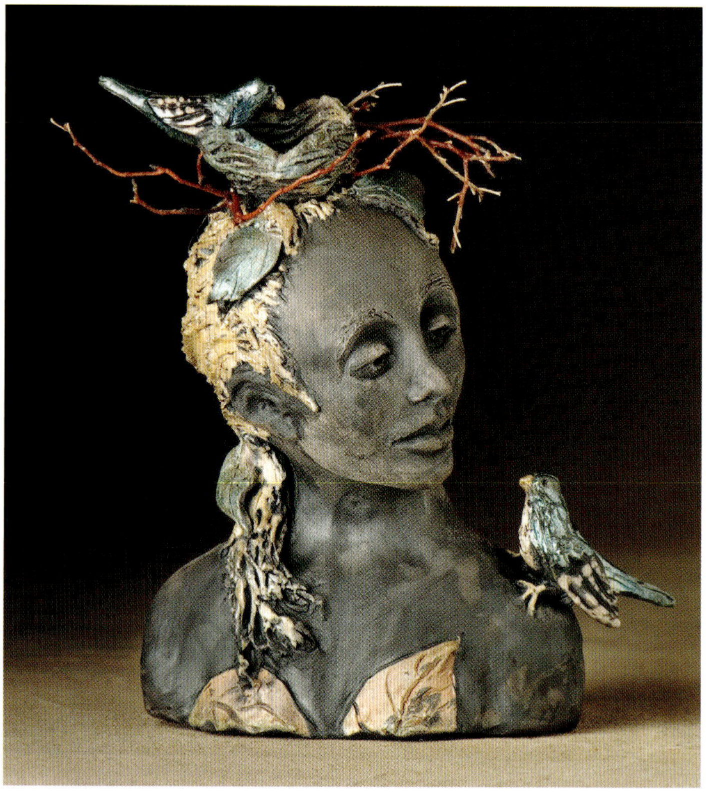

2

1 *Rachel's Secret,* 2010. Raku fired clay, 11" x 11" x 8". *Photo by artist.*

2 *Nesting Instinct,* 2010. Raku fired clay, 8" x 8 x 5". *Photo by Bill Nellans.*

3 *Who Would Not Change a Raven for a Dove,* 2010. Stoneware clay, 13" x 18" x 9". *Photo by artist.*

4 *Finding Her Voice,* 2009. Stoneware clay, 14" x 15 x 9". *Photo by artist.*

5 *Last Nuba of Kau,* 2009. Stoneware clay, 21" x 18 x 12". *Photo by artist.*

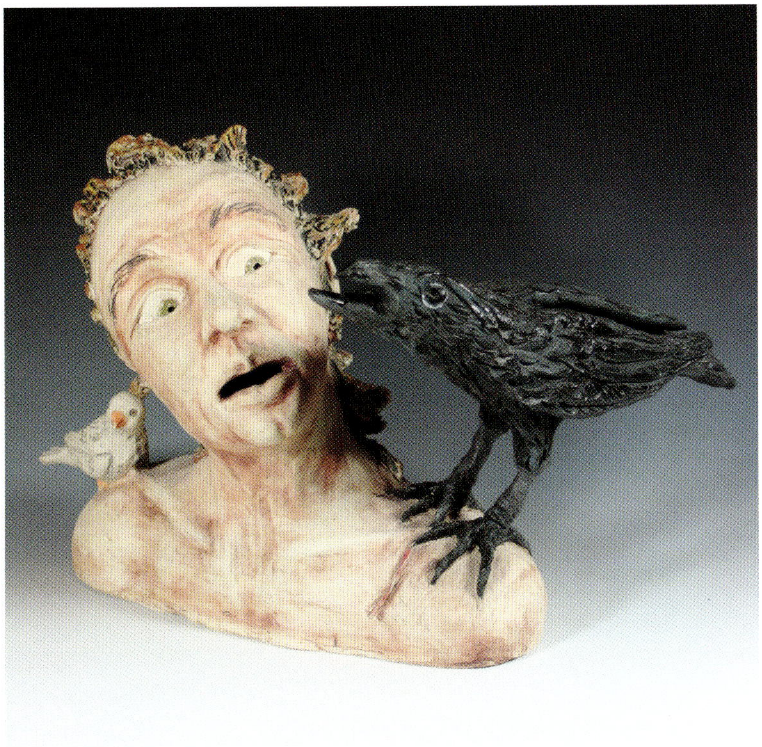

3

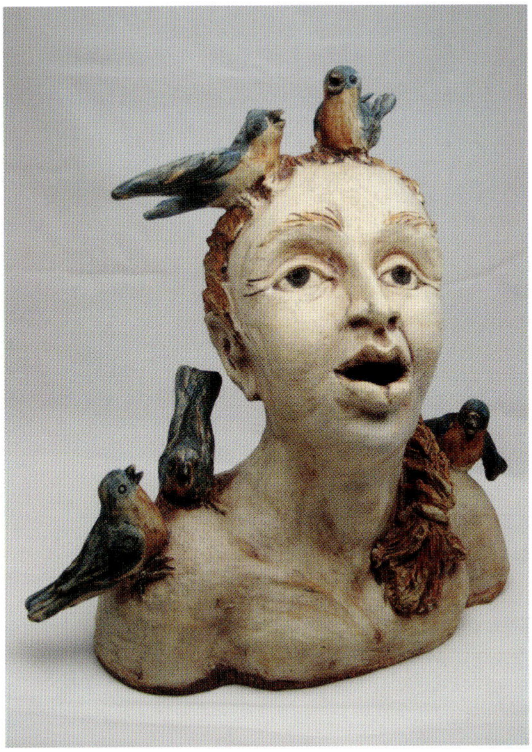

4

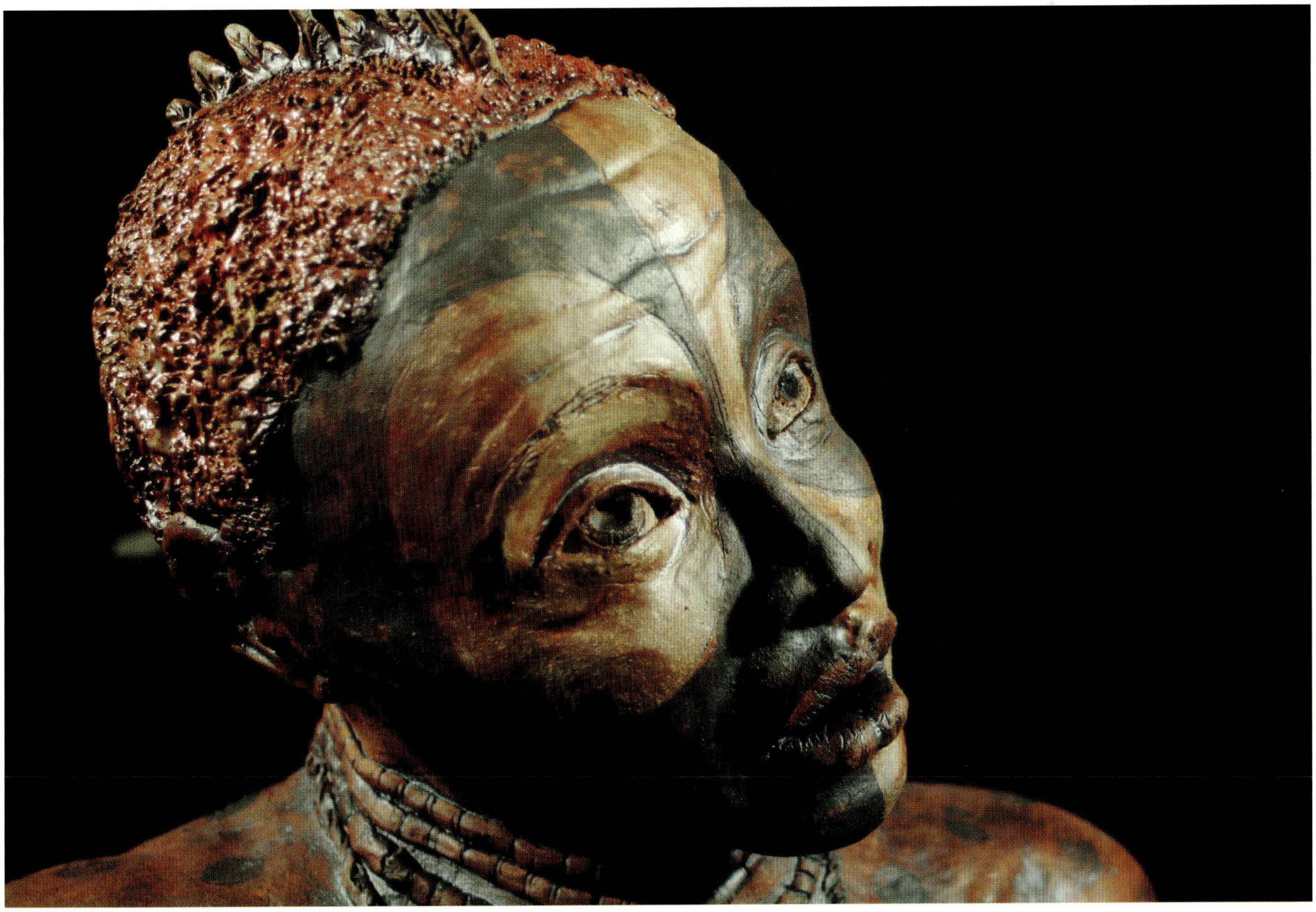

5

# Curt Brill

Tucson, Arizona, USA
www.curtbrill.com

*I am a sculptor whose work, for the past 35 years, has focused on the figure and been primarily cast in bronze. I am constantly reassessing my relationship with the figure in terms of both style and materials. The figure has remained central to my work and even though the understanding of the underlying realism holds the work together, the imagery has evolved. The intent of the work has shifted from just portraying the physicality of being Human to a more gestural, looser expression of what the Human experience is. Along with this, is the commitment to the creative process, so that the marks and the forms created also portray to the viewer the speed and aliveness with which I view each figure that I create. Rather than hide the energy that exists in each figure, the work strives to let this energy flow to and from the work. Lately many of the new pieces have been created in wood and fiber.*

*My work is housed in many private and public collections including Grounds for Sculpture, Mint Museum, Tucson Museum of Art, Skokie Sculpture Park.*

1

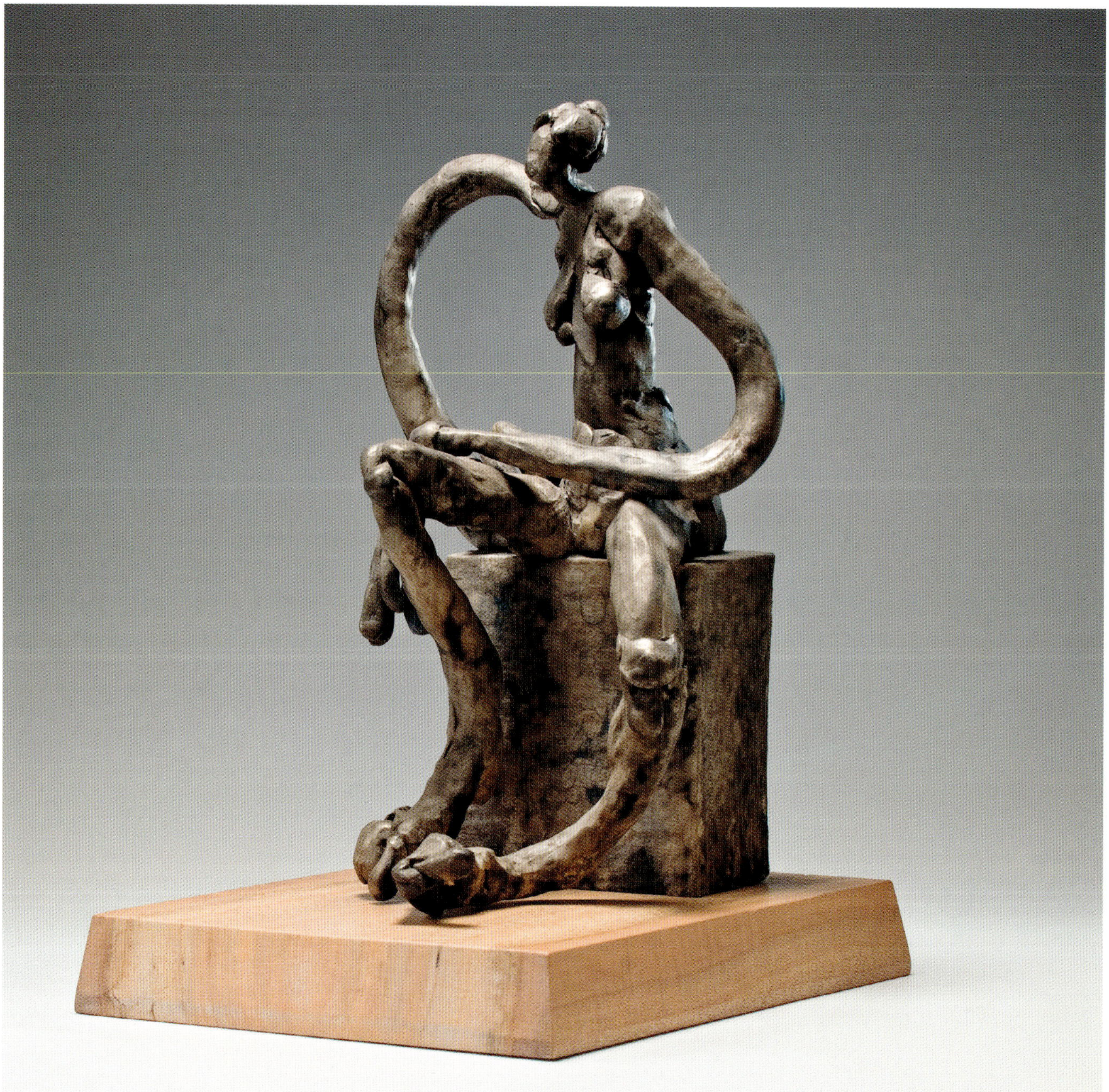

3

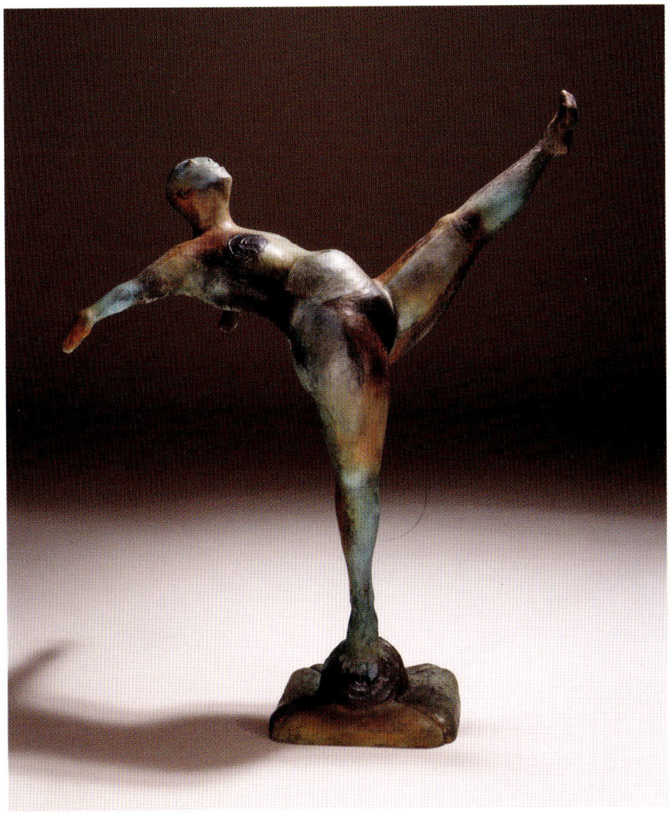

1 *Study 186*, 2011. Bronze, wood, 24" x 12" x 12". *Photograph by John Sartin.*

2 *Yoko,* 1991. Bronze, 64" h. x 54"w. x 32" d. *Photograph by Don Winston.*

3 *Amy,* 2001. Bronze, 48" x 70" x 84". *Photograph by Keith Schreiber.*

2

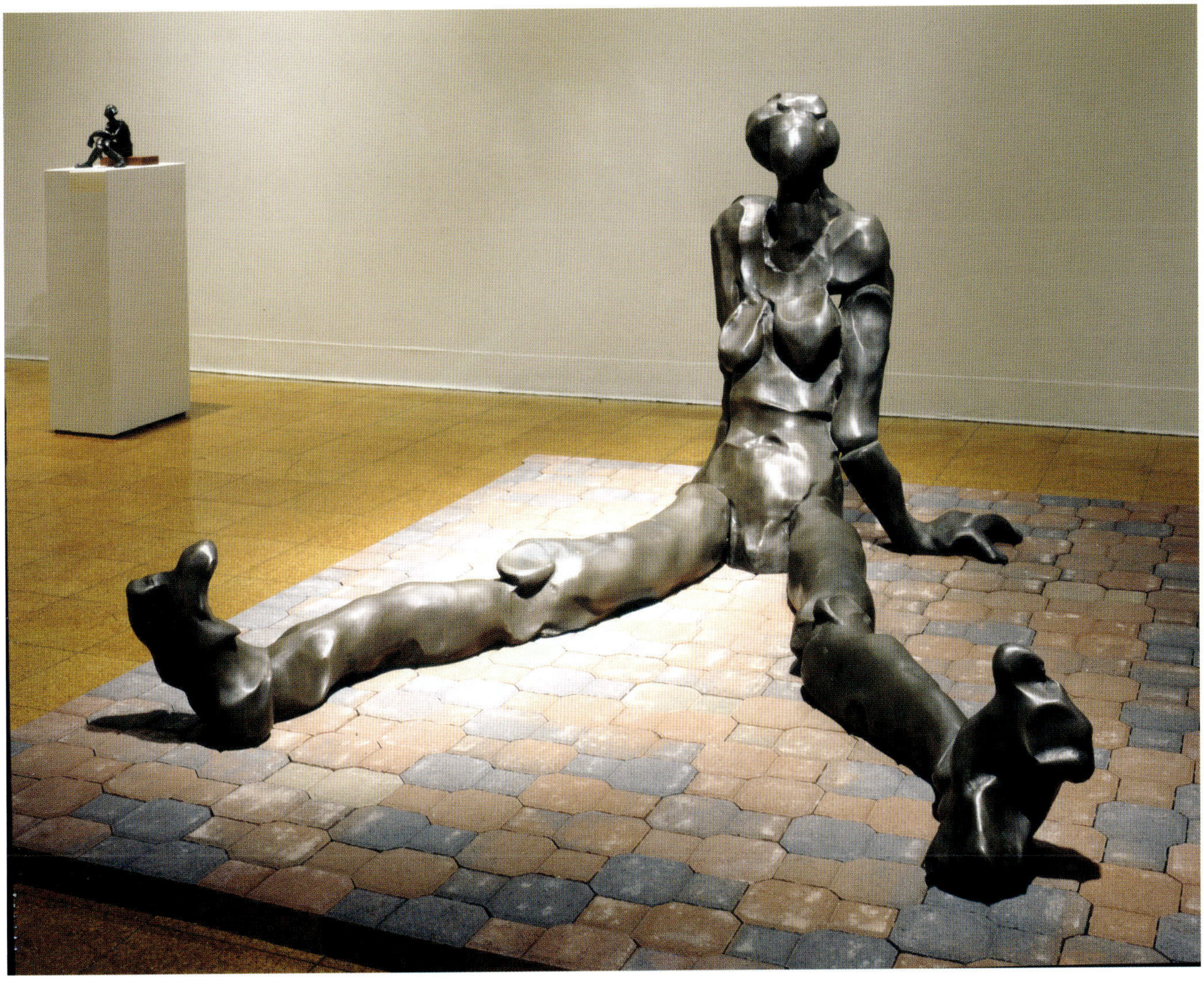

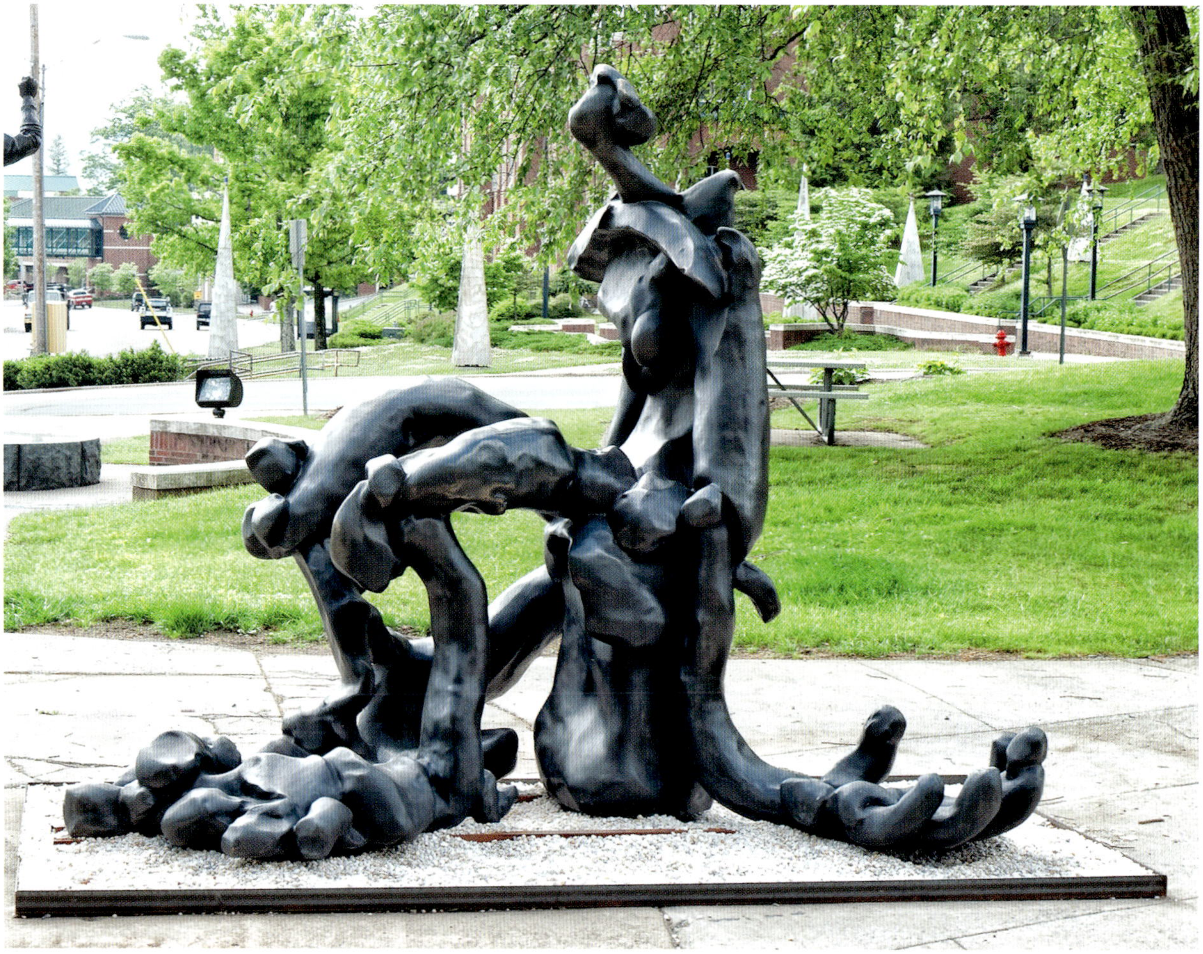

4

5

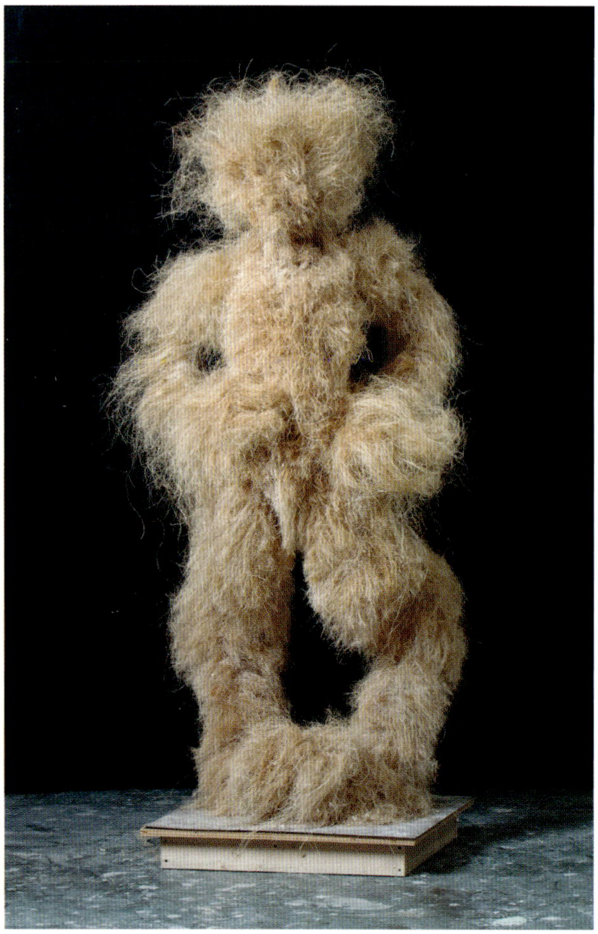

4 *Seated Diana,* 2009. Bronze, 96" x 72" x 112". *Photograph by Troy Tuttle.*

5 *Faiba Niozo,* 2011. Sisal fiber, 82" x 36" x 36". *Photograph by John Sartin.*

6 *Diana*, 2011. Bronze, 26" x 15" x 10". *Photograph by John Sartin.*

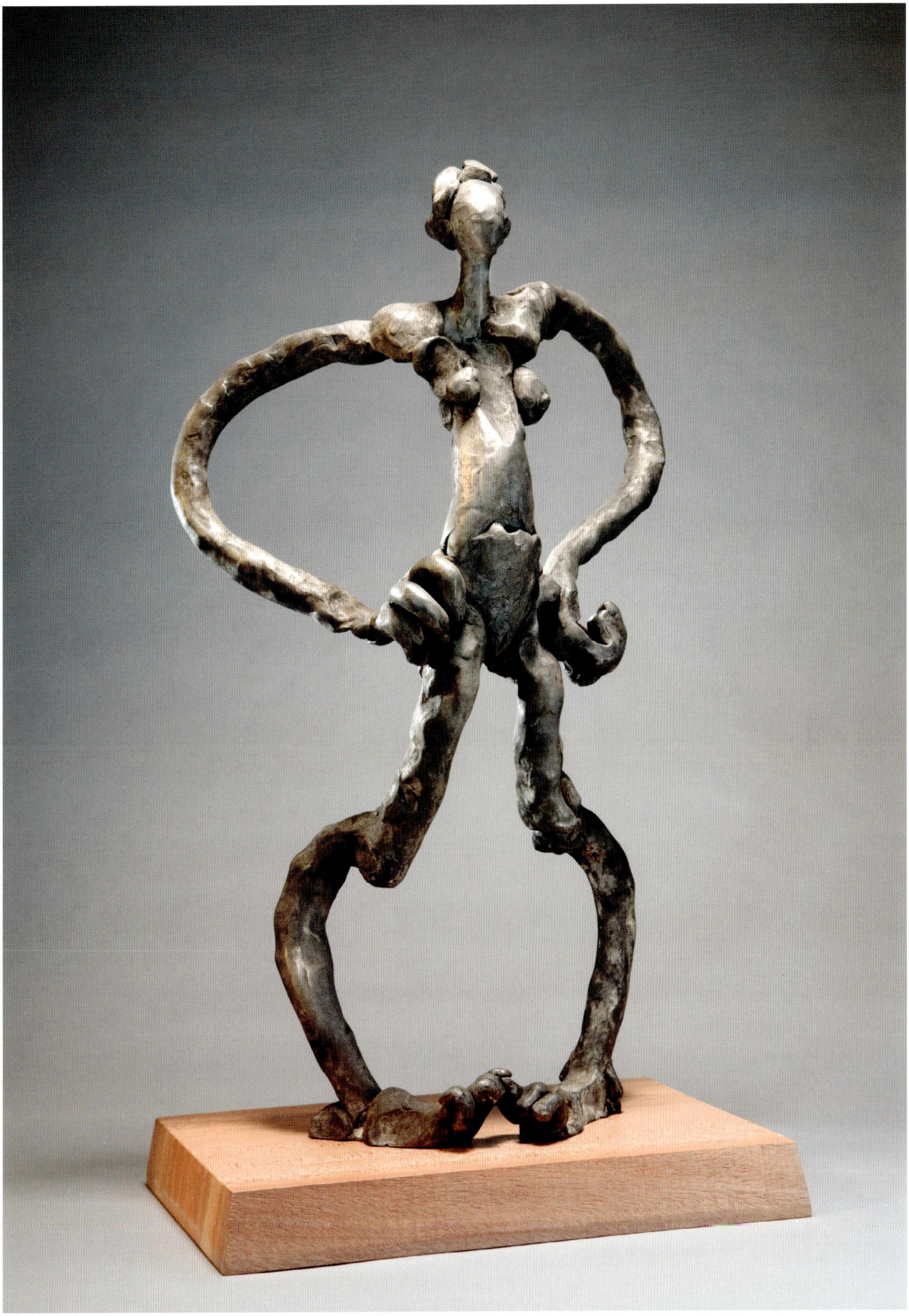

6

# MJ Bronz
# Jenny Authement
# Michael w. Howes

Louisiana, USA
www.mjbronz.com

MJ Bronz is the collaborative team of sculptors Michael w. Howes and Jenny Authement. Howes holds the MFA from the University of Alabama and is a retired Professor of Art at Nicholls State University in Thibodaux, Louisiana. He exhibits with the Ward-Nasse Gallery in New York City and the Baton Rouge Gallery in Baton Rouge, Louisiana. Authement holds the MFA from the University of Georgia and is the recipient of a Louisiana Division of the Arts Fellowship for 2003. Authement is an Art Instructor at Fletcher Technical Community College. She has exhibited throughout the southeastern U.S., in New York City at the Viridian Gallery, and at the Palazzo Vagnotti in Cortona, Italy. She is a member of the Baton Rouge Gallery. MJ Bronz created the "Salt Mine Rescue Memorial" in St. Mary Parish, Louisiana, in 1998. Internationally, MJ Bronz exhibited in the 2003 and 2005 "Biennale Internazionale Dell'Arte Contemporanea" in Florence, Italy. They were awarded the Grand Prize in the "Online Global Artoteque Art Now 2005" in London, England and are published in the *Famous 100 Contemporary Artists* book. They exhibited in the "Essence of Asia: Eastern Influence in Western Art" and the Broadway Gallery in New York.

Their installations explore links between the natural and spiritual worlds using a variety of materials, sound, and light.

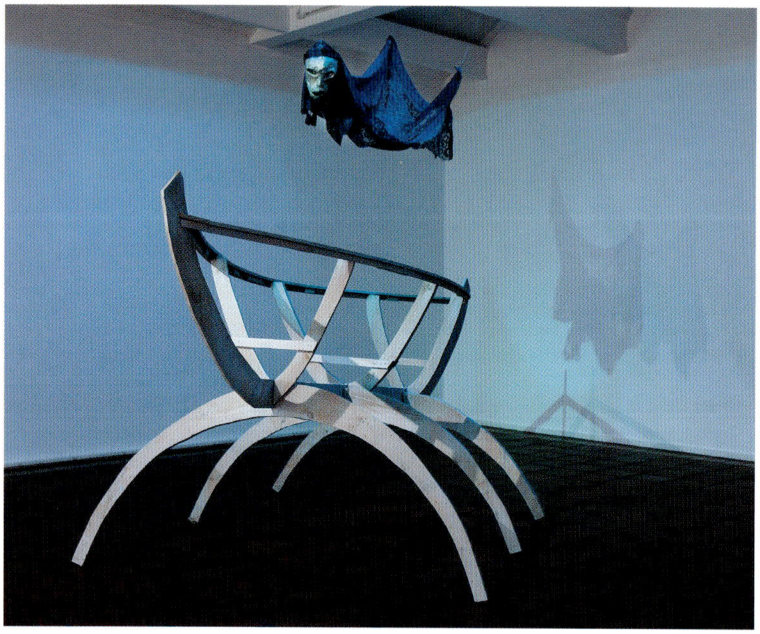

1

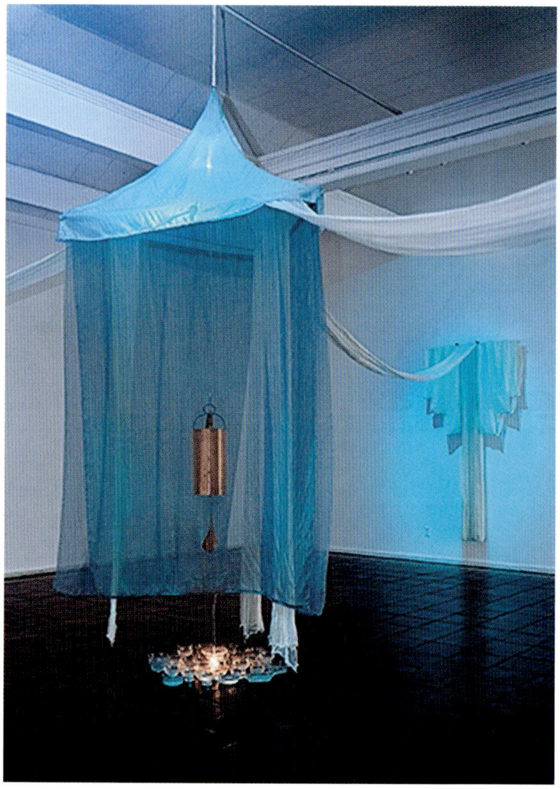

2

3

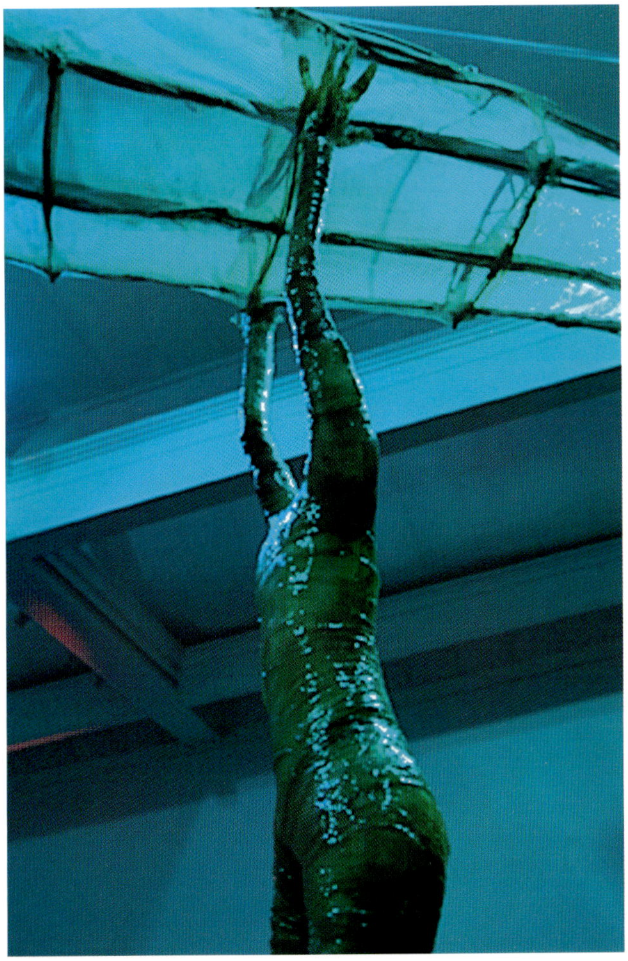

4

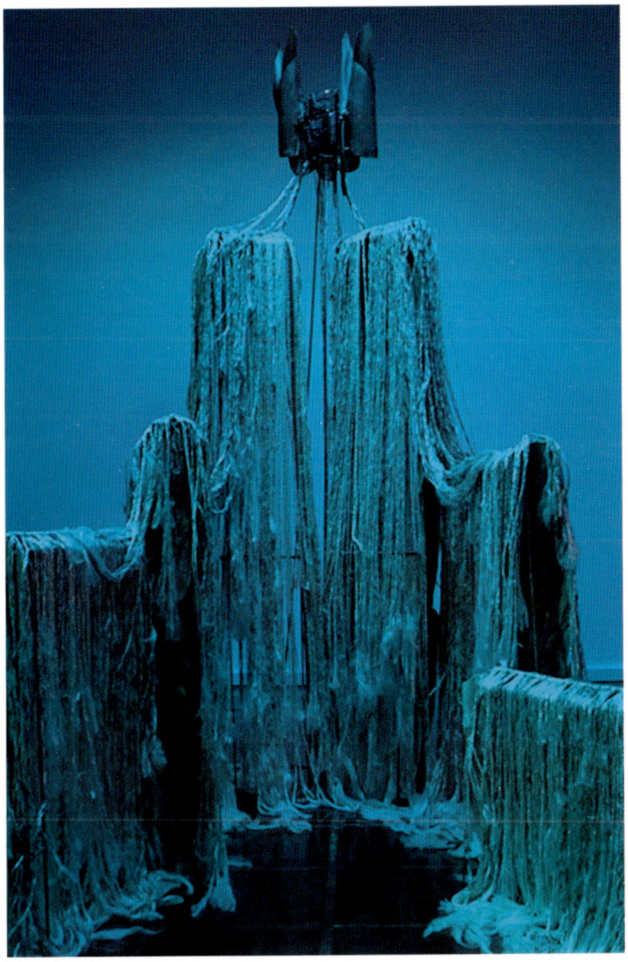

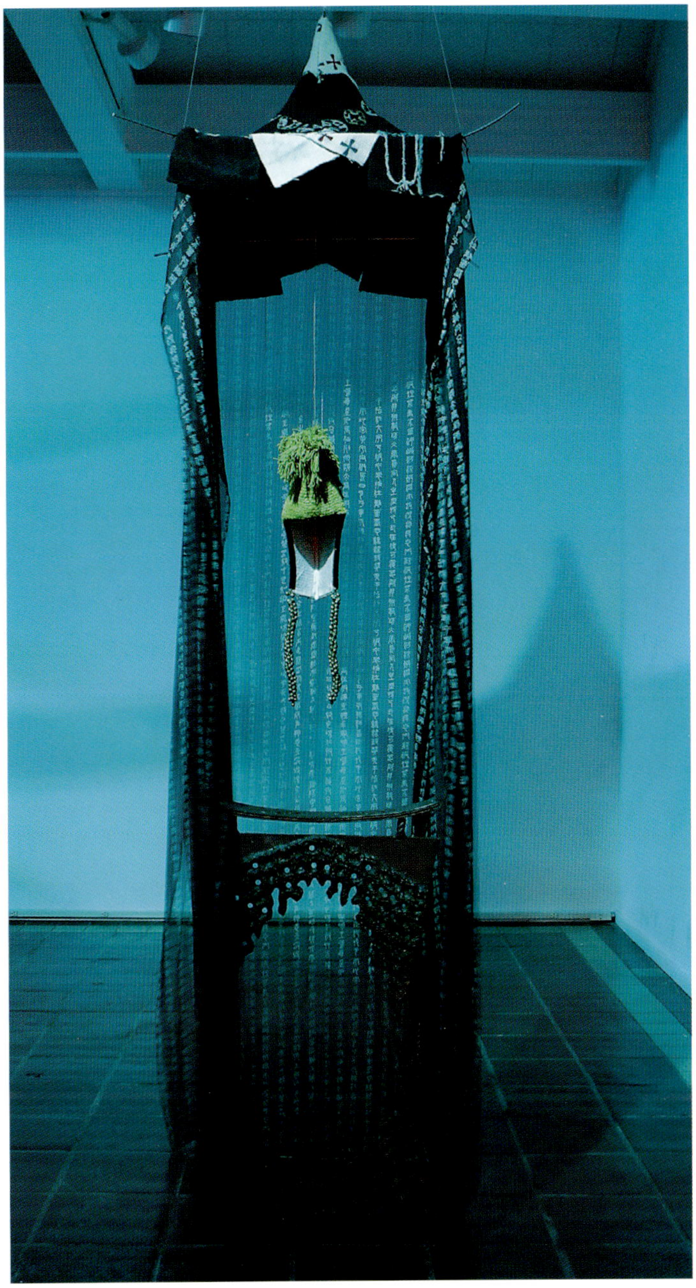

5

1 *Voyage of Spiritual Starvation,* 2010. Wood, resin, fabric, 14' l. x 11' h. x 7' w. *Photograph by Kevin Duffy.*

2 *Temple of the Human Spirit*, 2007. Stainless steel, fabric, bronze, glass; room size 15' h. x 15' d. x 15' l. *Photograph by Kevin Duffy.*

3 *Everyman's Journey,* 2006. Bamboo, resin, mixed, 15' h. x 10' l. x 3'w. *Photograph by Kevin Duffy.*

4 *Venerable Dwells,* 2005. Rope, bamboo, stainless steel, glass, copper, 8' h. x 6' l. x 6' d. *Photograph by Kevin Duffy.*

5 *Journey of Transition: Tibet,* 2003. Cast bronze, fabric, mixed, 3' l. x 3' d. x 10' h. *Photograph by Kevin Duffy.*

# Leah Brown

Fort Lauderdale, FLorida, USA
www.leahbrownart.com

Leah Brown is a south Florida-based artist and a graduate of the Rhode Island School of Design. She has completed multiple residency programs and exhibits nationally.

Brown's works form a language with which to connect the fragments of fairy-tales, folklore, history, and dreams that make up her personal mythology. The resulting narrative inspires paintings as well as sculptures and installations. These in turn become character and landscape studies to aid in the organic continuation of the same narrative, a project that Brown has spent the past 10 years researching, mapping, sculpting, painting, and composing.

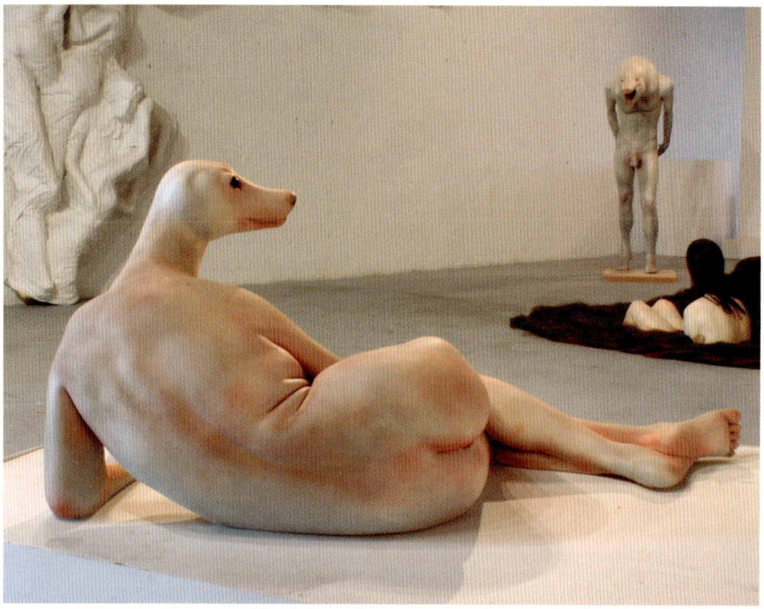

1

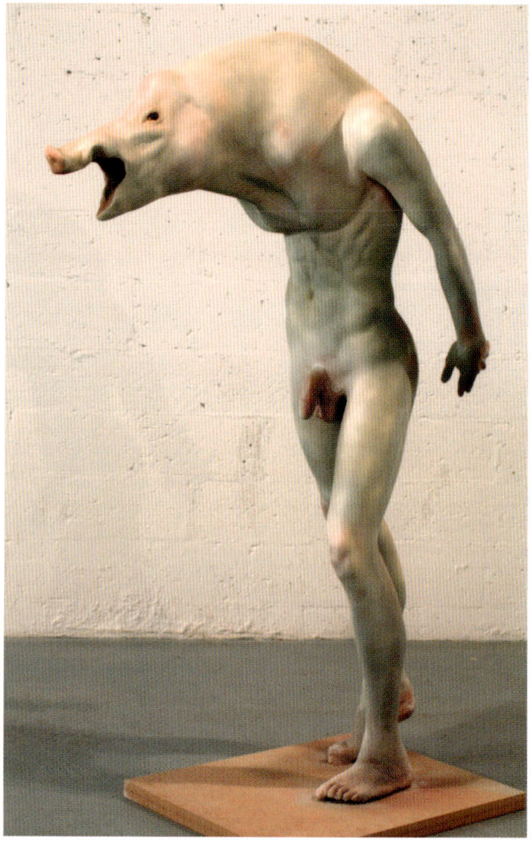

3

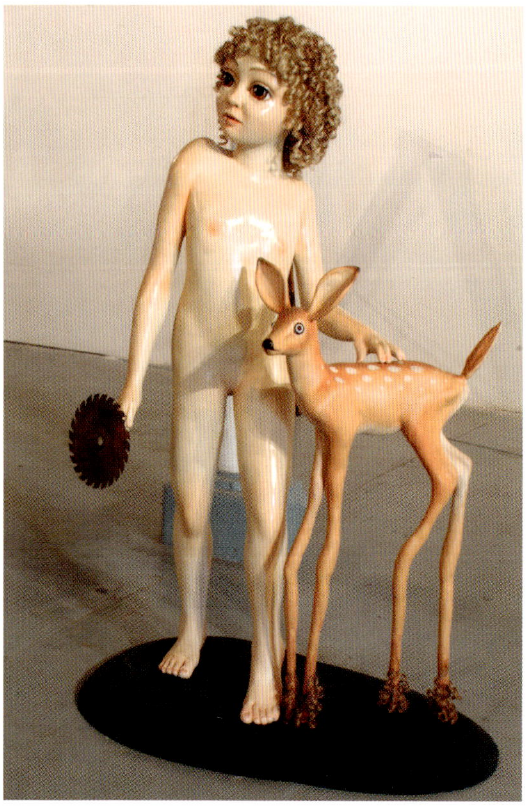

2

1 *Wolfie*, 2010. Aquaresin, glass eyes, paint, 7'. *Photograph by Leah Brown.*

2 *She Kept Her Head and Now She Had This*, 2010. Aqua-resin, hair, paint, 4'. *Photograph by Leah Brown.*

3 *Pigman*, 2010. Aquaresin, glass eyes, paint. 6'. length. *Photograph by Leah Brown.*

4 *Clinging Vines*, 2011. Aquaresin, paint, dress, hair; dimensions variable. *Photograph by Leah Brown.*

5 *Caterbaby*, 2006. Plaster, synthetic hair, paint, 3'. *Photograph by Leah Brown.*

6 *Lavinia and the Birdman*, 2007. Cotton and found objects; dimensions variable. *Photograph by Leah Brown.*

7 *Sutherland*, 2010. Aqua-resin, paint, hair, olive branches, inflated vinyl gloves, acetate; dimensions variable. *Photograph by Leah Brown.*

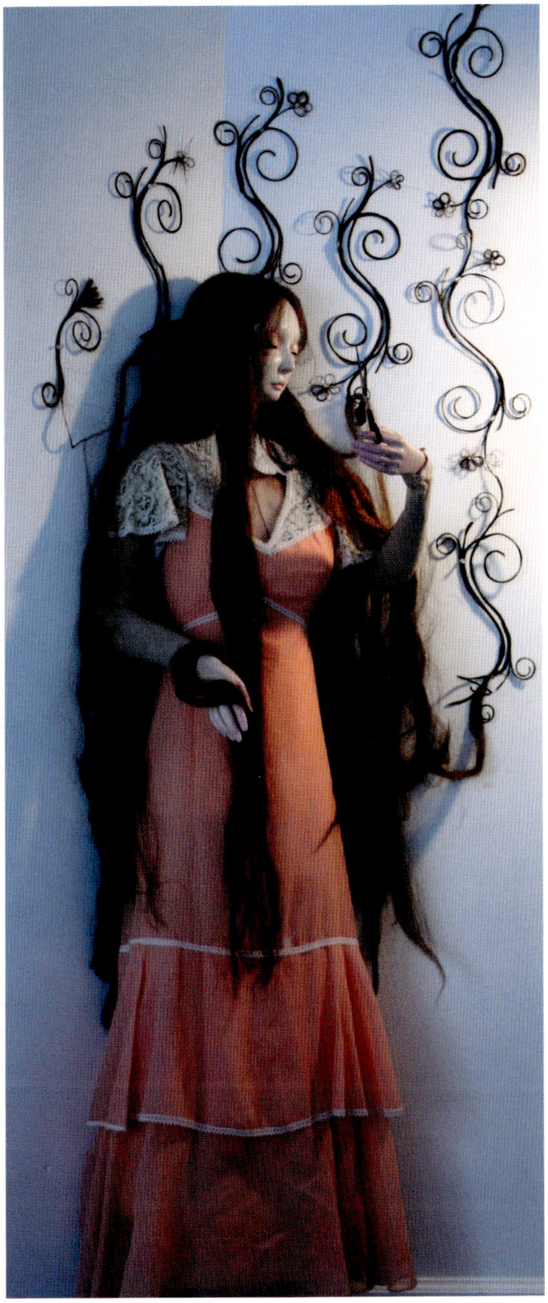

4

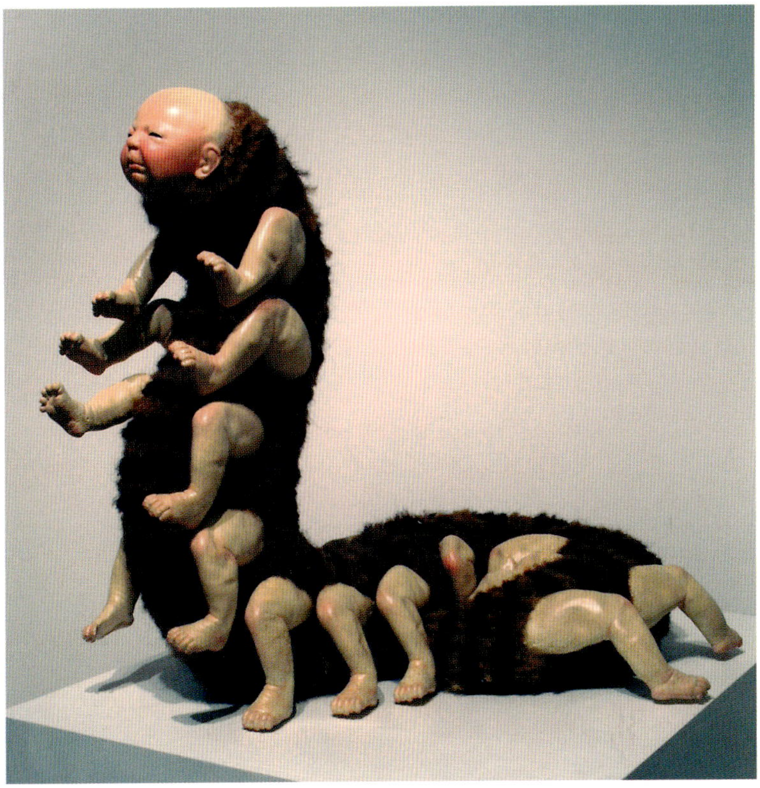

5

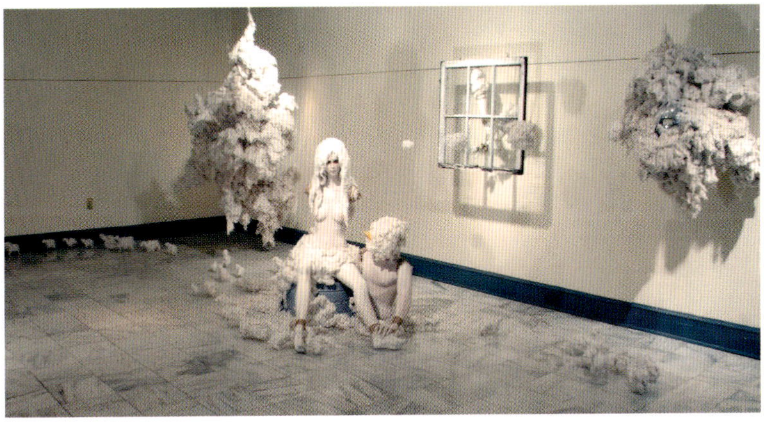

6

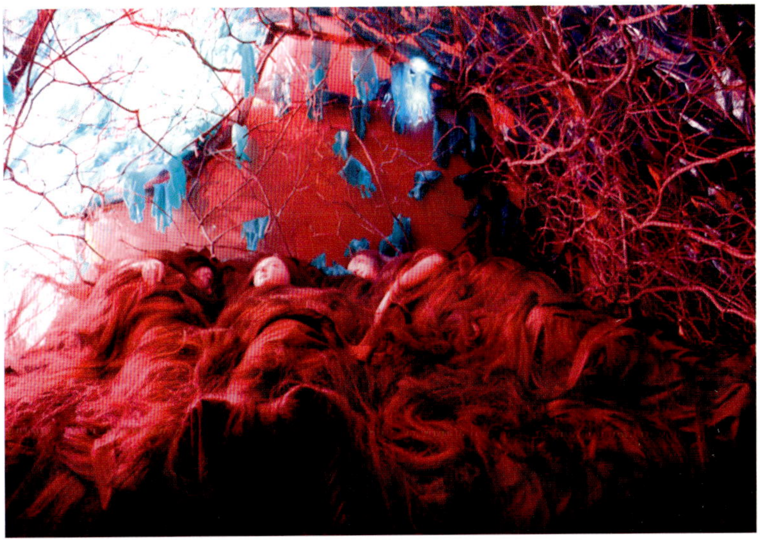

7

# Ken Butler

Brooklyn, New York, USA
www.mindspring.com/~KBhybrid

Ken Butler is an artist and musician whose hybrid musical instrument sculptures, performances, collage drawings, and installations explore the interaction and transformation of common and uncommon objects, altered images, and sounds, as function and form collide in the intersections of art and music.

Created primarily from urban detritus, the hybrids express a poetic spirit of re-invention and hyper-utility as hidden meanings and associations momentarily create a striking and re-animated cultural identity for common objects.

His works have been featured in numerous exhibitions and performances throughout the U.S., Canada, and Europe including The Stedelijk Museum in Amsterdam, Mass MoCA, The Kitchen, The Brooklyn Museum, Lincoln Center, and The Metropolitan Museum of Art in New York City, as well as in South America, Thailand, and Japan. His works have been reviewed in *The New York Times, The Village Voice, Artforum, Smithsonian*, and *Sculpture Magazine* and have been featured on PBS, CNN, MTV, and NBC, including a live appearance on "The Tonight Show." Awards include fellowships from the New York Foundation for the Arts, the National Endowment for the Arts, and the Pollock-Krasner Foundation.

He has performed with John Zorn, Laurie Anderson, Butch Morris, The Soldier String Quartet, Matt Darriau's Paradox Trio, The Tonight Show Band, and The Master Gnawa musicians of Morocco.

Works by Ken Butler are represented in public and private collections in Portland, Seattle, Vail, Los Angeles, Toronto, Montreal, Washington, and New York City, including the permanent collection of The Metropolitan Museum of Art.

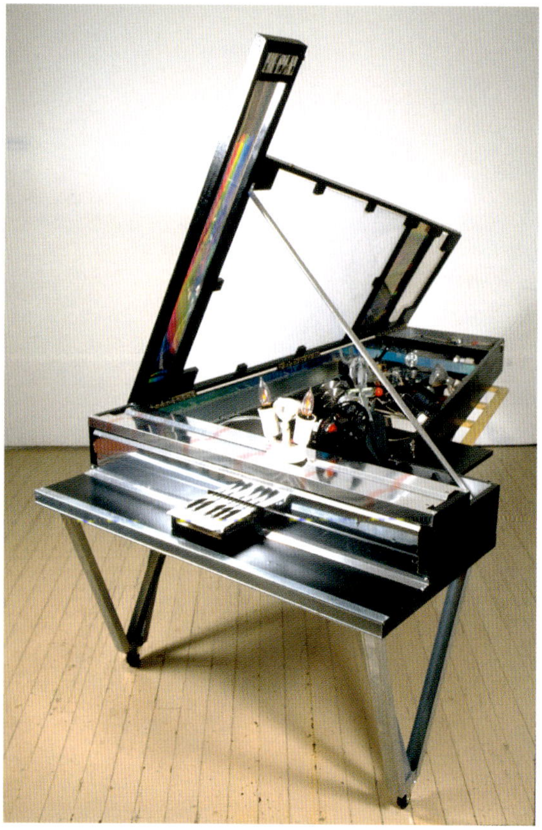

1

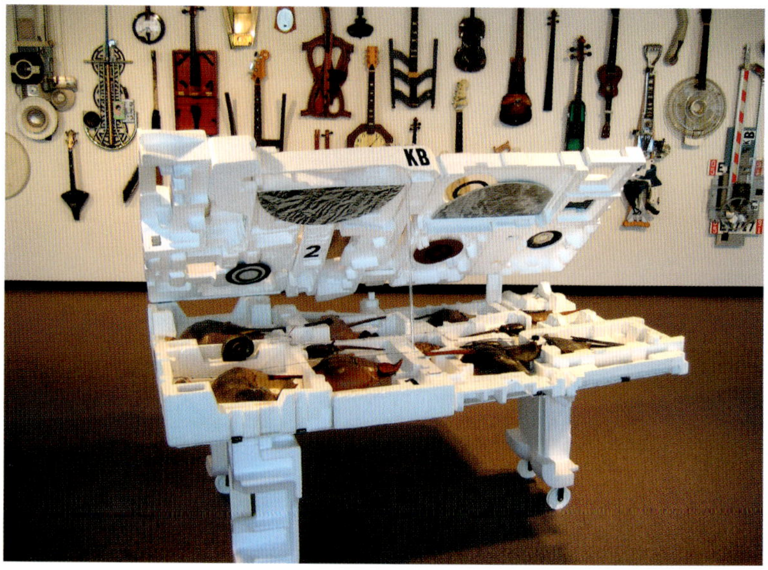


2

1 *Urban Grand Piano*, 1998. Assemblage, 72" x 48" x 89" (with top open). *Photograph by Ken Butler.*

2 *Styro-tone Grand Piano: A Rhythm Reliquary*, 2005. Assemblage, 62" x 42" x 73" (with top open). *Photograph by Ken Butler.*

3 *Card Extractor Aluminum*, 2002. Assemblage, 40" x 14" x 5". *Photograph by Ken Butler.*

4 *Blue Windscreen Exersizer*, 2002. Assemblage, 70" x 26" x 9". *Photograph by Ken Butler.*

5 *Red Lawnmower Guns*, 1999. Assemblage, 80" x 25" x 5". *Photograph by Ken Butler.*

6 *Bent Arm Violin*, 2002. Assemblage, 18" x 7" x 3". *Photograph by Ken Butler.*

7 *Rocking Chair Organ Pipe Bass*, 2002. Assemblage, 69" x 42" x 9". *Photograph by Ken Butler.*

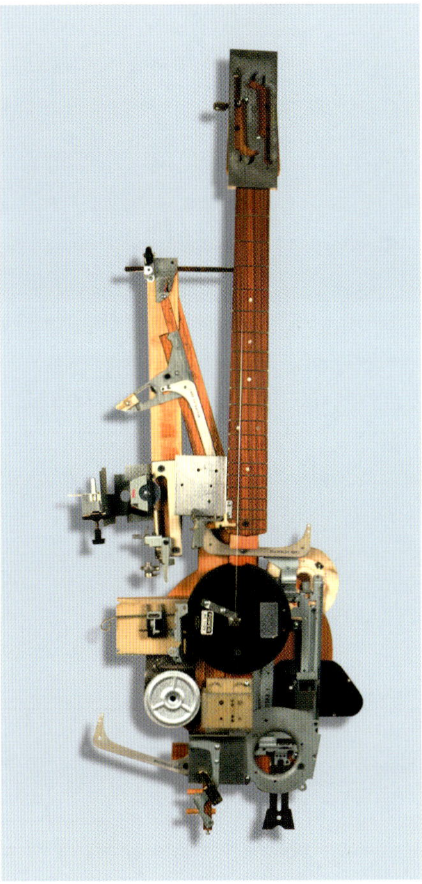

3

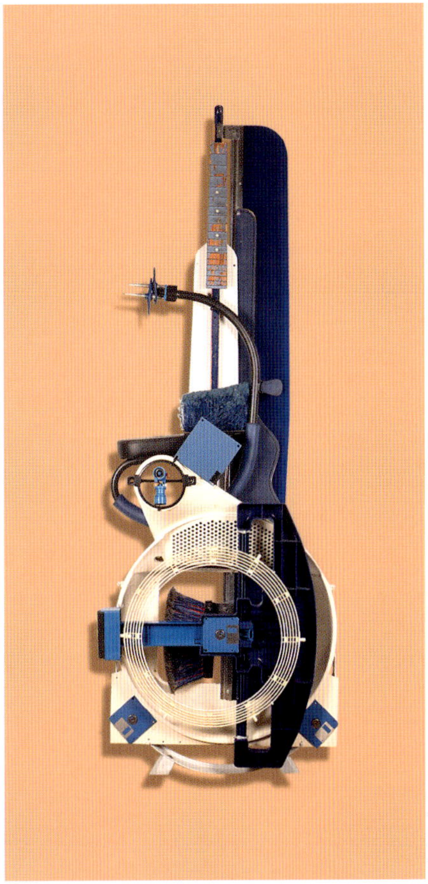

4

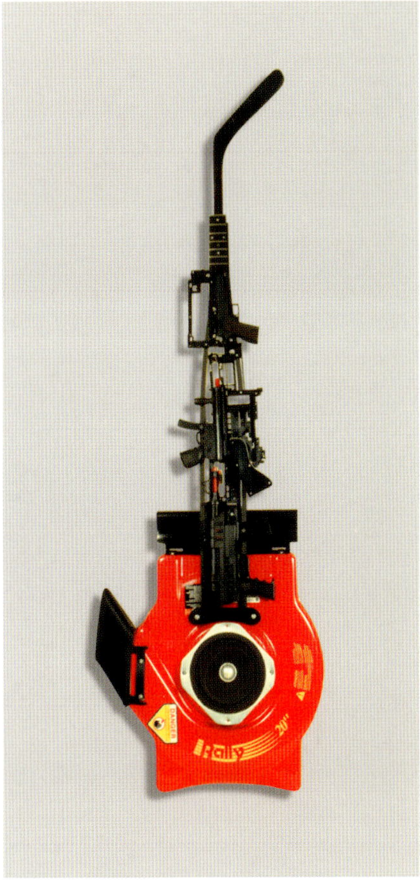


5

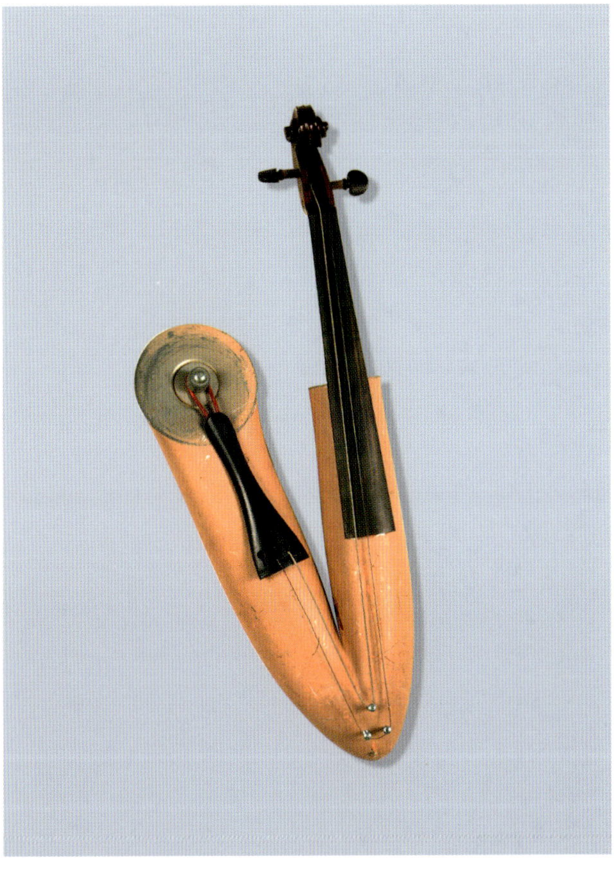

6

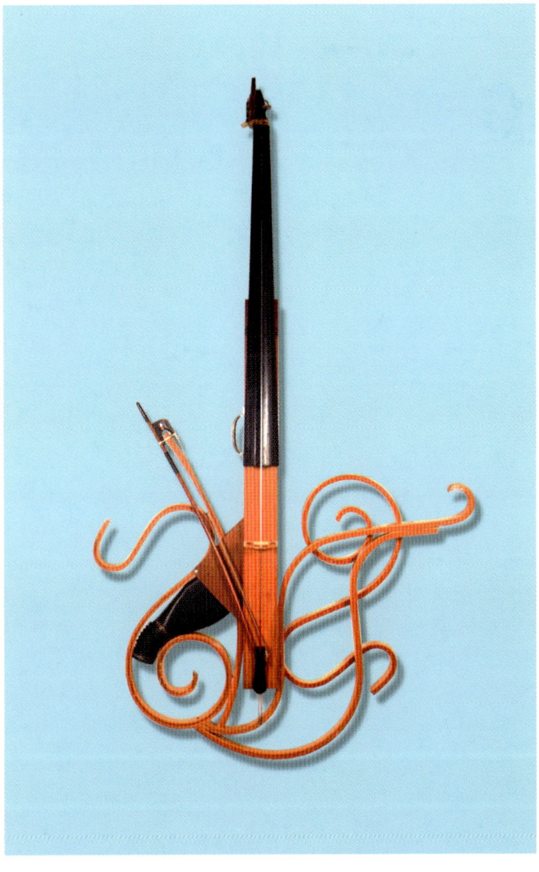

7

# Giancarlo Calicchia

Cleveland, Ohio, USA
www.Giancarlocalicchia.com

*From the ancient quarries of Carrara to the most advanced bronze and glass casting facilities, I've worked directly with the finest craftsmen in the world in my chosen fields of stone, wood, metal, bronze, glass, mosaic, ceramic, and oils. A background of traditional techniques and classical training has enabled a spiritual and psychological fluidity in the concepts and approaches that guide my work. The timeless techniques of the ancient world integrated into the powerful technologies developed so dramatically during the last few decades have given me the tools and the inspiration to create new worlds on very sound foundations that will withstand the ravages of time and exalt our humble limitations.*

*The nature of my work is closely related to one of my favorite words:* Gravitas. *Like gravity, it takes its root from the Latin language, meaning to be serious or to be taken seriously. Gravitas is a state of being heavy with creation, thoughts, feelings, and responsibilities. It is also the gravitation toward mental and physical awareness. Gravitas is experienced through wisdom, humility, empathy, and accountability. It is seen in the form of leadership, confidence, trust, sacrifice, and discipline. The highest degree of humanity exists in the psyche of our folklore, as a reminder of our true purpose. Gravitas represents the metamorphoses we must experience to achieve truth.*

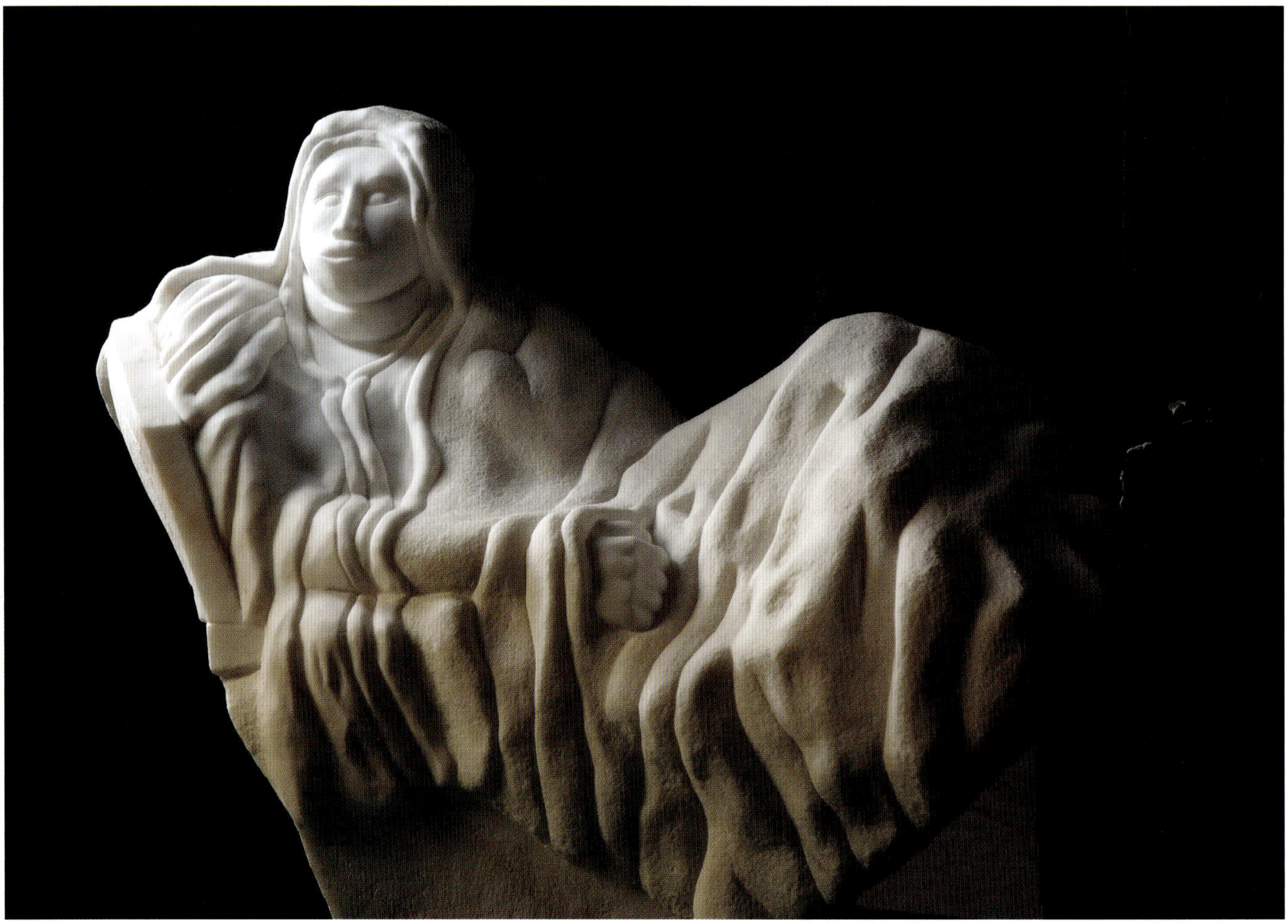

1

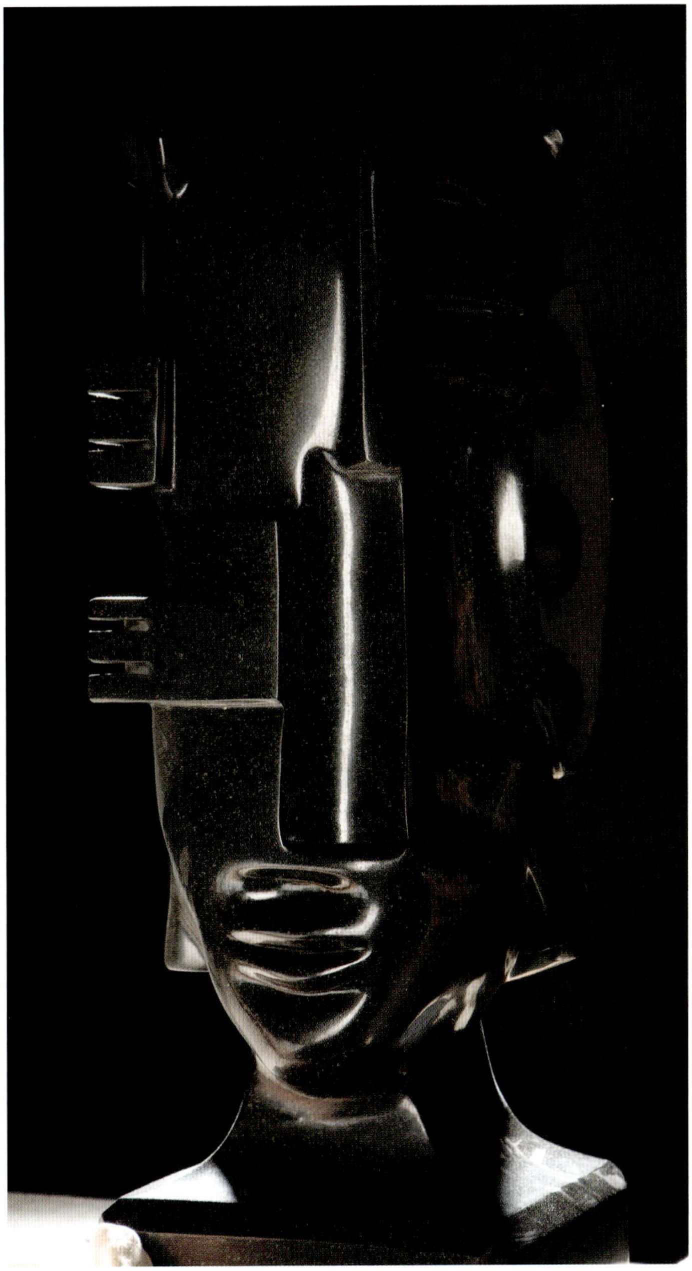

3

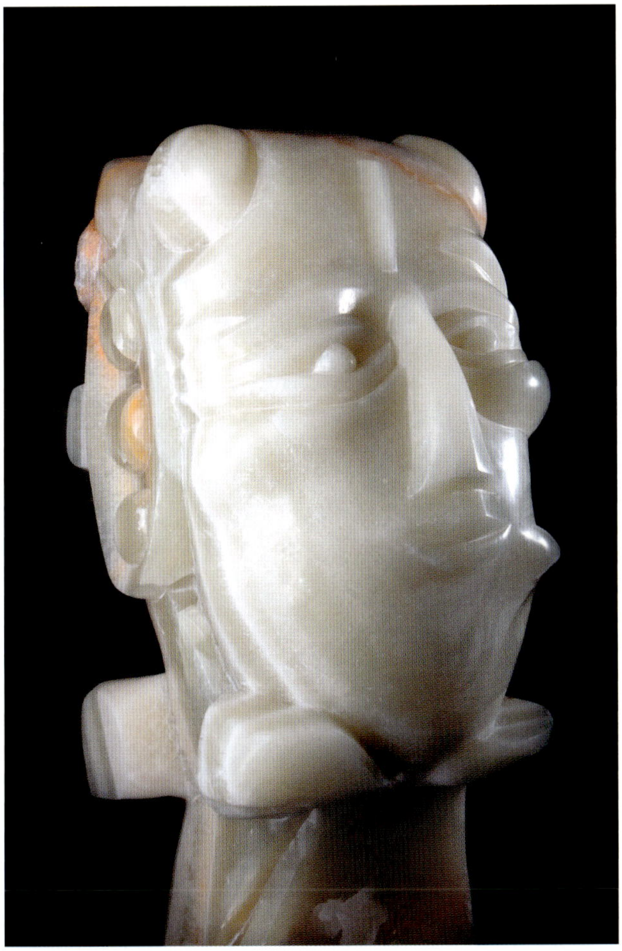

2

1 *Maya*, 1996. White alabama marble, 33" h. x 45" w. x 22" d. *Photograph by Michael Levy.*

2 *Inca*, 2009. Pakastani green onyx, 31" h. x 13" w. x 14" d. *Photograph by Michael Levy.*

3 *Thoughts,* 2007. Black granite (African Absolute), 48" h. x 16" w. x 16" d. *Photograph by Michael Levy.*

4 *Gravitas*, 2009. Glacial granite, 51" h. x 36" w. x 49" d. *Photograph by Michael Levy.*

5 *Athleta*, 2009. Glacial granite, 79" h. x 54" w. x 36" d. *Photography by Michael Levy.*

6 *Genesis*, 2010. Sapele, 330" h. x 66" w. x 5" d. *Photography by Michael Levy.*

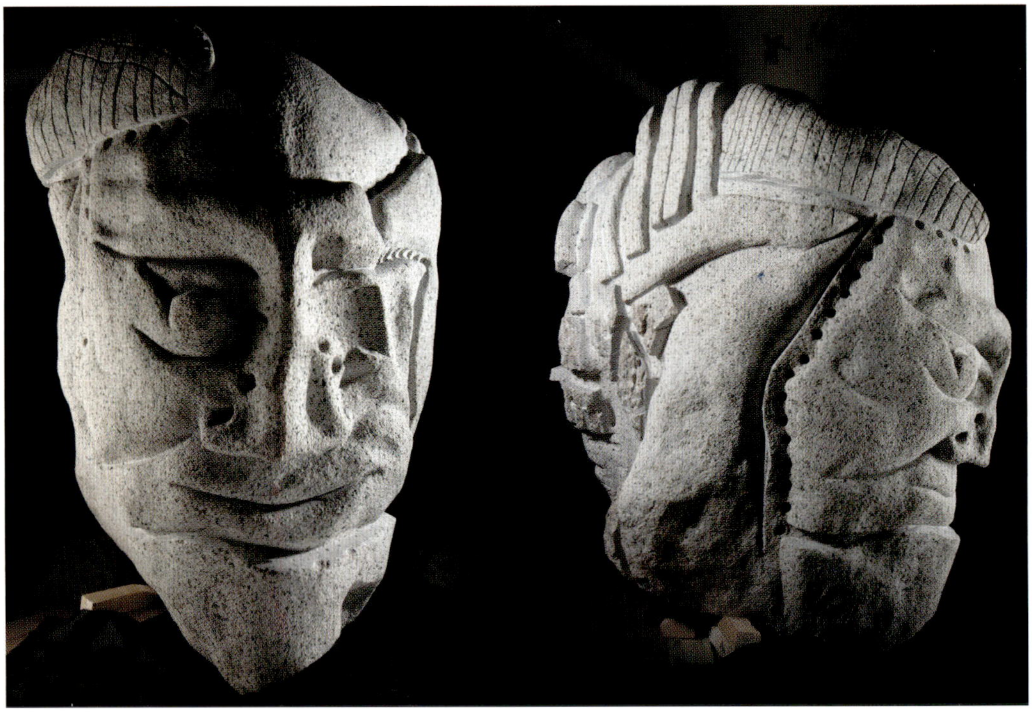

4

5

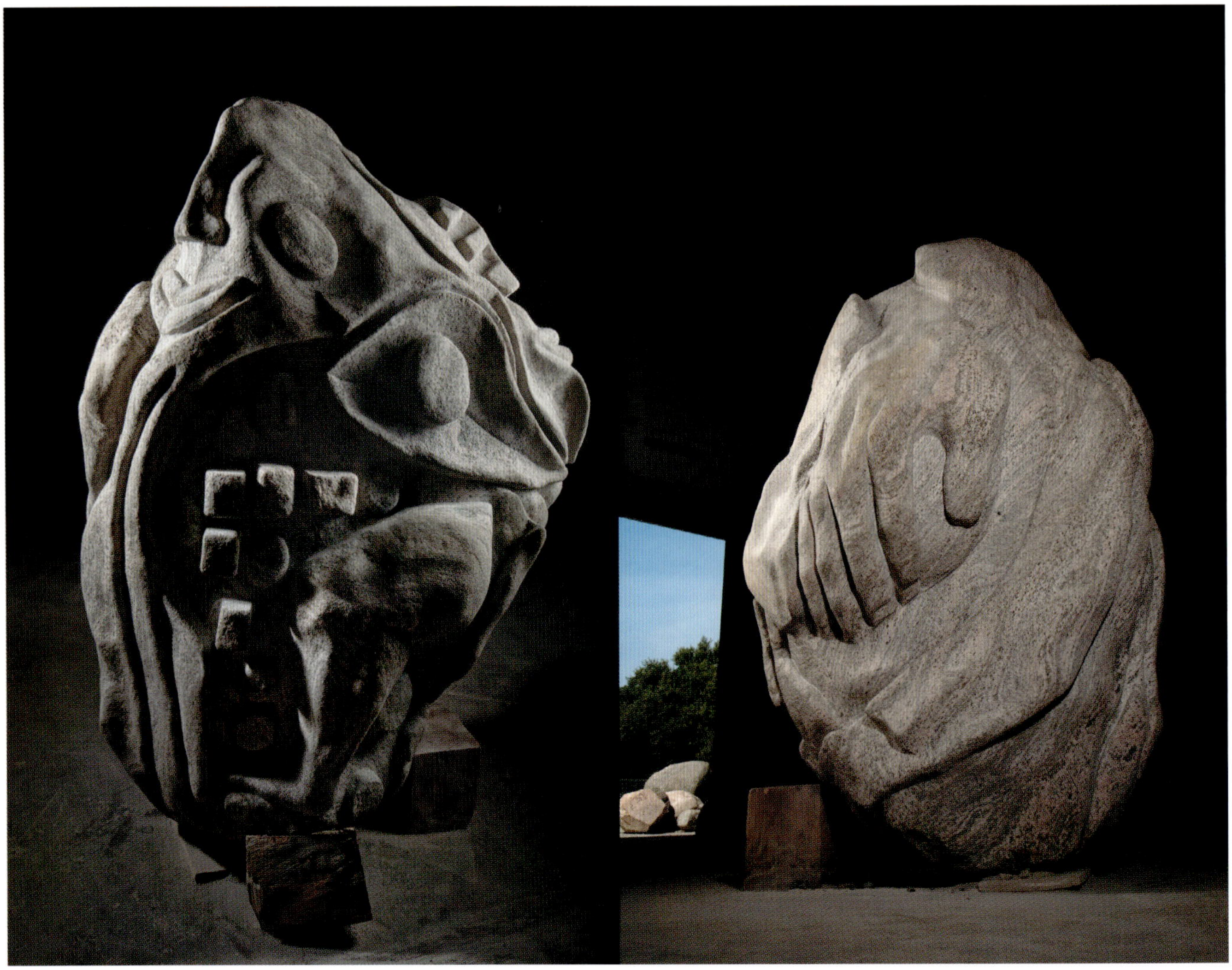

6

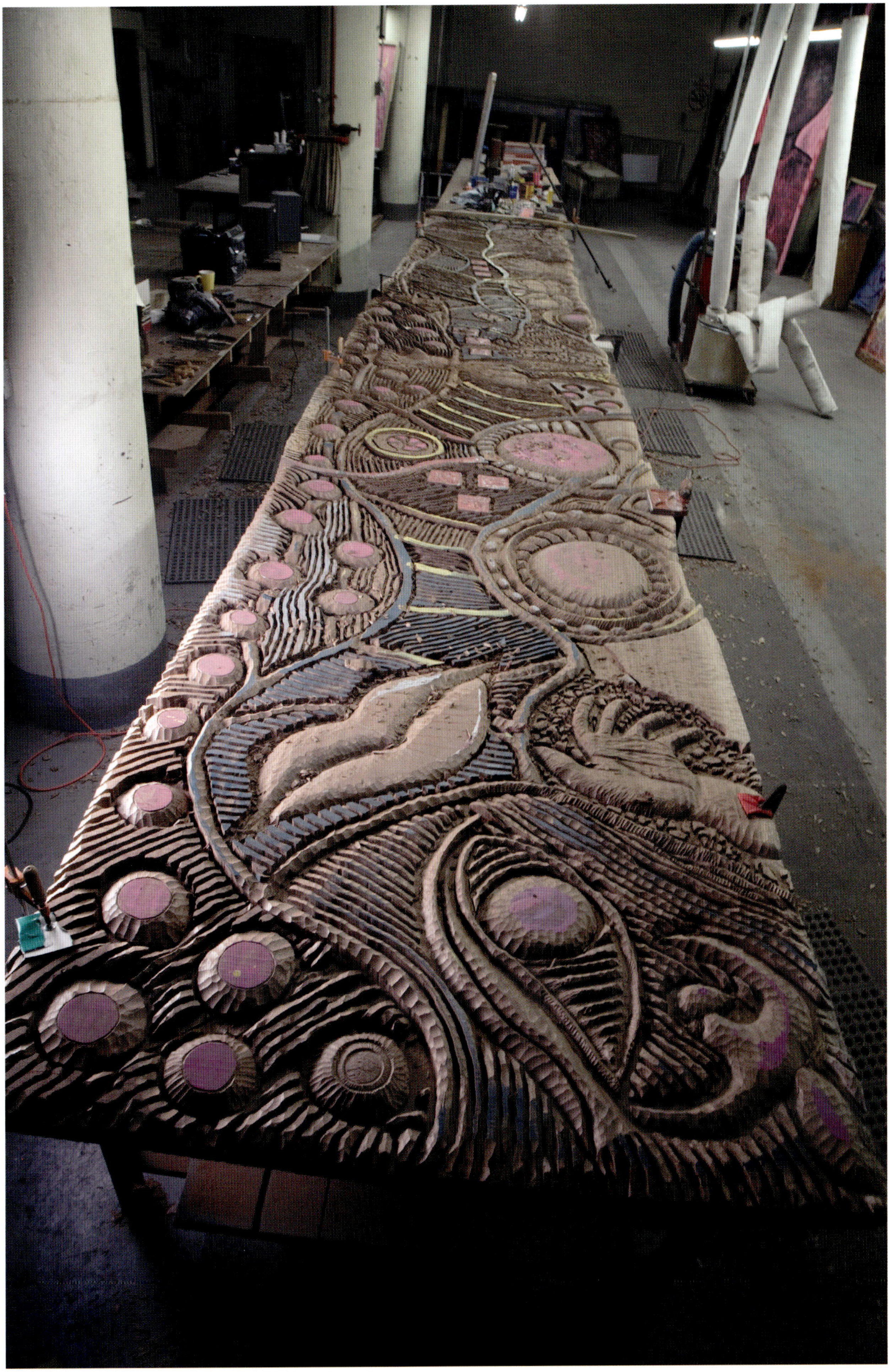

# Rachel Betty Case

Easton, Pennsylvania, USA
www.ThatWomanMakesCrazyArt.com

Rachel Betty Case was born in 1985 and raised in Lopatcong, New Jersey. As a child, she had a deep appreciation of art. Both of her parents were very supportive of her creativity and gave her complete artistic freedom within the parameters of her bedroom. The walls were quickly covered with doodles, messages, and image clippings, and the room was full of collected objects from the woods behind her house and elsewhere. The freedom to experiment with materials and collect inspiring objects is a large influence on Rachel's work today.

Rachel was trained as a traditional fine artist at the Delaware College of Art and Design, then as a fine artist and teacher at the Maryland Institute College of Art. In 2008, Rachel presented her graduate thesis project. On a small pedestal, covered by a vitrine, stood ten small skeletons made of nail clippings. This was the beginning of Human Ivory.

Rachel currently resides in Easton, Pennsylvania. Her work has been viewed in newspapers, magazines, and blogs, and featured on radio and television shows across the globe.

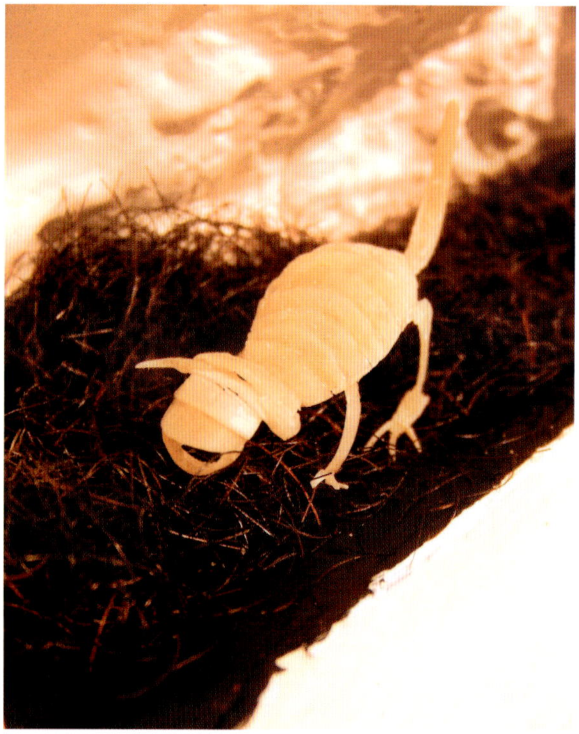

1

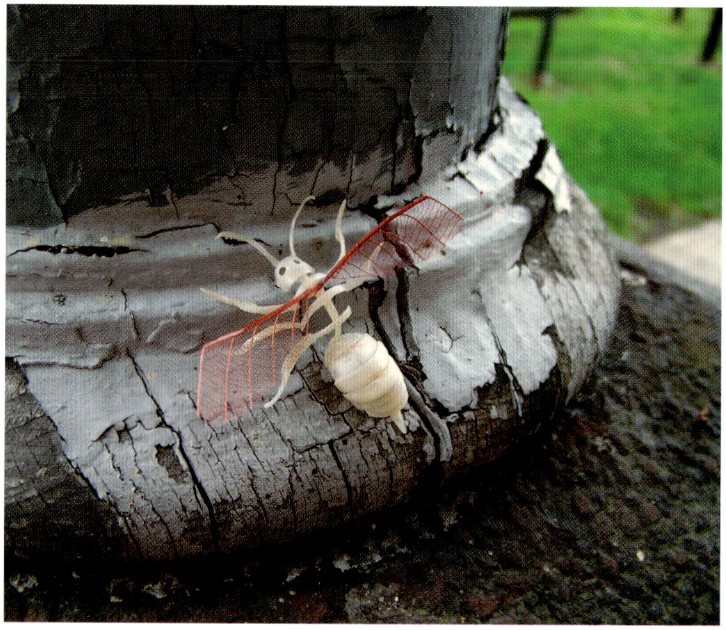

2

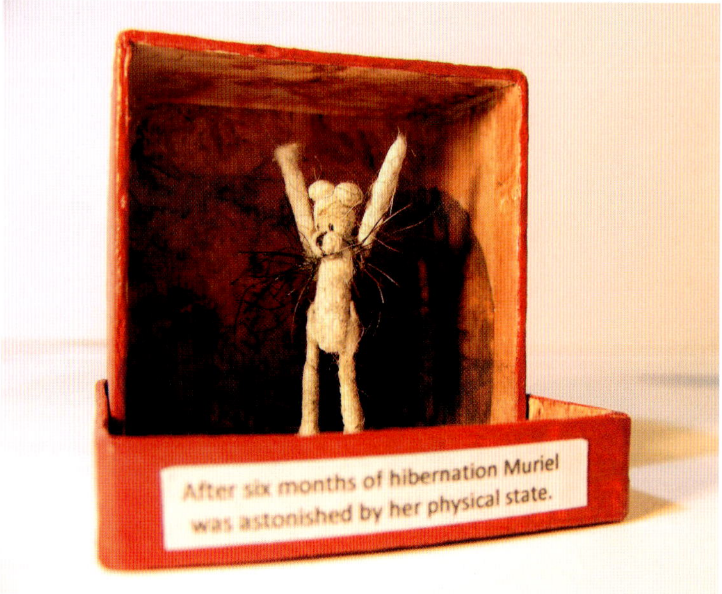


3

4 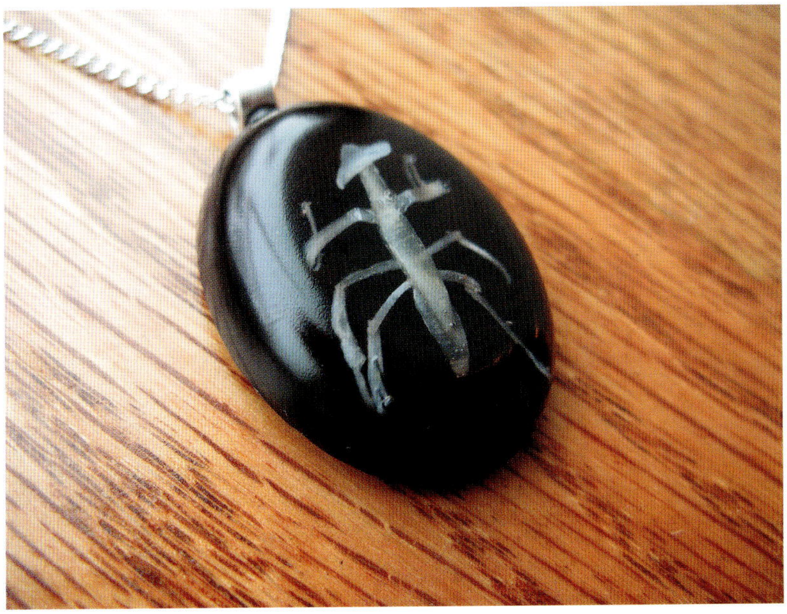

5 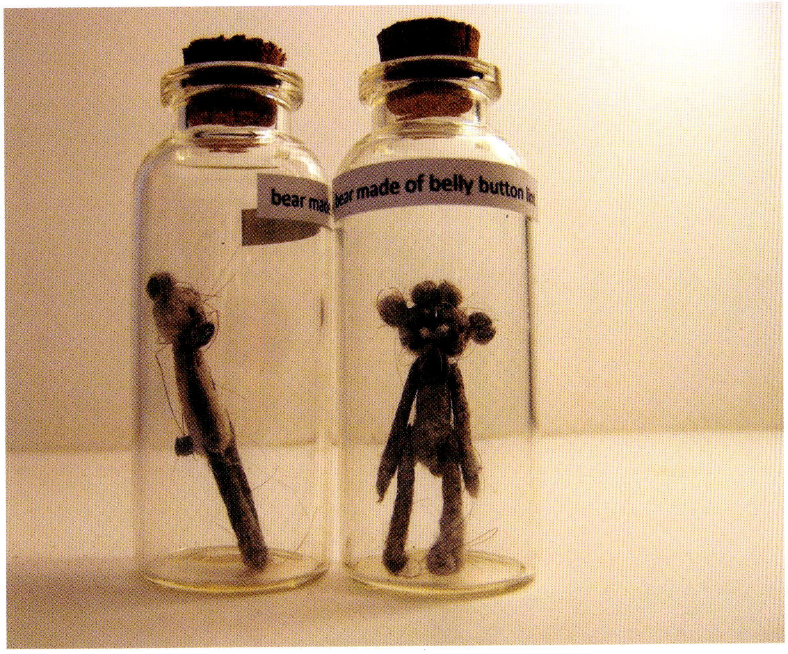


6 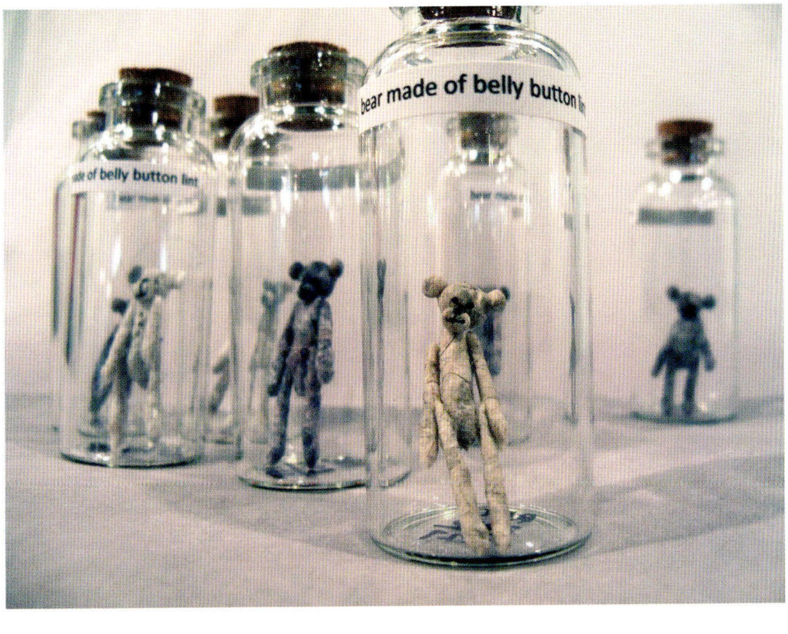


1 *Rho Beast of Lille O*, 2009. Human ivory (nail clippings), .75" tall. *Photograph by Rachel Case.*

2 *Honey Wasp,* 2009. Human ivory (nail clippings), 2.25" wingspan. *Photograph by Rachel Case.*

3 *Hibernation Diorama,* 2010. Belly button lint, beard hair, paper, paint, 2.5" tall. *Photograph by Chuck Nyce.*

4 *Mantis Pendant,* 2011, Human ivory, resin, sterling silver, 1.5" tall. *Photograph by Rachel Case.*

5 *Bear made of Belly Button Lint gawking at a Siamese Bear made of Belly Button Lint,* 2010. Belly button lint, glass jars, 2.5" tall. *Photograph by Rachel Case.*

6 *Bears made of Belly Button Lint,* 2011. Belly button lint, glass jars, 2.5" tall. *Photograph by Rachel Case.*

# Susan Case

Santa Fe, New Mexico, USA
www.bit.ly/nrPMYK

*Born in Brooklyn, New York, I was raised on Long Island. I studied drawing and painting at the Art Student League in New York City before coming to Santa Fe, New Mexico. My work has been shown locally and nationally. Venues include: The Center for Contemporary Arts, Santa Fe, New Mexico; Soho20 Chelsea Gallery, New York, New York (a woman-run gallery for several years); Arc Gallery, Chicago, Illinois; The Art Center of New Jersey; The Museum of Art, Santa Fe, New Mexico; Stables Gallery, Taos, New Mexico; The Capital Collection, Santa Fe, New Mexico; Museum of Contemporary Art, Fort Collins, Colorado; and The Santa Fe Community Gallery, Santa Fe, New Mexico.*

*Maybe it's the altitude, the cultural diversity, or the vast open spaces of New Mexico that has increased my awareness that life could have a spiritual dimension. I want to create art that has a timeless feeling of the past, yet has the urgency of and a relationship to the present. My concerns are with materials and how they relate to the idea of the work. I work in an open ended way through much trial and error. Using everyday materials like string or window screen in the process of making the sculpture can provide a connection to our individual and collective histories.*

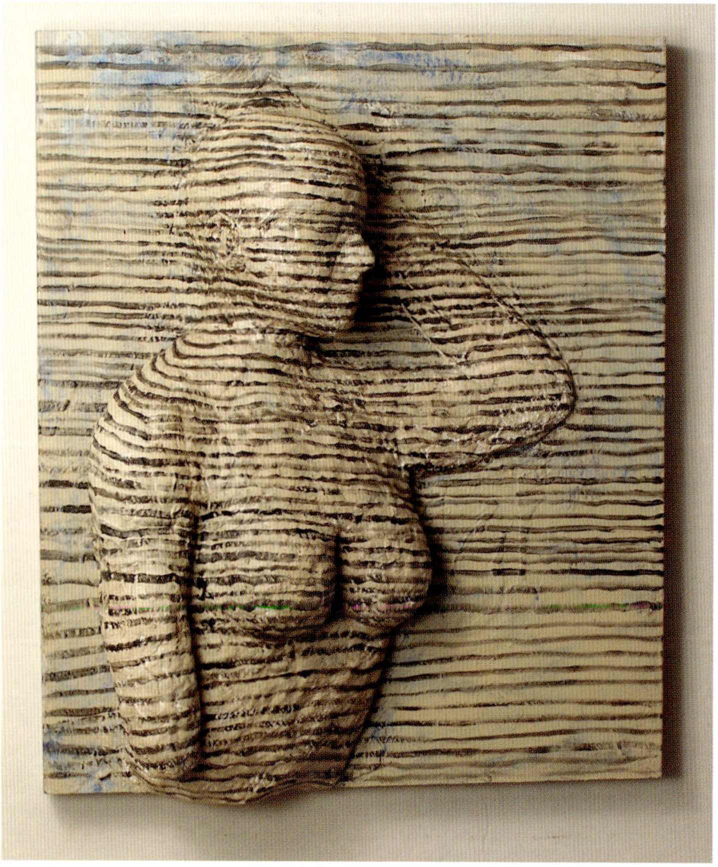

1

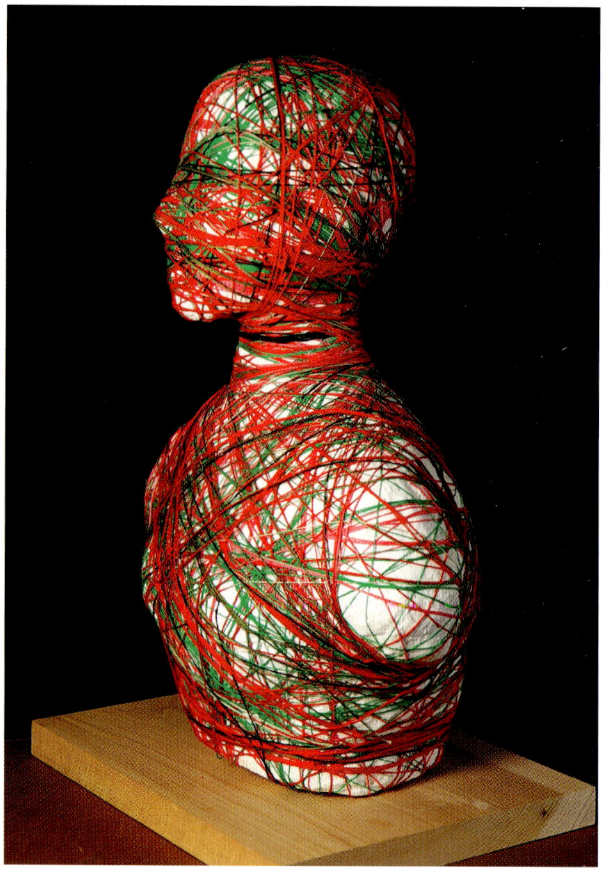

2

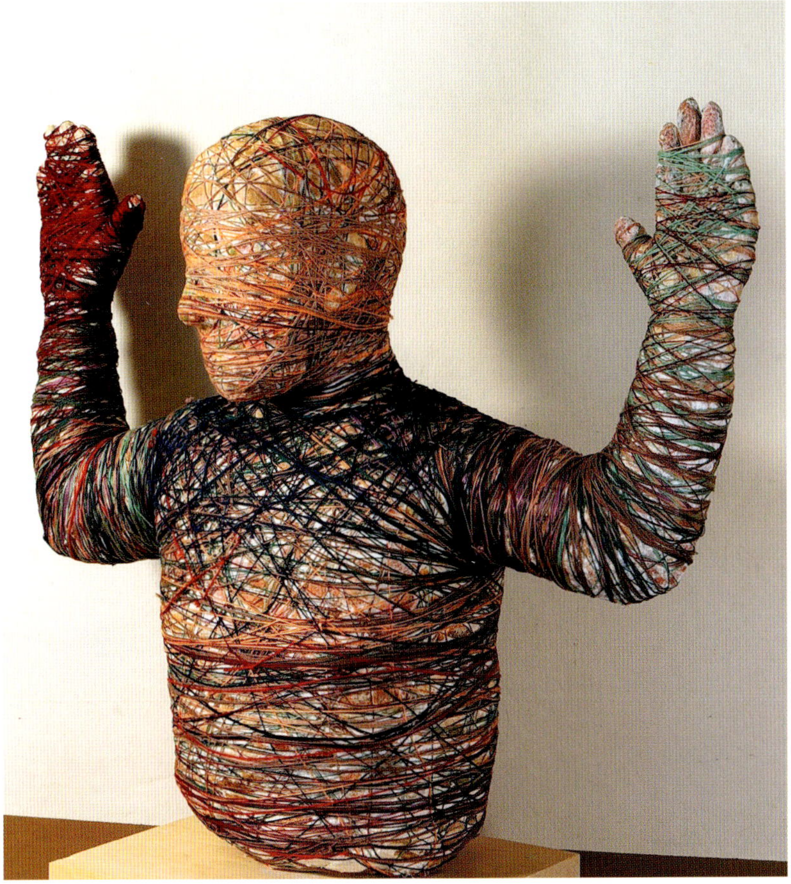

3

1 *Ancient Lines,* 2008. Plaster, fabric, acrylic, on a wood and masonite base, 30" x 26" x 9*". Photograph by Susan Case.*

2 *Wrap Around,* 2007. Plaster, fabric, acrylic, cotton cord, 23" x 16" x 12"*. Photograph by Sherwood Case.*

3 *Hands Up,* 2007. Plaster, fabric, acrylic, cotton cord, 28" x 30" x 12"*. Photograph by Sherwood Case.*

4 *Body Thorns,* 2007. Plaster, fabric, oil, shoe polish, steel nails, 20" x 16" x 10"*. Photograph by Sherwood Case.*

5 *Screen Play,* 2007. Fiberglass screen, paper collage on a plaster base; wood and masonite base, 24" x 20" x 17" . *Photograph by Sherwood Case.*

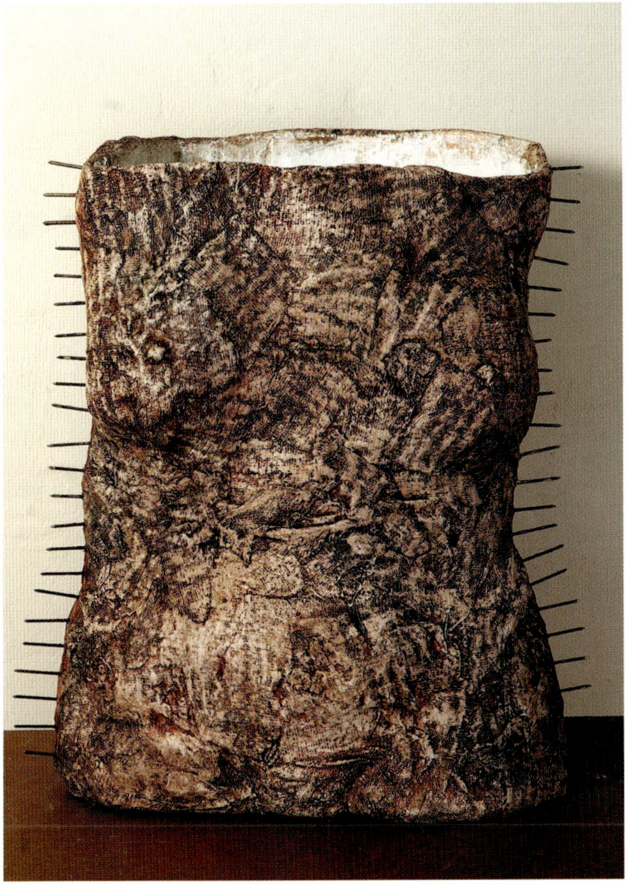

4

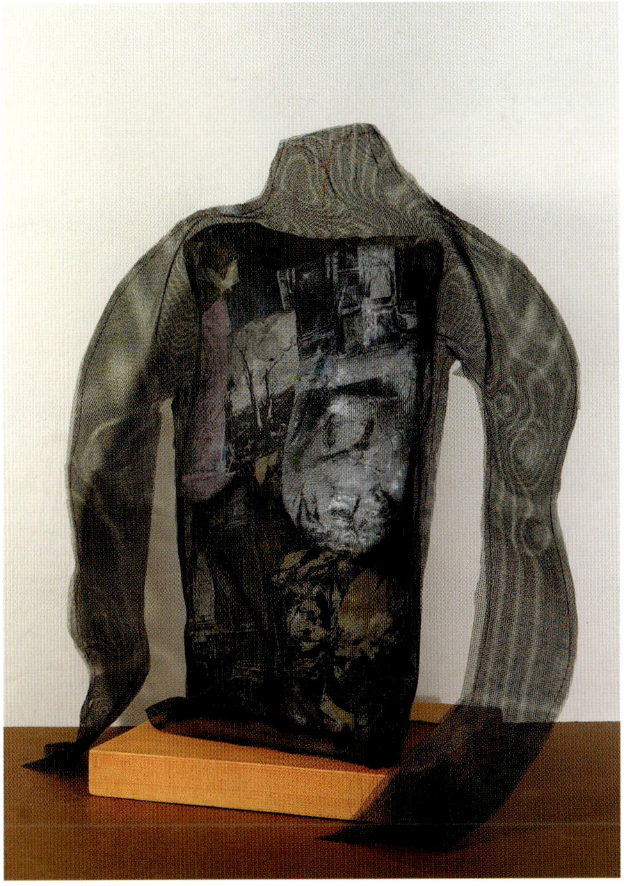

5

# Mark Chatterley

Williamston, Michigan, USA
www.chatterley.com

Chatterley's hand-built, ceramic creations appear to be our counterparts from another time…another world, but distinctly familiar. The Michigan native has received over twenty awards from both national and international exhibitions including the Fletcher Challenge Ceramics Award in Auckland, New Zealand and the Taiwan Golden Ceramics Award in Taipei. He was a participant in the JINRO International Ceramic Art (JICA) Workshop Invitational at the Hong-ik Ceramic Research Institute in Seoul, Korea.

Since receiving his Masters in Fine Arts from Michigan State University in 1981, Chatterley has exhibited his works widely – across the nation and abroad.

*My work is about traveling in the dream world. The place that exists between wakefulness and sleep. Betwixt and between. I am interested in conscious thoughts and the space between thoughts. My work allows me to get to these spots. I try to make pieces that are timeless yet contemporary. As if the sculpture was dug up from a civilization yet to exist.*

*Everything is either moving toward or away from nothingness. Life, death, creation and destruction – this is the world I find myself in. I want my art to echo these thoughts, everything in a state of flux, changing and reforming. A sense of decay along with life. Nothing is permanent and nothing stays the same. I also try to show thoughts and feelings of the human condition. Beauty in the malformed, acceptance of the inevitable. I am doing work of our time for our time, even though I look to the past, the dead for inspiration.*

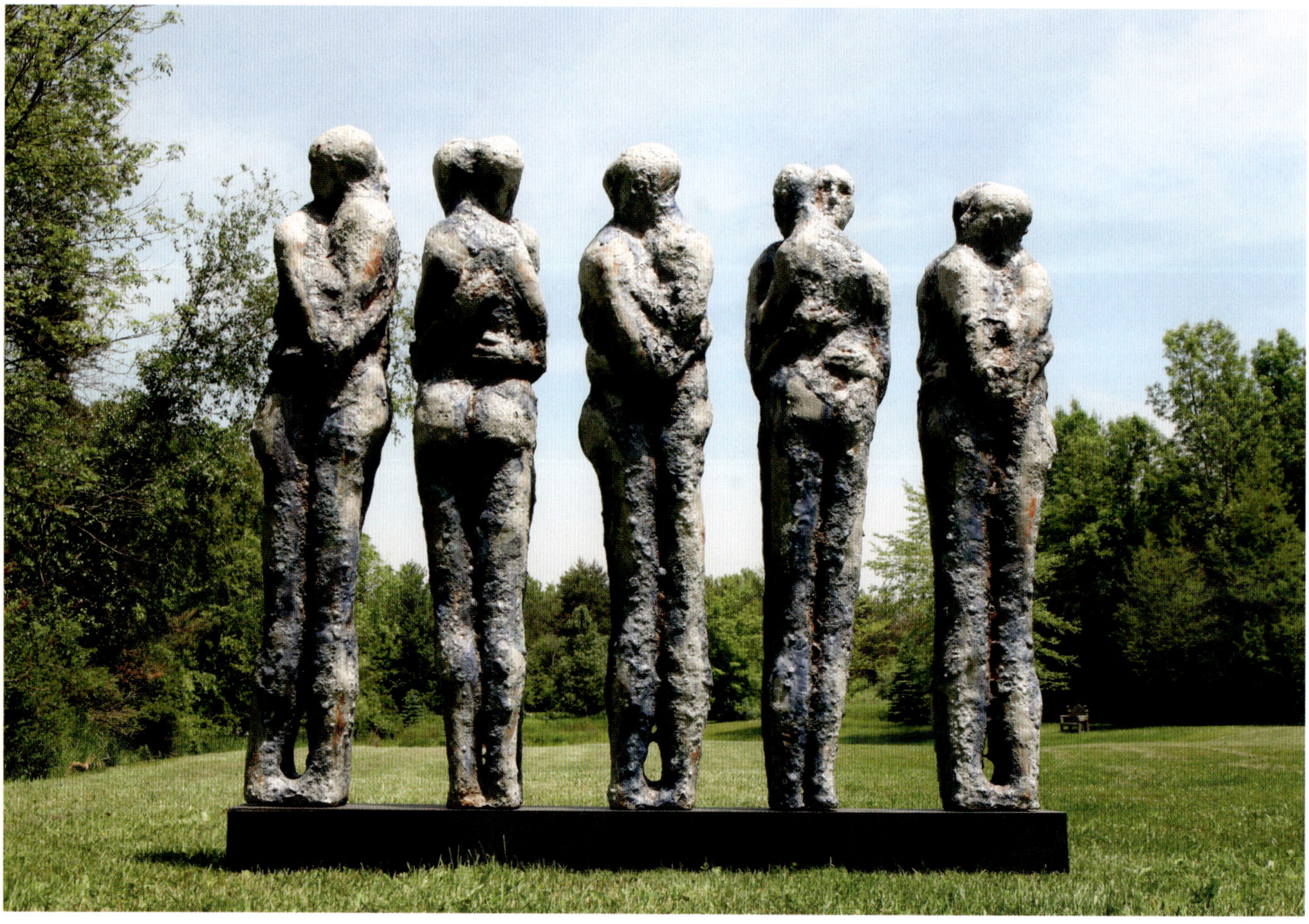

1

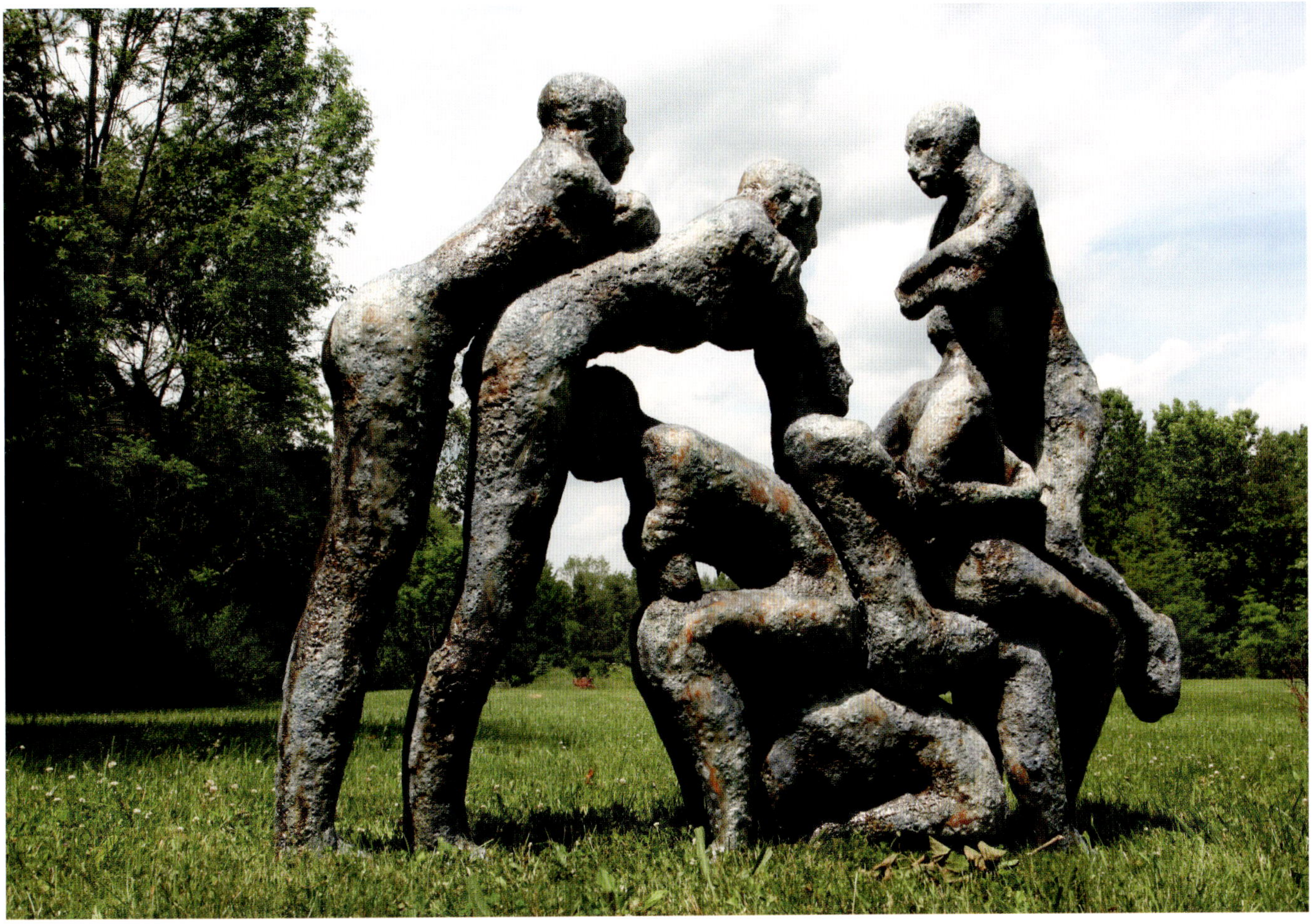

2

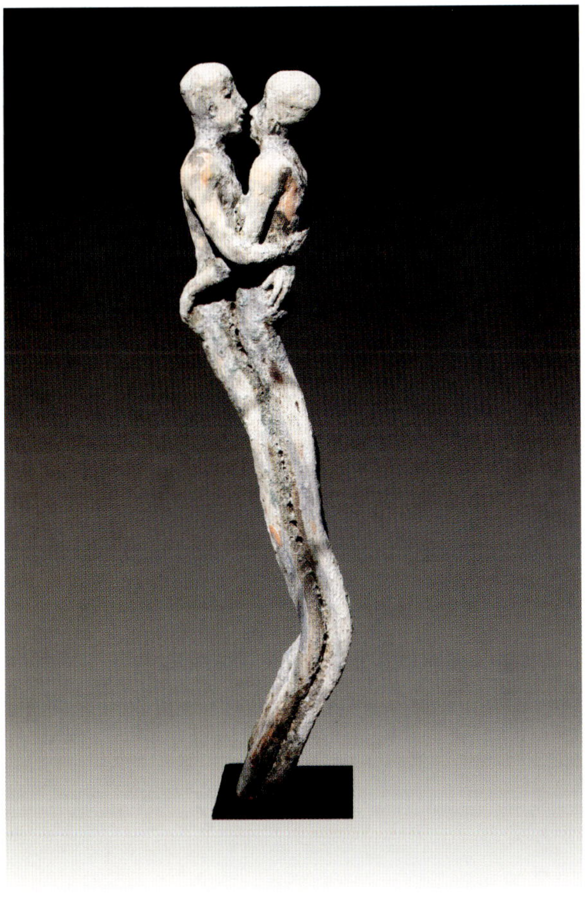

1 *All you need is Love,* 2009. Clay, 6' x 6' x 12".

2 *Layers of different dictions,* 2008. Clay, 72" x 61" x 16".

3 *Dirty Dancing,* 2009. Clay, 14" x 14" x 7'.

4 *Grouping,* 2009. Clay, 42" x 77" x 20".

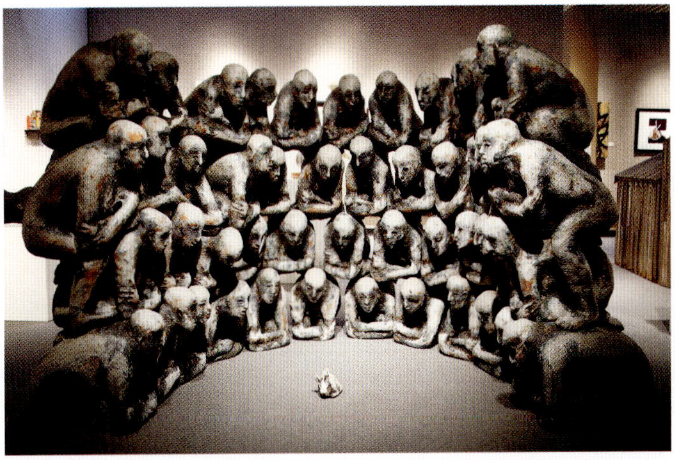

3

4

# Kim Chavez

Terrebonne, Oregon, USA
www.kimchavez.com

Kim Chavez is a bronze artist whose career began over 25 years ago. This Oregon artist is inspired by nature. Her sculptures reflect a fascination with the high desert, wildlife and sensitivity to the environment.

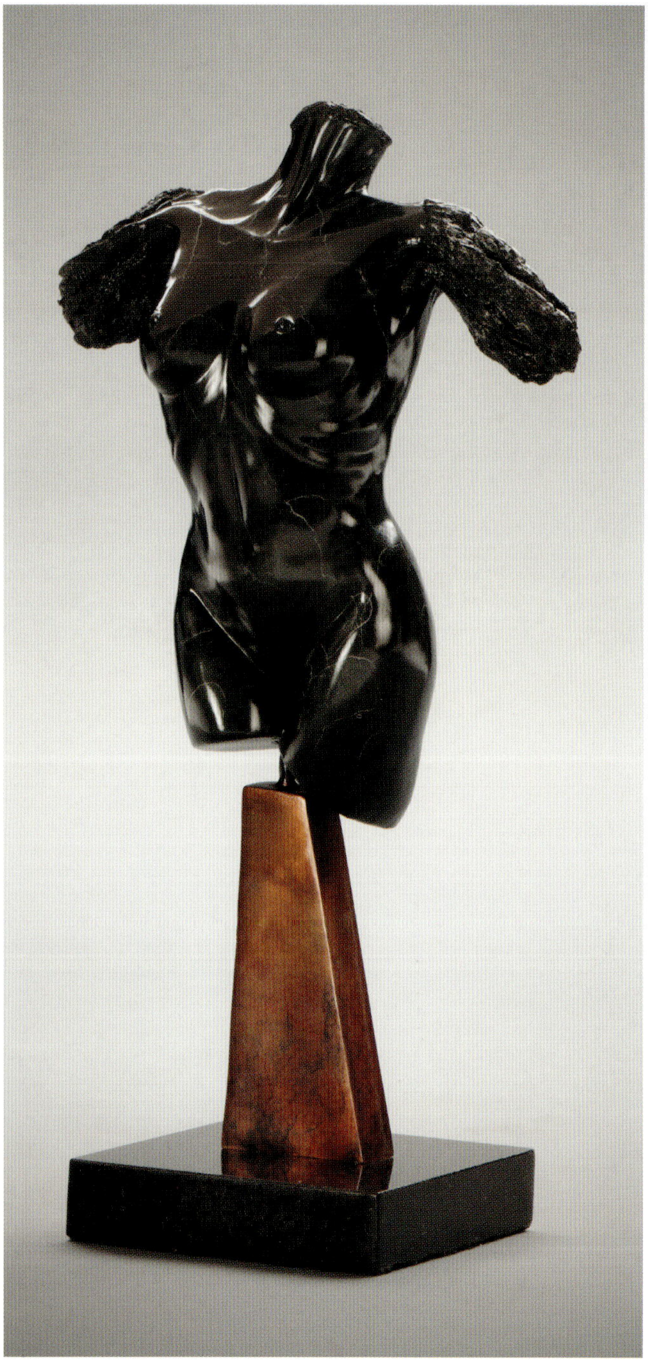

1

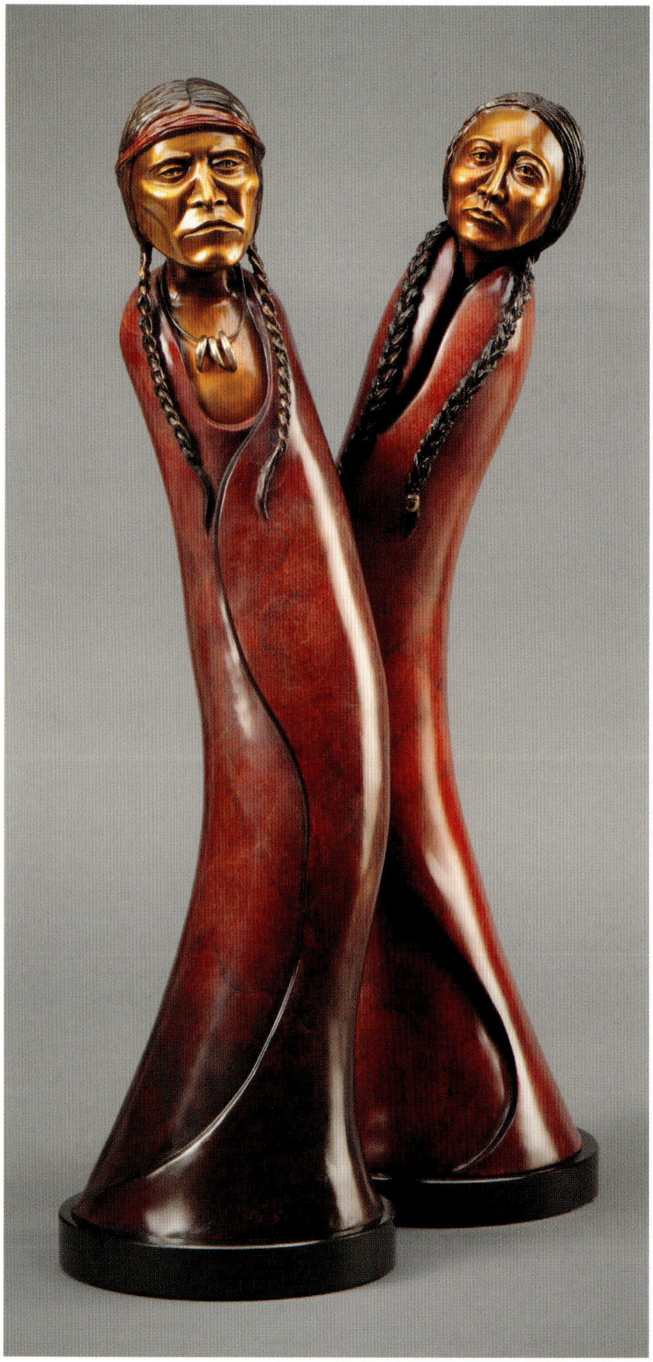

2

1 *Fledge,* 2010. Bronze, 16" x 5" x 5". *Photograph by Gary Alvis.*

2 *Hunter*, 2004, and *Gatherer,* 2004. Bronze 31" x 9" x 9". *Photograph by Gary Alvis.*

3 *Balance,* 2007. Bronze, 23" x 20" x 5". *Photograph by Gary Alvis.*

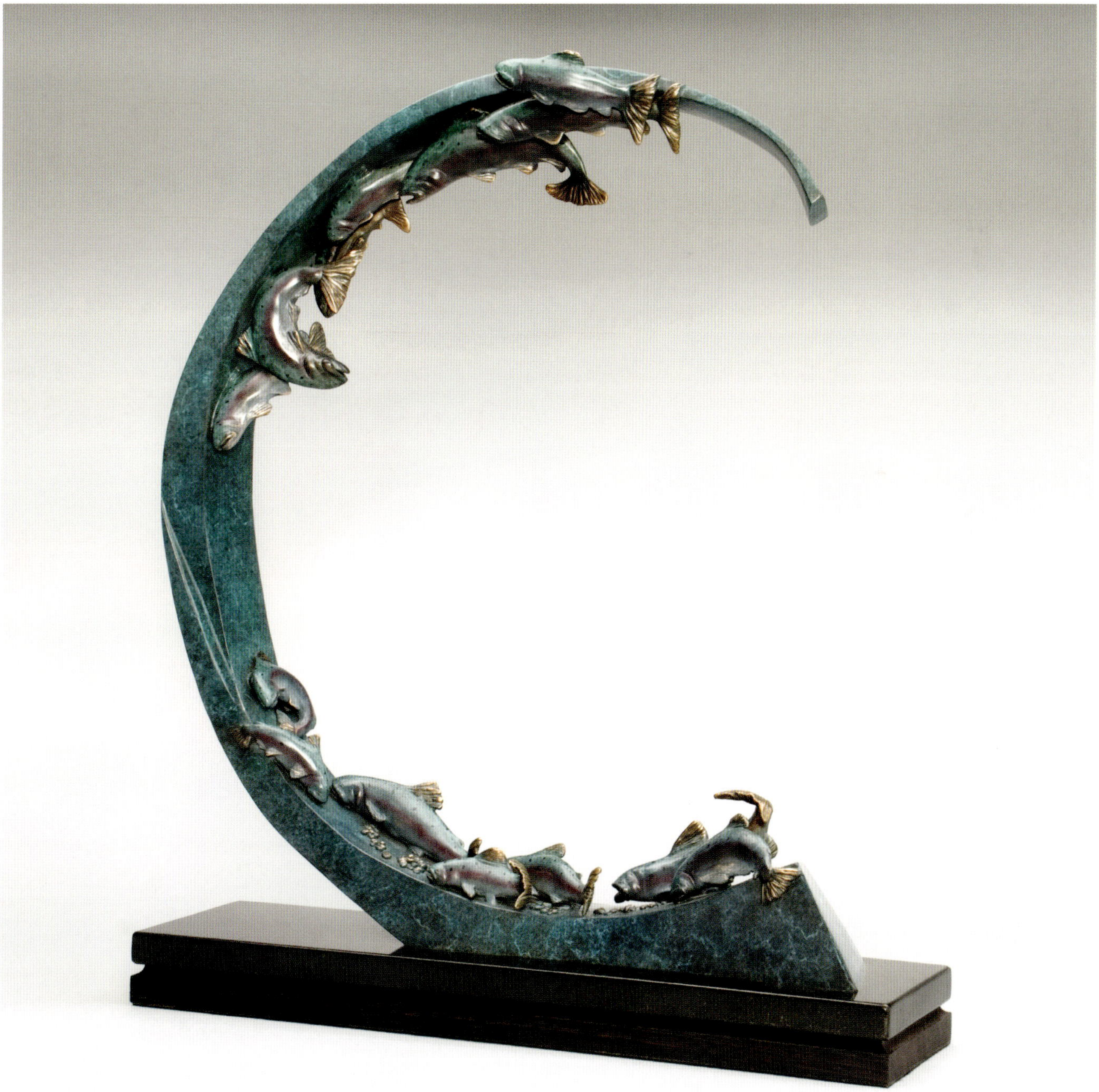

3

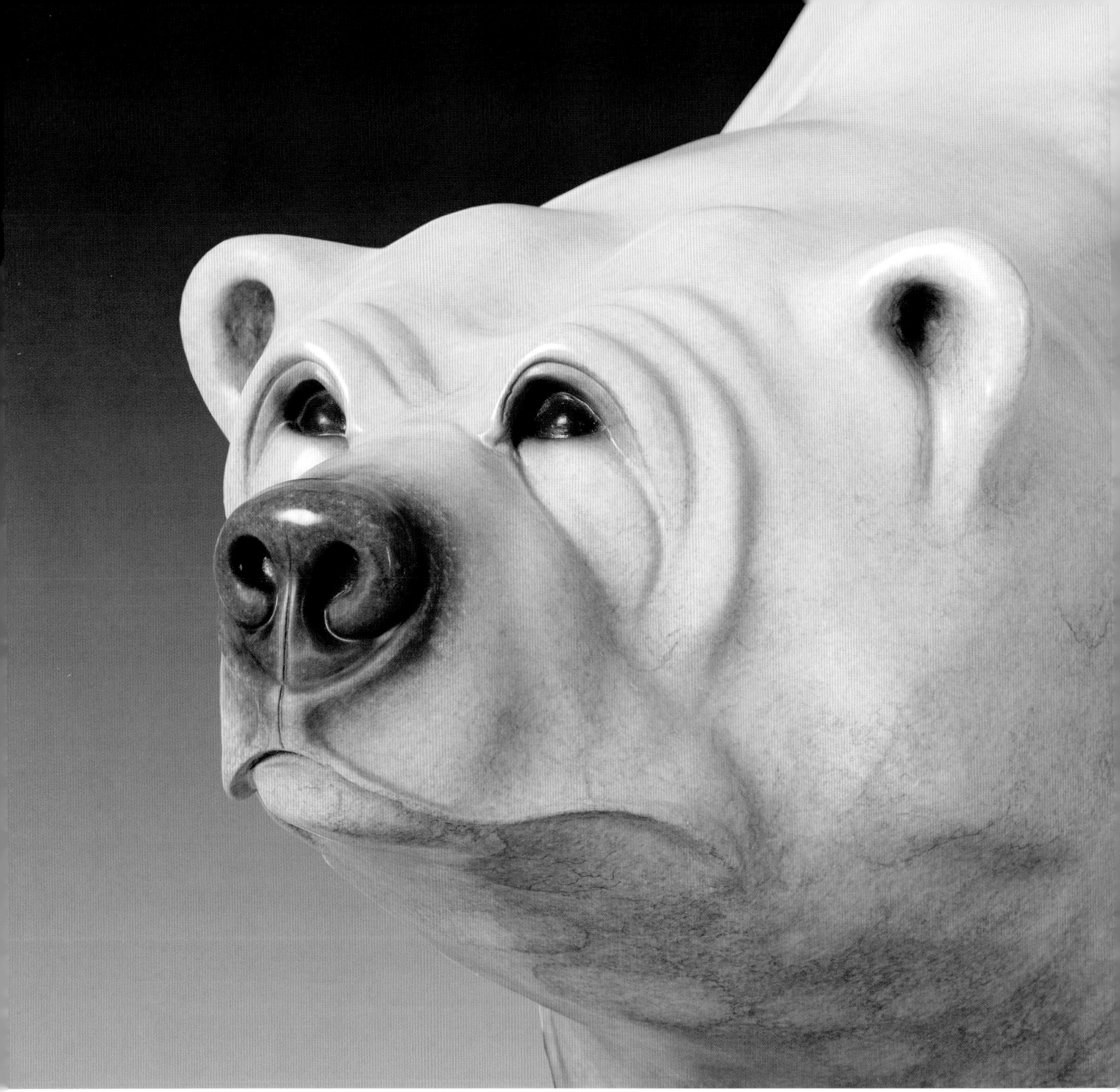

4

4 *Daydreamer* (detail). *Photograph by Gary Alvis.*

5 *Daydreamer,* 2004. Bronze, 31" x 23" x 60". *Photograph by Gary Alvis.*

6 *Constable of Ravens,* 2010. Bronze, 27" x 20" x 16". *Photograph by Gary Alvis.*

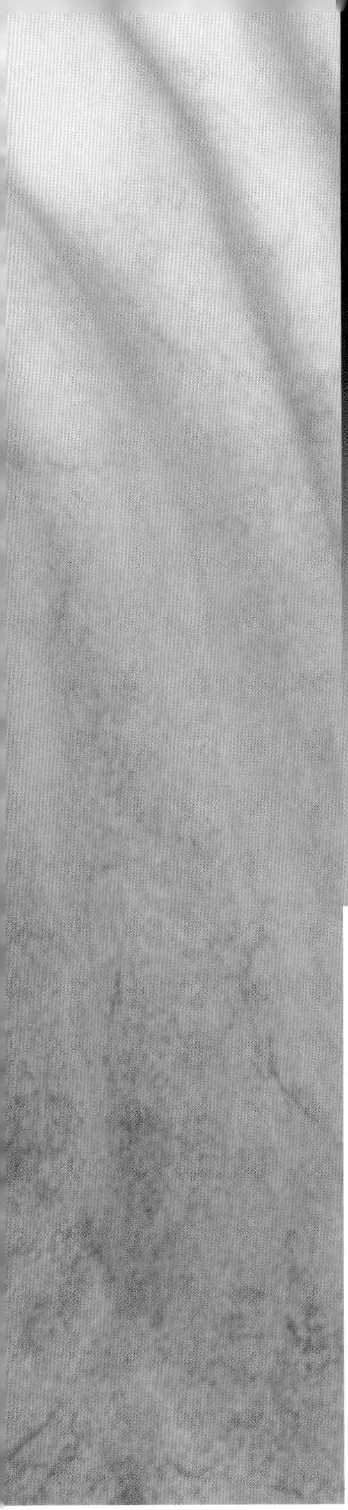

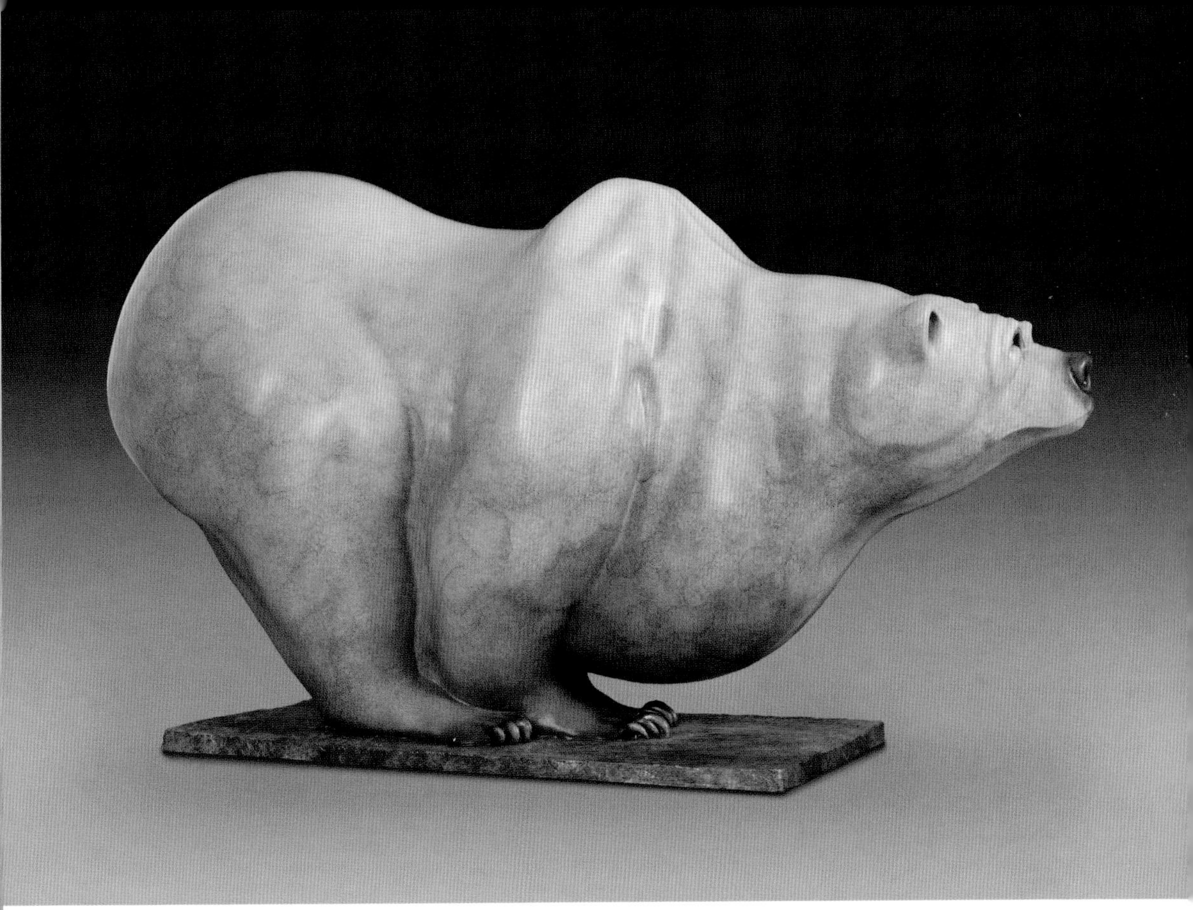

5

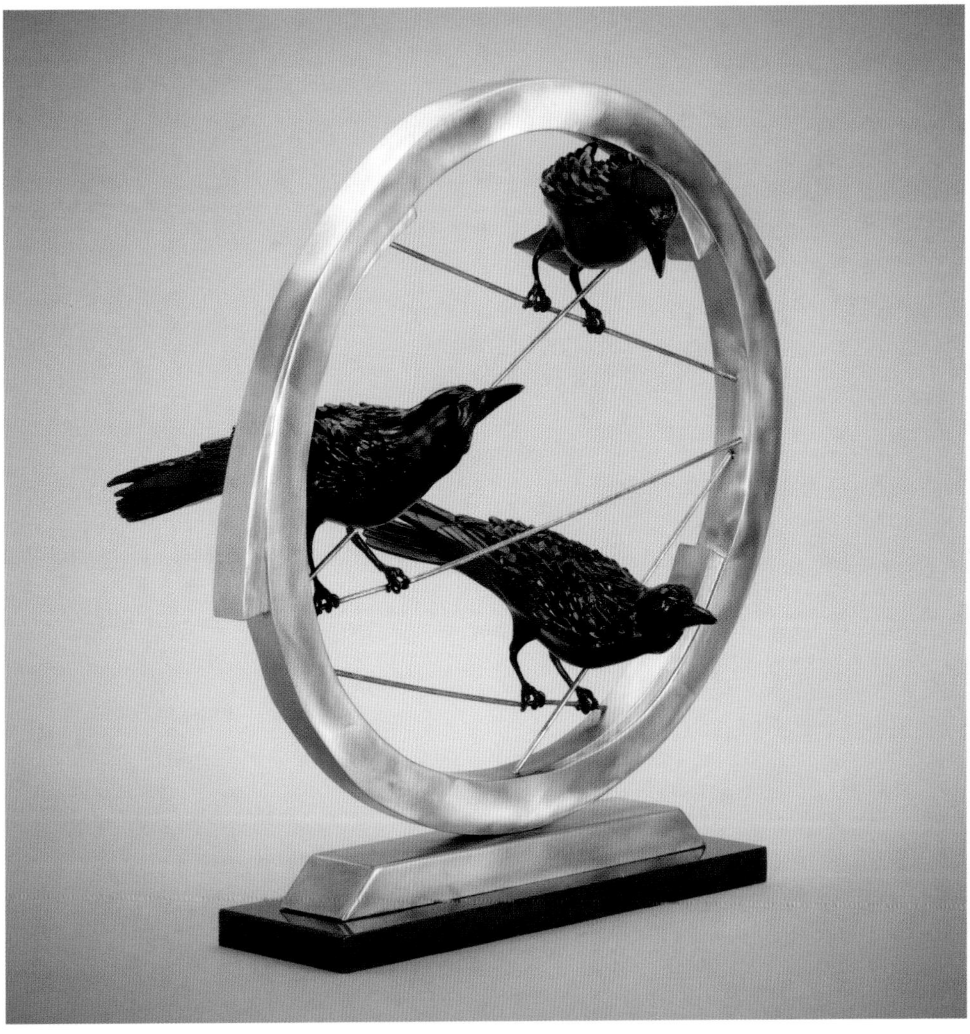

6

# Bob Clyatt

Rye, New York, USA
www.clyattsculpture.com

Bob's initial medium was photography; as a teen in northern California he created narrative and figurative works in a darkroom he built, and several prints were juried into regional Photographic Society of America shows. Bob was fortunate to be mentored for several years by western photographer Challiss Gore. After a brief career as a software entrepreneur and founder of a digital design firm, (both sold to public companies), Bob returned to studying and creating art full-time. His formal sculpture education centered on his years with Barney Hodes at the Art Student's League in New York. He also has degrees from U.C. Berkeley and MIT.

Bob's work has been featured multiple times in *The New York Times,* and is published in several books including Lark Books *500 Raku* (2011). Works have been included in invitational and solo shows throughout the U.S. Bob is represented by six galleries in North and South America including An American Craftsman Gallery in New York City.

*My work is to explore ancient knowledge and somehow embody or encode it in my sculptures and make it available to people today. In support of this, I am drawn to create my sculptures using ancient materials and methods, combined of course with modern technology. The result is contemporary art that at root is just earth, fire, water.*

*For me a successful sculpture is a mystery-object, gathering and amplifying whispers from the edges of awareness — maybe even giving us a glimpse of Creation.*

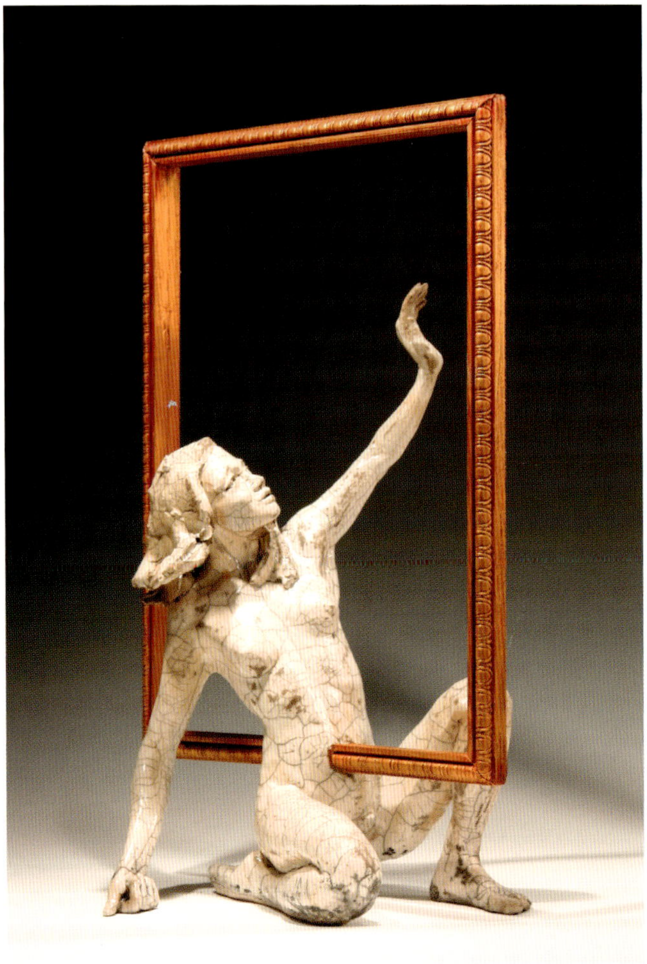

1

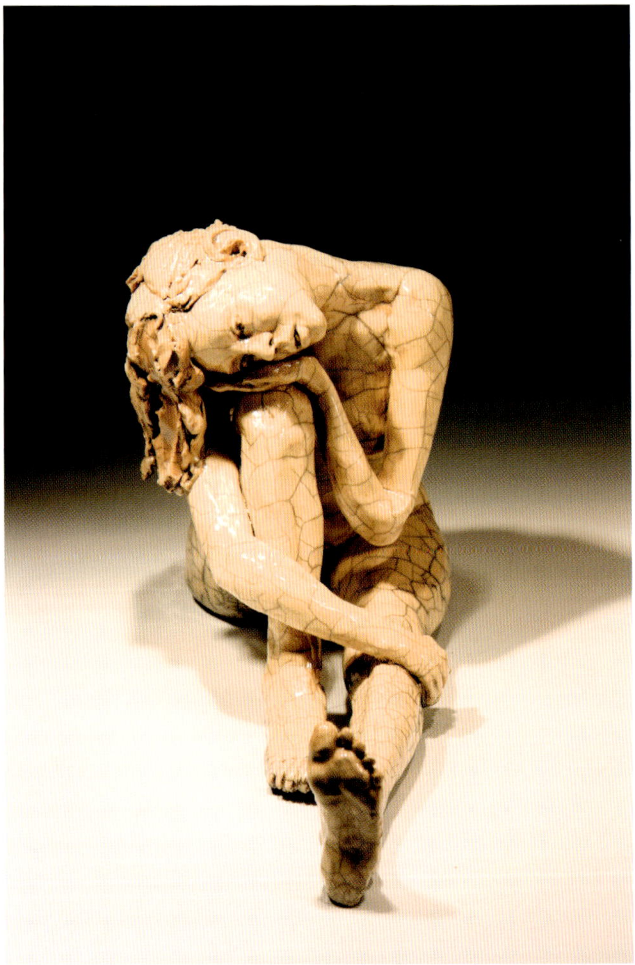

2

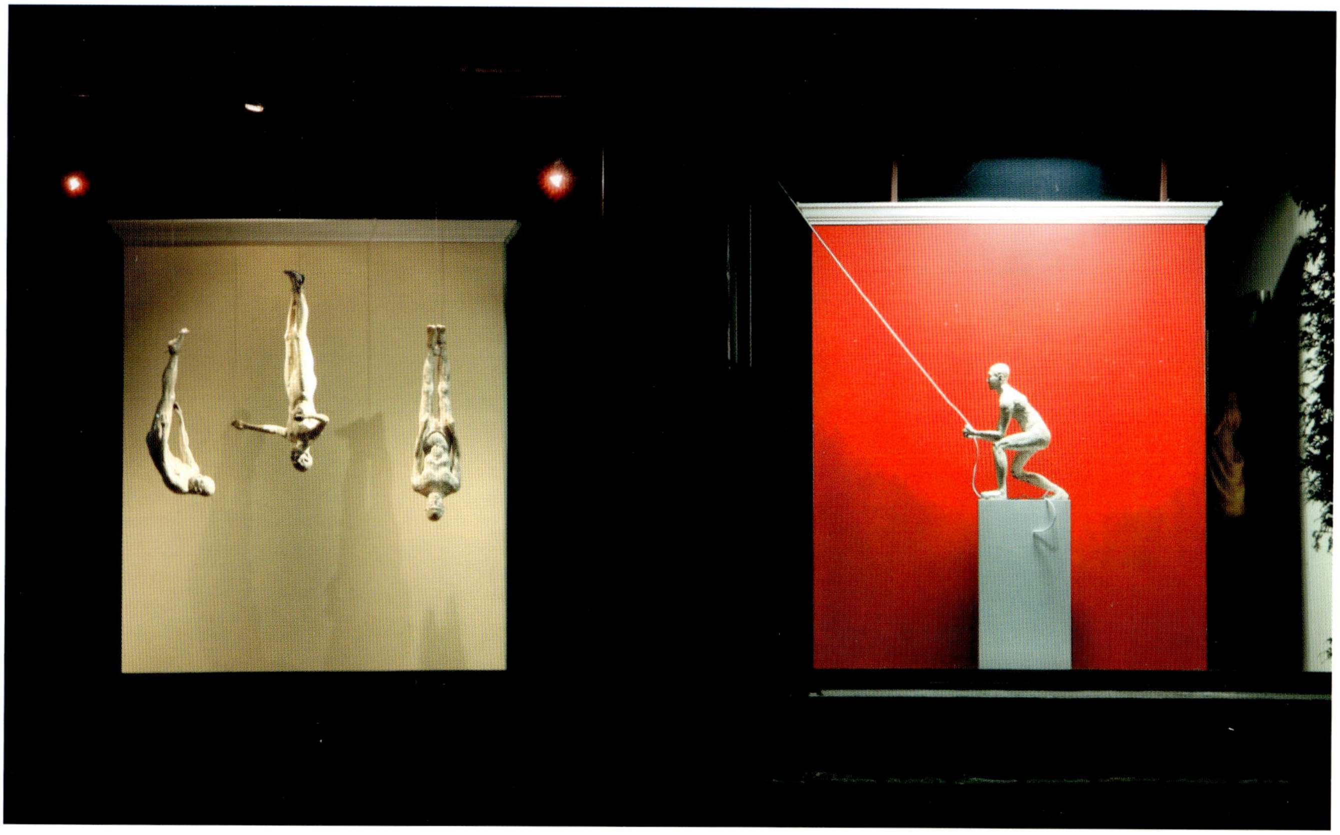

3

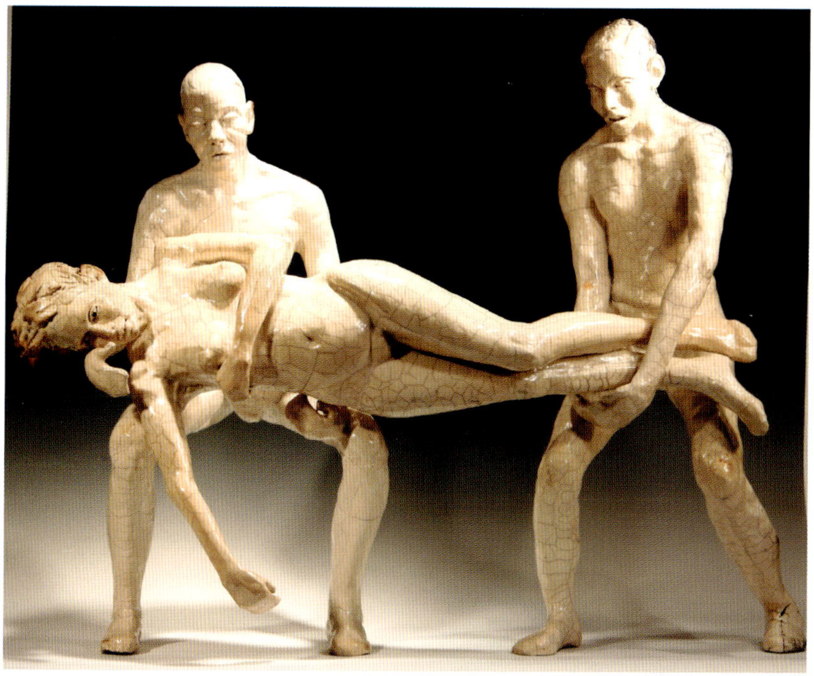

4

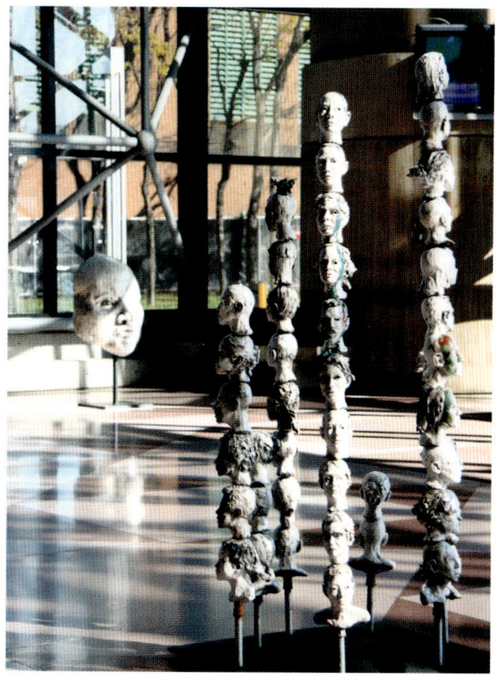

5

1 *Frame Series #2*, 2011. Raku-fired stoneware, 20" h. x 12" d. x 9" w. *Photograph by the artist.*

2 *Woman Head on Knee*, 2011. Raku-fired stoneware, 18" l. x 14" h. x 8" w. *Photograph by the artist.*

3 *Hanging Men*, 2011. Raku-fired stoneware, steel cable, rope. Four figures 34" h.; dimensions variable. *Photograph by the artist.*

4 *Dream Carriers*, 2010. Raku-fired stoneware, three interlocking figures, 30" h. x 33" w. x 16" d. *Photograph by the artist.*

5 *Our Institutions Fail (Us)*, 2010. Raku-fired stoneware, steel, umbrella element (not shown), 108" h. x 32" w. x 28"d. *Photograph by the artist.*

# Greg Coffelt

Riverside, California, USA
www.gregcoffeltsculptures.com

Metal Sculptor Greg Coffelt creates stunning, totally unique figurative masterpieces crafted from steel. Physically worked by hand and welded into place with an artisan's passion for recreating the graceful essence of the human form, his medium, primarily steel, is some of the hardest material in the world to sculpt.

Completely self-taught, Coffelt was inspired by the works of Rodin and Michelangelo, who are primary influences on his style and composition. He received an award from the Pacific Arts Foundation for the "Best of the Best" contest for a drawing he created. Eschewing the path taken by many metal sculptors who work in cast bronze, Coffelt was seduced by the challenge and beauty of working in steel which allows him to create his unique signature style. Like many great artists before him, a thorough study of human anatomy has given him insight into the human form and, when combined with application of his practical experience and creative vision, the artistic results are nothing less than awe inspiring.

Coffelt began to sculpt seriously in steel in 2000 with the "Evolution of Eve" series.

A single sculpture can take the artist up to 9 months to create. When finished, it is plated in nickel. Each sculpture is an original. An exact copy would be impossible. Therefore, every Coffelt creation is truly "one-of-a-kind." To the best of our knowledge, nothing quite like his art exists anywhere in the world.

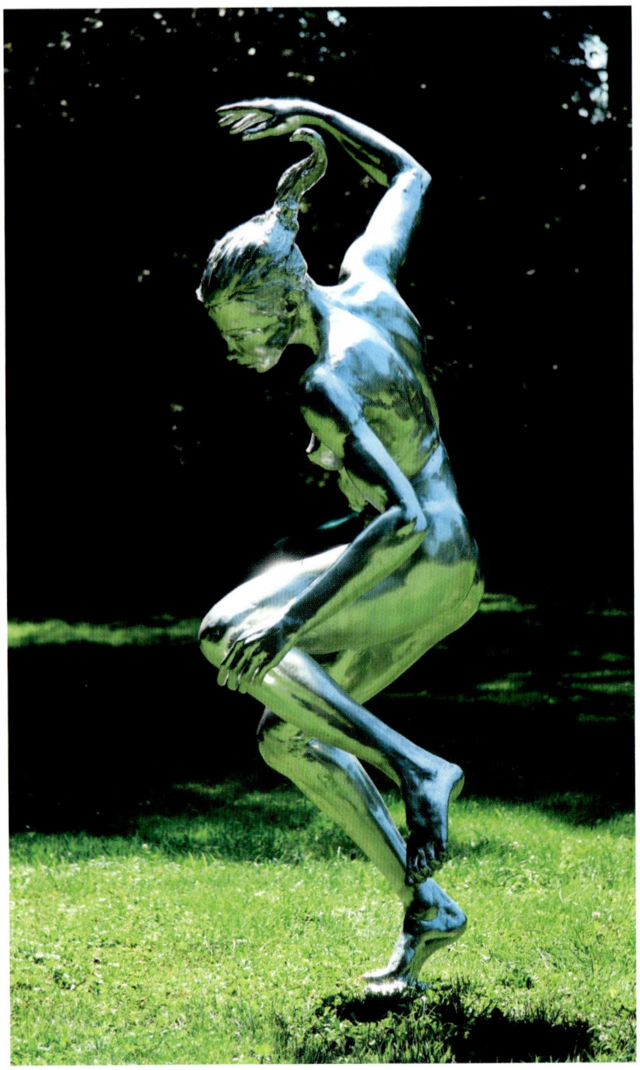

1

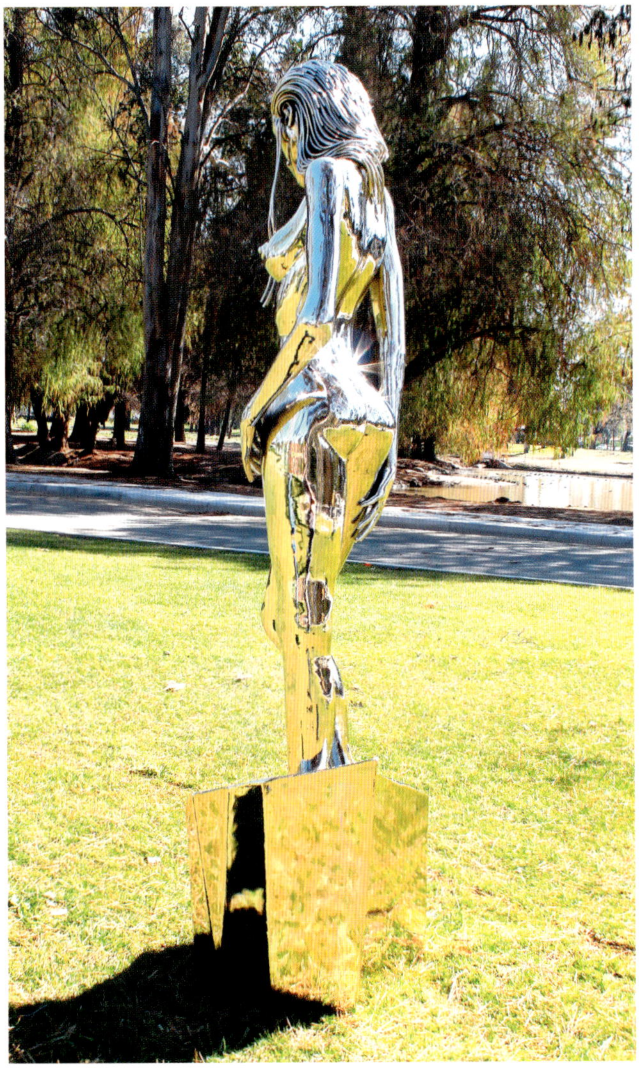

2

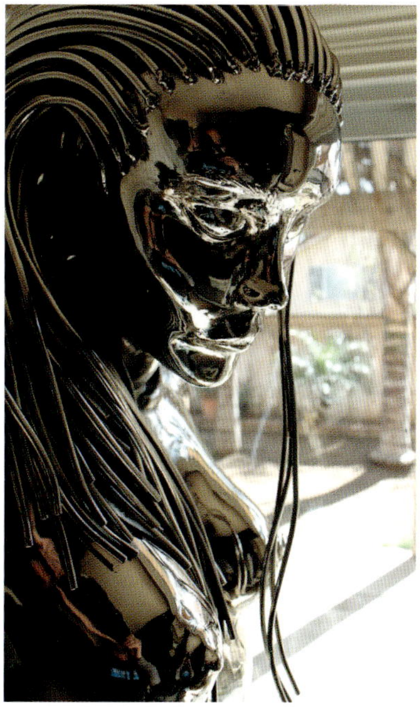

3

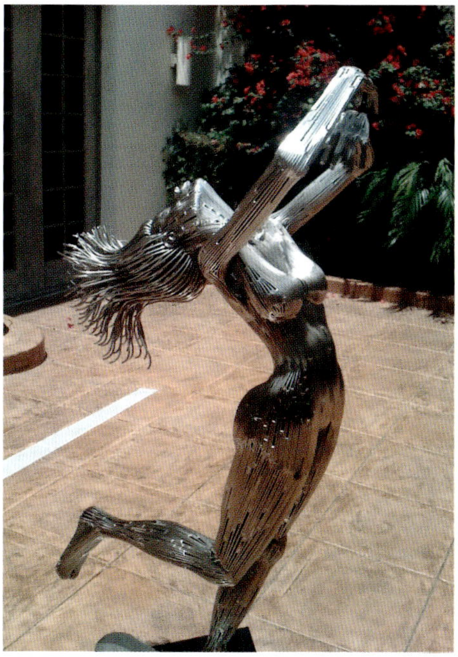

4

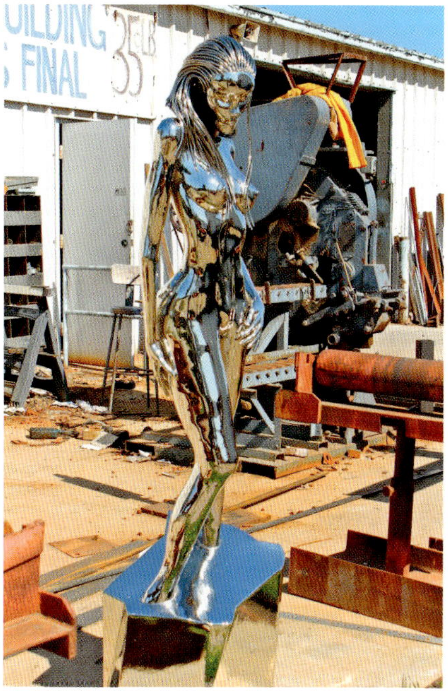


5

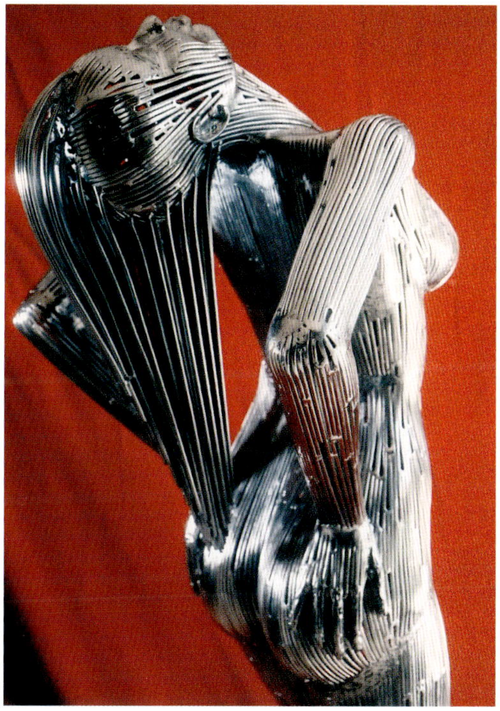

6

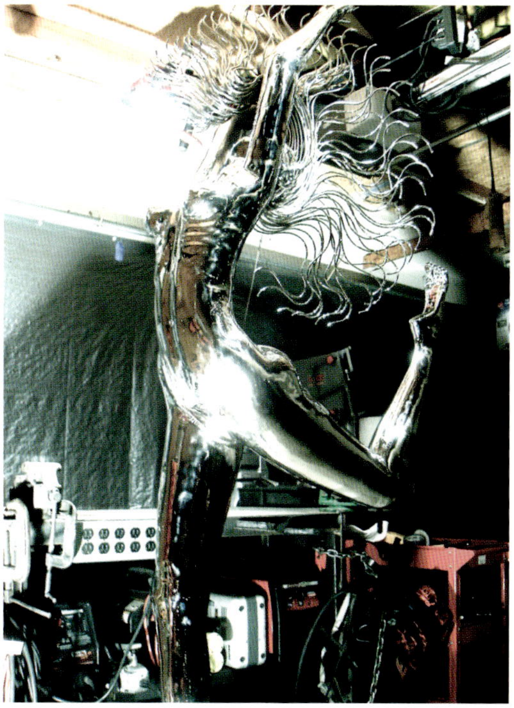

7

1 *Dance of Life*, 2009. Gelcoat, fiberglass resin, chrome finish, 83" h. x 36" w. x 24" d. (lifesize). *Photograph by the artist.*

2 *Evolution of Eve, figure 4* (detail). *Photograph by Greg Coffelt.*

3 *Evolution of Eve, figure 4* (detail). *Photograph by Greg Coffelt.*

4 *Evolution of Eve, figure 2*, 2002. Nickel-plated round steel, 78" tall. *Photograph by Greg Coffelt.*

5 *Evolution of Eve, figure 4*, 2011, Nickel-plated steel, 76" tall. *Photograph by Greg Coffelt.*

6 *Evolution of Eve, figure 3*, 2004, Nickel-plated round steel, 74" tall. *Photograph by Greg Coffelt.*

7 *Divina Natura,* 2009, Nickel-plated steel, 96" tall. *Photograph by Greg Coffelt.*

# Claudia Cohen Studios

Sausalito, California, USA
www.claudiacohen.com

Like beauty, truth lies in the eye of the beholder – and in the mind of the artist. The bronze and ceramic creations of California artist Claudia Cohen are not realistic in any strict sense of the term, but they are precise renditions of her imagination, engaging articulations of the ruminations of her subconscious. With her dazzling style of meticulous detail and feeling for form, the work brings to life a magical cast of characters – human, animal, and are a fantastical progeny from a different and inviting universe.

Claudia received her art education at The School of The Museum of Fine Arts in Boston, Massachusetts and then moved to the West Coast and opened her studio in the artist community of Sausalito, California, on the San Francisco Bay. In the book *Humor in Art*, by Nickolas Roukes, the work was described as Comic Surrealism, which aptly sums up her feel for humor and pathos. Magic Realism is another term often used to characterize her narrative creations – a style that blends objective reality with mythology and flights of fancy. In 2008 Sculptor Claudia was featured in Turin, Italy, at the MIAAO Museum as representative of The School of California Funk Ceramics.

Her magic-surreal style, unique colored patinas and mixture of humor and pathos cause art-lovers worldwide to seek-out the mysterious-visions that her sculptures evoke.

1

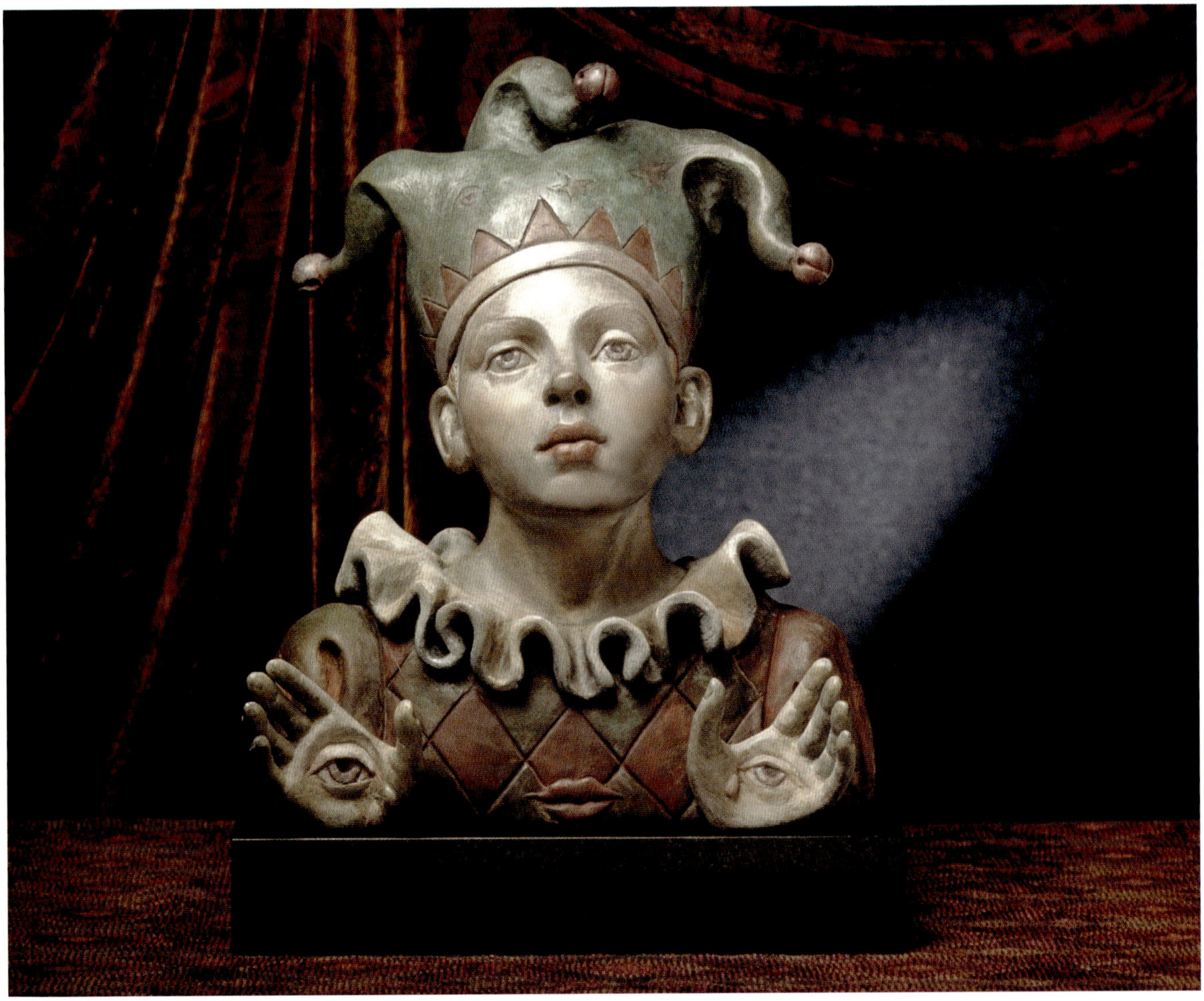

1 *Making Magic*, 2006. Bronze, 18" x 13" x 8". *Photograph by Kim Harrington.*

2 *The Hands of Time,* 2010. Ceramic, mixed media. *Photograph by Karen Strange.*

3 *Road Warriors,* 2008. Ceramic, mixed media, 11" tall. *Photograph by Kim Harrington.*

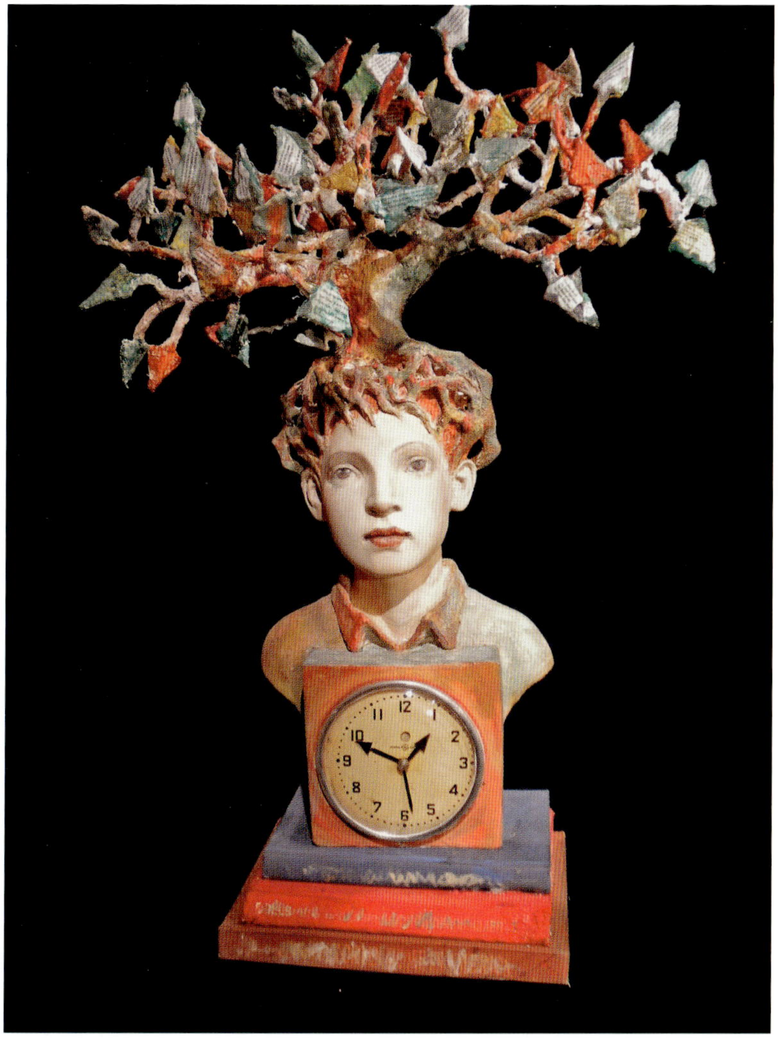

2

3

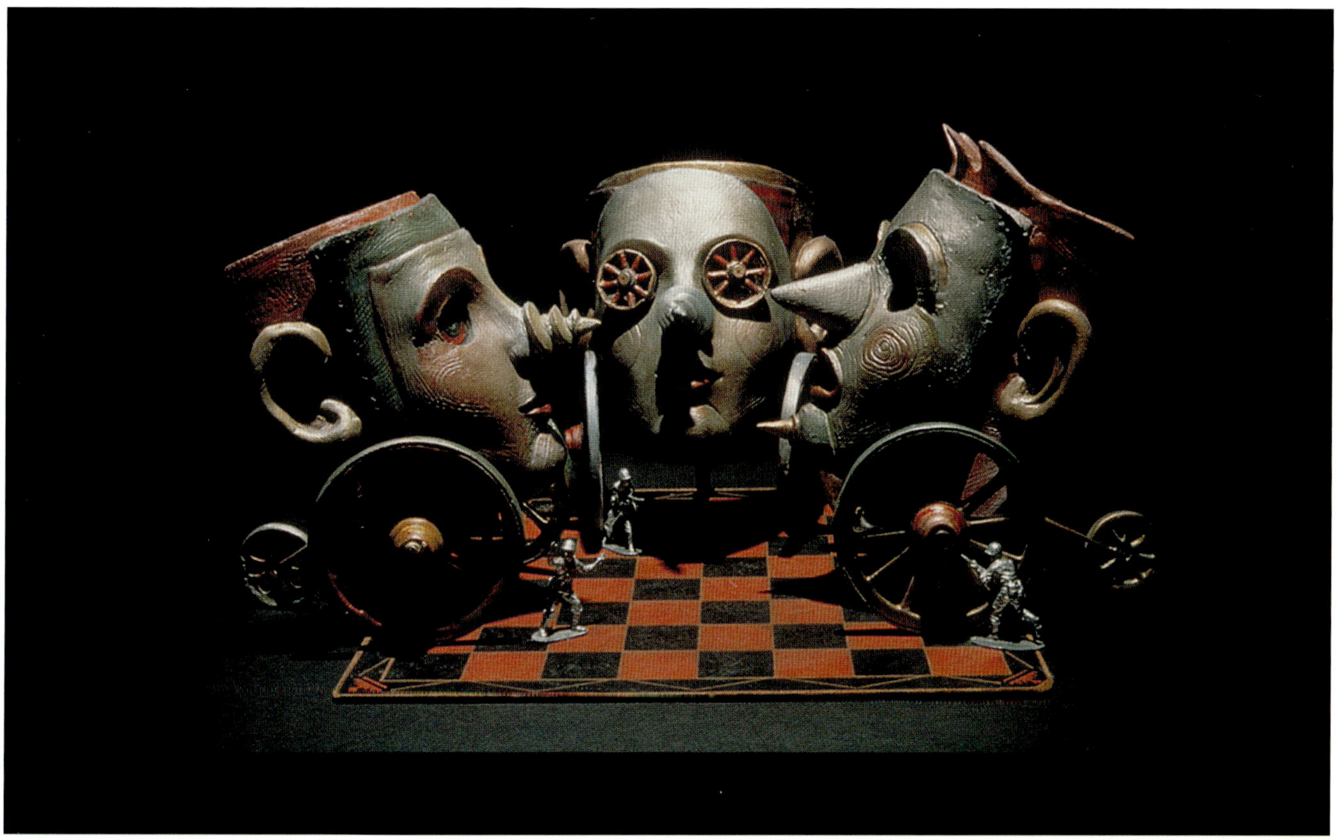

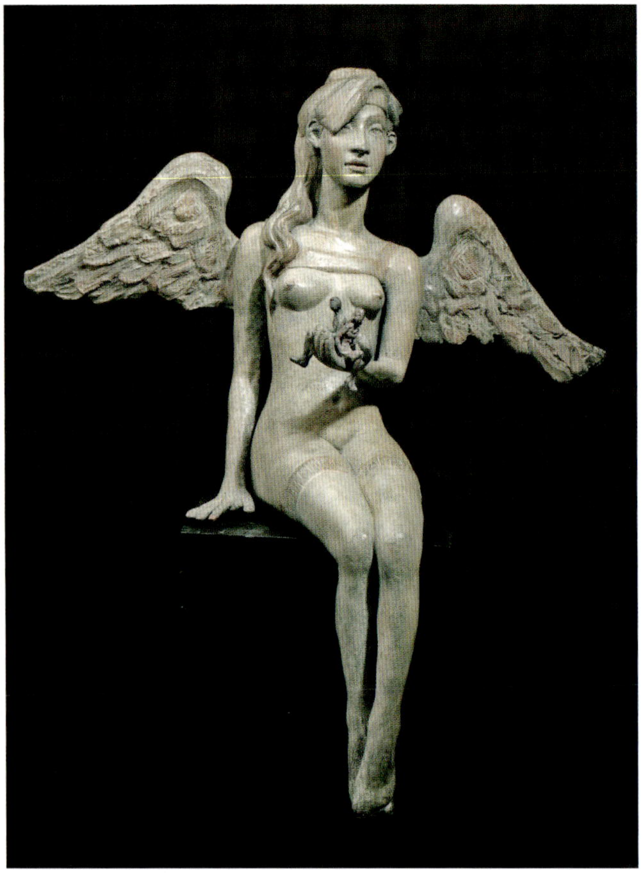

4

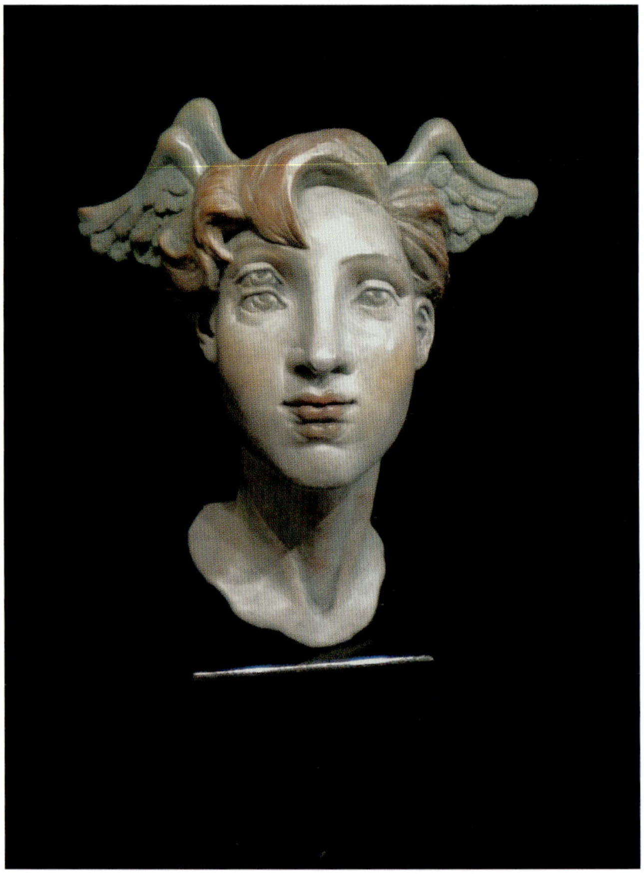

5

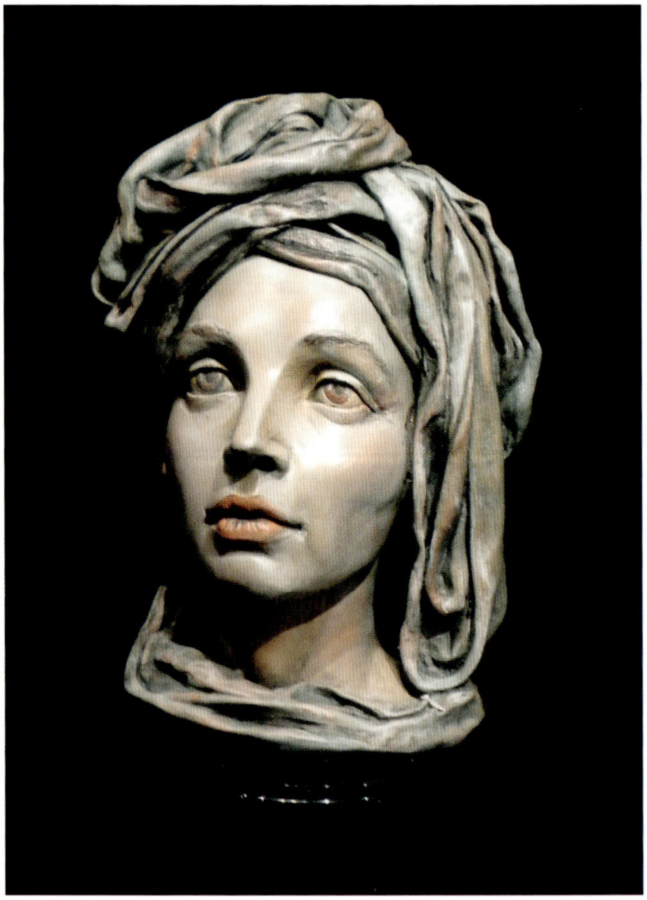

6

4 *The Eternal Conversation,* 2009. Bronze, 19" x 20" x 12". *Photograph by Kim Harrington.*

5 *Doubletake*, 2005. Bronze, 12" x 9" x 8". *Photograph by Kim Harrington.*

6 *Cassandra,* 2006. Bronze, 15" x 9" x 10". *Photograph by Karen Strange.*

7 *Screwball,* 2005. Bronze sculpture on wheels, 10" x14" x 8". *Photograph by Kim Harrington.*

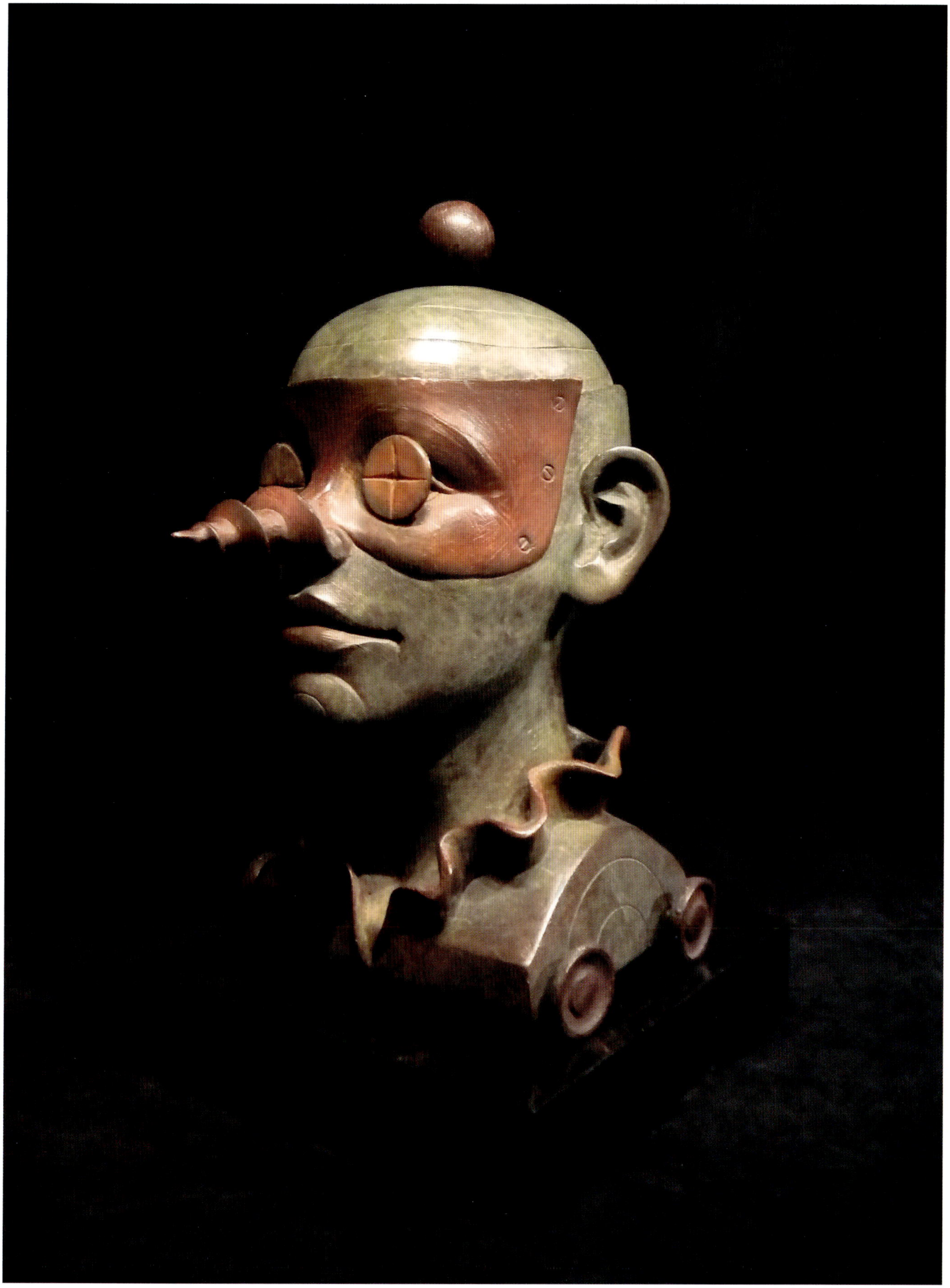

7

# Keri Joy Colestock

Pingree Grove, Illinois, USA
www.walldancers.com

*I create fun, funky original art. My journey began with my "Wall Dancers," polymer dolls. I have sold 1400 of them – each made one at a time. I have now been playing with found objects and I am having a riot! I truly am loving turning "junk" into masterpieces. Most recently my husband and have been collaborating on "KeRicTures" which are 26"-29" whimsical wood sculptures. Their faces are 5-6 layers of masonite assembled and painted to create very bright, funky sculptures!*

*I was diagnosed with Lyme disease in February 2002 and that kept me literally bed-bound. The first 300 "Wall Dancers" were made in bed. I was told it was impossible for me to do much of anything because I was severely damaged neurologically. I can confidently say that they were wrong! Actually the worse I feel, the more art I make! I truly believe everything happens for a reason and I accept that I am exactly where I am supposed to be today. I am blessed with a beautiful family and friends. I have met great people and learned great lessons on my journey.*

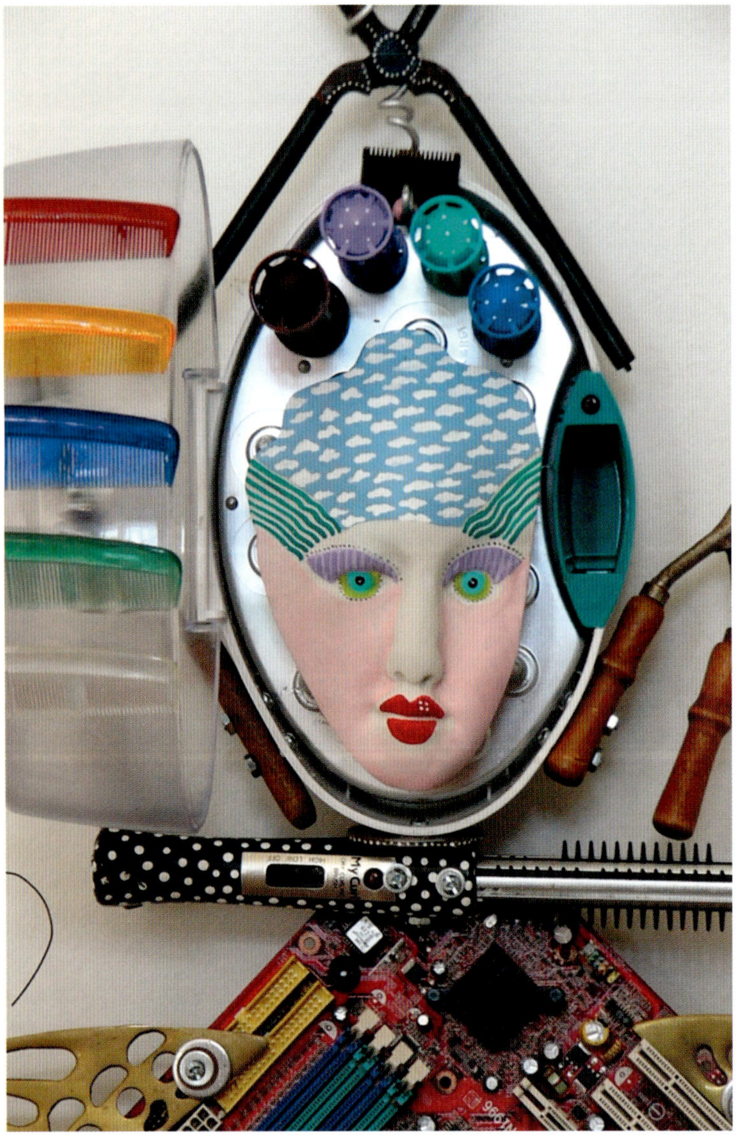

1

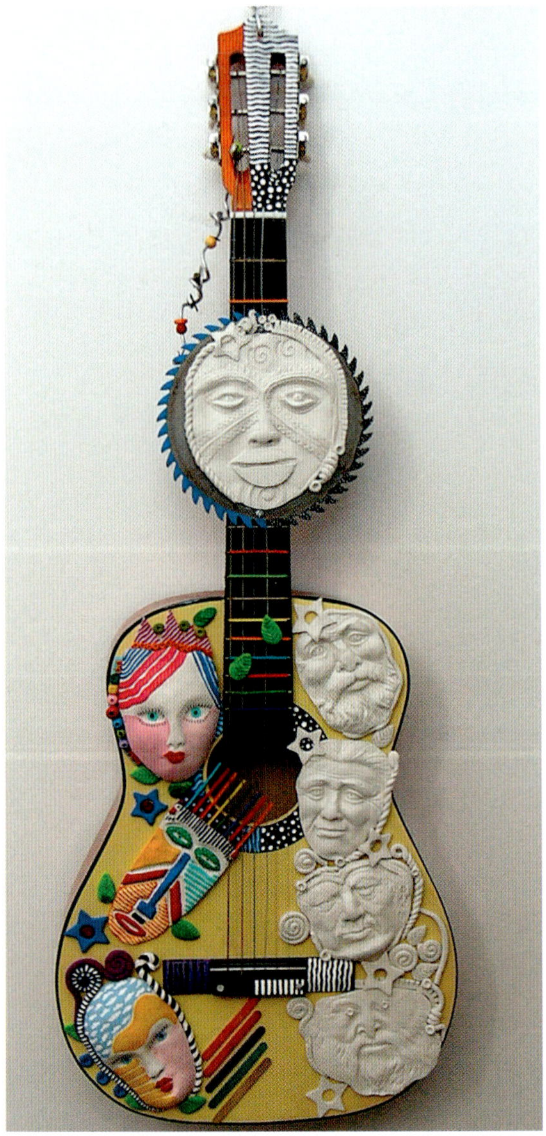

2

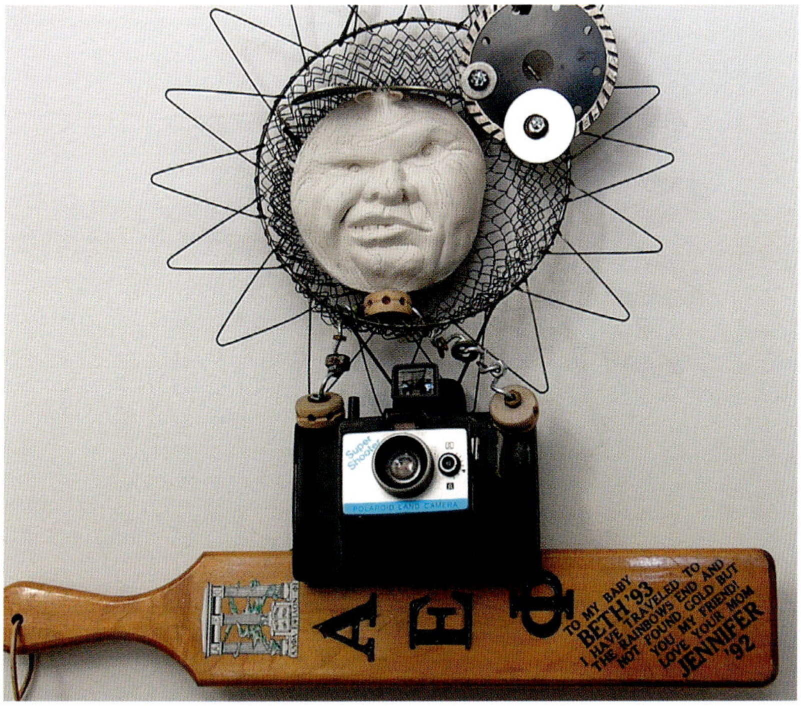


3

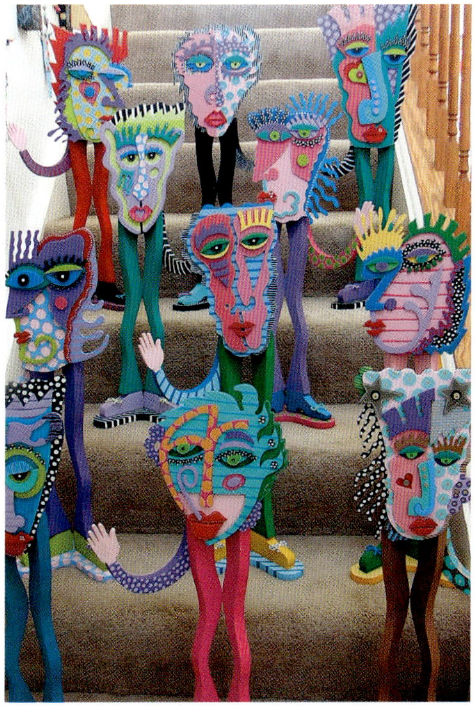

4

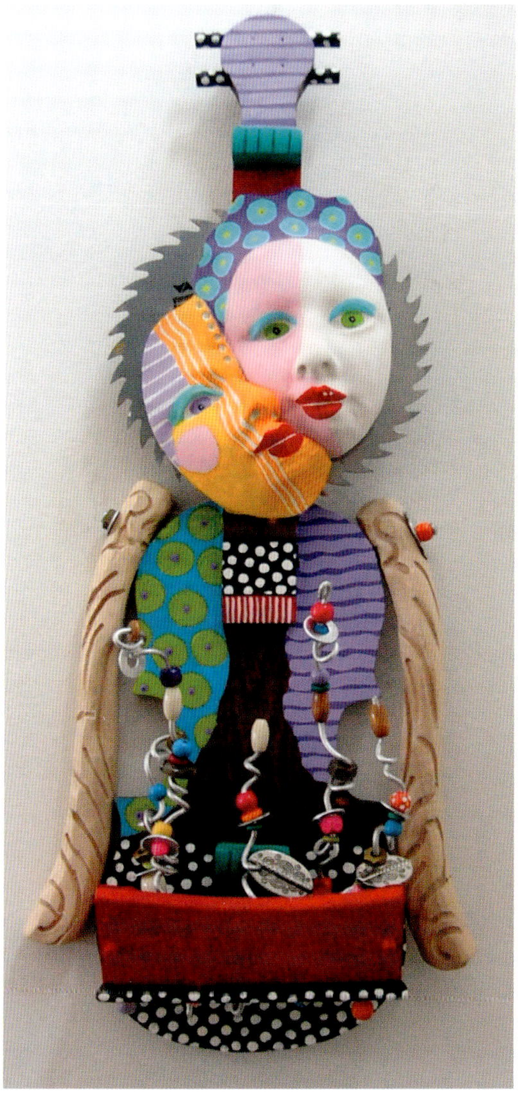

5

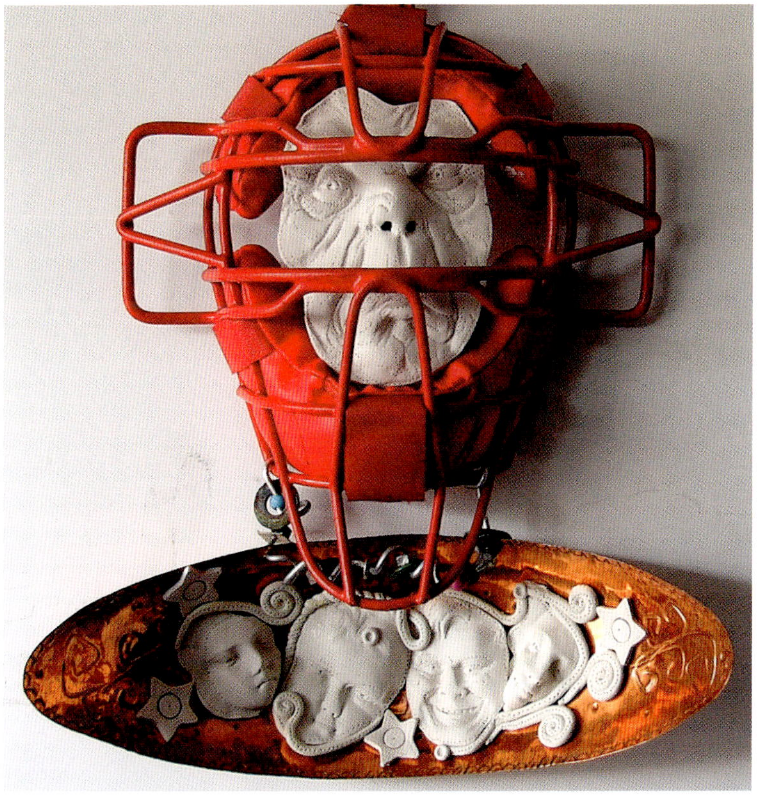

6

1 *My Daughter's Xmas Present* (detail), December 2010. Mixed media, 42" x 29" x 12".

2 *Play Your Heart Out*, December 2010, January 2011. Mixed media, 50" x 20" x 5".

3 *Cheap Sunglasses,* January 2011. Mixed media, 27" x 21" x 8".

4 KeRicTures, 2011. Mixed media.

5 *Time To Smell The Flowers,* April 2011. Mixed media, 24" x 10" x 5.5".

6 *Dream Catcher*, November 2010. Mixed media, 20" x 13" x 9".

# Mindy Z. Colton

Orlando, Florida, USA
www.mindycolton.com

Originally from New York City, Mindy was classically trained in all the traditional arts. She pursued a career in graphic design and illustration. She eventually left behind her successful career to follow her true passion as a fine artist. Her focus in recent years has been on sculpture from table top to monumental. Involved with horses her entire life, she chose to combine her passion for both art and equine in her unique sculptural works.

Mindy is a two-time State of Florida Grantee and three-time United Arts of Central Florida Grant recipient. "Renewal," a monumental sculpture exhibited at Epcot, received Best of Show and People's Choice Award in the 2006 Kissimmee Sculpture Experience. Colton's award-winning fine art has been exhibited in numerous solo and two-person shows and over 100 juried and group shows.

*I create one-of-a-kind and limited edition sculptures in ceramic, mixed media, bronze, aluminum, and other permanent media. My horses are unique figurative abstractions with a decidedly expressionistic aesthetic. I use the horse and other symbols to elicit a feeling or mood or to create a story. Using the horse as vehicles for concepts, metaphors, and more human emotions. With my unique mixed-media sculptures, I can indulge my artistic passion to both sculpt and paint. The long striding legs of my "Unbridled Spirit" horse sculptures are carved tree limbs, copper wires, and the textured body, various permanent composite materials. I strive for my works to intrigue the viewer, invite a closer look, and exhibit strength, determination and vulnerability.*

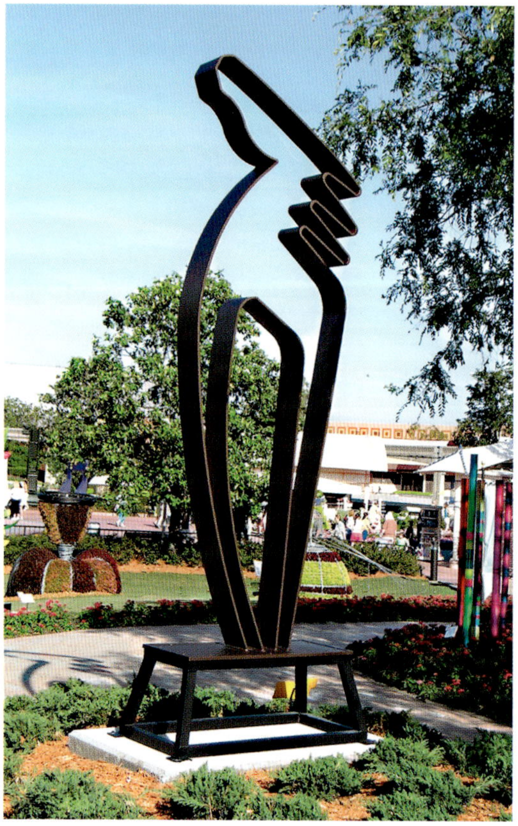

1

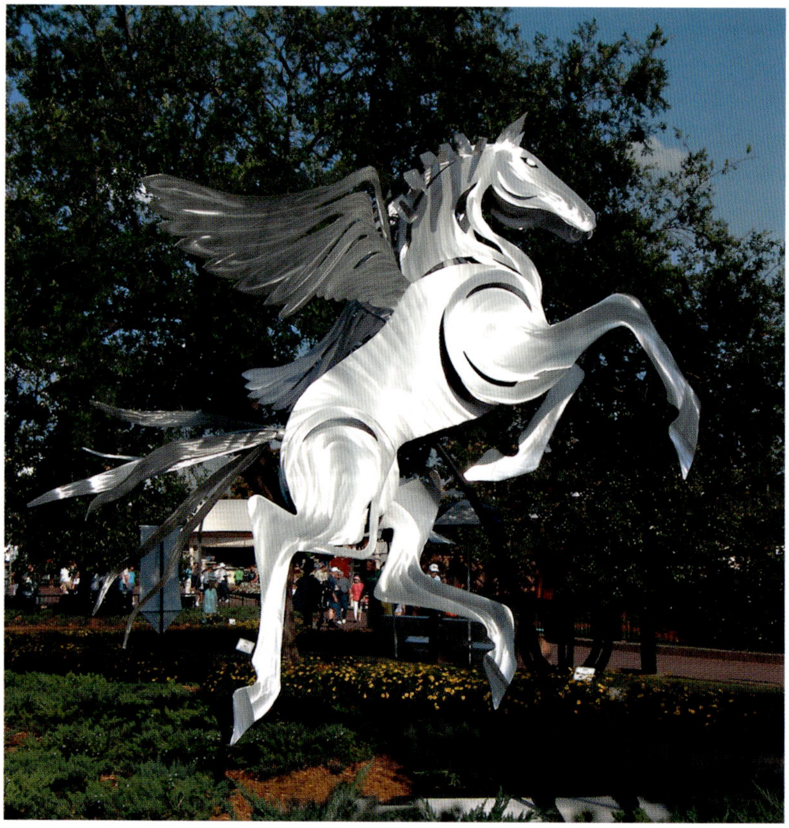

2

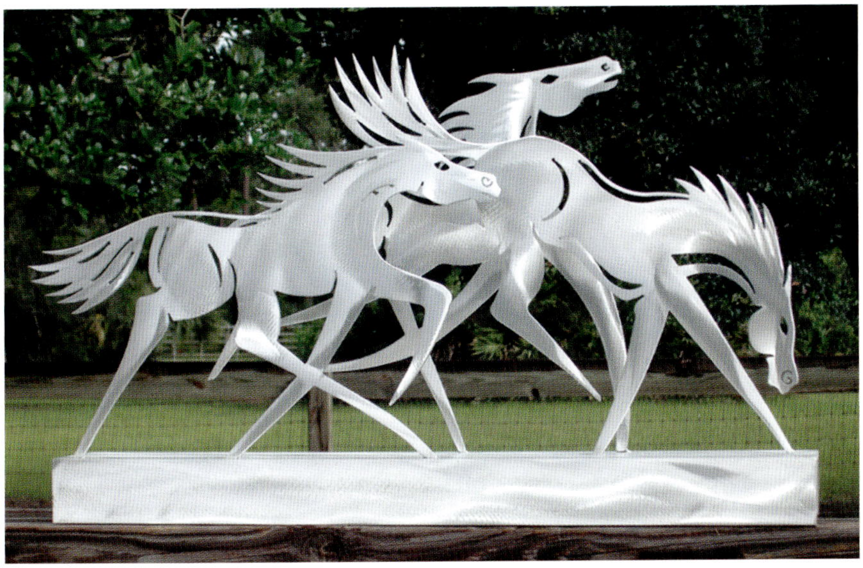

3

1 *Renewal*, 2005. Marine grade aluminum, 12'. *Photograph by Mindy Z. Colton.*

2 *Wind Dancer,* 2006. Marine grade aluminum,10'. *Photograph by Mindy Z. Colton.*

3 *Race the Wind*, 2006. Marine grade aluminum, 18". *Photograph by Mindy Z. Colton.*

4 *Unbridled Spirits: The Conversation,* 2010. Ceramic, mixed media. *Photograph by Randall Smith.*

5 *Close Encounter*, 2006. Bronze, 9". *Photograph by Randall Smith.*

6 *Nature's Gift,* 2009. Mixed media, 36". *Photograph by Randall Smith.*

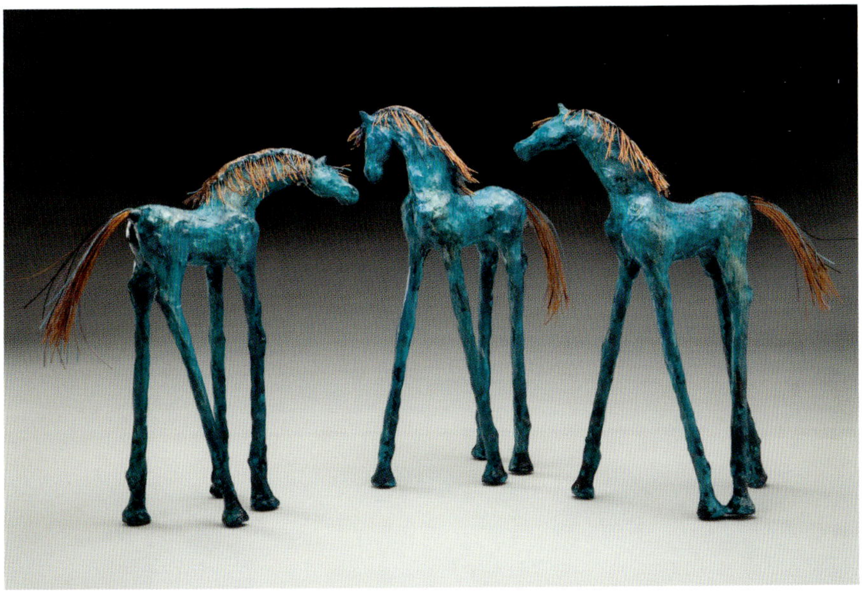

4

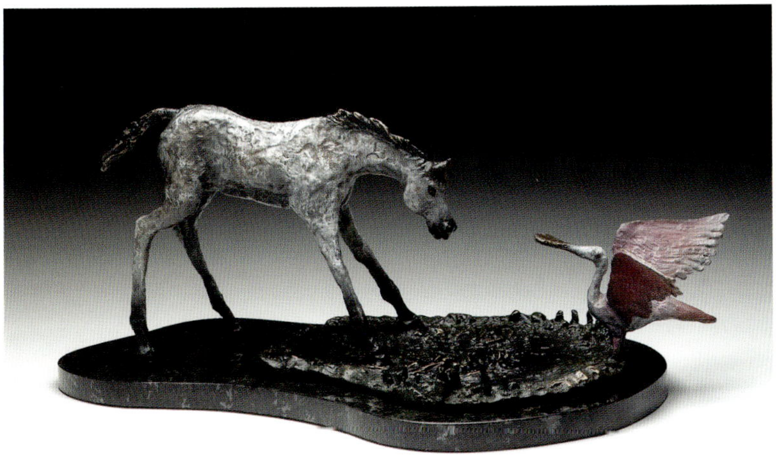

5

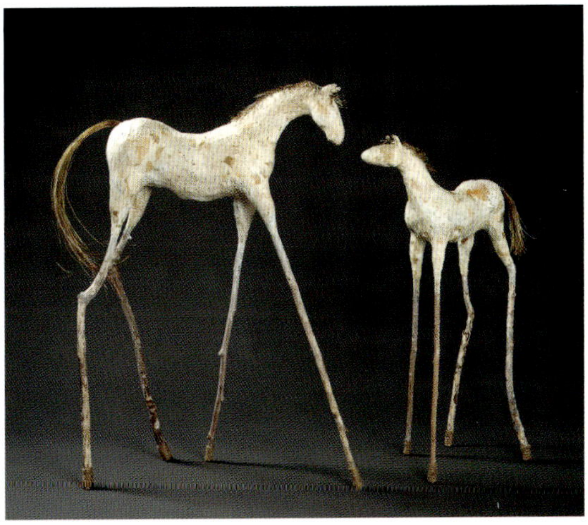

6

# Delayne Corbett

Vancouver, British Columbia, Canada
www.delayne.ca

Delayne Corbett is an award-winning sculptor admired by artists and the public alike. Born in Nelson, British Columbia, he grew up traveling across Canada as a member of the art world since his youth. Delayne has always worked with his hands, imaginatively rearranging his environment to engage his body and mind. Throughout his life he has continued to explore many media, always working on something new. His passion is working with stone to create sensual sculptures that invoke strong emotional responses. He studies sculpture through in-depth, self-guided research, superb mentorship, and attending workshops and competitions. Delayne resides in Victoria, British Columbia, and continues to sculpt. He is a sought after ice, snow, and sand sculptor, and often travels abroad to work on large projects. His home time is consumed by working either as a stonemason or in his studio.

Delayne's work explores the natural beauty of the environment by manipulating and rearranging the essence of that beauty in stunning, thought-provoking ways, making the common extraordinary. Stone sculpting allows him to take cues from the rock itself and create unique designs through the melding of nature and man. By accentuating the stones' inherent properties, his sculpture reflects the sensuality of nature. With the use of line, curve and negative space, the visual and tactile aspects of his work evoke a strong emotional and physical reaction.

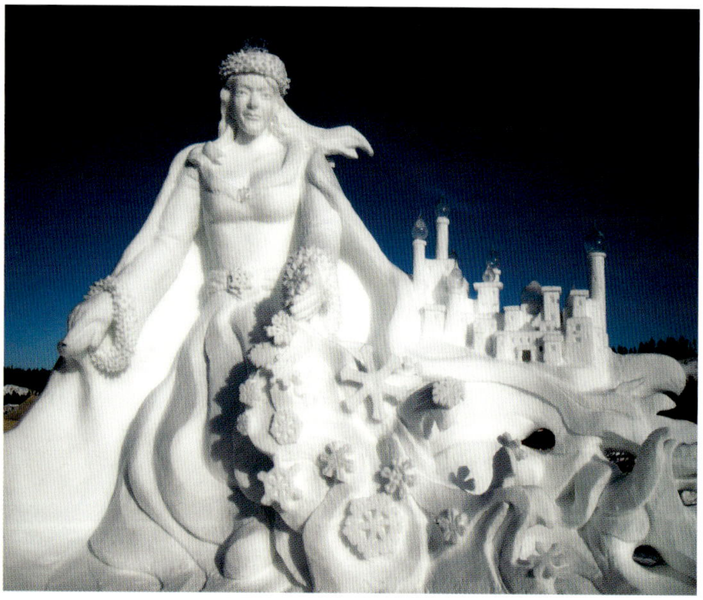

1

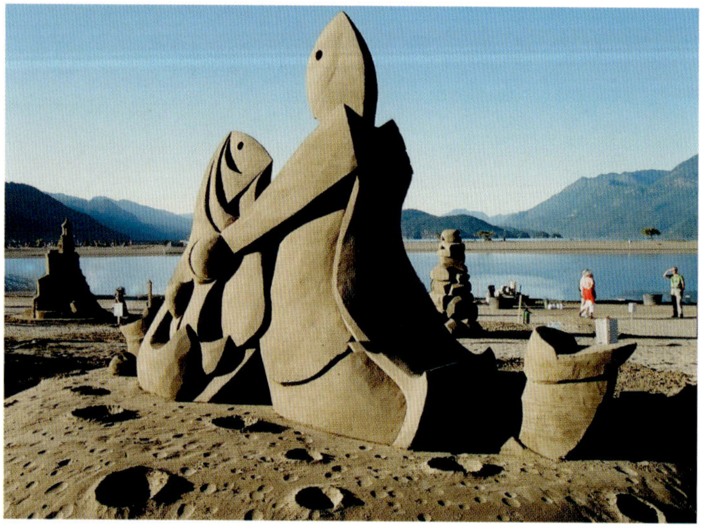

2

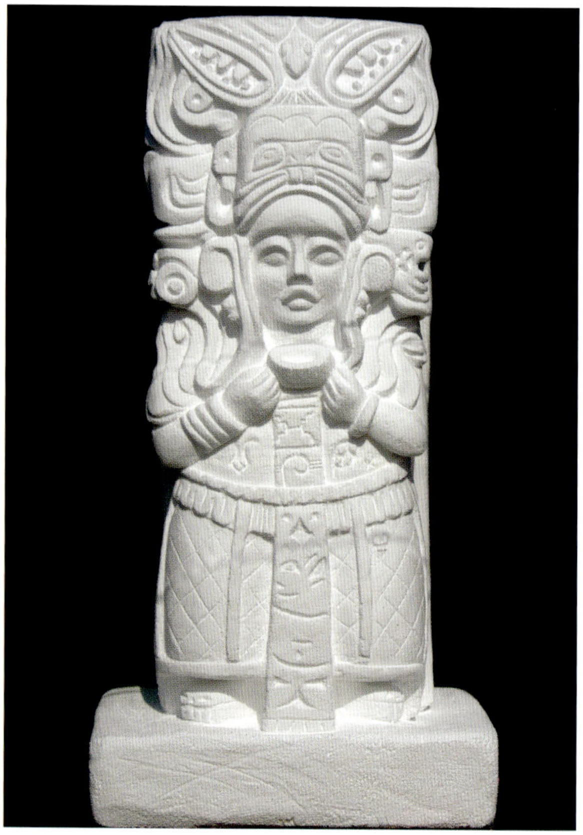

3

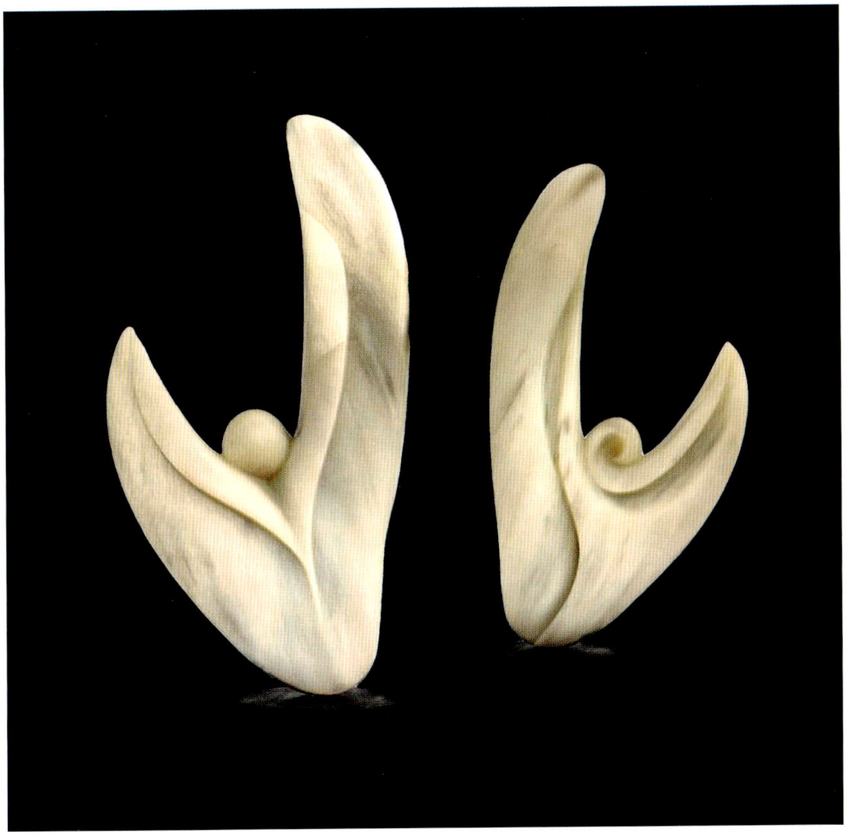

4

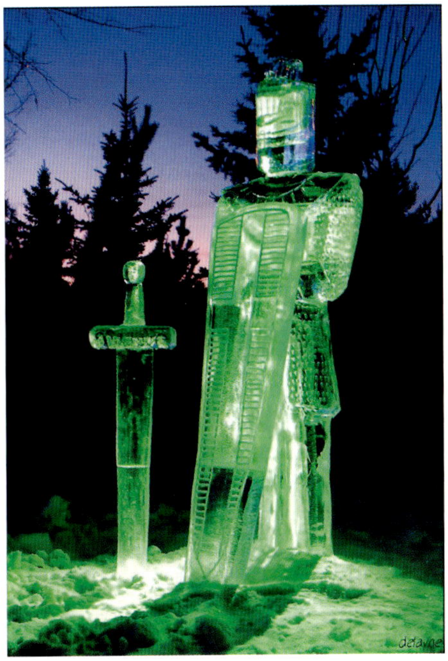


5

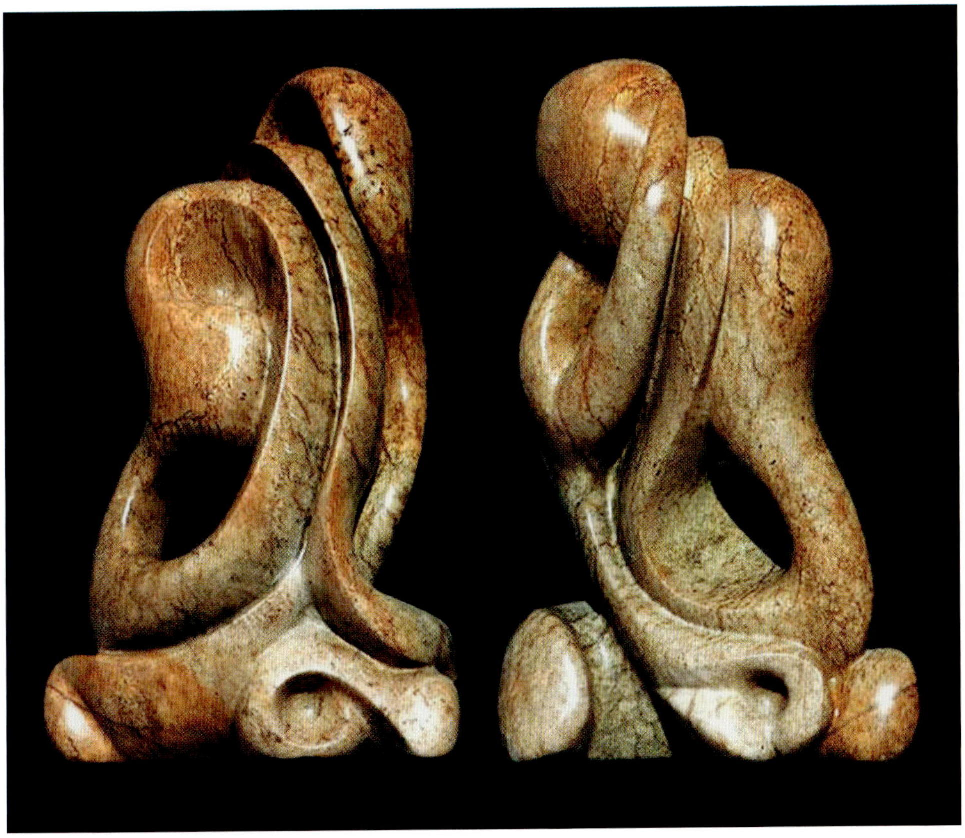

6

1 *Snow Queen*, 2009. Snow, 16' tall. *Photo by Delayne Corbett.*

2 *Moon Dancers*, 2007. Sand, 14' tall. *Photo by Delayne Corbett.*

3 *Mayan Stele*, 2009. Styrofoam, 8' tall. *Photo by Delayne Corbett.*

4 *Aspire,* 2005. Stone, 24" tall. *Photo by Delayne Corbett.*

5 *Ice Knight*, 2007. Ice, 6' tall. *Photo by Delayne Corbett.*

6 *Sensual Odyssey*, 1999. Stone, 16" tall. *Photograph by Delayne Corbett.*

# Josh Brooke Coté

Blachly, Oregon, USA
www.cotesculpture.blogspot.com

*A son of a watercolorist, I grew up surrounded by art, artists, and immense creativity. I spent my youth painting with my father and traveling with the family to art fairs on the east coast. Later, after studying painting and drawing at the University of Michigan School of Art, I became a self-taught sculptor. I soon became interested in Alexander Calder and wire sculpture as it bridges both linear drawing and sculpture, the two and three dimensions.*

*I create sculptures utilizing hand-modeled resin, cold-worked wire, found objects, glass, welded steel, and negative space. Each sculpture is unique. Resin is hand-modeled and painted, then integrated with found objects, glass, and recycled wire. With only needle-nosed pliers, the wire is cold-worked, painstakingly hand-manipulated, wrapped, and woven to itself. Natural patinas are obtained with acids.*

*My sculpture attempts to explore the boundaries and relationships between man, woman, and nature, centered on our relationship to the environment. Fusing elements of folk art, surrealism, and realism, ideas arise from dreams, observation, and nature. I often work with themes of transformation, nurturing, and regeneration. My creative energy is about growth and perceiving this energy with intuition. The challenge, the art, is attempting to translate this mystery through the process of my sculpture. My work resides in private and corporate collections worldwide.*

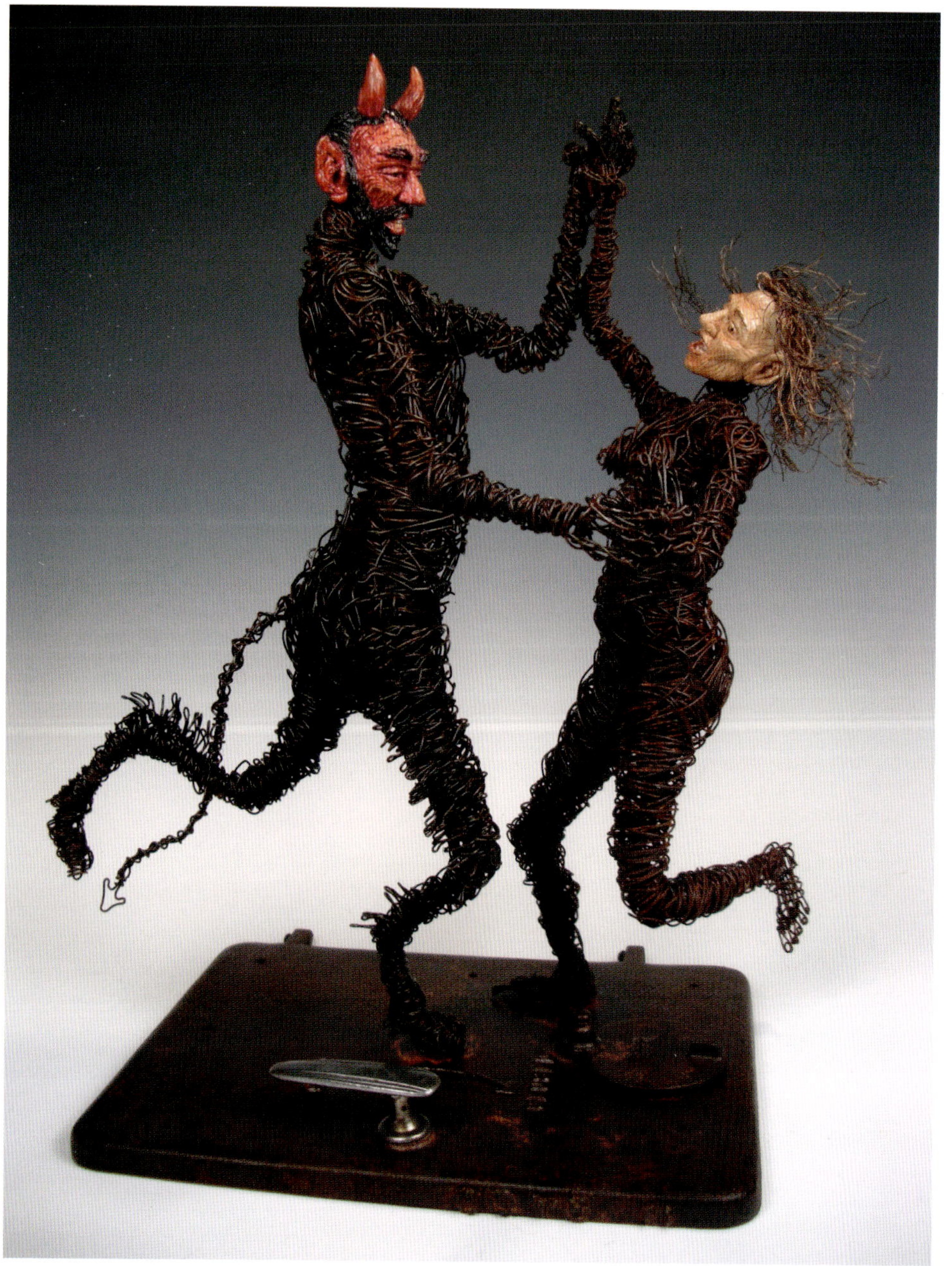

1

1 *Tarantella On Hell's Door*, 2011. Mixed media, 24" h. x 18" w. x 13" d. *Photograph by Josh Brooke Coté.*

2 *Begging Monkey*, 2010. Mixed media, 26" h. x 21" w. x 19" d. *Photograph by Josh Brooke Coté.*

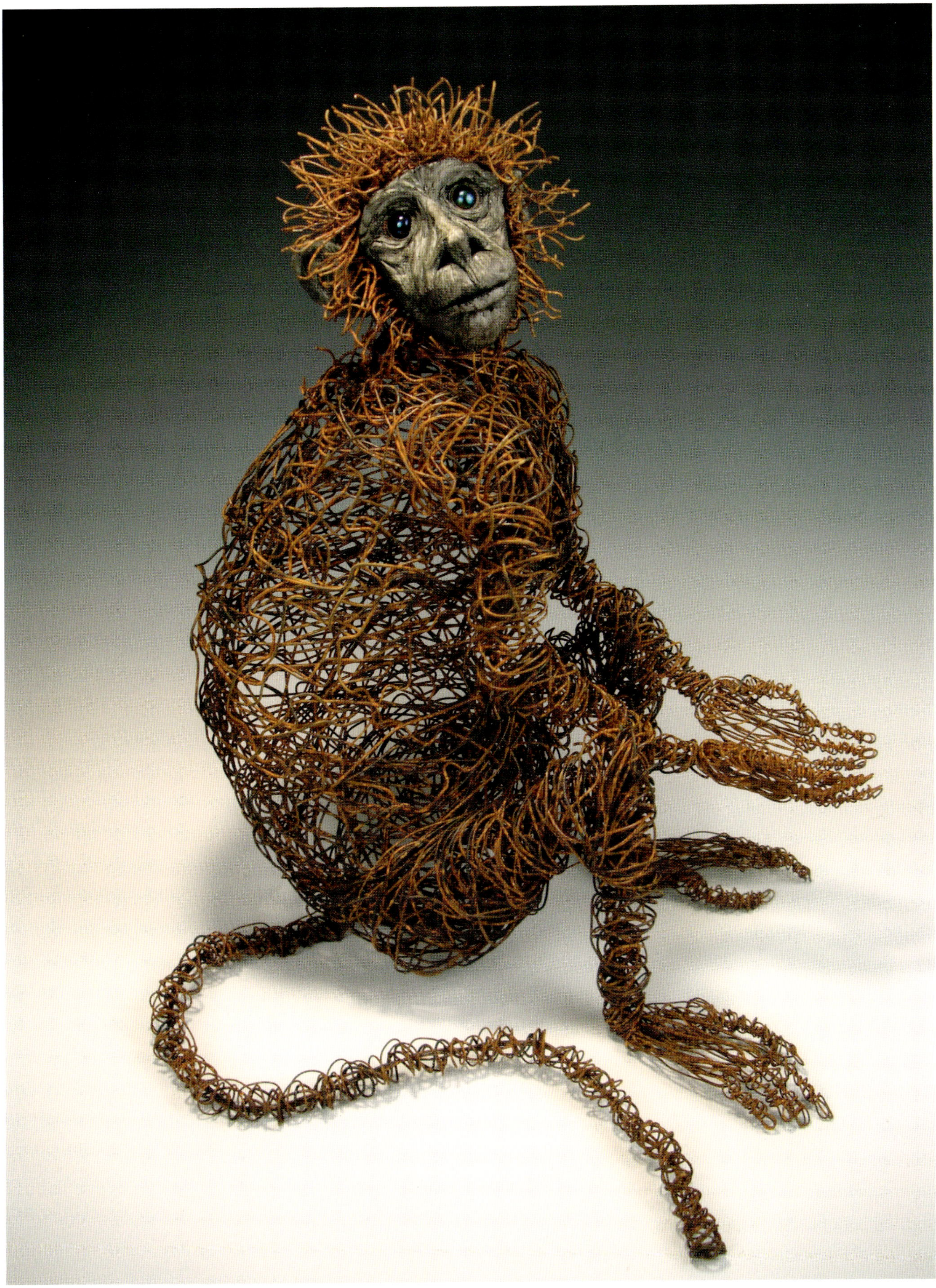

2

3

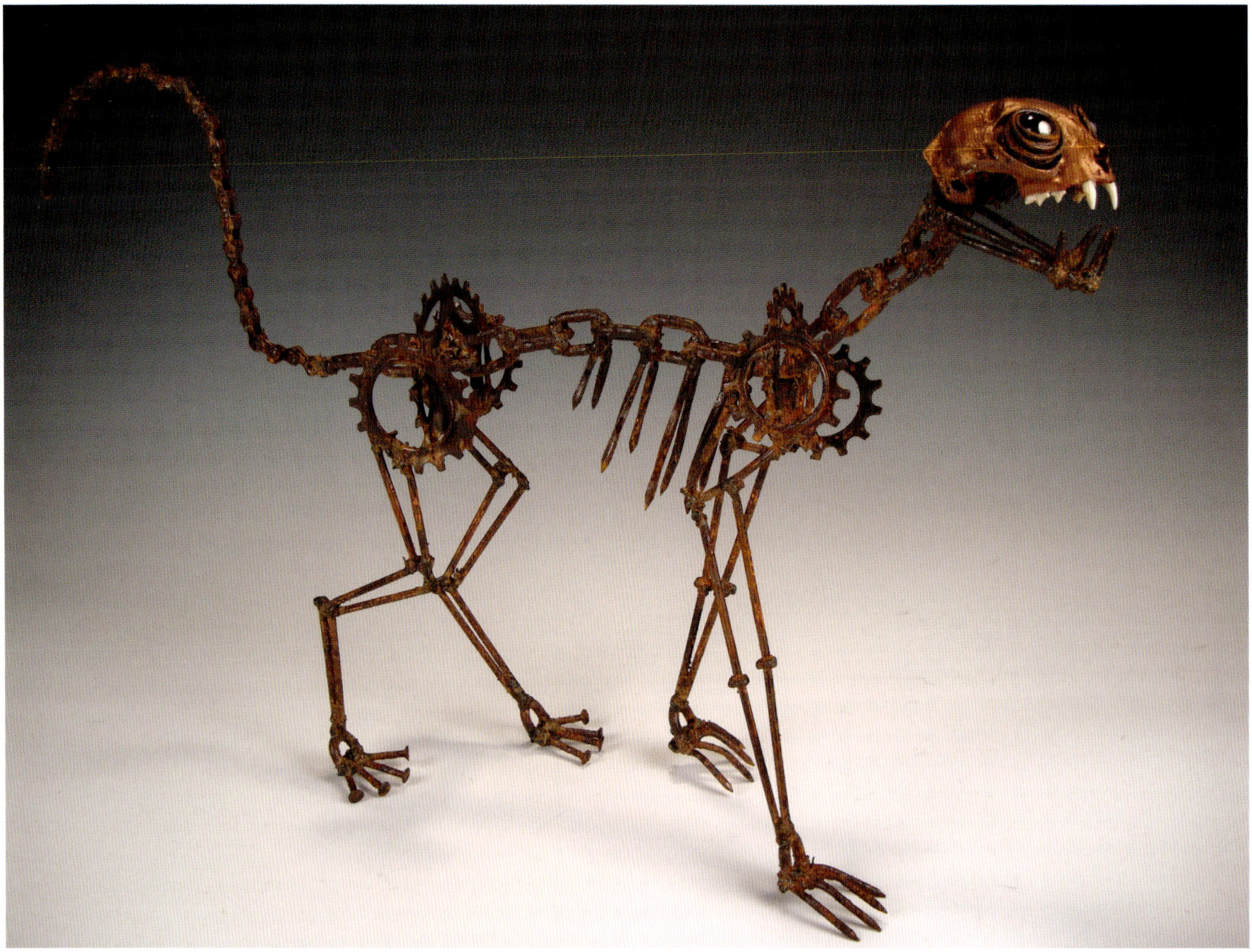

4

5

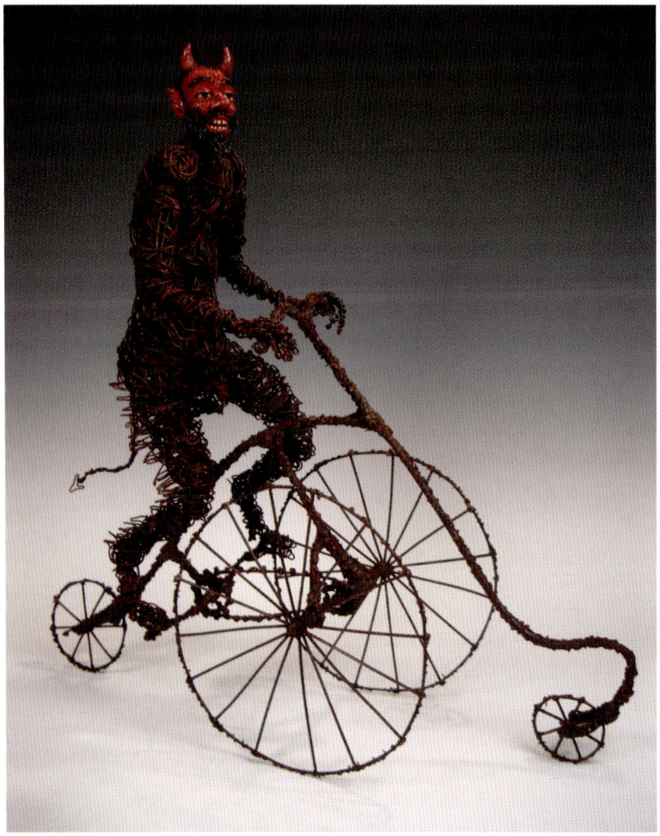

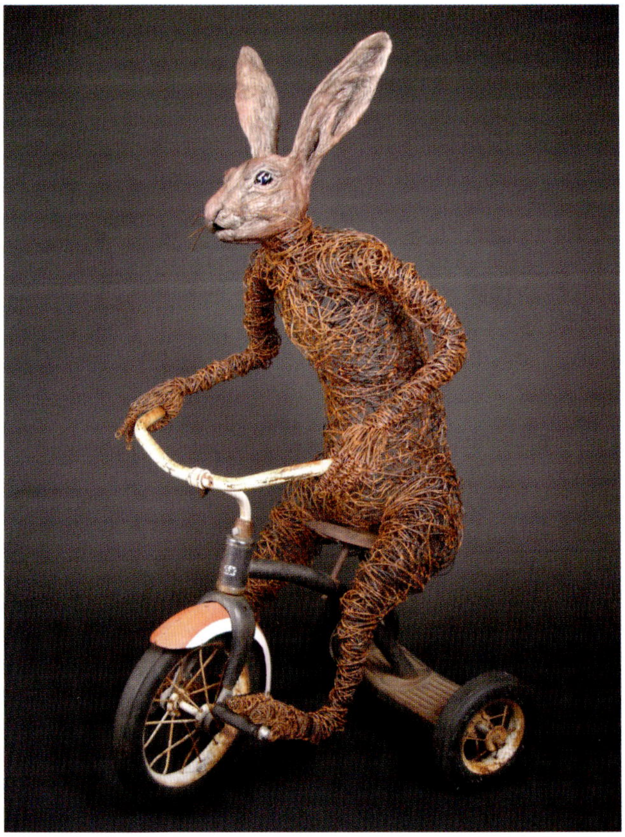

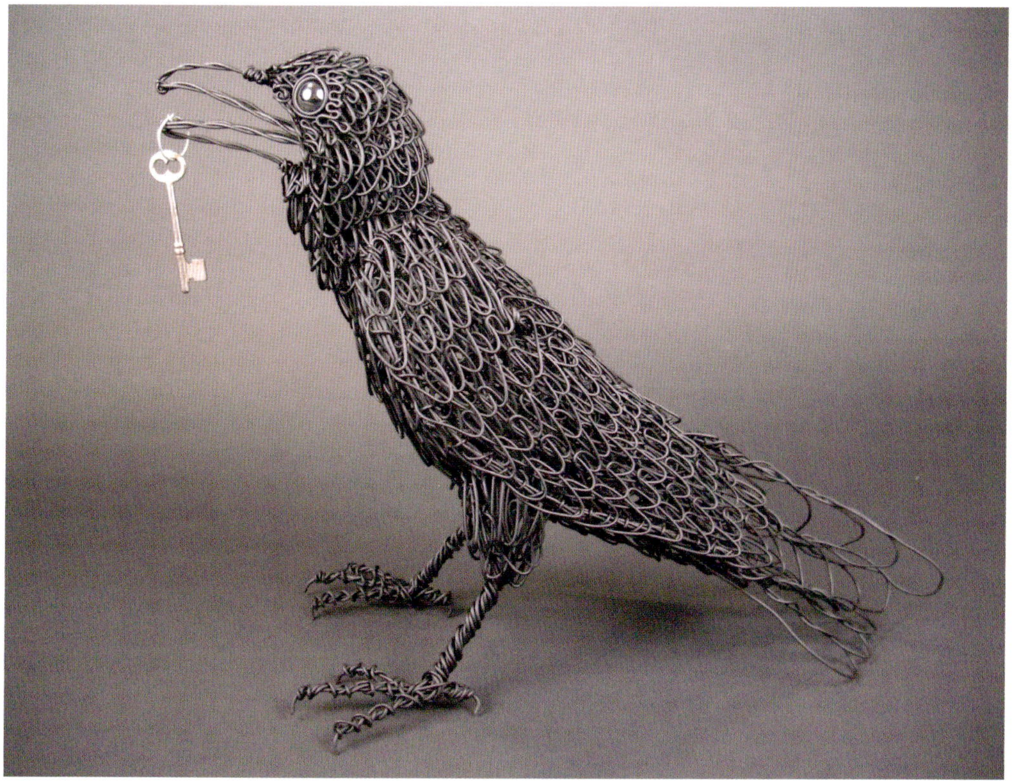

3 *Clockwork Cat*, 2011. Mixed media, 20" h. x 29" w. x 10" d. *Photograph by Josh Brooke Coté.*

4 *Devilocipede*, 2011. Mixed media, 22" h. x 26" w. x 14" d. *Photograph by Josh Brooke Coté.*

5 *Mobile Bunny*, 2010. Mixed media, 47" h. x 28" w. x 21" d. Photograph by Josh Brooke Coté.

6 *Crow With Skeleton Key*, 2011. Mixed media, 13" h. x 14" w. x 7" d. *Photograph by Josh Brooke Coté.*

7 *Woolly Mammoth*, 2010. Mixed media, 24" h. x 31" w. x 18" d. *Photograph by Josh Brooke Coté.*

6

7

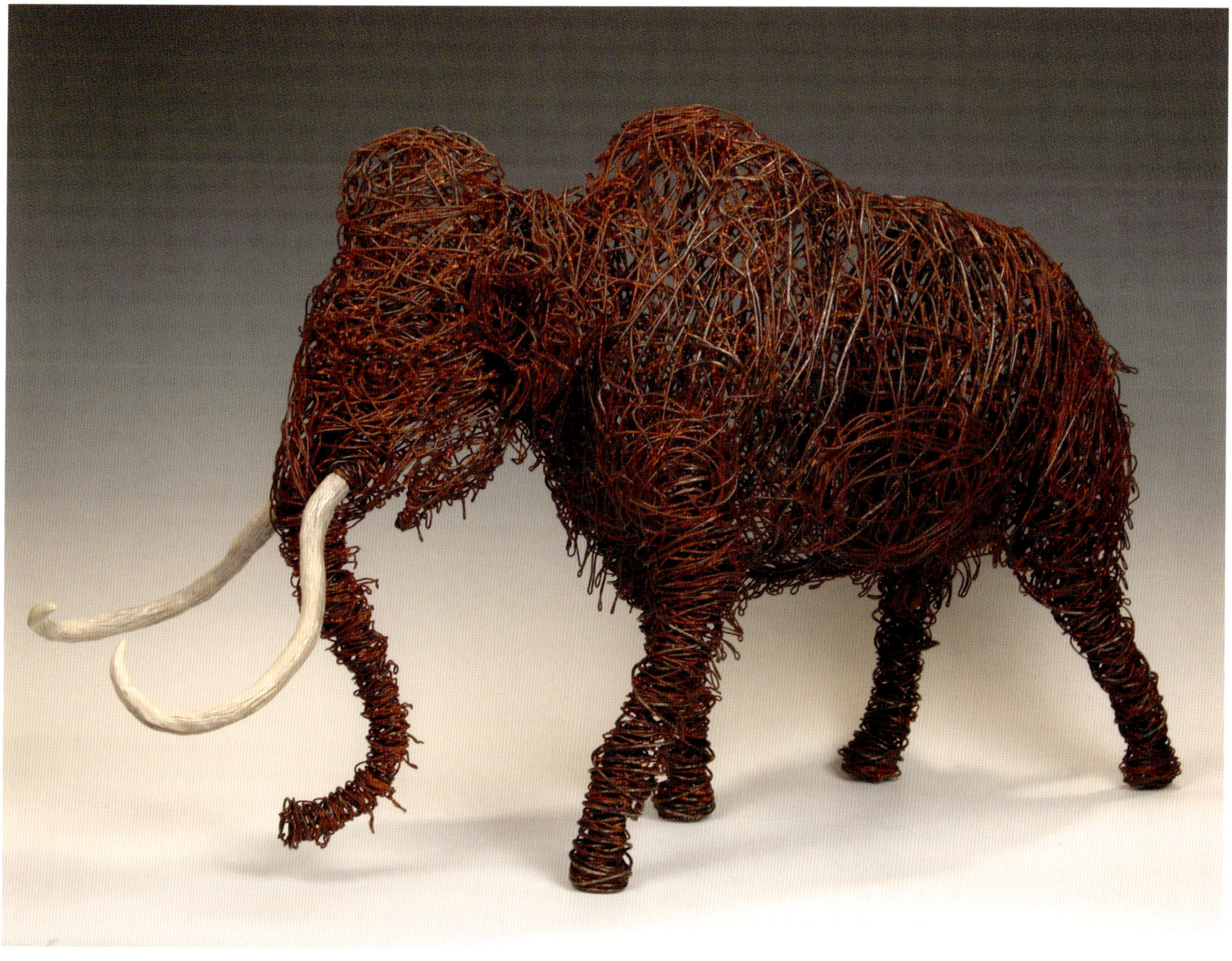

# Bill Czappa

Burbank, California, USA
www.czappa.com

*I was born on July 22, 1947, in Los Angeles California and grew up in Culver City. I graduated form Venice High and got an AA degree in art from Santa Monica College. I began building sculptures when I was 14, using found objects that my dad would bring home from work, as he was a machinist. Some of my earliest aesthetic influences were the old Venice canals, then inundated with oil derricks. I found the canals and the old bridges crossing them interesting and mysterious. In the sixties I started making surfboards and later built a cabin cruiser, which I lived on in Marina Del Ray for many years. I opened my first studio in North Hollywood, California, in 1976, and moved it to Burbank in 1983.*

*My work is made from found objects of all kinds, ranging from spaghetti sauce to concrete, and often includes sculpted wood. I seldom make a series; each sculpture is different from the next, although you may find some connecting links in style, content, or humor. I am also a writer and have incorporated text into some of my work. My goal in art is to make people feel better, uplift them, and make them think about things in a new way.*

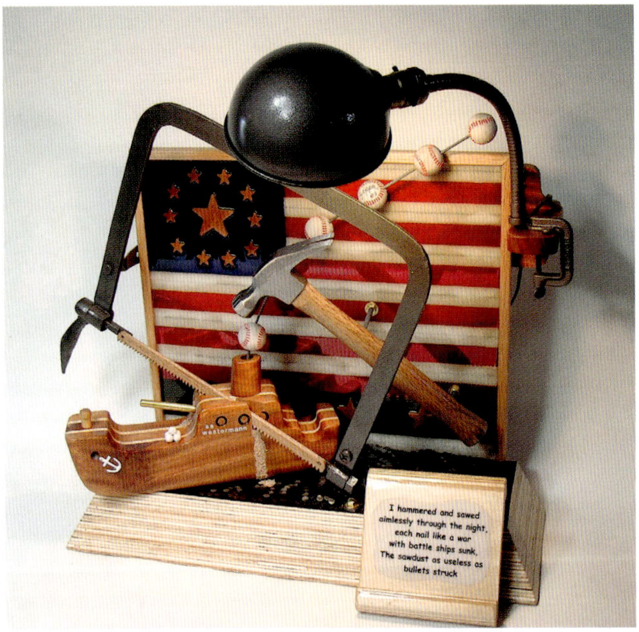


1

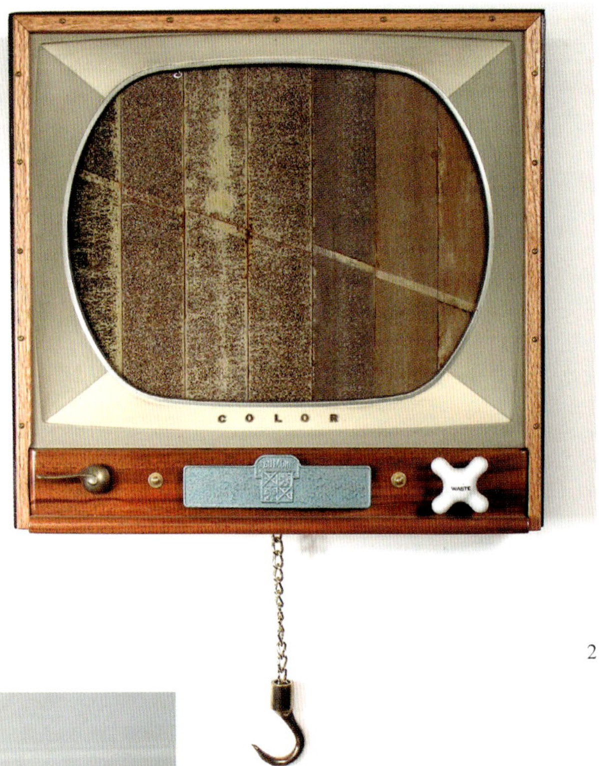


2

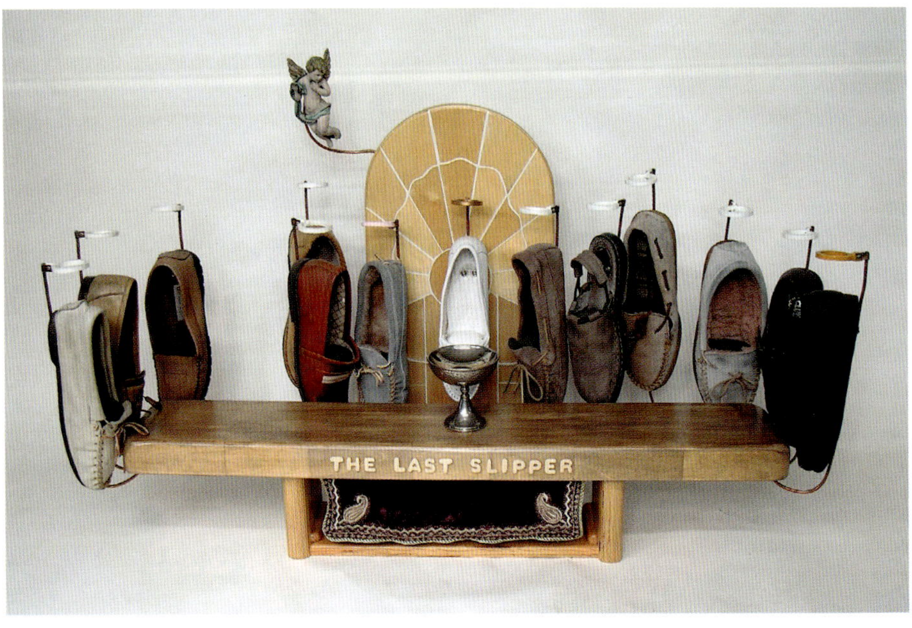


3

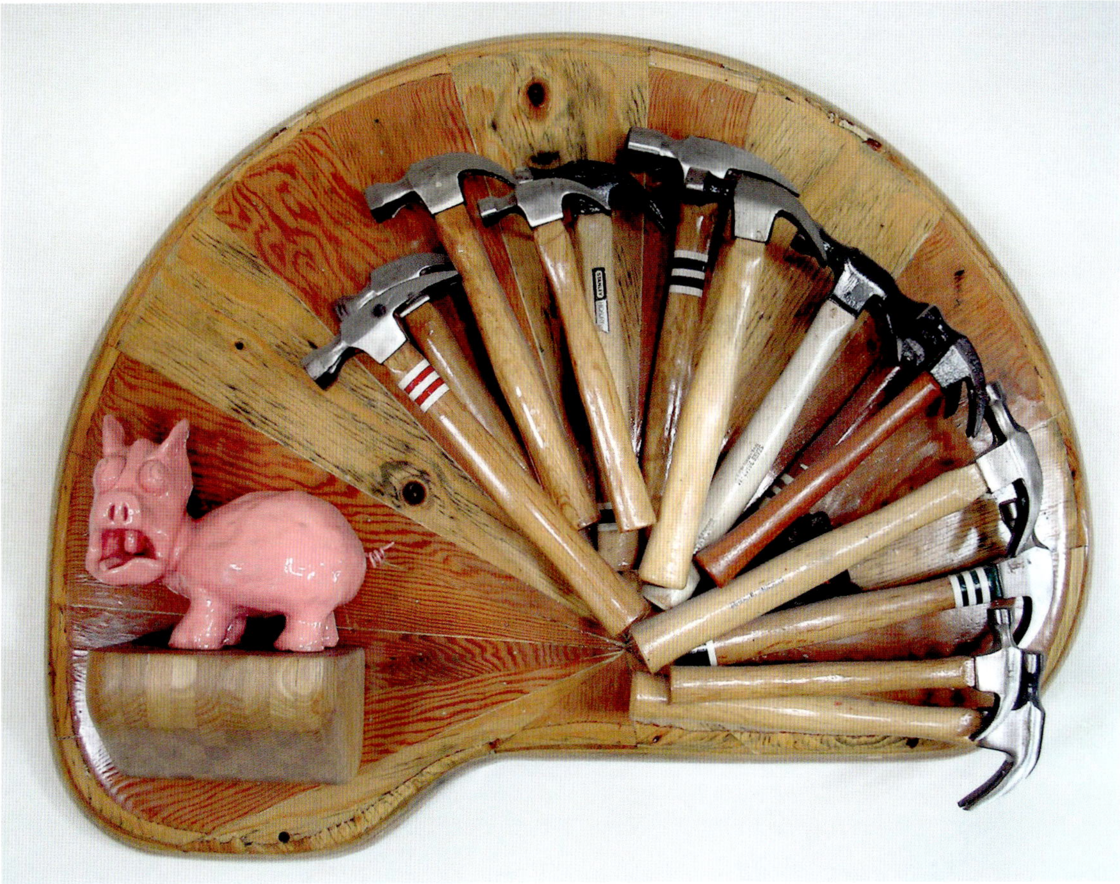

4

5

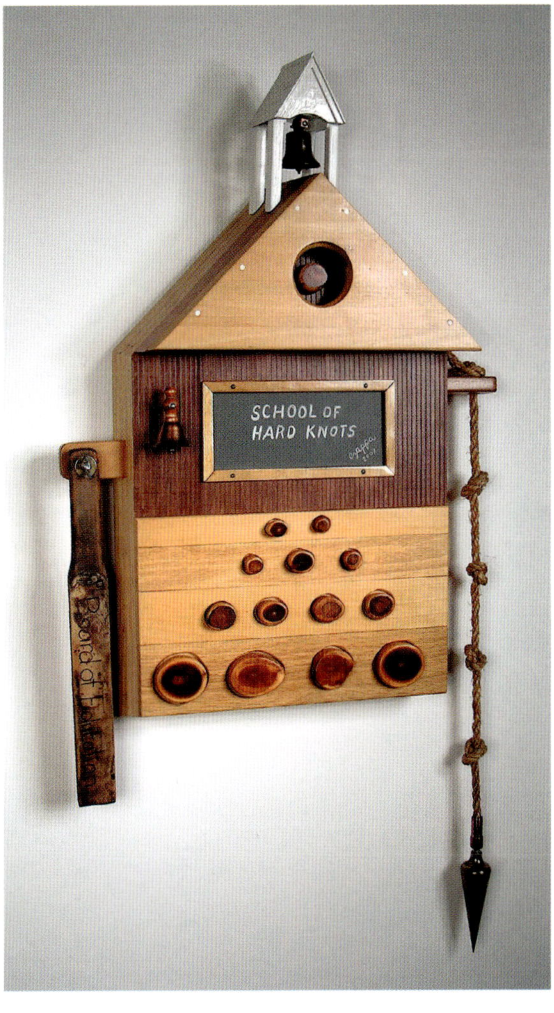


1 *The Never Ending War,* 2008. Mixed media, 26". *Photography by Bill Czappa.*

2 *Four Arguments for the Elimination of Television*, 2010. Mixed media, 36". *Photography by Bill Czappa.*

3 *The Last Slipper,* 2004. Mixed media, 31". *Photography by Bill Czappa.*

4 *A Pig's Interest,* 1998. Mixed media, 30". *Photography by Bill Czappa.*

5 *School of Hard Knots*, 2007. Mixed media, 42". *Photography by Bill Czappa.*

# Carole A. Feuerman

New York, New York, USA
www.carolefeuerman.com

Born in Connecticut, raised and trained in New York, Carole A. Feuerman is acknowledged as one of the world's most prominent hyperrealist sculptors. She has had six museum retrospectives to date and has been included in exhibitions at the State Hermitage, The Palazzo Strozzi Foundation, the Kunstmuseum Ahlen, and the Circulo de Bellas Artes, among others. Her work is included in the selected collections of His Majesty the Emperor of Japan, President Bill Clinton and Secretary of State Hillary Clinton, former Secretary of State Henry Kissinger, Soviet statesman Mikhail Gorbachev, the Forbes Magazine Art Collection, and the Caldic Collection.

Feuerman's prolific career has spanned four decades and across a variety of media. Working in resin, marble, and bronze, Feuerman has distinguished her skill in each medium by defining and recreating the human condition. She sculpts life-size, monumental, and miniature works, painting them with hundreds of layers before achieving human-like tones. Her resin sculptures employ her signature trompe-l'oeil technique to construct all clothing and accessories used to achieve her hyperrealist perfection. Eyes, teeth, hair, wrinkles and skin texture are meticulously rendered to give the viewer the impression of a living, breathing human being. Separate to her resin works, Feuerman has also introduced her own unique methodology of sculpting with molten metal that she calls "Painting with Fire."

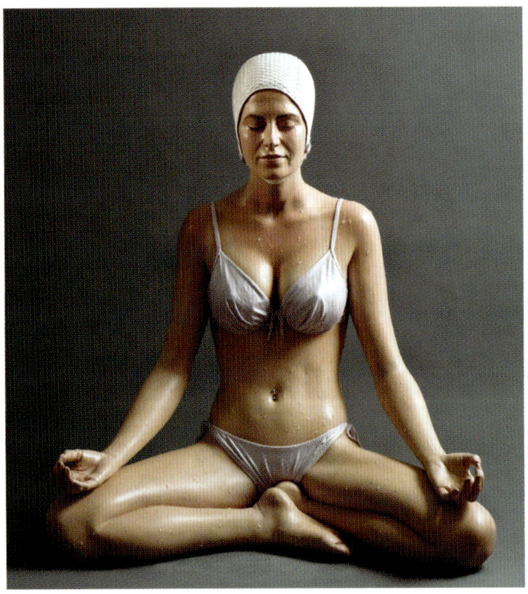

1

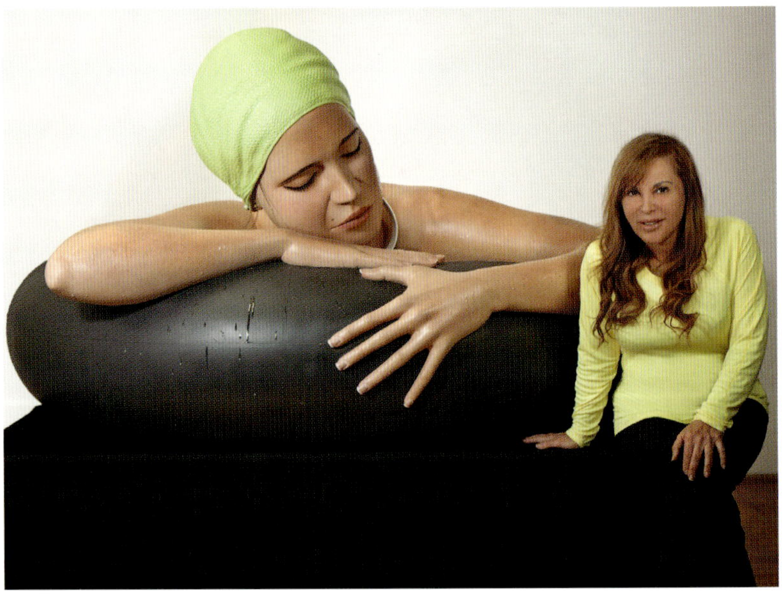

2

1 *Balance*, 2008-2010. Oil, resin, 36" x 32" x 18". *Photograph by Ellen Page Wilson.*

2 *Survival of Serena*, 2006-2010. Oil, resin, 38" x 84" x 32". *Photograph by Alvaro Corzo V.*

3 *Butterfly*, 2008-2011. Oil, resin, 21" x 22.5" x 21". *Photograph by Alvaro Corzo V.*

4 *Lady Neptune*, 1999-2011. Oil, resin, 46" x 28" x 38". *Photograph by Alvaro Corzo V.*

5 *Tree*, 2009-2011. Oil, & resin, 37" x 29" x 62". *Photograph by Ellen Page Wilson.*

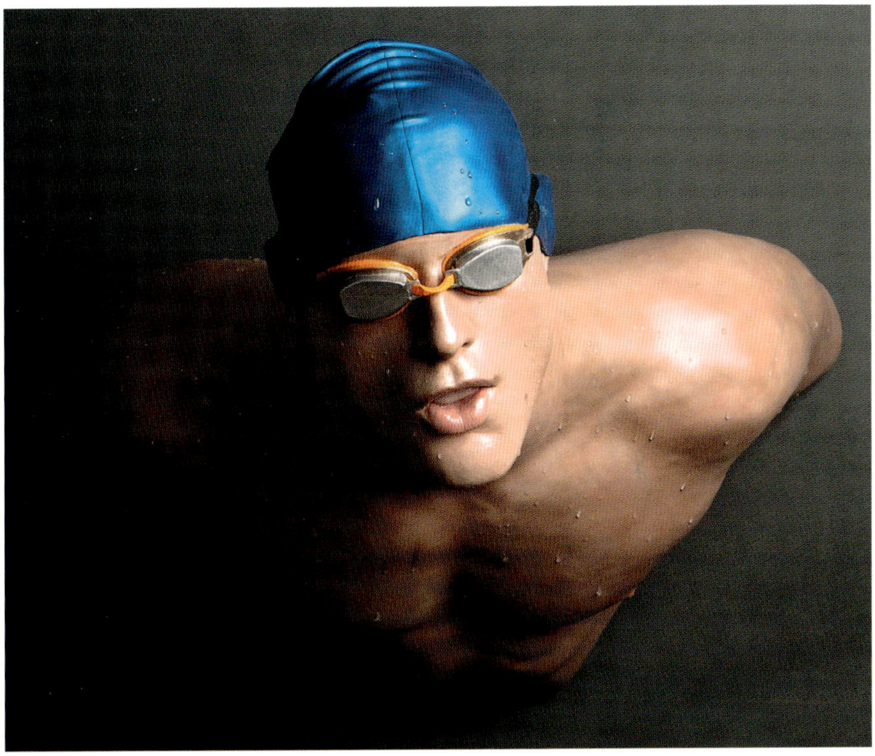

3

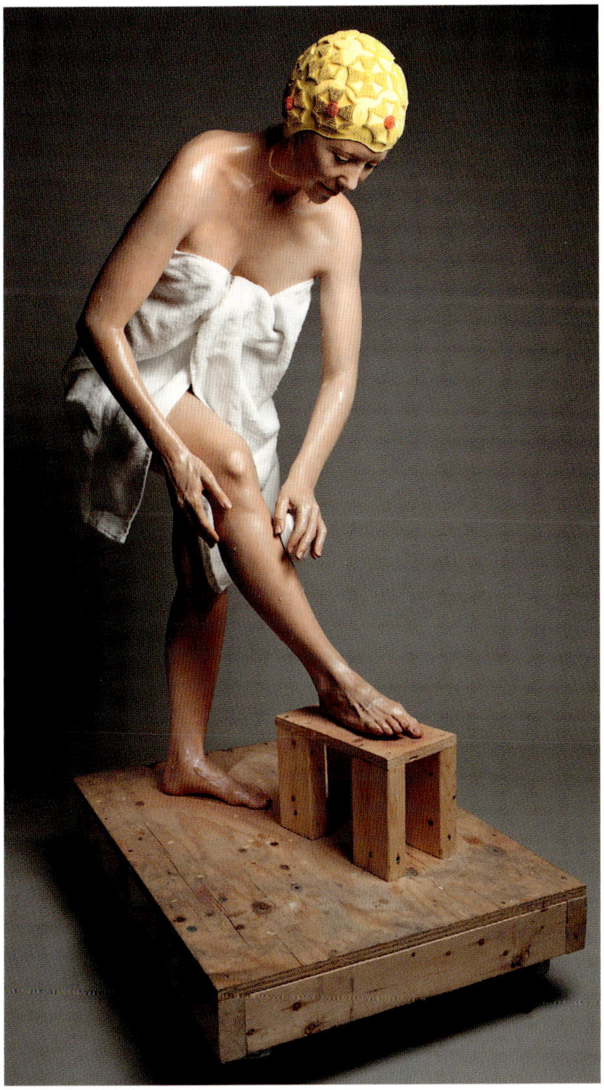

4

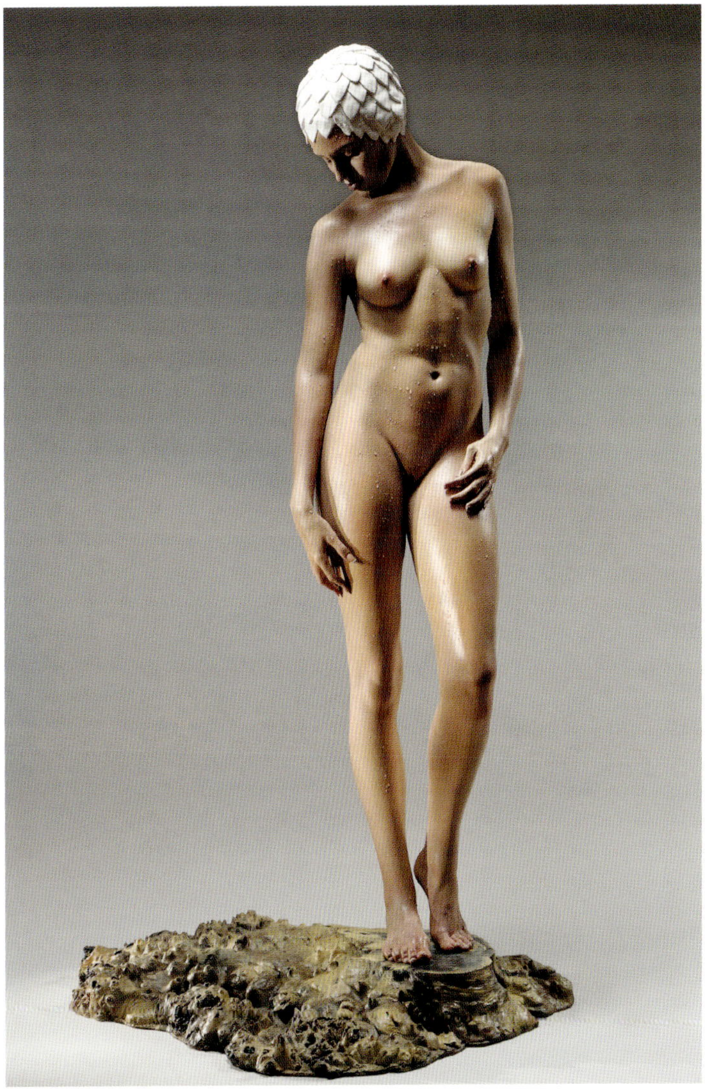

5

# Devin Laurence Field

Portland, Oregon, USA
www.devinlaurencefield.com

Devin Laurence Field grew up in New Zealand and lived in many countries throughout his youth. After New Zealand he studied art in England, France, Japan, and the United States, graduating Summa Cum Laude with a Master's degree in sculpture. The son of a zoologist, his travels as a child formed the basis for a keen perspective on the relationship between the built environment and the natural world. Devin specializes in large-scale public art commissions fabricated in metal. They are often site specific, synthesizing elements from the site, local tradition or history, and the artist's own form vocabulary. He has been honored by the National Academy of Design in New York, included in International Biennales, and chosen to build monumental sculptures for the Olympics. Devin's sculptures grace the permanent collections of museums, cities and sculpture parks around the world.

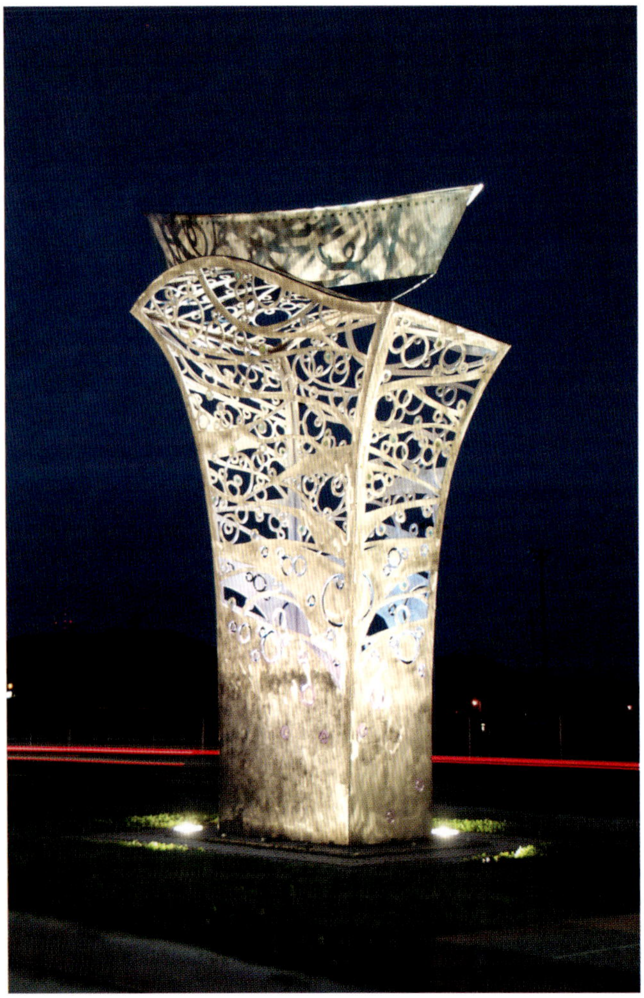

1

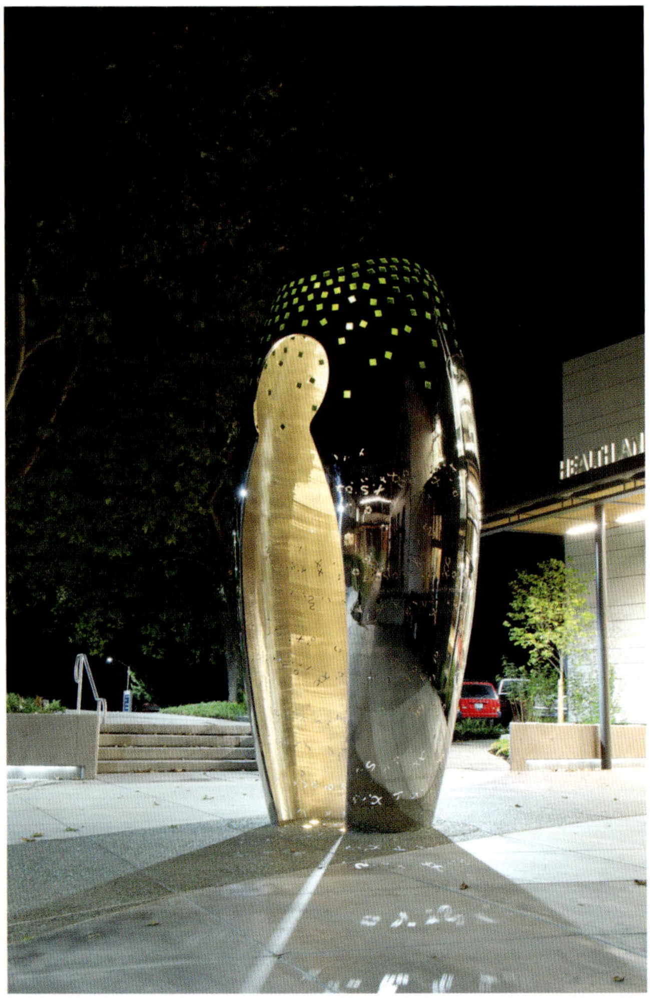

2

3

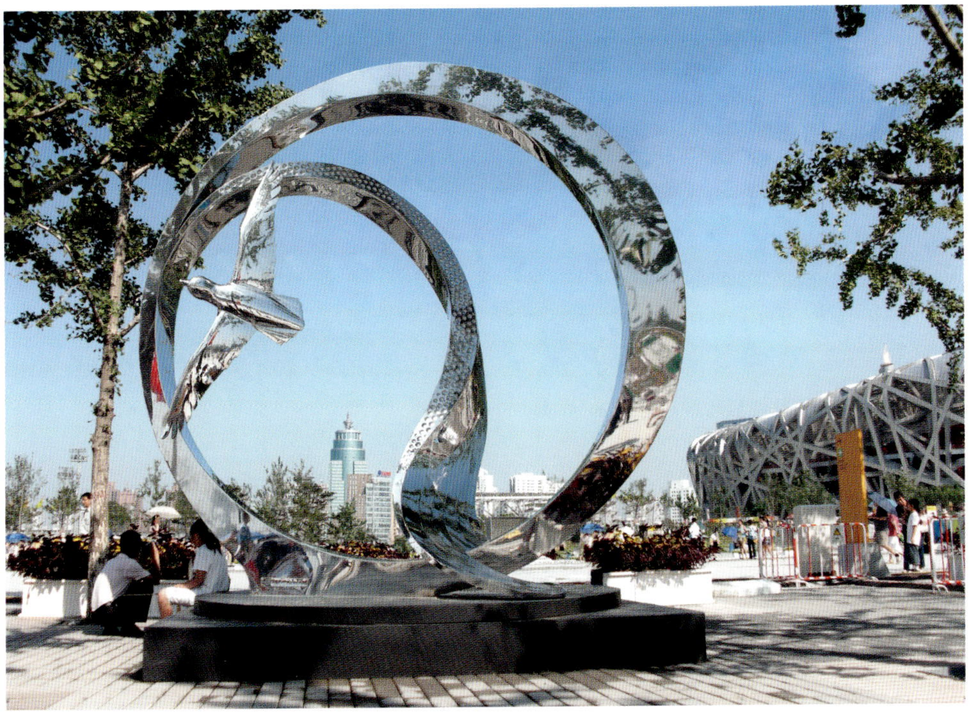

4

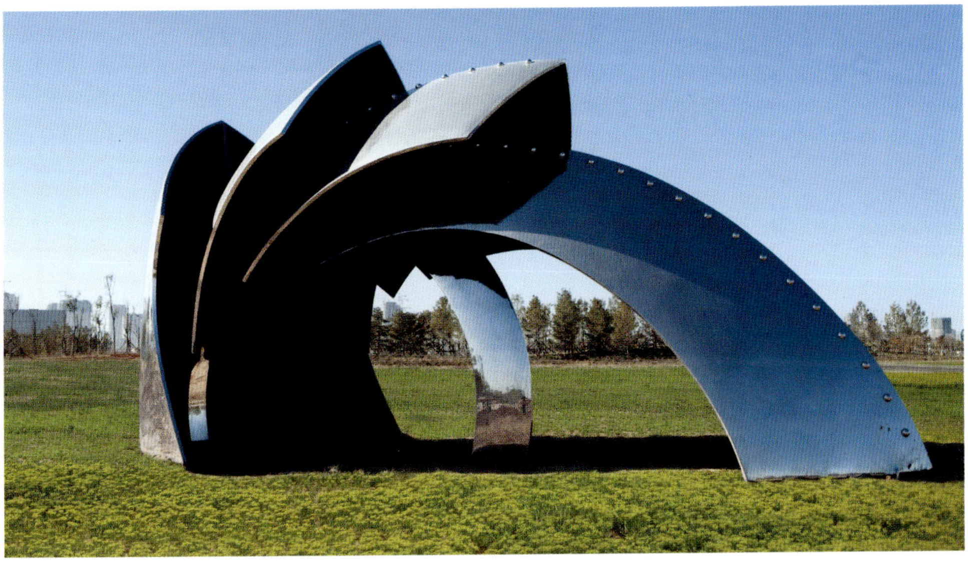

5

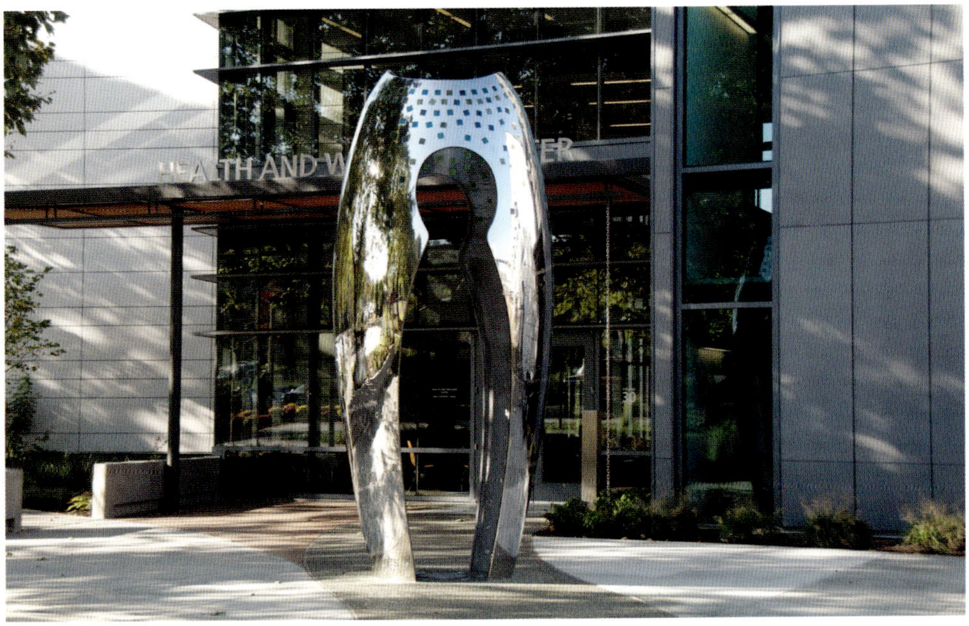

1 *McKenzie Drift*, 2010. Stainless steel, glass, light, 16' x 10' x 6'.

2 *Living Vessel* (night), 2010. Stainless steel, glass, light, 14' x 6' x 6'.

3 *One World One Dream*, 2008. Stainless steel, 14' x 16' x 16'.

4 *Sunsight*, 2009. Stainless steel, 14' x 21' x 8'.

5 *Living Vessel*, 2010. Stainless steel, glass, light, 14' x 6' x 6'.

# Pam Foss

Worton, Maryland, USA
www.pamfosssculpture.com

*I have discovered that using cast paper to create my abstract bas-relief sculpture underlines and accentuates the essence of my design concepts.*

*Working with cast paper, I am able to incorporate an infinite variety of form, texture, and color to convey the unbridled expression of power, movement, and emotion that for me, defines what sculpture is all about.*

*The ethereal qualities of cast paper sculpture are endlessly fascinating to explore. I'm drawn to the challenge of creating three-dimensional surfaces that enliven light and appear to float, as if suspended in space itself.*

*I began my career as a sculptor in 1980, creating a series of bronze sculptures portraying the beauty and excitement of thoroughbred racing. I soon expanded the scope of my work to include bronzes of Great Blue Herons and Bald Eagles, many of which were large works for public placement. I continue to create bronzes to this day with my work now including both figurative and bas-relief sculpture.*

*My work with cast paper began just two years ago and coincided with my long held desire to enter the realm of modernism by experimenting with the creation of abstract bas-relief sculpture in hand-made cast paper*

*I had no formal training as a sculptor, learning instead by studying the masters and working with other sculptors. I was born in Atlantic City, New Jersey. I am married, and the mother of three children and six grand-children.*

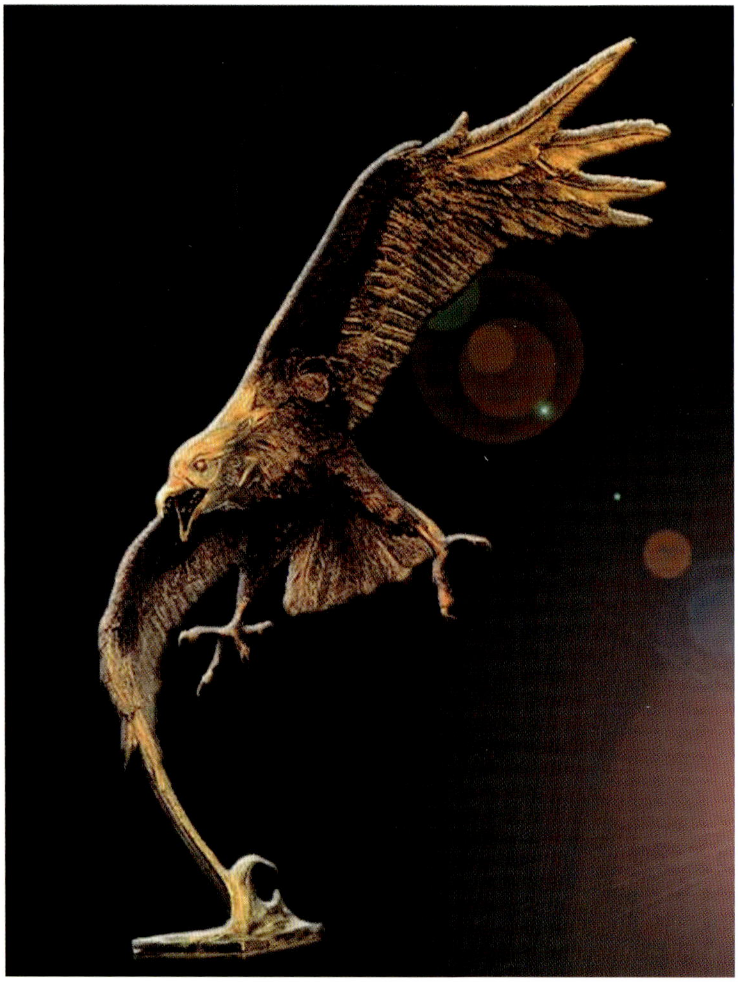

1

2

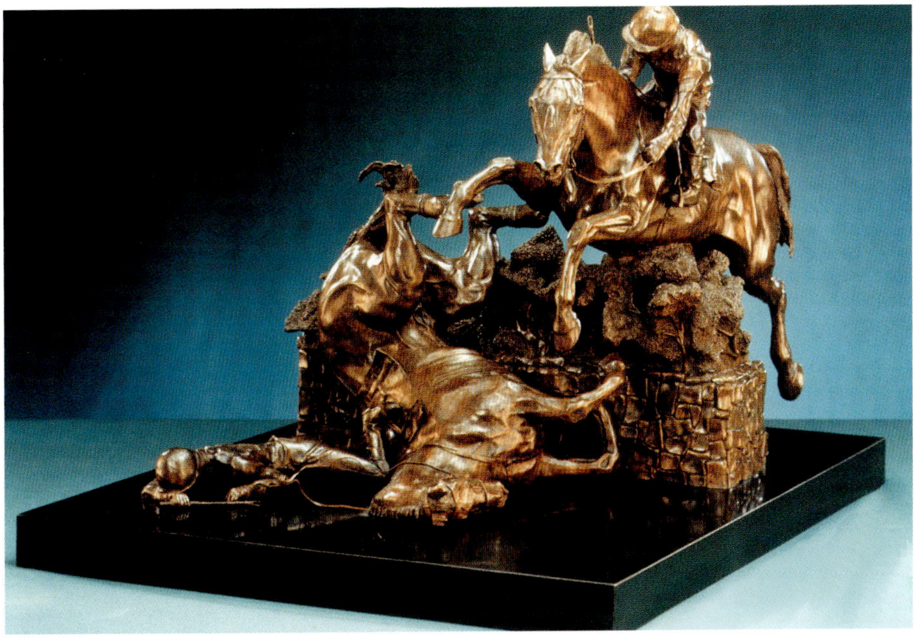

3

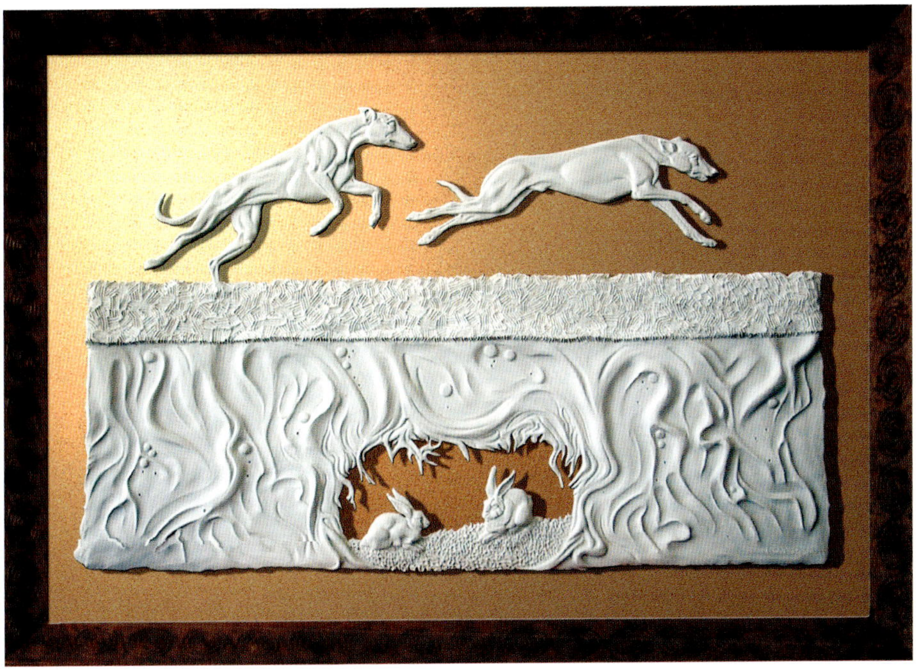

4

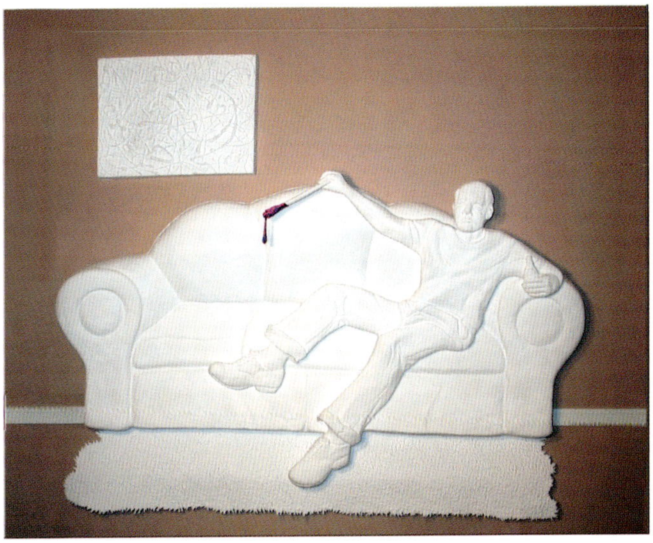

1 *Angle of Attack*, 1985. Bronze, 54" span x 30" high. *Photograph by Pam Foss.*

2 *Point to Point,* 1980. Bronze, 29" x 27" x 19" high. *Photograph by Pam Foss.*

3 *Hide N' Seek*, 2006. Cast paper, 27" x 42" x 4" deep. *Photograph by Pam Foss.*

4 *Jack the Dripper*, 2008. Cast paper, 30" x 40" x 4" deep. *Photograph by Pam Foss.*

# Tamae Frame

Gresham, Oregon, USA
www.tamaeframe.com

This Japanese-born artist studied calligraphy, drawing, and jewelry design in her youth. Later she worked as a jewelry and accessory designer in Tokyo, Japan. Tamae immigrated to the U.S. in the early 1990s and began producing one-of–a-kind art jewelry, focusing on figurative work.

She switched artistic mediums from metal to ceramics in 2004, in order to respond to the great need of expressing new creative urges, which emerged from the deeper layers of the self.

*My sculptures represent the images of ordinary women who have mysterious inner dimensions, where their meaning and emotions subtly play out. Sometimes I depict them as mystical creatures or bald headed women, depending on how I like to convey the psyche of the subject. My main medium is clay and it has opened the door to create my work in an intuitive way. The clay's plasticity allows my hands to have a dialogue with my inner vision, resulting in a piece that becomes both deeply personal and soulful.*

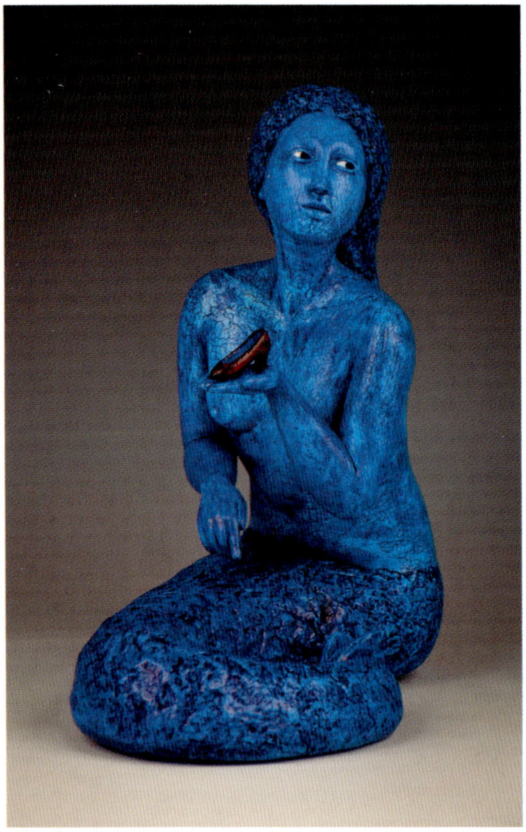

1

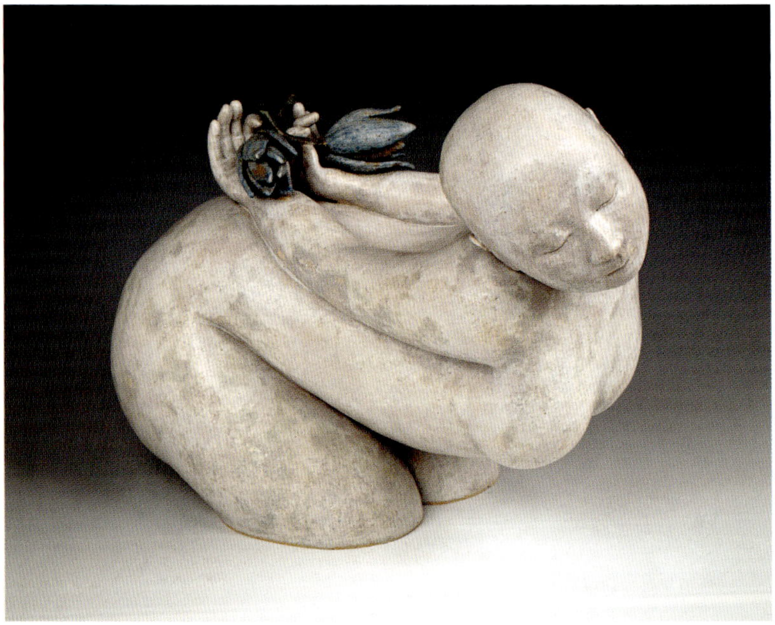

2

1 *A New Desire*, 2009. Ceramic, mixed media, 10". *Photograph by Dale C. Frame.*

2 *Embodiment of Lotus*, 2011. Ceramic, 13". *Photograph by Dale C. Frame.*

3 *Listening* (back view), 2009. Ceramic, mixed media, 15". *Photograph by Dale C. Frame.*

4 *Listening* (front view), 2009. Ceramic, & mixed media, 15". *Photograph by Dale C. Frame.*

5 *Personas* (front view), 2009. Ceramic, 16" *Photograph by Dale C. Frame.*

6 *Personas* (back view), 2009. Ceramic, 16". *Photograph by Dale C. Frame.*

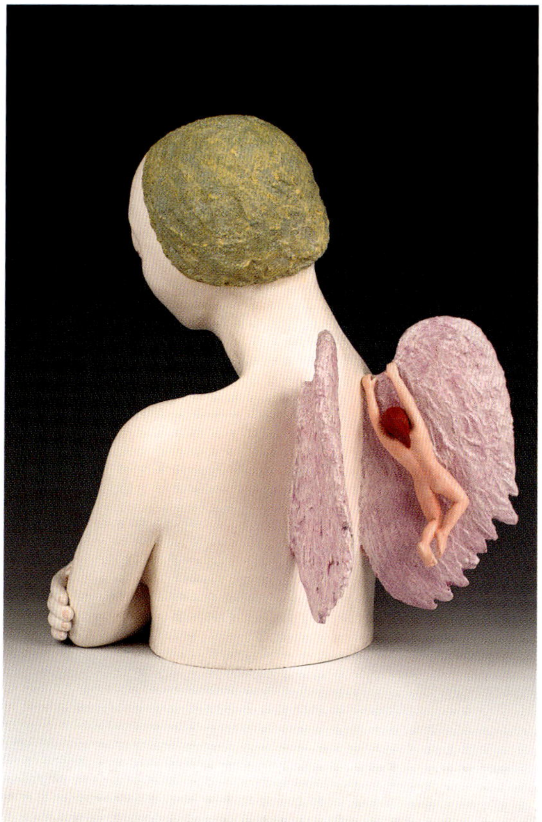

3

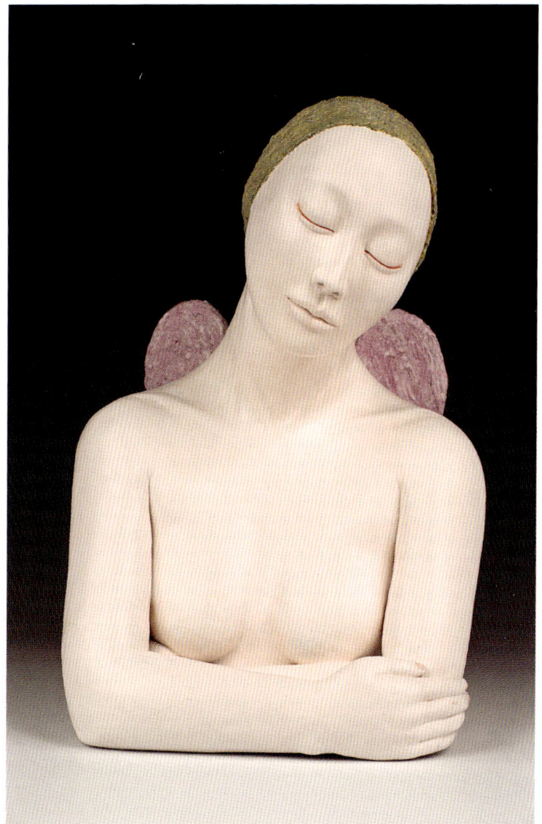

4

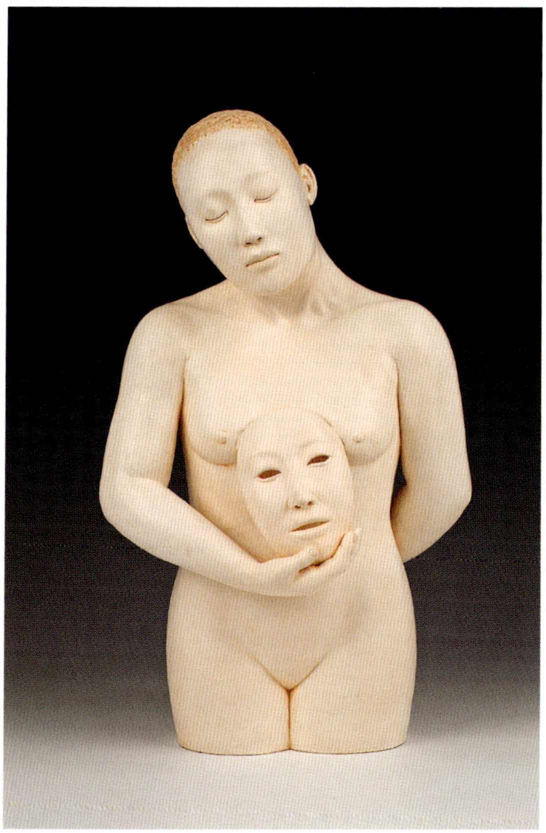

5

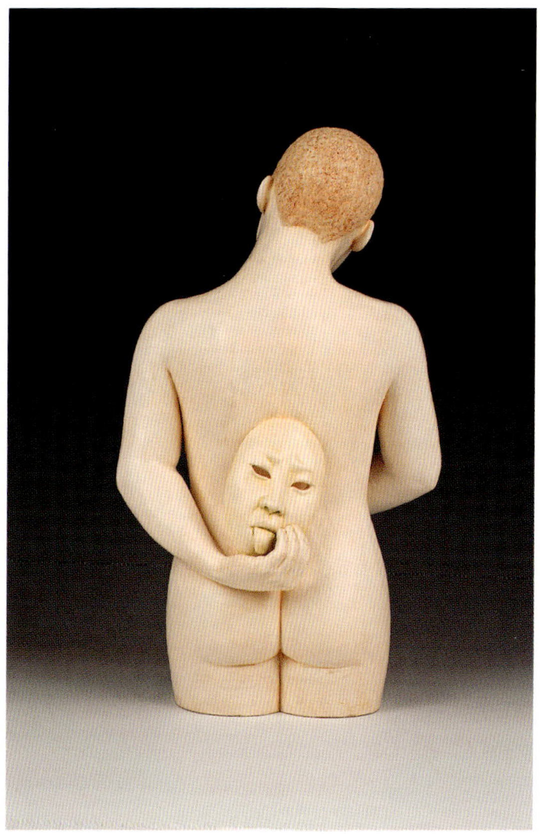

6

# Frank's Kitchens

Philadelphia, Pennsylvania, USA
www.frankskitchens.org

Frank's Kitchens (FK) is a Philadelphia based artistic design and fabrication collaborative. Founded in 2007 inside a small warehouse on North Hancock Street in Kensington, FK got its start primarily as a place to build massive human-powered kinetic sculptures for the annual sculpture derby during the Trenton Avenue Arts Festival. Today, now in a much larger space off North 5$^{th}$ Street, Frank's Kitchens is a fiery collective of passionate creativity, hosting artists who breathe to think and dream, and live to collaborate and build. Keeping its membership to a strict number of 12, including a fictitious figurehead in Frank R. Rosen himself, FK is comprised of a myriad of personal backgrounds from engineers to designers to metal smiths to electricians to carpenters to filmmakers.

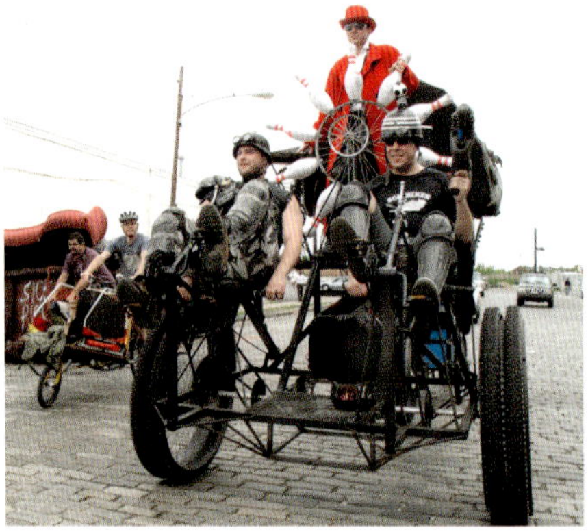

1

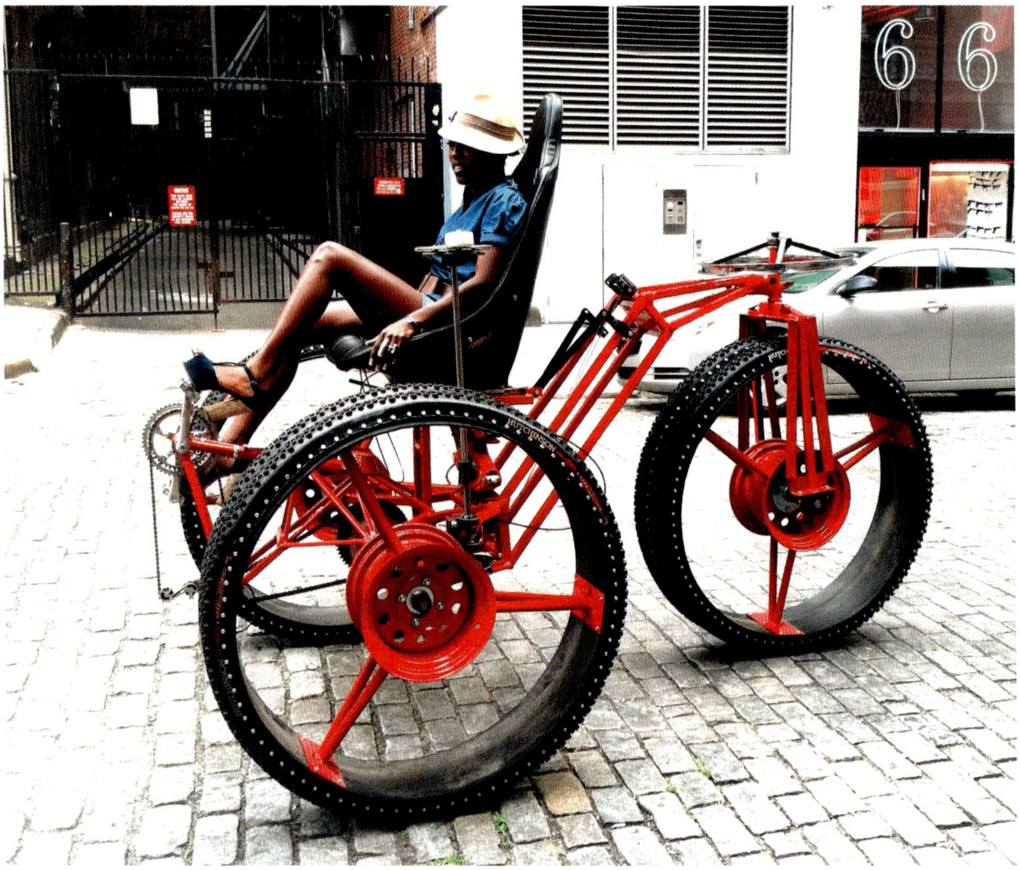


2

1 *The Sand Reckoner,* 2009. Steel. *Photograph by Douglas DiBella.*

2 *Le Velo Rouge*, 2011. Steel. *Photograph by Erik Silverson.*

3 *The Bluff Runner*, 2010. Steel. *Photograph by Phyllis Vetter.*

4 *The Negotiator*, 2010. Steel. *Photograph by Samantha Isom Photography.*

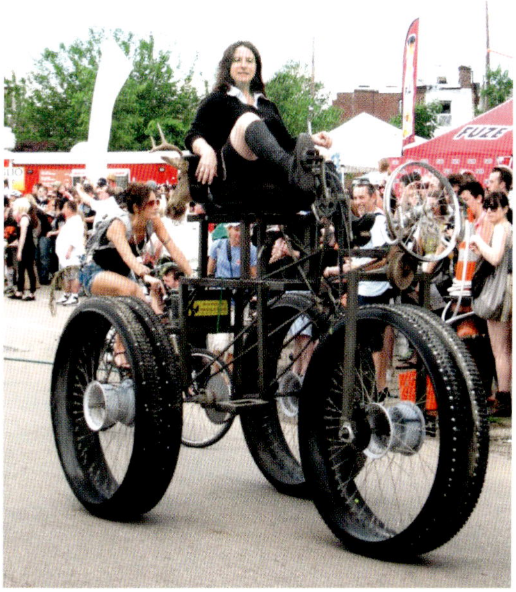


3

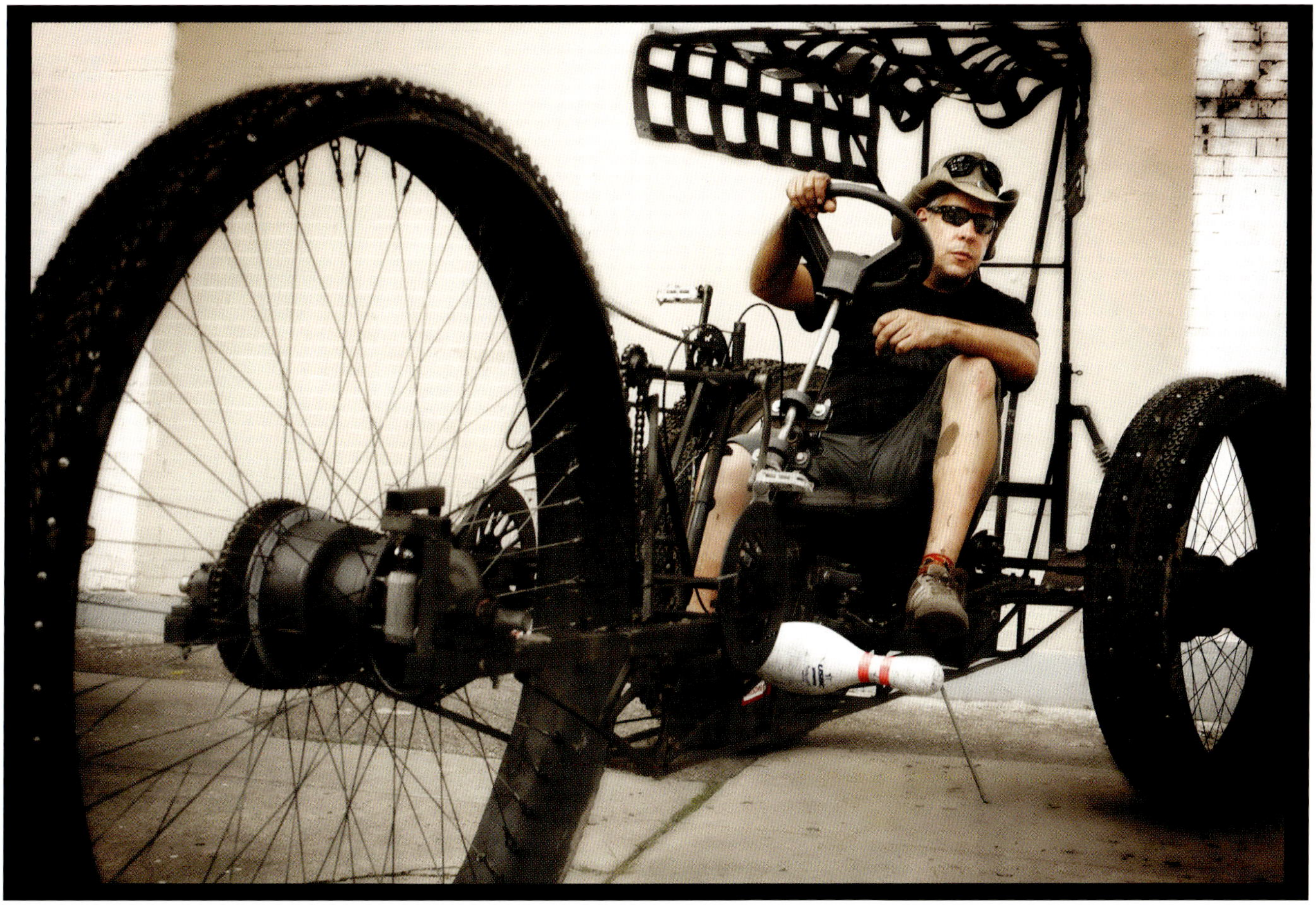

4

# Patricia Gapske

Kalamazoo, Michigan, USA
www.patriciagapske.com

*Early in my life I fell in love with sketching shadows made by objects set on white paper. I attended different colleges around my home state of Michigan exploring different art programs. I graduated from Western Michigan University with a degree in fine art in printmaking. I stumbled upon my love of clay many years later when I took my first figurative sculpture class and realized that it was my passion. I enter my sculptures in juried art competitions and sell my work. I recently had the great pleasure of exhibiting my art for a month at Midtown Gallery here in Kalamazoo and I have a piece in the permanent collection at the Carnegie Center for the Arts. I have been commissioned to create pieces for specific purposes such as a memorial, several for the healthcare field and other private collectors.*

*Clay is my favorite medium and for the past 10 years I have concentrated on sculpting the figure. Depending on what I'm trying to express determines whether it will look realistic or not. I am striving to evolve personally and through my art. Part of this evolution is using flight or birds integrated into the sculpture as a symbol of freedom. Birds have wings to soar above the earth, using their will as direction, yet need to be grounded to survive. I like to visualize my figures as being half human, half bird, as I feel a connection to birds and their ability to soar at a moments notice.*

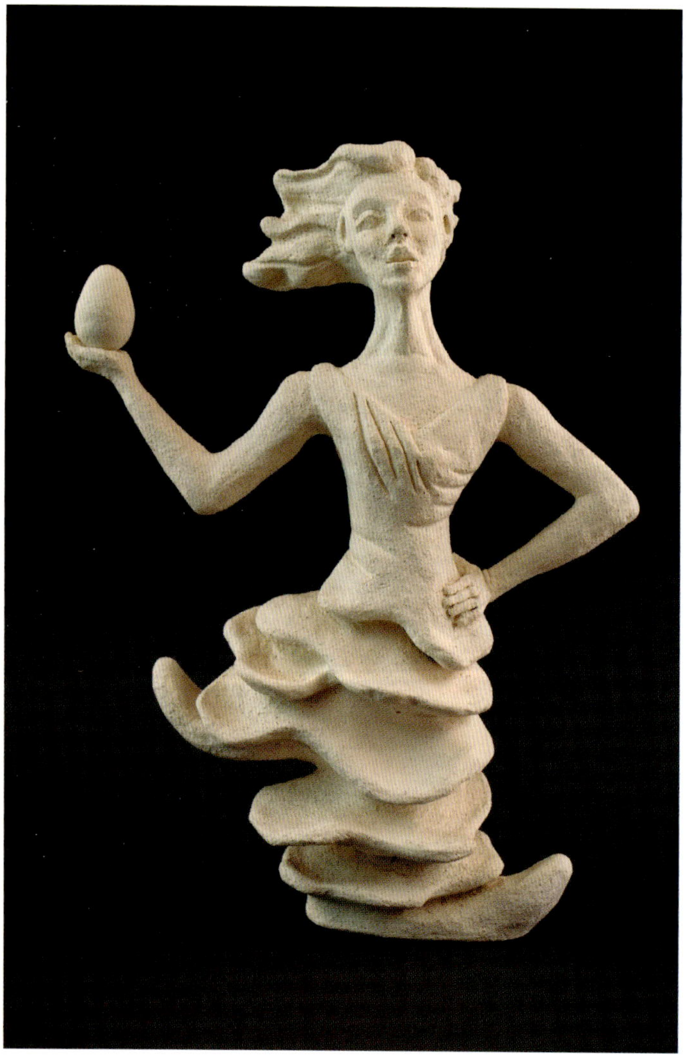

1

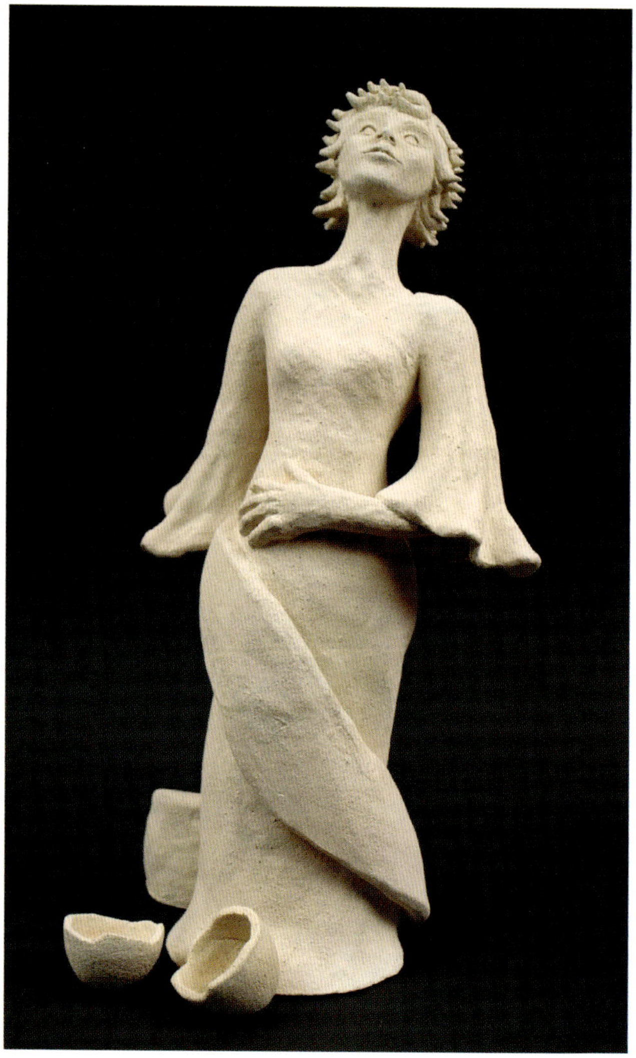

2

3

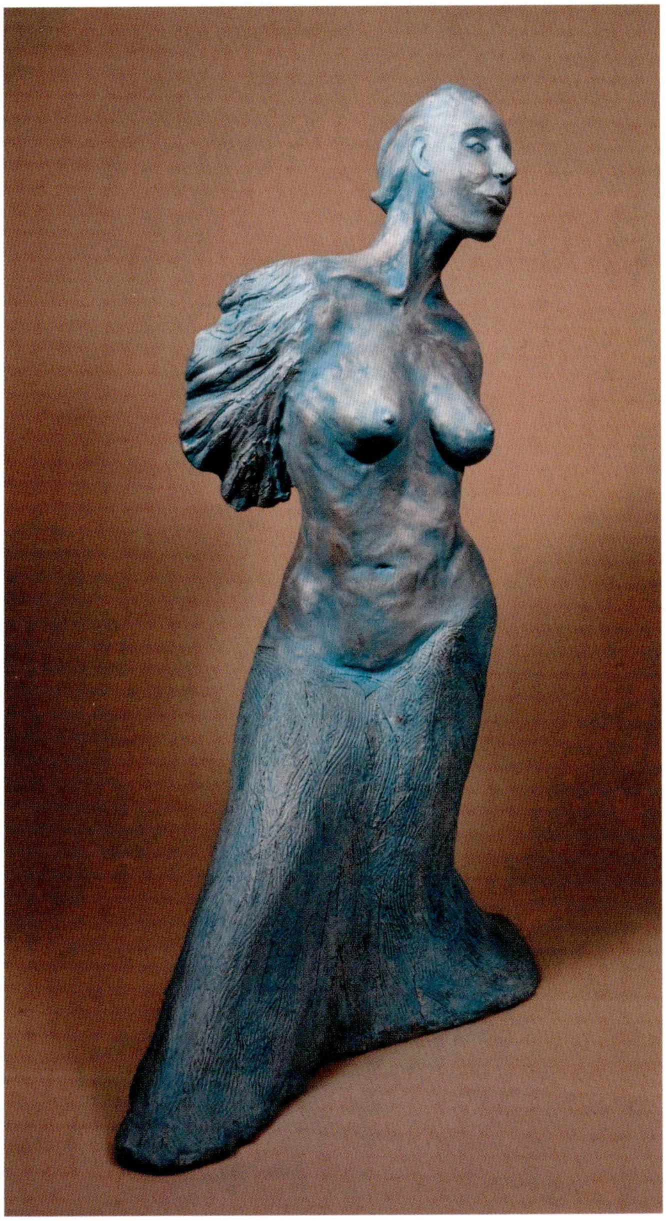

1 *Winds of Change*, 2010. Ceramic, 15". *Photograph by Patricia Gapske.*

2 *Free at Last*, 2010. Ceramic, 16". *Photograph by Patricia Gapske.*

3 *Rara Avis I*, 2002. Ceramic, 19." *Photograph by Patricia Gapske.*

4 *Brigit*, 2001. Ceramic raku, 9". *Photograph by Patricia Gapske.*

5 *Dryad's Long Winter*, 2011. Ceramic, 19". *Photograph by Patricia Gapske.*

4

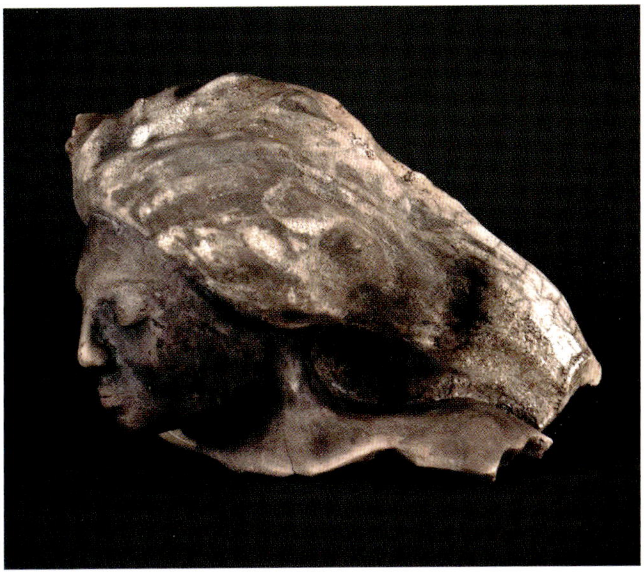

5

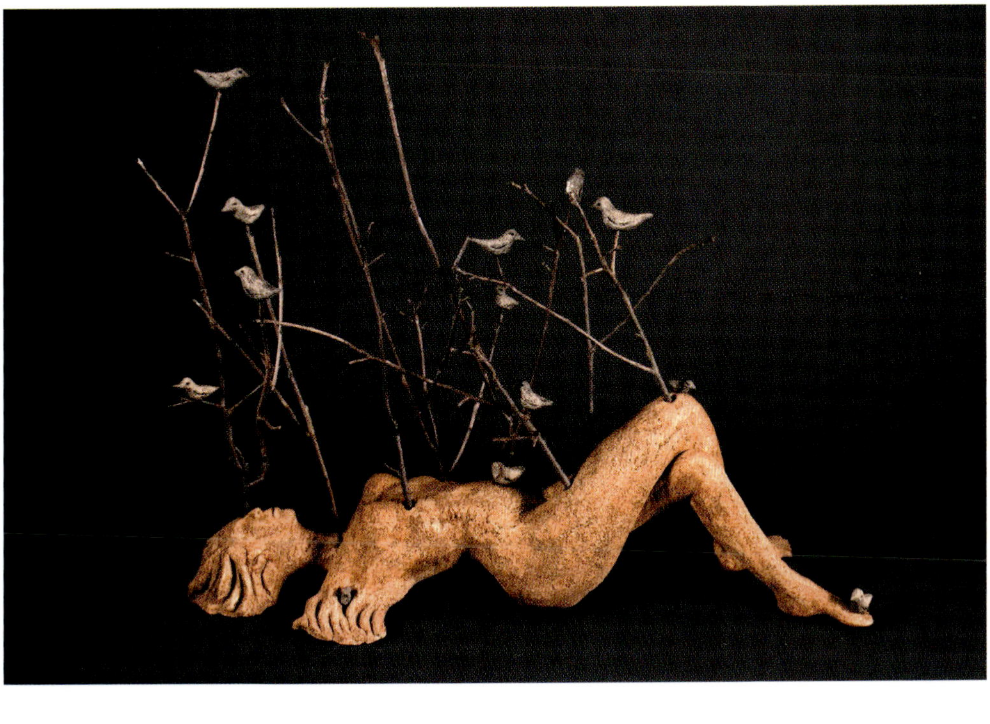

# Antonin Gauthier

Harrow, Ontario, Canada
www.agauthiermetalart.com

*I'm a minimalist metal sculptor. I present only the essential details in a sculpture.*

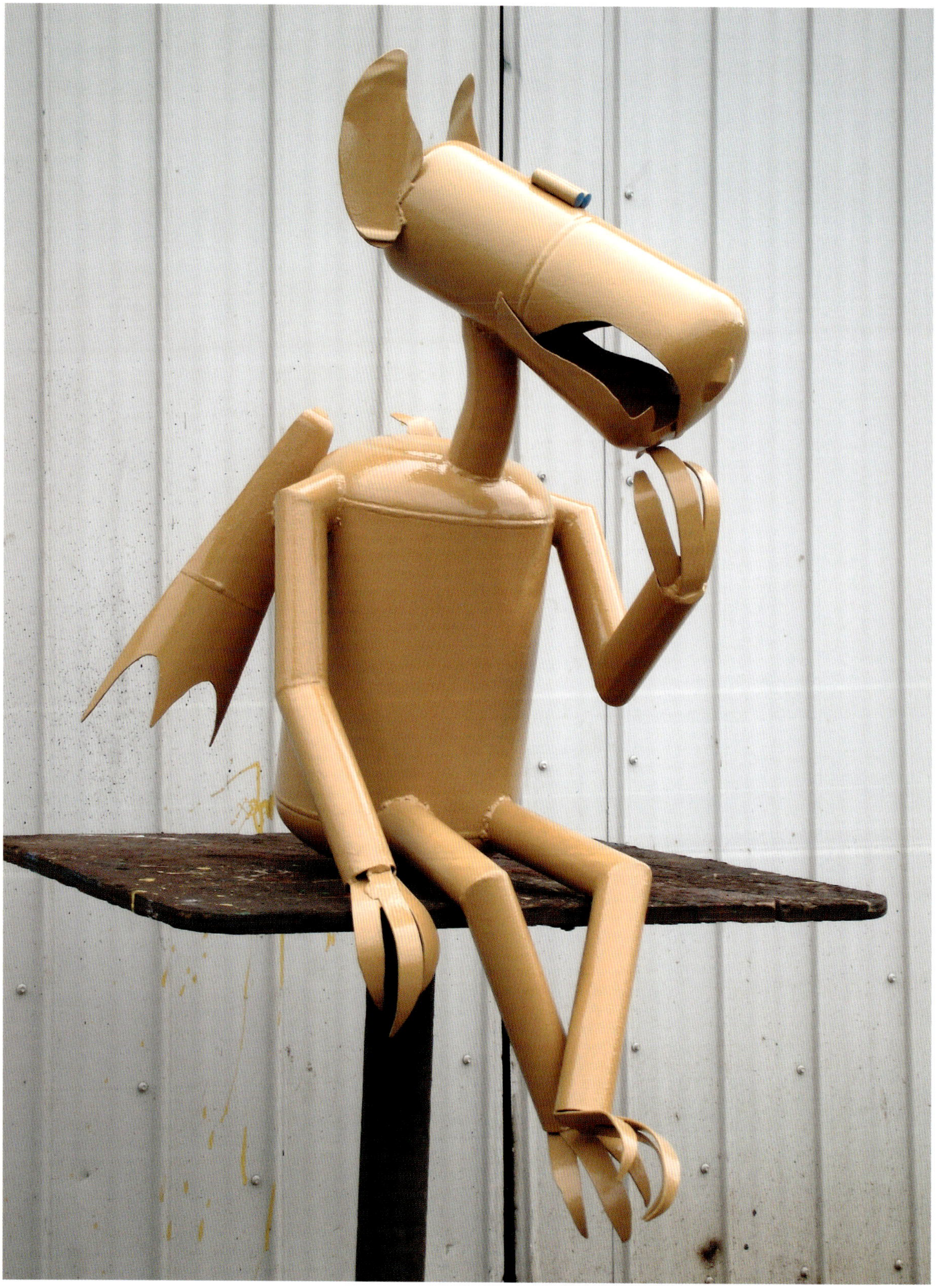

1

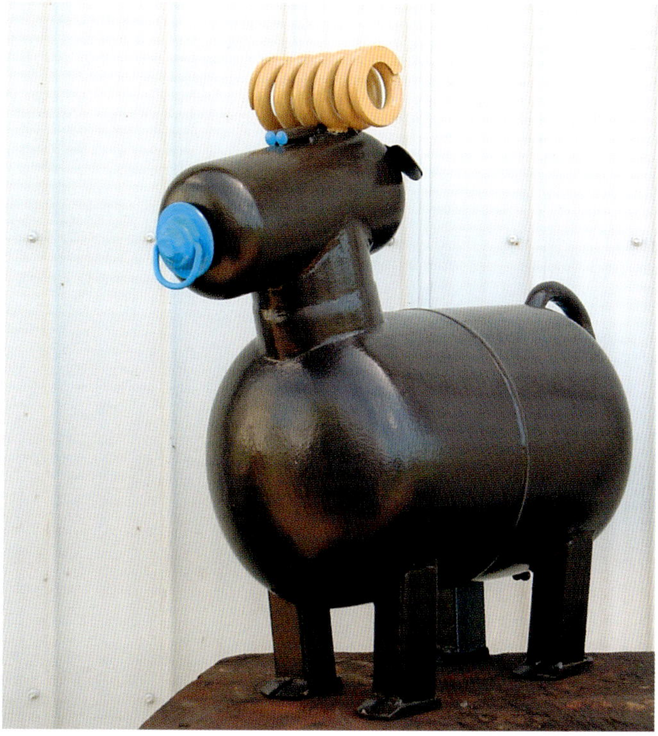

2

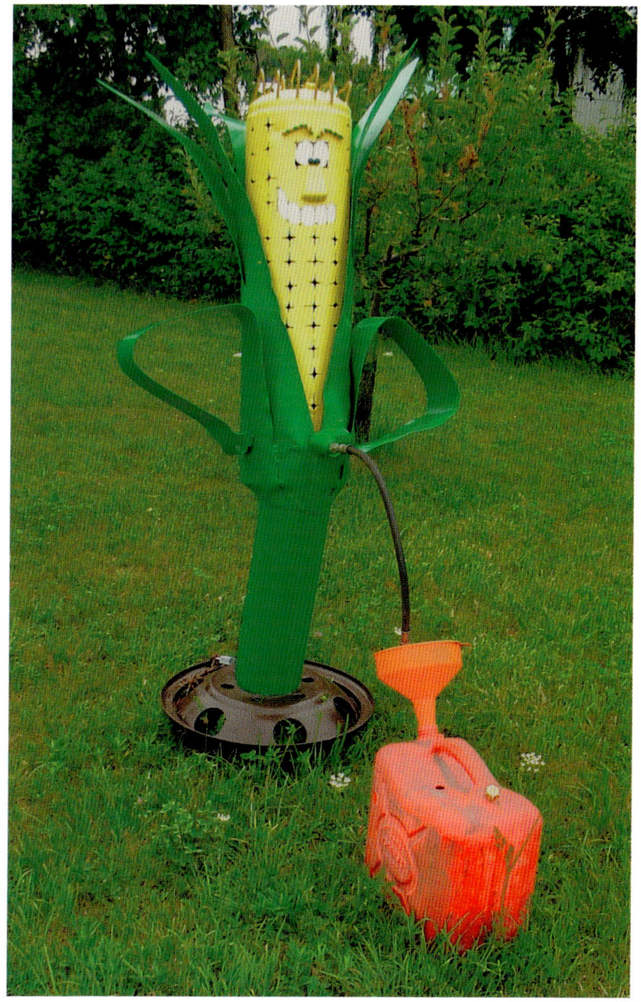

4

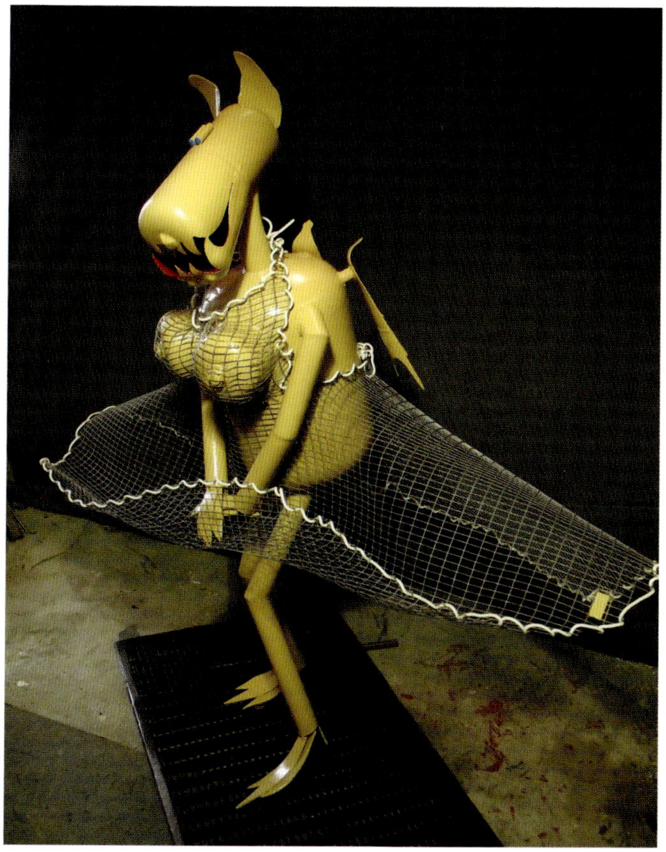

3

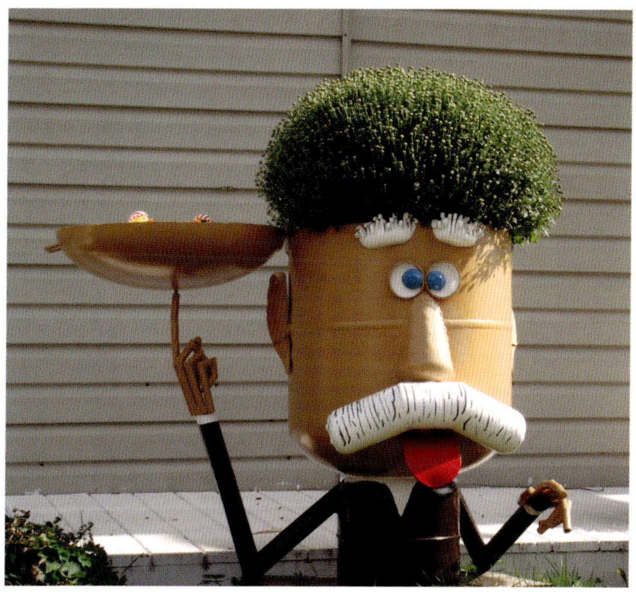

5

1 *The Thinker Gargoyle*, 2011. Recycled steel, 68" x 62" x 45".

2 *The new heavy-duty ram*, 2010. Recycled steel, 12" x 28" x 29".

3 *Marilyn Gargoyle*, 2011. Recycled steel, 68" x 62" x 45.

4 *The Canadian pis*, 2009. Recycled steel, 33" x 69" x 30".

5 *It's all about (what you grow in your head)*, 2010. Recycled steel, 40" x 42" x 28".

# Robert E. Gigliotti

Bow, Washington, USA
www.robertegigliotti.com

*I approach sculpture from two different perspectives. First, I try to make each piece interesting on a purely visual level. Second, I use symbolism from the physical world, mythology, and spiritual practices to challenge the viewer's paradigms about our relationship to each other, to our environment, and to the universe. In my opinion, the unveiling of the true Self and, consequently, nondual Spirit is the ultimate goal of art. You can substitute the word God, Tao, or whatever, for Spirit, but it's basically about the realization that "All is One" that I'm getting at. I think that this is intuitively what artists are doing when they create art. It represents an attempt to go from the finite self to the timeless Self. This type of art is sometimes called transpersonal art. It occurred to me that what I am attempting could be called "visual koan." The intent of a koan is to instill the understanding that the separation between subject and object is an illusion. Purely representational art can expand ones consciousness as well, if it captures a timeless moment because Spirit itself is timeless; meaning not time everlasting, but beyond time. I believe that any art that disarms you, makes you smile, or makes you think is successful. At the very least, most artists hope for an emotional response to their work; I love it, I hate it, it makes me feel...etc. I hope my work inspires you in some way.*

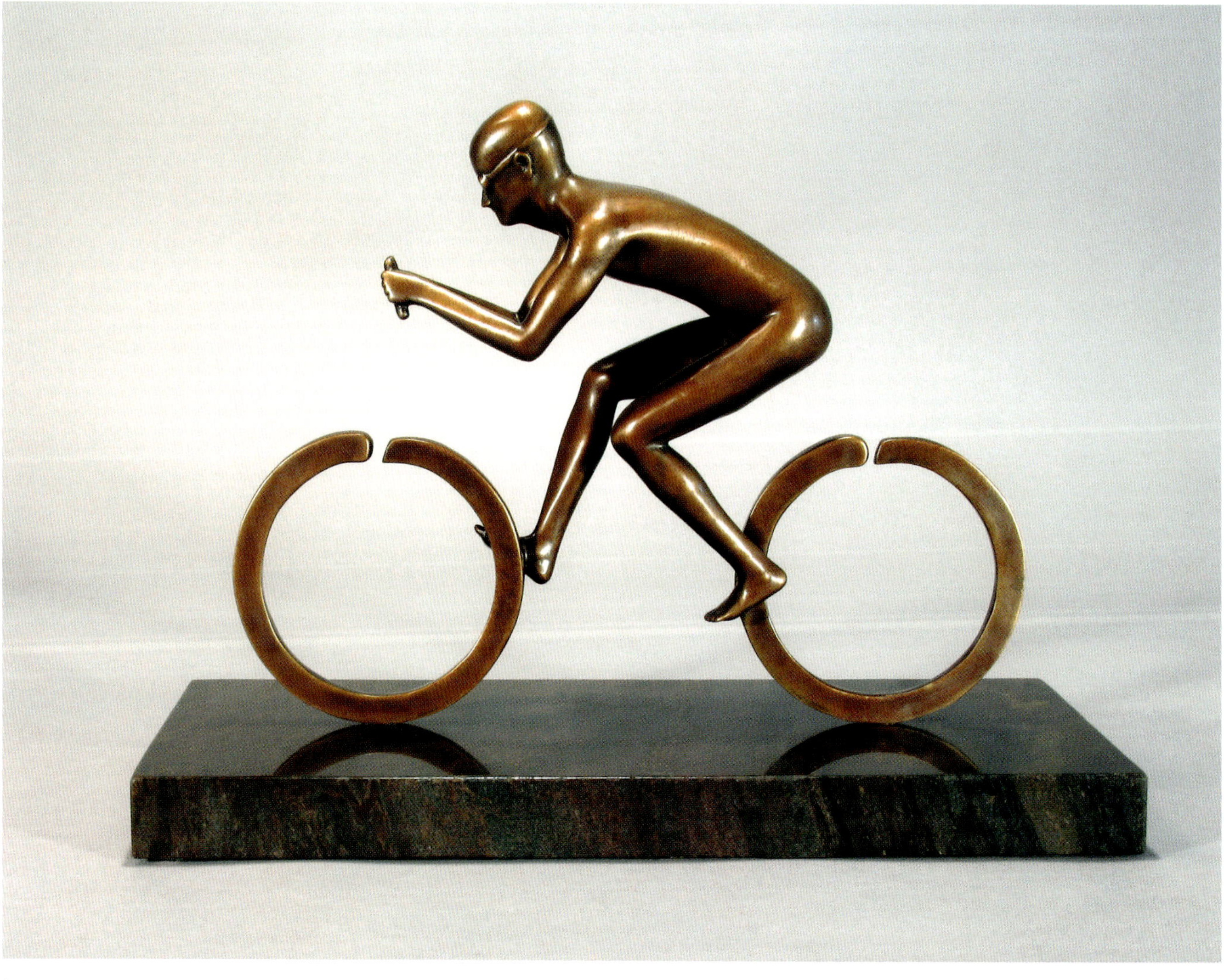

1

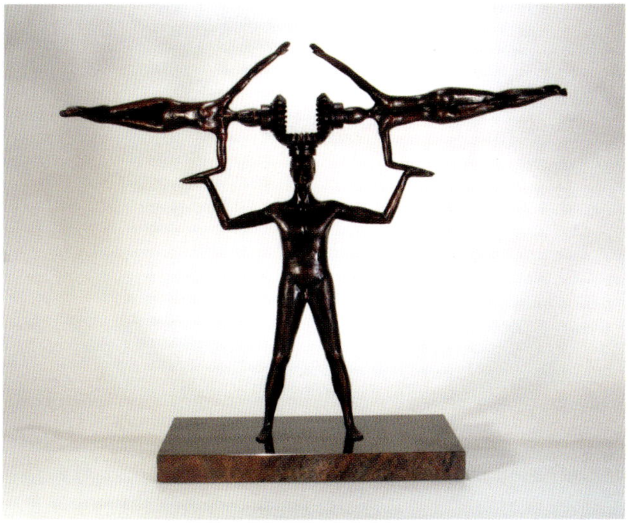

2

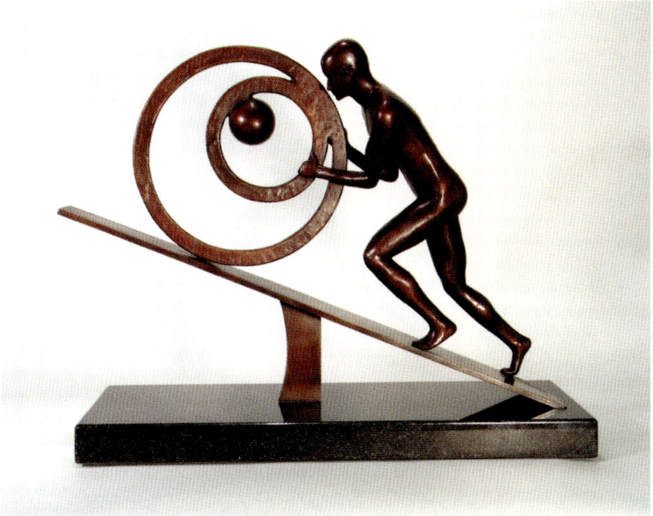

4

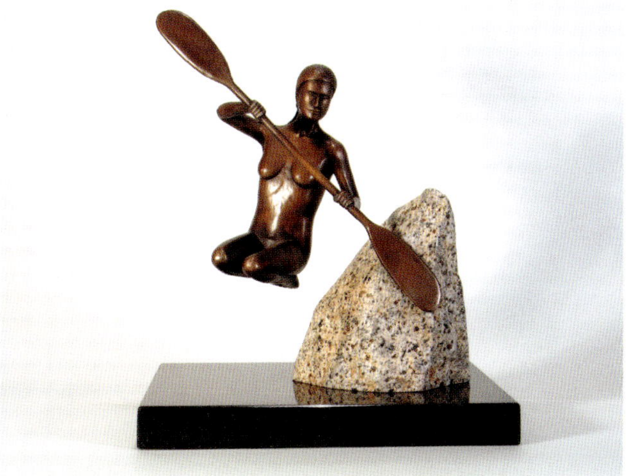

3

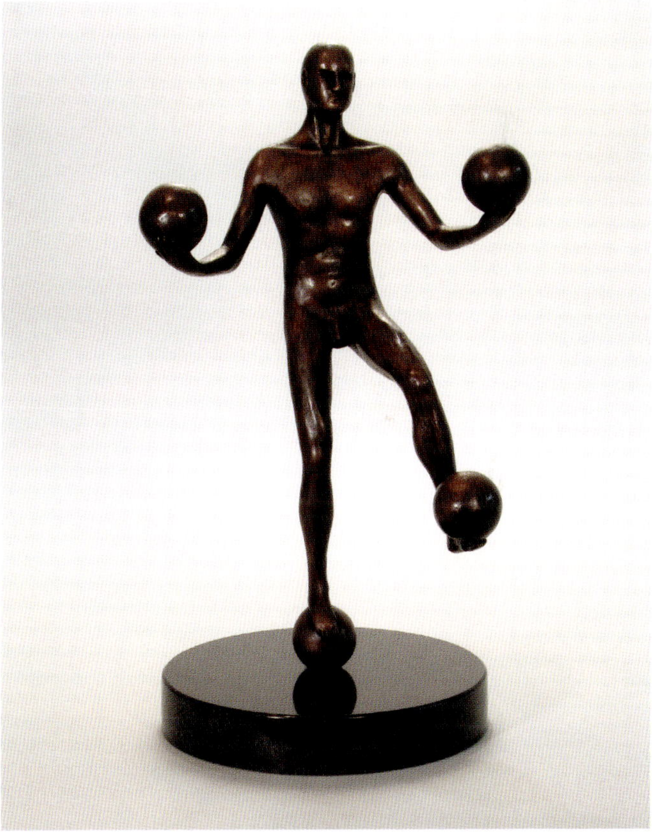

5

1 *Cyclist*, 2010. Cast bronze, 9" h. *Photograph by the artist.*

2 *Aerial Ballet*, 2001. Cast bronze, 18" h. *Photograph by the artist.*

3 *Paddler*, 2009. Cast bronze, 9" h. *Photograph by the artist.*

4 *Sisyphus*, 1987. Cast bronze, 10" h. *Photograph by the artist.*

5 *Four Noble Truths*, 1995. Cast bronze, 15" h. *Photograph by the artist.*

6 *Rower*, 2008. Cast bronze, 7" h. *Photograph by the artist.*

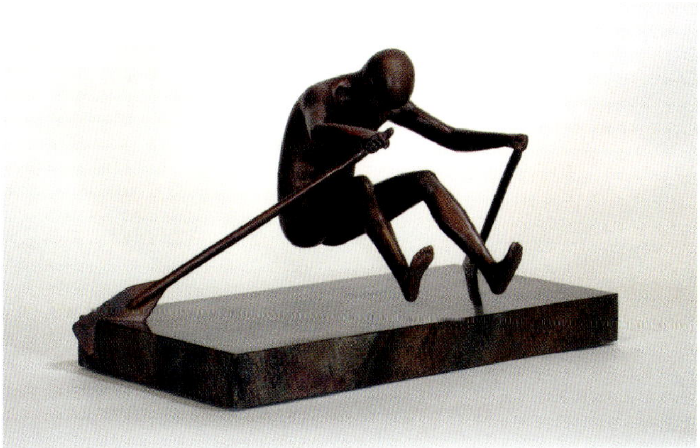

6

# Denis Grace

Eugene, Oregon, USA
www.denisgrace.com

*With degrees in architecture and structural engineering, I was drawn to historical restoration and, eventually, sculpture, my one true passion in life.*

*Over time I began to think of sculpture in terms of artistic anatomy and poetic impact. As I worked, I would look back in history to try to understand how other sculptors dealt with these issues. This led me to the Hellenistic Greeks. They developed the fundamental concepts of gravity, muscle, bone, and psychology. From there I studied the Romantics and the Symbolists. My work, then, is based on a classical structure that is layered with emotion, symbolism, and romance, in the sense that I believe that beauty, feeling, and mystery take precedence over rational thought..*

*My studio is located in the hills overlooking Eugene, Oregon.*

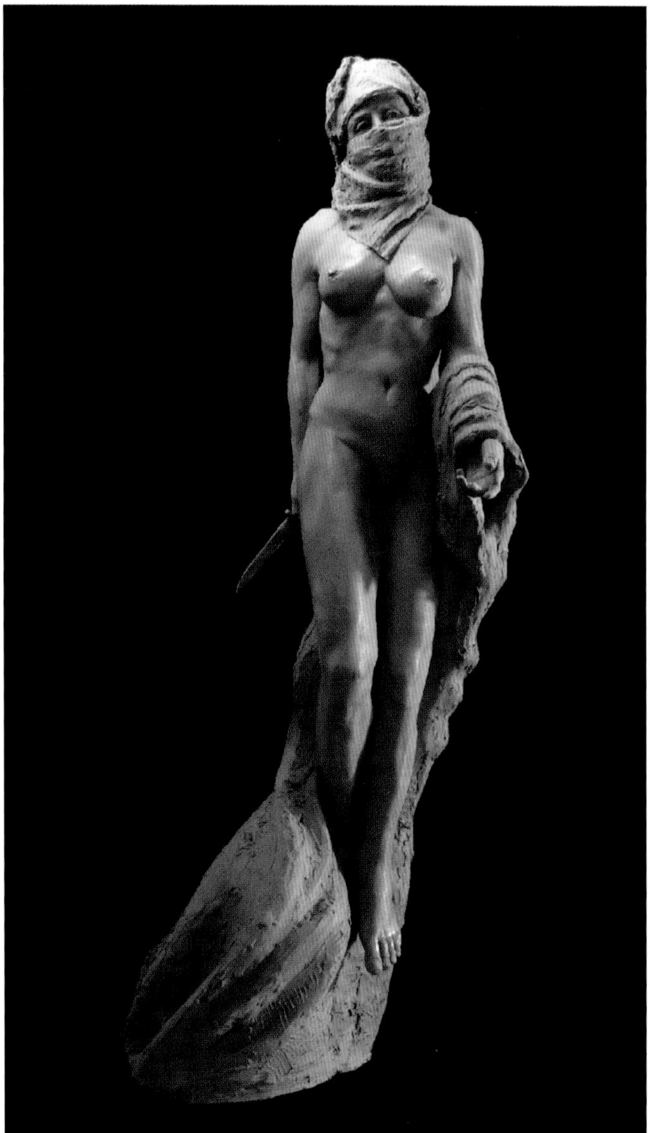

1

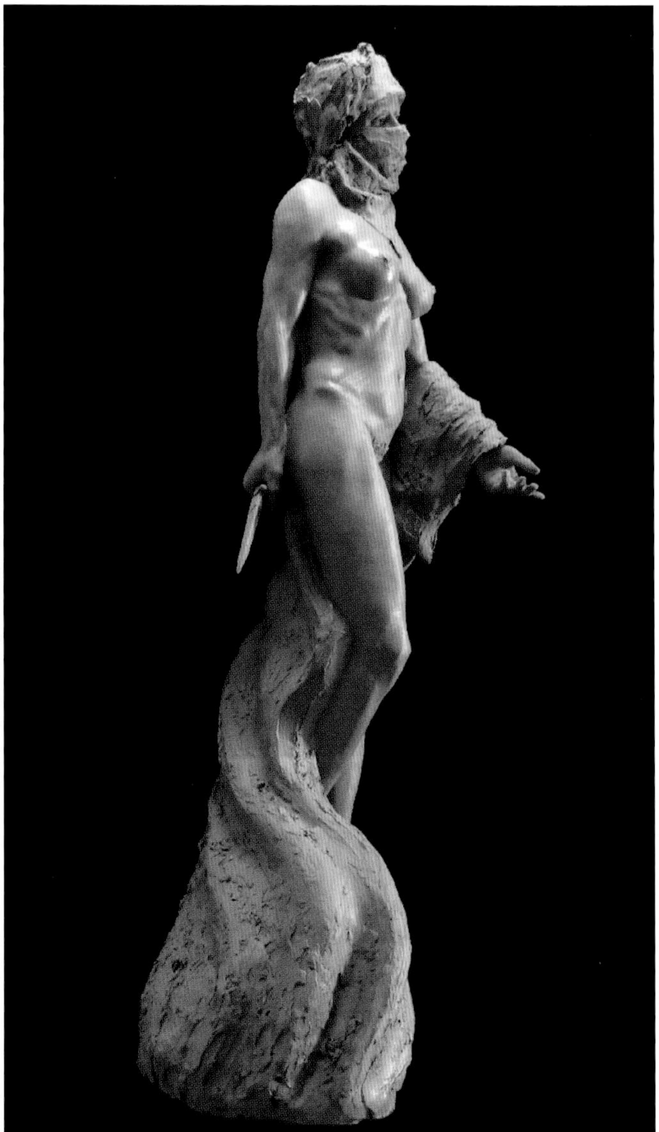

2

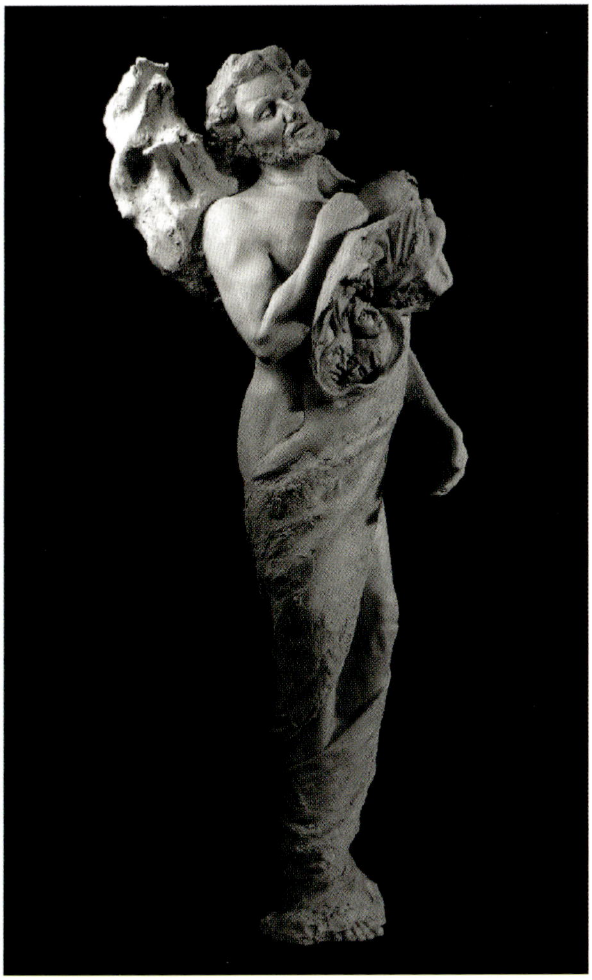

3

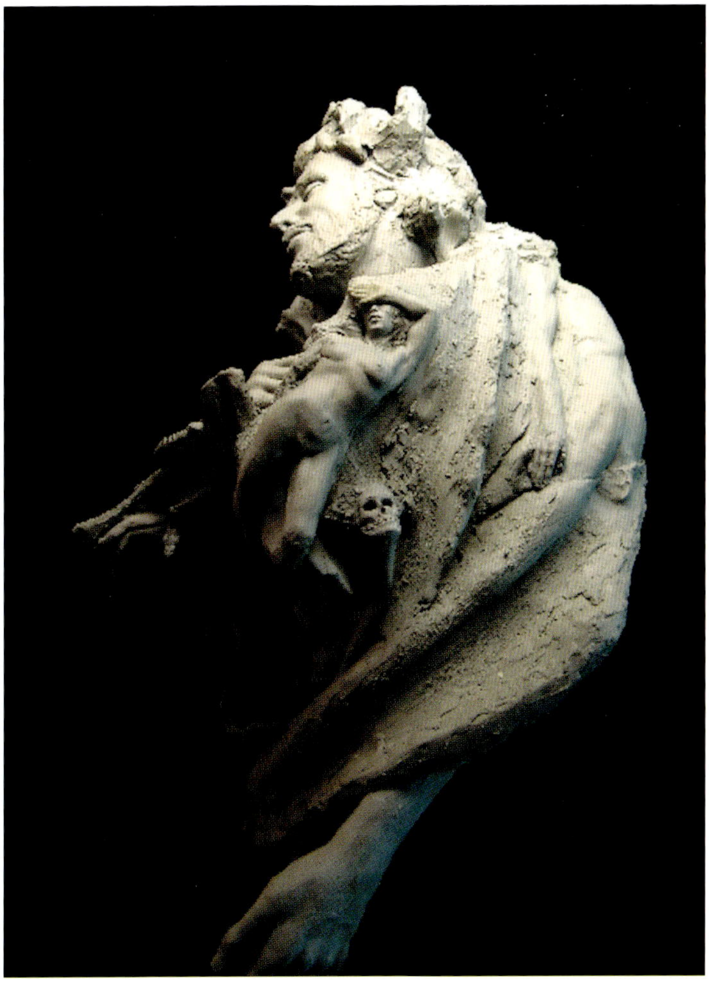

4

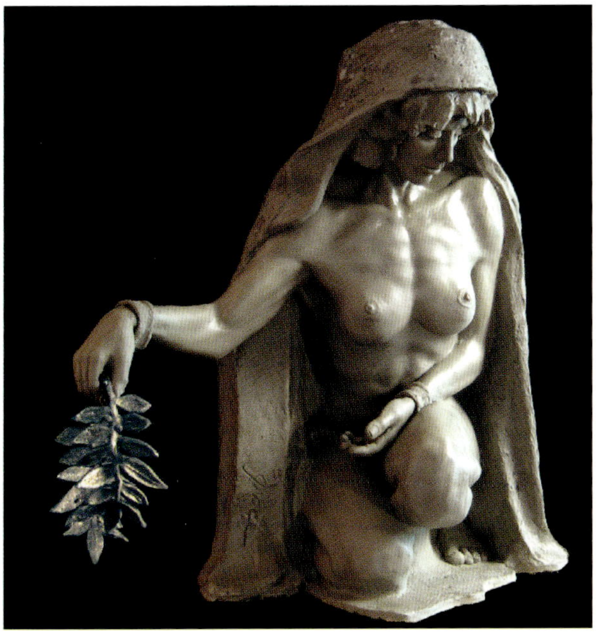

5

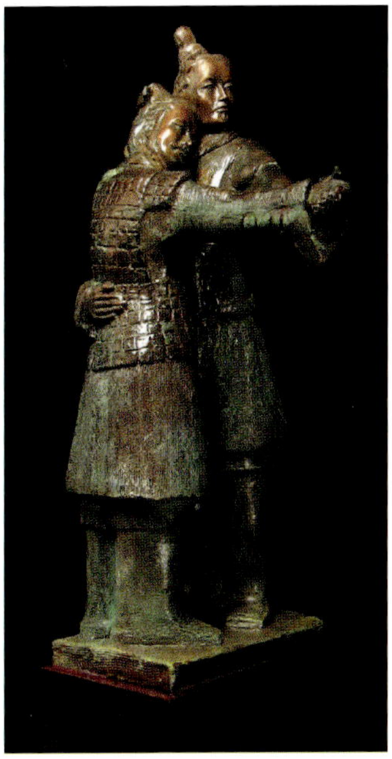

6

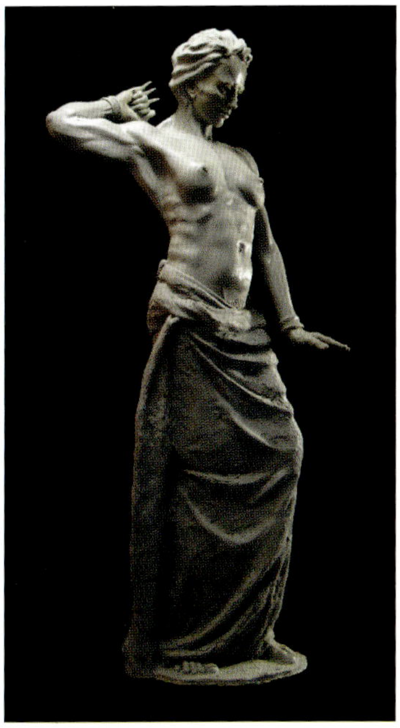

7

1 *The Terrorist*, 2009. Clay, 32". *Photograph by Denis Grace.*

2 *The Terrorist* (detail), 2009. *Photograph by Denis Grace.*

3 *Letting go*, 2010. Clay, 39". *Photograph by Denis Grace.*

4 *Letting go* (detail), 2010. Clay, 39". *Photograph by Denis Grace.*

5 *Defeat*, 2010. Clay, 18". *Photograph by Denis Grace.*

6 *Tango Warriors*, 2009. Clay, 14". *Photograph by Denis Grace.*

7 *Victory*, 2010. Clay, 36". *Photograph by Denis Grace.*

# Ed Haddaway

Albuquerque, New Mexico, USA
www.edhaddaway.com

Ed Haddaway has been building things since his early childhood in Fort Worth, Texas. His talent was first acknowledged when he was in the third grade and was placed in a citywide art program for exceptional students. Graduating from the University of New Mexico with a BFA in 1972, he traveled and did a variety of construction work. After attending graduate school at North Texas University in 1976, Haddaway worked at Delahunty, a prestigious contemporary gallery in Dallas. Soon after, he returned to New Mexico and began seriously producing his sculpture.

He received an NEA grant in 1979/80, has taught and exhibited his work widely in galleries and museums over the years. His work is in many private collections and he has completed a number of large public commissions.

"My work is somewhat autobiographical, but with a smattering of angst," Haddaway says. Critics often perceive a hint of darkness under the work's uplifting and happy demeanor. "It's like the witch's candy-covered house…it looks wonderful and you want to eat it, but you know that the witch is around somewhere." His recent works often involve mechanical elements and Haddaway sees himself as an inventor, something he aspired to as a child. Indeed, the work grows out of his active childhood imagination, which Haddaway has worked to retain through the years. His dreams and Carl Jung's ideas of the collective unconscious have greatly influenced him and he accepts the role of a poet and storyteller. "I'm exploring the intangible," Haddaway says," and my sculptures are just leftovers, scattered along the path."

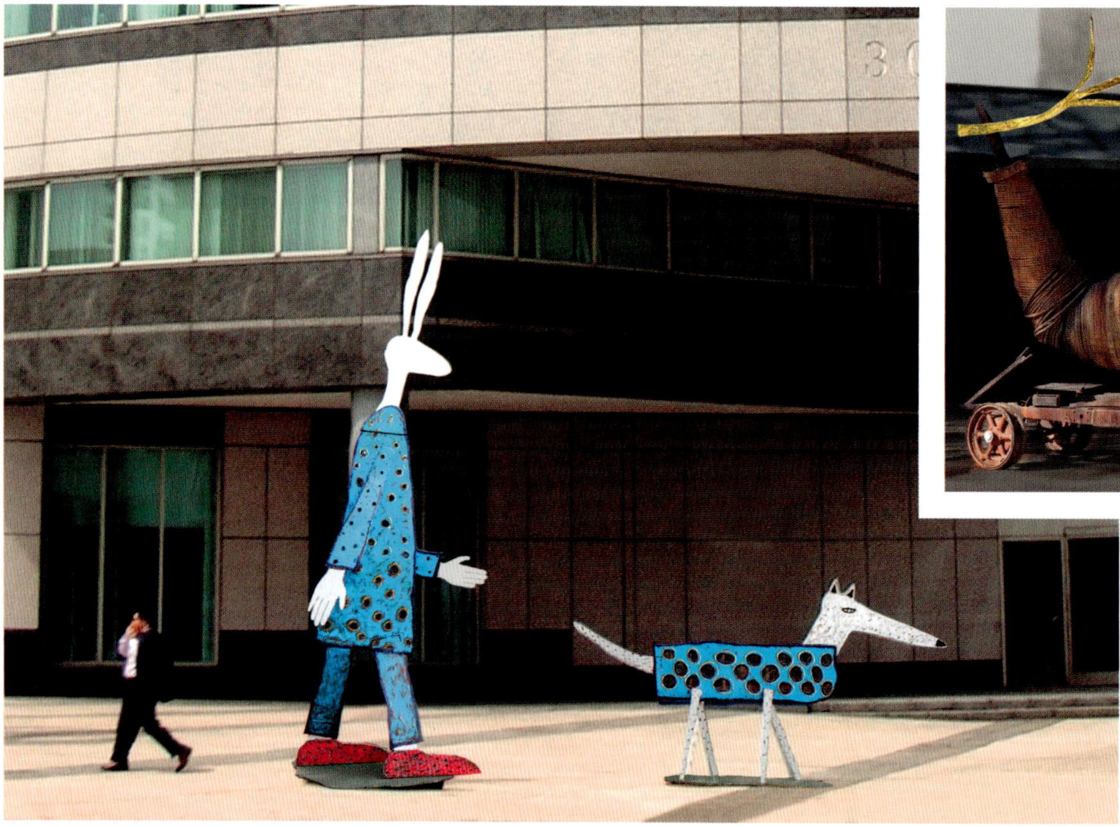

1

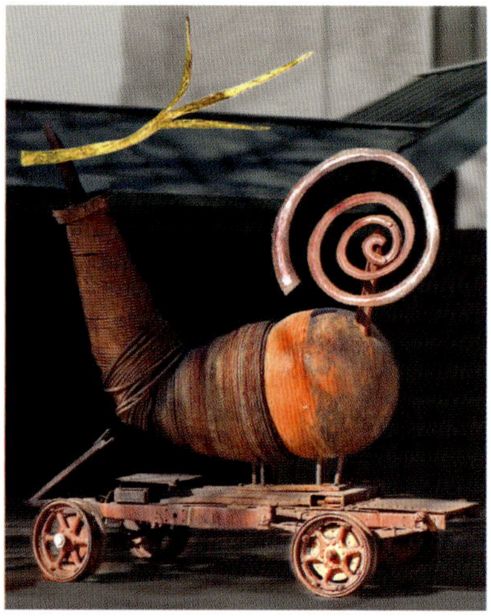

2

1 *Early Morning Walk*, 2010. Painted steel, 19' x 26' x 6'. *Photograph by Margot Geist.*

2 *So Happened Before Dream*, 2008. Painted steel, found object, 12' 6" x 11' x 5' 6". *Photograph by Margot Geist.*

3 *Old Mama Fern*, 2008. Painted steel, 37' x 10' x 10'. *Photograph by Margot Geist.*

4 *Allegory By The Numbers*, 2009. Painted steel, found object, 87" x 41" x 27". *Photograph by Margot Geist.*

5 *Burr Tangle and Axis Mundi*, 2008. Painted steel, 10' x 7' x 2'. *Photograph by Margot Geist.*

6 *Shadow Night Device*, 2009. Painted steel, marble, found objects, 55" x 22" x 24". *Photograph by Margot Geist.*

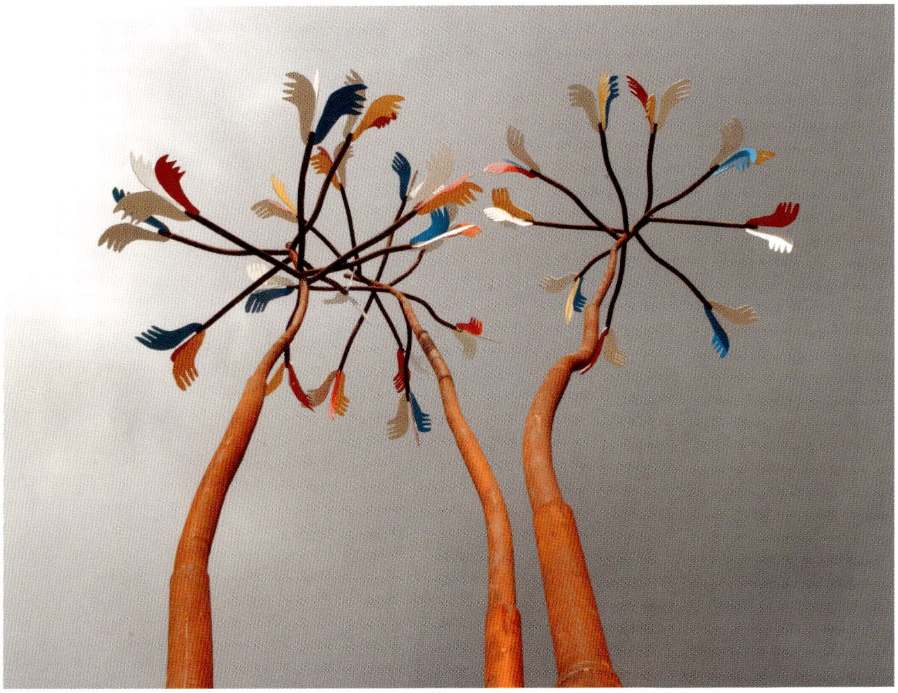

3

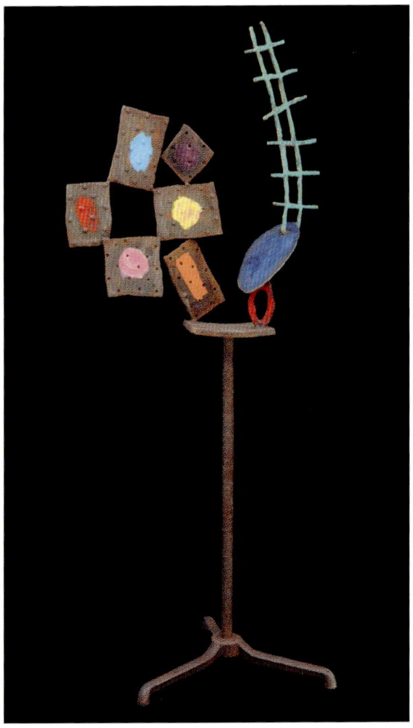

4

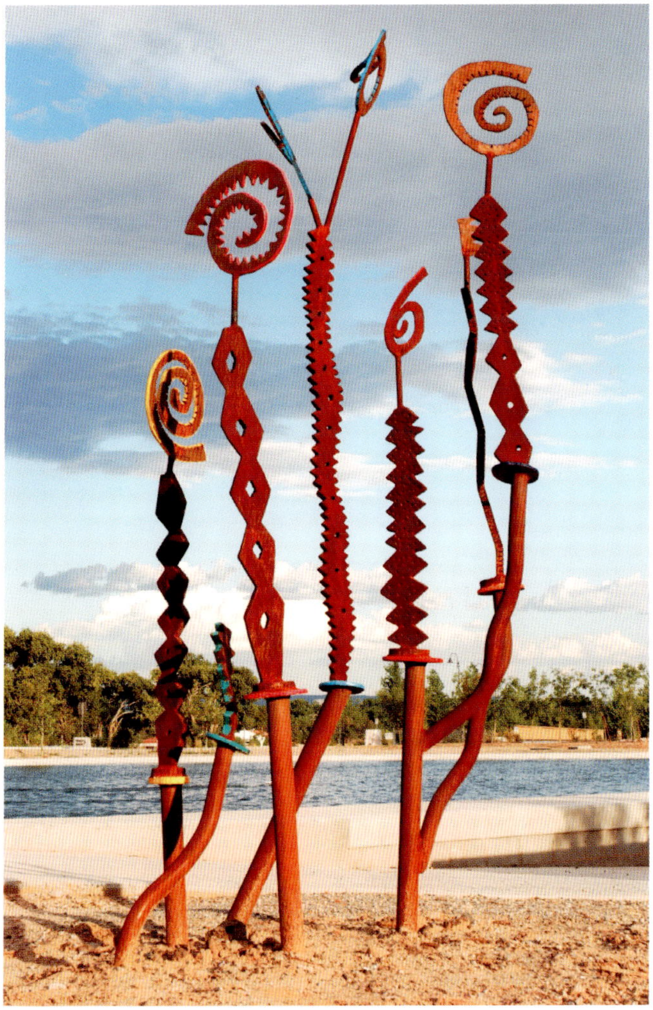

5

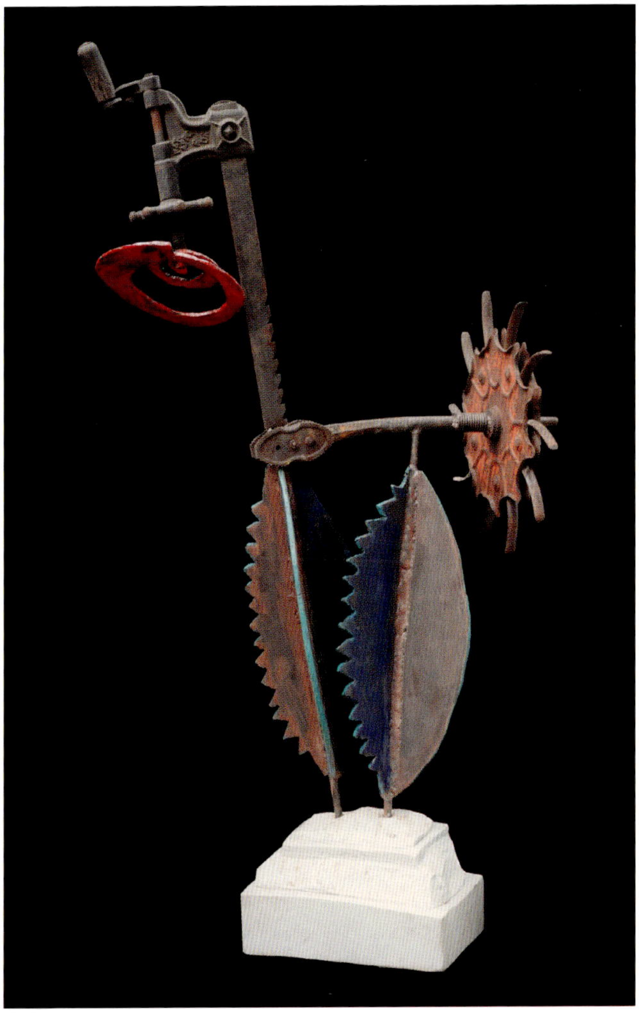

6

# Hoss Haley

Asheville, North Carolina, USA
www.hosshaley.com

*The foundation of my aesthetic and creative process can be traced back to growing up in the stark farmland of western Kansas. The land there is flat and vast, interrupted only by an occasional fence or grain elevator. There is no middle ground; everything is either macro or micro. I think there is a certain purity to this extreme. This, more than anything else, informs my aesthetic. I choose to work with materials from industry and agriculture—steel, concrete, stainless steel—and techniques borrowed from basic fabrication—cutting, forming, and welding. The inherent qualities of these materials and processes, their weight, strength, color, and marks, become an essential part of the work.*

*Life on a farm requires a good deal of self-reliance and the ability to solve problems under any conditions. The highest currency is a general handiness and the ability to make do with what's at hand. In my studio, I apply this general philosophy to my creative process. Each new project starts with "what if…?" For example, what if I could roll large sheets of flat steel into a coil the way I roll a strip of paper around a straw? I set out to emulate this process in steel. If a method for doing so doesn't exist, I create it. There is a problem to solve and a process developed to solve the problem. The form is the by-product of this system and is equally informed by material, process, and aesthetic decisions made along the way.*

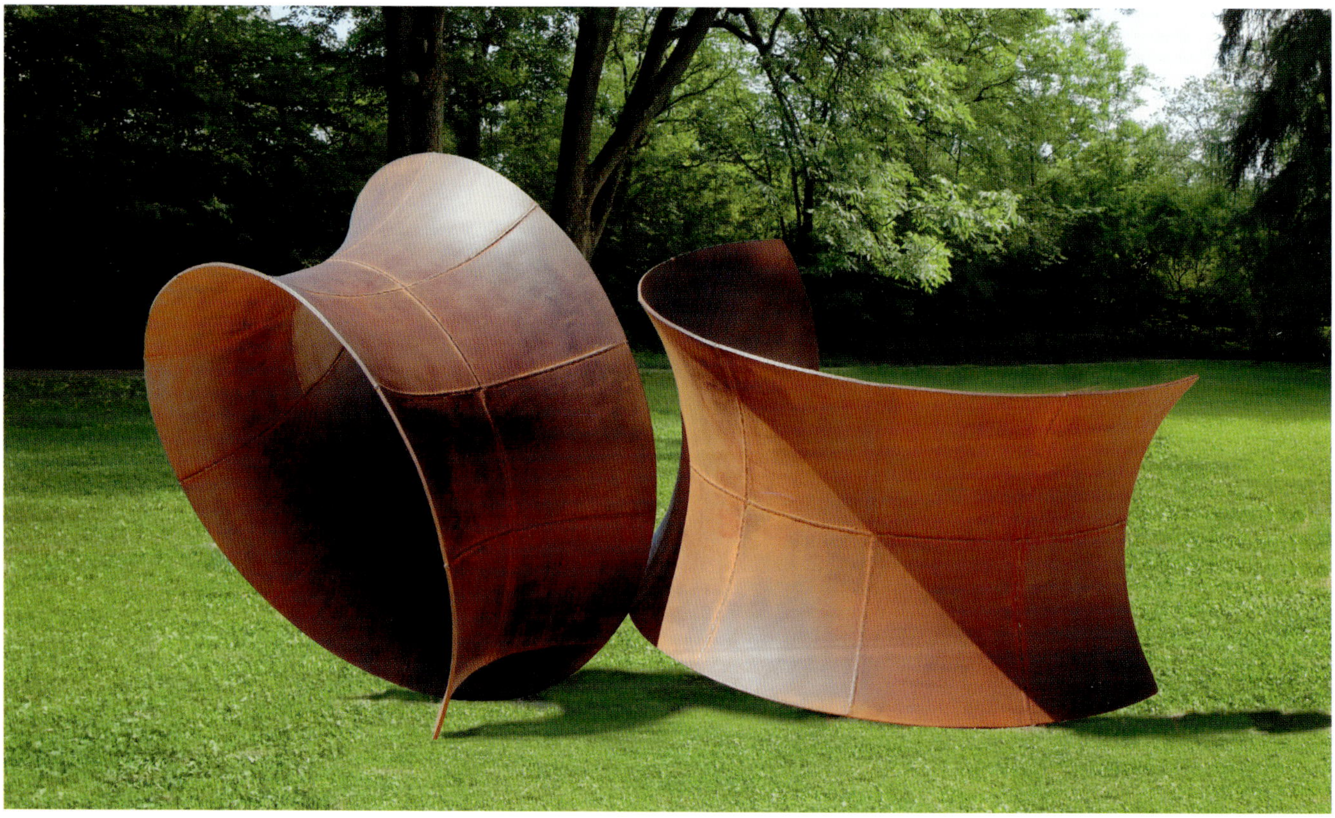

1

1 *Warped Grid,* 2008. Cor-Ten steel, 8.5' x 18' x 10'. *Photo courtesy of Hoss Haley Studio.*

2 *Architectural Coil* (maquette), 2011. Cor-Ten steel, 9" x 9" x 16". *Photograph courtesy of Hoss Haley Studio.*

3 *Conical Coil* (maquette), 2011. Cor-Ten steel, 9" x 8" x 14". *Photograph courtesy of Hoss Haley Studio.*

4 *Integrity,* 2006. Fabricated bronze, 8' h. x 12' x 4". *Photograph courtesy of Hoss Haley Studio.*

5 *Toric Large* (arch), 2007. Formed and fabricated Cor-Ten steel, 10' x 12' x 8'. *Photo courtesy of Hoss Haley Studio.*

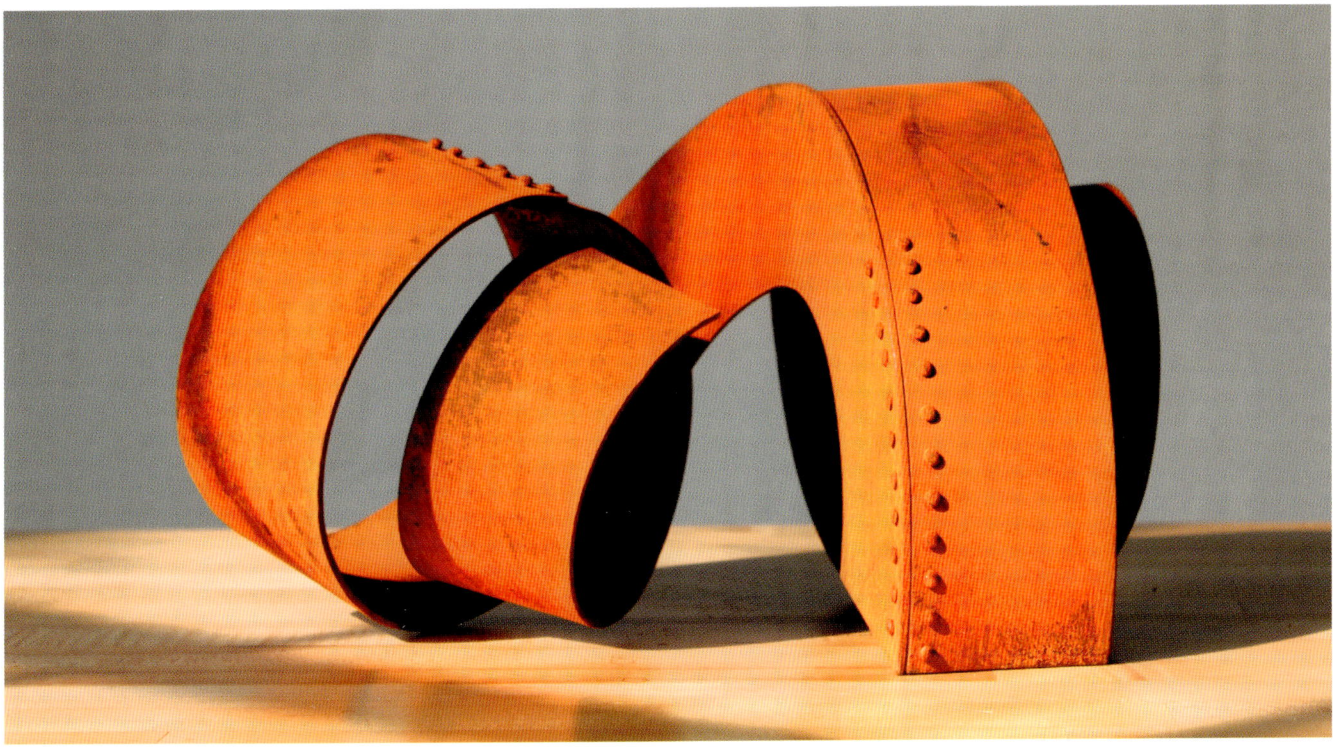

2

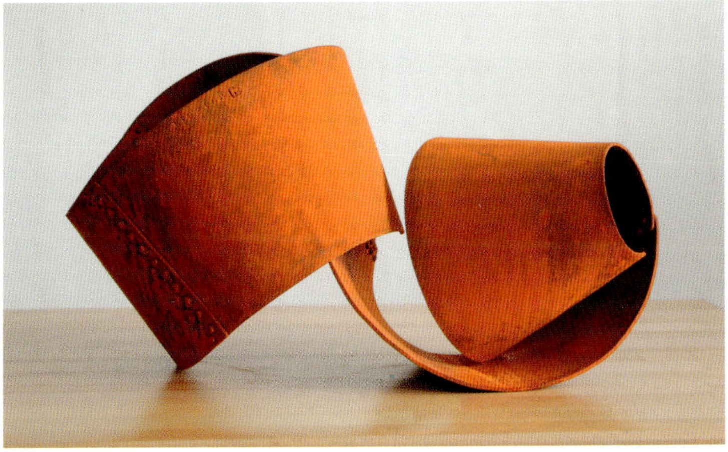

3

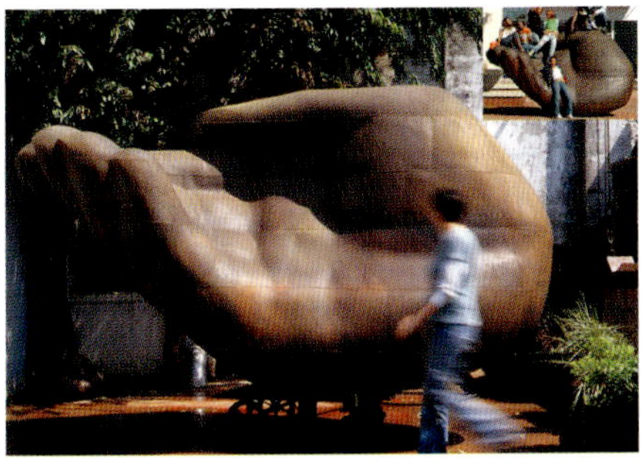

4

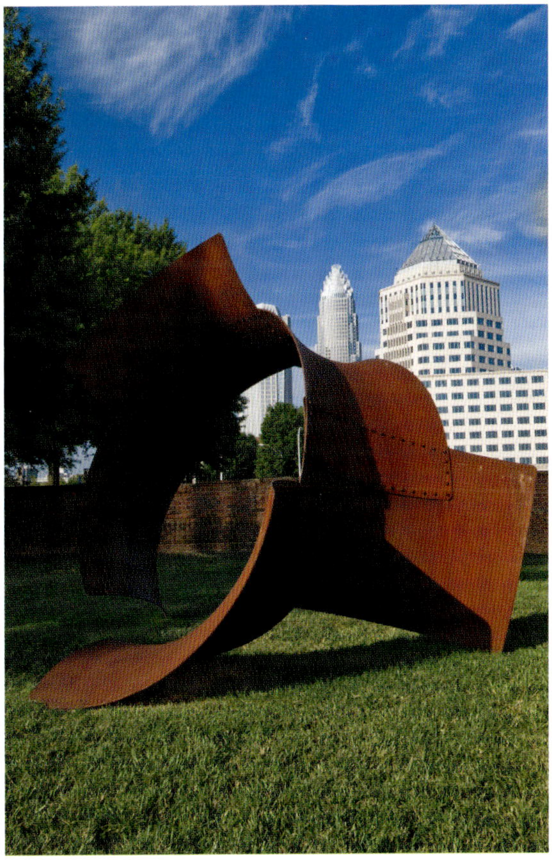

5

# David Hamlow

Good Thunder, Minnesota, USA
www.davidhamlow.com

David Hamlow received an MFA in painting and drawing from the University of Minnesota in 2005. He has shown work in regional, national, and international venues, including the Minneapolis Institute of Art, the Roy C. Moore Gallery at Gainesville State College, Georgia, and The Ferencvarosi Gallery in Budapest, Hungary. He currently lives in Good Thunder, Minnesota, with his wife, artist Liz Miller, and he teaches 2- and 3-dimensional art at Minnesota State University, Mankato.

*My work addresses daily life – particularly those daily experiences that, through repetition and homogeneity, are rendered invisible. Quotidian activity in contemporary culture creates an overlooked energy. This energy has the potential to be creative or destructive and, due to its incremental nature, can be difficult to qualify or quantify.*

*My goal is to reveal this energy as an objective experience with measurable impact. Through a variety of media– ranging from drawing series and video to performance and installation – I strive to expose the habit in creativity and the monumental in the mundane.*

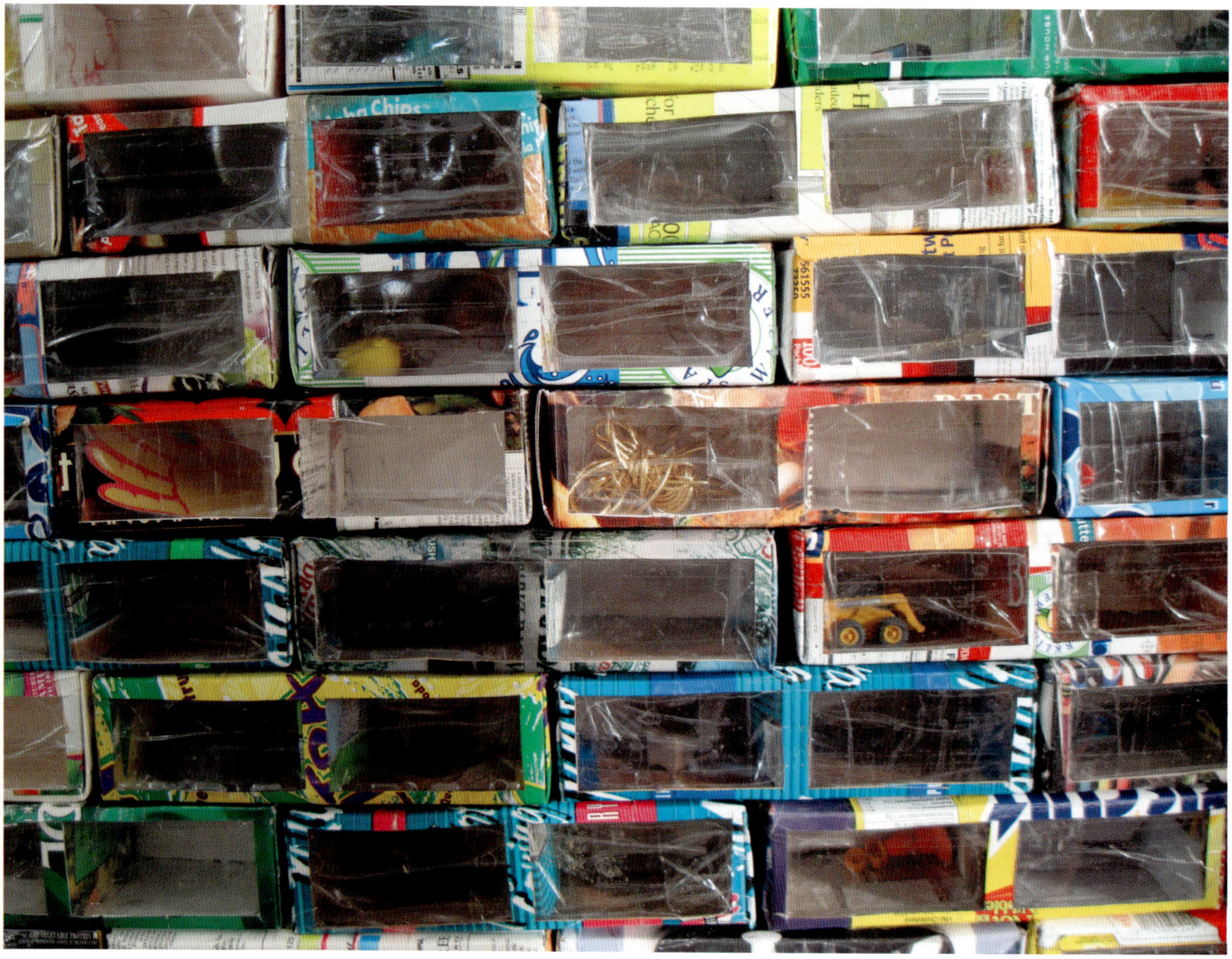

1

2

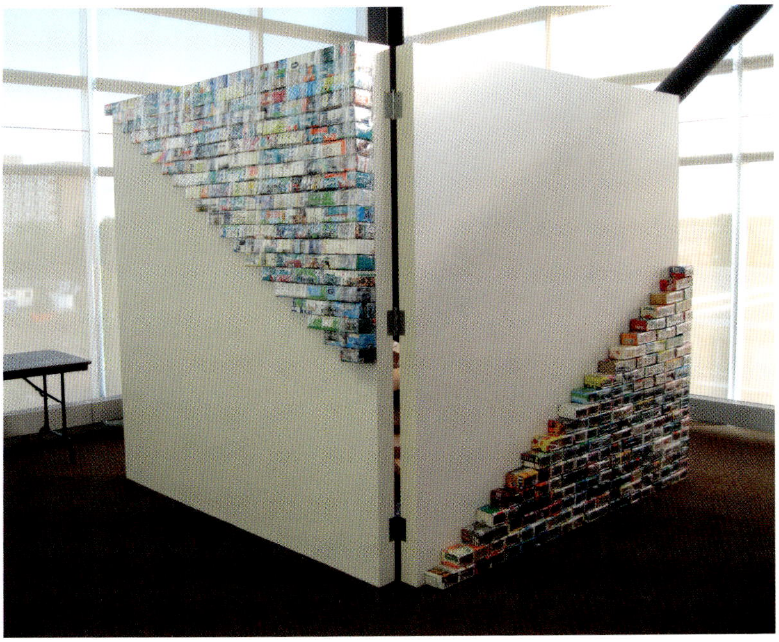

3

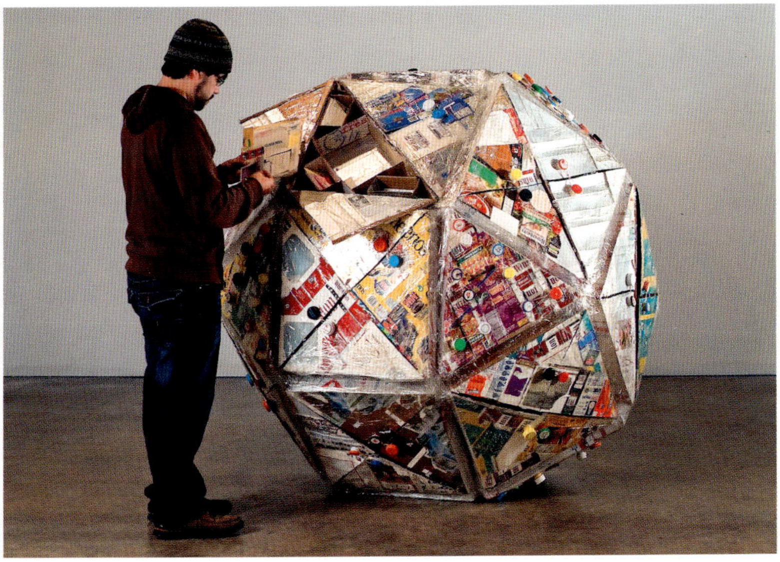

1 *Archival Structure Five: Bricks* (detail), 2011. *Photography by David Hamlow.*

2 *Archival Structure Five: Bricks*, 2011 (on-going). Conserved cardboard, plastic, personal detritus; dimensions variable. Location: University of Wisconsin, Osh-Kosh. *Photography by David Hamlow.*

3 *Archival Structure Four: Rhombacubeoctahedron: Version 1*, 2009. Conserved cardboard, personal detritus. 60" x 60" x 60". *Photograph by Richard Roche.*

4 *Archival Structure Four – Box 8* [closed view], 2009. Conserved cardboard, personal detritus. 15.5" x 29" x 2.5". *Photography by David Hamlow.*

4

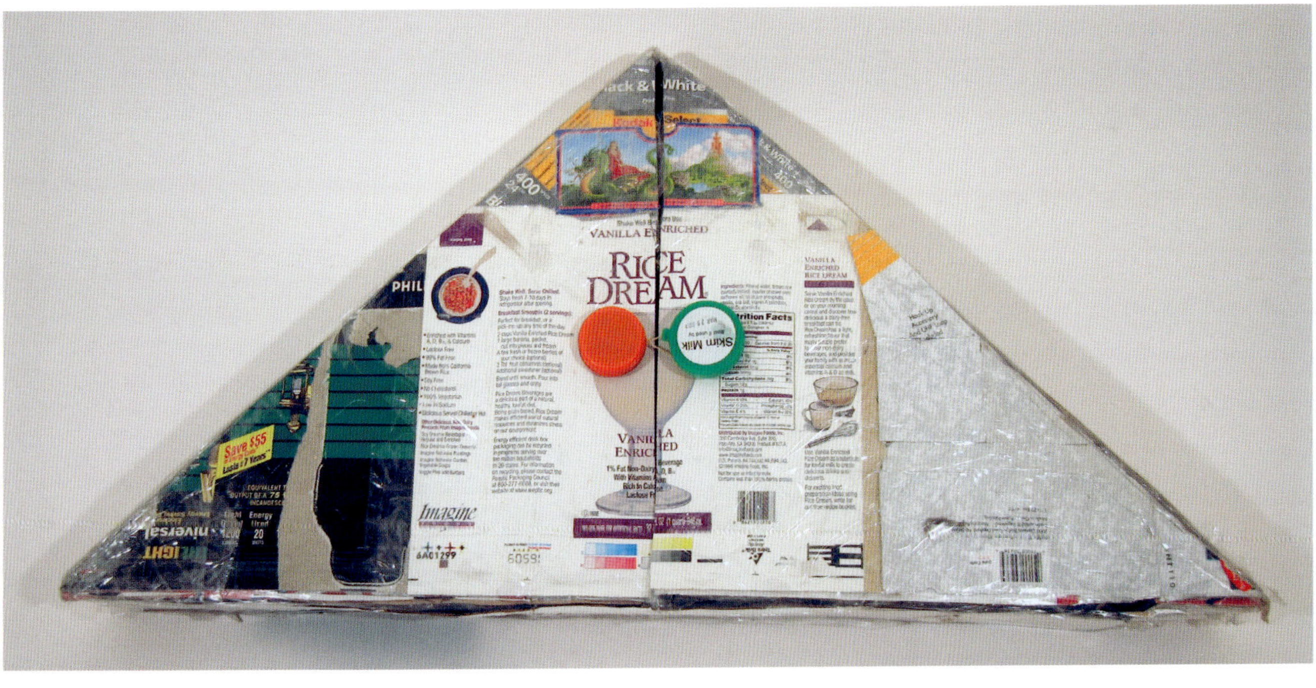

# Mark Yale Harris

Santa Fe, New Mexico, USA
www.markyaleharris.com

*Born in Buffalo, New York, I spent my childhood enthralled in a world of drawing and painting. Though honored for my creative endeavors, I was encouraged to pursue a more conventional career. After finding conventional success, the artistic passion that existed just beneath the surface was able to present itself. I began sculpting and have since created an evolving body of work in alabaster, marble, limestone, and bronze, often combining different elements to bring forth a duality in the sculpture that I make. My sculpture is now featured in public collections, museums, and galleries worldwide, including: Booth Western Art Museum, Cartersville, Georgia; the Four Seasons Hotel, Chicago, Illinois; and the Open Air Museum, Ube, Japan.*

*The purpose of my artwork is to provoke a perceptual, internal, and intellectual response for the viewer, a visual that speaks to life's experiences. To create symbols of universal connection and the relationship that one has to another and to nature.*

*Furthermore, art conveys my nonverbal view of life. An ongoing portrayal of myself, my behavior, adventure, exploration, risk taking, and my non-acceptance of convention and the status quo. I am continually in search of the new, the different, and I am fascinated with the unconventional. Life has a hard, aggressive side, as does much of my work, represented by rigid, angular lines. However, the soft side is also apparent, visible as curves and soft forms.*

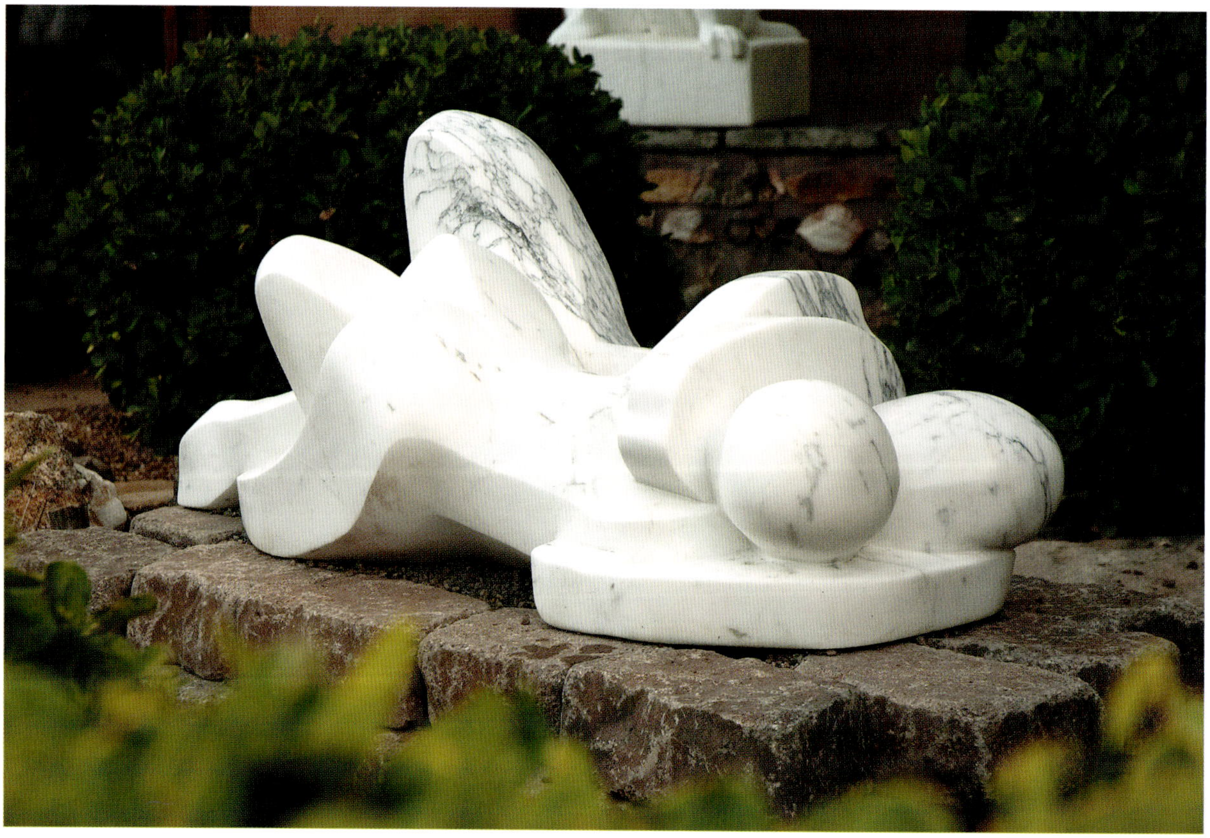

1

1 *As One*, 2008. Italian Carrera marble, 46" x 19" x 22", *Photography by Steven Yadzinsky.*

2 *Crush*, 2007. Bronze, 61" x 80" x 20.5". *Photography by Jim Lincoln.*

3 *Lost*, 2011. Steel, limestone, 7" x 6" x 19". *Photography by Alex Irvin.*

4 *Recoil*, 2003. Bronze, 46" x 33" x 42". *Photography by Larry A. Falke.*

5 *Chaos*, 2010. Italian translucent alabaster, 22" x 10" x 10". *Photography by Steven Yadzinsky.*

6 *Whirlwind in the Thorn Trees*, 2008. Bronze, 42" x 10" x 10". *Photography by Steven Yadzinsky.*

7 *Surface*, 2008. Marble, steel, 21" x 14" x 9". *Photography by Steven Yadzinsky.*

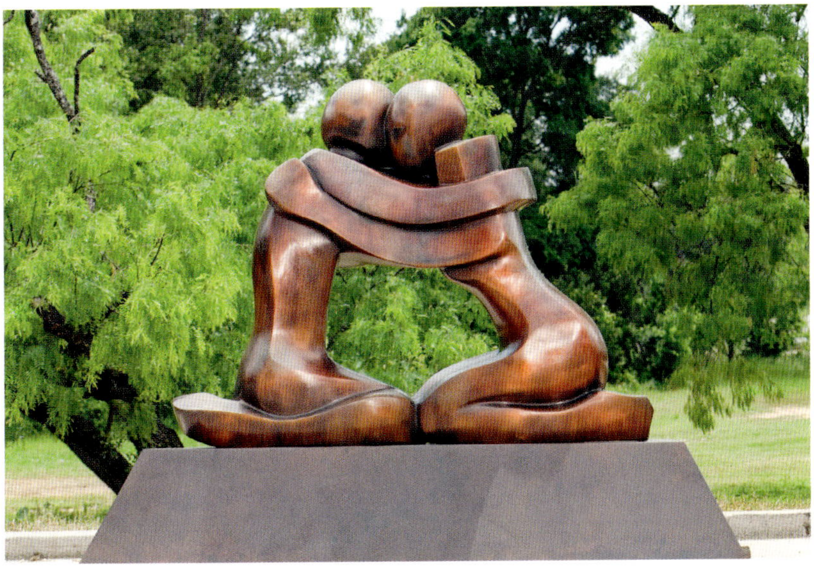

2

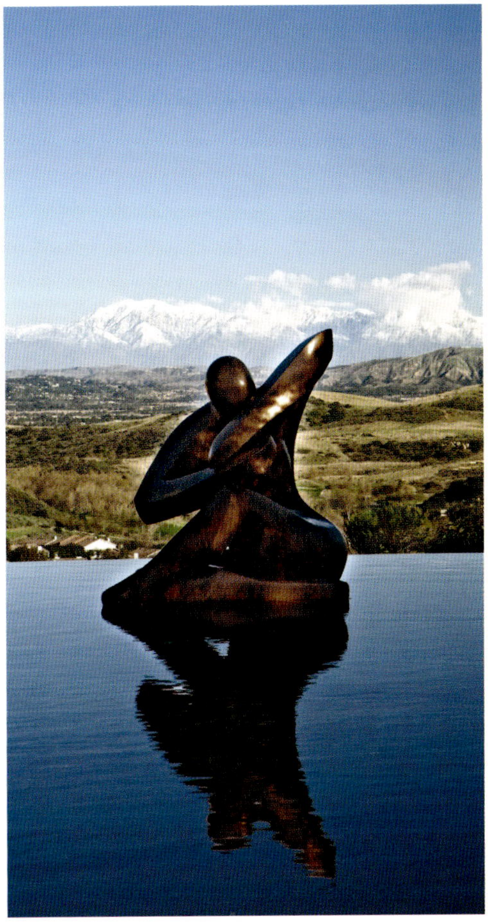

4

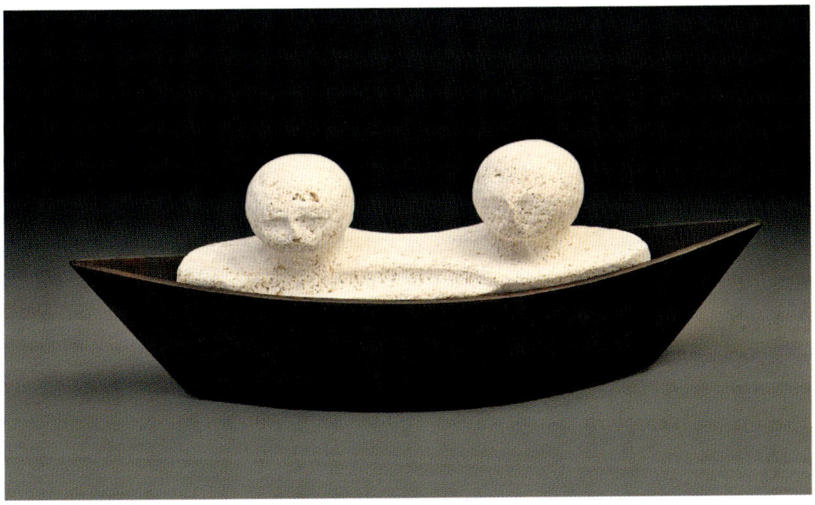

3

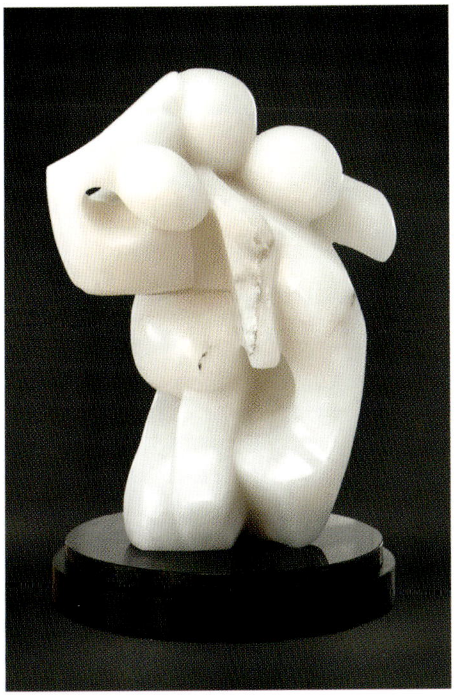

5

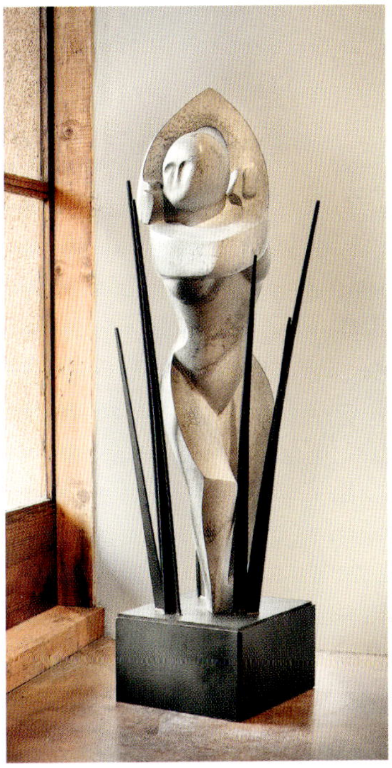

6

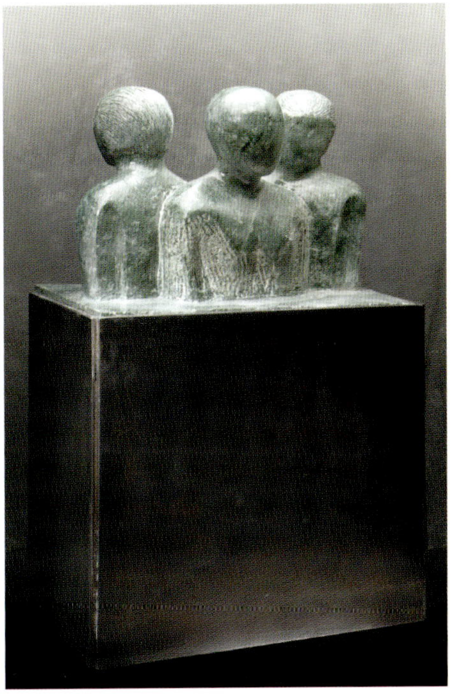

7

# Sabin Howard

New York, New York, USA
www.sabinhoward.com

A conductor of universal energy, sculptor Sabin Howard taps into the source to create works of shocking beauty. These modern classical bronzes confirm Sabin as a master of 21st century figurative sculpture and illuminates why classicism and its embrace of the human body endures so powerfully. Bucking the trends and banking on beauty, Sabin's aesthetic, both minimalist and sumptuous, is rich with timeless appeal and harmony, conjuring an uplifting alchemy that transforms the viewer with the art of possibility and spirit.

He grew up surrounded by the visual splendor of Italy and the urban hotbed of New York City in the 1960s and 70s. This dual upbringing is the basis of his vision to create classical art with a modern vision of self expression. The result is an art that is unique and individual to the artist's experience and universal in its narration of the visual themes. The *New York Times* wrote "Sabin Howard, a sculptor of immense talent, has created some of the last decade's most substantive realistic sculpture. When viewing his works, visitors may be reminded of the time when Donatello and Rodin walked the earth."

After twenty-eight years of practicing art and over 40,000 hours of sculpting from life, Howard creates a shift in the art world with his revolutionary vision challenging what is possible today.

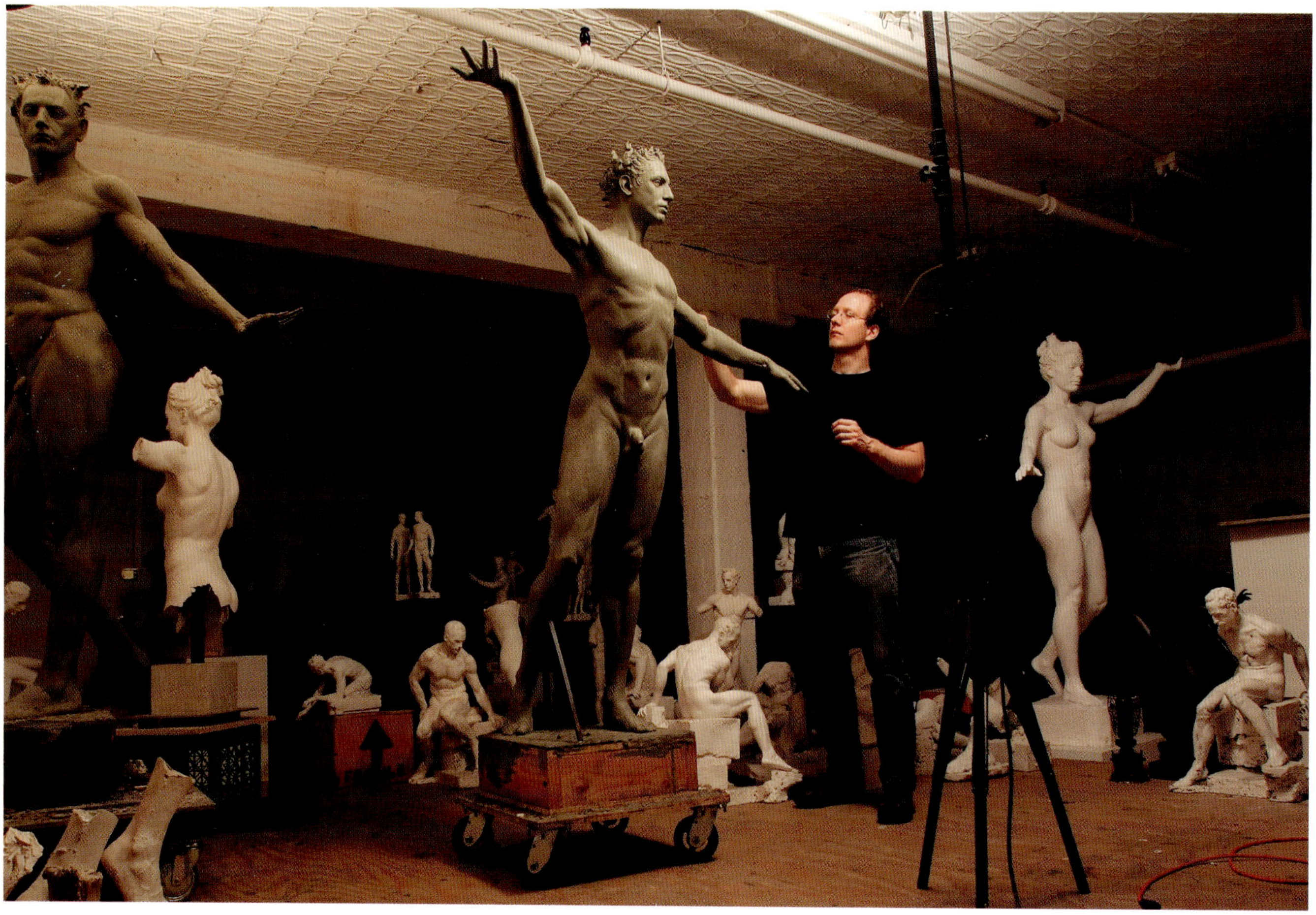

1

1 Studio with completion of *Apollo*, 2010. Original clay, 6'3". *Photograph by Kristina Willianson.*

2 Studio with completion of *Aphrodite*, 2006. Hydrocal-plaster, 6'3". *Photograph by Kristina Willianson.*

3 *Persistence* and *Stubbornness*, 1997. Bronze, 28" high. *Photograph by the artist.*

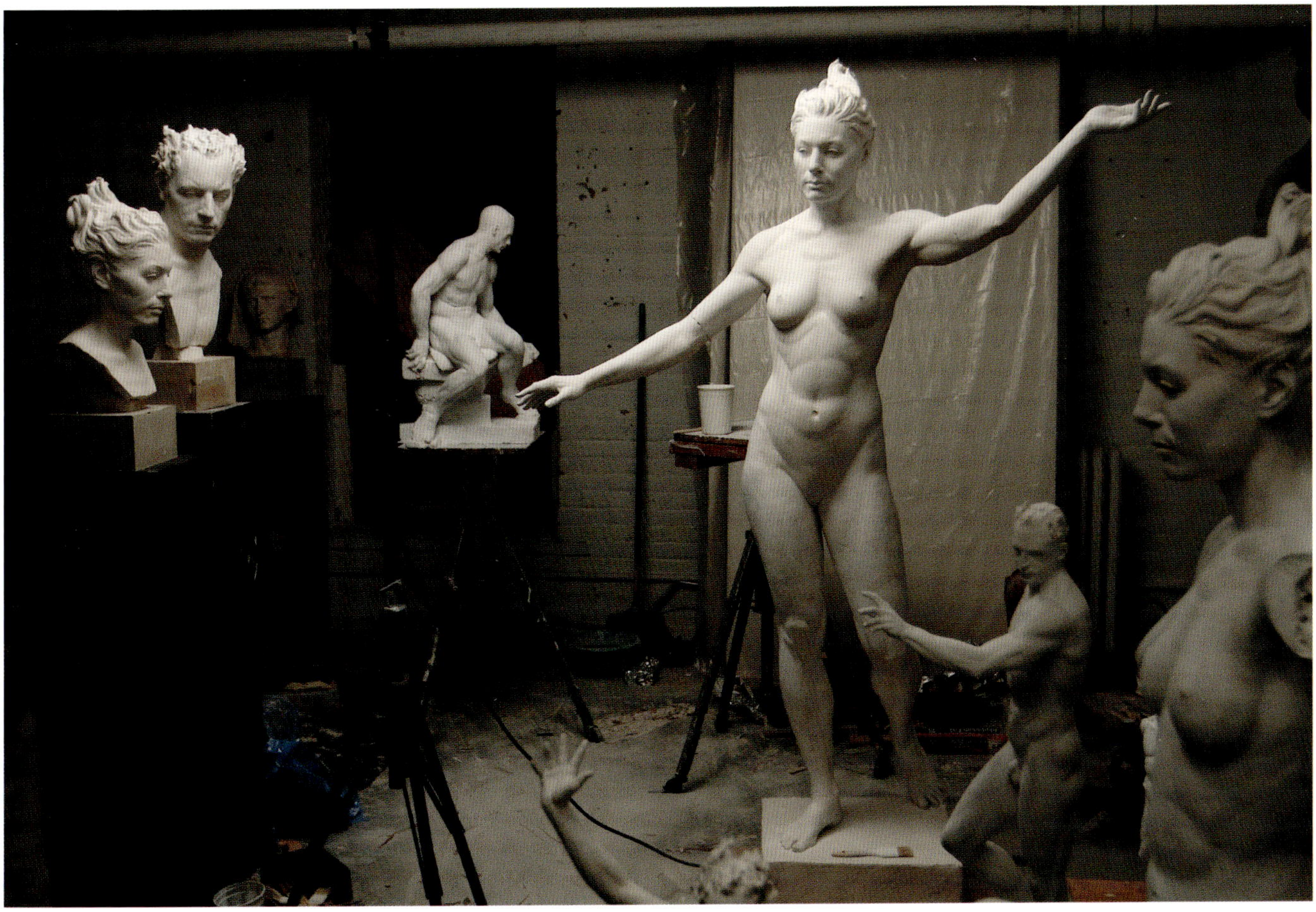

2

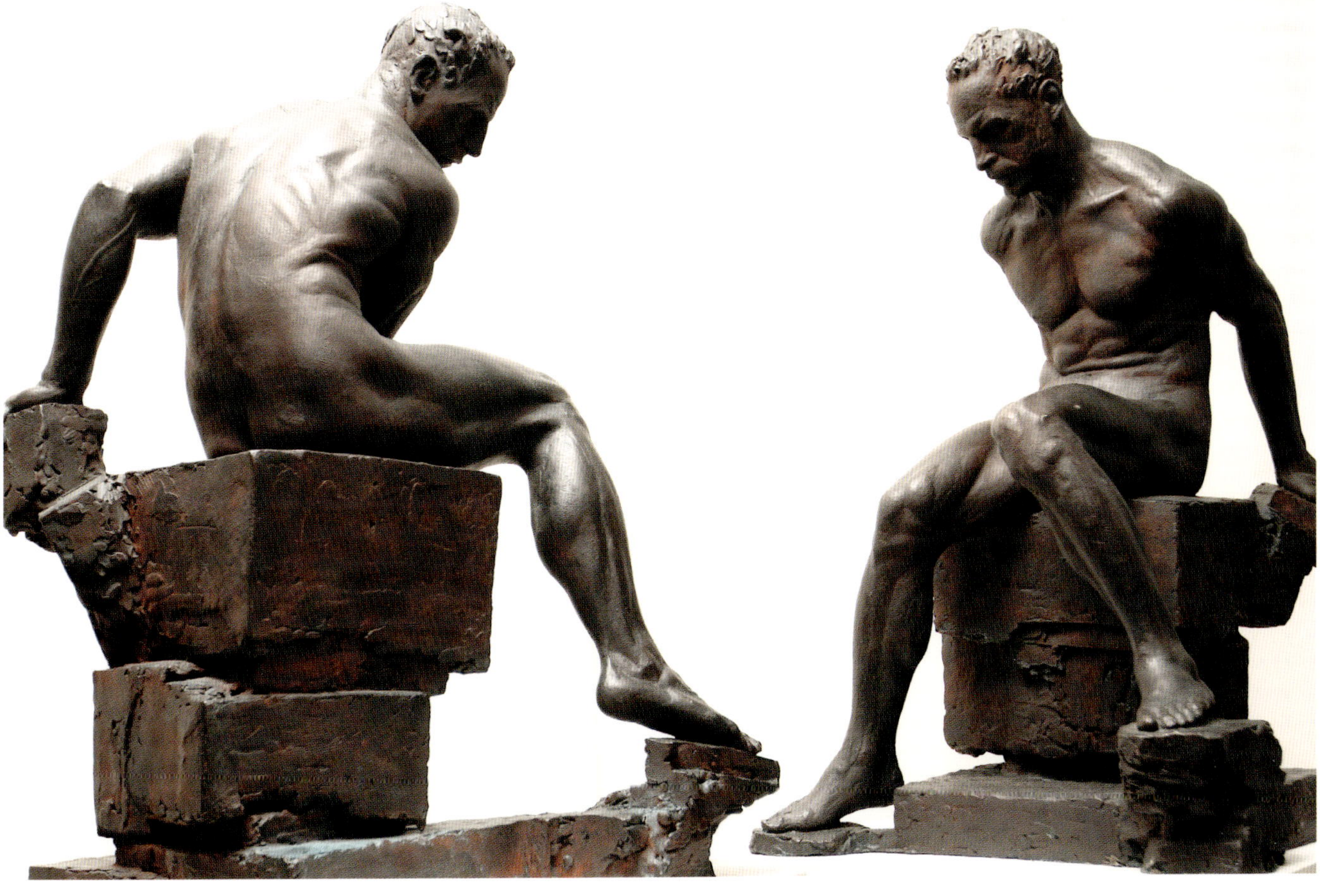

3

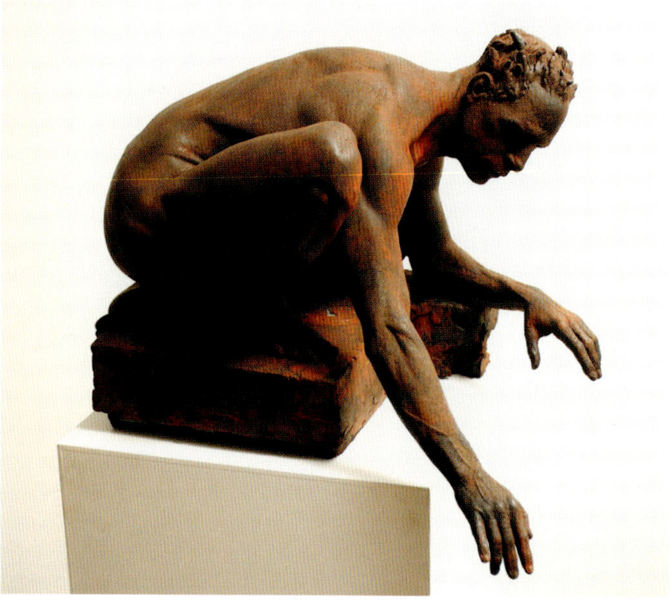

4

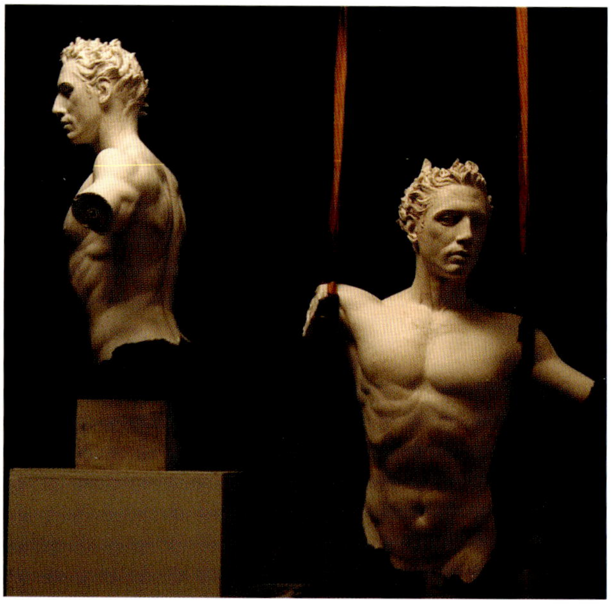

5

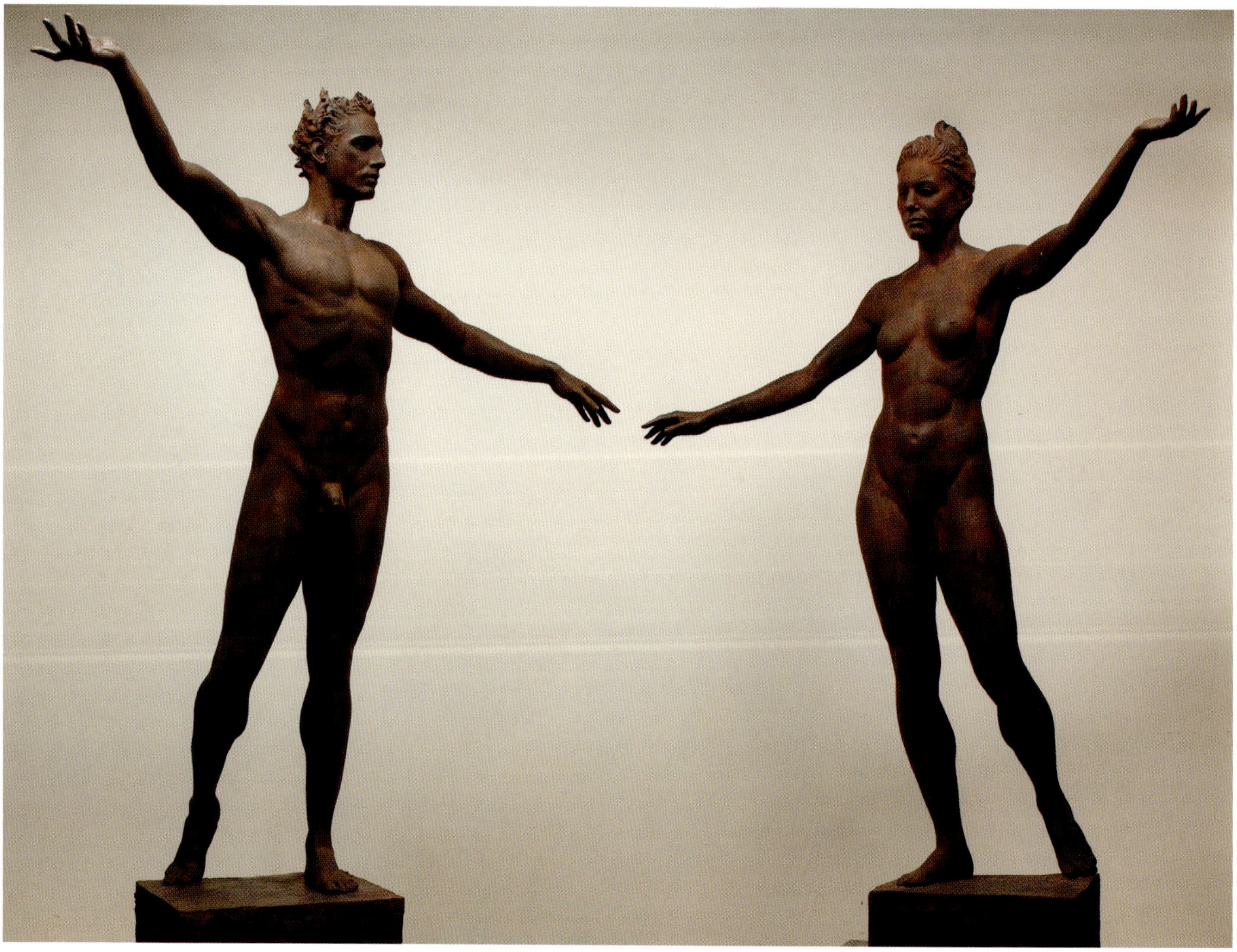

6

4 *Armor*, 2005. Bronze,14" high. *Photograph by Kristina Willianson*

5 Fragment of *Apollo.* Hydrocal-plaster, 36" high, *Photograph by the artist.*

6 *Apollo* and *Aphrodite*, 2005-2010. Both 6'3" high. *Photograph by Kristina Willianson*

7 *Hermes*, 2005. Bronze, 7'3" high. *Photograph by the artist.*

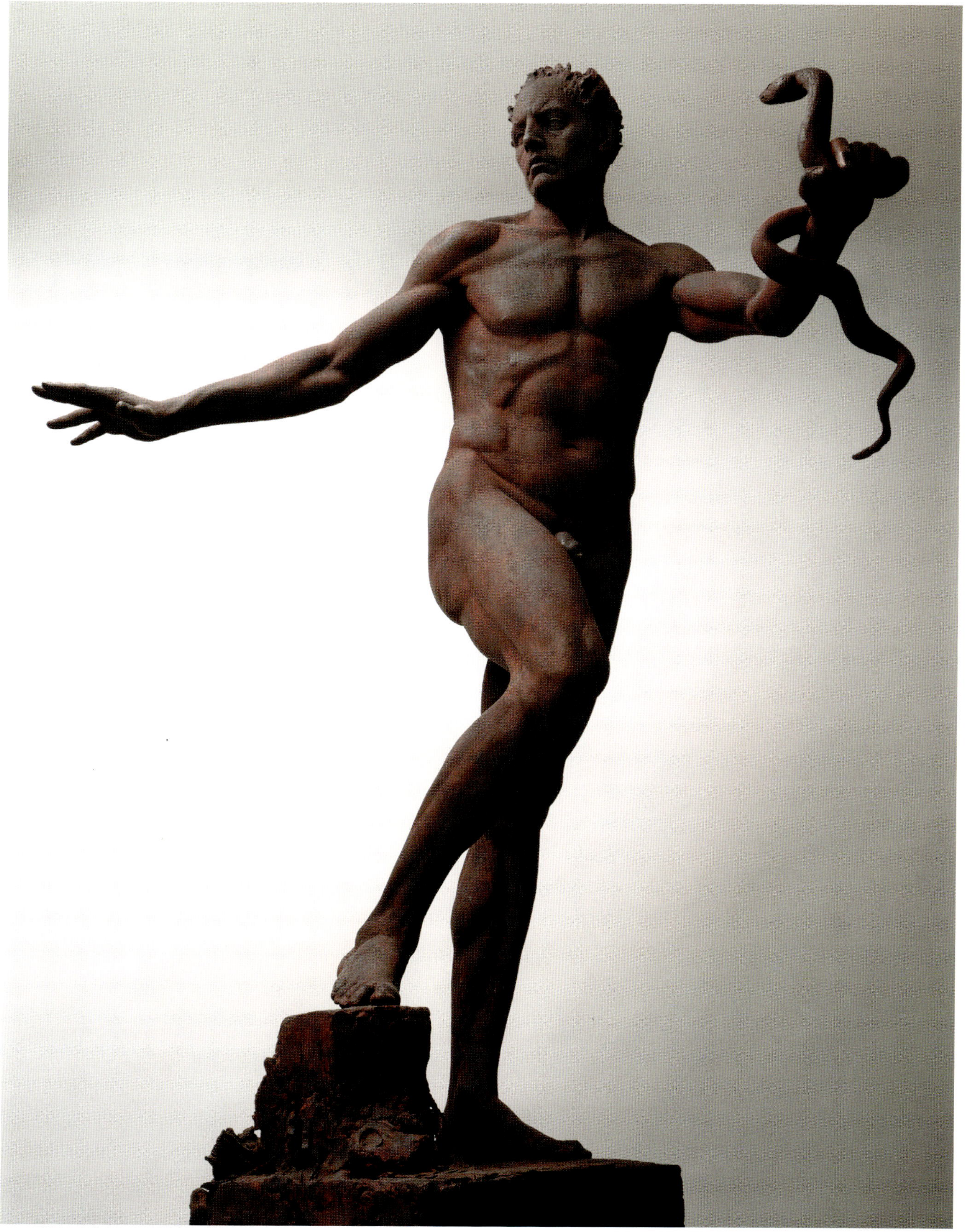

7

# Nadia Iliffe

London, UK
www.ndigallery.com

Nadia Iliffe started her artistic career working for graphic design agencies in Paris before moving to Chicago, where she discovered a passion for sculpture. She currently lives in London, where she develops and exhibits her unique metal sculptures and paintings.

Exploring the relationship between ourselves and the technologies we create is the central theme behind Nadia's mixed media artwork. She now specializes particularly in sculptures that blend metals such as titanium or copper with reclaimed objects like antique clocks or old computer parts.

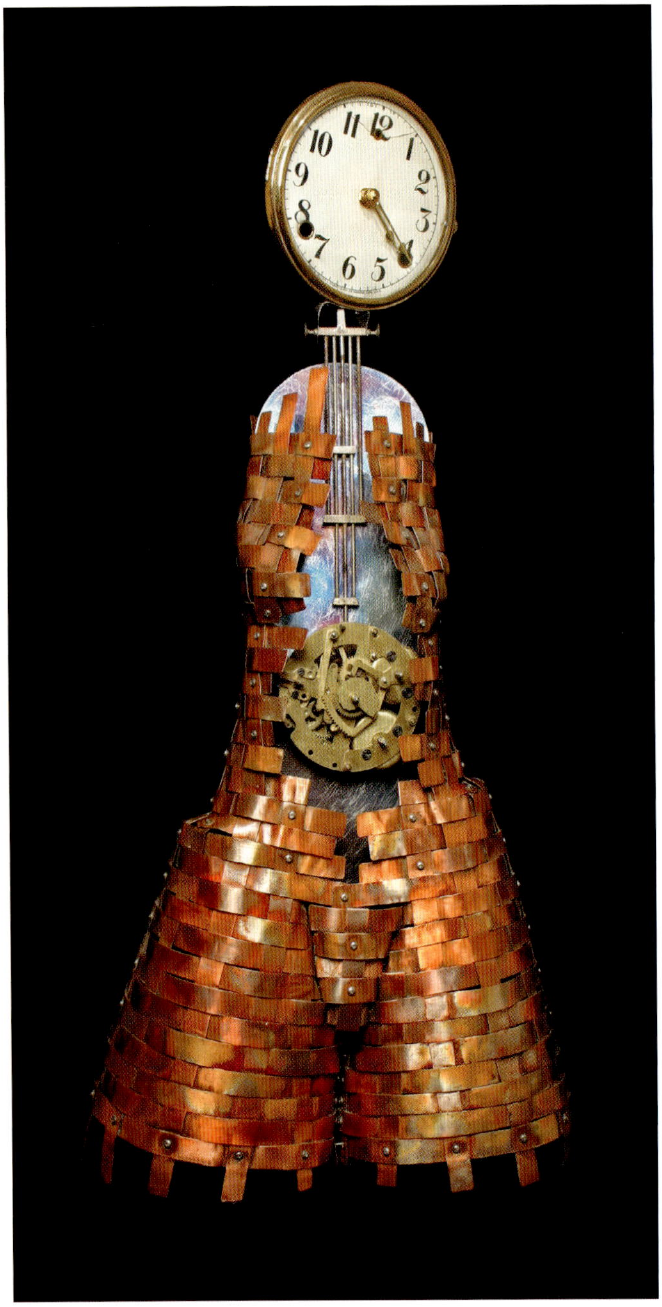

1

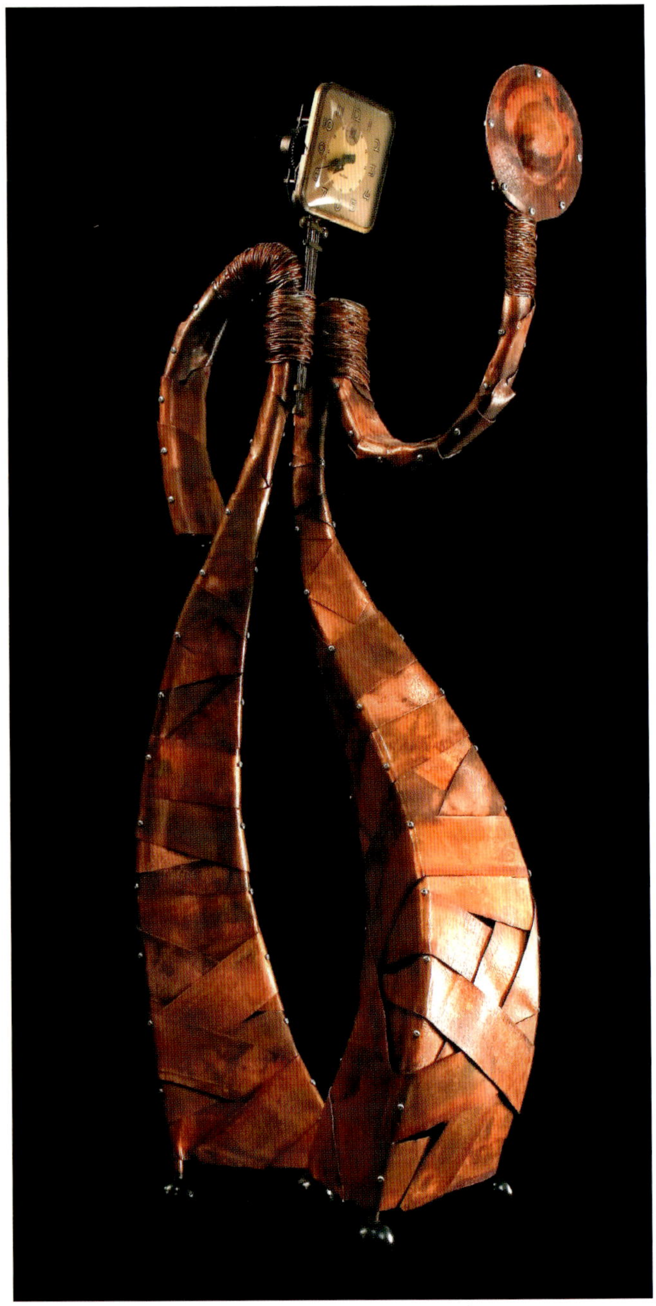

2

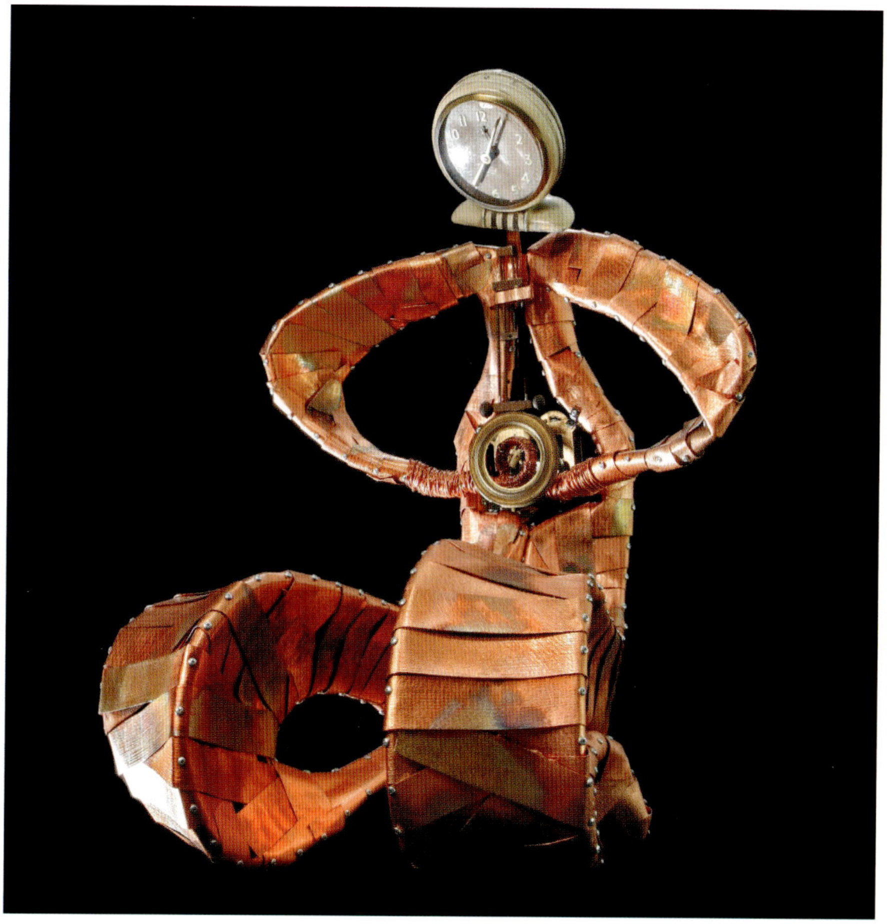

3

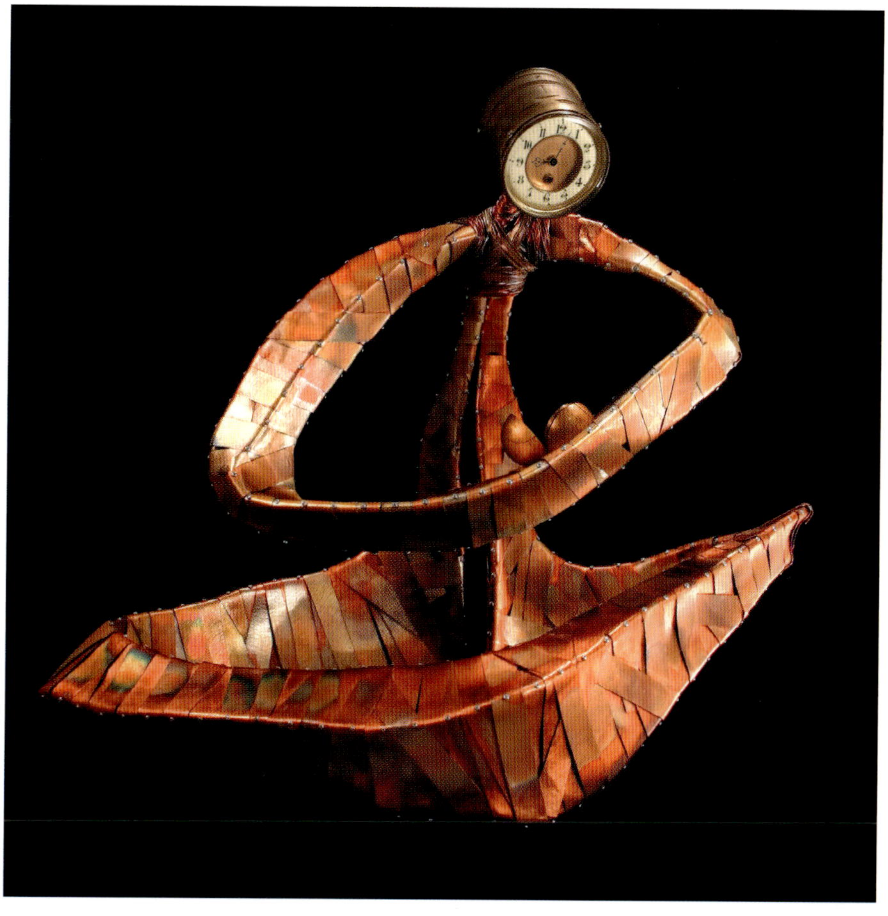

4

1 *Dame Horloge*, 2003. Copper, titanium, clock parts, 26". *Photograph by Nadia Iliffe.*

2 *Miroir… dis moi*, 2004. Copper, clock parts, 37". *Photograph by Nadia Iliffe.*

3 *Chronos,* 2004. Copper, clock parts, 29". *Photograph by Nadia Iliffe.*

4 *La Maternité*, 2005. Copper, clock parts, 21". *Photograph by Nadia Iliffe.*

# Jane Jaskevich

Atlanta, Georgia, USA
www.atlantasculpture.com

Jane carves her dreamy sculptures in her studio behind her home. There are piles of boulders and lots of dogs and cats, a few fish, a turtle, and frog that surround her. It is a busy place and full of life. She carves from her experiences. A large body of her work portrays women.

Her inspiration to become a sculptor happened when an art professor told the class to create a vessel and give a lecture about it. Jane, taking ceramics at the time, made a pinch pot that resembled a female. The figure was hollow. When it came time for her to talk about her "vessel" Jane said, "This is a vessel that holds the spirit." Hundreds of sculptures have followed that vessel. Jaskevich has always been interested in the spiritual and mystical side of mankind.

*My stone sculptures are mystical in nature. They have been referred to as "dreams in stone."*

*I am a direct carver. With an idea in mind, I draw directly on the stone and start chiseling. Primarily a figurative sculptor, I carve both human and animal forms, sometimes combined.*

*Combining various materials is of special interest to me. I pay homage to the Greco-Roman roots of stone in sculpture. I combine contemporary bodies with Greek faces. From the Romans, I borrow the process of combining different stones in one figure. Sometimes an object inspires me. I have added interesting found objects that suggest parts of the body.*

*My stone sculptures invite the viewer to interpret thus creating their own stories.*

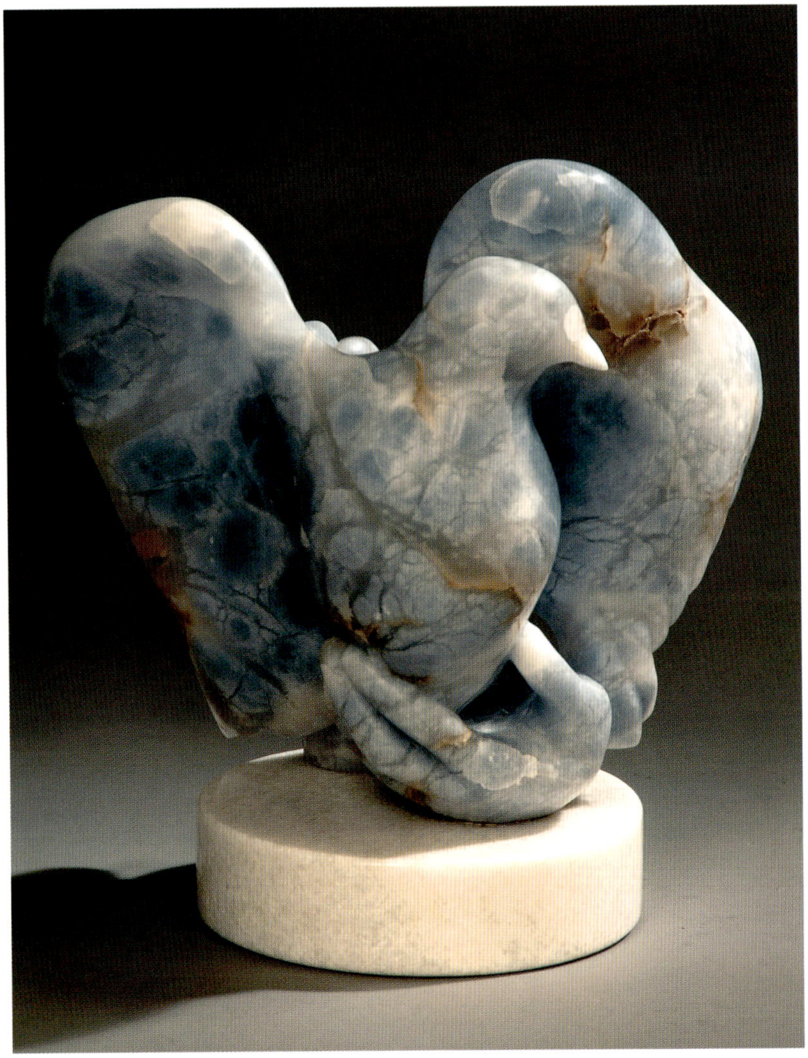

1

1 *Capturing Happiness*, 2011. Blue alabaster, marble, 13" x 8" x 14". *Photograph by John Dale.*

2 *Apollo*, 2009. Utah alabaster, limestone, 20" x 11" x 7". *Photograph by John Dale.*

3 *Warrior.* Chloride, Virginia steatite, found object, 16" x 14" x 7". *Photograph by John Dale.*

4 *Daphne*, 2010. Alabaster, red oak, limestone, 11" x 11" x 57". *Photograph by John Dale.*

5 *Swimmer.* Canadian blue marble, 17" x 5" x 14". *Photograph by John Dale.*

6 *Millie's Dream.* Alabaster, 12" x 6" x 11". *Photograph by John Dale.*

7 *Forgotten Angel*, Firefly brucite, quartz, 9" x 10" x 13". *Photograph by John Dale.*

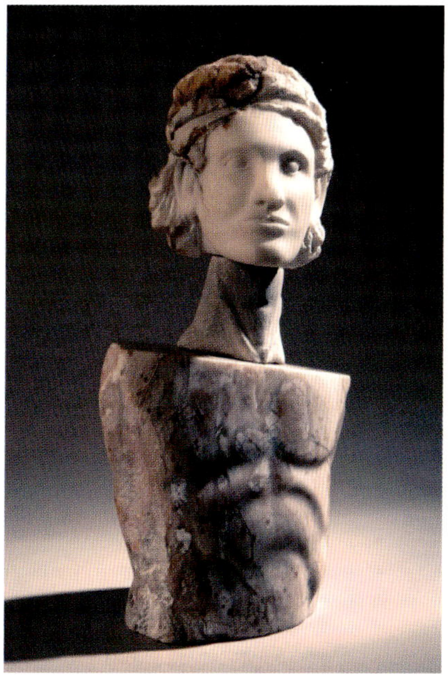

2

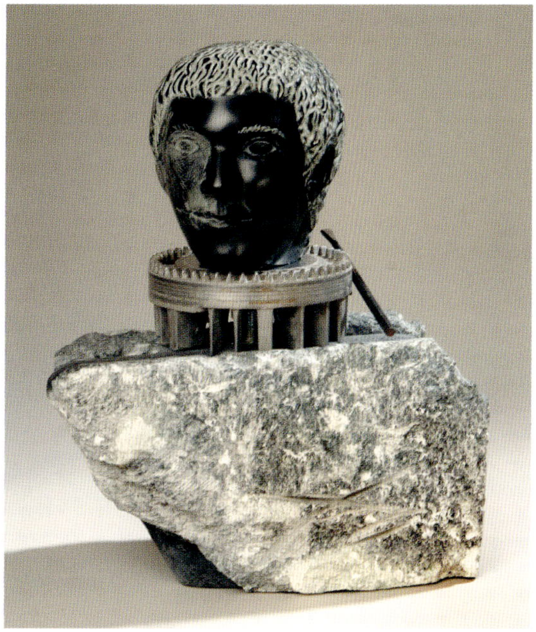

3

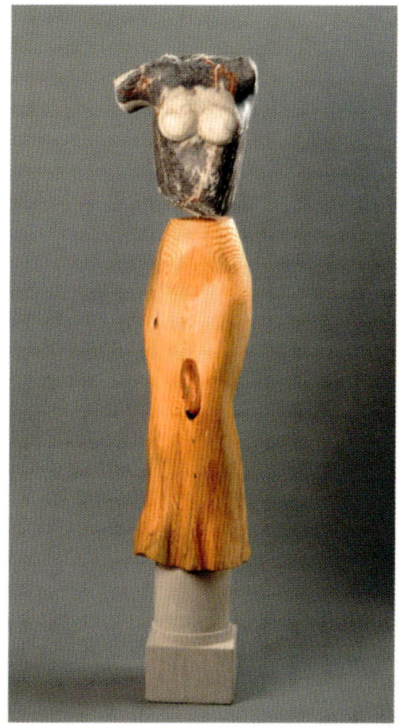

4

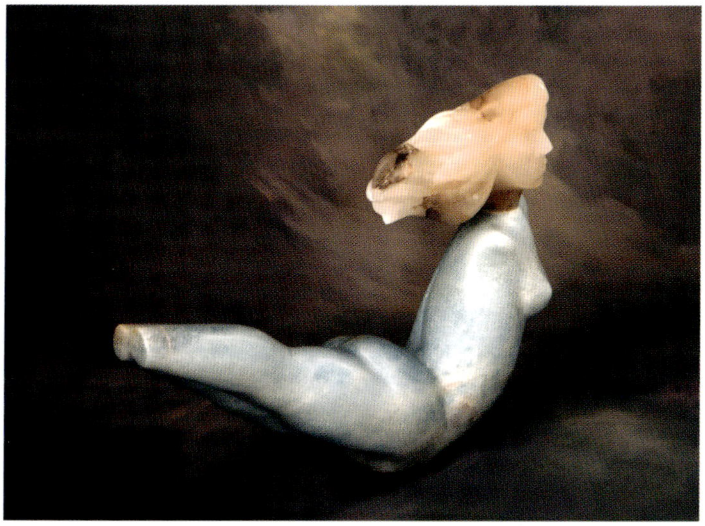

5

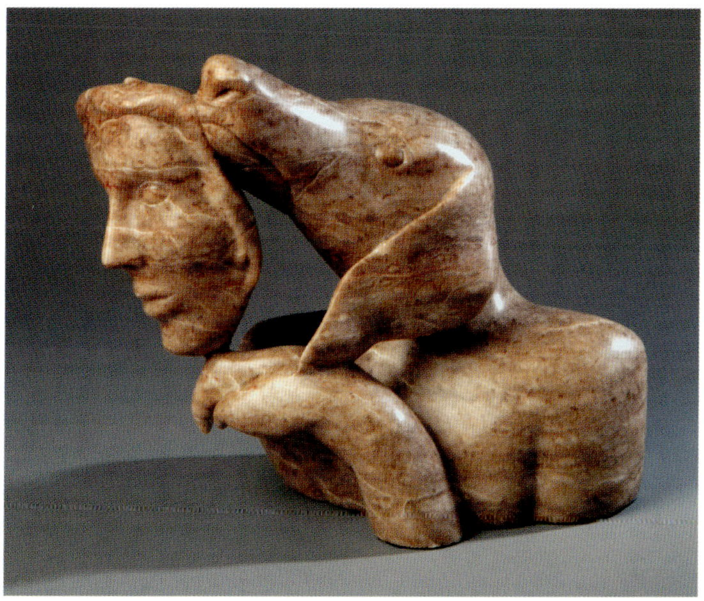

6

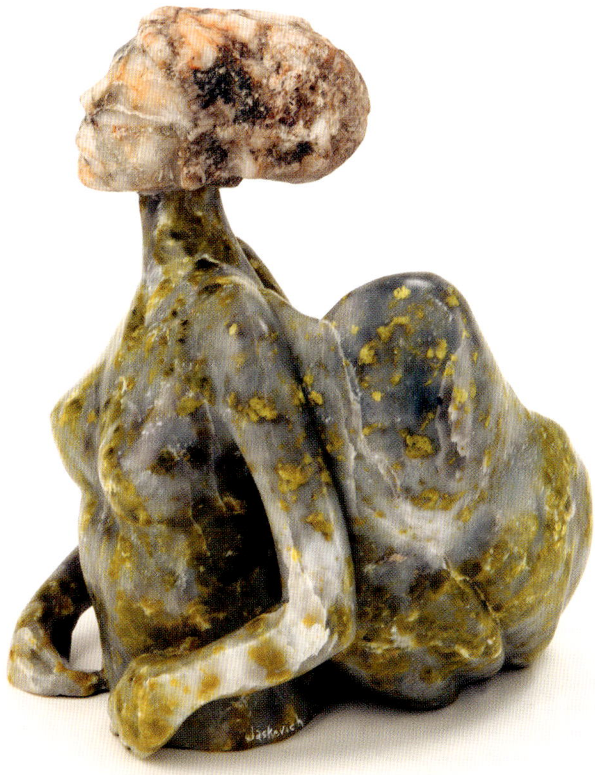


7

# Gregory Johnson

Cumming, Georgia, USA
www.gregoryjohnson.biz

*Whether a memorial sculpture, historic recreation, or commemorative figurative work, I cull the composition that will capture the "presence" of the figure in the "moment," that will dovetail with the "mission." These feelings must blend seamlessly together.*

*A somewhat more thoughtful onlooker might delve a few layers down, into other implications. The story lies in the gestures these figures make and content depicted. My goal is not a photographic rendering, but rather an active, fluid sculpture, which presents the moment, allowing the art to tell its own story as it might.*

Artist Gregory Johnson was born on January 30, 1955, in Chicago, Illinois. His early training includes the Art Institute of Chicago and tutoring by several world-class artists. He traveled through Europe and the Mediterranean, touring major art museums for an entire summer through an International Studies Program.

He has created over four hundred public art works that are located in numerous museums, corporate and private collections throughout the United States, Canada, Europe, Costa Rica, and the Middle East.

Currently, the artist resides with his wife Jane and family in Forsyth County, Georgia, where he professionally pursues his career of making art.

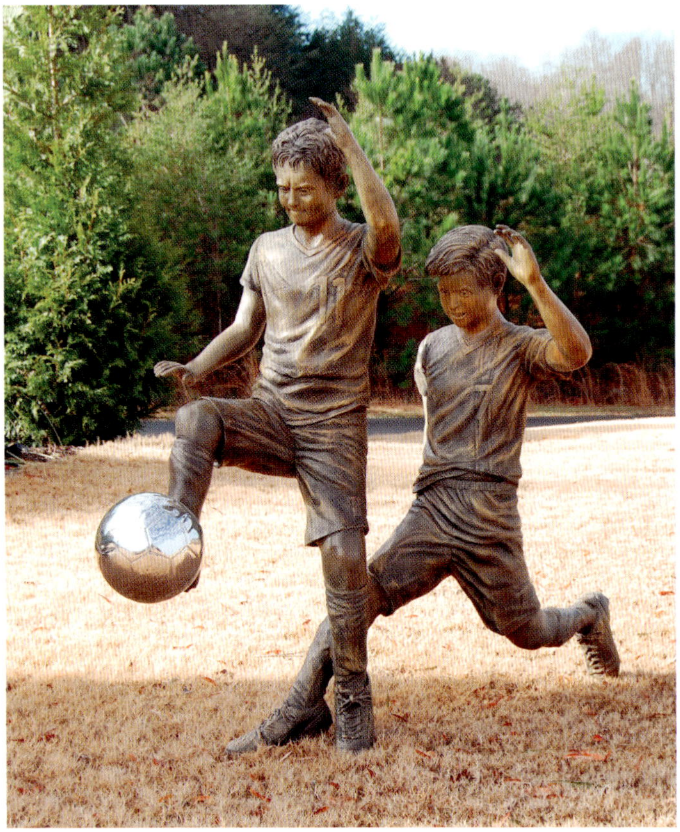

1

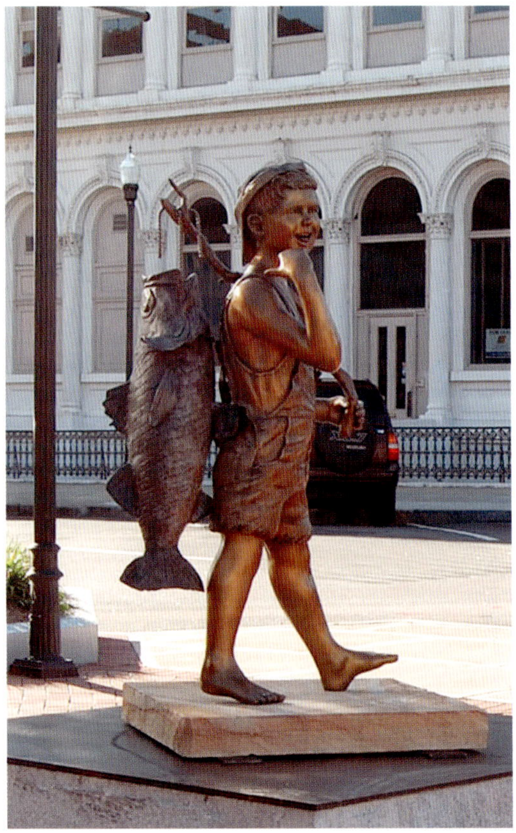

2

1 *Bringing on the Heat,* 2011, Bronze, stainless steel, 64" h. x 54" d. x 35" w.

2 *Fishtale*, 2008, Bronze, stone, 46" h. x 28" d. x 22" w.

3 *Little Professor,* 2008. Bronze, 48" h. x 30" d. x 28" w.

4 *Cabin Fever*, 2009. Bronze, granite, 52" h. x 28" w. x 36" d.

5 *Bookworm*, 2010. Bronze, walnut, 32.5" h. x 10" d.

6 *Tidal Temptation*, 2010. Bronze, walnut, 28" h. x 17" w. x 9" d.

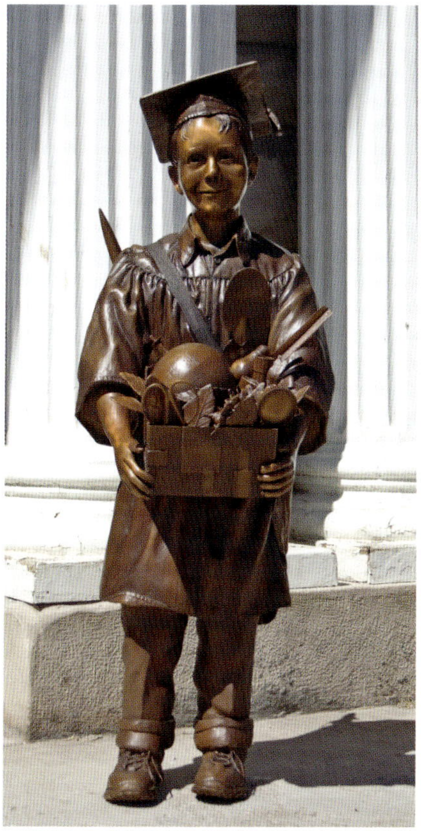

3

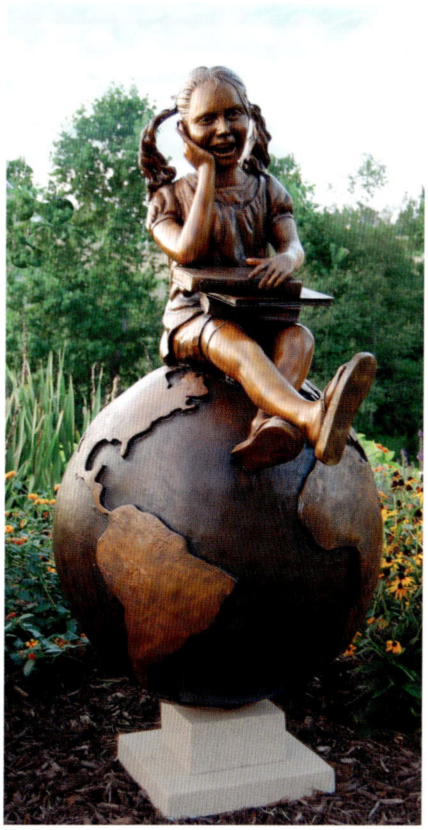

4

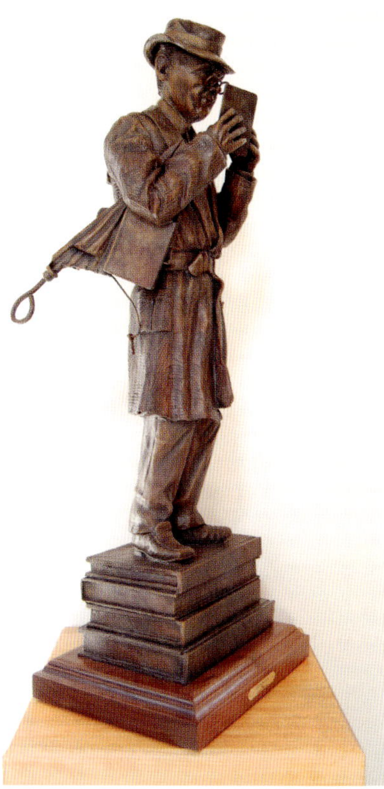

5

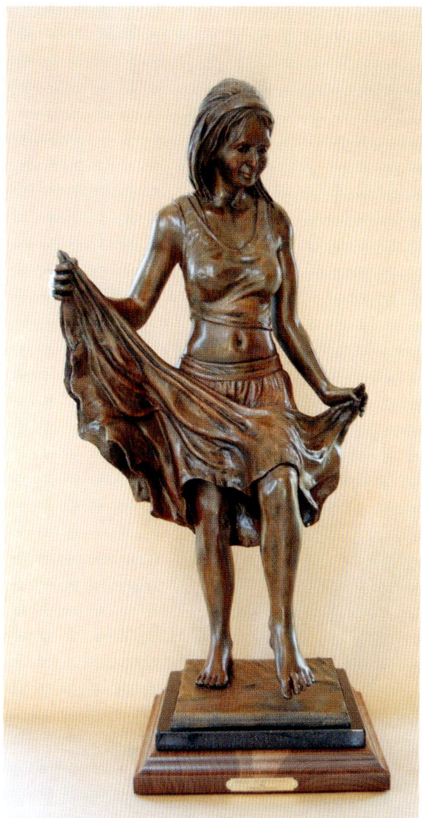

6

# Jeffrey Kennedy

Palm Coast, Florida, USA
www.jeffreykennedyart.com

*After graduating from the Ringling School of Art , I set out on a long, colorful journey to pursue art in the most creative form. I believe we all need to surround ourselves with humor in one form or another. The power of humor has been my life buoy and I am very fortunate to make a living doing what I truly love. Having this style of art on my menu for others to enjoy has elevated my passion for art to an all time high.*

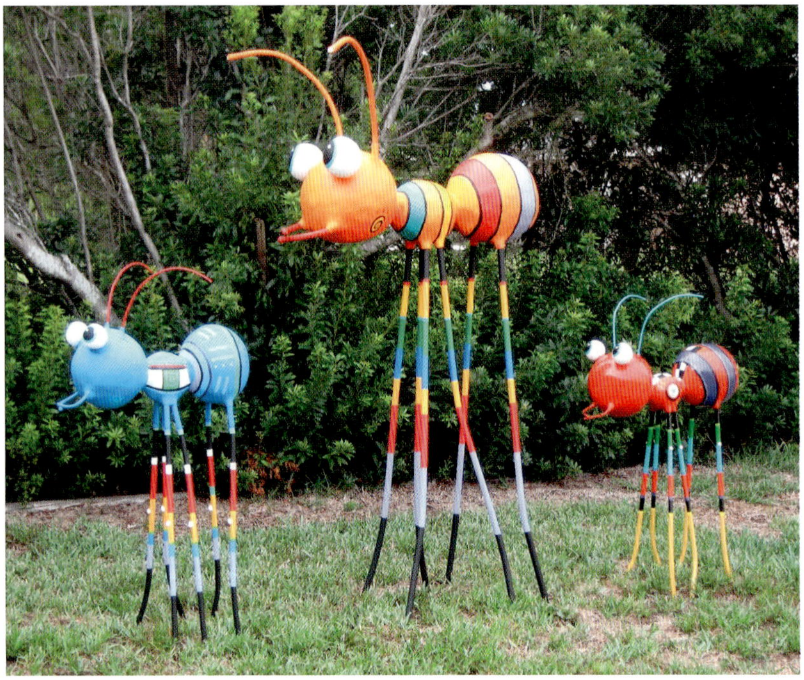

1

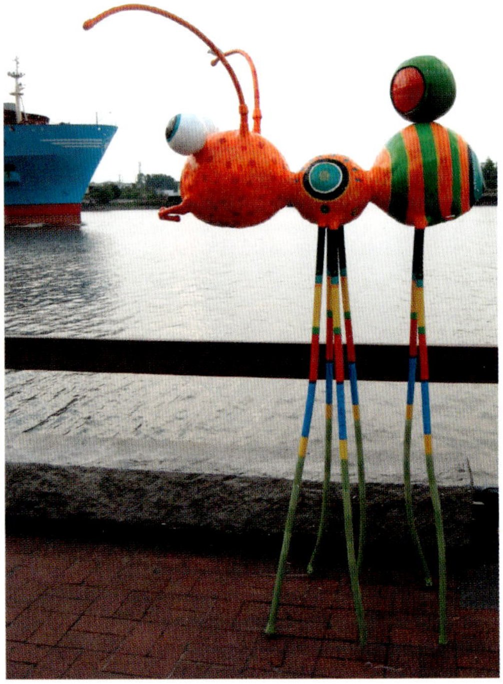

2

1 *Ant Family*, 2011. Fiberglass, metal, 4' to 7' tall. *Photograph by Jeffrey Kennedy.*

2 *Bigger Than Me!*, 2010. Fiberglass, metal, 7' tall. *Photograph by Jeffrey Kennedy.*

3 *Spikie the Guard Dog*, 2011. Fiberglass, metal, 7' tall. *Photographed by Jeffrey Kennedy.*

4 *Face Off*, 2011. Fiberglass, metal, 7' tall. *Photograph by Jeffrey Kennedy.*

5 *Spoonbill Eating Fruitloops*, 2010. Clay, metal, 36" tall. *Photograph by Jeffrey Kennedy.*

6 *Dog Versus Machine*, 2010. Fiberglass, metal, 7' tall. *Photograph by Jeffrey Kennedy.*

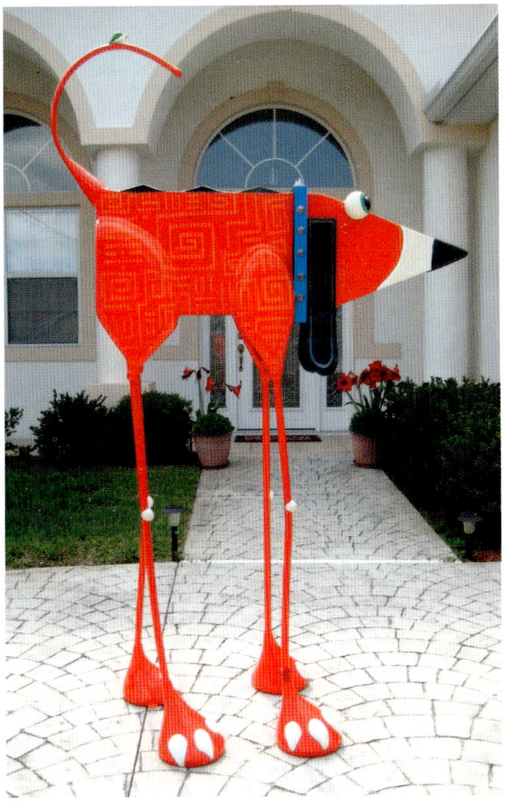

3

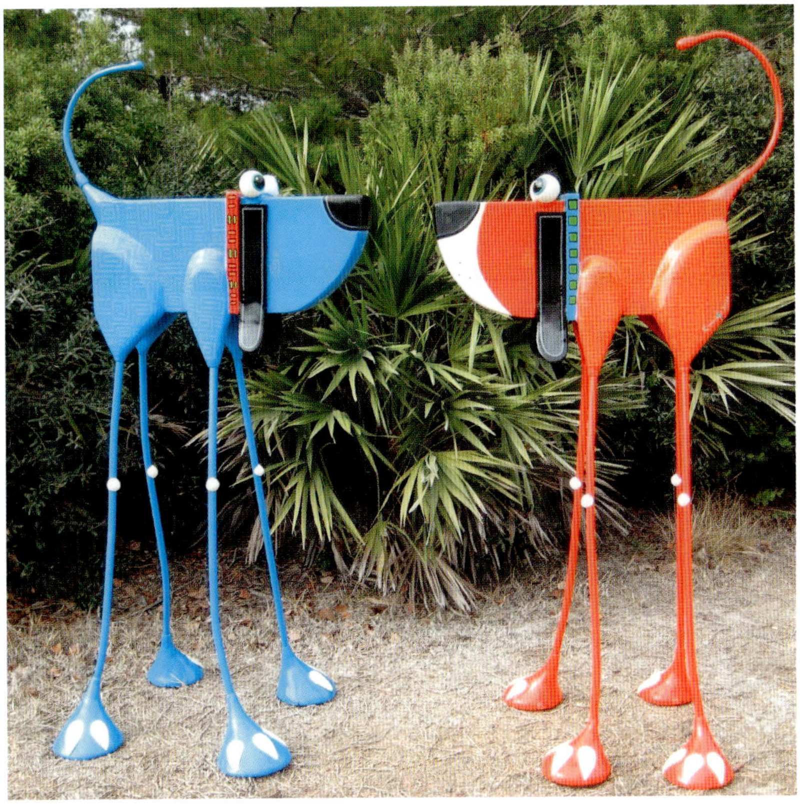

4

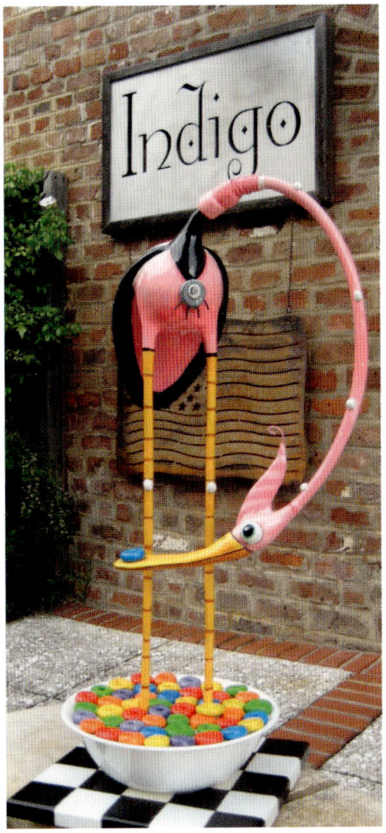


5

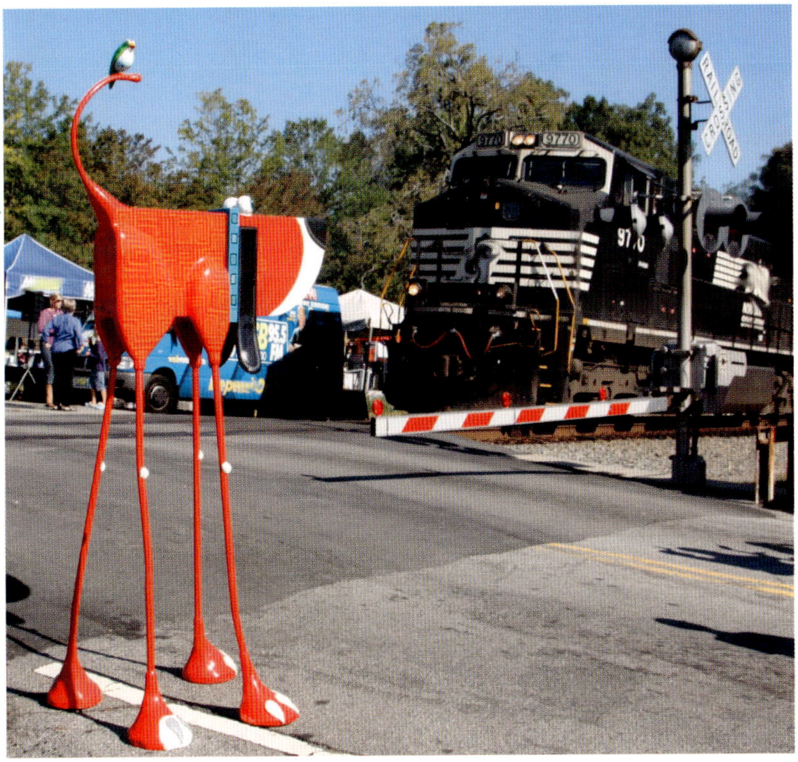

6

# Suprina Kenney

Brooklyn, New York, USA
www.2ndsouls.com

Born on Long Island, New York, and raised in the suburban sprawl, Suprina never felt at home until she discovered a junk yard. Her collections of odd items started at a very young age and she always had a quirky idea about what was beautiful and valuable. "I never 'got' the thrill others seemed to get from the new car, the diamond ring, or success measured in money" she says. Her thrill came from helping lost animals, being in nature, seeing something wonderful in the rotten banana peel in the gutter. Suprina graduated with a BFA in sculpture from Philadelphia College of Art. This is where she created her first found object work of art. She has sculpted professionally for high profile clients like, Annie Leibovitz, Apple Computer, Bloomingdales, and the Bronx Zoo. Specializing in large sculpts, Suprina learned her craft and brought those talents to her own personal art. Her studio is now in the Brooklyn Navy Yard, which jibes with her style very well, as the Navy yard was left to rot for years before its current renaissance and new found popularity.

*What I have realized is that my work is focused on the figure, its movement, and its archetypical predicament. I work with the figure because it seems the best form for communicating the human condition. Movement is also extremely important to me. A figure without movement has no life, no story.*

*Worth is a matter of context. Whether something is deemed ugly, unworthy, or socially unacceptable can turn on a dime. It depends on where it is, who is looking at it, what it means to them. I strive to be the alchemist of that change, to "turn that dime."*

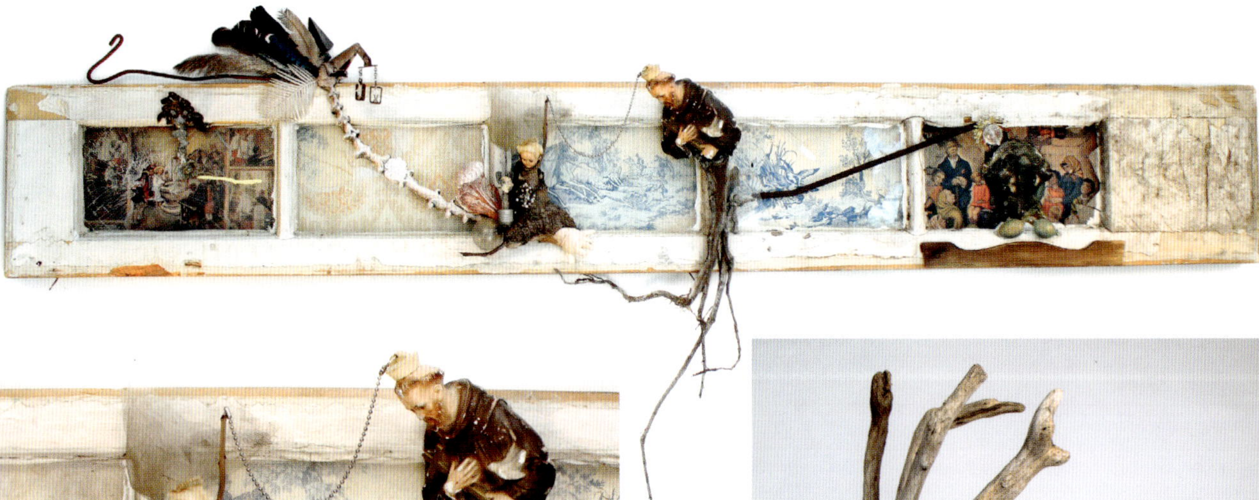

1

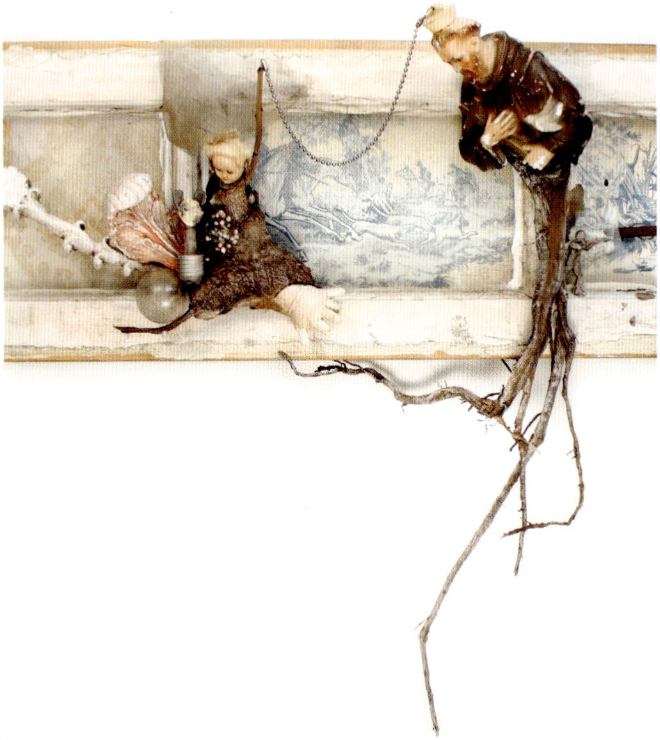

2

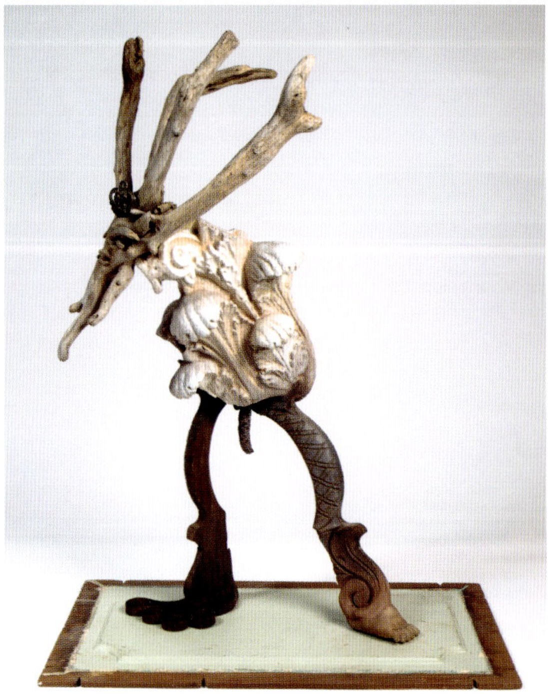

3

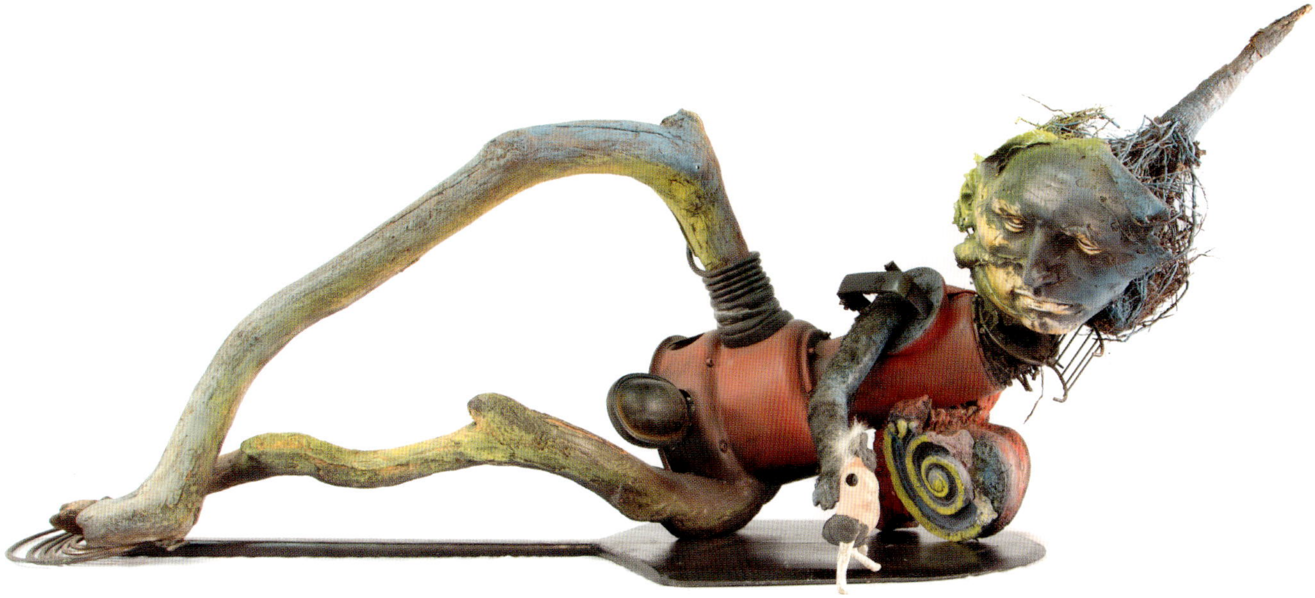

4

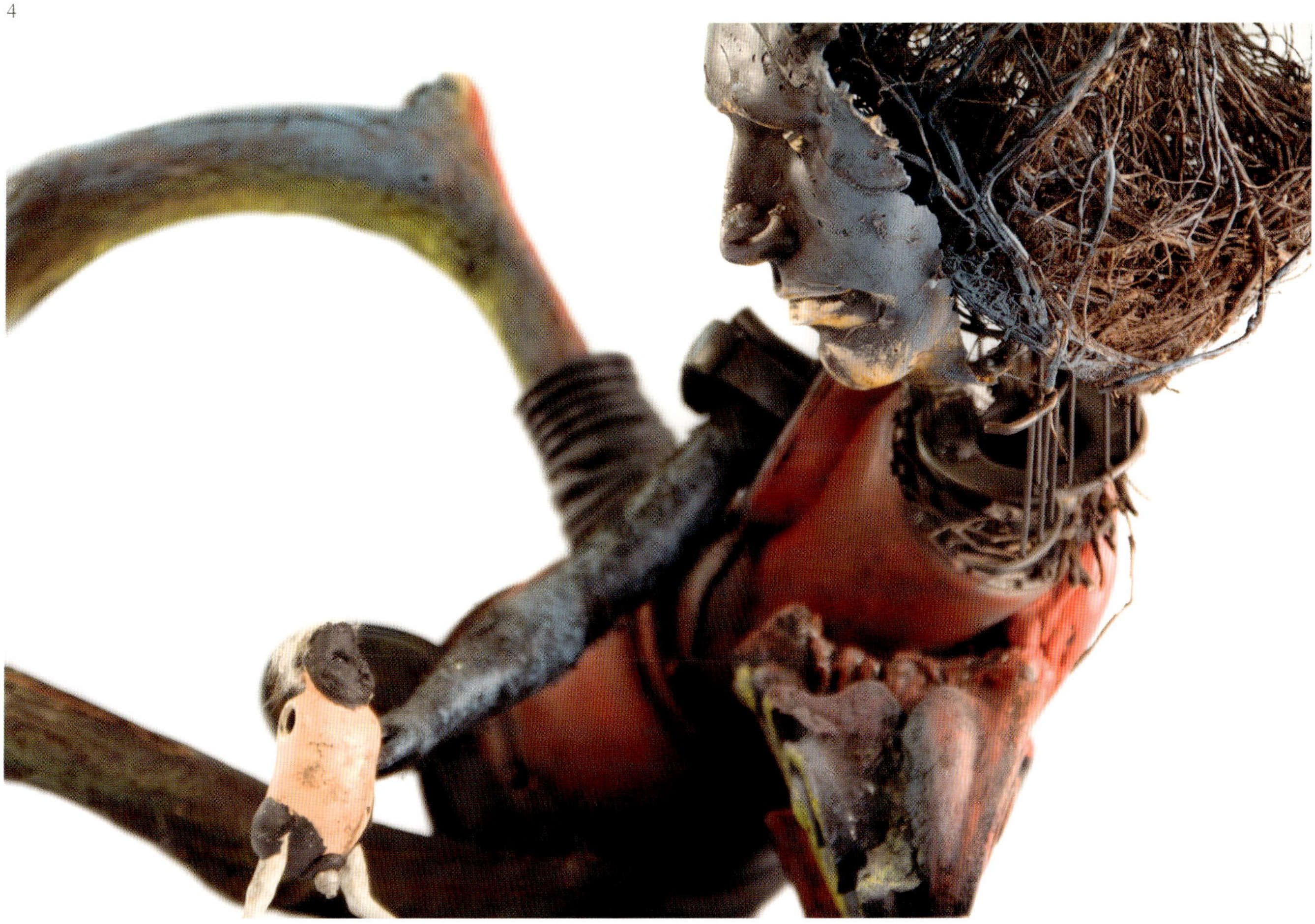

5

1 *Union*, 2010. Epoxy, found objects, paint, 96" w. x 30" h. x 6"d., wall relief. *Photograph by Suprina Kenney.*

2 *Union* (detail), 2010. *Photograph by Suprina Kenney.*

3 *Angry Guru*, 2008. Epoxy, found objects, paint, 28" h. x 24"w. x 18"d., wall mount. *Photograph by Suprina Kenney.*

4 *Seduction*, 2011. Epoxy, found objects, plaster, paint, 60" w. x 30" h. x 28" d. *Photograph by Suprina Kenney.*

5 *Seduction* (detail), 2011. *Photograph by Suprina Kenney.*

# Linda Lewis

West Des Moines, Iowa, USA
www.lindalewisart.com

Like many artists, Linda got a bachelors degree in art and also something more practical, like teaching, to insure she could support herself. For the next 34 years she worked as an educator in the public schools until a workshop given by a narrative sculptor in Santa Fe, New Mexico, reignited her passion for creating objects. She now works full time as an artist creating figurative sculptures from clay. Since then, Linda has exhibited her sculptures at nationally recognized juried art festivals, galleries, exhibitions and most recently at SOFA Chicago. She has received several awards including best of show, first place in sculpture, as well as recognition in national print media.

The clay sculptures Linda creates deal with common themes between people: love, parenthood, family, and the search for happiness and fulfillment. Instead of focusing on the figure, she tells the story through the use of facial expressions, the tilt of the head, or perhaps the shifting of the stance, texture of the surface, and the use of symbols. Titles are added to each piece to support the narrative, anything from "The harassed housewife" to "Daydreaming" to "Just between us." A recent series focused on the challenges of being a mother – both the humorous and the more serious aspects. The pieces are coilbuilt with a combination of surface applications of glazes, slips, terra siggillatta, oxides, and overglazes. She multi-fires her pieces to cone 04.

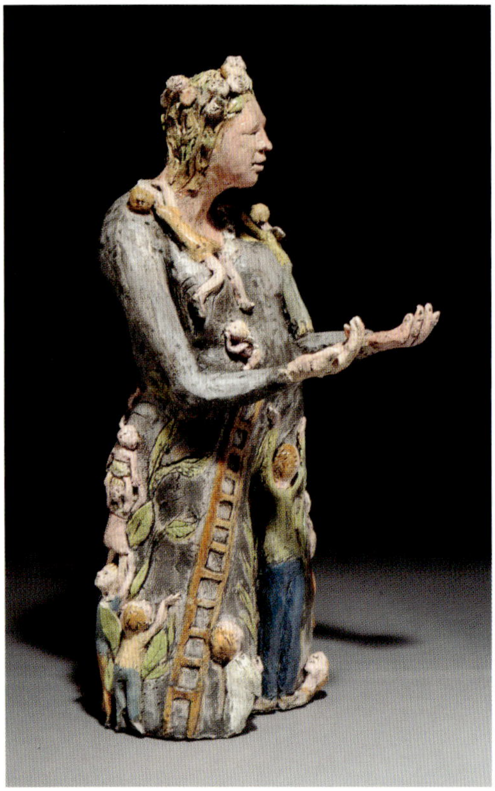

1

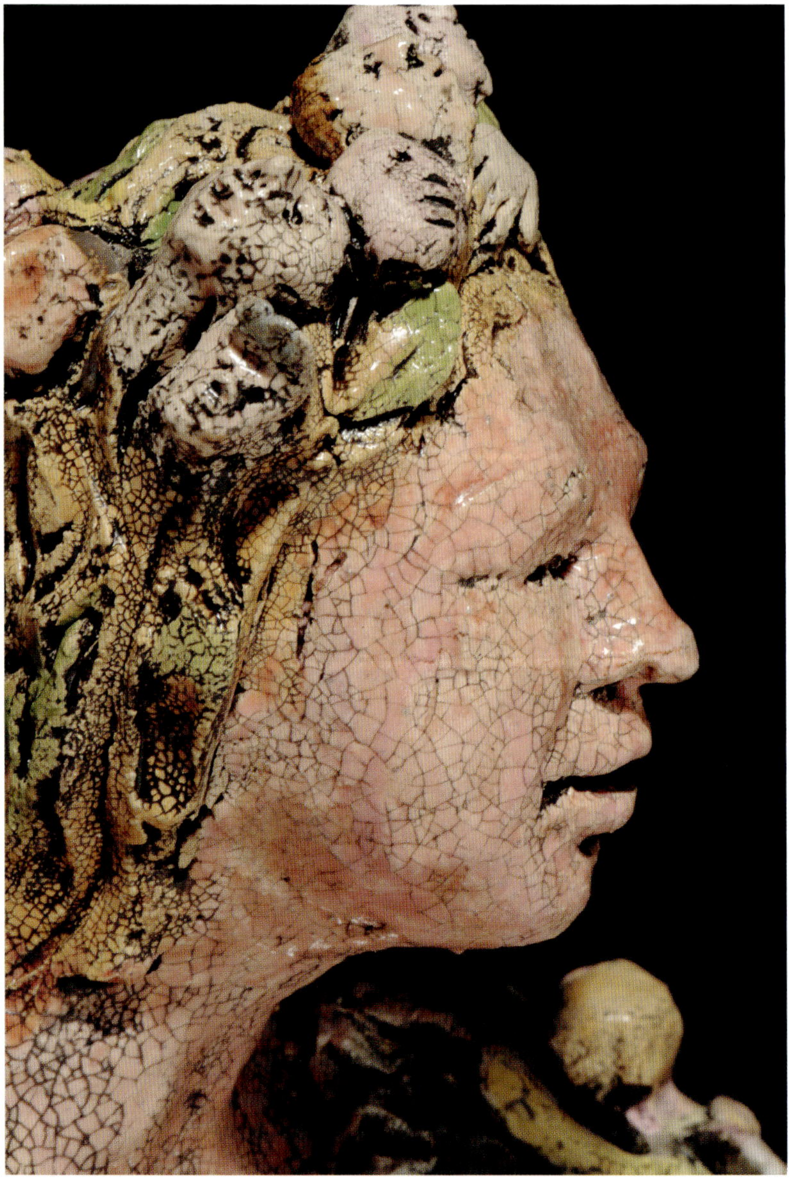

2

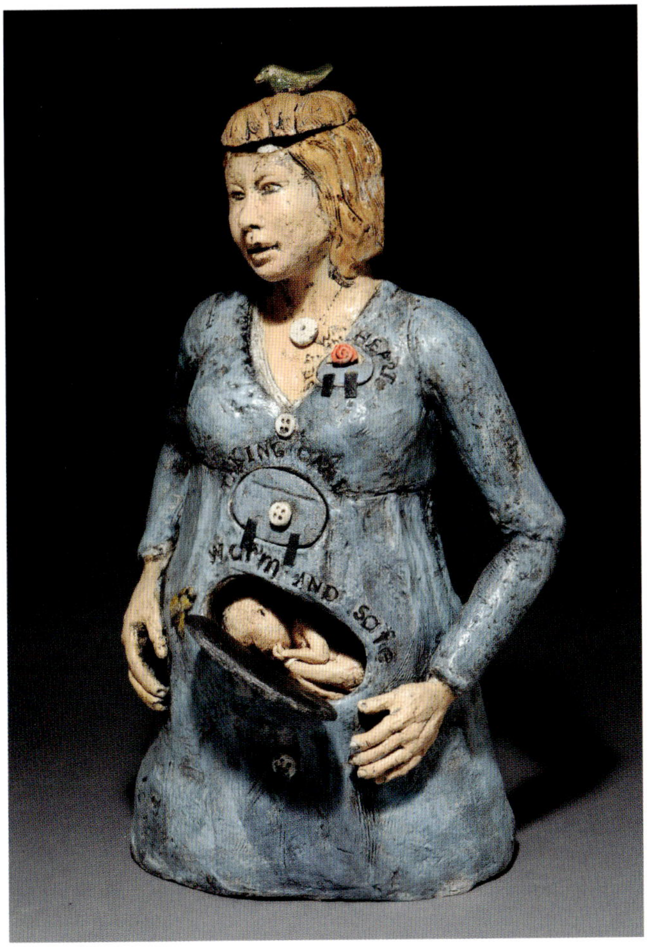


3

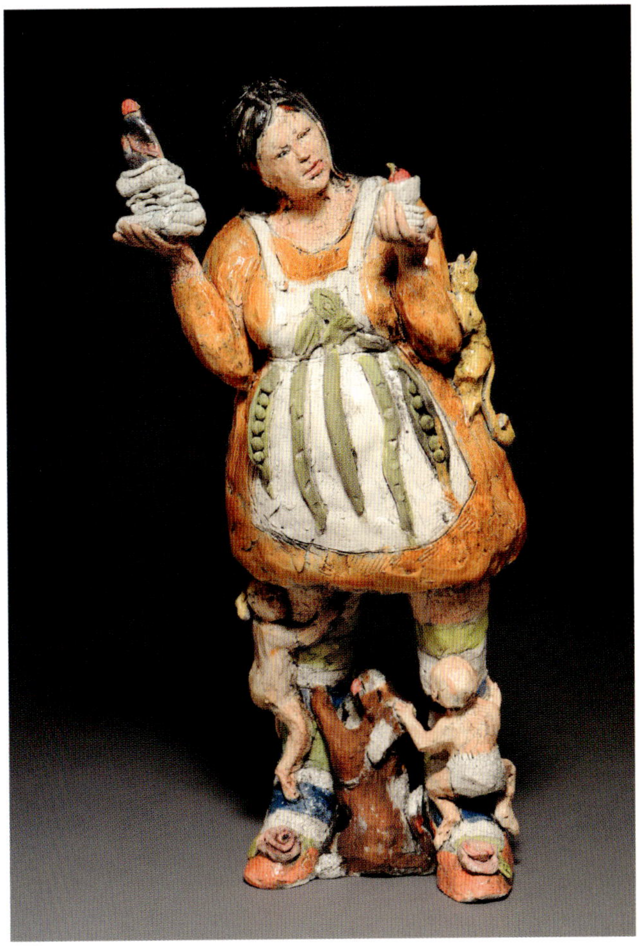

4

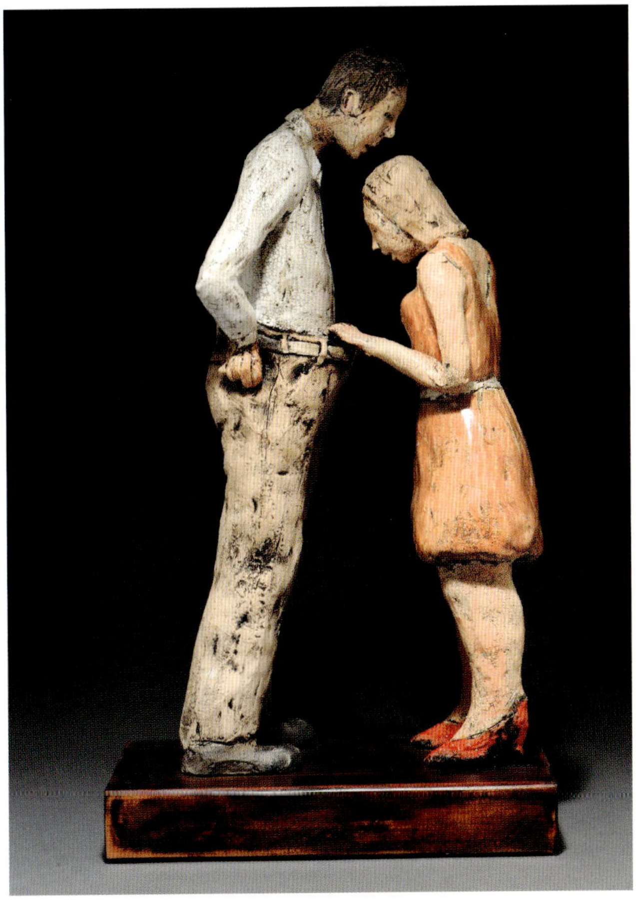

5

1 *Their life is my life*, 2010. Clay, 35". *Photograph by the artist.*

2 *Their life is my life* (detail), 2010. *Photograph by the artist.*

3 *The making of a mother*, 2010. Clay, 33". *Photograph by the artist.*

4 *The daily juggle*, 2010. Clay, 18". *Photograph by the artist.*

5 *Looking for love in all the wrong places*, 2010. Clay, 17". *Photograph by the artist.*

# Jacob Linn

Ormond Beach, Florida, USA

*I'm nearly nineteen years old and enjoy what I do. I like making these sculptures and thinking about what is next in the creation process. I like making things that might shock people or make them think differently about something that's so common in their lives or question their opinions on certain things. I don't know if my art work is even that influential on people, but I get a kick out of them asking me if I'm on some sort of hardcore drug and getting to show them you don't have to be on narcotics to make something weird. I find most of my inspiration from children's stories, things in the trash, cartoons, throwing up, road kill, and religion, all of which are some of my favorite things. I like the idea of being lost in my own train of thought with nothing else bothering me and I think that's how I'm able to stay focused and motivated with my artwork. I like paints and crazy bright colors that pop out and poke you in the eyeball like a cool shirt from the 80s. My name's Jake and this is my work I hope it makes your brain laugh.*

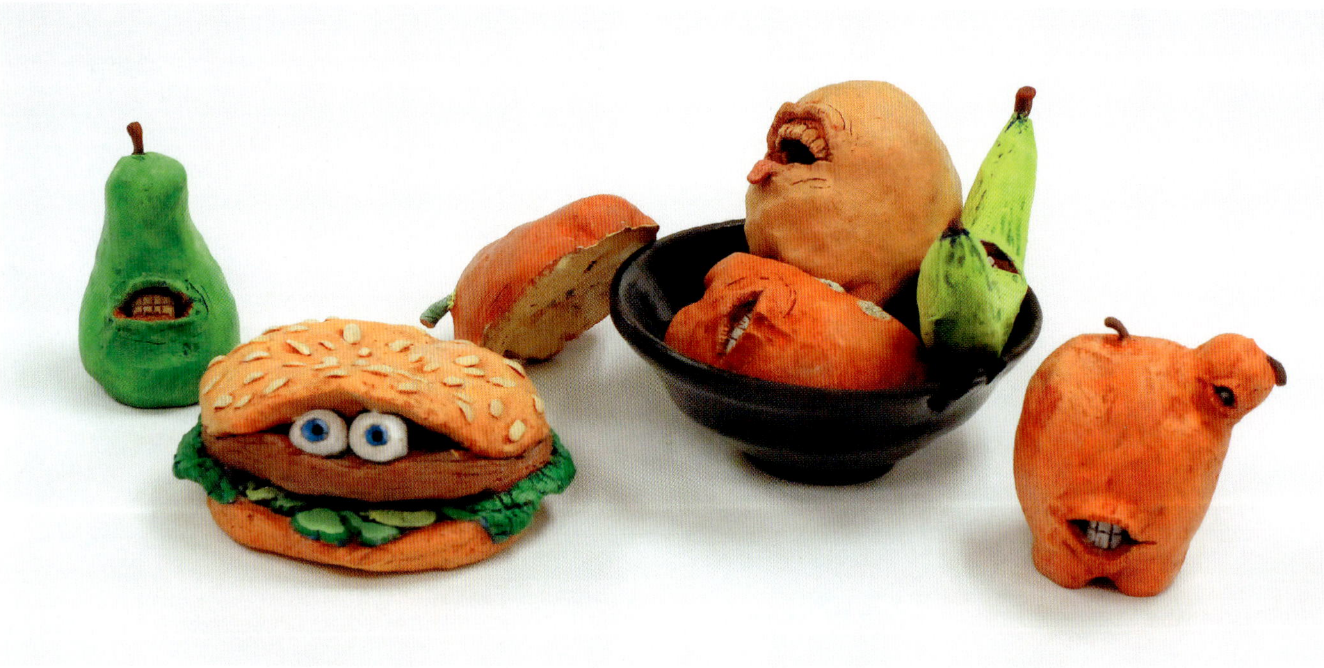

1

1 *Liquid Diet*, 2010, Acrylic, clay, each piece roughly 5" x 5". *Photograph by Richmond.*

2 *My God is a Cyclops*, 2010. Acrylic, clay, 36" x 12". *Photograph by Richmond.*

3 *Self Portrayal*, 2010. Acrylic, clay, 24" x 9". *Photograph by Richmond.*

4 *Reptilian*, 2010. Acrylic, clay, 5" x 2". *Photograph by Richmond.*

5 *"I'm not your father I'm your gym coach,"* 2010. Acrylic on clay, 5" x 7". *Photograph by Richmond.*

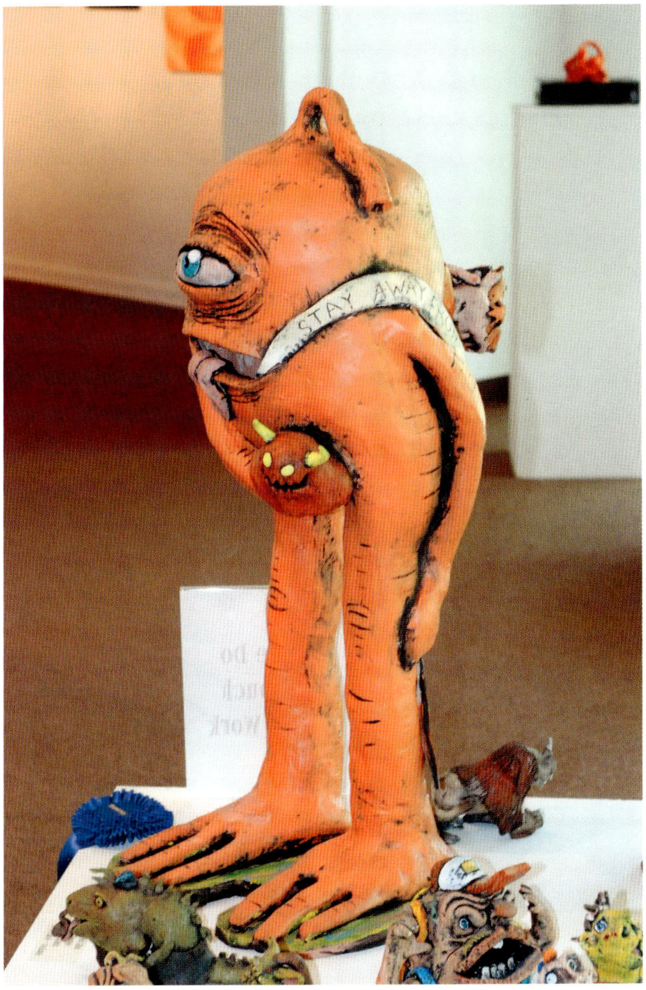


2

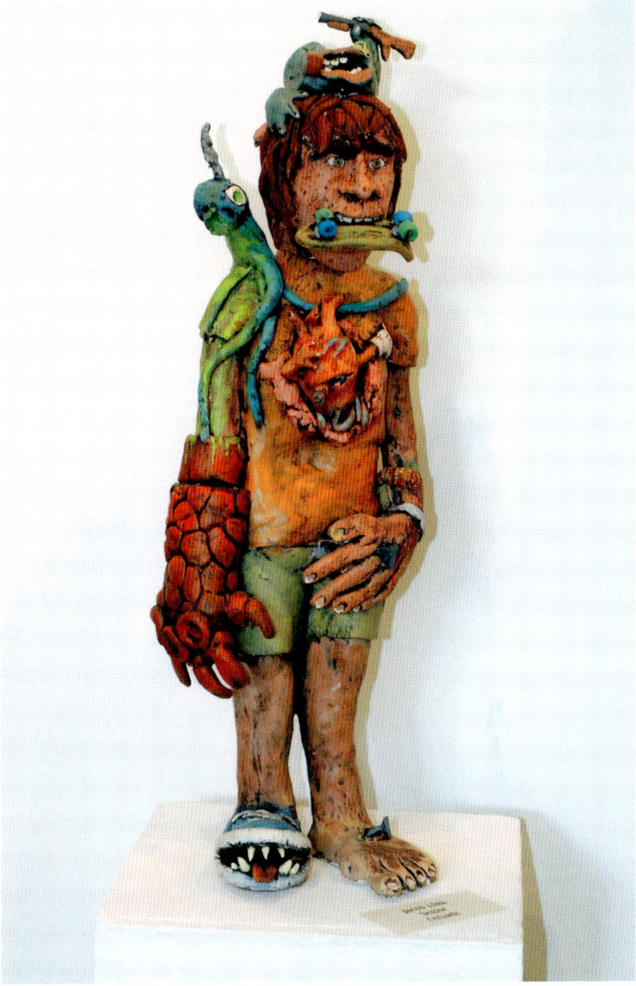

3

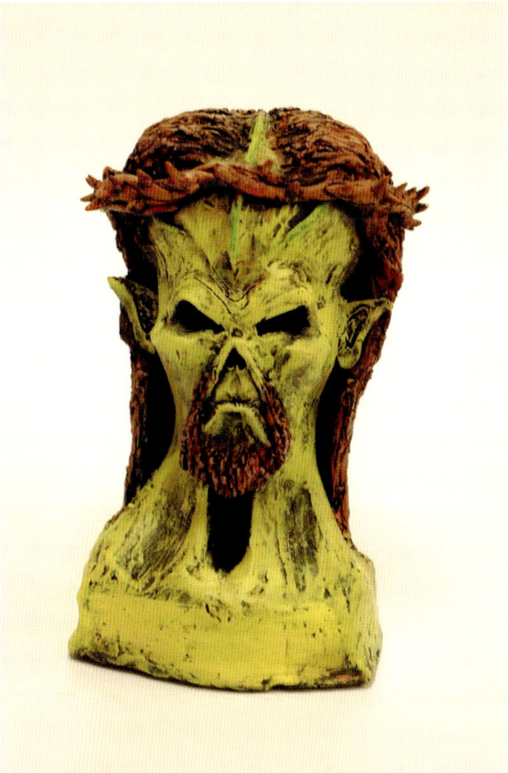

4

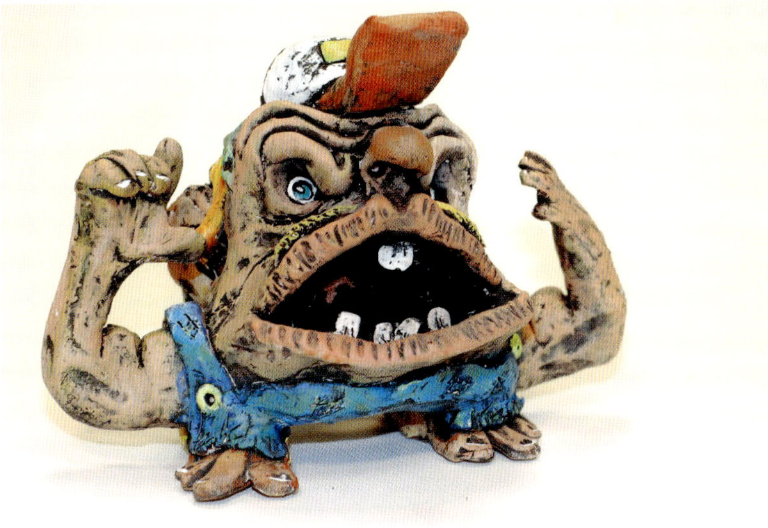

5

# D. Dominick Lombardi

Valhalla, New York, USA
www.ddlombardi.com

*For the past 30-plus years I have dedicated my life to making art, curating, and writing criticisms and essays. My gallery representation is with the Kim Foster Gallery, New York, New York. Reviews of my exhibitions have appeared in such publications as Sculpture, ARTnews, artnet, NY Art Beat, Time Out New York, Zing, and the New York Times. My criticisms and features have appeared in Art Experience NYC, d'ART, The New York Times, Sculpture, culturecatch, Art in Asia, and Public Art and Ecology among others. As a curator, I have worked on numerous exhibitions with various themes including Anonymous, Monkey Spoon, Nature Calls, The Intelligent Design Project, Critics Select, Over the Top – Under the Rug, Speaking in Strings, The Tradition of Icons and Champions of Modernism.*

*Urchins, scamps, rascals have often been used as a sympathetic symbol of the marginalized. They develop uncanny survival skills living outside the masses. My sculptures, which represent those "hidden" individuals, are a sort of reverse double entendre in the way they combine two intentions for one meaning. The discarded objects that constitute the core of the human, and more recently, animal forms include toys, furniture parts, and construction materials. They are castaways, just like the lost souls that are represented in the sand and acrylic medium. As these objects are repurposed as an armature, I continue my process of reusing materials – a valuable lesson taught to me by my grandfather who survived both the Spanish influenza and the Great Depression.*

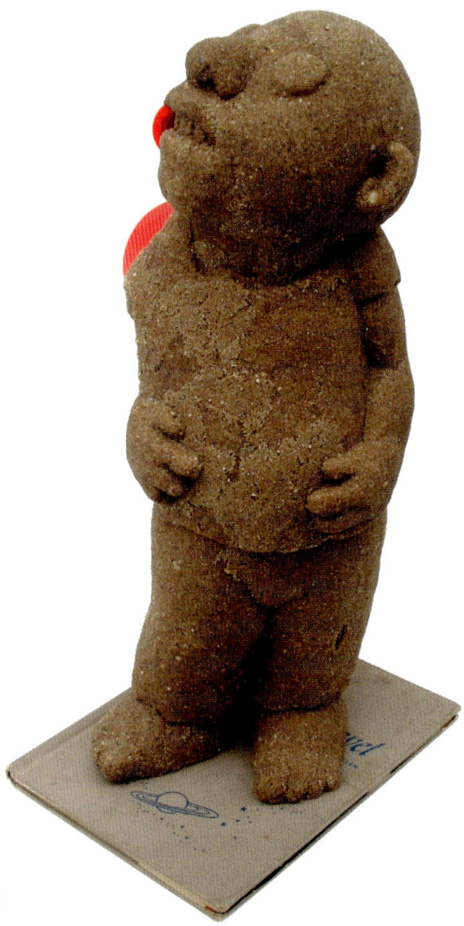

1

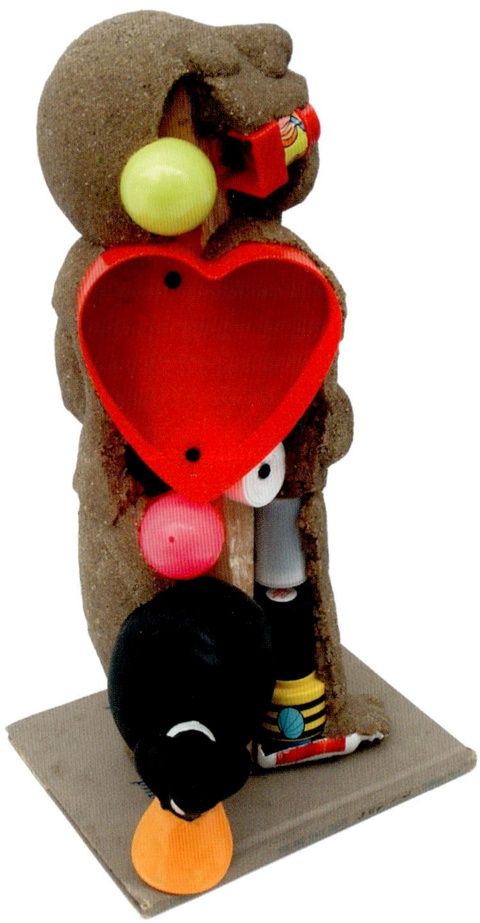

1 *Urchin #4,* 2009. Sand, acrylic medium, objects, 17" x 9" x 7". *Photograph by D. Dominick Lombardi.*

2 *Urchin #12,* 2009. Sand, acrylic medium, objects, 26" x 14" x 16". *Photograph by D. Dominick Lombardi.*

3 *Urchin #7,* 2009. Sand, acrylic medium, objects, 17.5" x 12" x 8.5". *Photograph by D. Dominick Lombardi.*

4 *Urchin #24,* 2010. Sand, acrylic medium, objects, 28" x 30" x 20". *Photograph by D. Dominick Lombardi.*

5 *Urchin #27,* 2011. Sand, acrylic medium, objects, 16" x 19" x 10". *Photograph by D. Dominick Lombardi.*

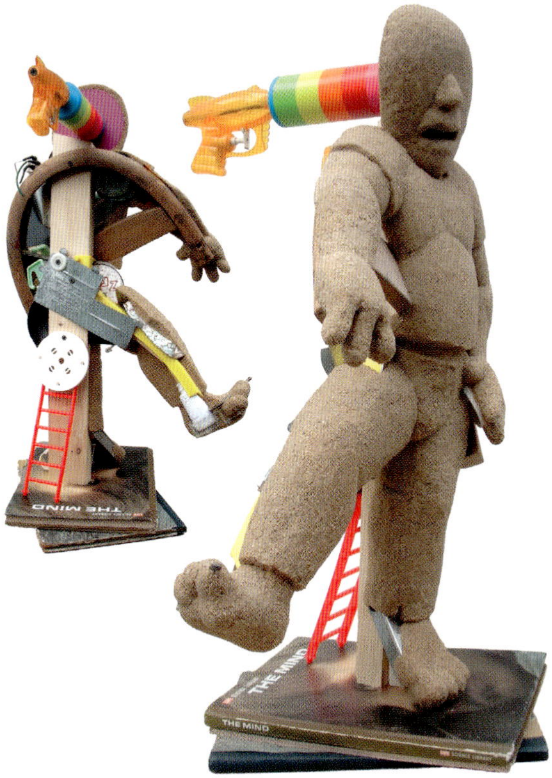


2

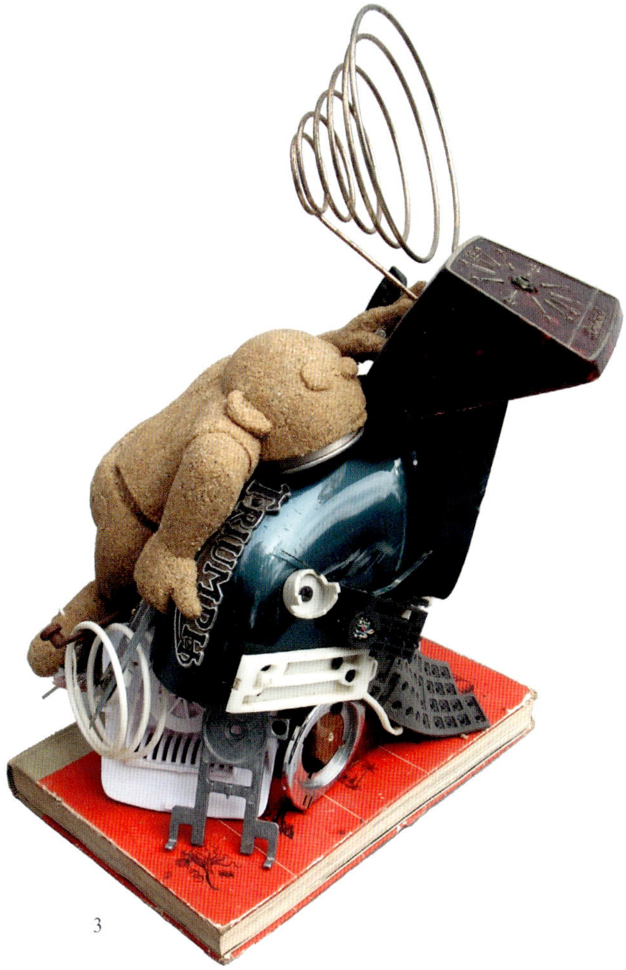

3

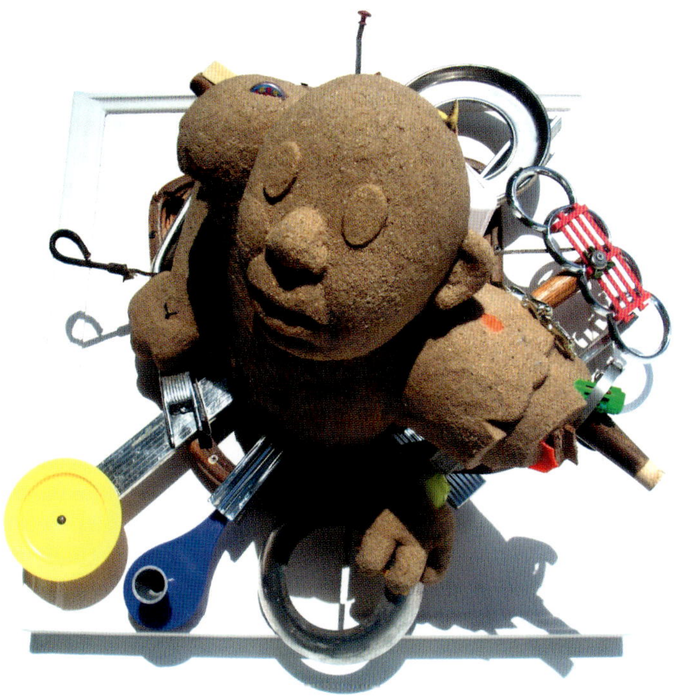

4

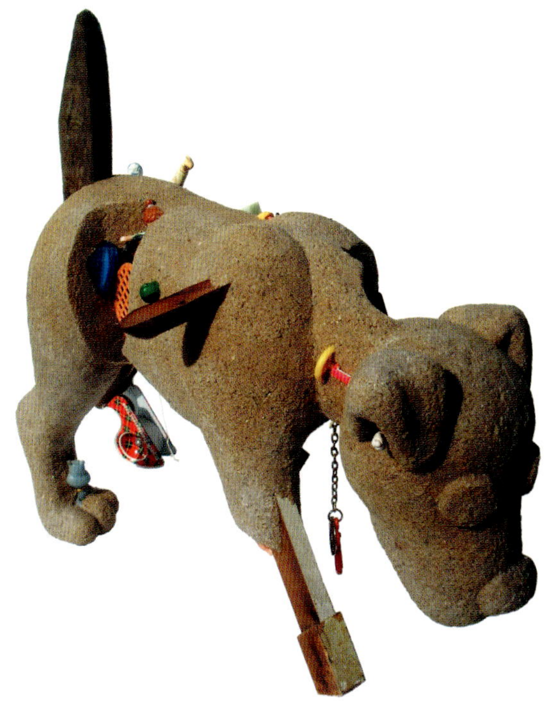

5

# Angel Olegario Luna

Yuma, Arizona, USA
www.fineartamerica.com/profiles/angel-luna.html

Angel Olegario Luna was born and raised in Prosser, Washington. He graduated from Whitworth University with a BA in history. He completed his BFA degree in ceramics/sculpture at Eastern Washington University in 1998 and MFA at the University of Idaho in 2002. He is a professor of fine art at Arizona Western College in Yuma, Arizona.

*My beliefs as an artist begin with my roots with my family. I am a Mexican-American and have worked in the fields with my hands. This has caused me to continue working with my hands in the medium of clay. I have been influenced by the figure through the majority of my creative process in sculpture. I have two major bodies of figurative work.* Gente Not Numbers *deals with farm worker social issues. The worker is replaceable, but experiences with the individual are irreplaceable. These figures are created using terra cotta clay.* Border Monsters *deals with immigration, the border culture, and traditional and contemporary masks of Mexico. The new immigrant is seen as the monster of our time. These figures are stoneware with china paint for the mask colors.*

1

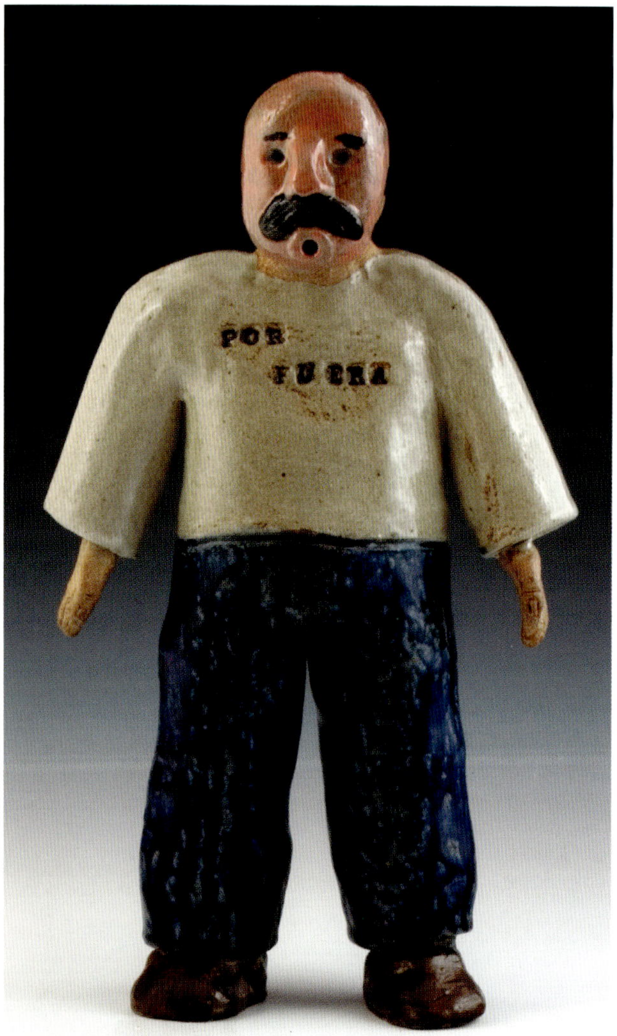


2

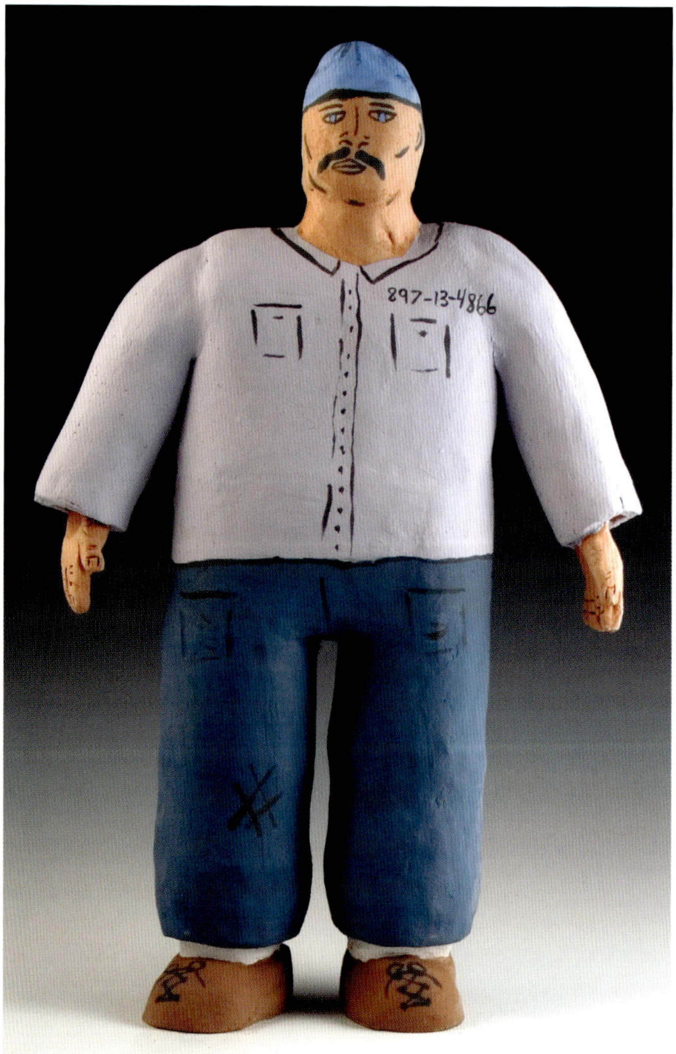


1 *Border Monster: Whistle Mask,* 2006. Ceramic, 14". *Photograph by the artist.*

2 *Gente Not Numbers: Farm Worker Purple Shirt,* 2006. Ceramic, 16". *Photograph by the artist.*

3 *Border Monster: Moon Mask,* 2006. Ceramic, 14". *Photograph by the artist.*

4 *Border Monster: Green Devil,* 2010. Ceramic, 16". *Photograph by the artist.*

5 *Gente Not Numbers: Flower Seller,* 2006. Ceramic, 13". *Photograph by the artist.*

6 *Gente Not Numbers: Lettuce Worker,* 2009. Ceramic, 16". *Photograph by the artist.*

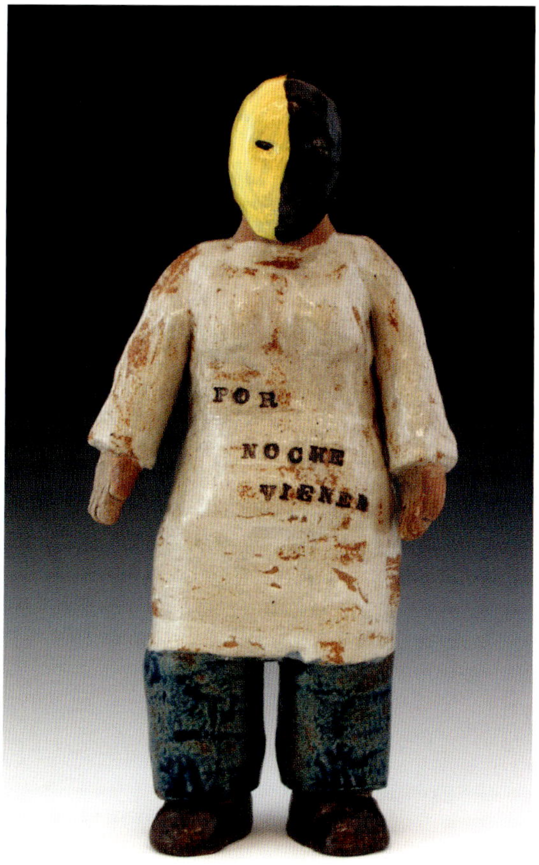


3

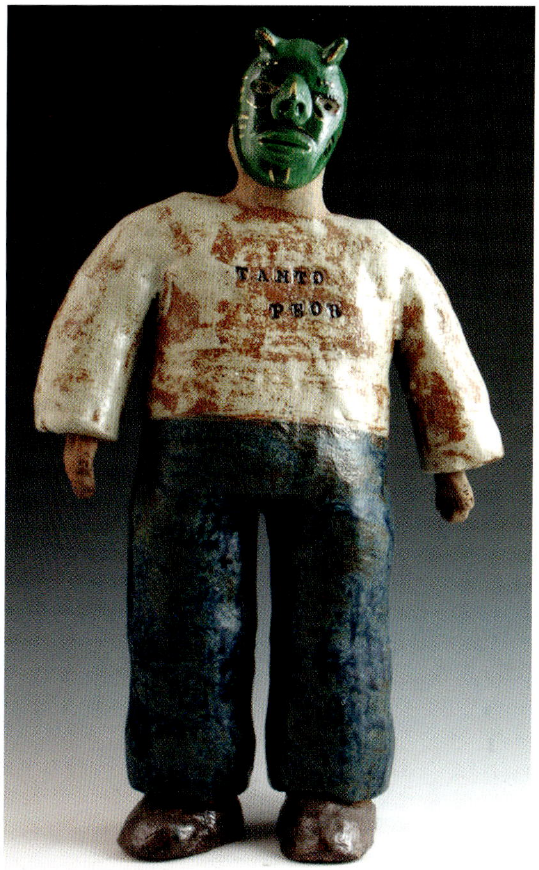


4

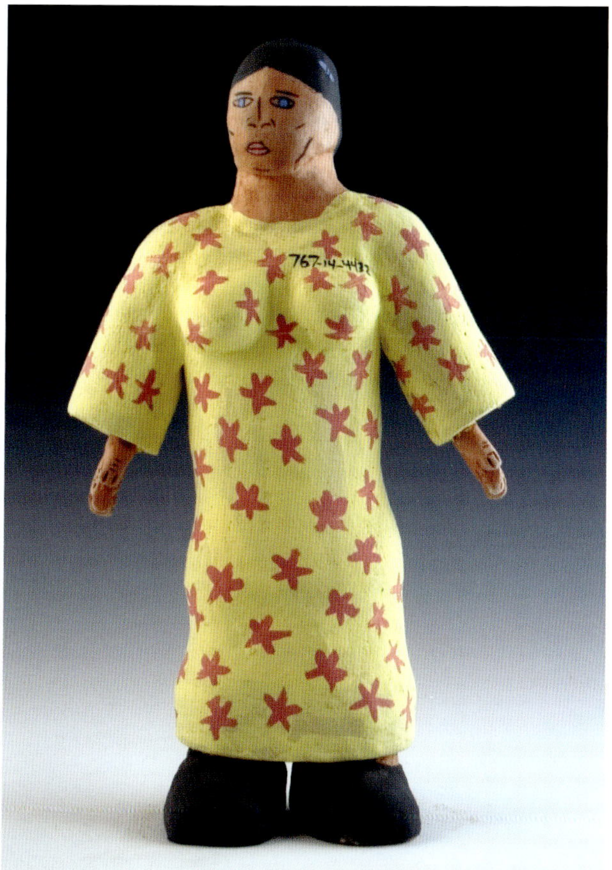


5

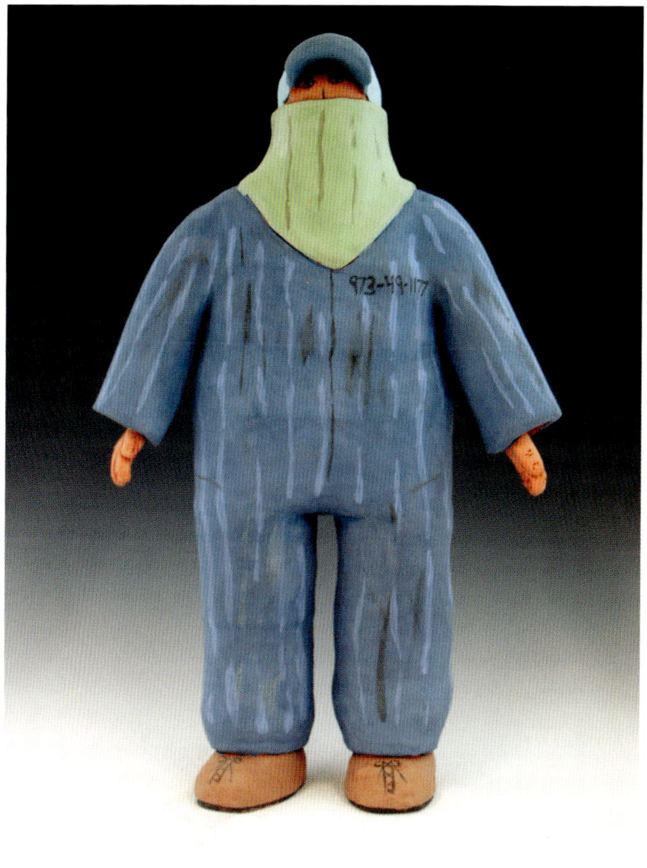


6

# Thomas Maes

TM-ART Gallery Café, Chania Crete, Greece
www.thomas-maes.artistwebsites.com

*Born in Belgium, Brasschaat, I started to discover art in my young years, drawing images making small sculptures. I never really did something with it, however, until I came to live in Greece 2005. My passion for creation started growing from that moment on. In 2007 I had my first one man show and exhibit where I sold more than 40 of my creations. I use my passion for and knowledge of science, design, painting, drawing, engineering, technologies, sculptures, and photography to create my art.*

*I make modern-classic sculptures out of many different materials. In a world full of hi-tech, I try to give each more soul and natural beauty, by designing and making them fit into a more natural environment.*

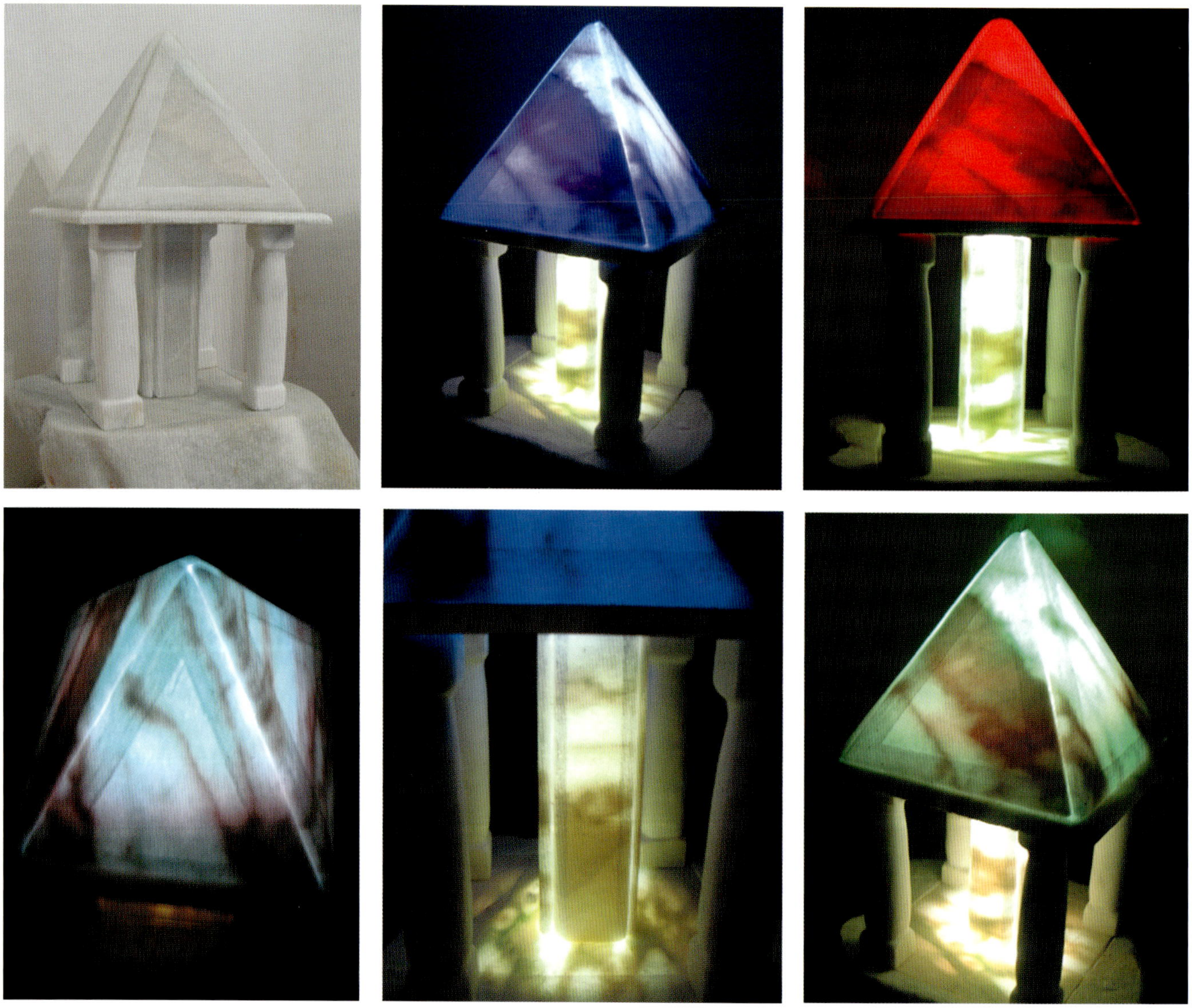

1

1 *The Two Civilizations*, 2010. Marble, 50cm x 30cm x 30cm. *Photograph by Thomas Maes.*

2 *Flowers of Memories*, 2009. Mixed media, marble, 70cm x 30cm x 20cm. *Photograph by Thomas Maes.*

3 *Sun Obelisk*, 2009. Marble, 85cm x 46cm x 46cm. *Photograph by Thomas Maes.*

4 *Weather Plant*, 2009. Mixed media, 75cm x 20cm. *Photograph by Thomas Maes.*

2

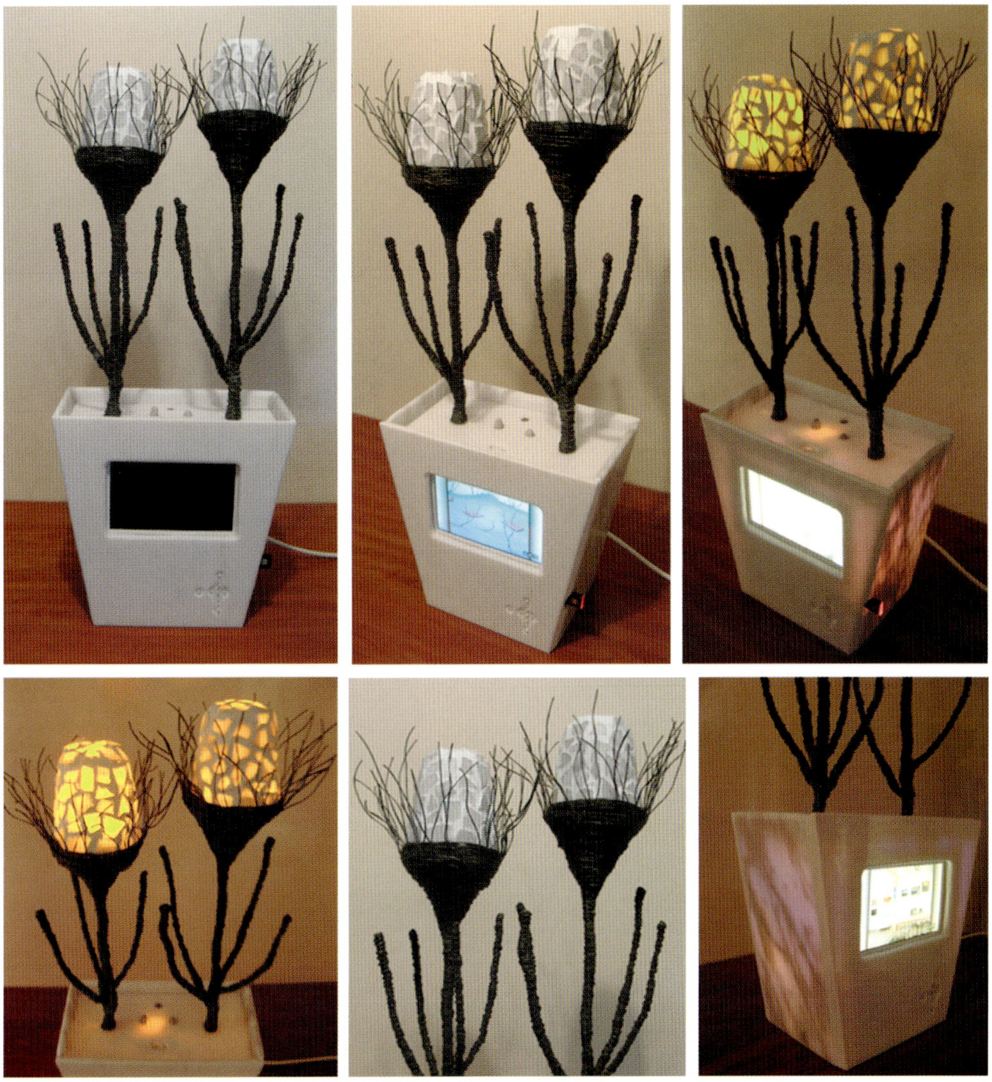

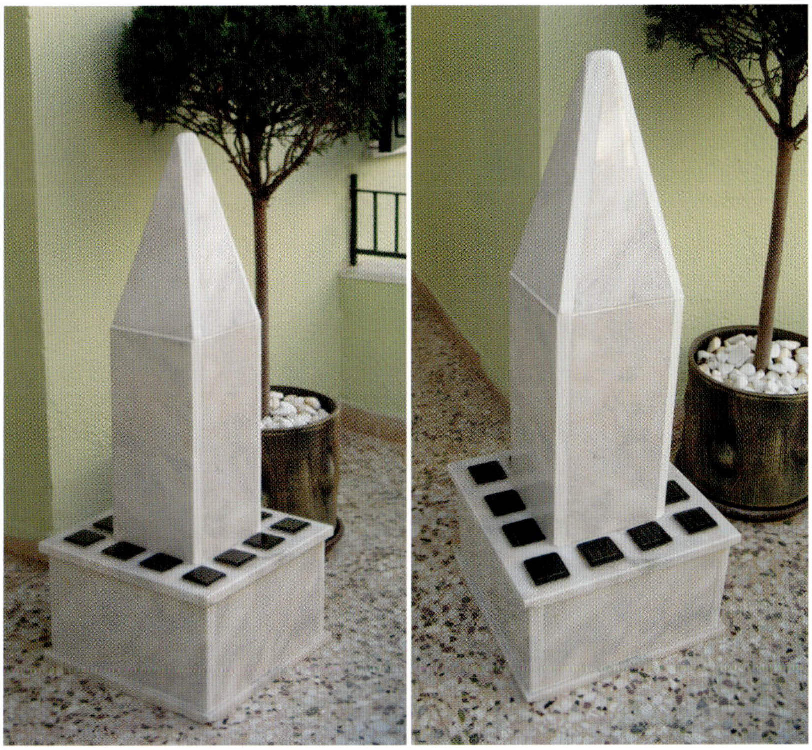

3

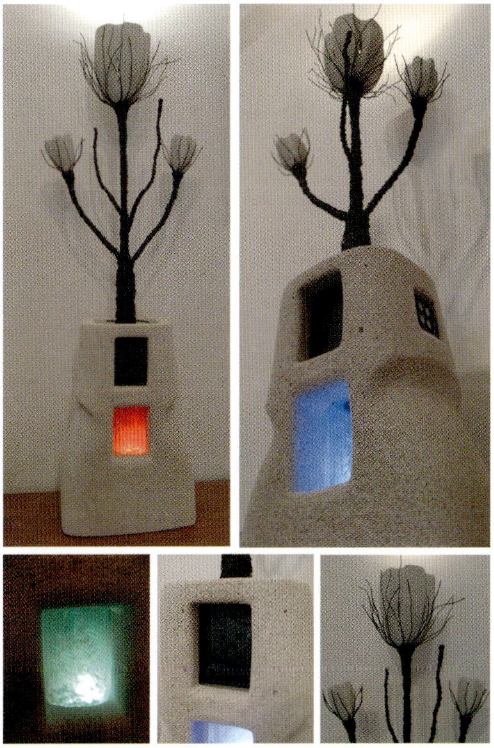

4

# Lauren Marems

Sherman Oaks, California, USA
www.maremsart.com

*I love to work in clay and have created these face jugs from high-fired stoneware clay. They are fired twice and glazed with high-fire glazes as well as low-fire glazes to achieve a more colorful look. I often add enamels and bake them a third time at lower temperatures when I need color that I can't get with standard glazes. They are hollow jugs that will hold liquid.*

*I love to create fantasy creatures because they allow me do create without limits. I have worked as a professional sculptor on films and television and a lot of my work reflects the influence of many years of creating creatures for Sci-fi.*

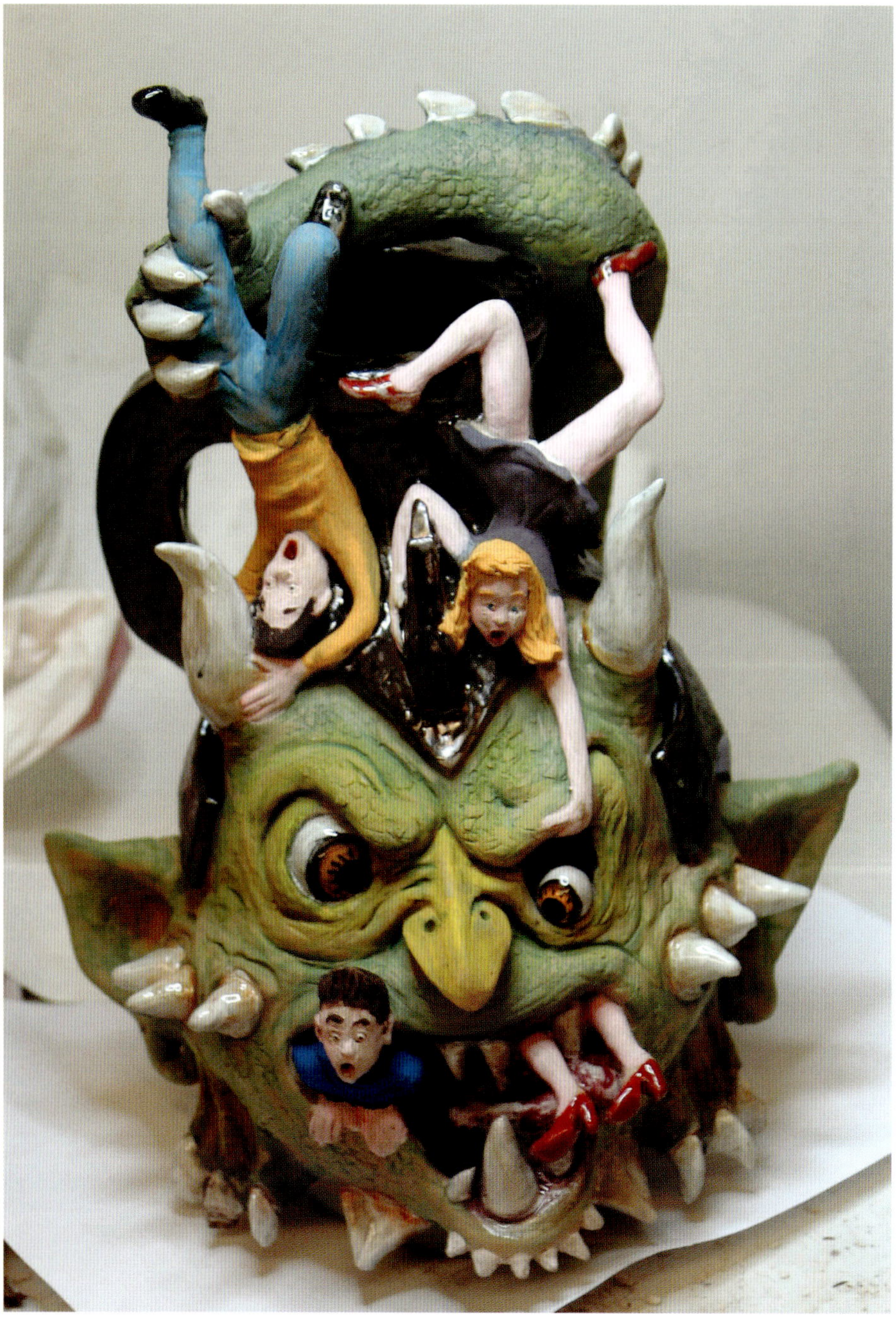

1

1 *People Eater,* 2010. Cone 10, stoneware porcelain mix, 10.5" high.

2 *Meg,* 2009. Cone 10, stoneware porcelain mix, 11.5" high.

3 *Lexi,* 2009. Cone 10, stoneware porcelain mix, 11" high.

4 *The Jailer "Unlock Your Inner Demons,"* 2011. Cone 5, stoneware iron oxide, 11".

5 *Jokula*, 2010. Cone 10, stoneware porcelain mix, 12" high.

4

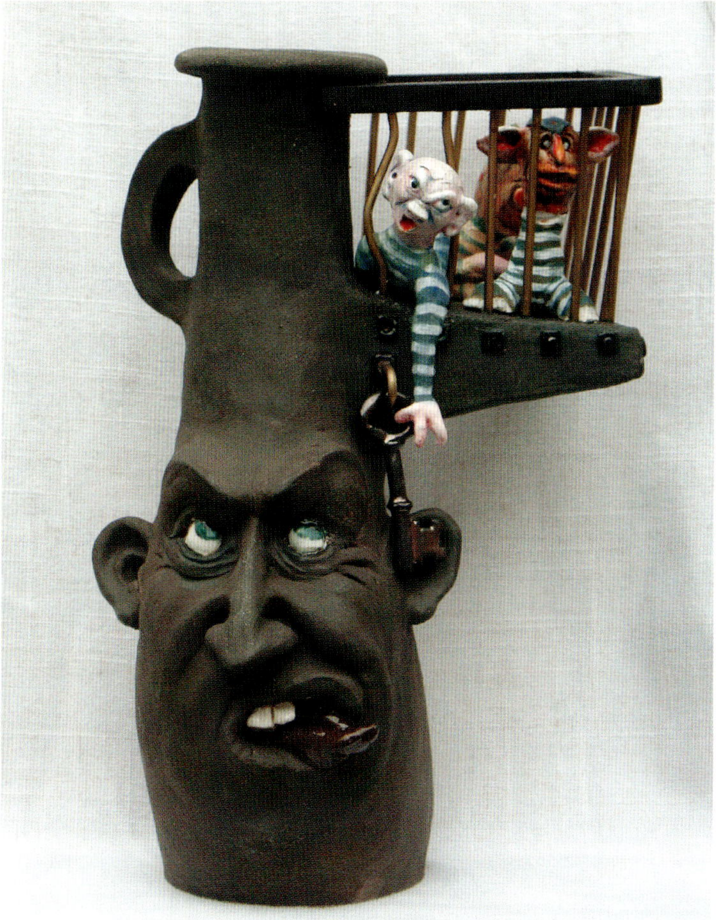

2

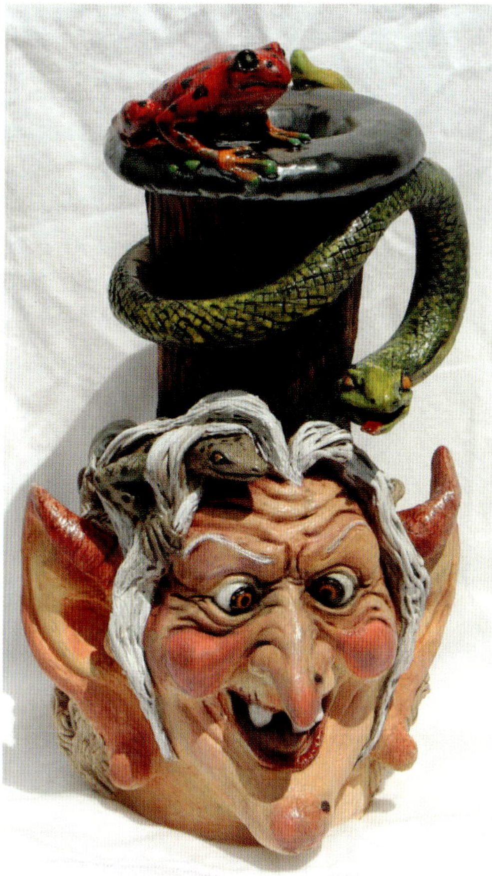

5

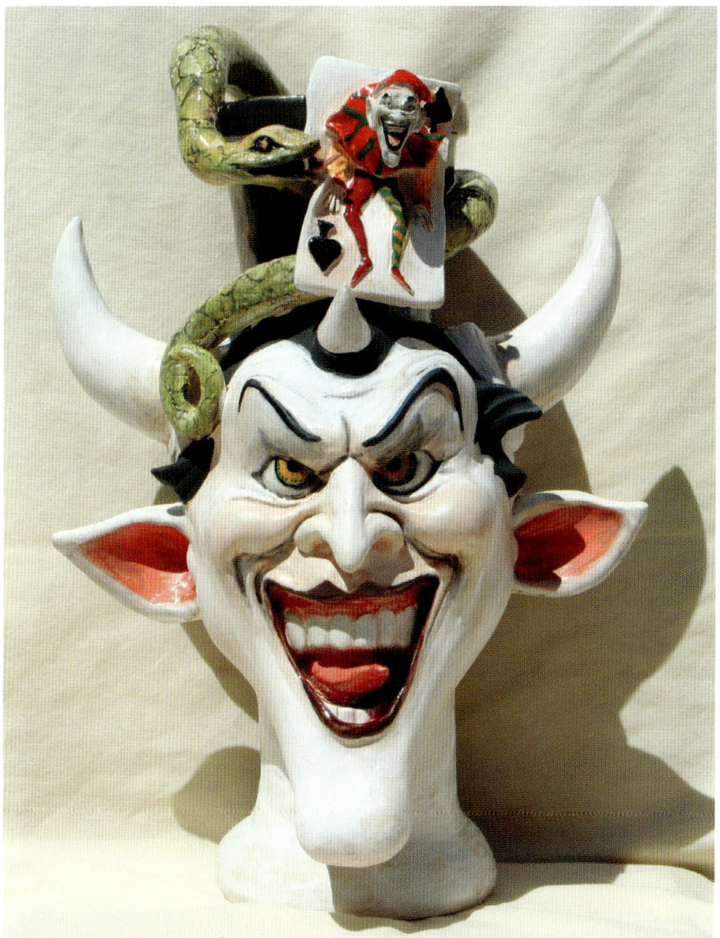

3

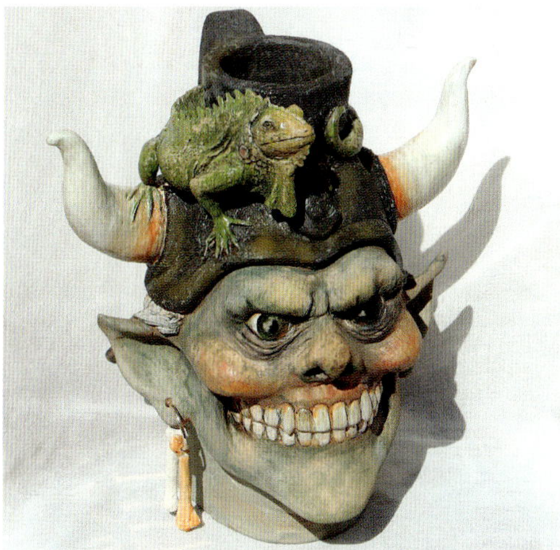

# Peter W. Michel

Fayetteville, New York, USA
www.petermichel.com

Peter W. Michel was born in Schenectady, New York. He received his AB degree in fine arts from Oberlin College in Ohio, and a degree in architecture from MIT in Cambridge, Massachusetts. He pursued further studies in sculpture at the Museum of Fine Arts School and Rice University in Houston, Texas. Michel has worked as an architect in Boston, Houston, and New York. In 1989, he began to use the computer as a tool to design and produce his sculpture.

His public sculpture has been shown in Chicago's Pier Walk, the Chesterwood Museum in Stockbridge, Massachusetts, the downtown Stamford, Connecticut, Art in Public Places exhibition, and the Federal Reserve Board in Washington, DC. His work has included commissions by the Houston Festival, the Houston Academy of Gymnastics, Texas Children's Hospital West Campus in Houston, the Thea Bowman House in Utica, New York, the City of Syracuse, New York, and a number of private individuals. His work is in Wandell Sculpture Garden in Urbana, Illinois, and The Oakton Sculpture Park in Des Plains, Illinois, and in private collections across the United States as well as in Germany, Japan, Korea and South Africa

His work is a celebration and exploration in symbols of self, relationship, and community, and represents a stand for the possibility art is, for the expression of joy, aliveness, love and relationship. Through color, humor, the play of ideas, the effects of light and space, the viewer is invited to access his/her own spirit of playfulness and relatedness.

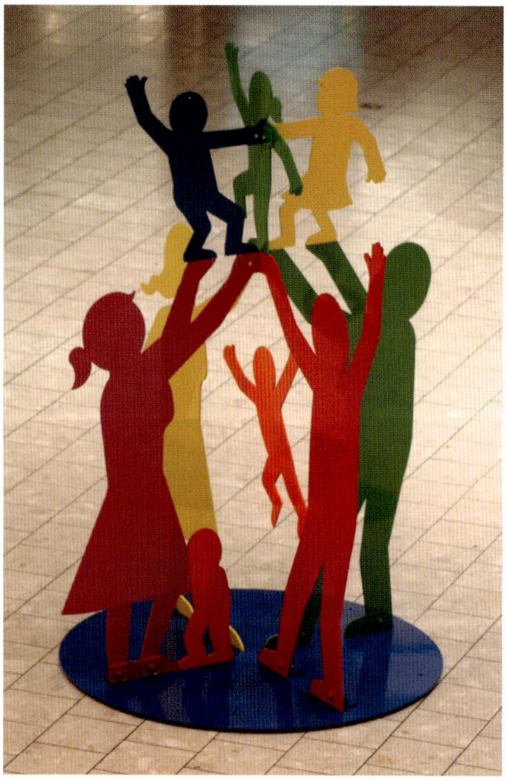

1

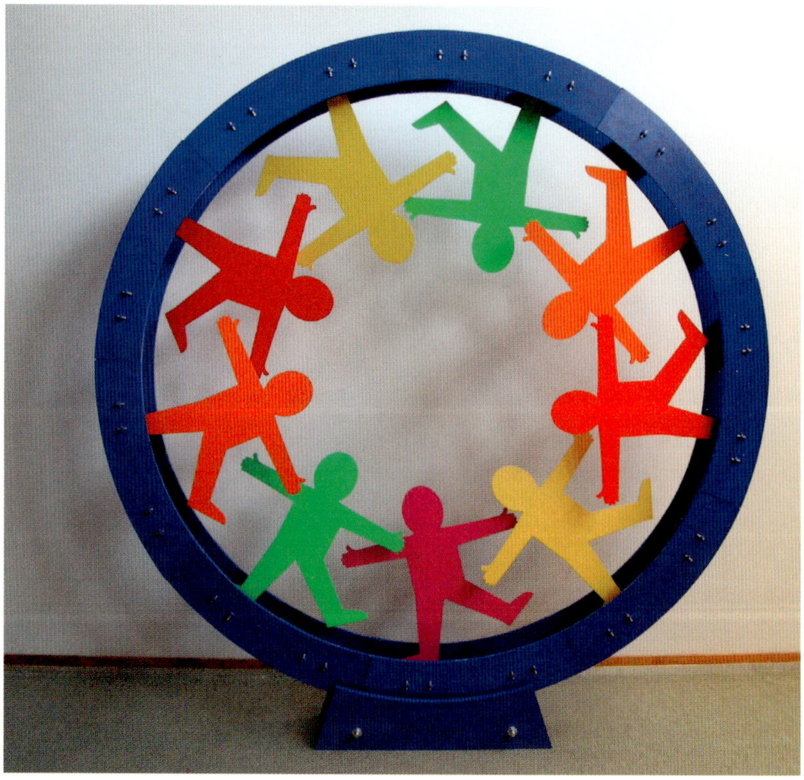

2

1 *Family Celebration*, 2006. Painted aluminum, 7' 9". *Photograph by Peter W. Michel.*

2 *Folk Circle Mandala*, 2002. Painted wood, 7' 5". *Photograph by Peter W. Michel.*

3 *Fathers and Sons*, 1999. Painted aluminum, 10'. *Photograph by Peter W. Michel.*

4 *Peace Garden Totem*, 2009, Painted aluminum, 12'. *Photograph by Peter W. Michel.*

5 *Two Are Halves of One*, 2006. Painted aluminum, 9' 9". *Photograph by Peter W. Michel.*

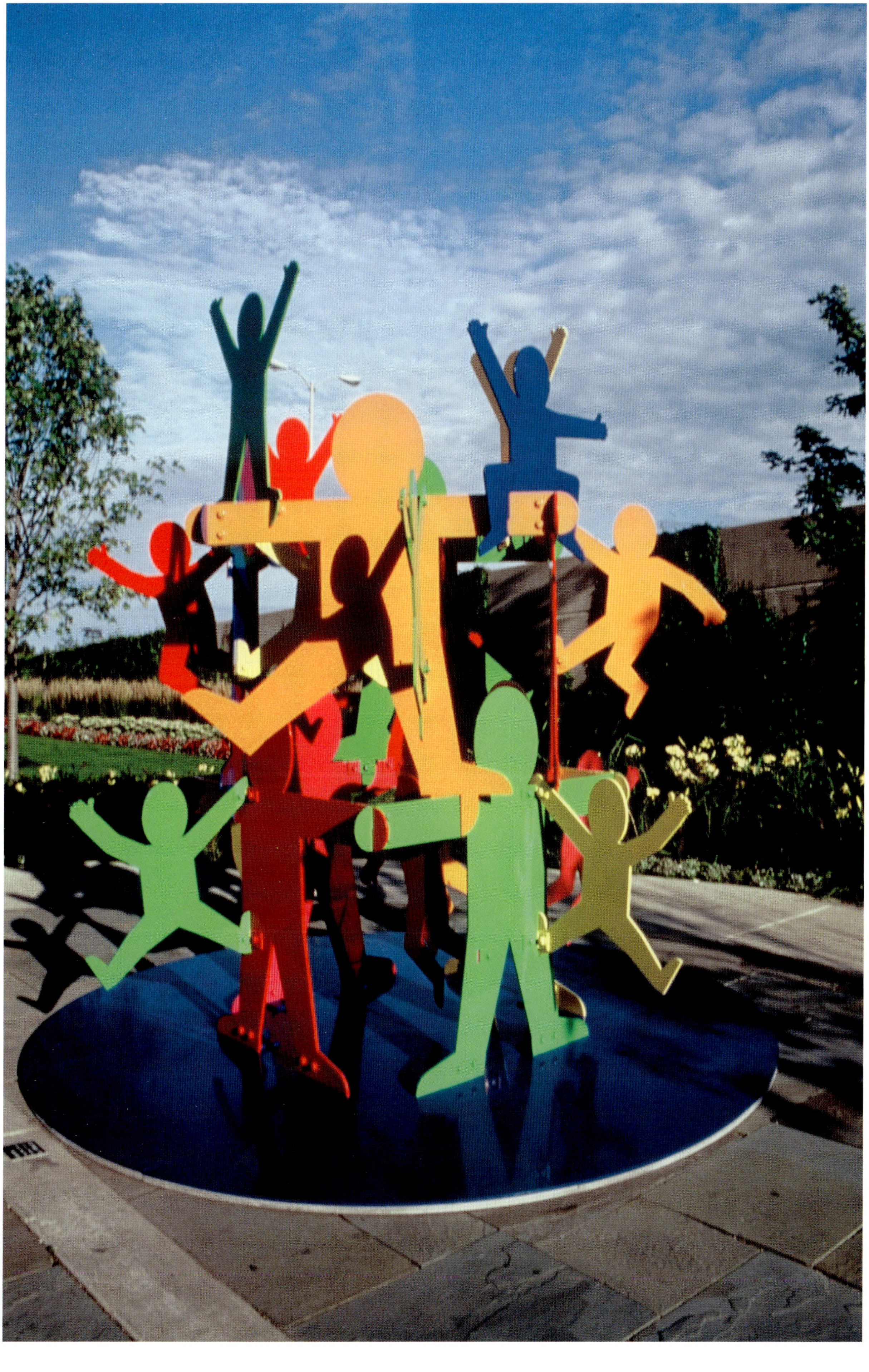

3

4

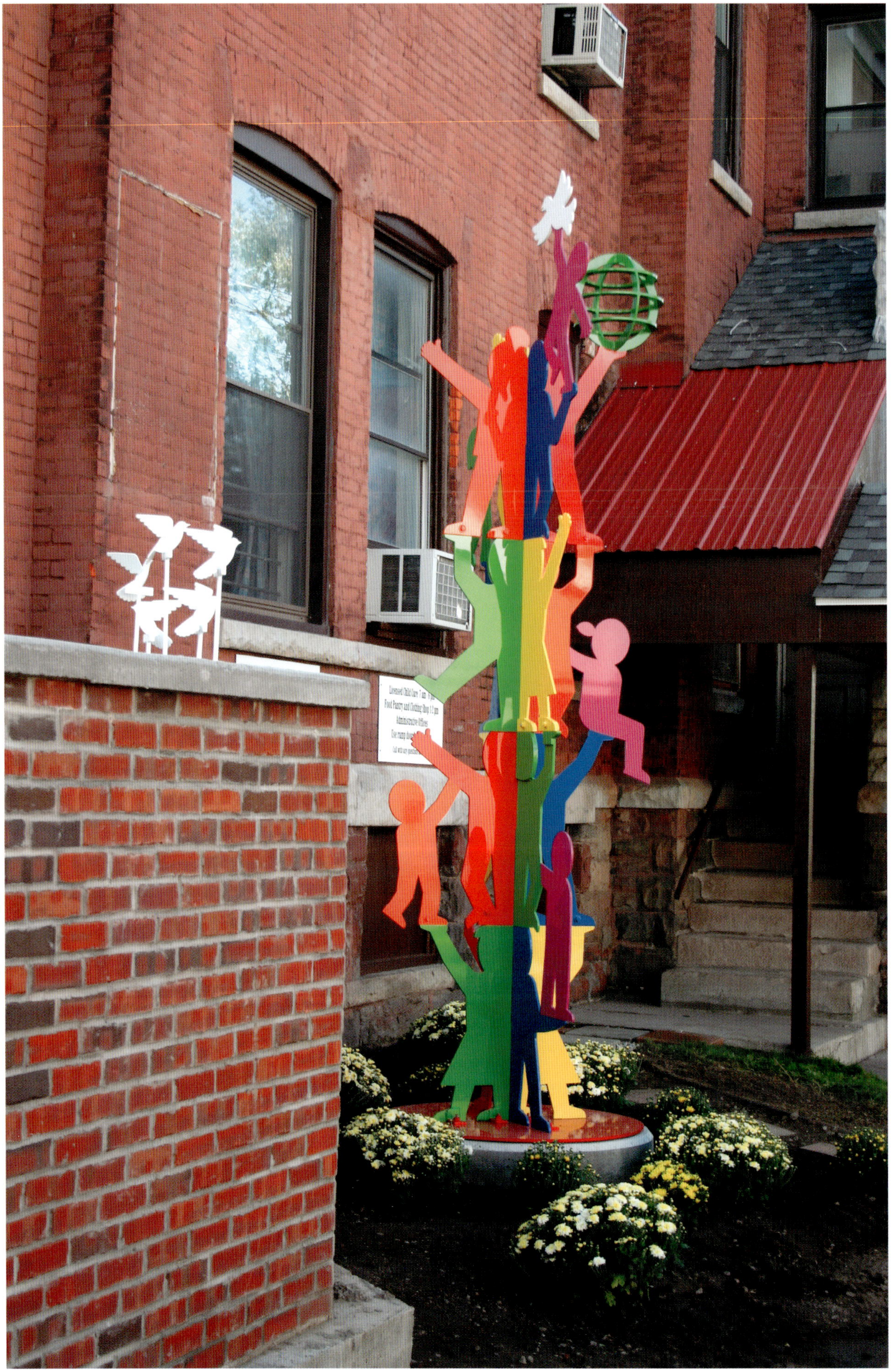

5

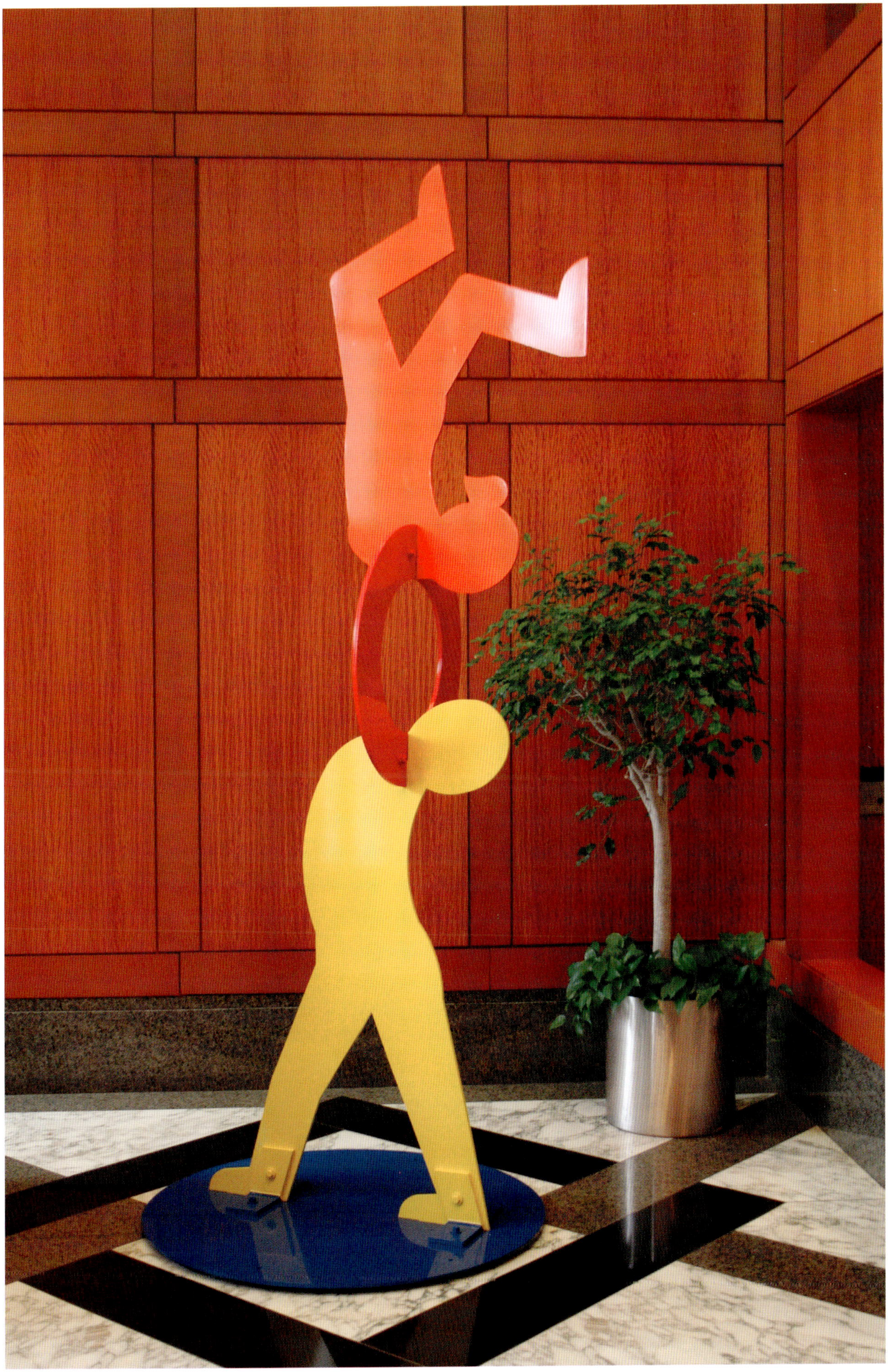

# Milo Mirabelli

Wenatchee, Washington, USA
www.milomirabelli.com

*From my early career in a sign shop to the 20 years I spent designing packaging equipment and the plants they operated in, and the past 15 years as an artist of wood, designing and creating have always played a central role in my life. My love affair with wood began in the early 1960s, after seeing one of Henry Moore's sculptures at the Seattle World's Fair. Ever since then I have been aiming to show it at its best by pushing its limits and combining it with other natural and man made materials, I am always striving to refine my techniques and to learn new ones.*

*I use my sense of design to work with various media and design elements to bring them to their simplest and most pure form. The combination of sight and touch are the only way the true beauty and depth of the wood and his various creations can be fully experienced. My creativity and design abilities marry with the integrity and personality of the various media to come together in a partnership that often leaves the viewer to ponder… "how did he do that?"*

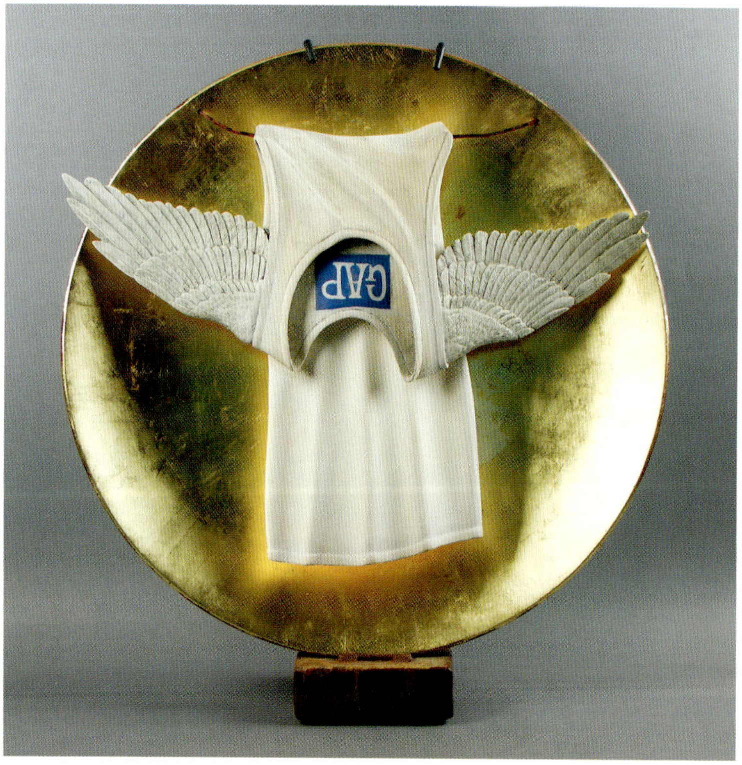


1

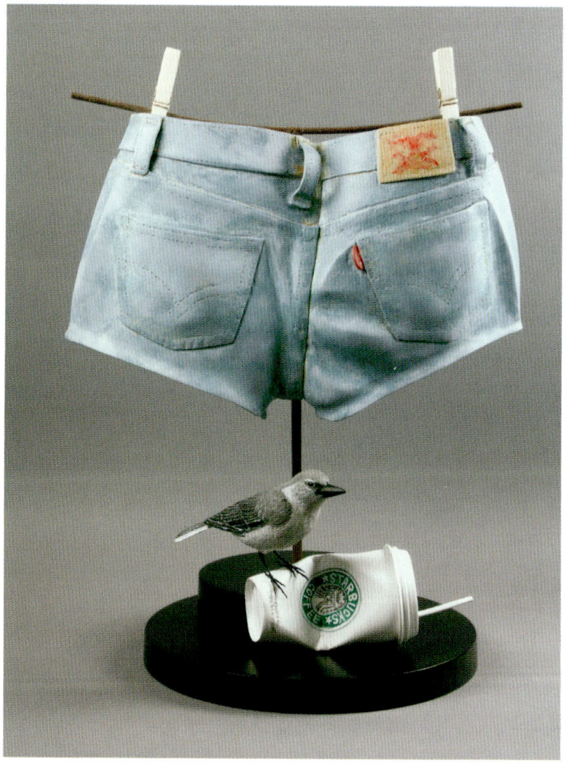

2

1 *Little Wings.* Hand turned and carved walnut, bass, acrylic paint, 22kt gold leaf, 25" t. x 23" w. x 6" d. *Photo by the artist.*

2 *Day at the Beach.* Hand carved bass, tupelo, ebonized maple, acrylic paint, 24" x 19" x 13.5". *Photo by the artist.*

3 *Trojan Koi.* Hand carved bass, tupelo, acrylic paint, bronze patina, 39.5" l. x 11.5" t. x 8" d. *Photo by the artist.*

4 *Classic.* Hand carved bass, ebony, maple, acrylic paint, lacquer, 23kt gold leaf, 19" l. x 9.5" t x 8" d. *Photo by the artist.*

5 *Surfin Sockeye.* Hand carved bass, maple, ebony, acrylic paint, 25.5" l. x 18.75" w. x 13" t. *Photo by the artist.*

3

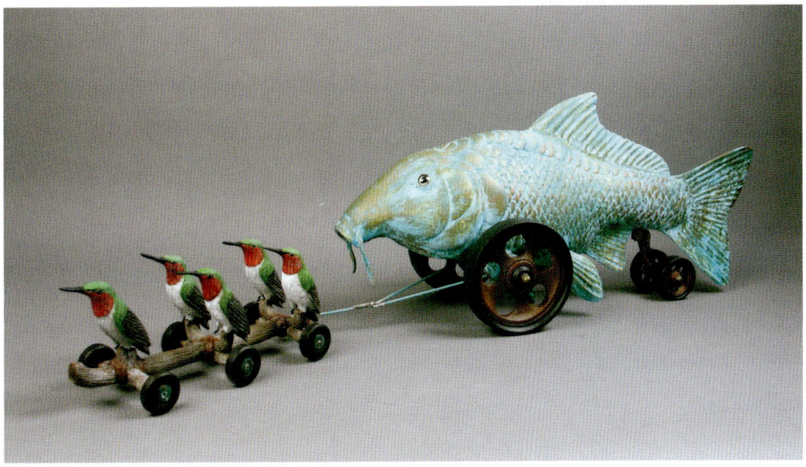

4

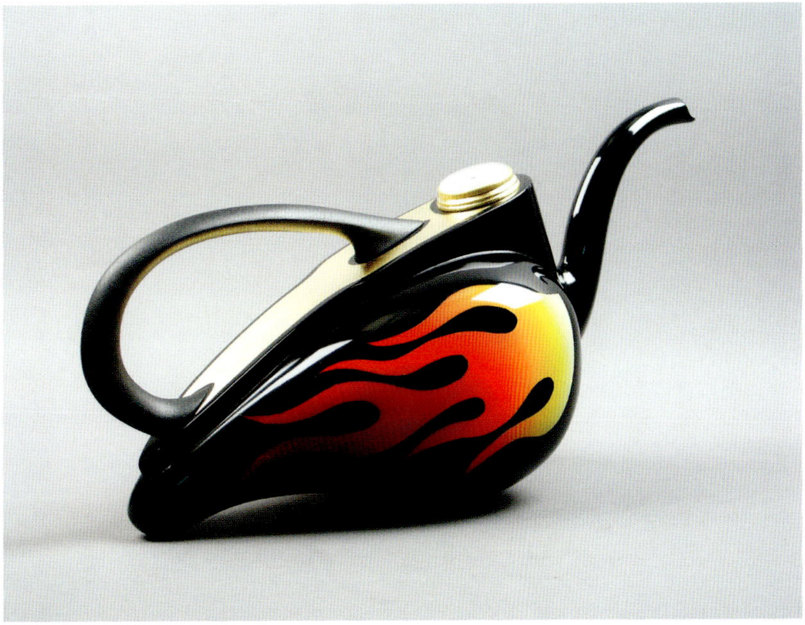

5

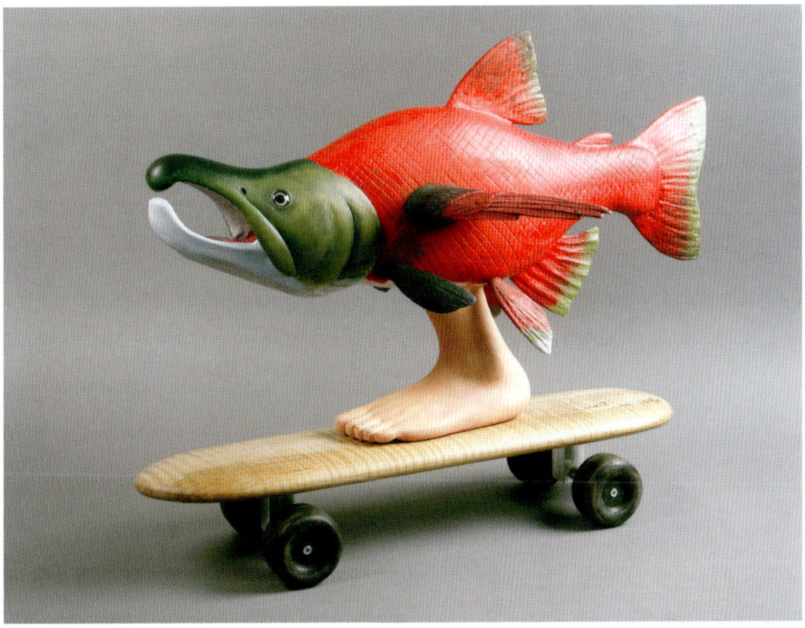

# Brian Mock

Portland, Oregon, USA
www.brianmock.com

*I grew up in Portland, Oregon. My artistic spark was ignited at an early age, fueled by the organic beauty of the Northwest. I excelled in a variety of artistic media throughout my youth and young adulthood, including drawing, wood carving, watercolor, and acrylic painting. My current work applies talents and passion from these multi-artistic disciplines.*

*The life of each piece begins by gathering reclaimed materials from scrap yards, industrial recycled bins, and various donations. Structures are then sketched to ensure individual components are complementary in form and aesthetics. Each piece of the sculpture, from frame to metal finish, need exact measurement and placement to ensure structural precision, technical excellence, and visual beauty. I am inspired by the challenge of creating something unique, fun, and inherently curious. I merge imagination with technical skill by incorporating reclaimed, found objects and everyday items into one-of-a-kind pieces. Work integrating welded, recycled materials is designed to be interactive, and pique the viewer's intrigues of how an eclectic collection of things can become an entirely different something else. I love the notion that there is something to learn in every day, and I try to incorporate this into my art by constantly exploring new avenues, and welcoming growth.*

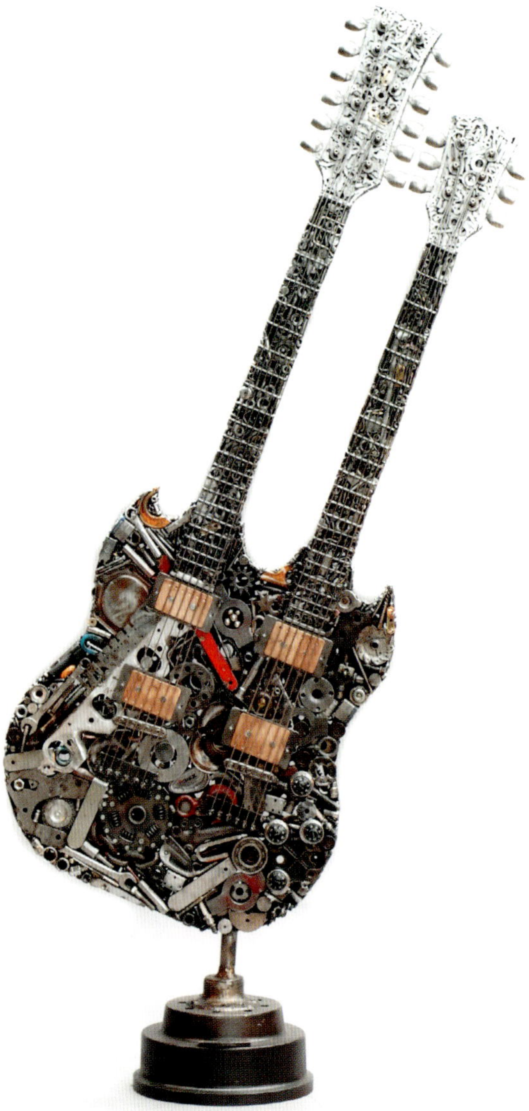

1

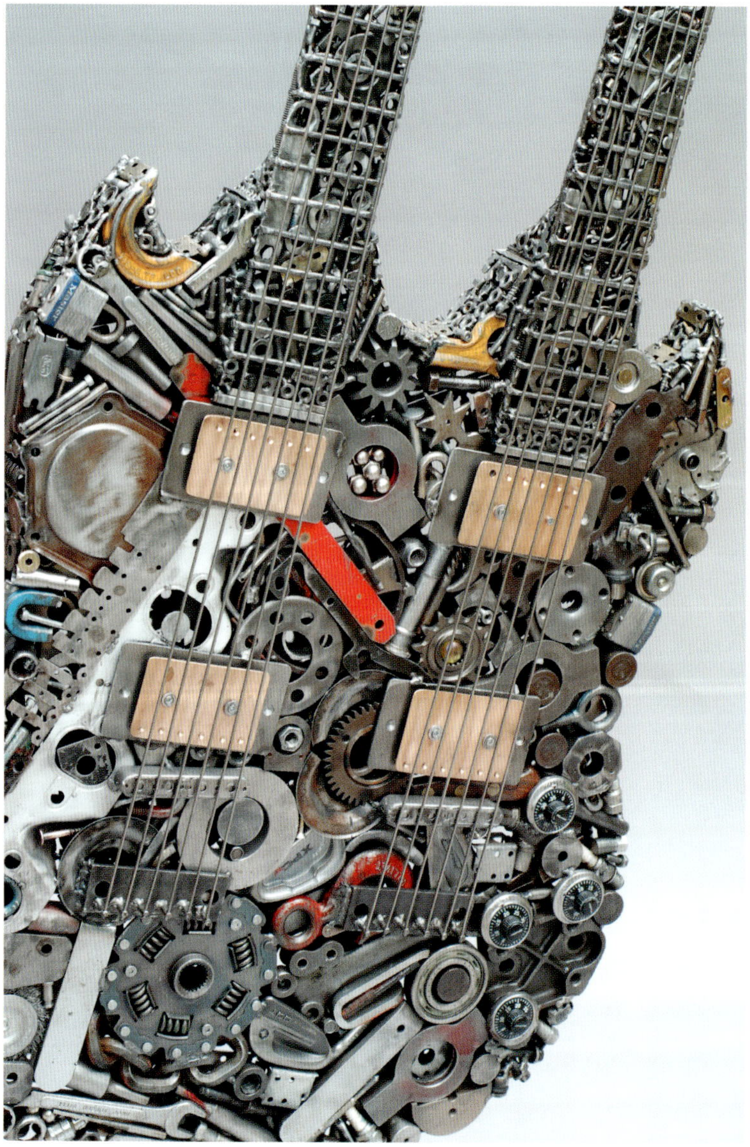

2

1 *Heavy Metal*, 2010. Recycled metal, 84". *Photo by the artist.*

2 *Heavy Metal* (detail), 2010. *Photo by the artist.*

3 *Mermaid*, 2006. Recycled metal, 78". *Photograph by Brian Mock.*

4 *Gurtrude*, 2007, Recycled metal, 96". *Photograph by Brian Mock.*

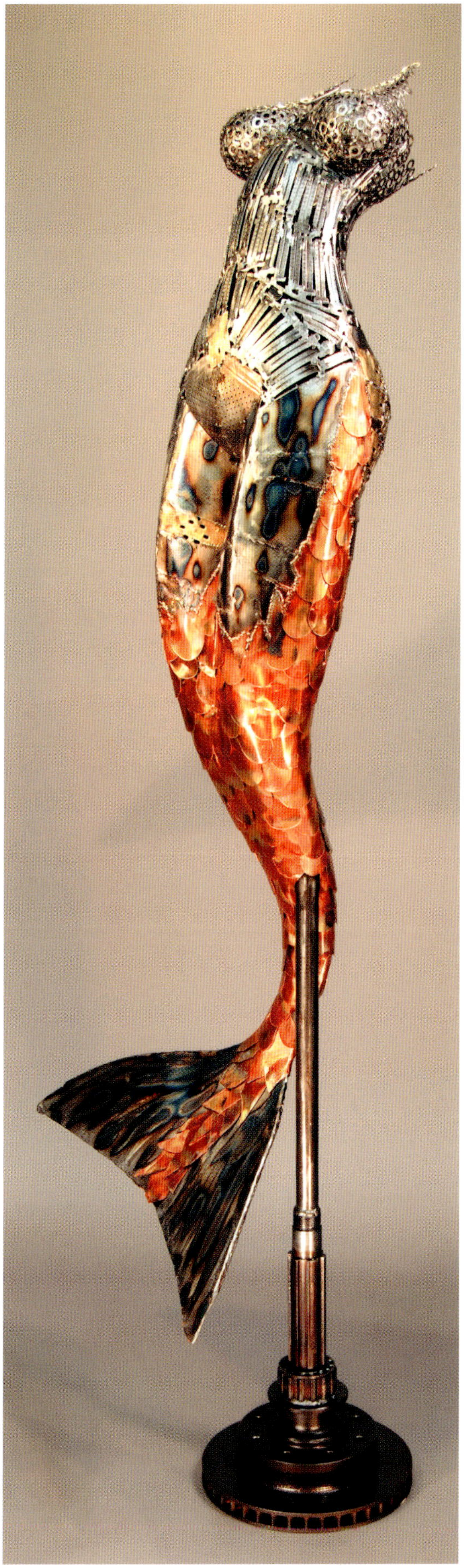

3

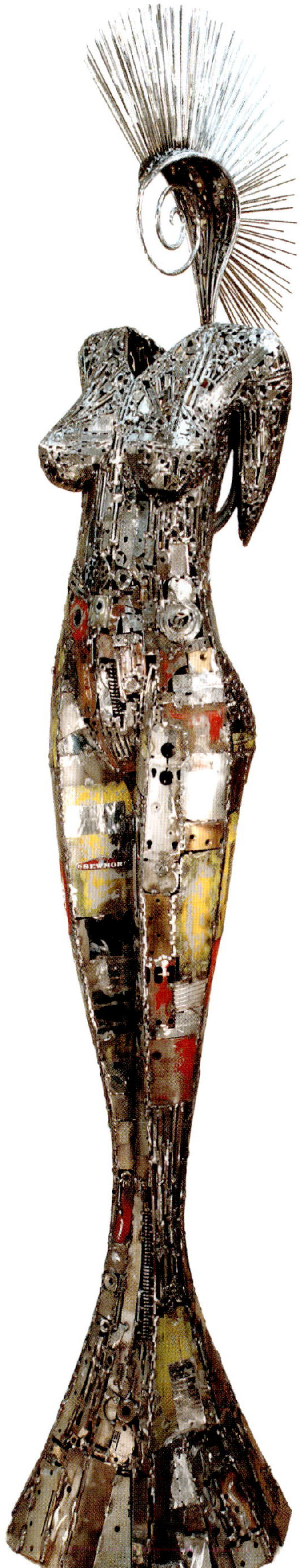

4

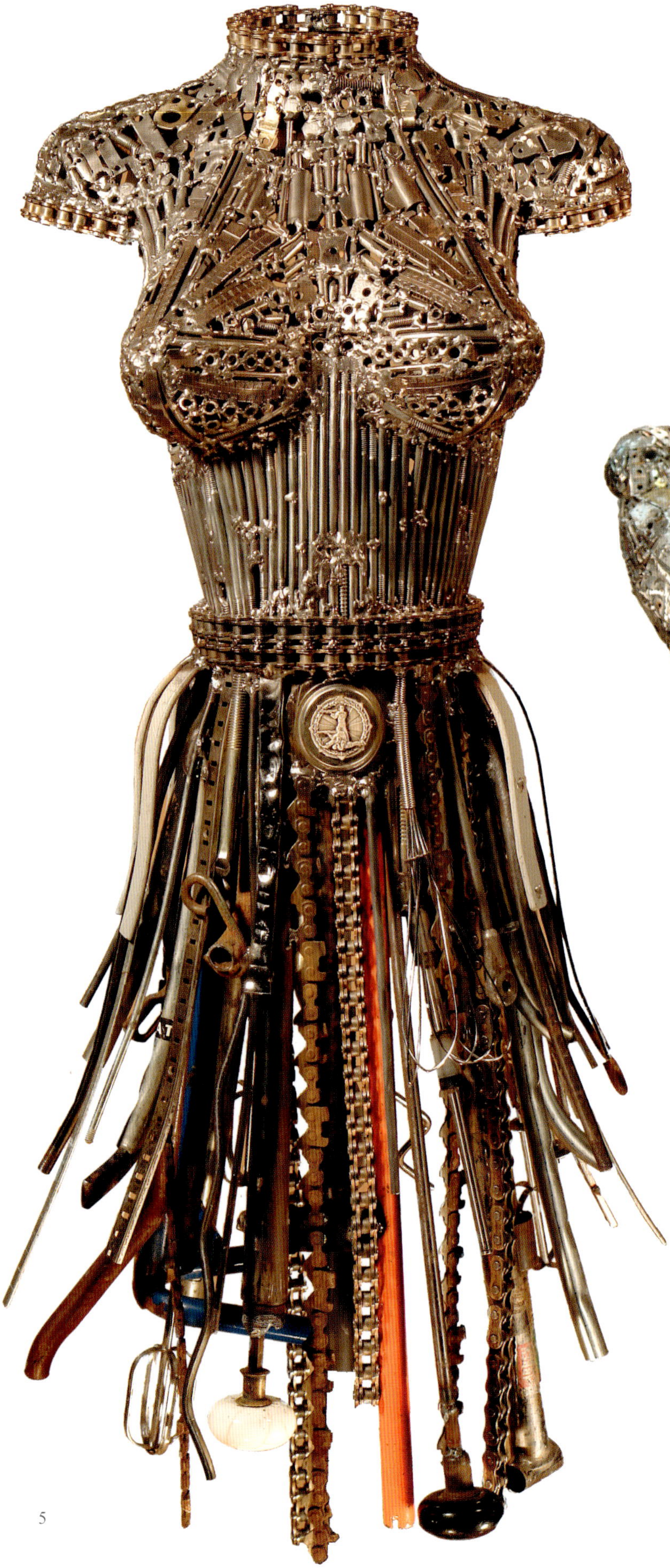

5

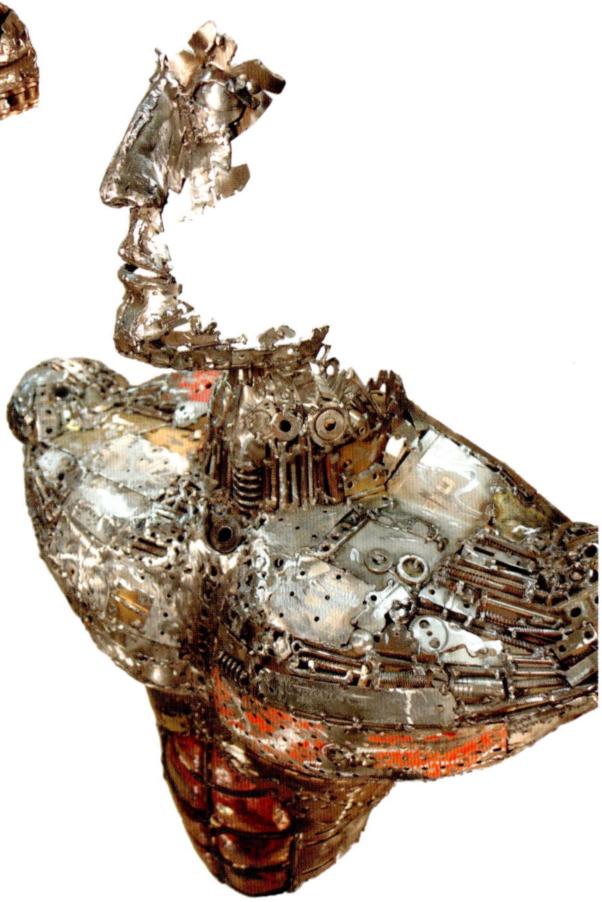

6

5 *Iron Maid'n*, 2006. Recycled metal , 60".
*Photograph by Brian Mock.*

6 *Metal-morphosis*, 2007. Recycled metal, 60".
*Photograph by Brian Mock.*

7 *Ripley's Dog*, 2010. Recycled metal, 60".
*Photograph by Charles Waugh.*

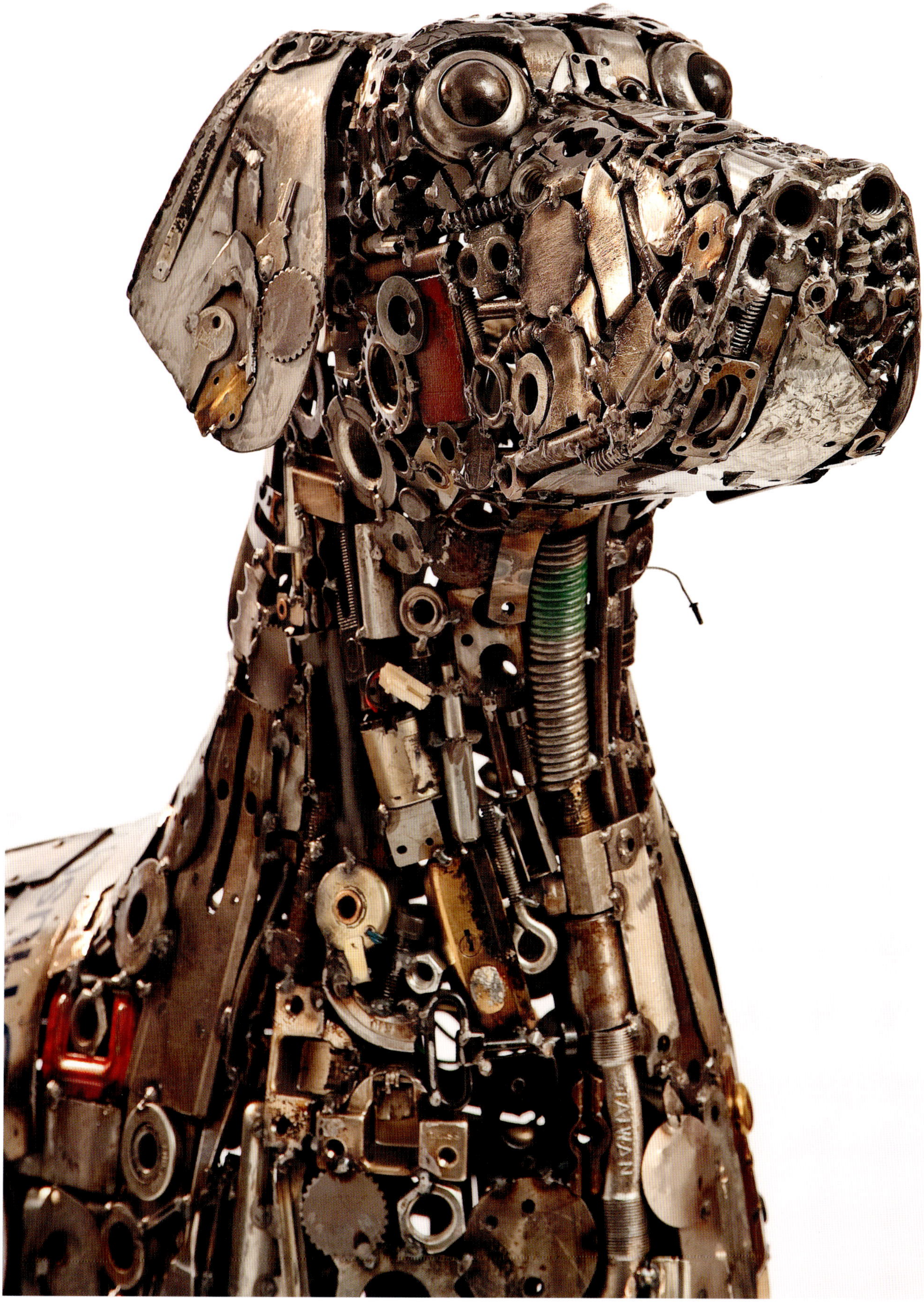


7

# Joe O'Connell & Blessing Hancock

Tucson, Arizona, USA
www.creativemachines.com
www.skyrimstudio.com

*Our work is about finding inspiration in the day-to-day encounter. We look for new ways to live with art – ways in which art solves problems, enriches the human experience, and creates an atmosphere of participation and curiosity. We often begin with the emotion we want to convey and then find ways to give it form. Interactivity lies at the heart of our sculpture and this sometimes takes the form of touch-sensitive circuitry, electronics, and lighting. We like to leave room for people to bring their own meaning to pieces in significant ways.*

As an artistic team, Joe and Blessing encompass both ends of the spectrum. Joe is a technologist with an interest in living systems; Blessing is an environmental designer with an interest in machines. Together they are drawn to the generative logic that underlies mechanical and natural structures. Their work spans public art, technological sculpture, and museum exhibition.

Joe grew up making things and turned that into a career. After a long liberal arts education that spanned four universities he began working for science museums where he designed and built exhibits. He founded Creative Machines in 1995 to design and fabricate interactive exhibits for museums around the world.

Blessing owns the collaborative art and design company Skyrim Studio which focuses on public art and creative consulting. Her background in sculpture and Landscape Architecture shaped her interest in public art. She specializes in site integration, ensuring that the experience of art extends beyond the boundaries of sculpture.

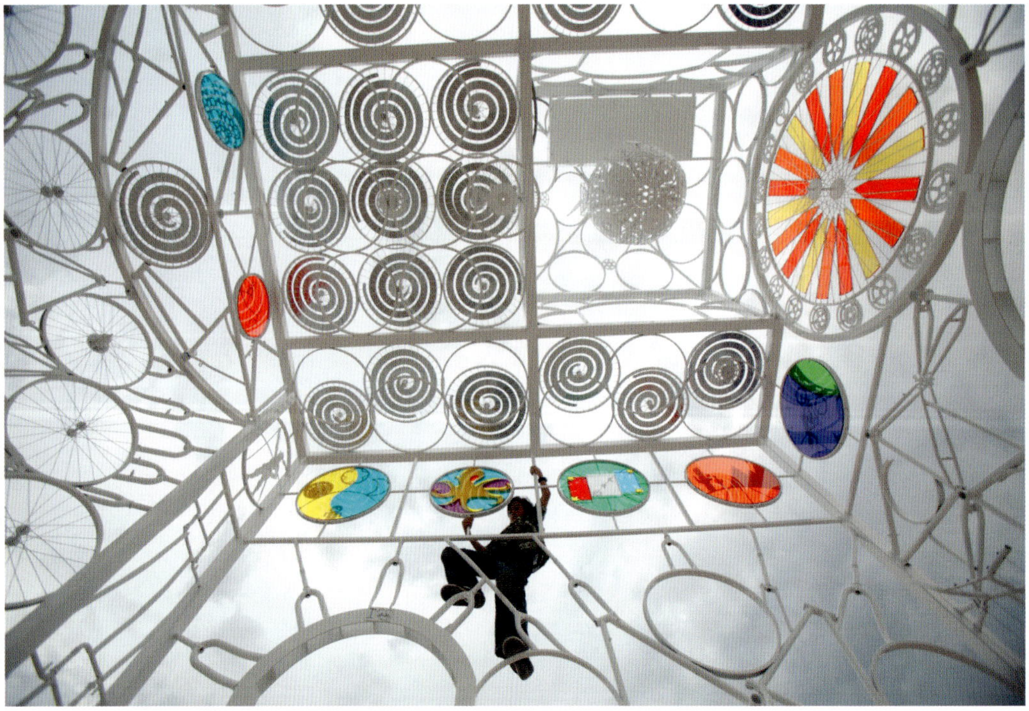

1

2

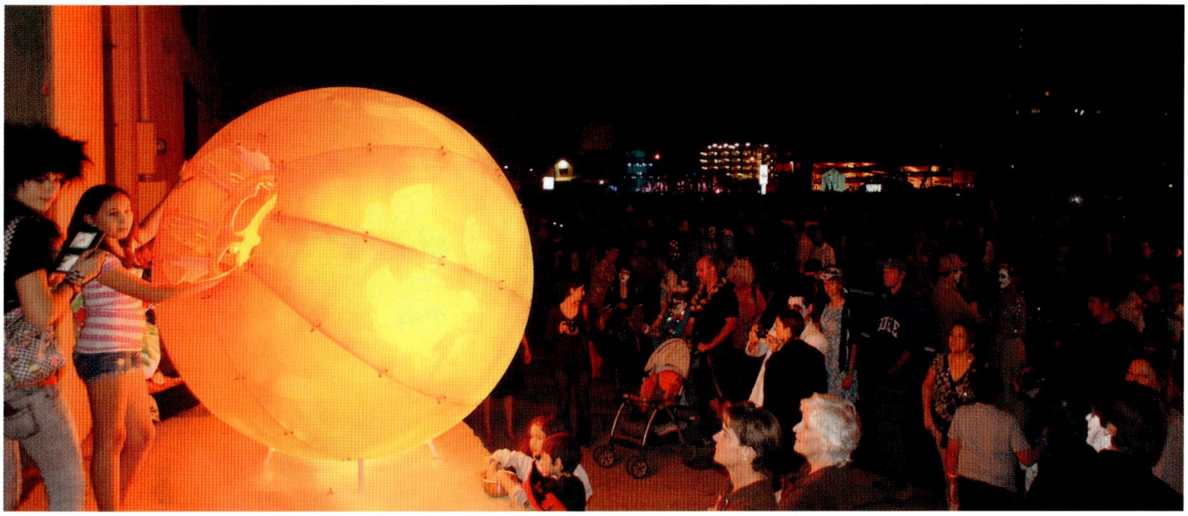

3

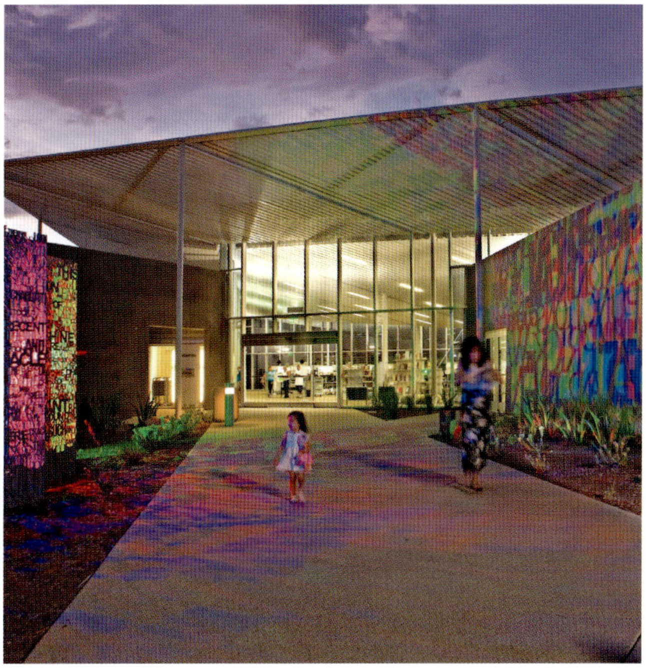

1 *Bike Church*, 2009. Steel, bicycle parts, acrylic, LED lighting, 12' x 12' x 22'. *Photograph by David Sanders.*

2 *SeedPods*, 2010. Steel, acrylic, LED lighting, 6' x 6' x 6', five sculptures total. *Photograph by Blessing Hancock.*

3 *Wondrous* (detail), 2008. Galvanized steel, LEDs, 9' x 19' x 3'. *Photograph by David Sanders.*

4 *Public Drums*, 2008. Bulletproof polycarbonate, LEDs, sounds, 30" x 21" x 21". *Photograph by Amy Haskell.*

5 *Desert O*, 2004. Steel, frosted acrylic, LEDs, electronics, secret button, 81" x 72" x 19". *Photograph by Amy Haskell.*

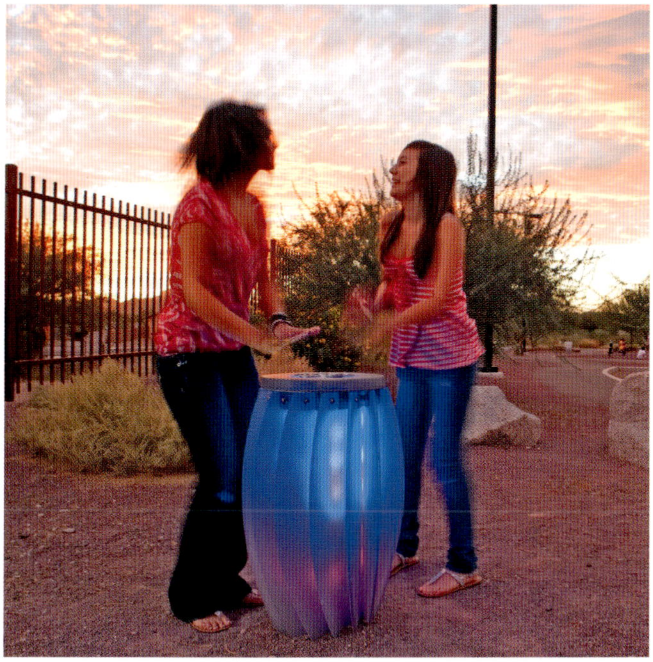

4

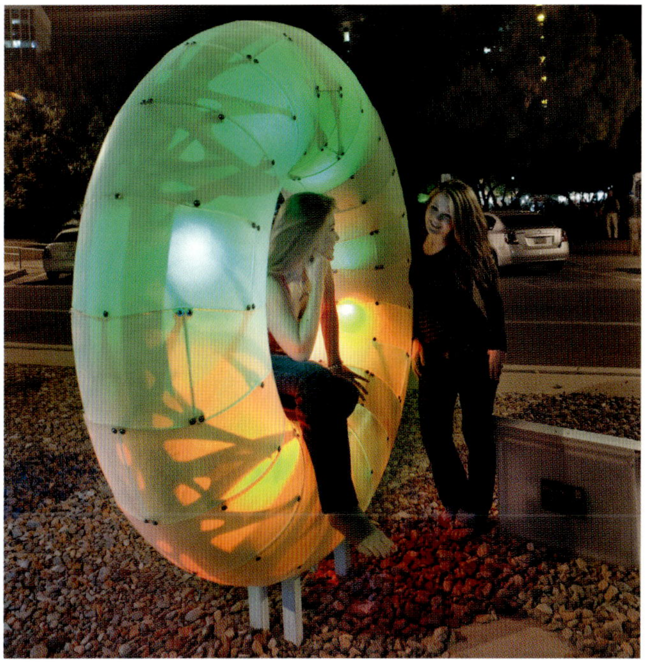

5

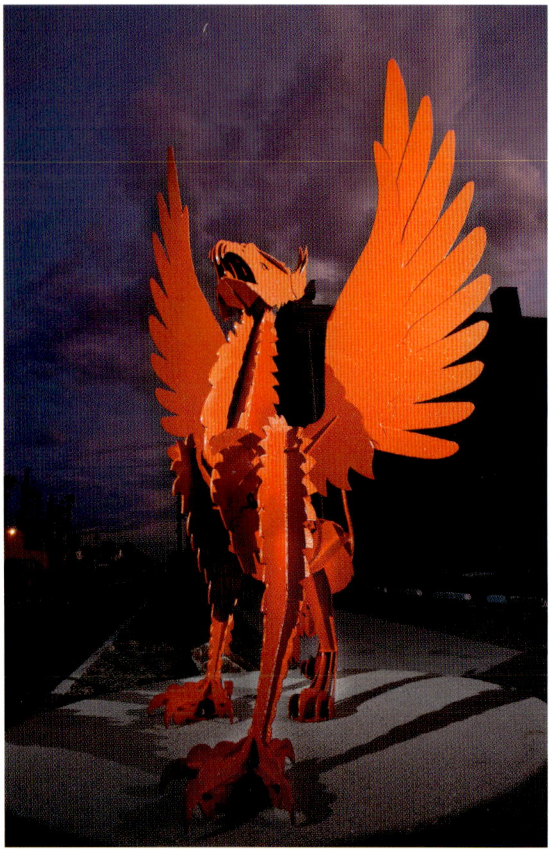

6

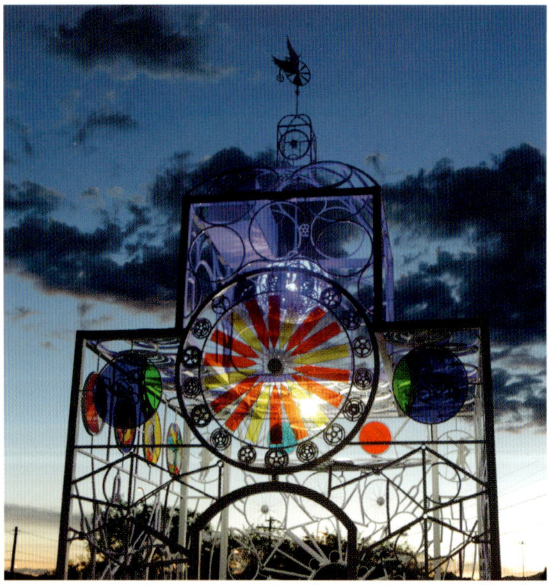

7

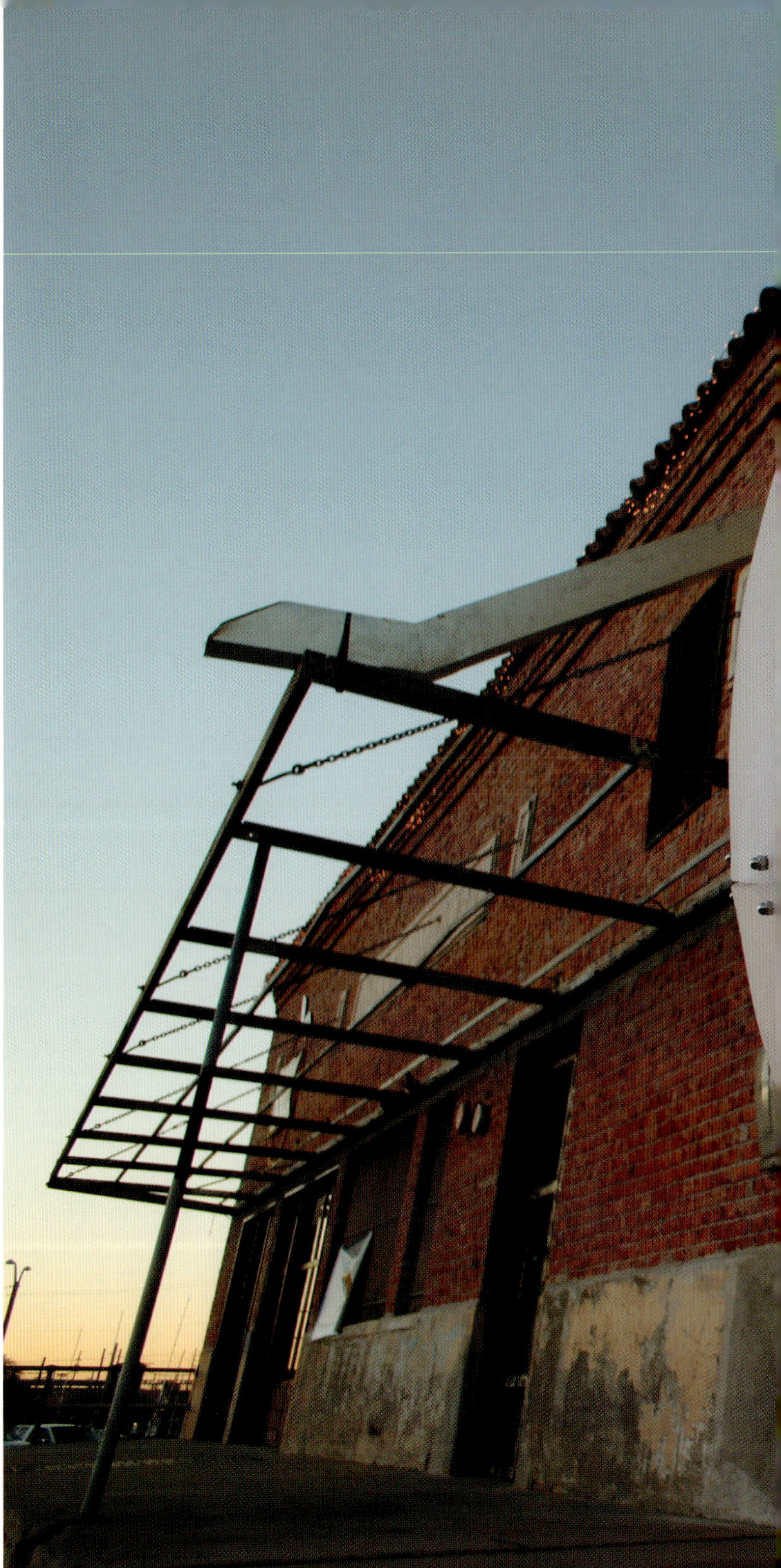

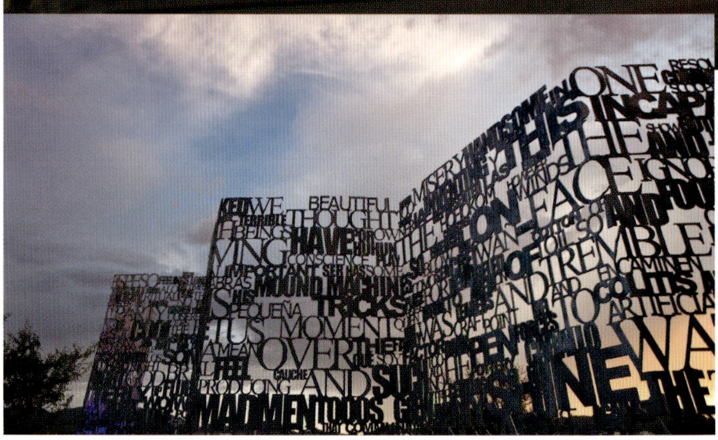
ONE
BEAUTIFUL
THOUGHT
HAVE
CONSCIENCE
MOMENT
OVER
FEEL
PRODUCING
AND

8

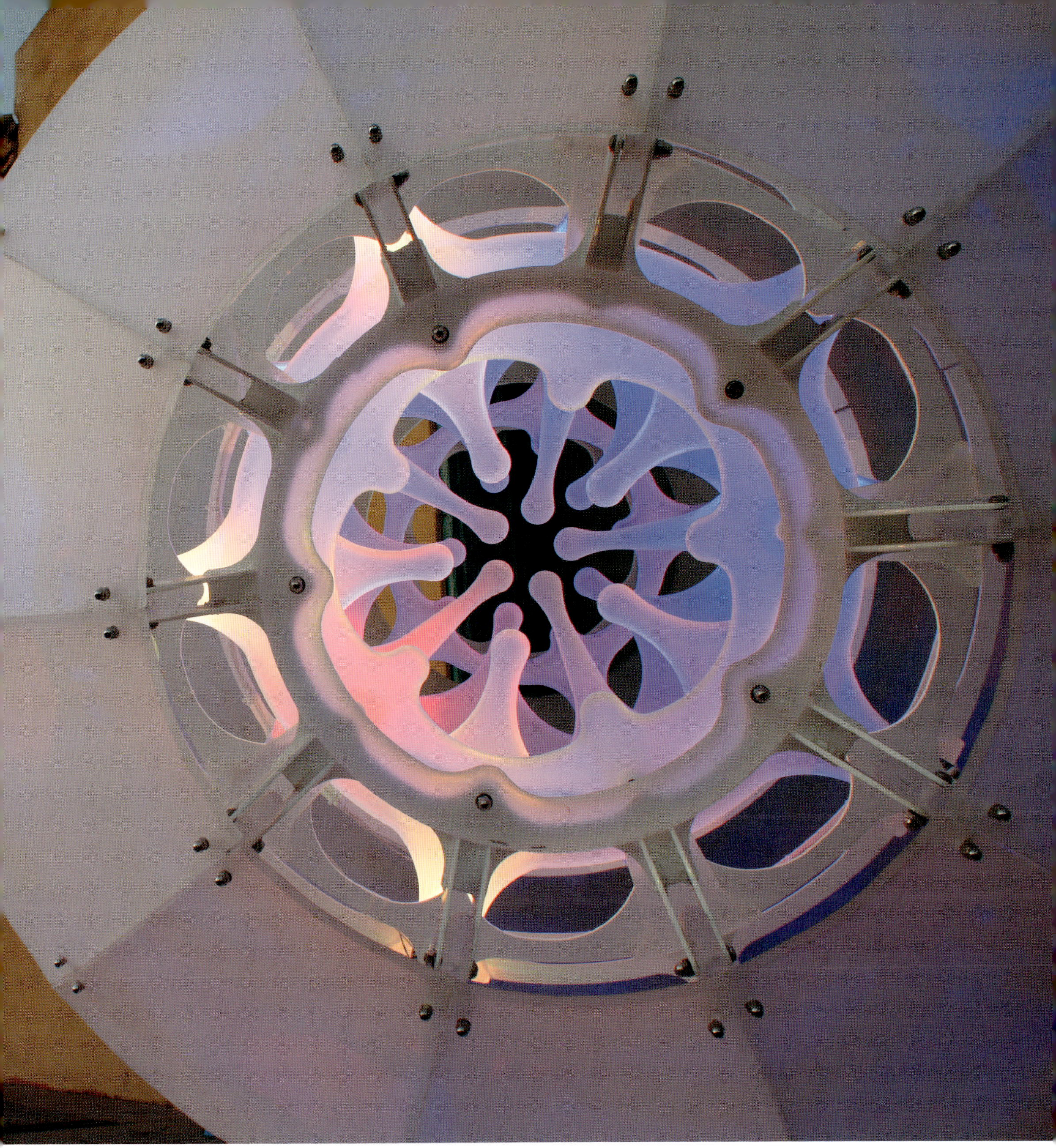

9

6 *Toby*, 2009. Welded steel, LEDs, concrete texture (footprints), 144" x 84" x 96". *Photograph by Amy Haskell.*

7 *Bike Church* (detail), 2009. *Photograph by David Sanders.*

8 *Wondrous,* 2008. Galvanized steel, LEDs, 9' x 19' x 3'. *Photograph by David Sanders.*

9 *SeedPods*, 2010. Steel, acrylic, LED lighting, 6' x 6' x 6', five sculptures total. *Photograph by Blessing Hancock.*

# James P. O'Neal

Bridgeton, New Jersey, USA
www.jamesonealwoodcarving.com

*Born and raised in Delaware, I graduated high school, served three years in the USMC, and then worked a variety of blue collar jobs; the last twenty plus years have been spent working at an oil refinery. I've always enjoyed working with wood and have always been intrigued with figurative sculpture. For the past five years I have lived in a wooded area of southern New Jersey and it was soon after moving here, in my late 40s, that the opportunity and inspiration came to finally attempt a sculpture from a large piece of wood.*

*My sculptures are about the wood. I sculpt in wood because I find that the beauty of the wood itself always captures the attention much more than the subject being portrayed in the sculpture. Though imperfect and difficult to sculpt, the amazingly diverse grain patterns, colors, knots, and assorted natural defects always combine to result in a totally unique piece.*

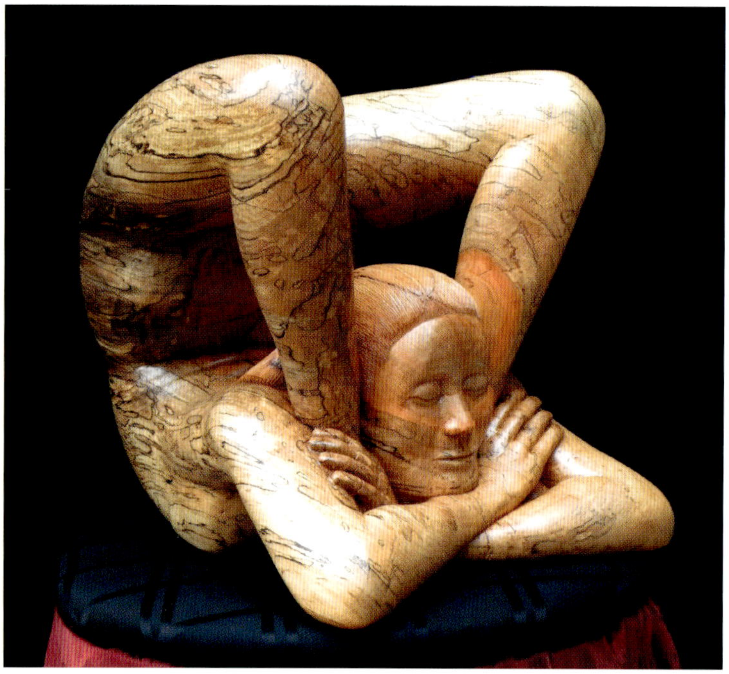

1

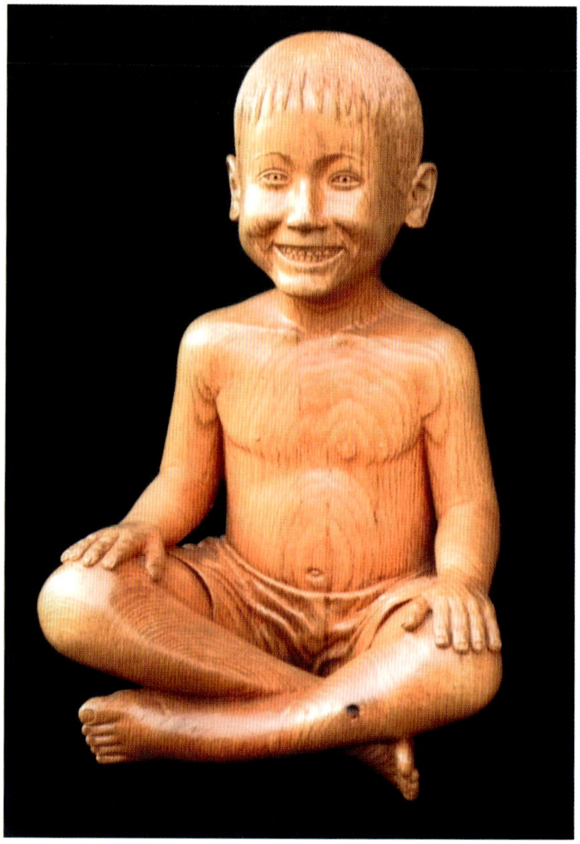

3

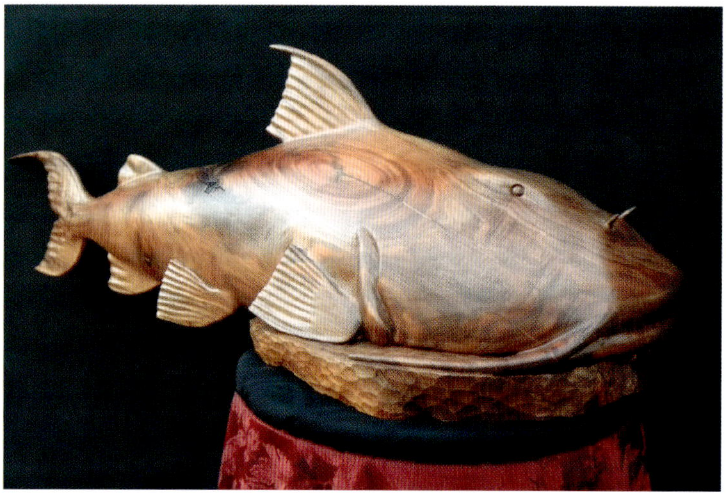

2

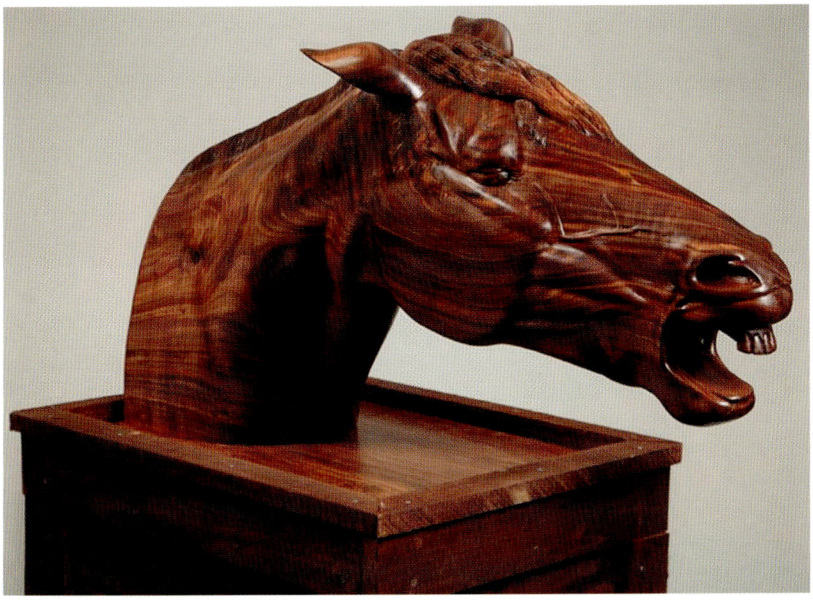

4

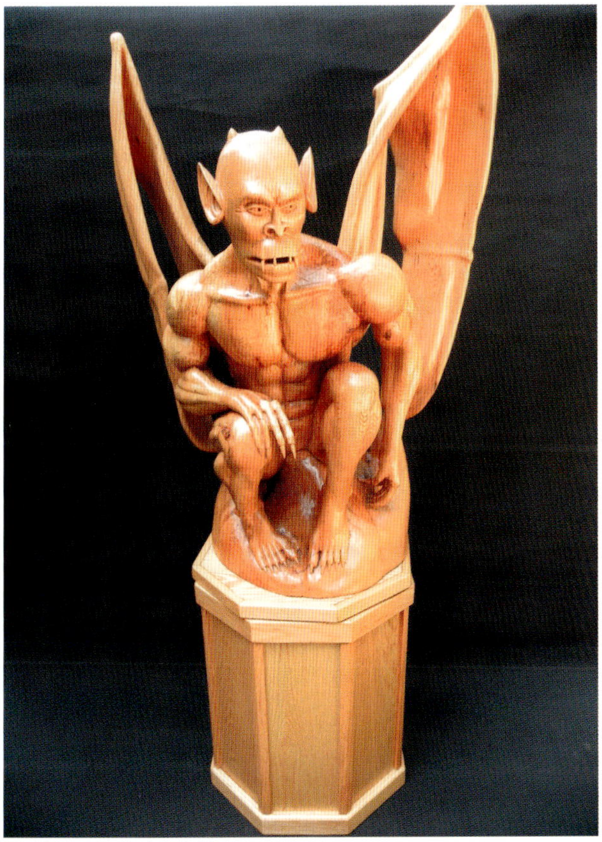

5

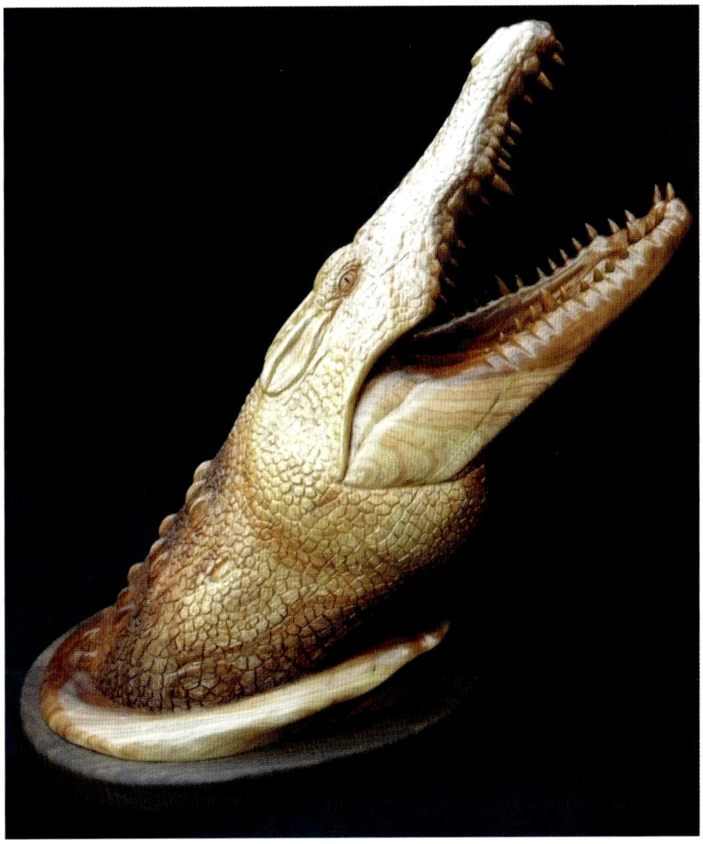

6

1 *Contortionist*, 2010. Sycamore, 18" h. x 25" w. x 17" d. *Photograph by James O'Neal.*

2 *Goonch Catfish*, 2010. Black walnut, 17" h. x 65" w. x 24"d. *Photograph by James O'Neal.*

3 *Bug*, 2010. Red oak, 24" h. x 16" w. x 16" d. *Photograph by James O'Neal.*

4 *Hobo,* 2010. Black walnut, 67" h. x 39" w. x 18" d. *Photograph by Jack Williams.*

5 *Gargoyle*, 2008. Red oak, 50" h. x 38" w. x 24" d. *Photograph by James O'Neal.*

6 *Croc*, 2010. Japanese zelcova, 31" h. x 37" w. x 18" d. *Photograph by James O'Neal.*

# Judy Onofrio

Rochester, Minnesota, USA
www.judyonofrio.com

*I have lived and worked in Rochester, Minnesota, for the past forty years. My career began in ceramic sculpture, transitioned into skeleton-like architectural structures and large-scale fire performances, and then, in the 1990s, I began working in large-scale figurative mosaic sculpture. I received the Bush Foundation Artist Fellowship in 1999, and the McKnight Foundation Distinguished Artist Award in 2005.*

*In the last four years, I have used my studio practice to process my experience of mortality, renewal, and healing after a cancer experience. My work through that time mirrored my journey to regain my health and, for me, was about my healing process and the celebration of being fully alive.*

*My current work has transformed into abstracted assemblages with an emphasis on animal bones. The process of working with animal bones revealed to me an increasing awareness of their organic beauty and the life they once supported, life that is still visible in the curves and surfaces of the bone. Through my intuitive studio practice, I sought to move toward a universal experience of beauty that would speak of the transitory nature of life.*

*In my work, fertility and eroticism live side by side with mortality and fragility. It is my hope that this work will evoke not only a memory of the Garden of Eden, but celebrate the ongoing cycle of ever-changing life, full of expectation and promise.*

1

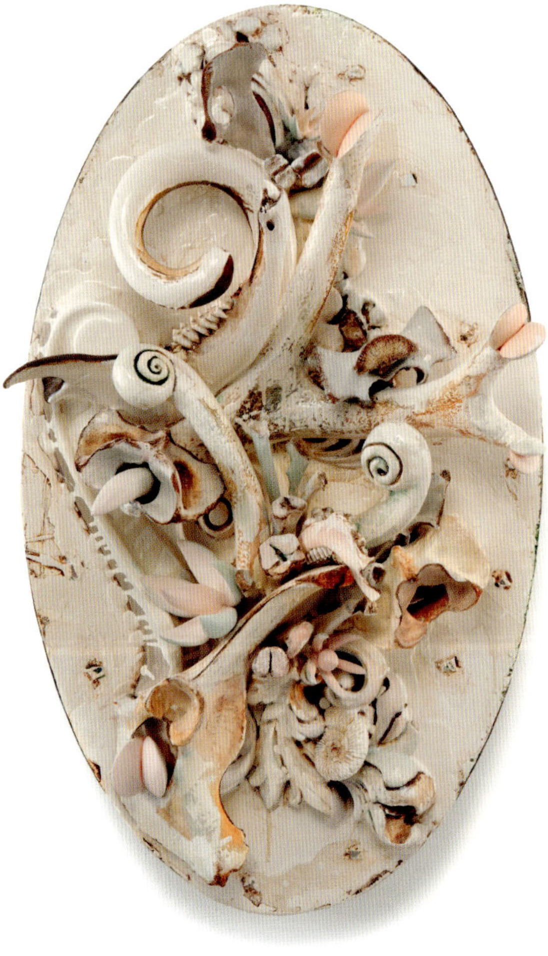

2

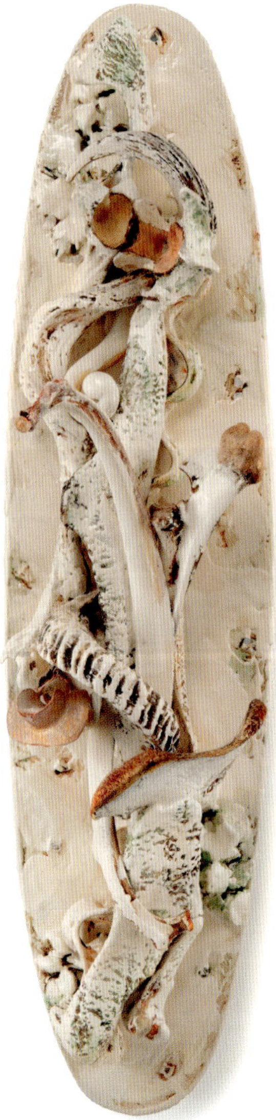

1 *Fern*, 2010. Mixed media, 42" h. x 28" w. x 18" d. *Photograph by Rik Sferra.*

2 *Vine*, 2010. Mixed media, 44" h. x 11.5" w. x 9" d. *Photograph by Rik Sferra.*

3 *Compote*, 2010. Mixed media, 21" h. x 24" w. x 17" d. *Photograph by Rik Sferra.*

4 *Bowl*, 2011. Mixed media, 22.5" h. x 30.5" w. x 26" d. *Photograph by Rik Sferra.*

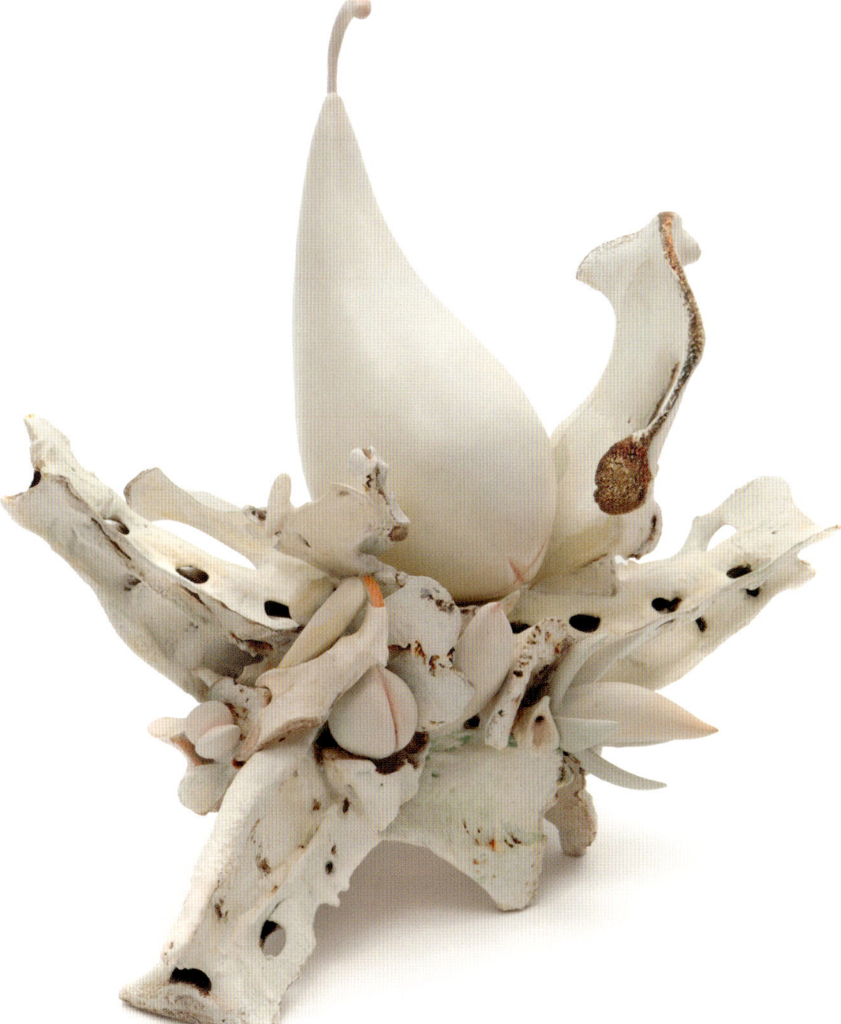

3

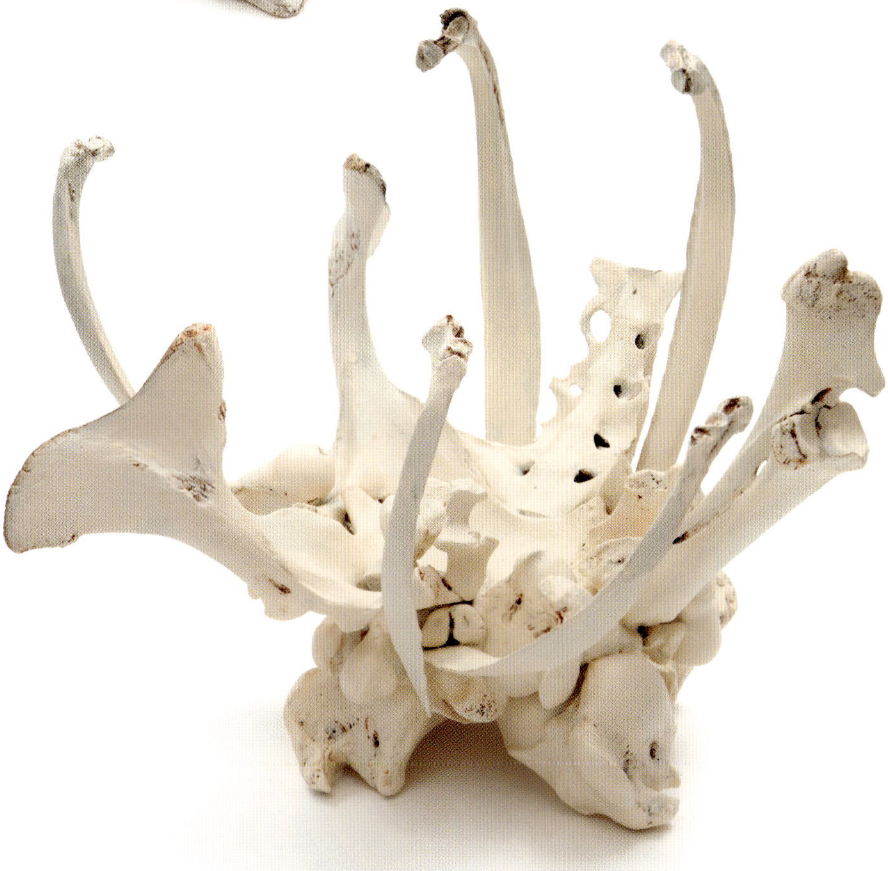

4

# Steven Panarelli

Homer, Alaska, USA
steven-panarelli.fineartamerica.com

Steven Panarelli grew up in a small town south of Boston surrounded by dense deciduous forests and colonial homes. When he wasn't exploring the woods, woodworking, or playing music he was studying the ancient art of bonsai. Wire trees were discovered by accident when one particular zero below night in his school bus home in Homer, Alaska, left his live trees frozen and lifeless. Using scrap wire pulled from an alternator to produce the first tree and his passion for the shapes took hold. Now many trees later and miles of wire behind him, Steven has work all over the world. Steven continues to make his trees in his home tucked amongst the spruce in Homer, where he works as a special education teacher.

Steven's work has been described as a meeting point between machine and nature. His style of wire trees is a totally self-taught process. It can be a very physical process in the creation of each tree and each piece is original. Wire has been the perfect medium to achieve the natural taper we see in each tree, from the base of the tree to the last leaf bud. Guided by the rules of traditional bonsai, he aims for a realistic yet stylized look of growth that was formed in the most extreme of natures elements, each telling their own story. The ultimate goal is produce the feeling of wabi, the inner stillness of being alone in the woods with truth, virtue, and beauty.

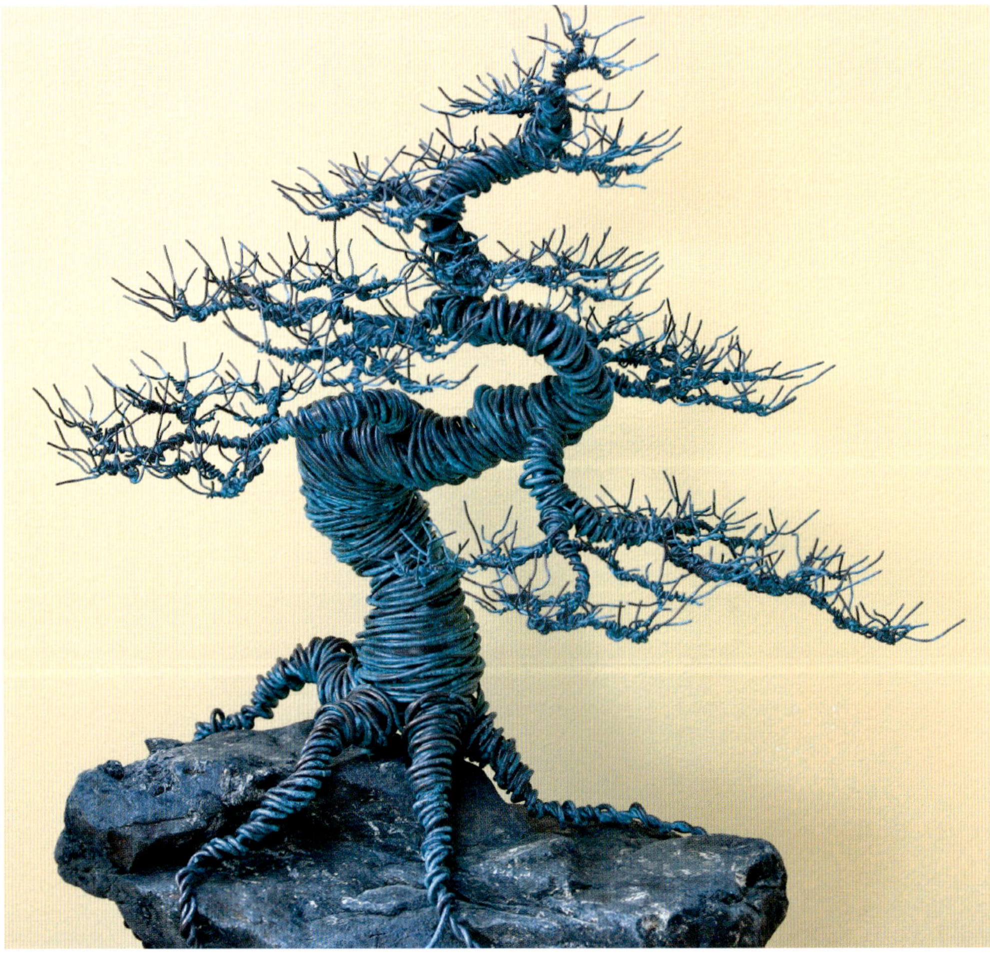

1

1 *Holdfast,* 2009. Copper, stone, 19" x 21" x 12". *Photograph by Steven Panarelli.*

2 *Naga*, 2010. Copper, stone, 31" x 25" x 22". *Photograph by Steven Panarelli.*

3 *Full Son*, 2008. Steel, stone, 11" x 15" x 10". *Photograph by Steven Panarelli.*

4 *Anna*, 2011. Steel, copper, stone,16" x 26" x 10". *Photograph by Steven Panarelli.*

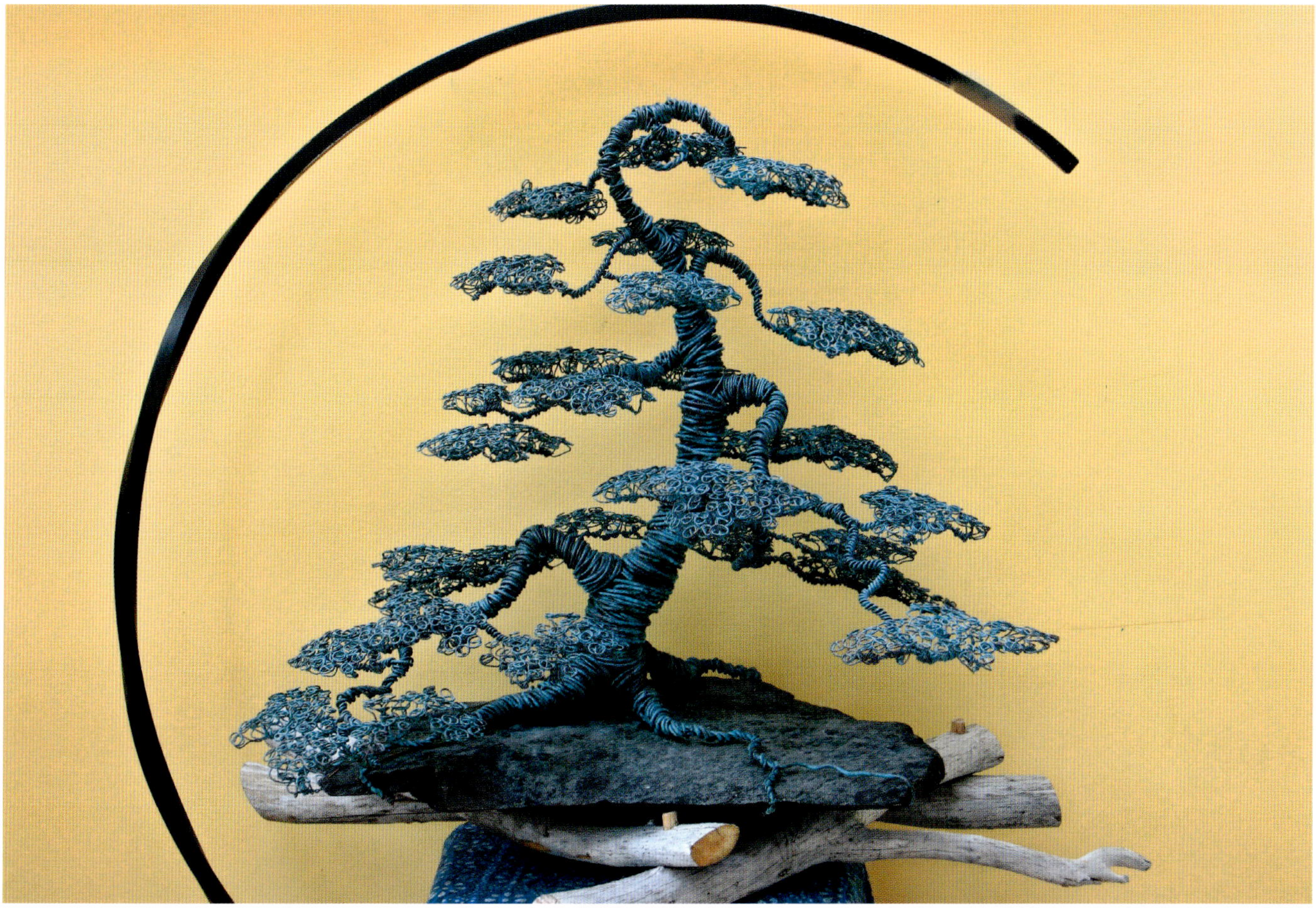

2

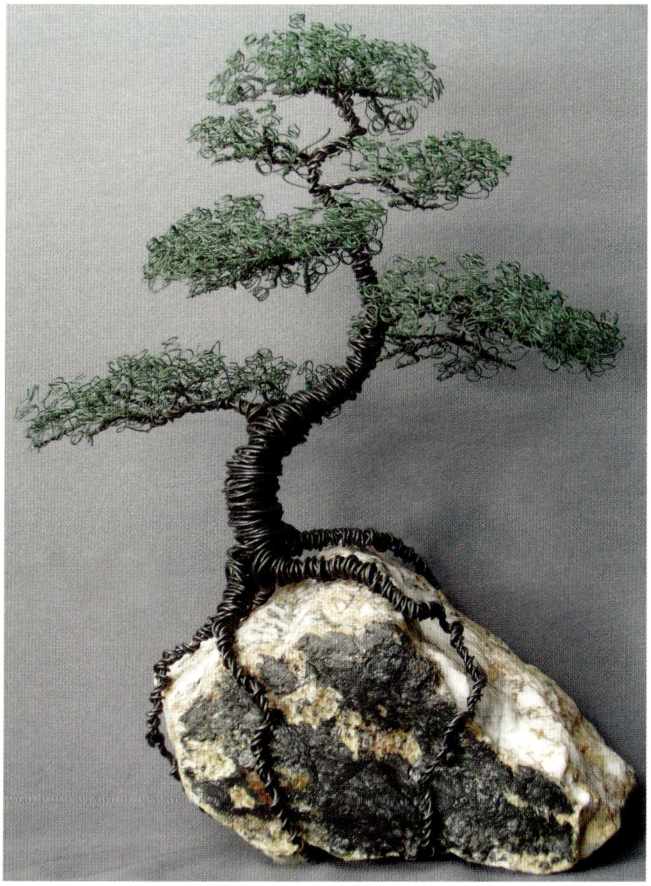

3

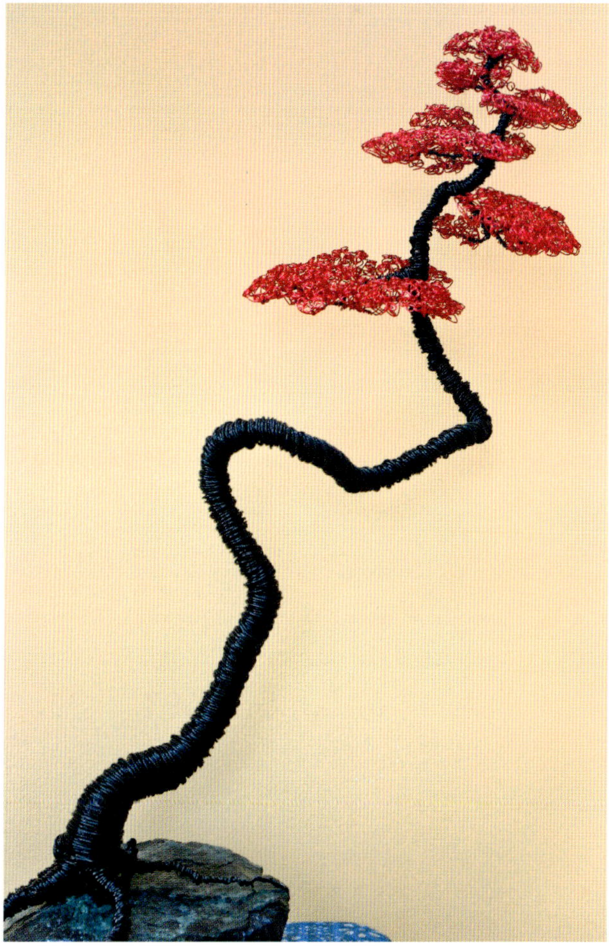

4

# Arimathea Noel Pappas

Kamloops, British Columbia, Canada
www.soulfulcreationart.com

Arimathea Pappas, a Canadian and British Columbian, began her artistic quest at an early age, exploring life through her love of sculpture, drawing, and photography. Her extensive travels both on land and as a Master Scuba Diver, have provided her a unique vision. Her present focus on the ceramic arts has been driven by participation in various workshops, ever improving her technique. An exhibiting member of the Thompson Valley Potters Guild, she has enjoyed considerable success amongst her peers and the art collecting community.

*As a sculptress, I like to feel a connection with my work and have devoted much effort into capturing the sensual beauty of the female form. The challenge of bringing the subject to life is ongoing making sculpting my most passionate medium. The inspiration for my work is purely from the soul using love and enthusiasm to harness the three dimensions. Each creation is an evolution of beauty, rhythm, and proportion that symbolizes passion, new beginnings, and the quest for spiritual evolution.*

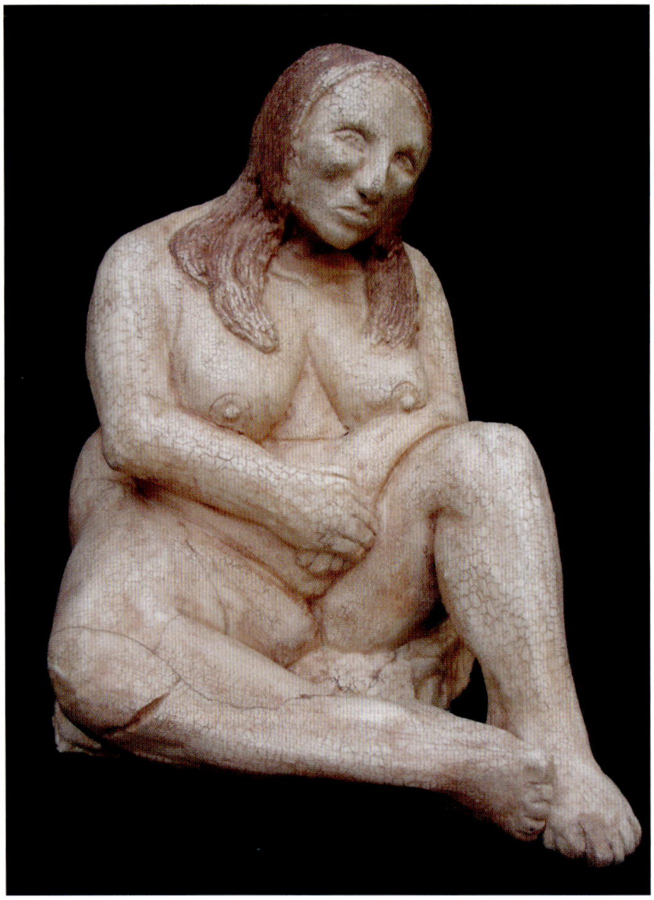

1

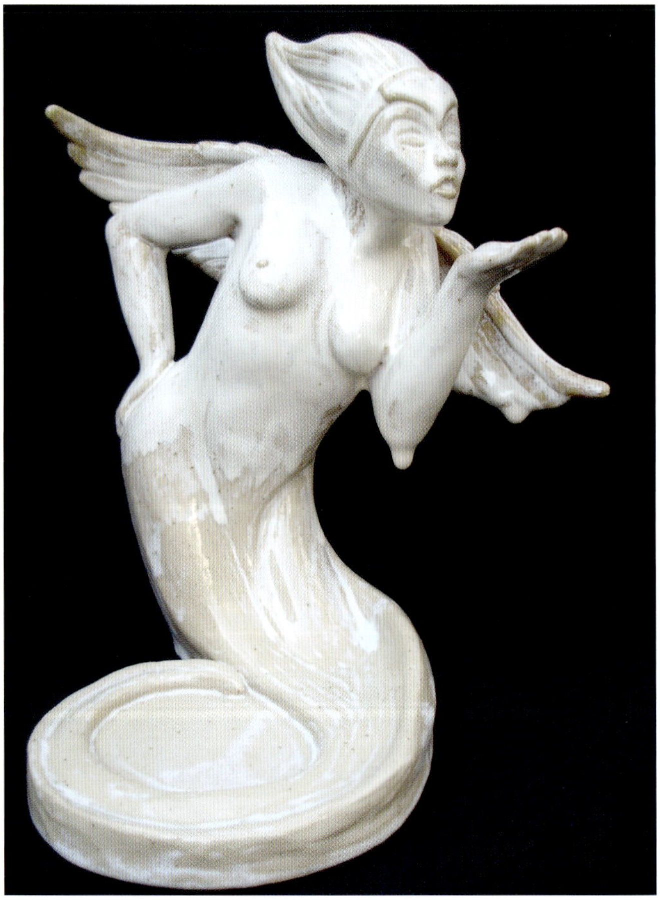

2

1 *Donii*, 1998. Ceramic, 9". *Photograph by Arimathea Noel Pappas.*

2 *Elemental Goddess of Wind*, 2010, ceramic, 9.5". *Photograph by Arimathea Noel Pappas.*

3 *Struggle and Peace*, 1997. Ceramic, 5.75". *Photograph by Arimathea Noel Pappas.*

4 *Earth Guardian*, 2010. Ceramic, 9". *Photograph by Arimathea Noel Pappas.*

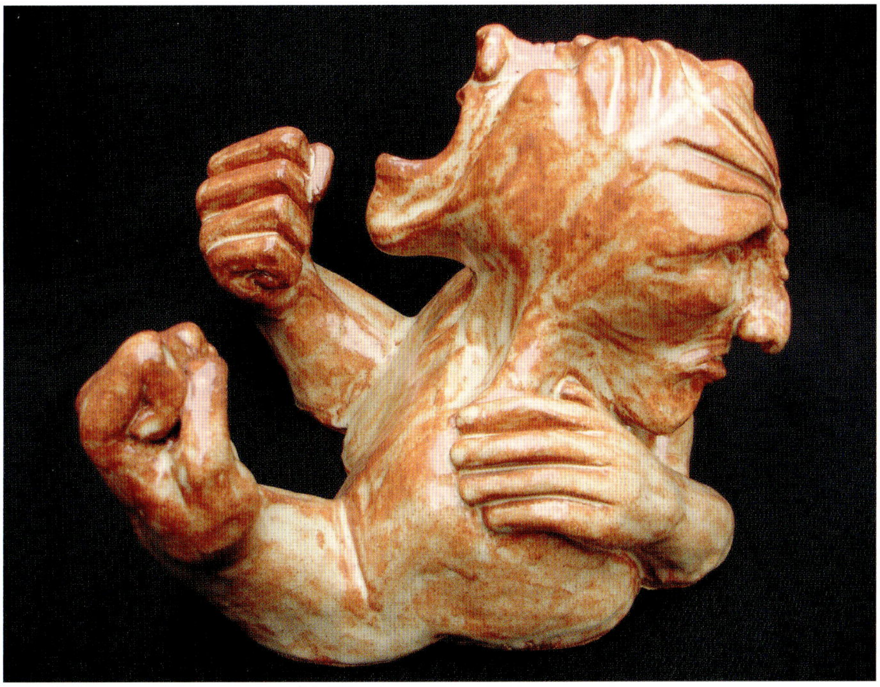

3

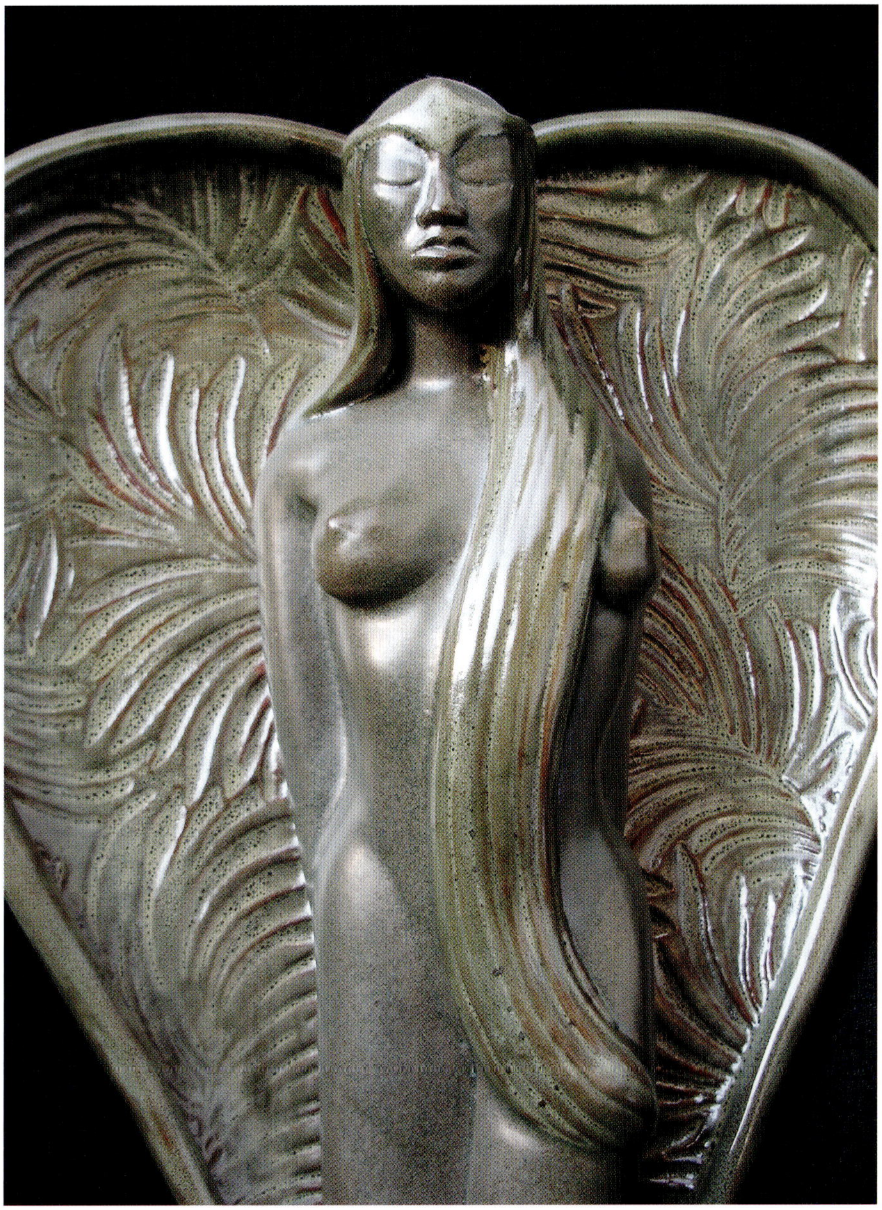

4

# Lane Patterson

Tucson, Arizona, USA
www.lanesart.com

*I was born in rural Illinois on November 7, 1943. My educational background includes degrees in art, design, and education. I taught design at Mankato State University (now Minnesota State) in Minnesota for about 20 years before moving to Arizona. I was an antiques dealer for about 8 years, retiring from that in 1999 and beginning to make art (lamps and figural sculpture) seriously. I show in assorted galleries throughout the Southwest, and do several art shows every year.*

*My father operated an auto salvage, so I grew up around lots of metal with rust or other patinas. I saw beauty and pattern in some of those surfaces, and naturally developed the ability to see forms as resembling objects other than what they what they were intended to be. Today, I look at junk and see body parts, lamp parts, or sculpture parts, so I'm what is known as a recycle artist. My figural pieces are all "anatomically complete," which often suggests humor or social commentary, since I often title them to have verbal/visual puns.*

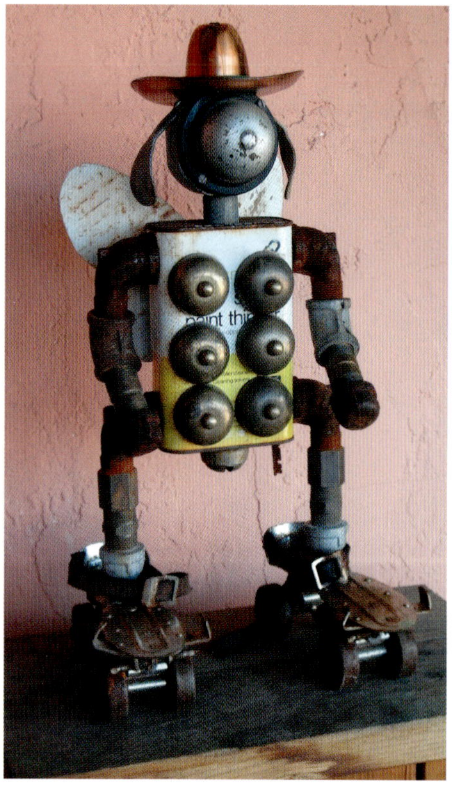

1

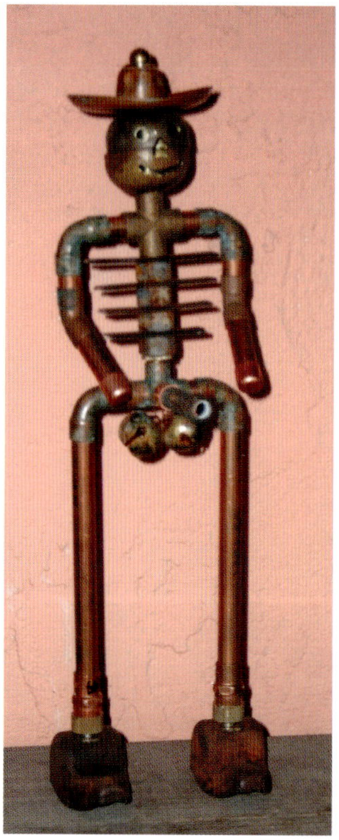

2

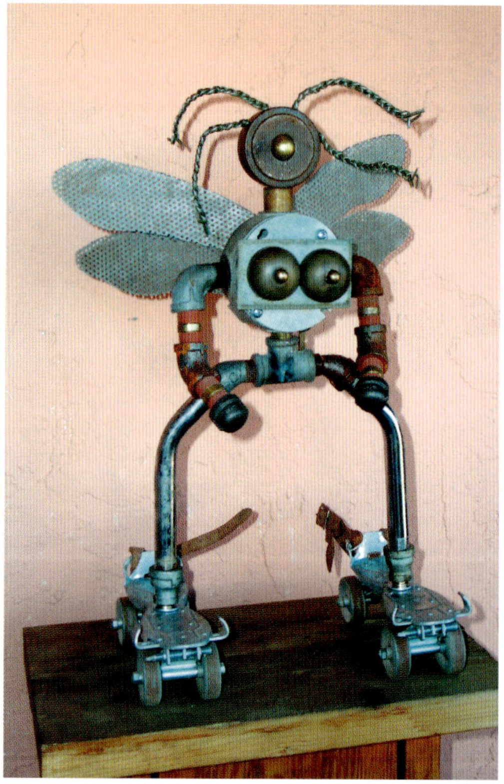

3

1 *Bitch on Wheels*, 2009. Recycled metal parts, 21" tall. *Photograph by Lane Patterson.*

2 *Dead Cowboy*, 2011. Recycled metal parts, 2". *Photograph by Lane Patterson.*

3 *Female with Dreadlocks*, 2005. Recycled metal parts, 15". *Photograph by Lane Patterson.*

4 *Kneeling Fairy*, 2010. Recycled metal parts, 14". *Photograph by Lane Patterson.*

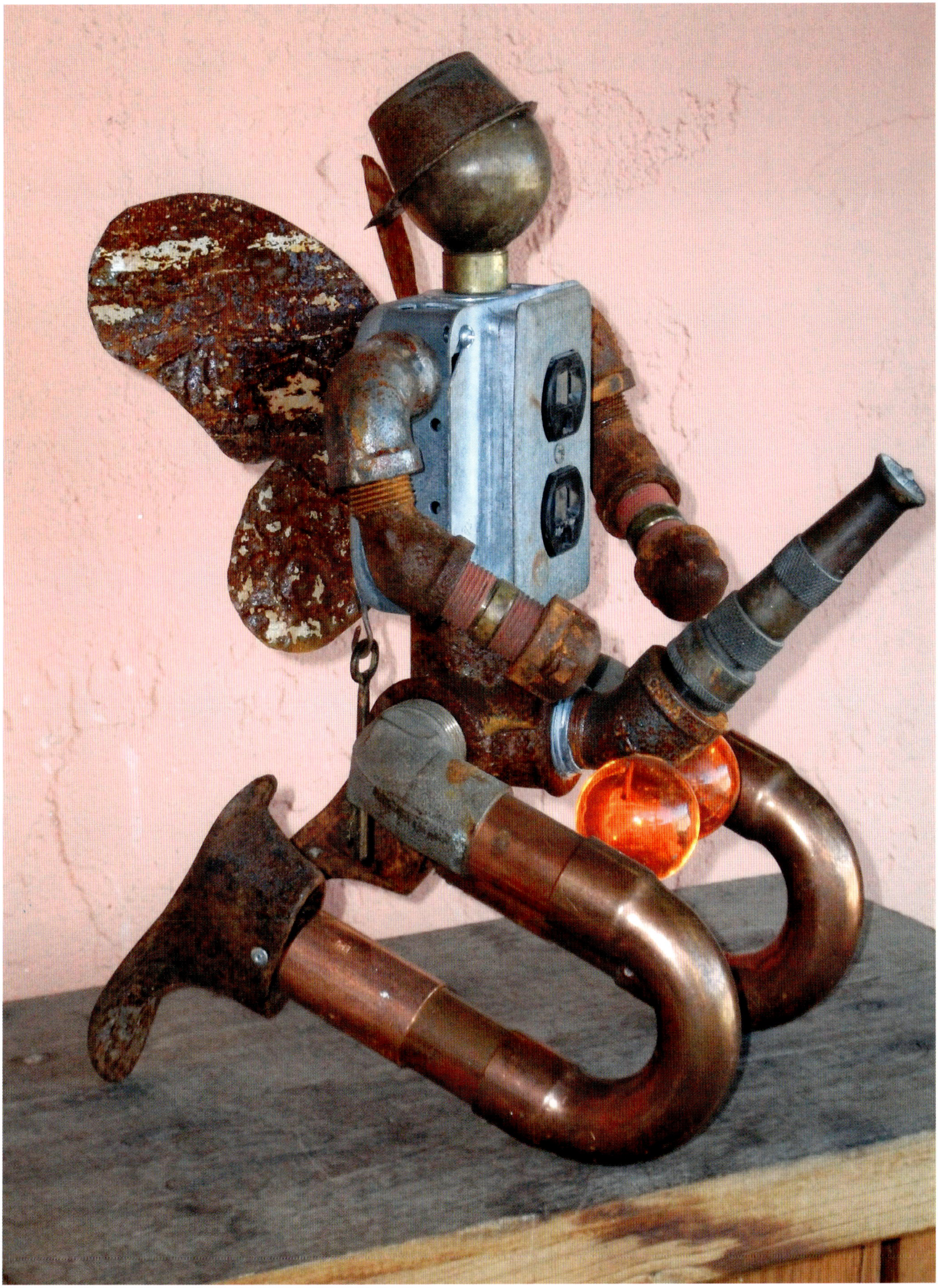

4

# Jolanta Izabela Pawlak

Chicago, Illinois, USA
www.jolantaizabela.com

*I was born in Poland and educated in Europe and the U.S. with double master's degrees in sculpture and photography from the Academy of Arts, Poznan, Poland. I am a professional member of the International Sculpture Association and have exhibited my work in museums and galleries throughout Europe, the U.S., and the Caribbean. For five years I had my own successful gallery on the island of Curacao in the Netherland Antilles.*

*I work consciously, employing both traditional and innovative techniques. Obsessed with texture, I work in various mediums: sculpture, jewelry, drawing, painting, photography, and mixed-media installations. I like to get deep and personal with my models' stories. This becomes a therapeutic experience as well as a social commentary, forcing contemplation of our connection to each other and the viewing of my work well beyond optical appearances. Each piece celebrates different aspects of a subject, creating a bridge between the intimate and public faces of an individual or object. The process of transforming a piece from clay into wax, from the inside out, acts as a translation of the inner vision into a new reality. I create small, sculptural necklaces in silver for the body, and large-scale pieces cast in bronze or iron to expand the scale for larger installation. I plan my exhibitions so the viewer has the freedom to experience a piece of my work from their own perspective, creating a lasting impression.*

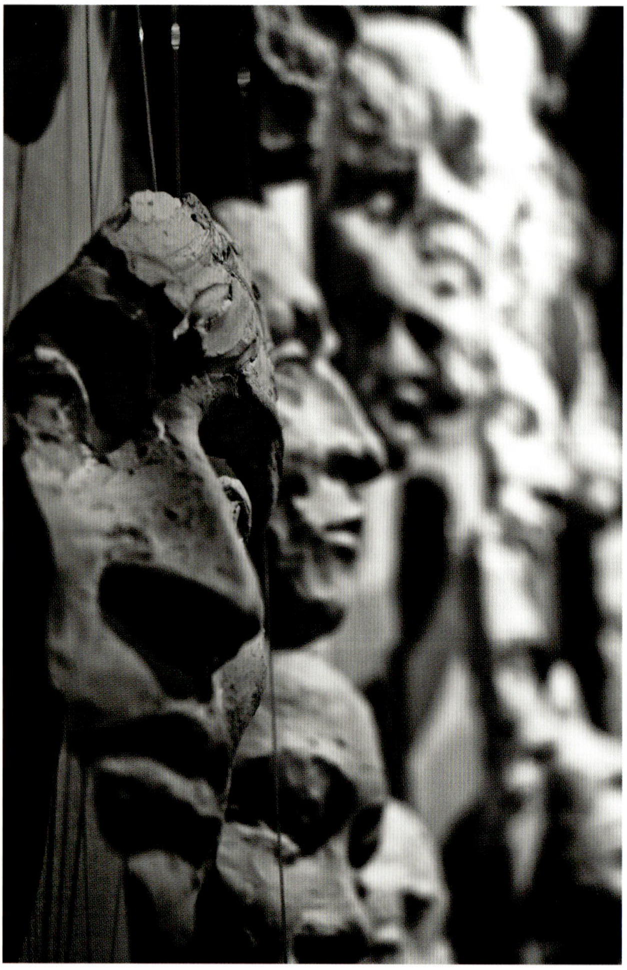

1

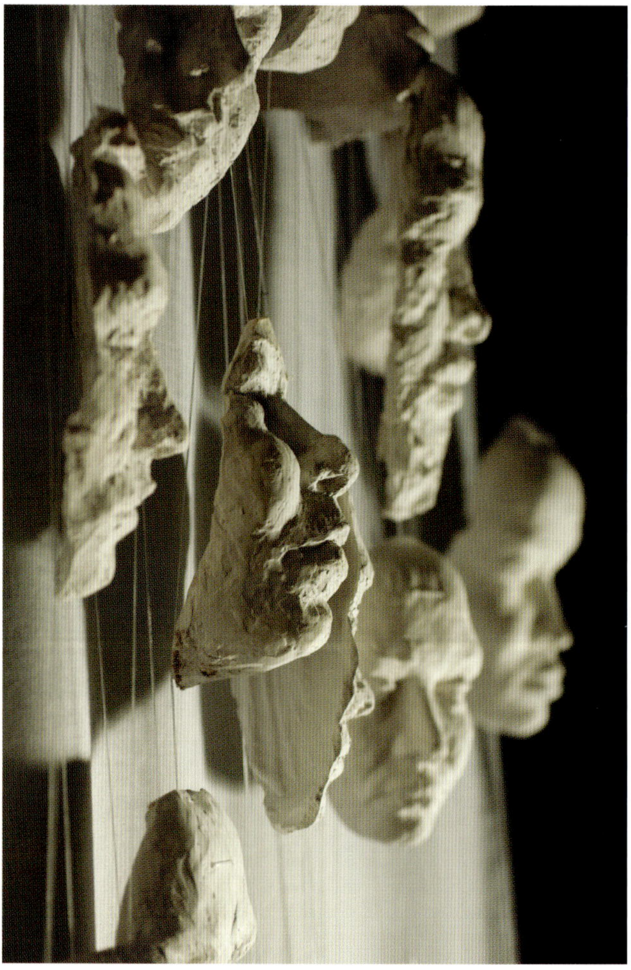

2

1 *You May Know Each Other*, 2011. Glazed ceramic, photography, digital projection, 58" w. x 16' h. *Photograph by Jolanta Izabela Pawlak.*

2 *You May Know Each Other*, 2011. Glazed ceramic, photography, digital projection, 58" w. x 16' h. *Photograph by Jolanta Izabela Pawlak.*

3 *You May Know Each Other*, 2011. Glazed ceramic, photography, digital projection, 58" w. x 16' h. *Photograph by Jolanta Izabela Pawlak.*

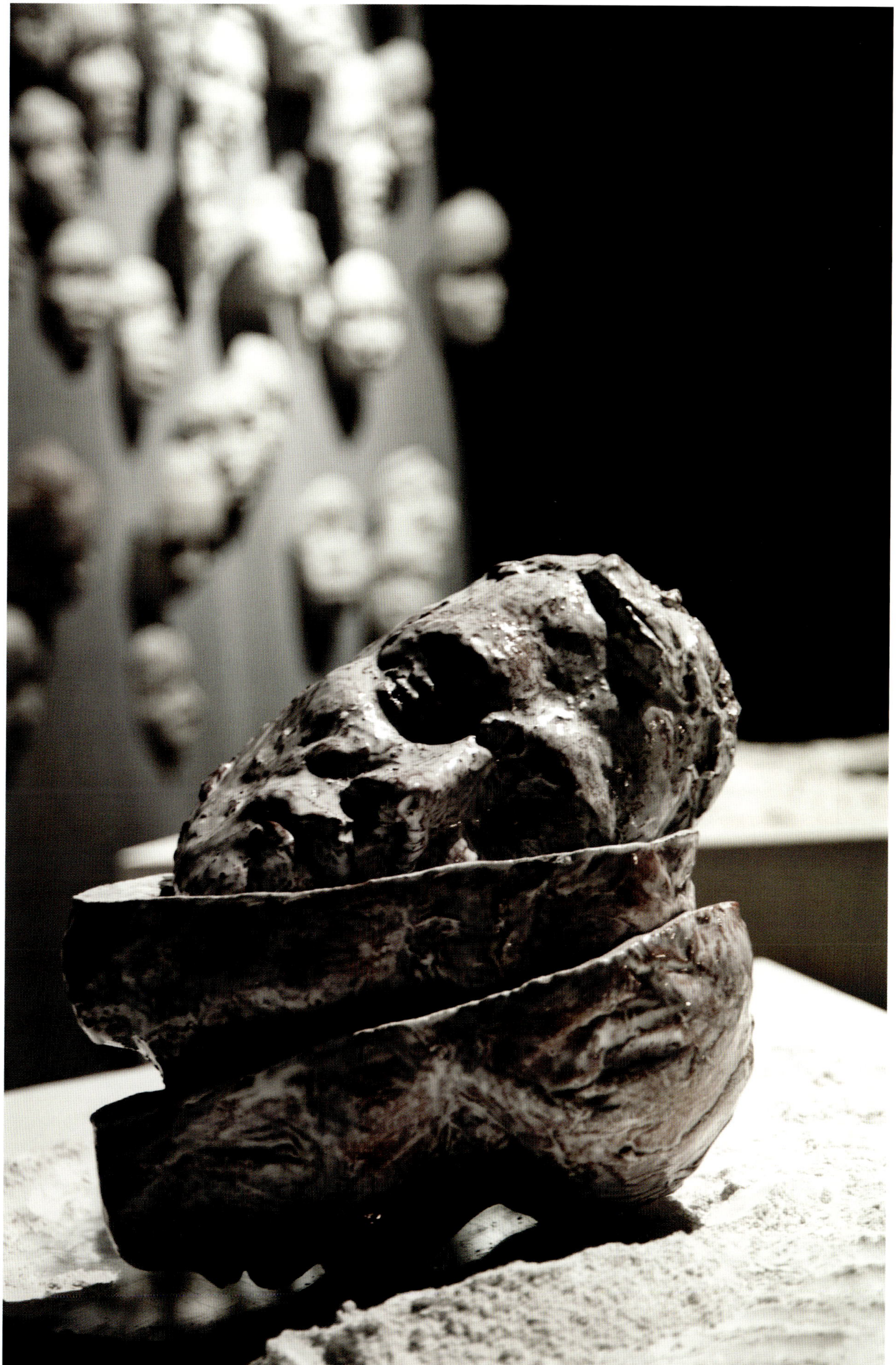

3

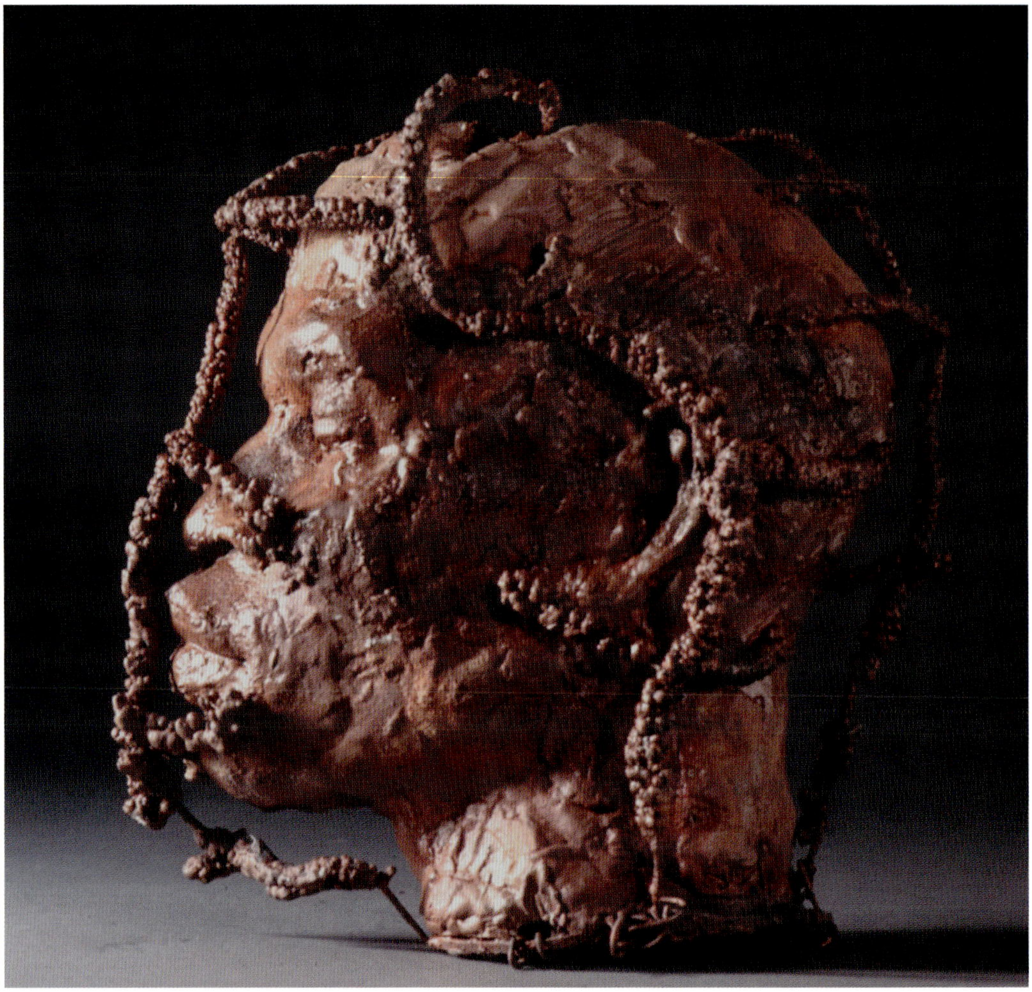

4

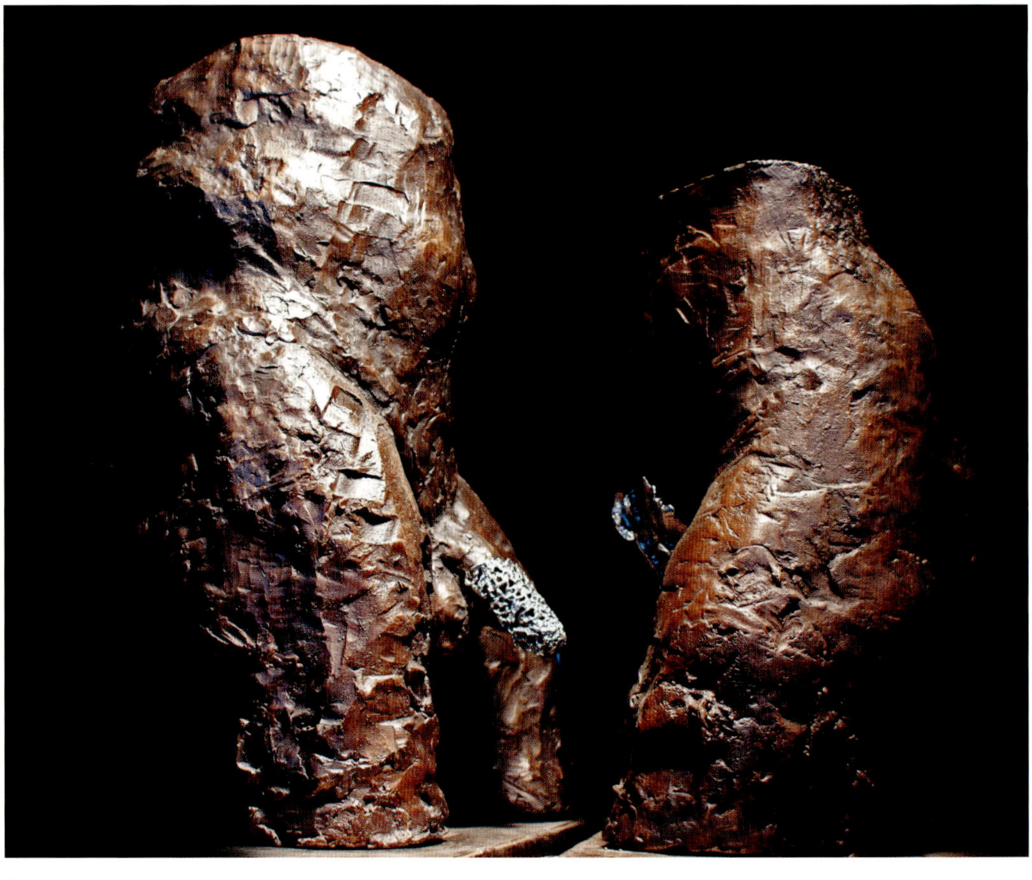

5

4 *Prison of My Mind*, 2002. Electroform technique, 13" x 11" x 13". *Photograph by Jolanta Izabela Pawlak.*

5 *Adam & Eve*, 2006. Cast bronze, silver, 24" x 16" x 15" & 19" x 14" x 9". *Photograph by Jolanta Izabela Pawlak.*

6 *You May Know Each Other*, 2011. Glazed ceramic, photography, digital projection, 58" w. x 16' h. *Photograph by Jolanta Izabela Pawlak.*

6

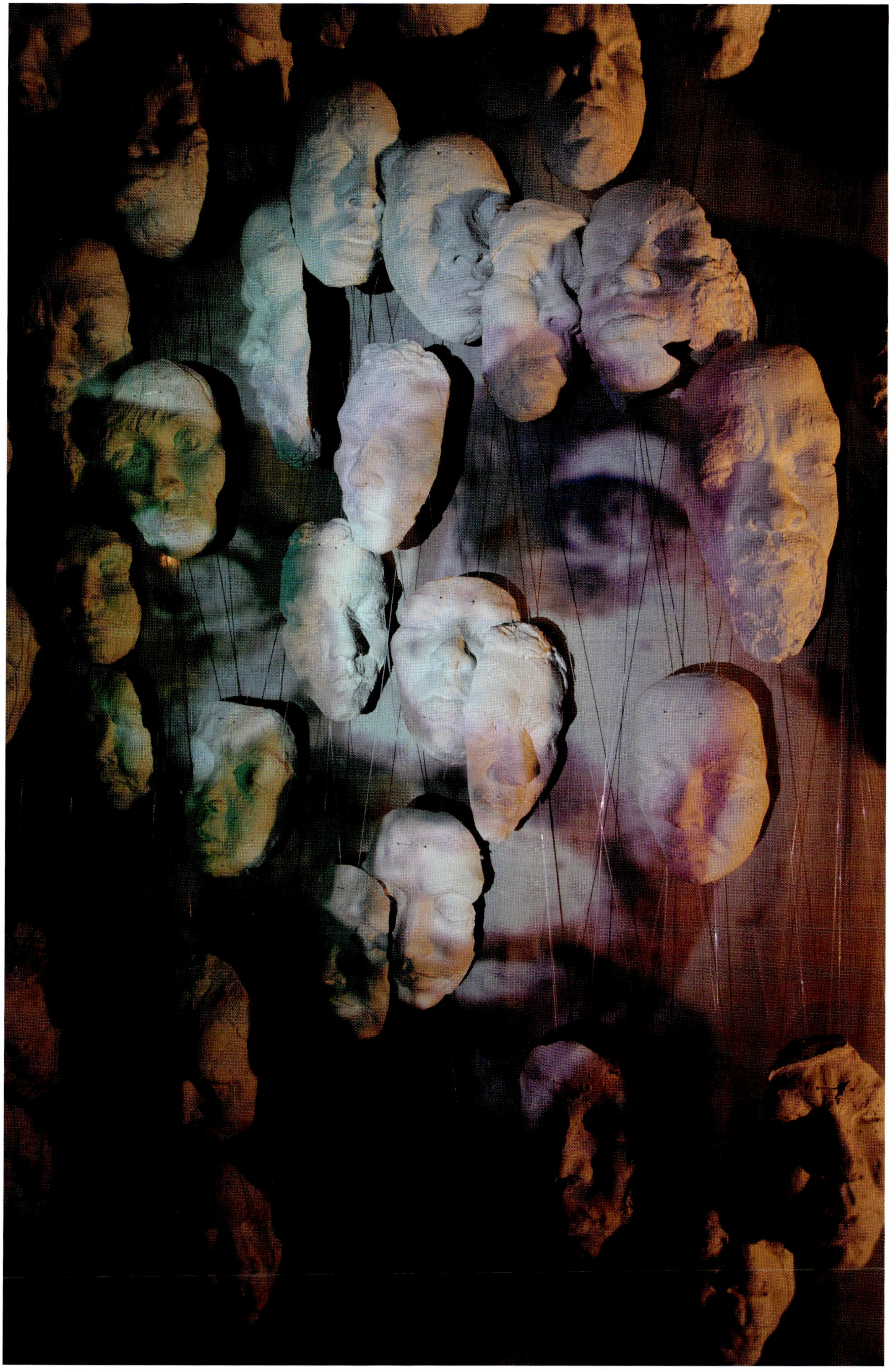

# Joshua Pennings

Grave, The Netherlands
www.joshuapennings.com

*As a modern blacksmith I make sculptures of iron and steel. In my smithy, I shape the cold metal to warm sculptures, going back to the basics, iron and fire, hammer and anvil. Forging like people did 2000 years ago, I use ancient techniques combined with modern metalworking, like welding. It is a great way to shape my ideas. Always driven and progressive, I'm working on my statues. My work is exhibited in sculpture parks, art fairs, galleries, and shows throughout the Netherlands, Germany, France, Russia, and Belgium. I take part in exhibitions and shows regularly. I do a lot of commissions for customers and municipalities. My sculptures are in private collections in the Netherlands, Europe, and the USA. My work is also more and more in public spaces.*

*Powerful animals and fantasy-creatures are a major theme in my work. Locomotion, like flying and travelling, are also very common in my sculptures. My sculptures are varied, sometimes full of humor and sweet, sometimes quite naughty, or strong and fierce looking. Often I am inspired by the material, but most of the time sculptures arise from my fantasy and dreams. My sculptures are made of new steel, cor-ten steel, and recycled metal, often old tools. My work can be indoors and outdoors. Every piece is handmade and unique.*

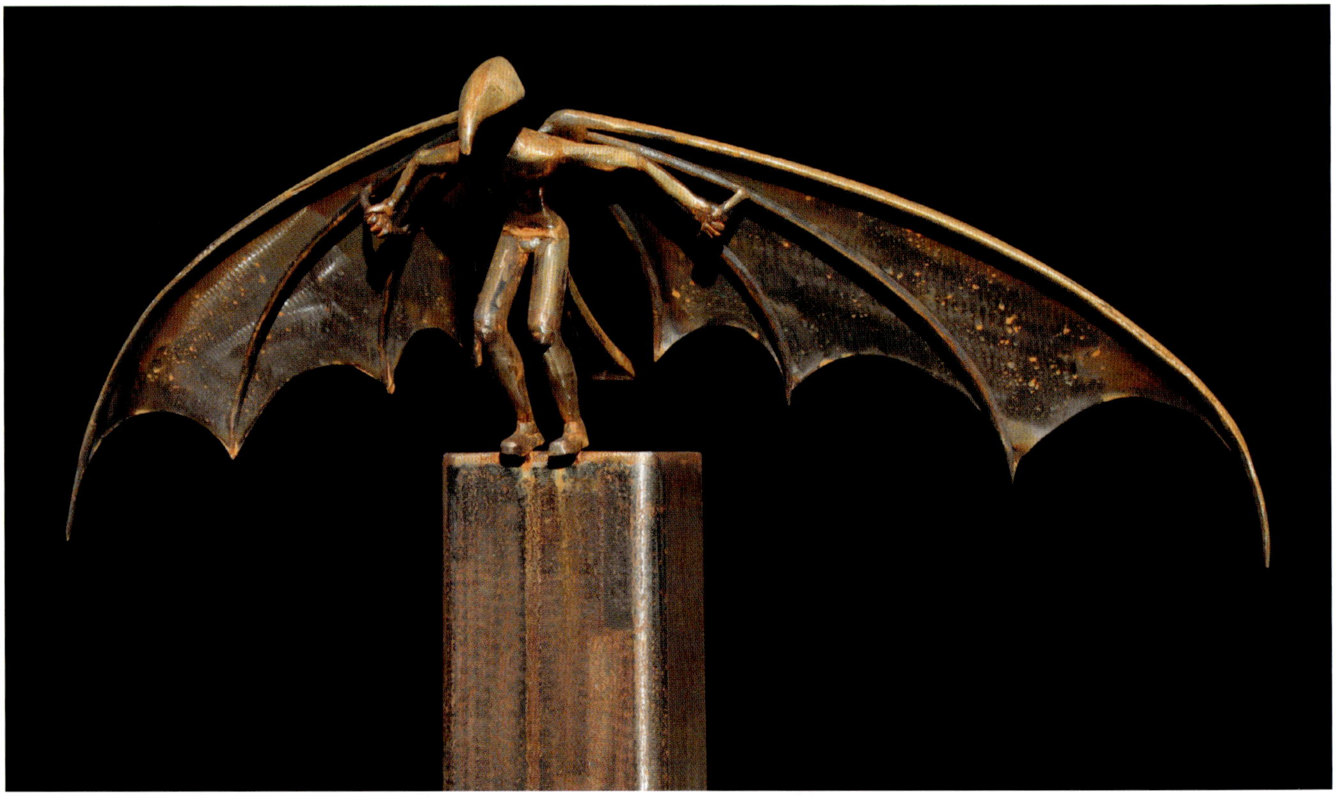

1

1 *Dreamflight.* Forged and fabricated steel, 175cm x 83cm x 44cm. *Photograph by Joshua Pennings.*

2 *Rhino.* Forged and fabricated steel, 135cm x 170cm x 35cm. *Photograph by Joshua Pennings.*

3 *Machine Fish.* Forged and fabricated steel, glass, 71cm x 68cm x 42cm. *Photograph by Joshua Pennings.*

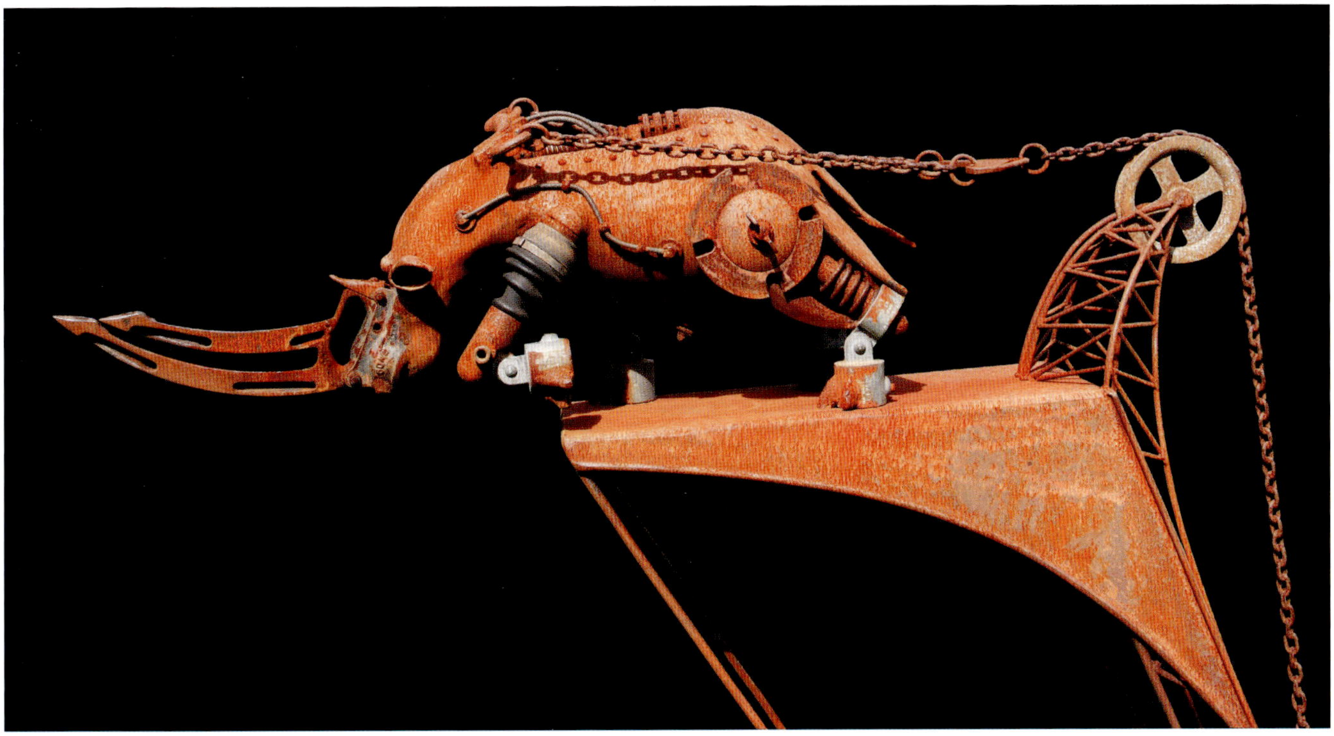

2

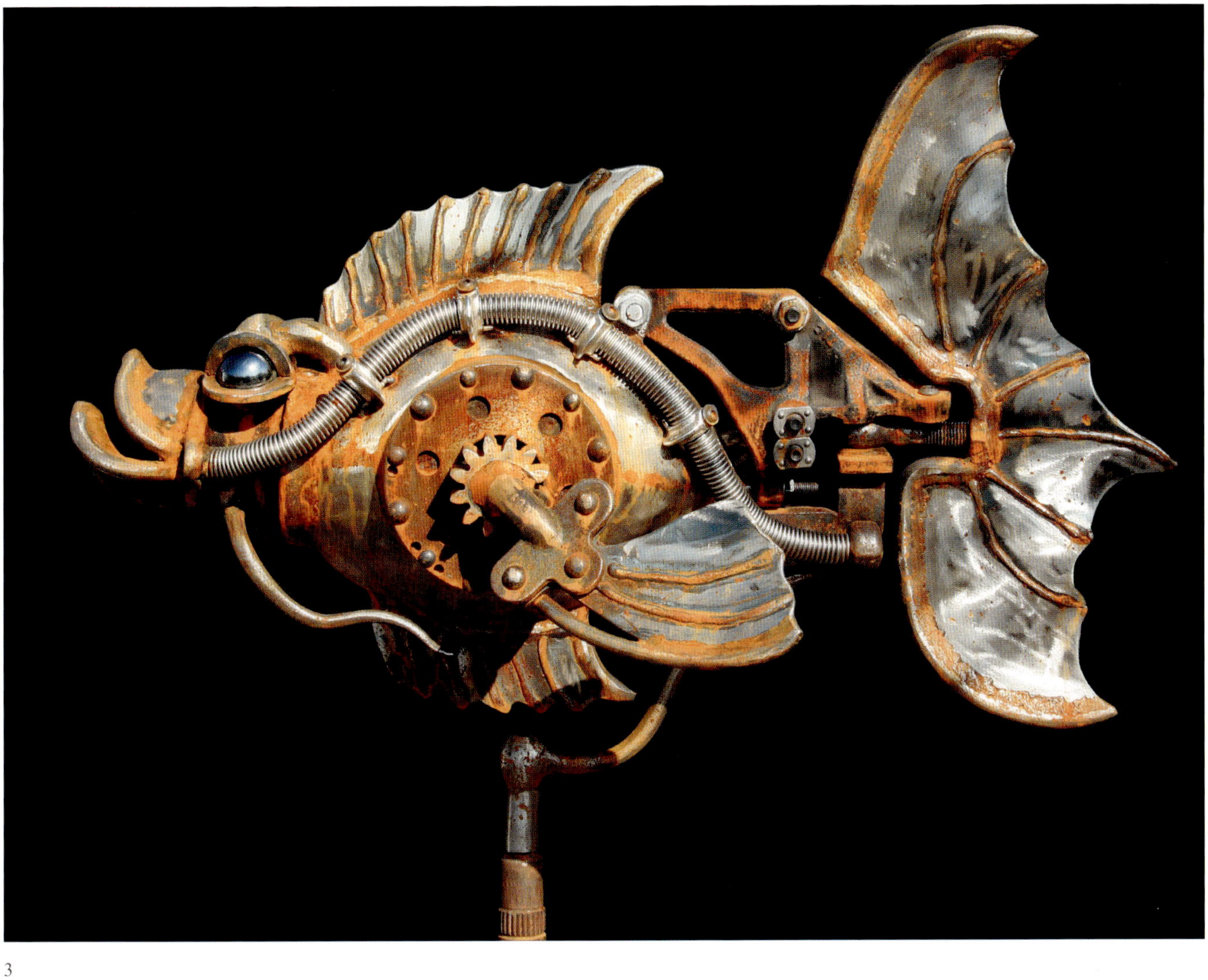

3

4 *Eagle.* Forged and fabricated steel, glass, 53cm x 39cm x14cm. *Photograph by Joshua Pennings.*

5 *Bison.* Forged and fabricated steel, 132cm x 26cm x 53cm. *Photograph by Joshua Pennings.*

6 *Raven.* Forged and fabricated steel, glass, 151cm x 46cm x 34cm. *Photograph by Joshua Pennings.*

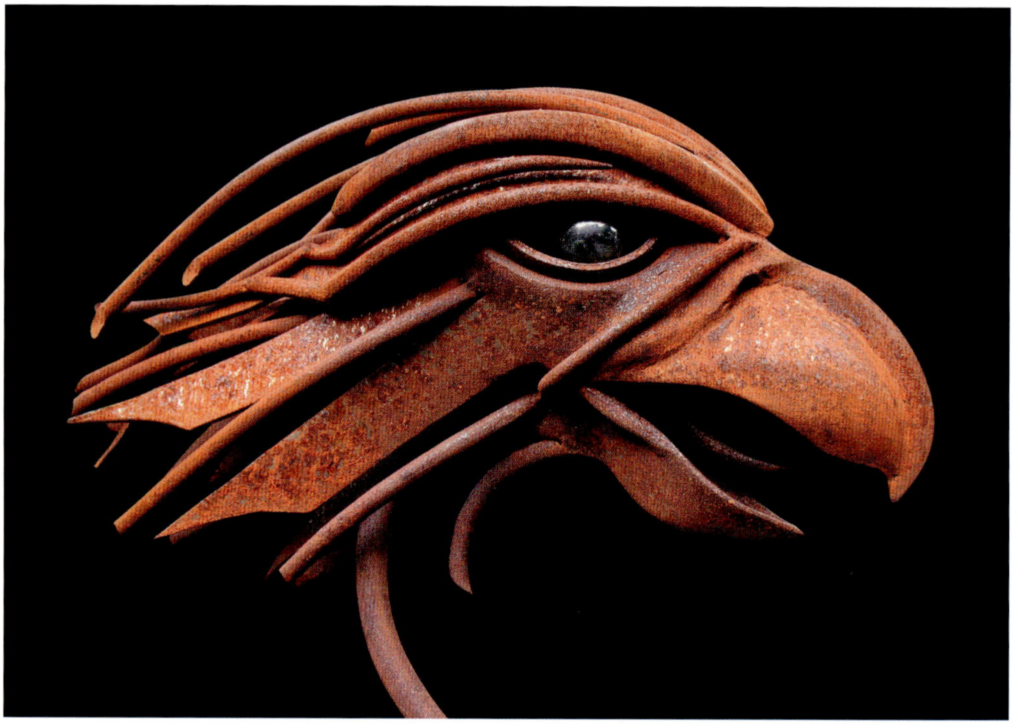

4

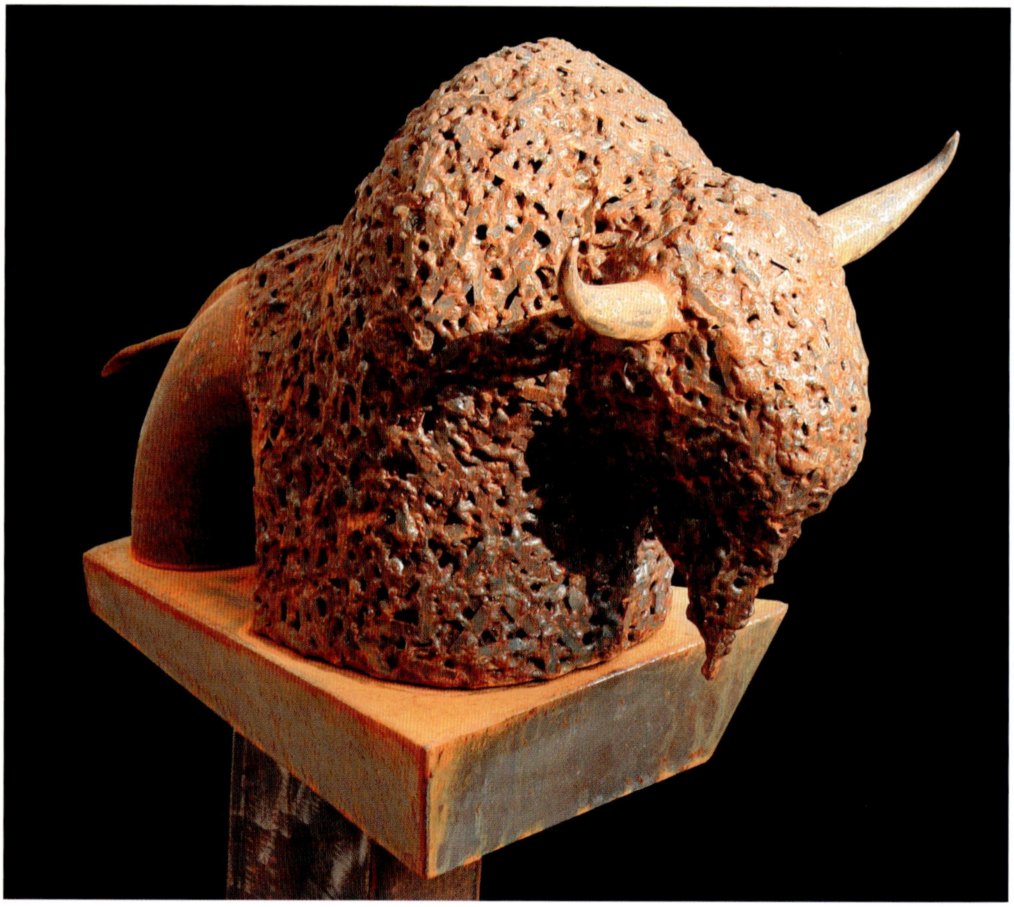

5

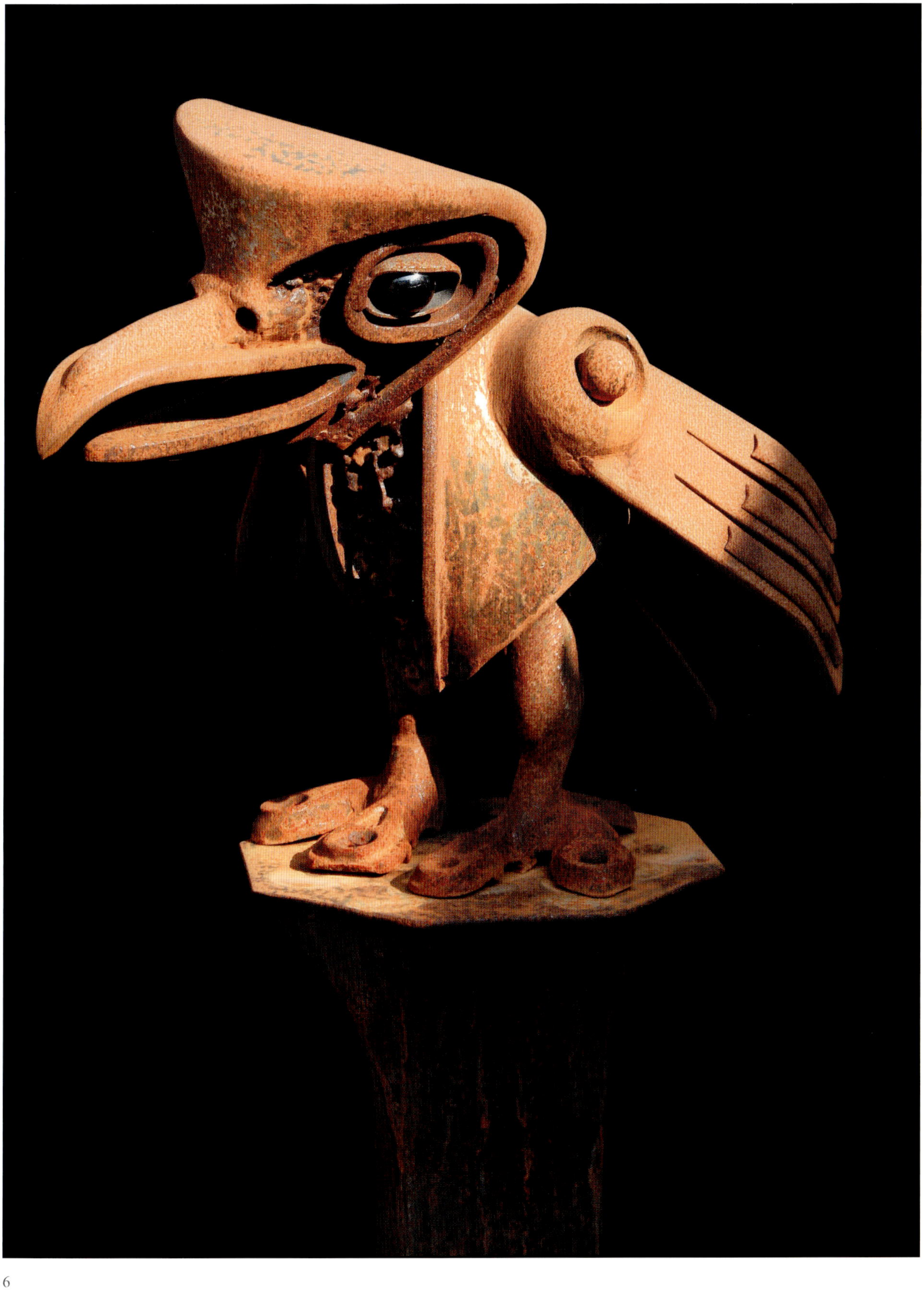

6

# Lauren Raine

Tucson, Arizona, USA
www.rainewalker.com

*I'm an intuitive visual artist, as well as a ritualist, choreographer, and mask maker. My collection of masks, The Masks of the Goddess, traveled throughout the U.S. for almost 10 years, celebrating the Divine Feminine through dance and storytelling. In 2007, I received a fellowship with the Alden Dow Creativity Center for "Spider Woman's Hands," a Community Arts Project based on the Native American creatrix story of Spider Woman (Thought Woman), who wove the world into being with what she imagined. I believe we are all weavers within the great Web, and, like the Spider Woman, we are creating the future with the stories we tell today.*

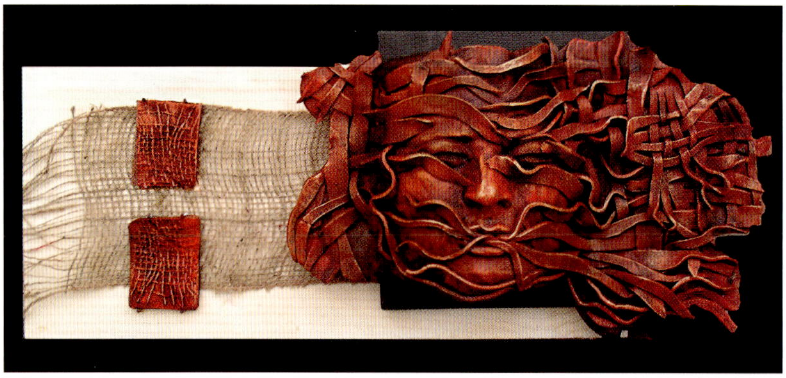
1

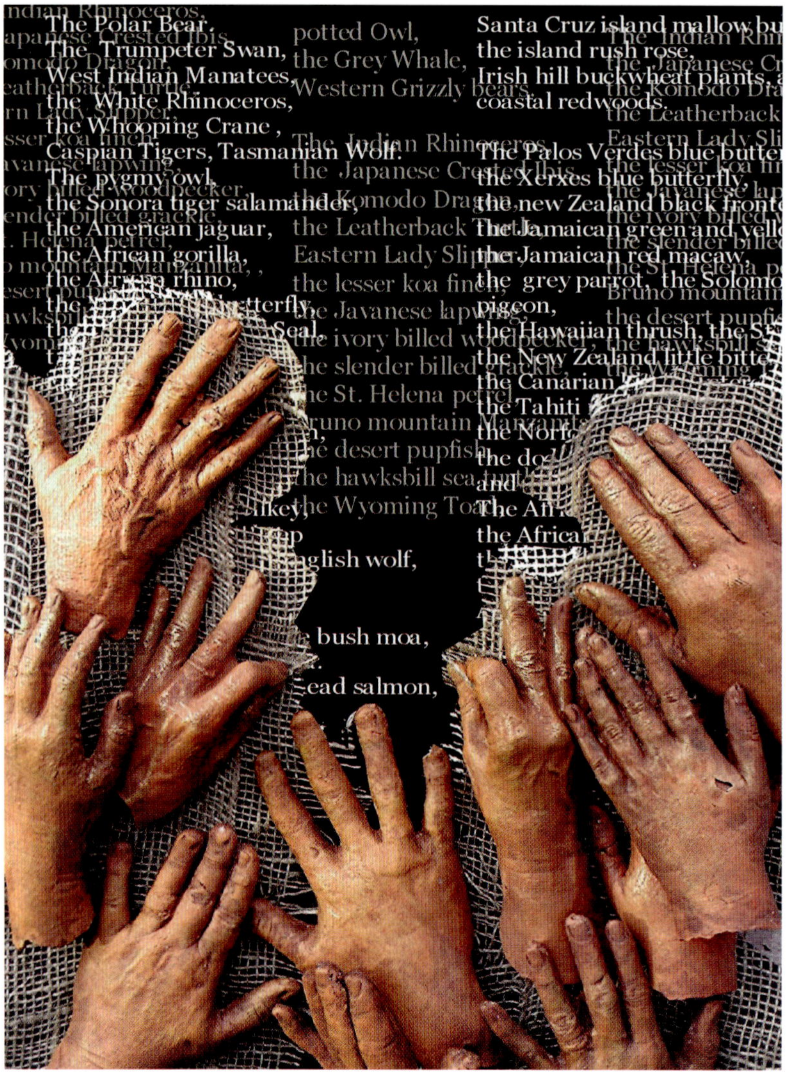

2

1 *Tse Che Nako Weaving the World into Being*, 2007. Mixed media, 40" x 24". *Photograph by Lauren Raine.*

2 *The Sixth Extinction*, 2007. Mixed media, 20" x 17". *Photograph by Lauren Raine.*

3 *Anima/Animus Shrine*, 2003. Mixed media, 20" x 12". *Photograph by Lauren Raine.*

4 *Non-Local Quontum Mandala*, 2009. Mixed media, 20" x 20". *Photograph by Lauren Raine.*

5 *Gaia*, 2005. Mixed media, 27" x 36". *Photograph by Lauren Raine.*

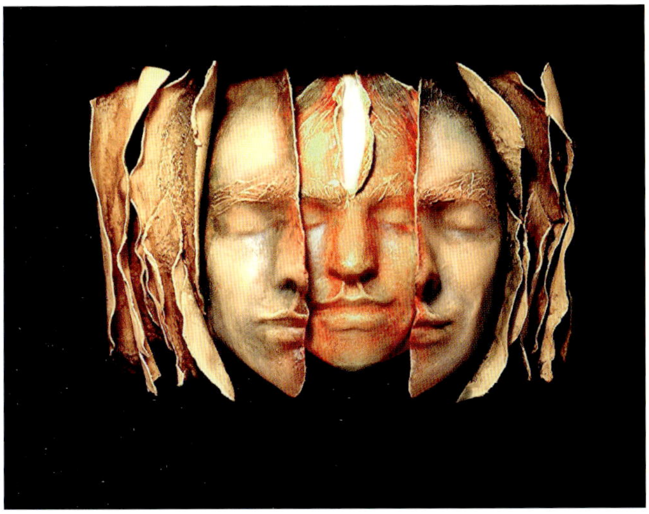

3

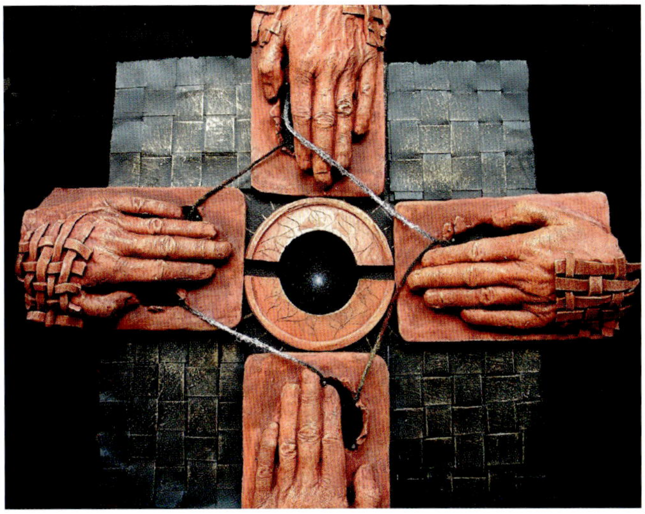

4

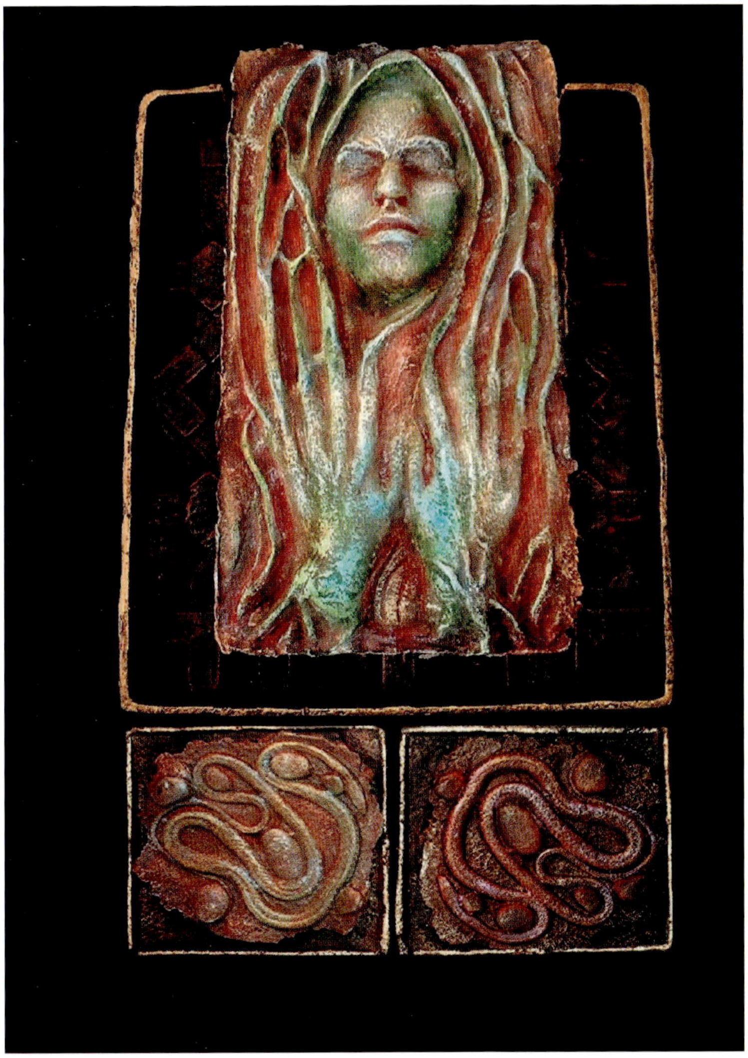

5

# Leisa Rich

Atlanta, Georgia, USA
www.monaleisa.com

Leisa Rich draws from art and fiber techniques and uses an array of new materials, detritus, and machine stitching to form her sculptures and installations. She holds MFA, BFA, and Bachelor of Edcuation in Art degrees. Leisa has been featured on the PBS artist special "In Context," in the books *Hand to Hand: 195 Artists Witness the Iraq War* (Cecelia Kane/Blurb Publishing), *The Best of America Sculpture Artists and Artisans,* (Kennedy Publishing), and *Quilt National 2009* (Lark Books), and exhibits internationally. She has won prestigious awards such as bestowments from The Barbara L. Kuhlman Foundation and Distinguished Juror Award from The University of Texas. She is on the Board of Directors of the South East Fiber Arts Alliance. Leisa teaches at colleges, arts centers, educational institutions, and her studio. Previous experience includes international fashion, set design, wearable art business, and art school director.

Growing up in Canada inspired a passion for nature in Leisa. In recent work, humans disappear due to their never-ending quest to conquer and consume, resulting in a post-Apocalyptic Reclamation state whereby the organic matter left unchecked morphs with the detritus left behind by humans. Leisa's Neo-Surrealist art quilts, massive installations and sculptures, fantastical gardens, and morphed trash creatures create a wonderful world… without us. Current work is viewer interactive; multiple pieces can be pulled off and placed on by viewers, giving them the satisfaction of entering Leisa's world and altering it to create their own story.

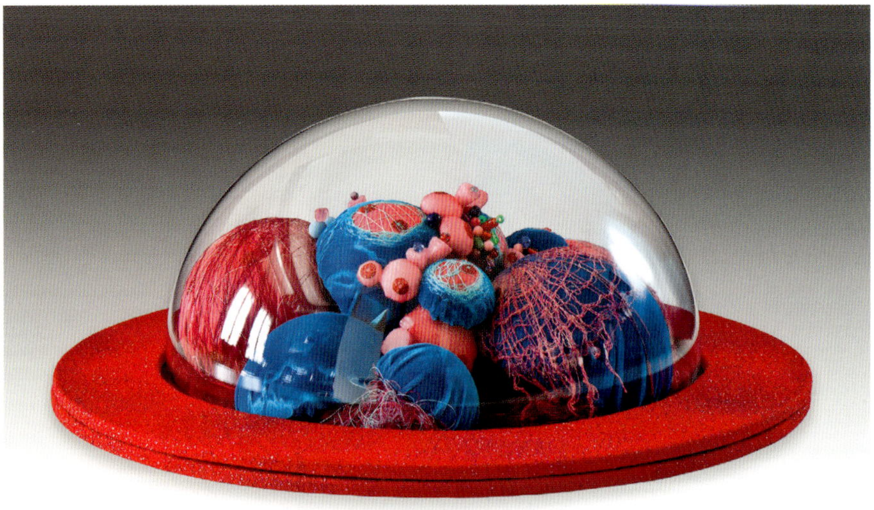

1

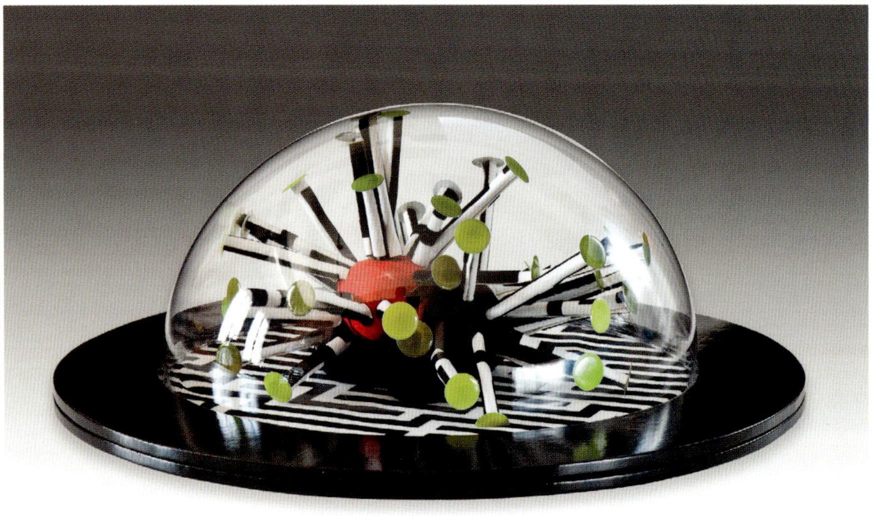

2

1 *Passive*, 2011. Various detritus, mixed media, each 12" h. x 22" diam. *Photograph by Michael West.*

2 *Aggressive*, 2011. Various detritus, mixed media, each 12" h. x 22" diam. *Photograph by Michael West.*

3 *The Three Muses*, 2003. Recycled detritus, metal fishing cages, thread, digital image transfers; dimensions variable-figures life size. *Photograph by David Wharton.*

4 *Beauty From the Beast*, 2009. Human detritus including bubble wrap, plant stakes, 1970s bed quilt, fabric, vinyl, acrylic paint, canvas; dimensions variable; garden view 5' x 20' x 25'. *Photograph by Michael West.*

5 *Cell*, 2010. Free motion machine embroidered, recycled plastic flower netting, vinyl, 10" x 24" x 24". *Photograph by Leisa Rich.*

3

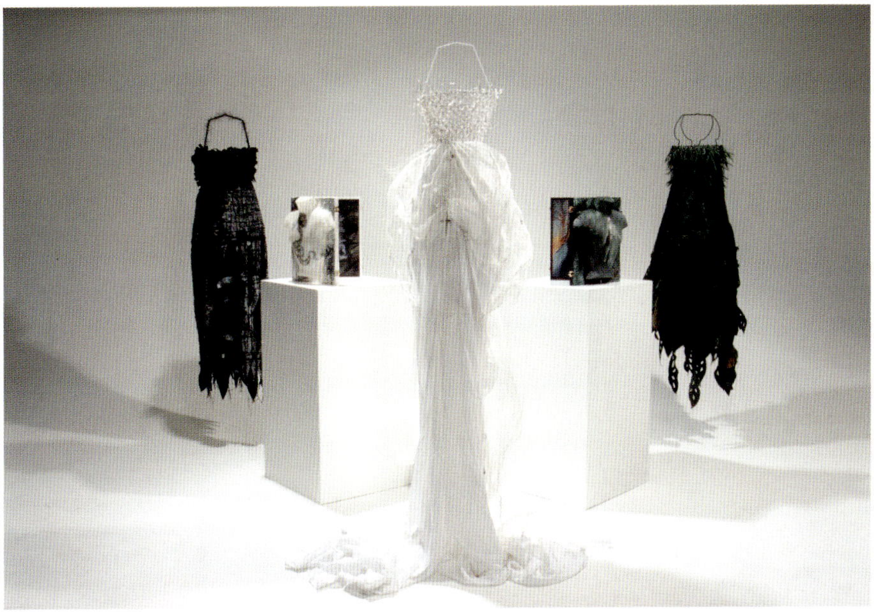

4

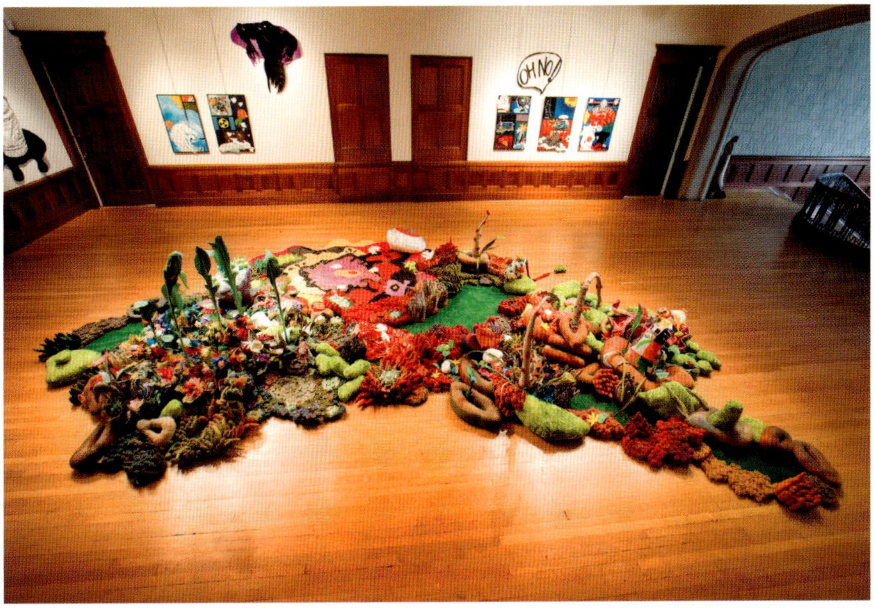


5

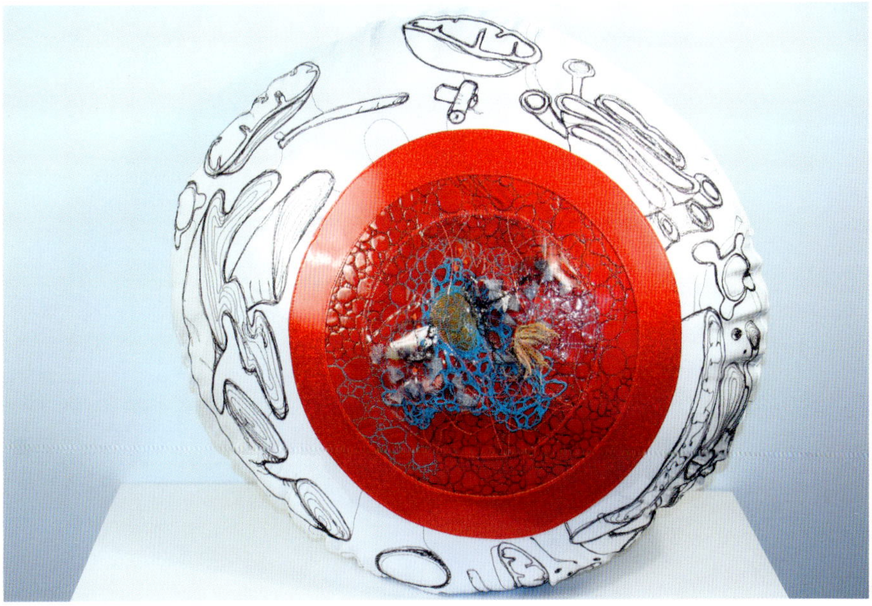

# Stefanie Rocknak

Oneonta, New York, USA
www.steffrocknak.net

Stefanie Rocknak has been sculpting for over 23 years. Her sculptures have been in over 40 shows, including the traveling show "Captive Passage," which was hosted by five major eastcoast museums, including the Smithsonian and the South Street Seaport Museum. She has been a member of the Sculptors Guild (New York, New York) since 2007, and her work has also been featured in five books and over 30 magazines and newspapers, including *Arts and Antiques, ROJO* magazine (Spain), *Craft Arts International* (Australia), and the cover of *Sculptural Pursuit*. Stefanie's work can be found in the mariner's museum, on the Hudson River sloop, the *Clearwater*, and in private collections across the United States. She is self-taught and is currently an Associate Professor of Philosophy and the Director of the Cognitive Science Program at Hartwick College in Oneonta, New York. Her teaching and research interests include the philosophy of art, the philosophy of mind, and the work of the Scottish empiricist, David Hume. She has presented her philosophical work in over thirty national and international venues and has published her work in a number of well-known journals.

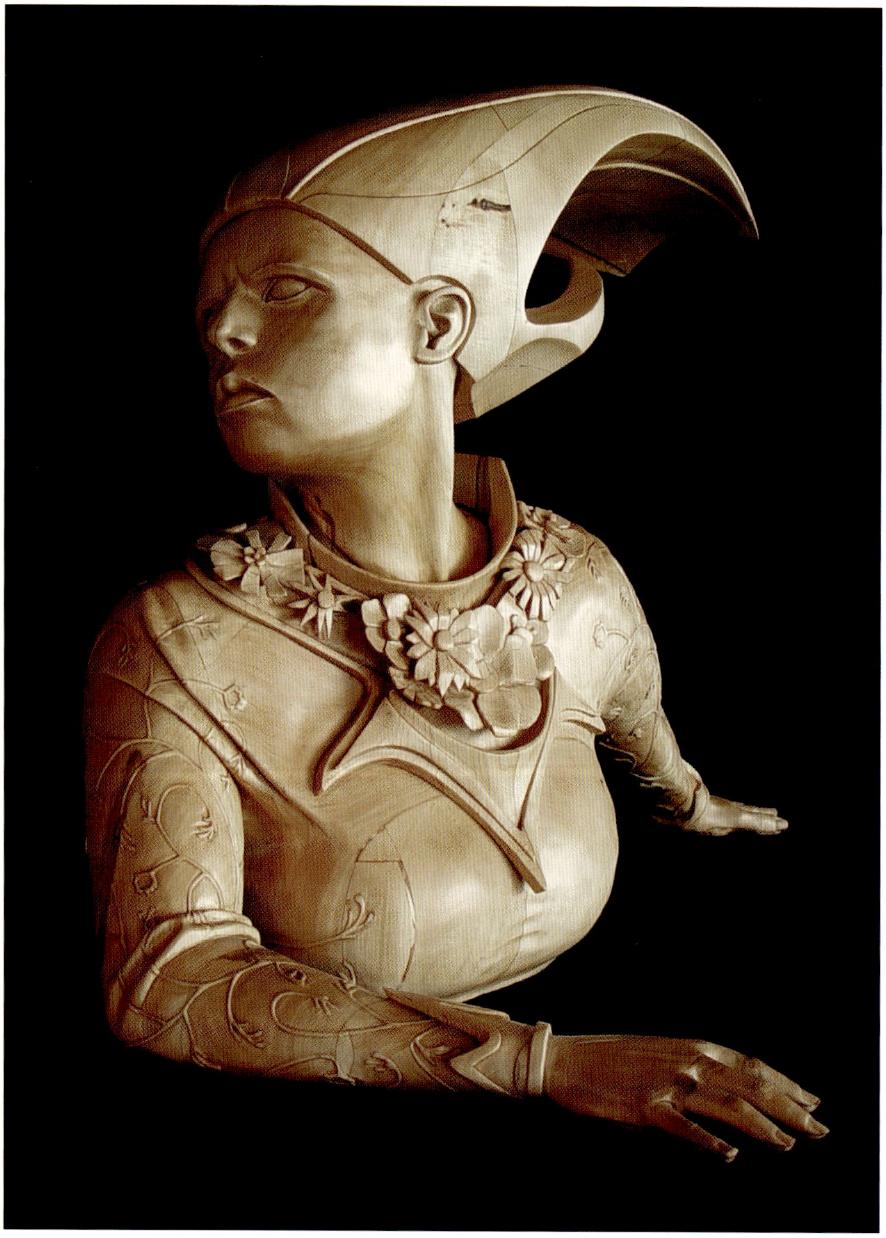

1

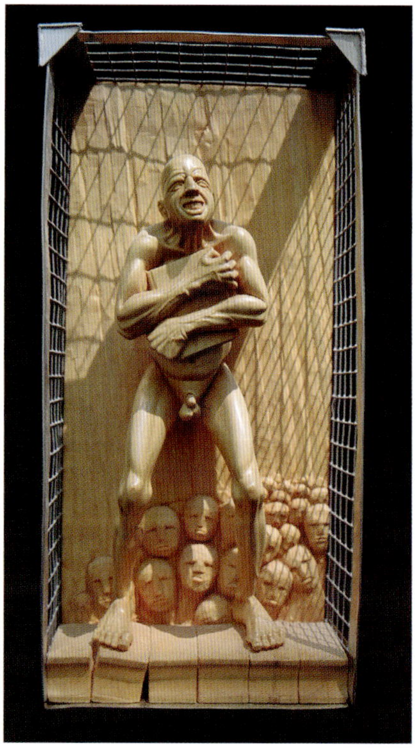

2

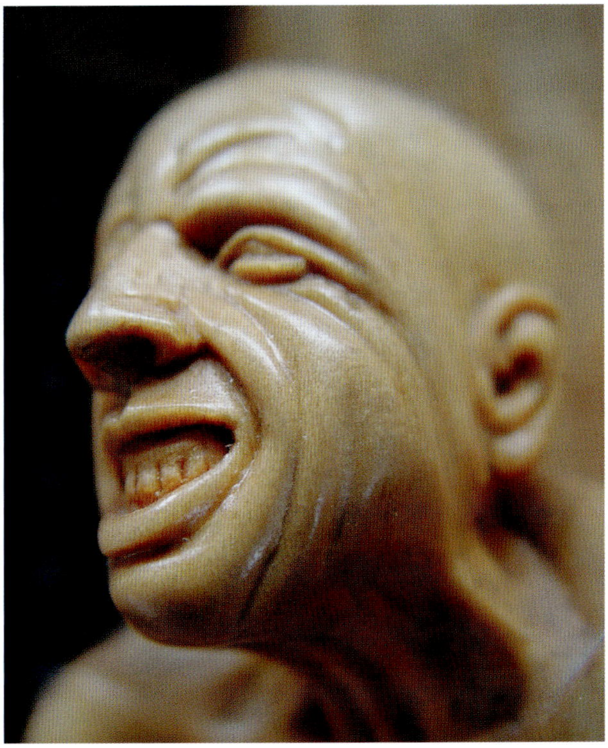

3

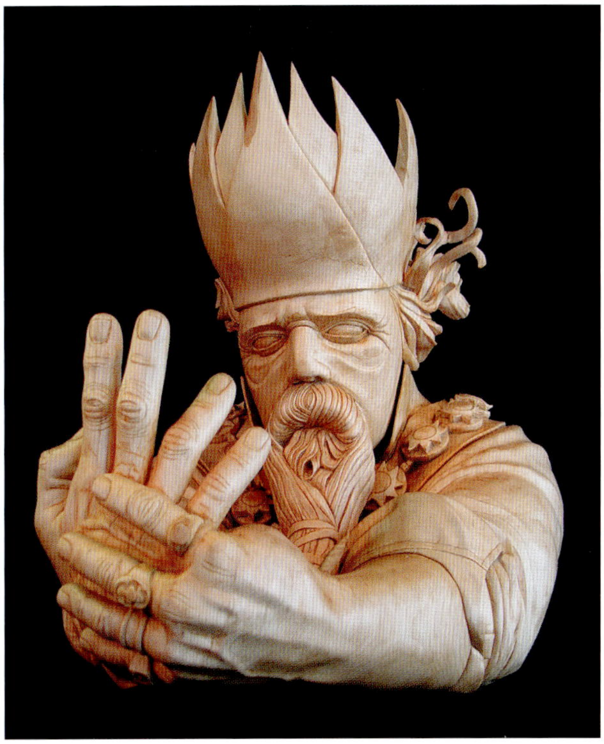

4

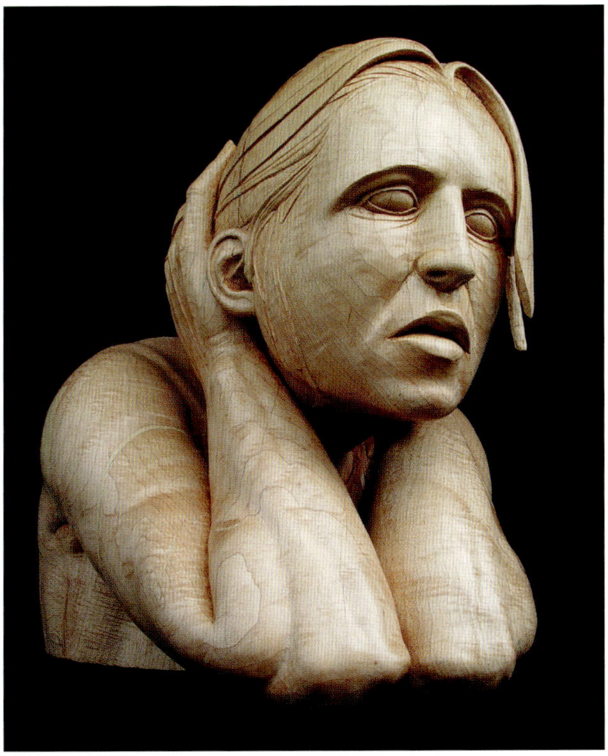

5

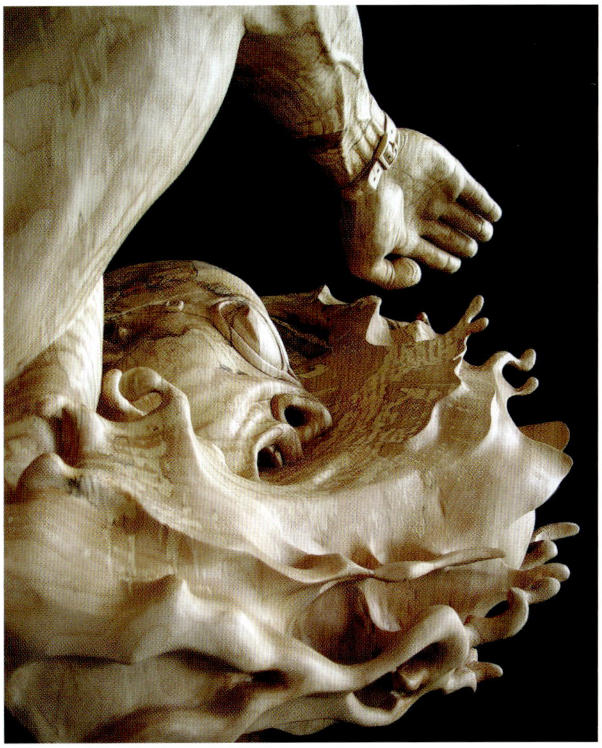

6

1 *The Queen*, 2010. Laminated basswood, lifesize. *Photograph by Stefanie Rocknak.*

2 *The Academic*, 2000. Limewood, 10" tall. *Photograph by Stefanie Rocknak.*

3 *The Academic* (detail), 2000. *Photograph by Stefanie Rocknak.*

4 *The King*, 2008. Basswood, lifesize. *Photograph by Stefanie Rocknak.*

5 *Ghastly Nights*, 2004. Maple, lifesize. *Photograph by Stefanie Rocknak.*

6 *The Swimmer*, 2006. Basswood, lifesize. *Photograph by Stefanie Rocknak.*

# Ron Rodgers

Sebastopol, California, USA
ronrodgersstudio@yahoo.com

Rodgers's work digs through and explores the history of art in order to spur the genesis of his own creations. With this inspiration, he goes beyond what came before and creates pieces that deliver a breakthrough into timelessness. His work represents not merely dots in the continuum, but a sort of stretching forward and back with the intent to bridge the past and bring forward a dynamic aesthetic voice relevant to our times.

The cultural influences mined from prehistory through the classical to the modern area, have resulted in dramatic sculptures with deep psychological overtones. Much of his work is steeped in Greek mythology, inflected with a more contemporary urban sensibility. The heroic-sized pieces offer an aspect of grandeur and classicism in elemental human themes. One can find depictions of earthly bondage, transcendence, and renewal referenced in one piece. It is in this way that he honors the human experience, expressing the infinite in bronze.

Through the years Rodgers's artwork has earned him a vast number of prizes, nominations, and noteworthy praise, from regional accolades to international recognition. Whether it be through direct competition or public art "events," his activities and creations in sculpture have piqued the public interest, as proclaimed in main stream newspapers, magazines, books, and every major television network in the United States.

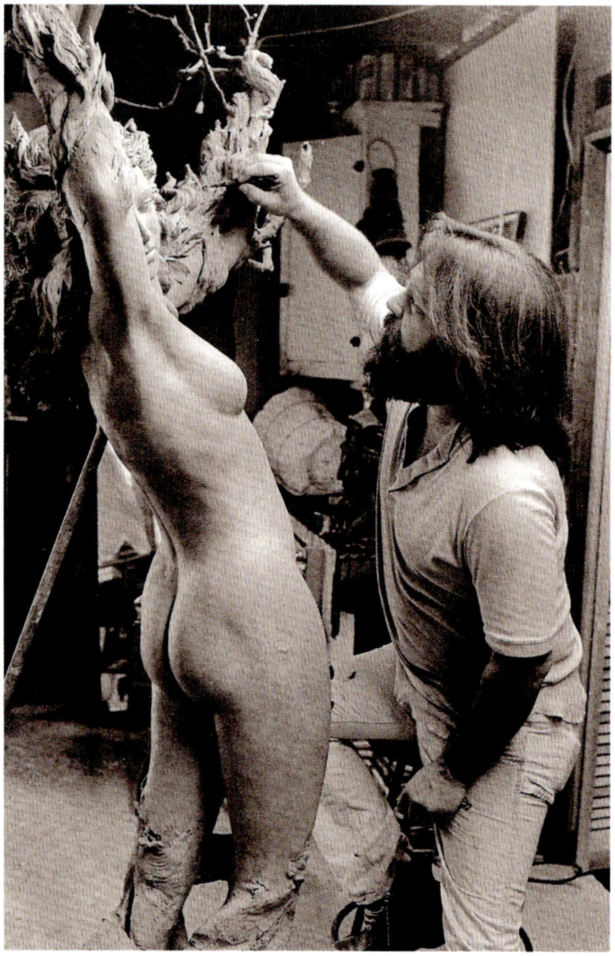

1

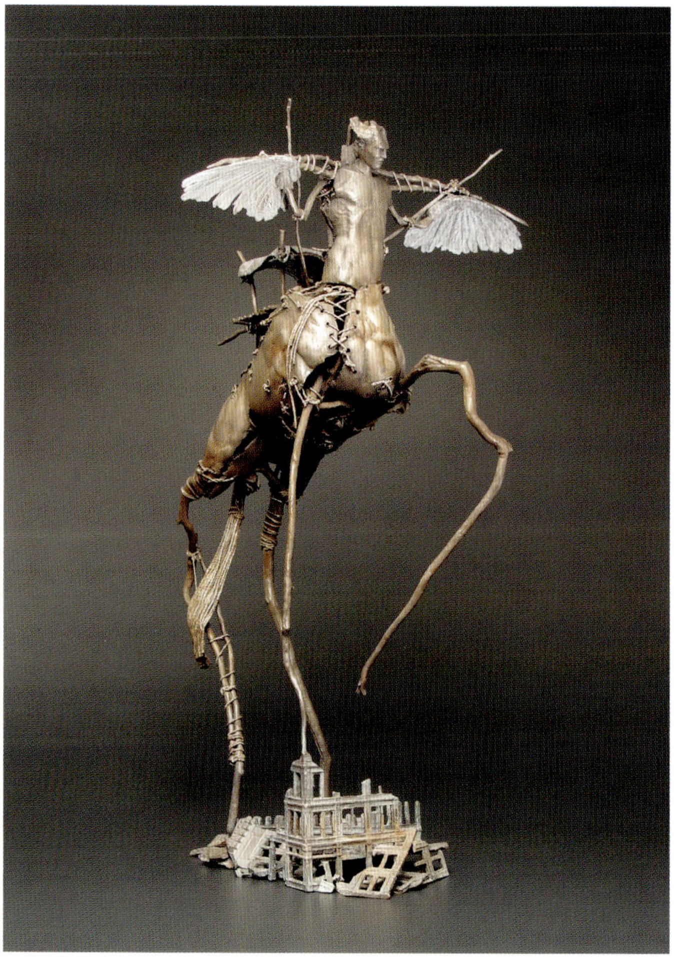

2

1 *Daphne*, 1988. Clay, 8'. *Photograph by San Jose Mercury.*

2 *Soulchaser*, 2006. Bronze, 21". *Photograph by Don Greenberg.*

3 *Diana* (detail), 1996. Bronze, 8.5'. *Photograph by Bent Severin.*

4 *Phoenix*, 2003. Bronze, 16.25". *Photograph by Kenn Ferro.*

5 *Harbinger Complex*, 2004. Bronze, 6.25'. *Photograph by Kenn Ferro.*

6 *Odyssey of Diana*, 1996. Bronzes, various. *Photograph by Bent Severin.*

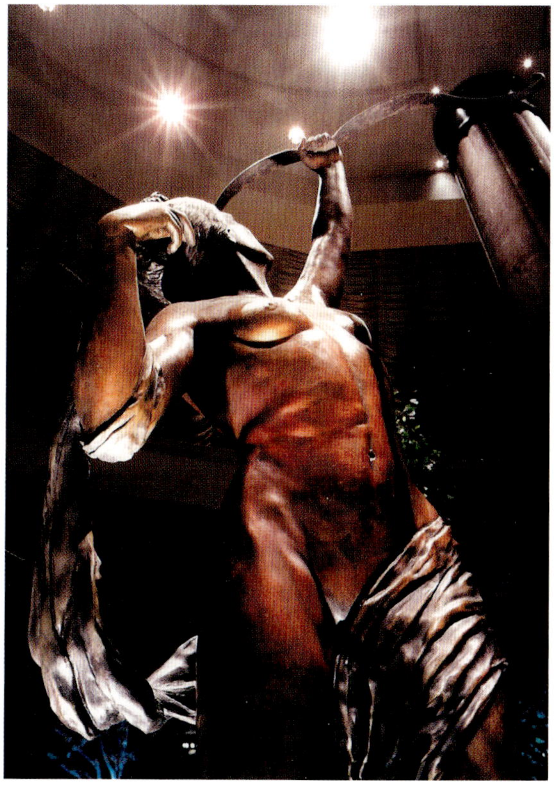

3

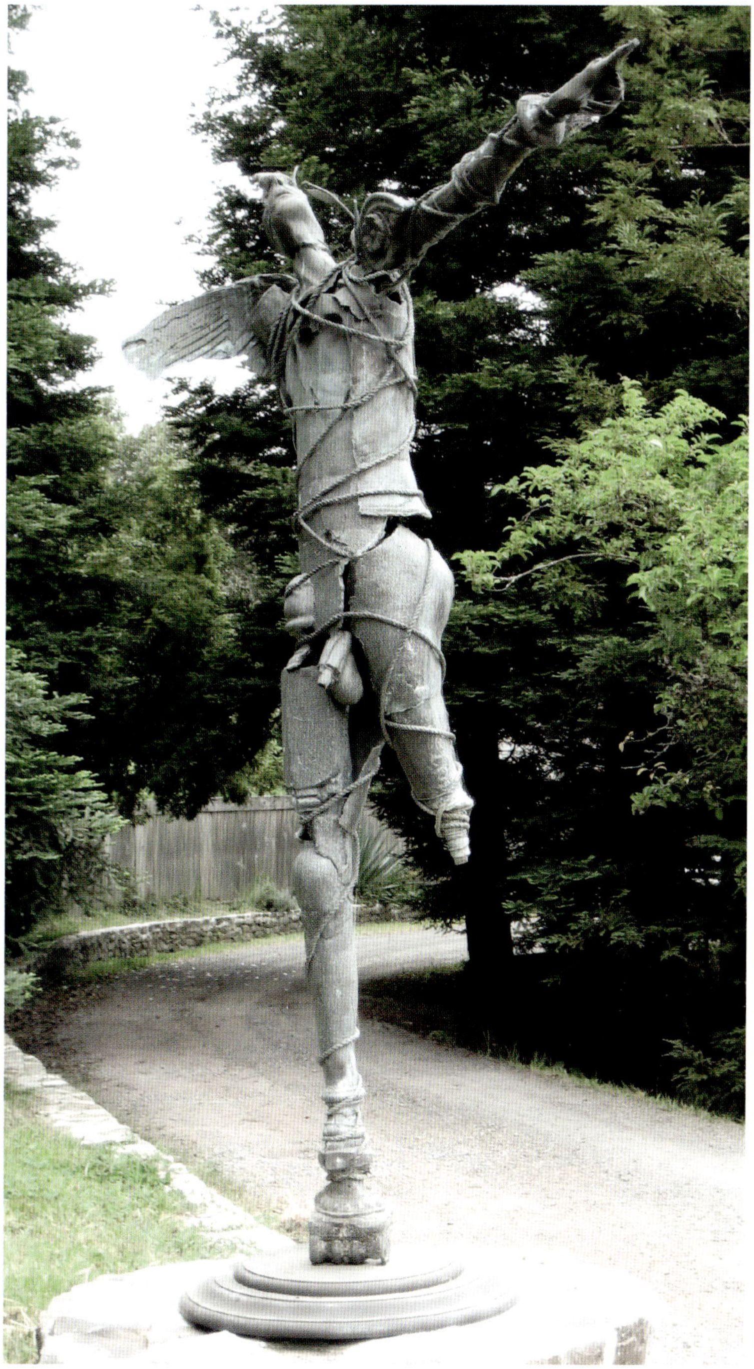

5

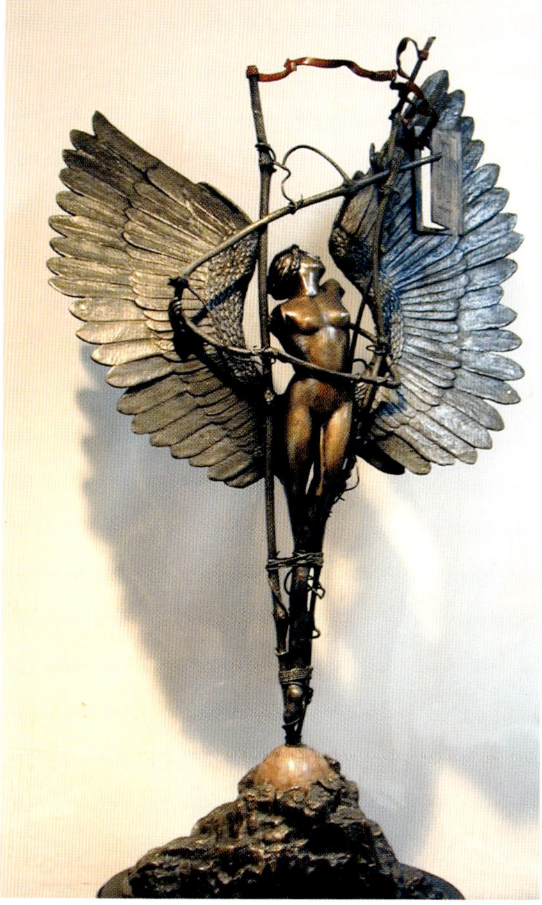

4

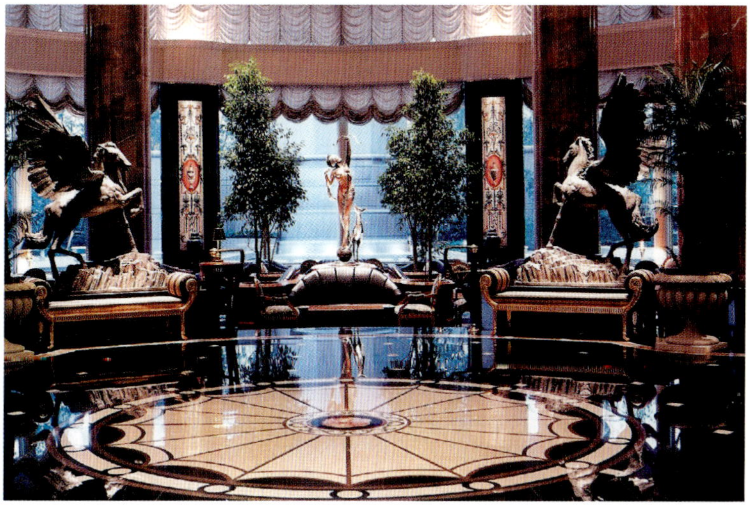

6

# Heath Satow

Los Angeles, California, USA
www.publicsculpture.com

As a contemporary art metal sculptor working primarily in steel and stainless steel, Heath Satow has been creating iconic scale public art pieces since 1989. Satow's formal training as a designer enables him to create sculpture that works harmoniously with its surroundings, while his artistic instinct provides inspiration and creativity to produce fresh and distinctive work. His art has been commissioned for many public sites including an airport, zoos, hospitals, corporations, and museums in locations as diverse as Palm Desert, Hong Kong, and Dubai. These works have become icons and points of reference for the communities in which they are located.

Satow's artistic focus is to utilize the natural qualities of metals and other materials to create contemporary yet inviting interpretive sculpture. He designs each sculpture specifically for its location and to meet the goals of the project. His forte in the public art arena is the ability to effectively communicate message of the institution/municipality and engage the viewer with his artistic and interpretive abilities. Passionately committed to environmentally sustainable design, all of Satow's materials are durable and virtually maintenance-free. His sculptures are created through direct fabrication, with all metals being 100% recyclable. Any waste generated during production is completely recycled.

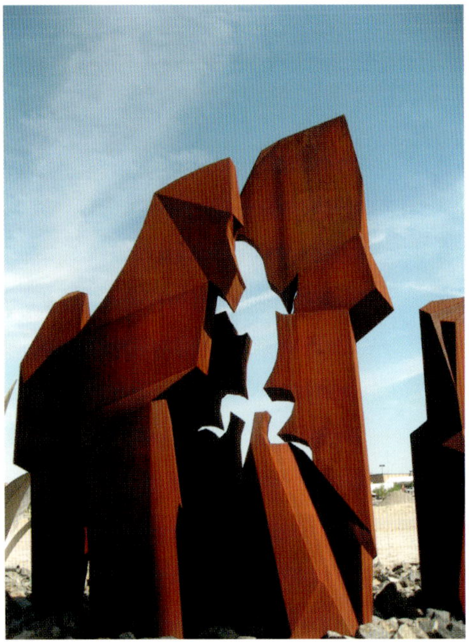

1

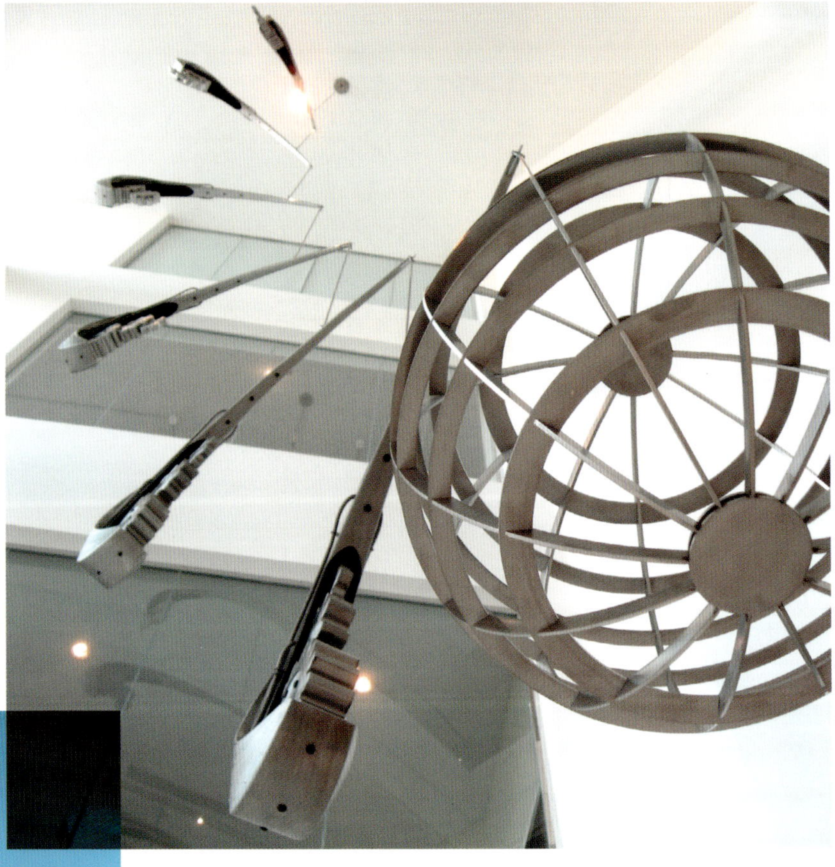

3

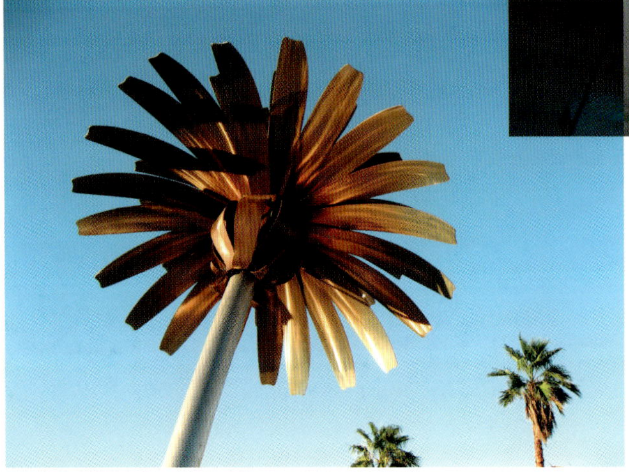

2

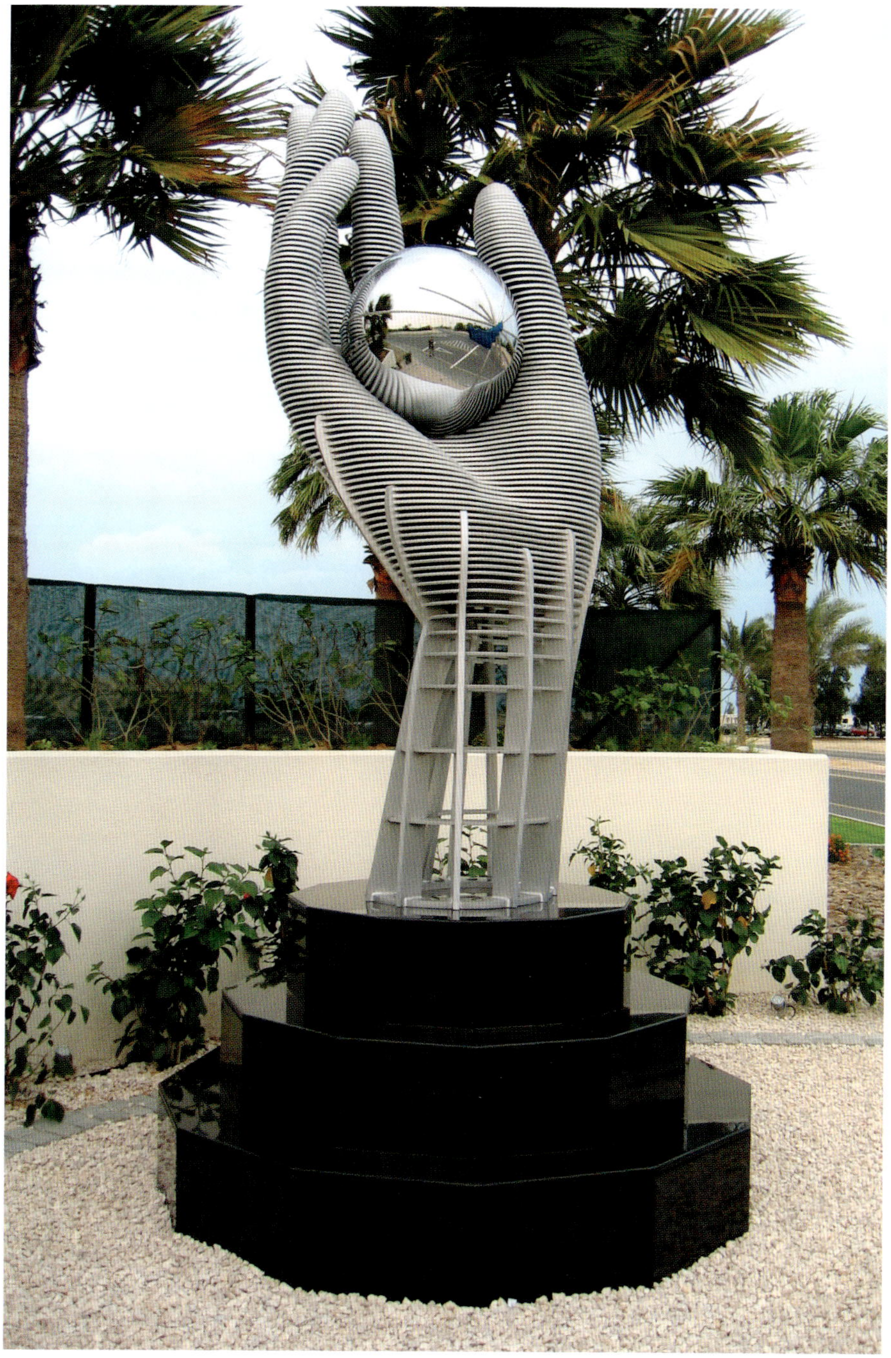

4

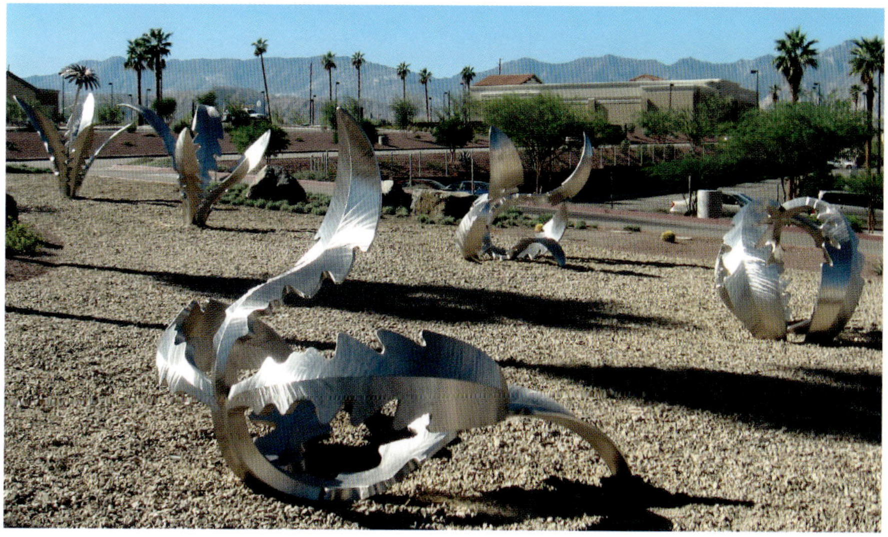

5

1 *Ce N'est Pas Une Lizard*, 2006. Oxidized steel, stainless steel, 30' x 11' x 6'. *Photograph by Heath Satow.*

2 *Tumbling Weed* (detail), 2008. *Photograph by Heath Satow.*

3 *Composure,* 2007. Stainless steel, 40' x 7' x 6'. *Photograph by Heath Satow.*

4 *Rising*, 2005. Aluminum, stainless steel, 12' x 6' x 6". *Photograph by Heath Satow.*

5 *Tumbling Weed*, 2008. Aluminum, stainless steel, 10' x 25' x 74". *Photograph by Heath Satow.*

# Leo Sewell

Philadelphia, Pennsylvania, USA
www.leosewell.net

Leo Sewell grew up in Annapolis, Maryland, and discovered the Navy dump by age 10. He has been picking trash and building with it ever since. By the late sixties, he had a masters degree in Art History and began a career as a junk sculptor. To date he has completed over 4000 assemblages.

The work is composed of recognizable objects of plastic, metal, and wood. The sculptures are representational, mostly animals and people.

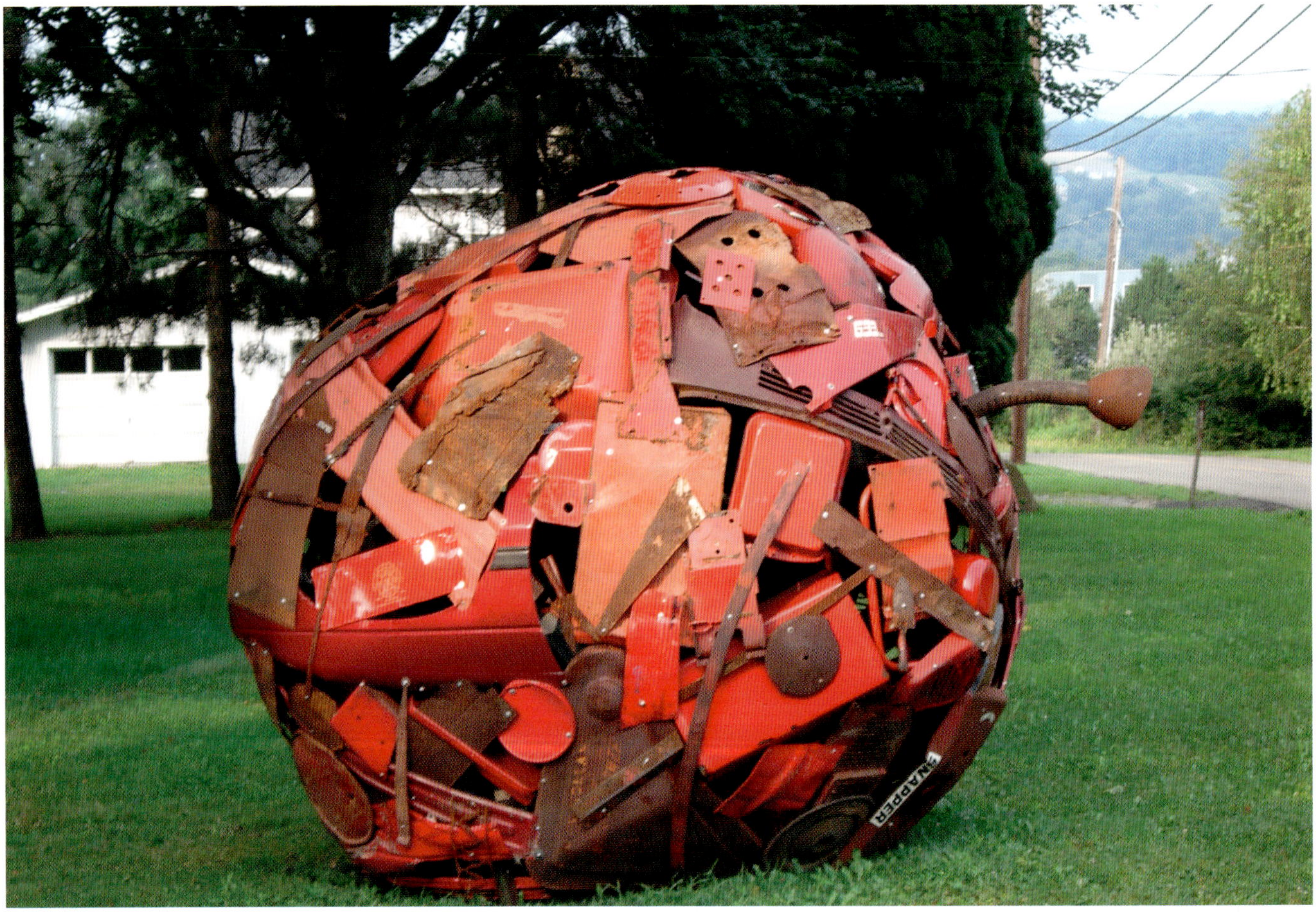


1

1 *Apple*, 2006. Reclaimed objects, 8' x 8' x 10'. *Photograph by Barbara Sewell.*

2 *Raven*, 2002. Reclaimed objects, 18" x 21" x 6". *Photograph by Barbara Sewell.*

3 *Duck*, 2003. Reclaimed objects, 16" x 8" x 16". *Photograph by Abby Sewell.*

2

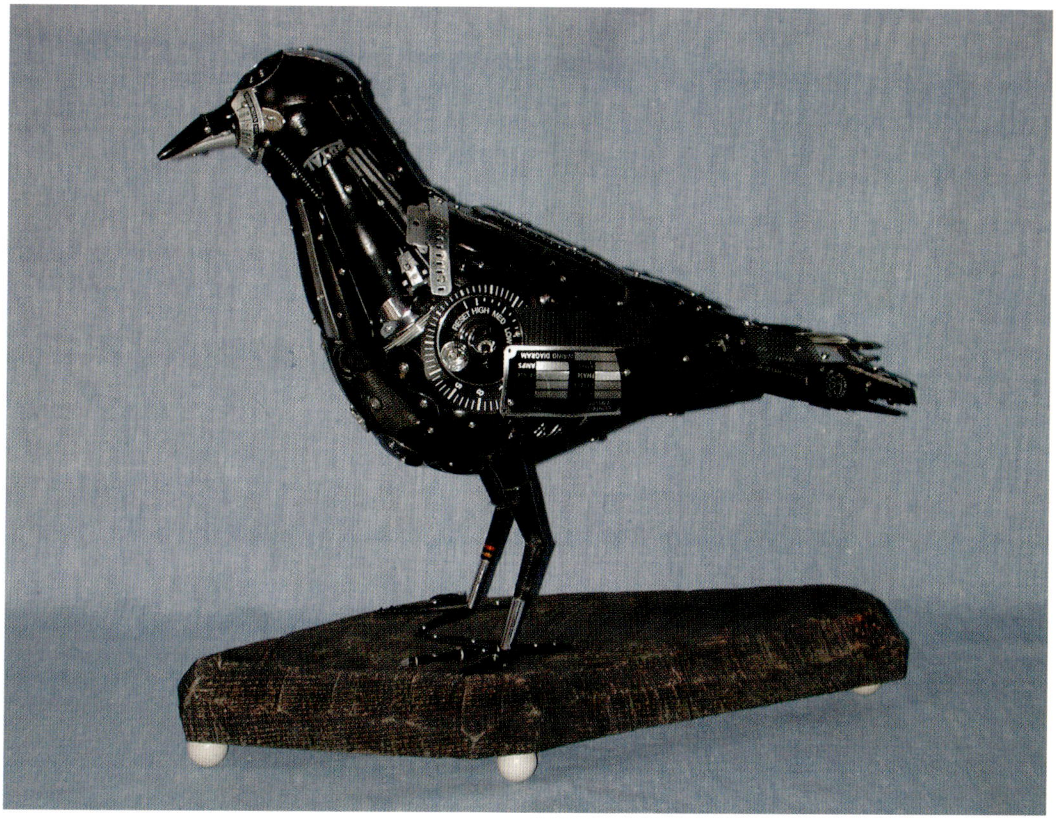

3

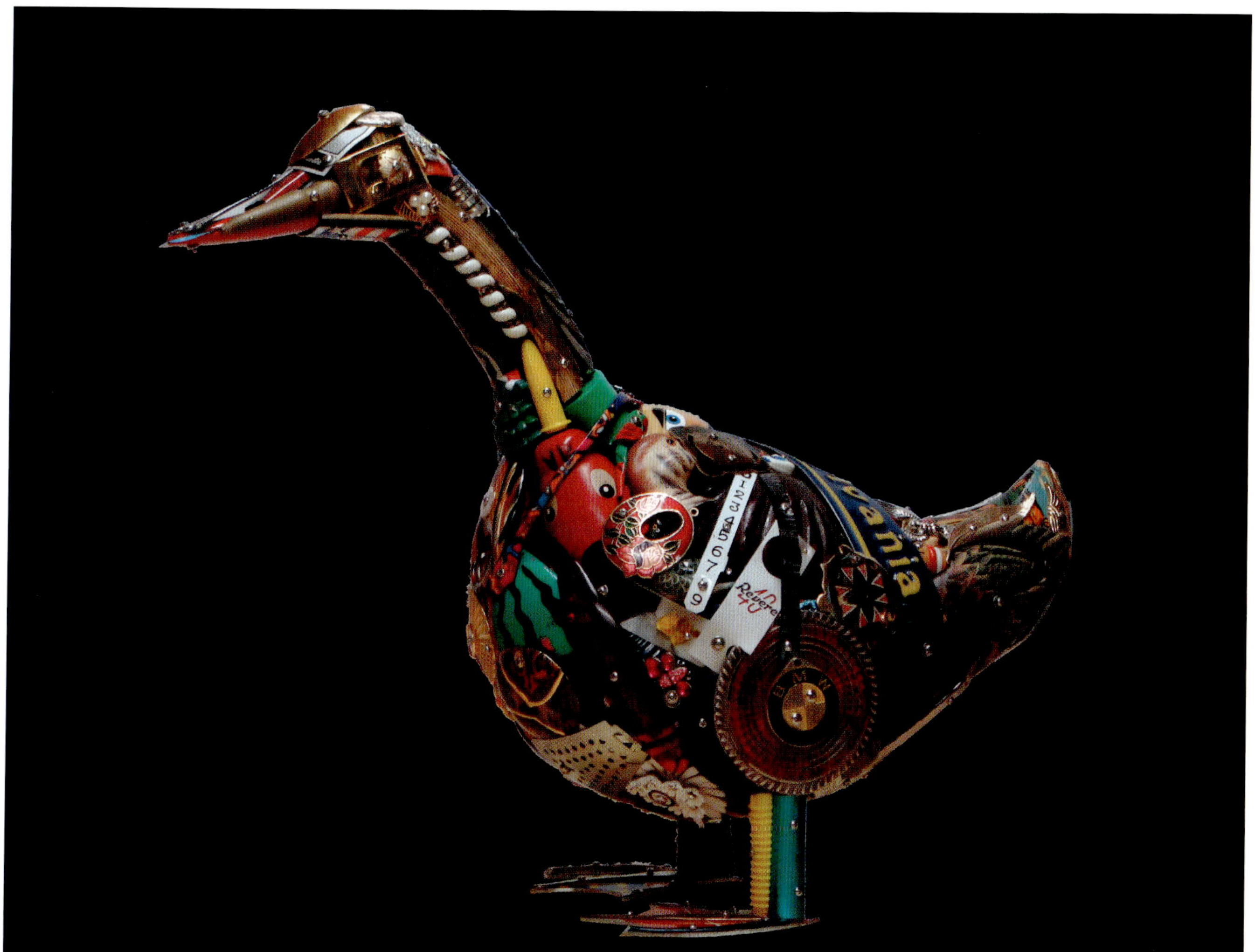

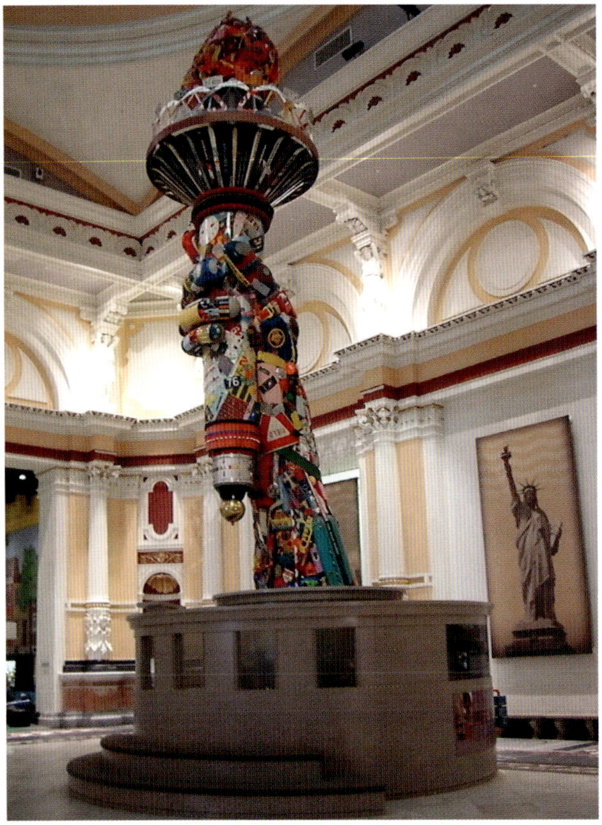

4

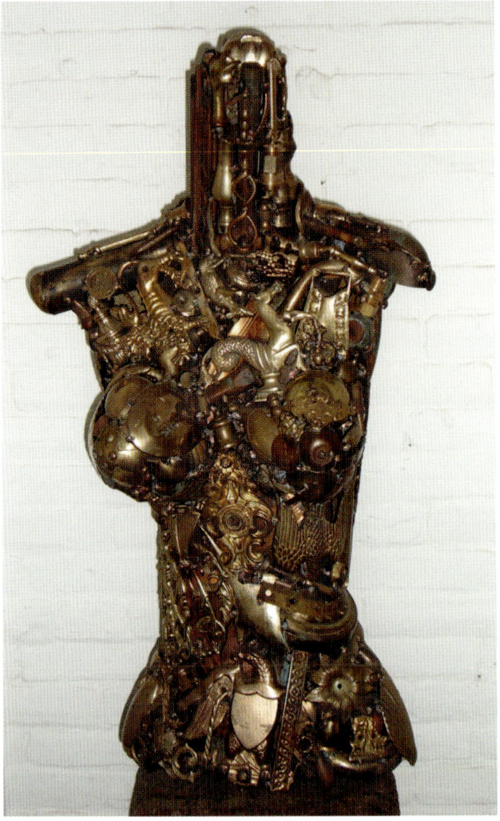

5

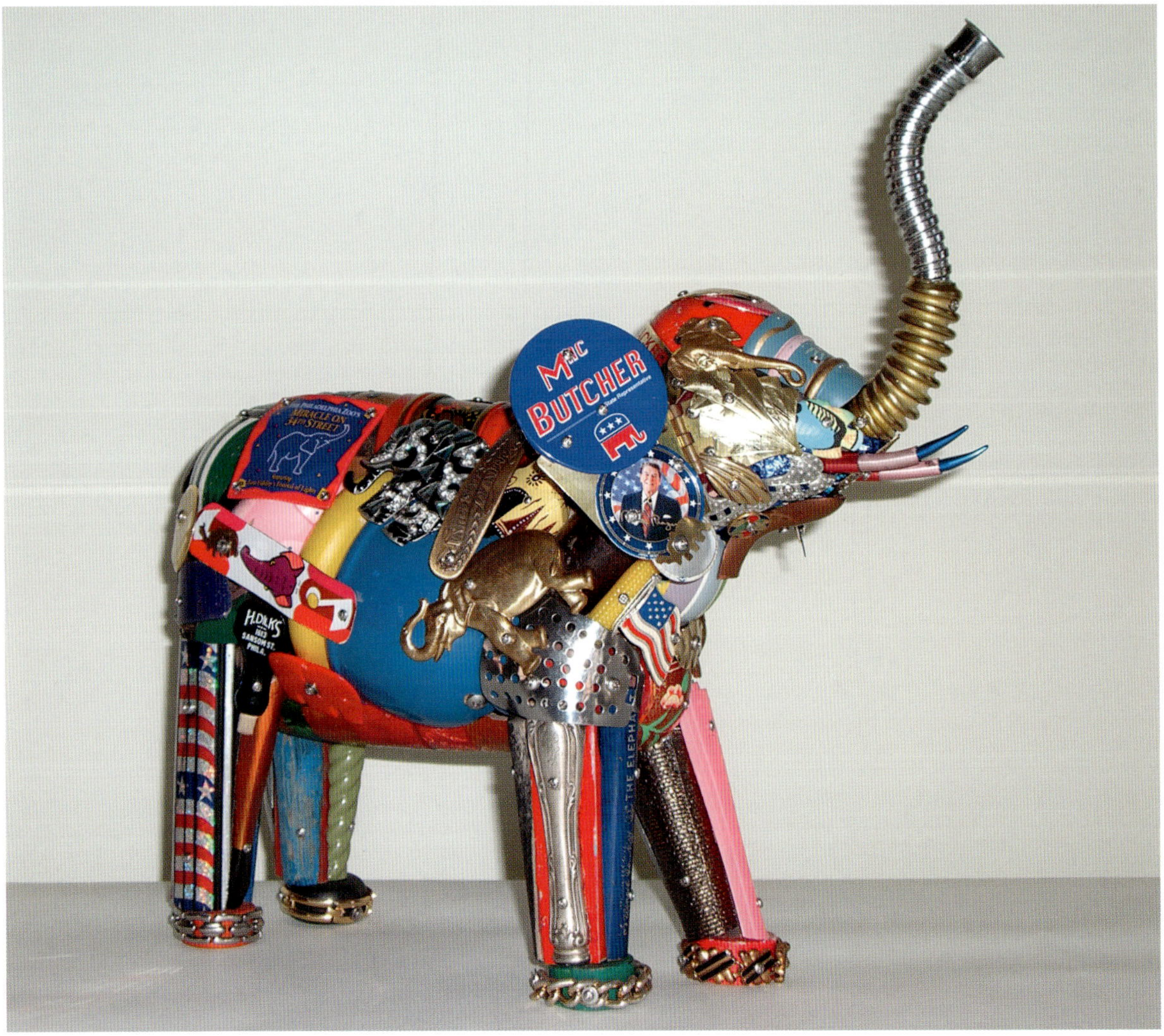


6

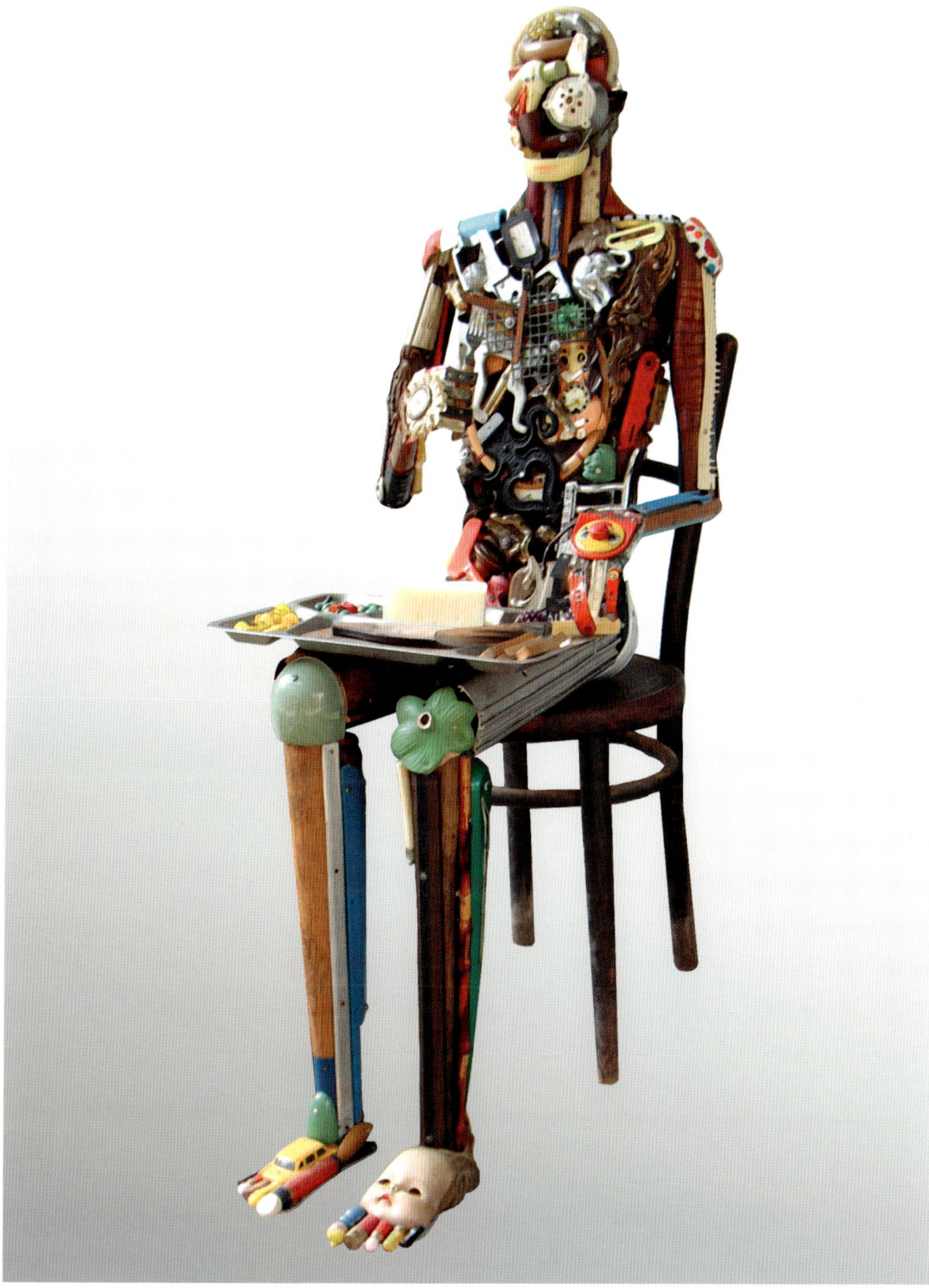

7

4 *Liberty Torch*, 2007. Reclaimed objects, 40' x 15' x 12'. *Photograph by Barbara Sewell.*

5 *Torso*, 2008. Welded brass objects, 31" x 18" x 9". *Photograph by Barbara Sewell.*

6 *Elephant*, 2005. Reclaimed objects, 14" x 7" x 13". *Photograph by Barbara Sewell.*

7 *Seated Man*, 1975. Reclaimed objects, 51" x 20" x 33". *Photographer unknown.*

# John E. Simms

Jackson, Wyoming, USA
www.johnesimms.com

*I live and work in Jackson Hole, Wyoming, where I have a studio and small sculpture garden. I have practiced as a sculptor for 22 years. Prior to that I was a professional skier as well as an inventor and product designer, and started several successful companies based on my various products. I have always been intrigued by geometric forms and this is born out in my designing as well as my sculptures.*

*I use the computer design program Rhino3d to develop large sculptures with geometric origins but unexpected results. All my sculptures are fabricated by cutting, forming, and welding steel, stainless steel, aluminum, or bronze into pieces as large as two tons. These pieces may be powder coated, painted, patinated or rusted. My sculpture Field of Red Bison is interesting in that each bison utilizes three perfect circles of equal radii. One full circle, two semi circles, and five arc sections. Imploding Cube shows a six-foot aluminum cube, each face of which rolls in to form a one foot negative space cube at its center. I mounted this piece on an apex and utilized sophisticated bearings that would allow the piece to be revolved to show differing aspects. Imagine my surprise when I discovered that the wind would cause the sculpture to revolve! This piece is now sited in a reflecting pool at the Indianapolis Center for the Arts*

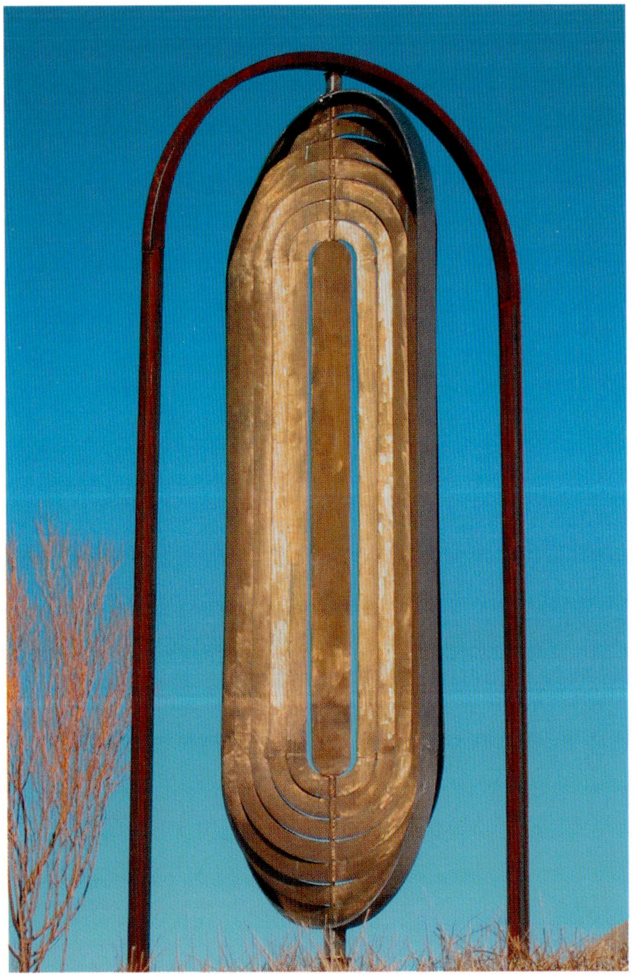

1

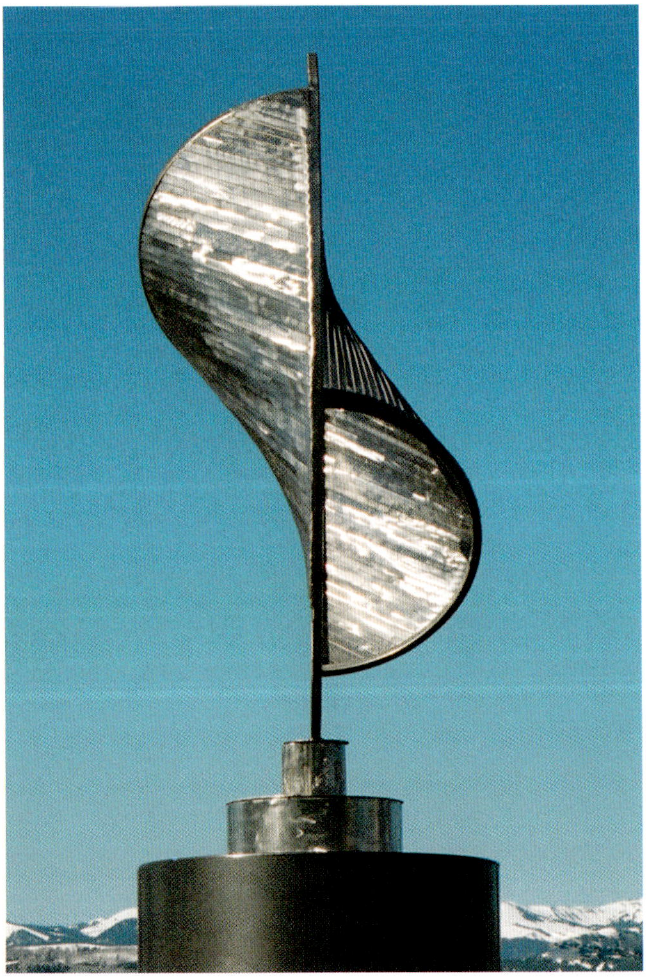

2

1 *Portal*, 2004. Bronze, steel, 12' h. x 8' x 4'. *Photograph by John Simms.*

2 *Ellipse Dynamo*, 2007. Bronze, stainless steel, 10' h. x 6' x 6' *Photograph Michael Clark.*

3 *Imploding Octahedron*, 2006. Powder-coated aluminum, 13' h. x 4' x 6'. *Photograph by John Simms.*

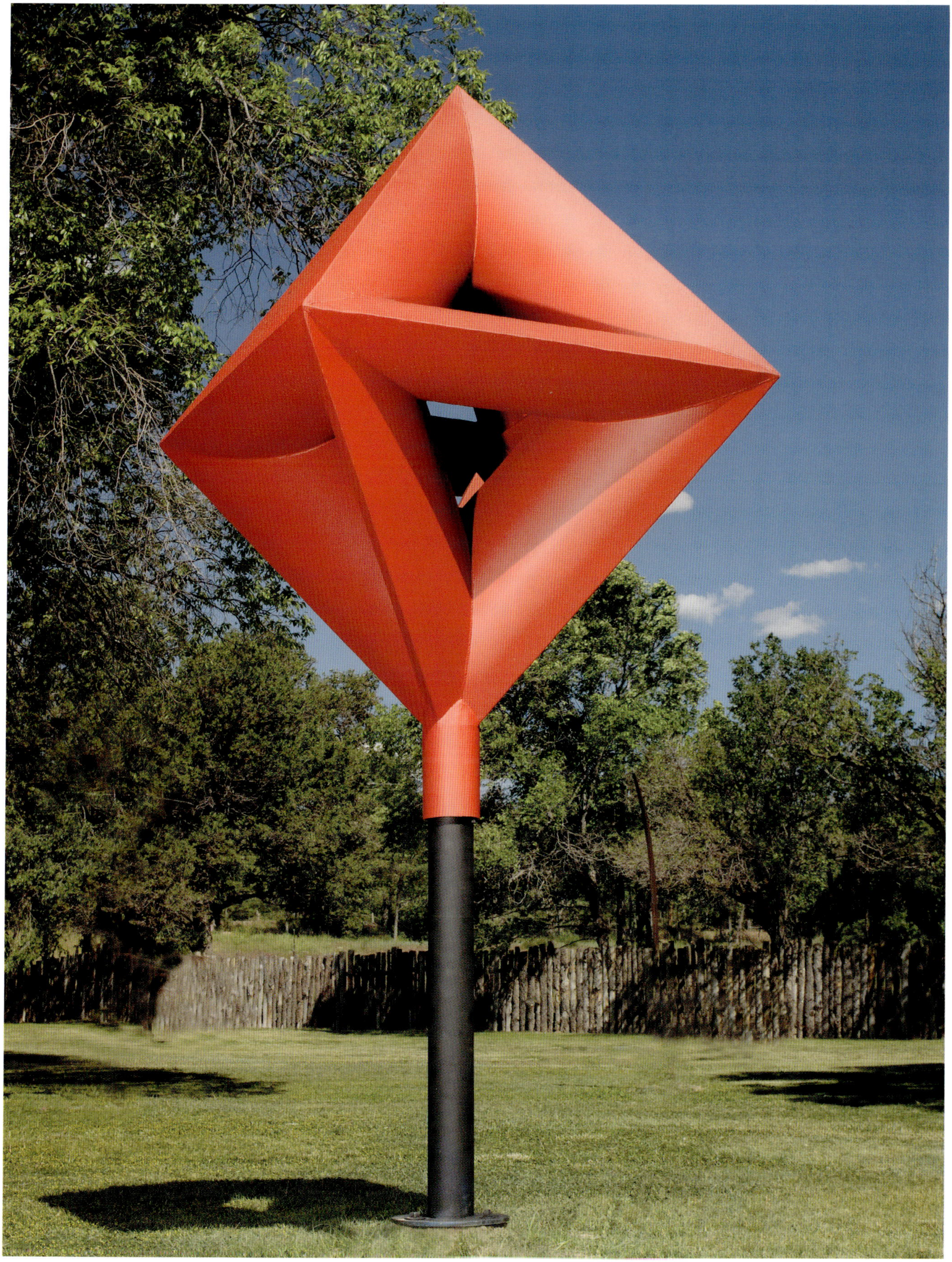

3

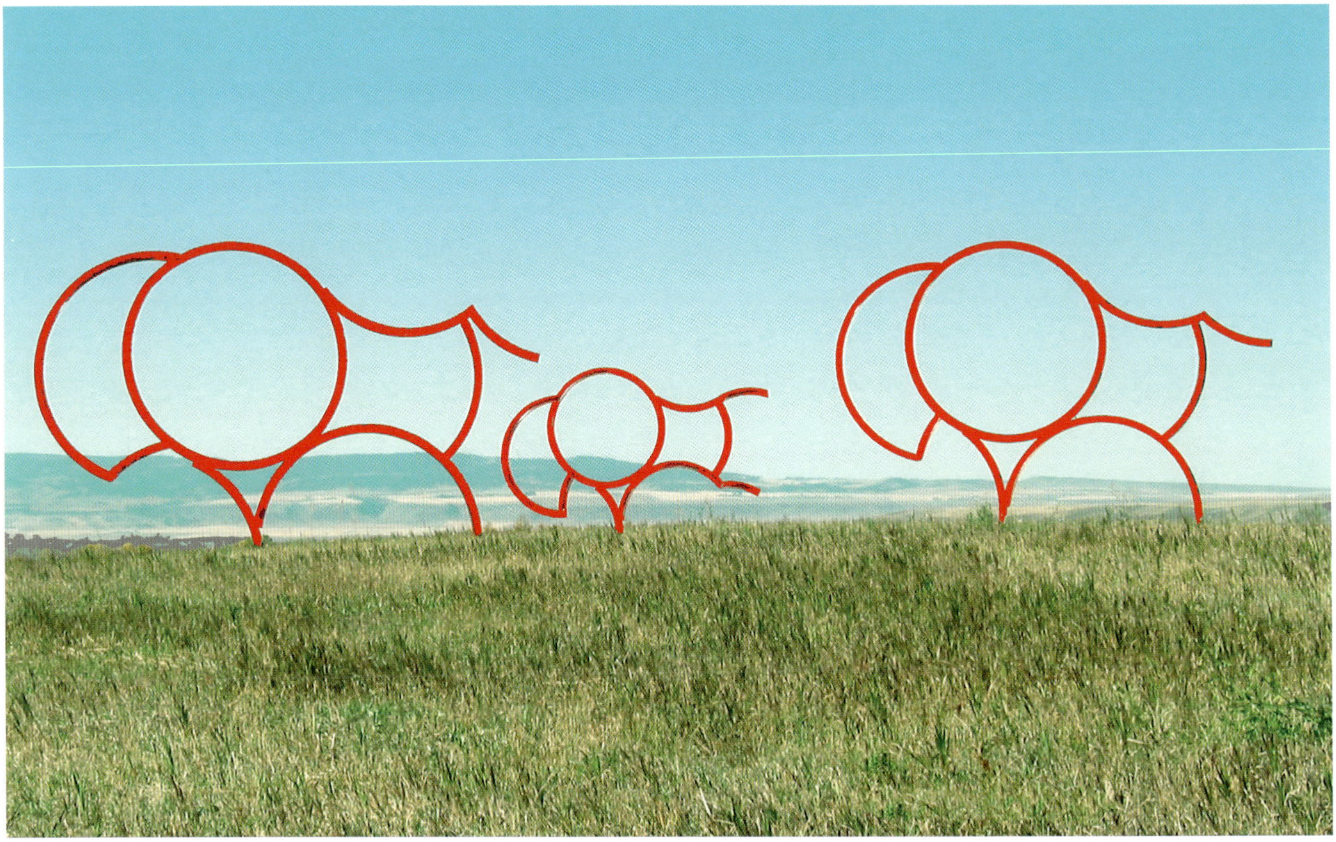

4

5

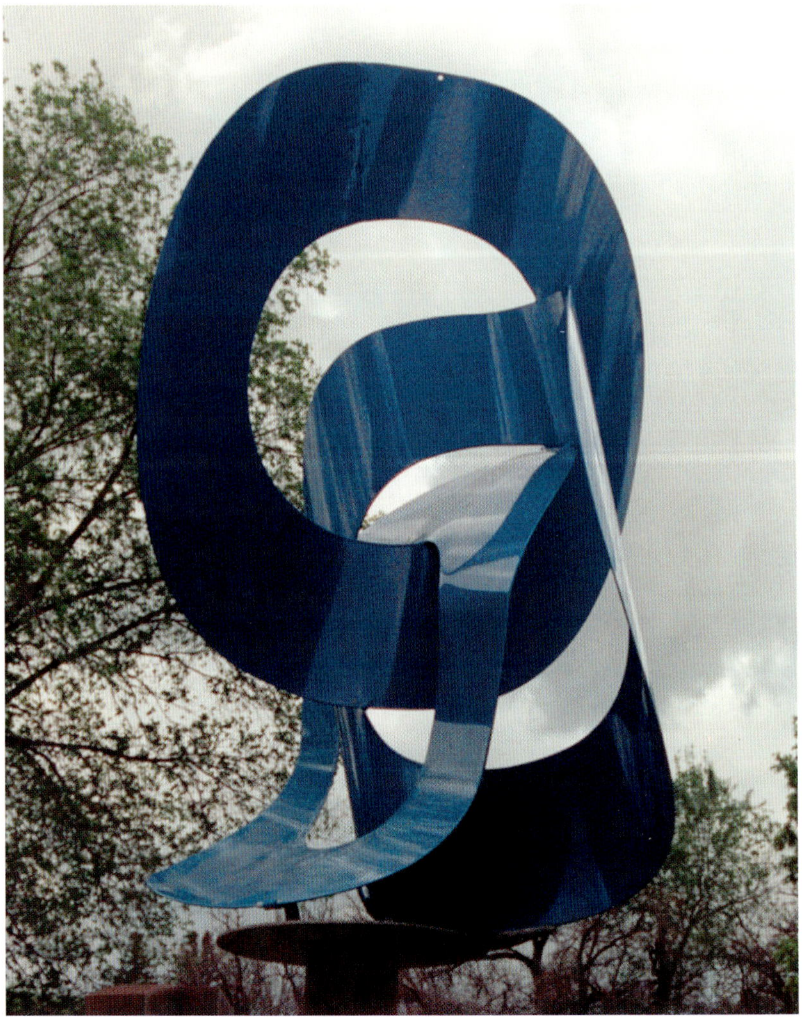

4 *Field of Red Bison*, 2002. Steel I-beam, 80' w. x 12' h. x 25' d. *Photograph by John Simms.*

5 *Cloud Form*, 2006. Powder-coated steel, 4' h. x 3' x 3'. *Photograph by John Simms.*

6 *Imploding Cube*, 2005. Burnished aluminum, 11' h. x 8' x 8'. *Photograph by John Simms.*

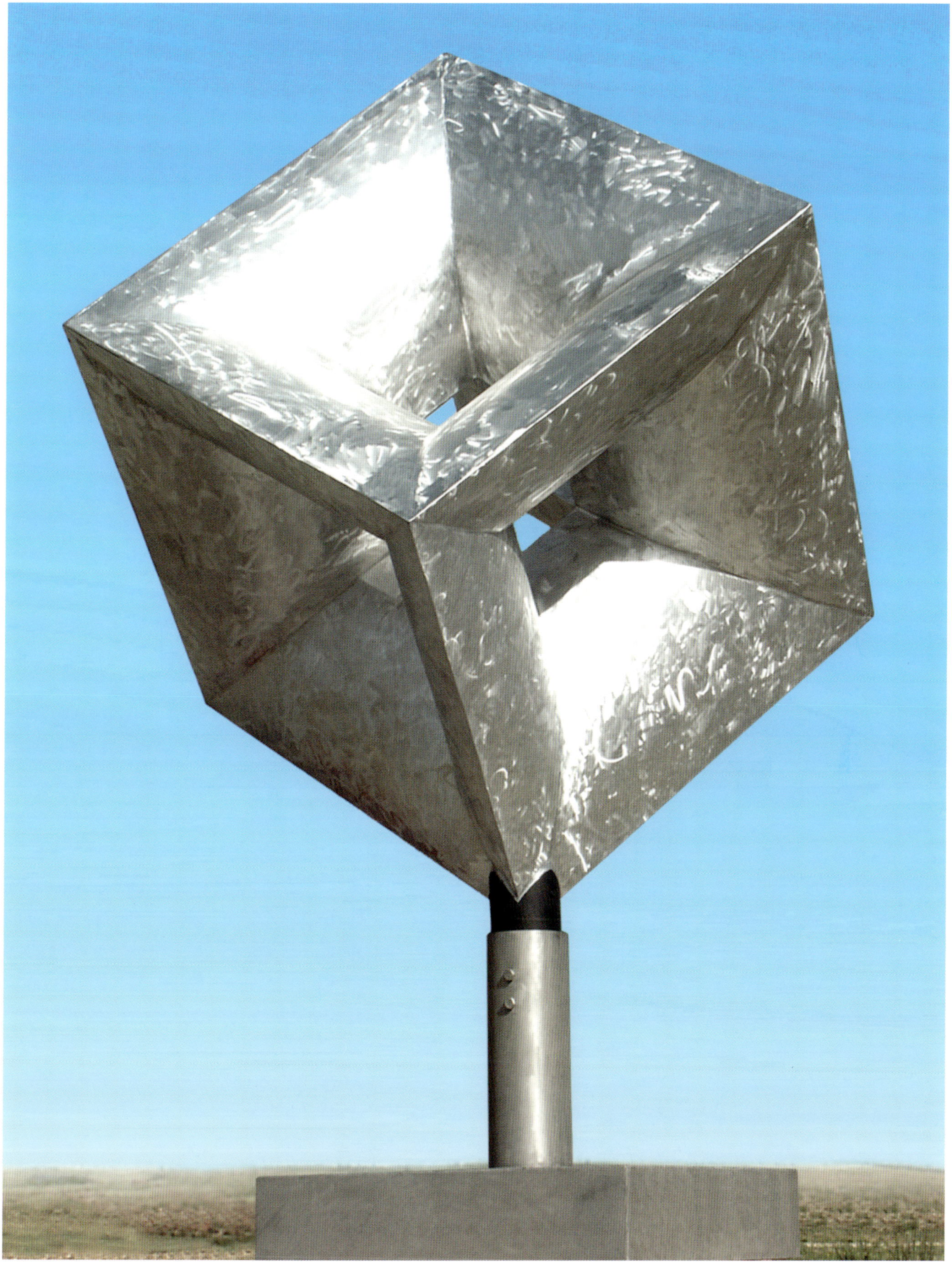

6

# Sandi Smith

Cantonment, Florida, USA
www.sandi-smith.artistwebsites.com

I am a self taught ceramic sculptor. I started in 2004 and all of my works are hand built.

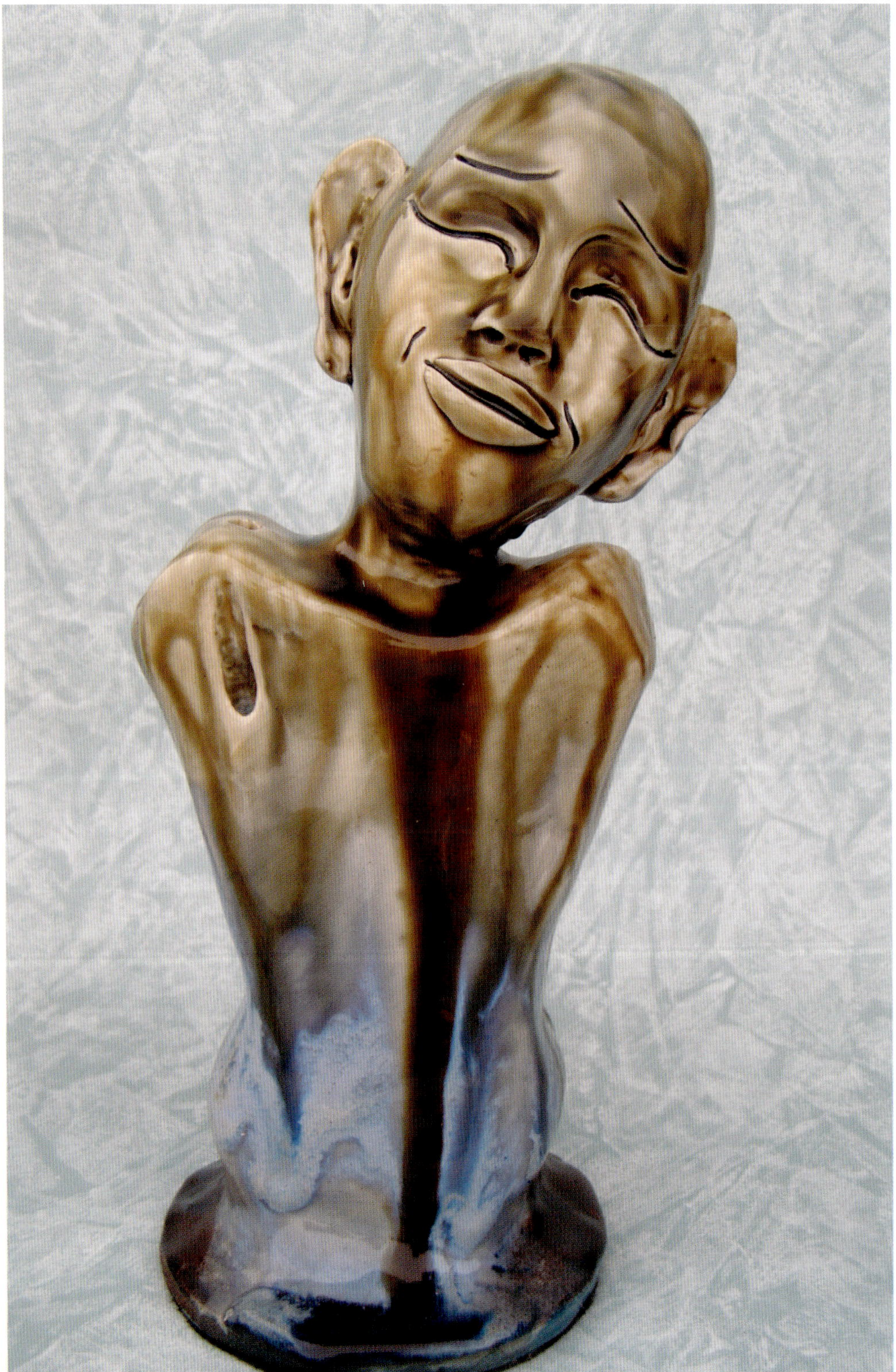

1

1 *Pride & Joy*, 2010. Ceramic, 4" x 10". *Photograph by SD Smith.*

2 *Be The Notes You Play.* Ceramic, 10.25" x7". *Photograph by SD Smith.*

3 *Love Being A Woman*, 2008. Ceramic, 4.25" x 10". *Photograph by SD Smith.*

4 *Madelyn*, 2011. Ceramic, 7" x 9.5". *Photograph by SD Smith.*

5 *Zen*, 2006. Ceramic, 5" x 10". *Photograph by SD Smith.*

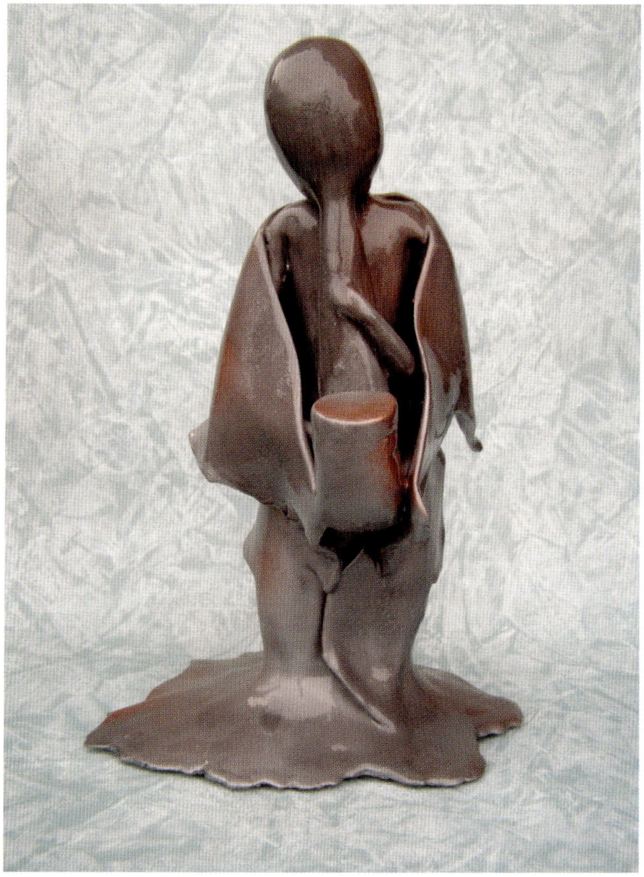

2

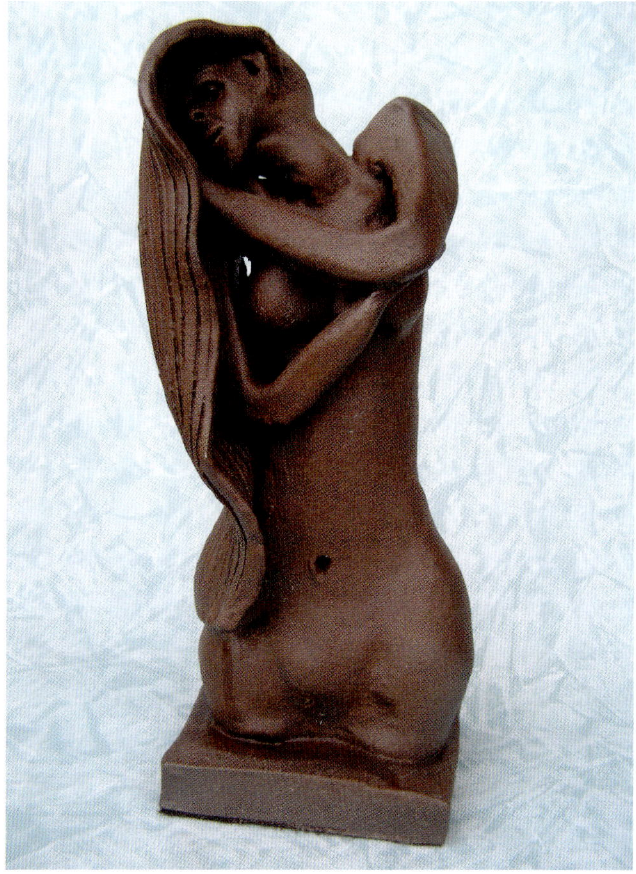

3

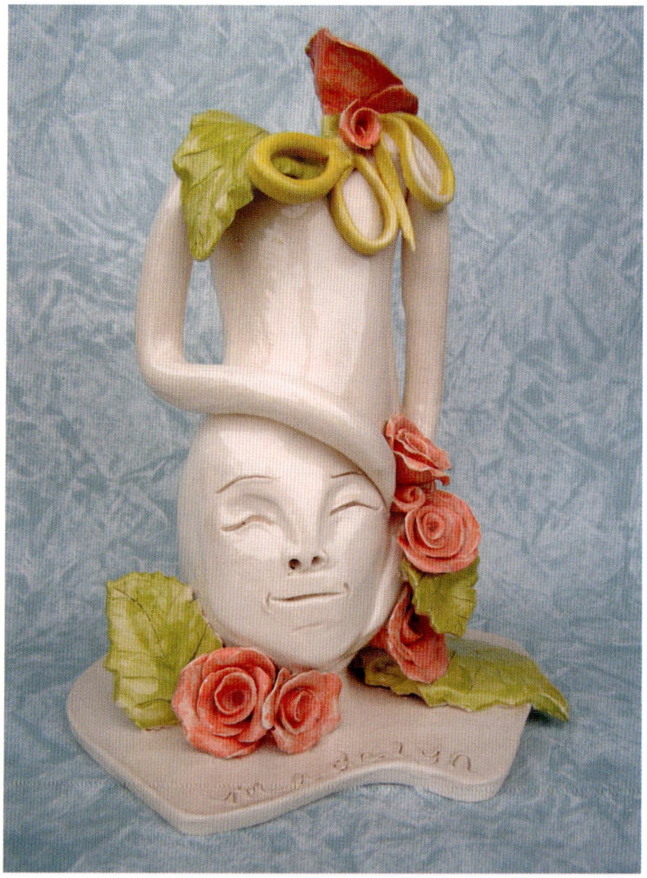

4

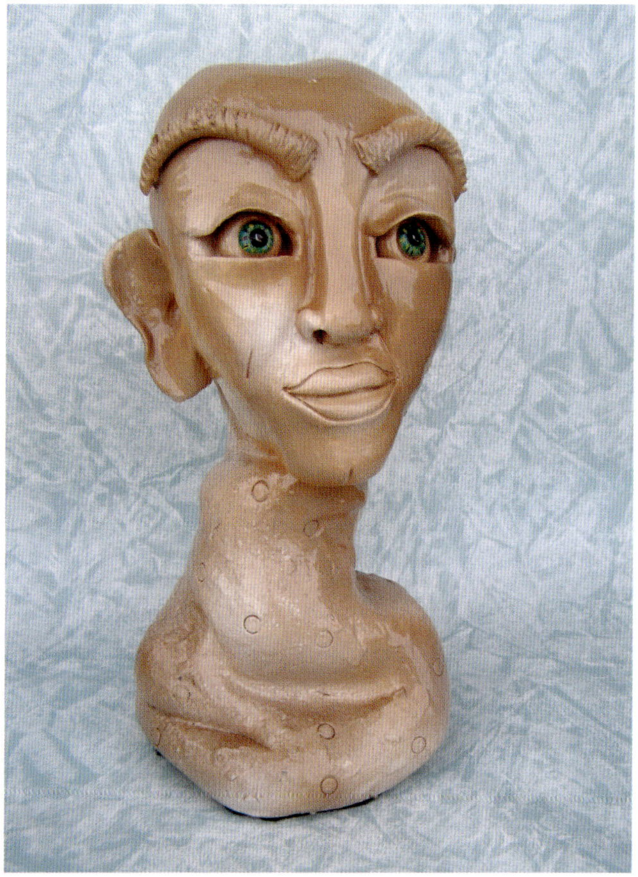

5

# Stan Smokler

Kennett Square, Pennsylvania, USA
www.stansmokler.com

*I have been making sculpture for the past 30 years. For me doing sculpture is an ongoing exploration of how material affects the space it occupies. I am always searching for new ways to invent and organize space. My welded sculptures, created from steel, are modeled in a spontaneous and improvisational manner. This style of modeling creates a lively sequence for discovery. Once I begin to work, I often see things unfold that I did not visualize before. Ultimately, I strive to breathe new life into discarded material, creating forms that deliberately deny their past history in order to serve a new formal purpose.*

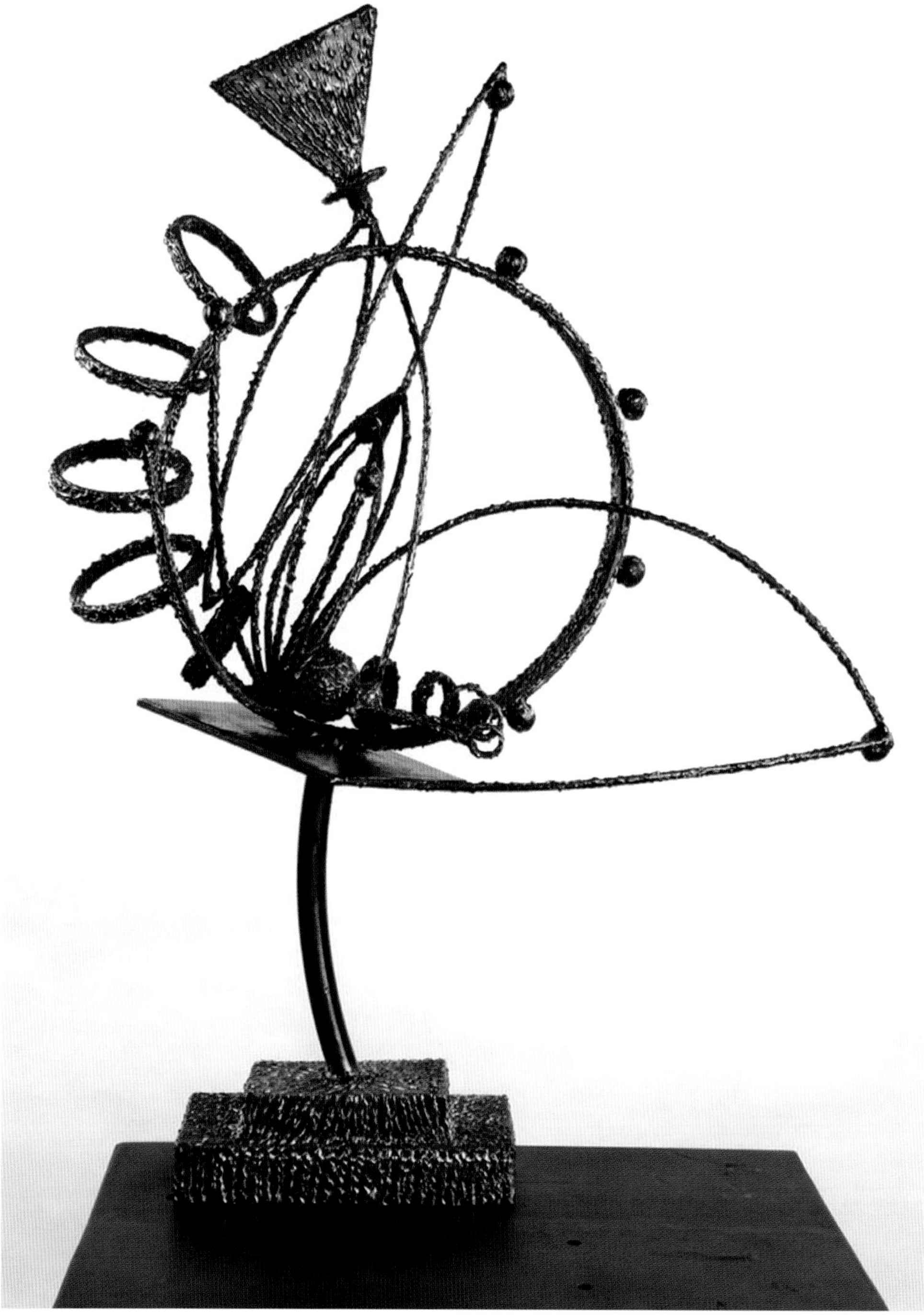

1

1 *Twin Echoes*, 2007. Steel, 38" h. x 20" w. x 20". *Photograph by D. R. Brignac of Supervova.*

2 *Tracking*, 2007. Aluminum, maquette, 15" h. x 18" w. x 24.5". *Photograph by D. R. Brignac.*

3 *Molecules*, 2011. Steel, wall hanging, 19" h. x 19" w. x 4.5". *Photograph by W. K. Bielicki.*

4 *Lazarus*, 2011. Steel, 30" h. x 35" w. x 11". *Photograph by W. K. Bielicki.*

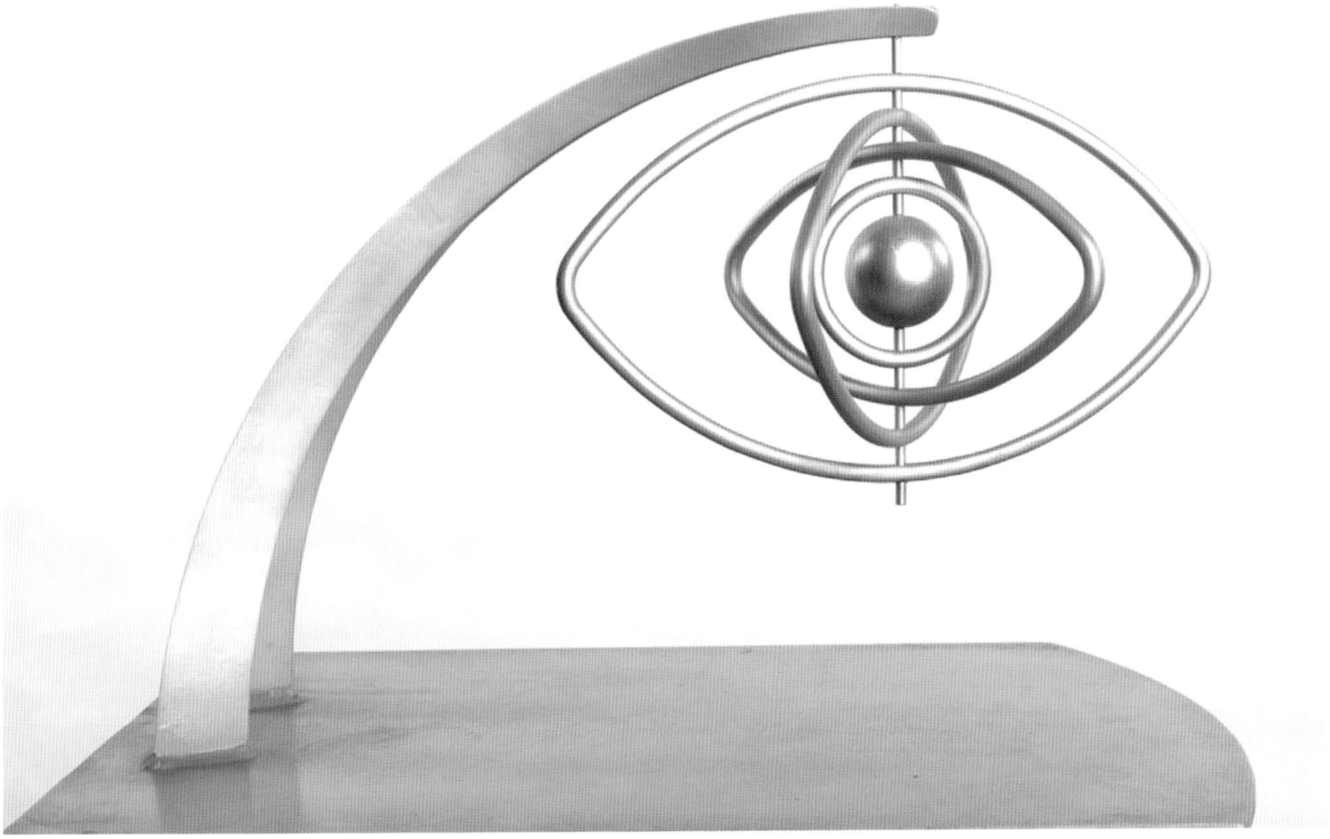

2

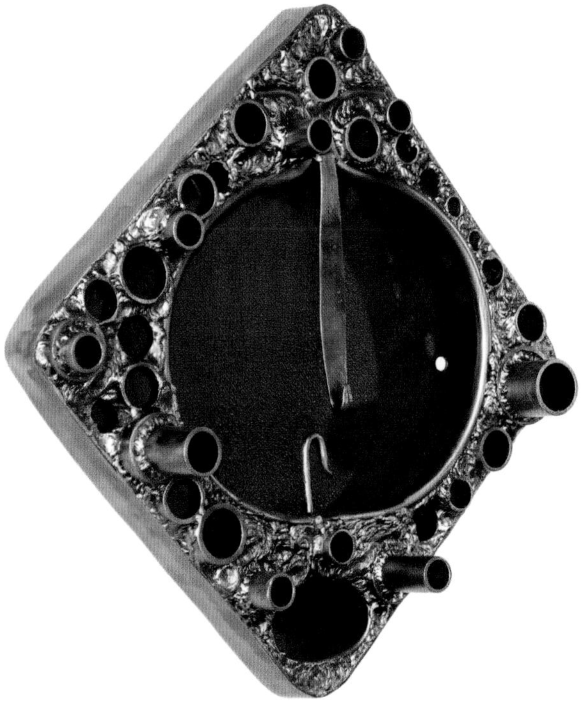

3

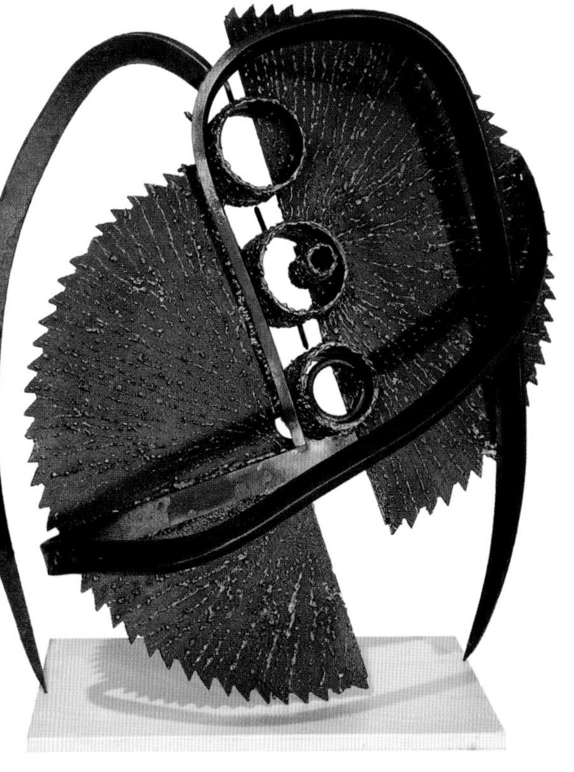

4

# Jözef Sumichrast

Lake Forest, Illinois, USA
www.jozef.com

*In the first phase of my artistic career as a painter, I drew realistically and three-dimensionally, but without a traditional form of perspective. My drawings resembled architectural blueprints. I would paint these flat, two-dimensional drawings as three-dimensionally as possible. The effect created a new perspective, similar to the way cubism saw an object from different perspectives. I then applied this thought process to my sculpture. On the same piece, I am working simultaneously with flat, two-dimensional surfaces and curved sculpted forms. More recently I have begun to experiment with transparent material, which allows the viewer to see inside and through the sculpture. Examples of this technique are M Theory and Hair. Also, I am sculpting separate parts of one sculpture and fabricating them back together, as in Narrow Horses II. Finally, I have started to suspend my sculptures from walls and ceilings, which shows the bottom of the sculpture in addition to the top and sides. Examples of this technique are Susan's Dance and String Theory.*

*I believe that, in addition to simple sensations like color, line and form, and simple emotions like pleasure, anger or curiosity, art should express a concept or idea beyond its obvious physical presence. I believe that there is more than three-dimensional space ,and as an artist I am attempting to express and transmit these feelings. There are phenomena in the world that cannot be measured in terms of length, breadth, and thickness. There are motions and functions that lay outside of our three-dimensional space. Though inaccessible to us, there is an assumption that beyond the three-dimensions known to our geometry, additional dimensions are possible.*

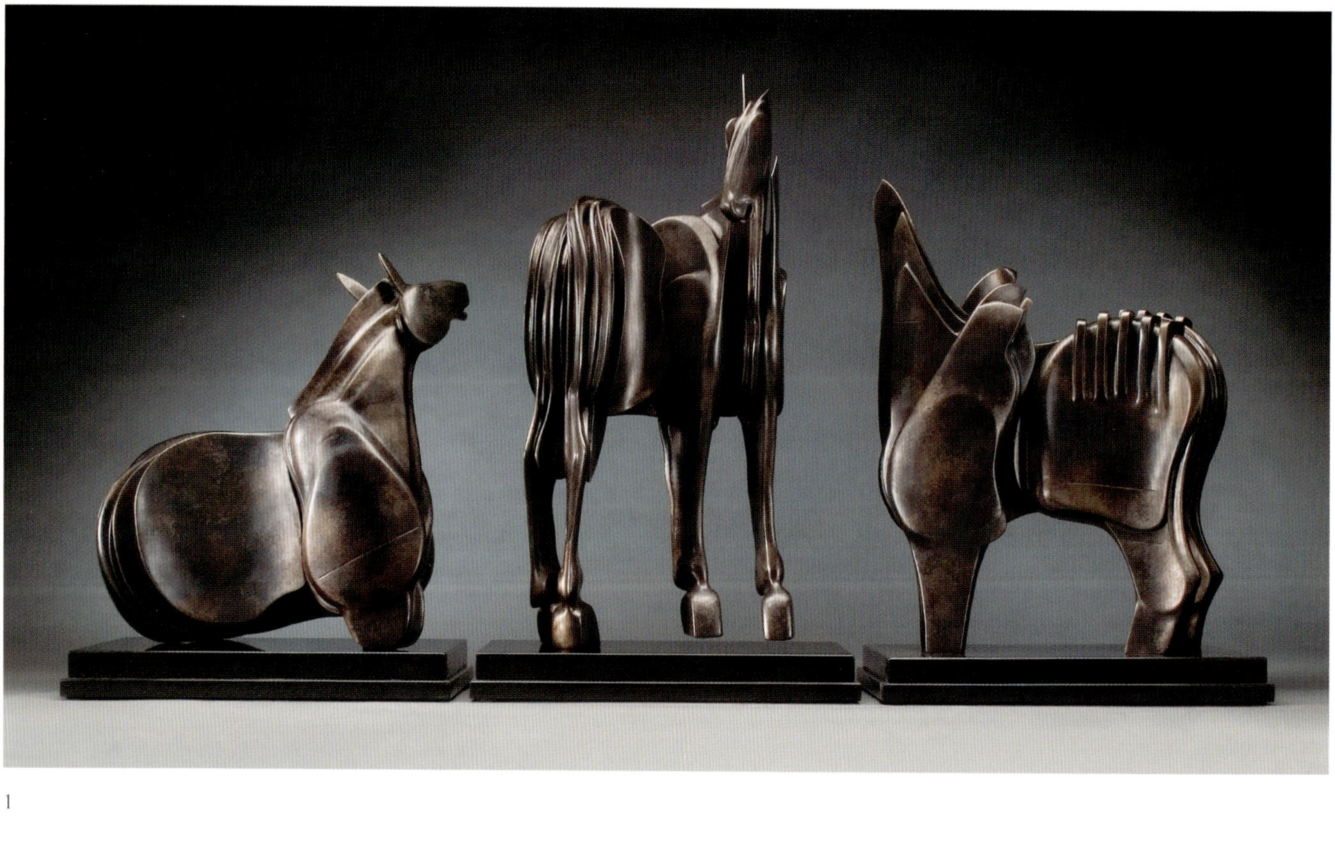

1

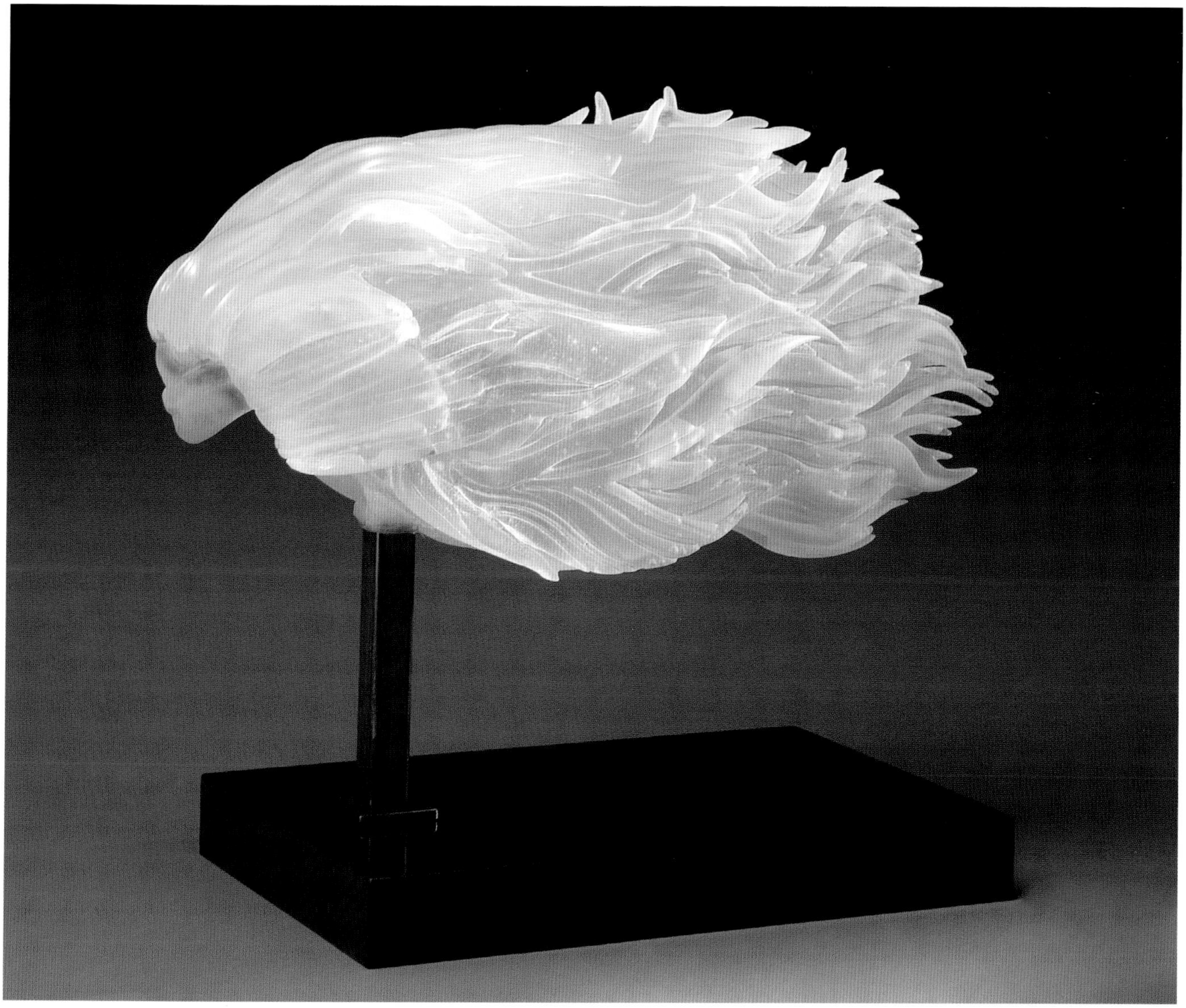

2

1 *Elevation Triptych,* © 2007. Bronze, 17" x 11" x 20", 17" x 11" x 28", 17" x 11" x 25". *Photograph by Mel Schockner.*

2 *Hair,* © 2007. Urethane, 18" x 24" x 10". *Photograph by Mel Schockner.*

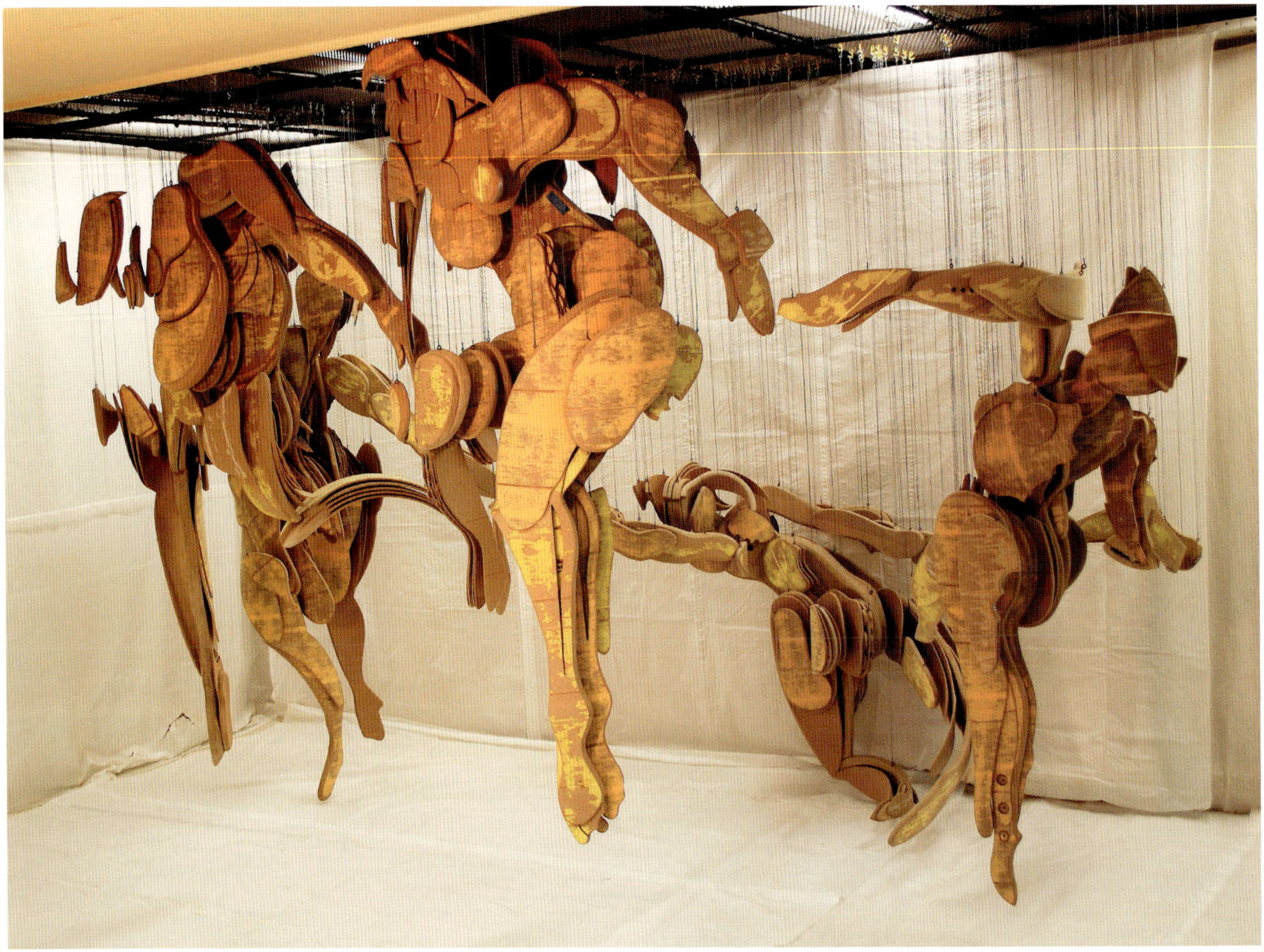

3

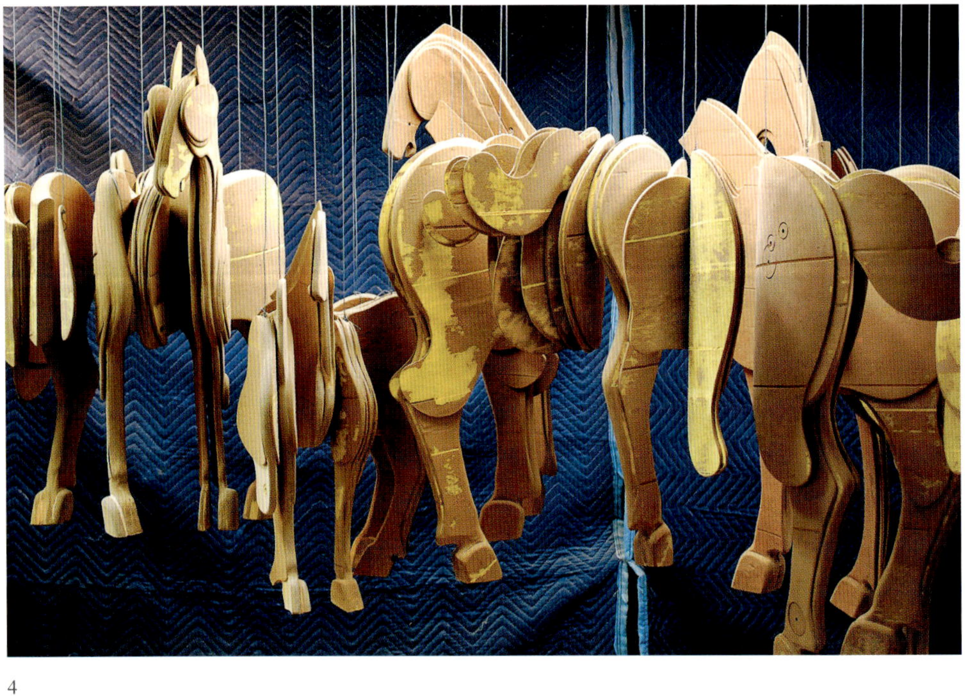

4

3 *Susan's Dance*, © 2011. Cardboard, 244" w. x 108" d. x variable height. *Photography by Susan Snyder.*

4 *String Theory* (detail), © 2010. Cardboard, 300" w. x 96" d. x variable height. *Photography by Susan Snyder.*

5 *Susan's Dance* (detail), © 2011. *Photography by Susan Snyder.*

5
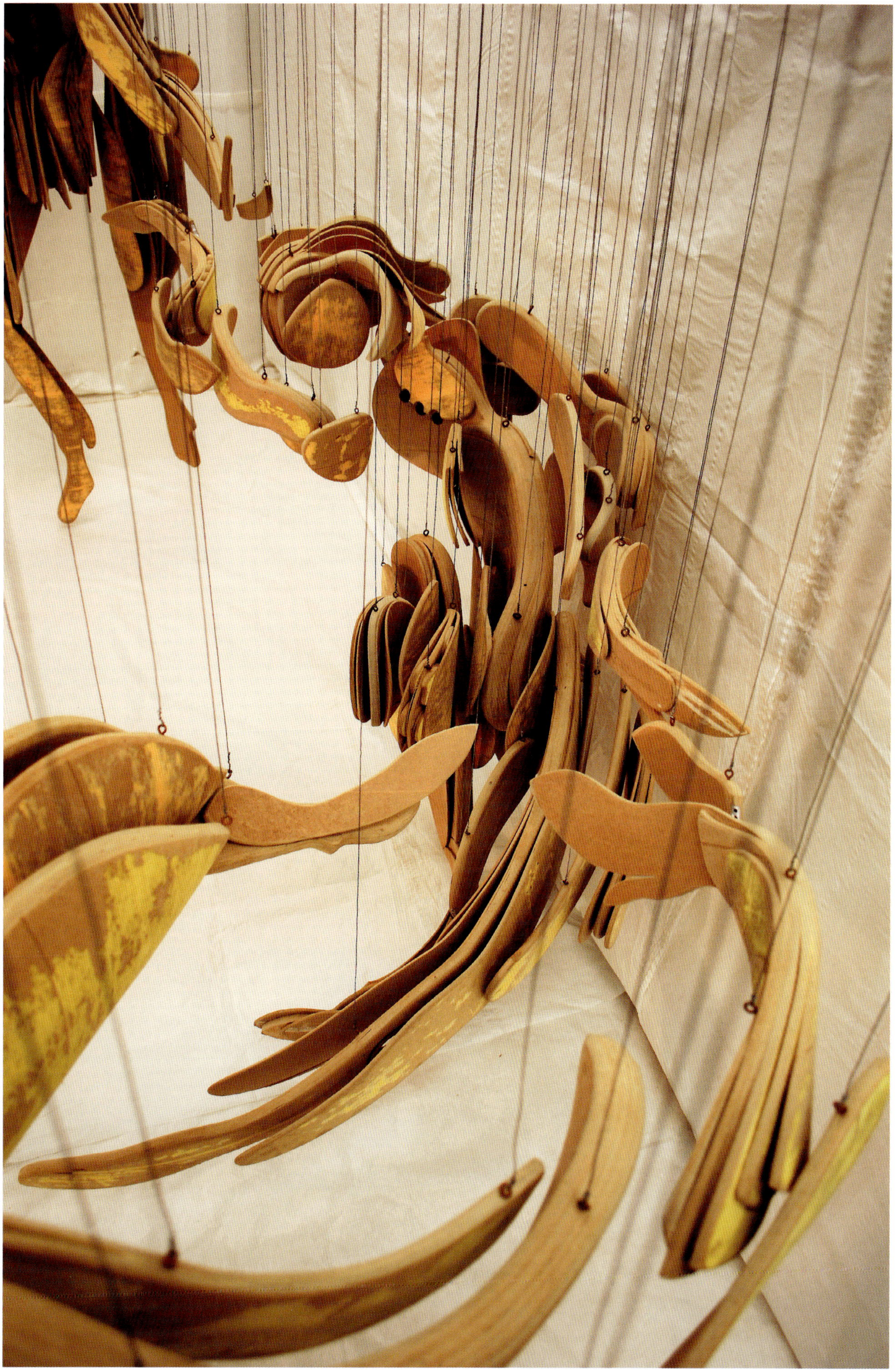

# Victor Tan Wee Tar

Singapore, Singapore
www.victortanweetar.com

*I began experimenting with wire in my first year at an art college in 1995. Due to a visual impairment, I had to find an alternative to pencil and paper for my life-drawing class, and I found wire. Space was the paper, and wires were the pencil strokes. And since graduating with a BFA in sculpture in 1997, I have not stopped focusing on using only wires and steel rods. Without using any equipment or adhesive, I employ a basic method of weaving and connecting the wires to form a sculpture strong enough to stand on its own. Unlike traditional concepts of sculpture as a solid mass, carved down or built up, my line works carve into the spaces, creating forms that draw weight from the space itself.*

*My works, through using the fundamental human forms, seek to highlight the mundane, the humble person that we are, caught in a certain journey, examining and releasing a variety of emotions and wonderings. Being a Buddhist, the practice of mindfulness or working in a meditative state helps me to be more acutely aware of each sensation that arises in the process of creation. I enjoy the process of creating, investigating existential ideas about humanity, the isolation of the human emotions in the moment and through the passage of time and life. Sculpting, to me, is a way of exploring and experiencing constant change and movement. Each change, each movement, each experience suggests a new possibility.*

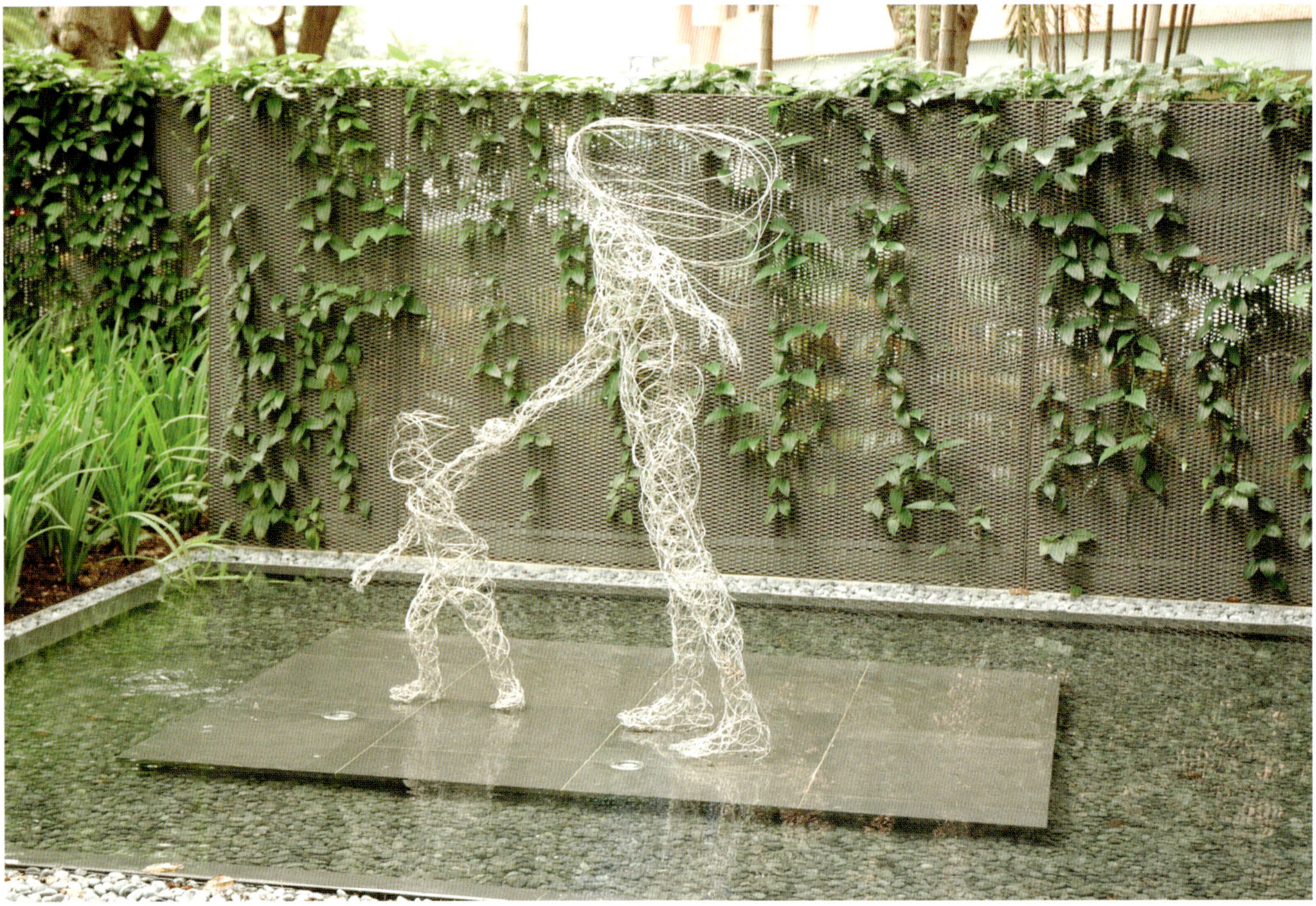

1

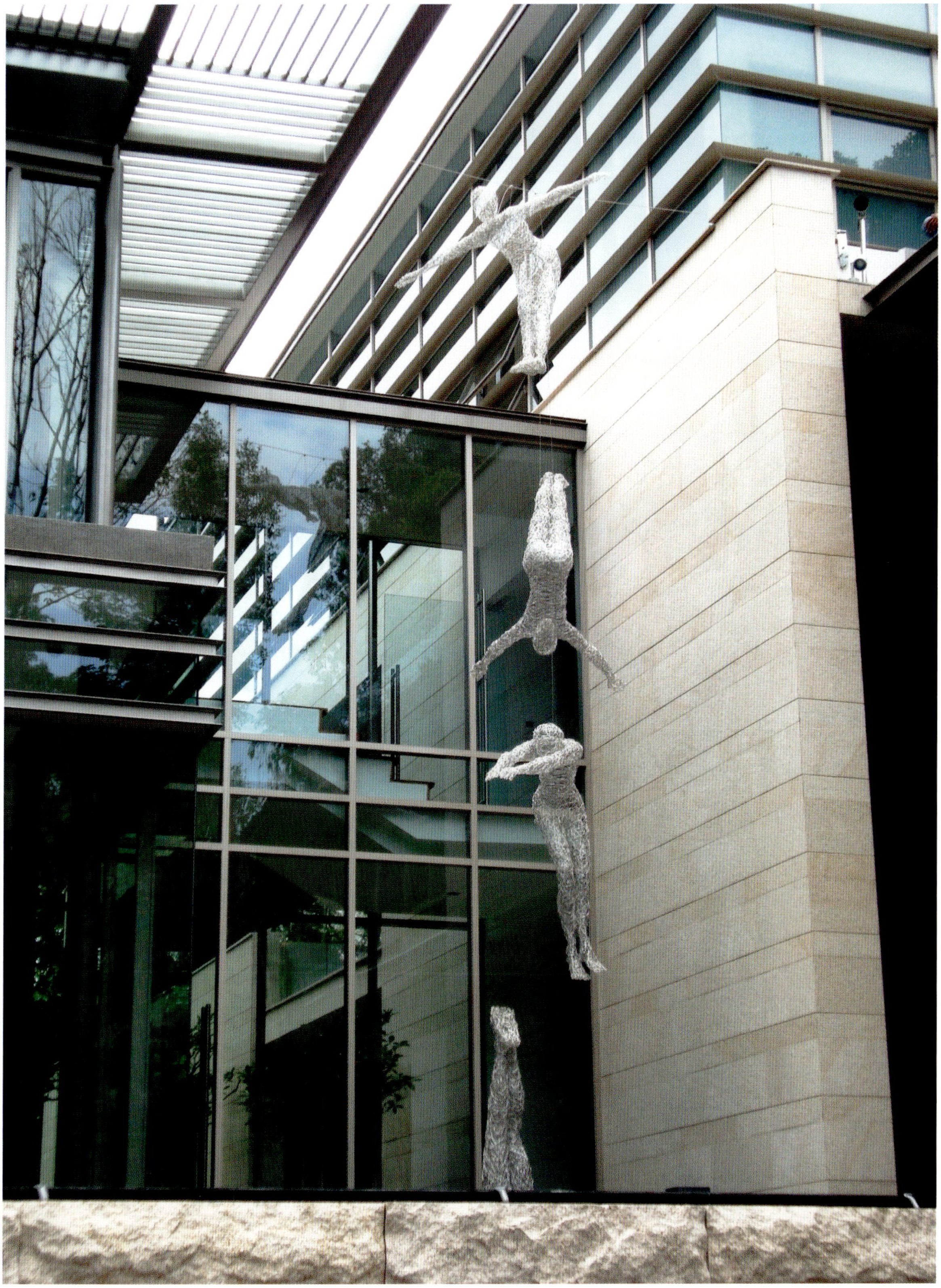

2

1 *Come*, 2007. Stainless steel wires, 1.6m. *Photograph by Clarence Chan.*

2 *Divers*, 2008. Stainless steel wires, 6m. *Photograph by Wendy Tan.*

3

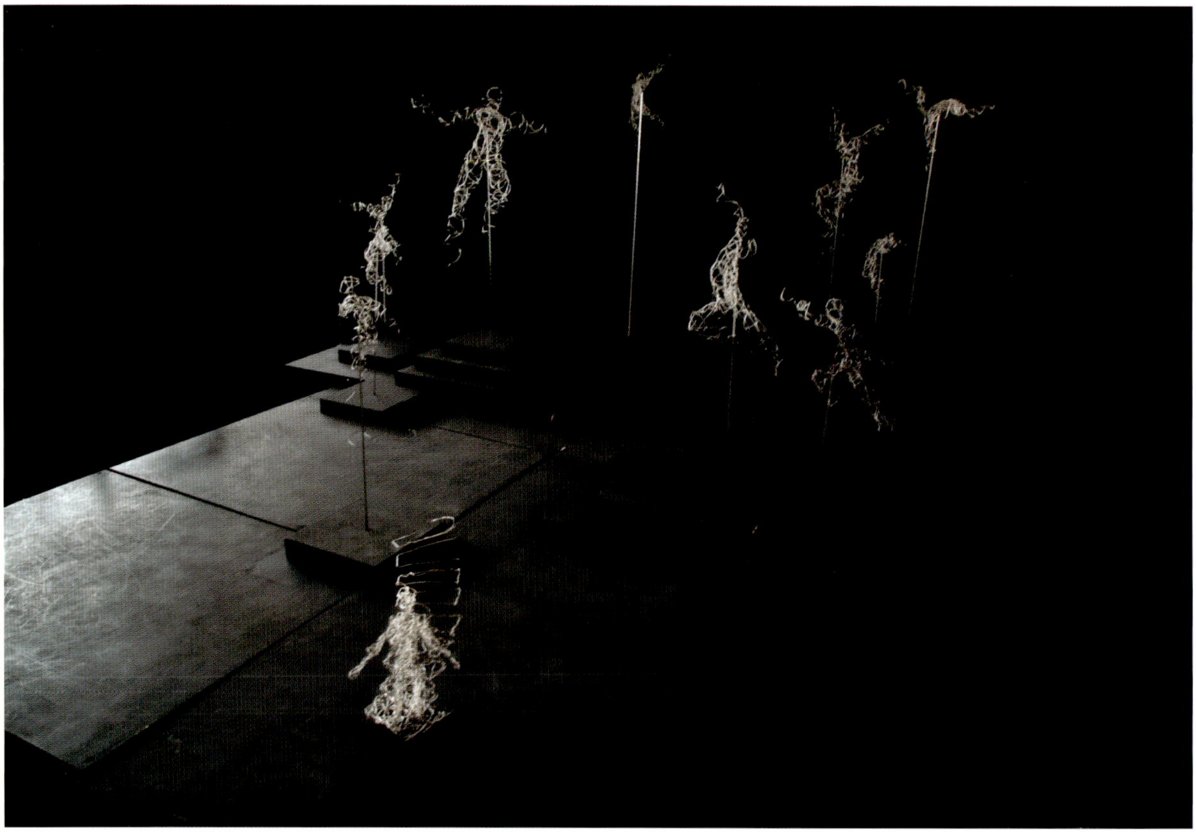

4

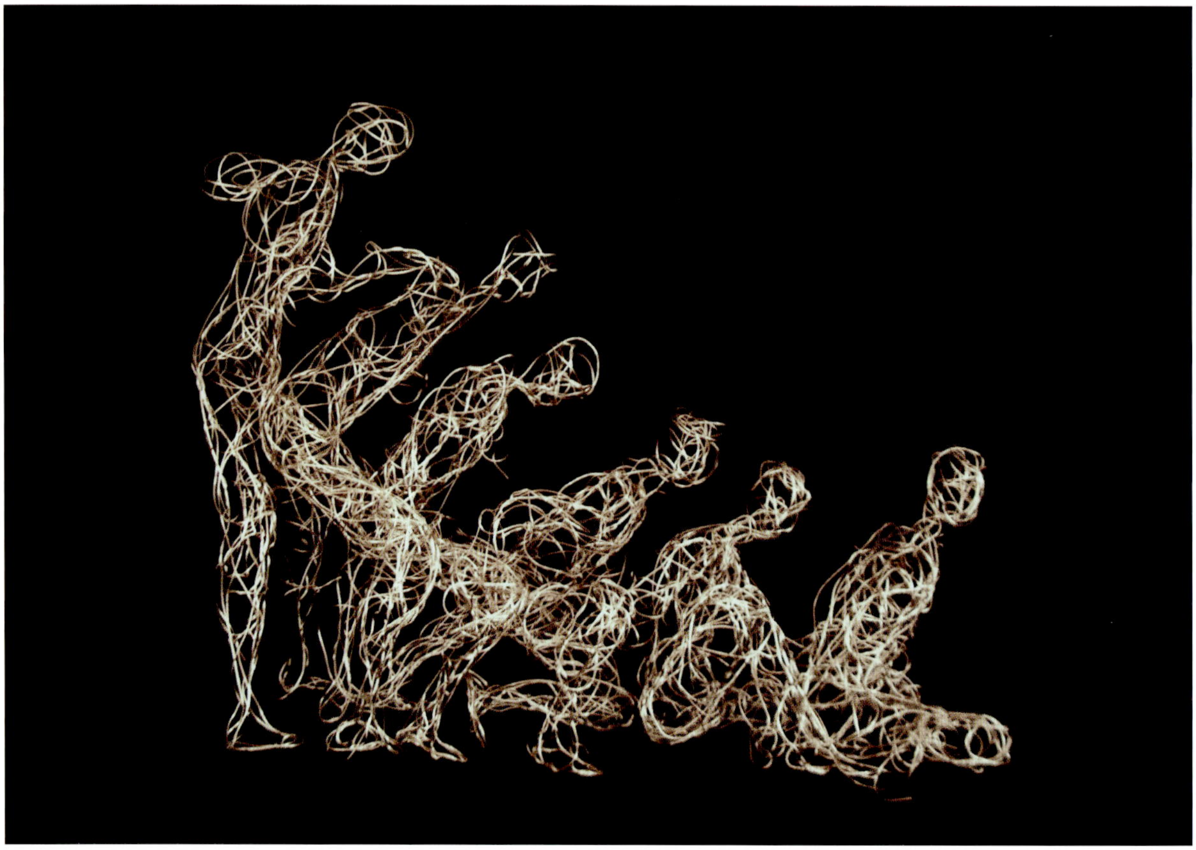

3 *The Stair, the Cloud, and the Sky (marquette)*, 2009. Stainless steel wire, various heights. *Photography by Sol Yan.*

4 *The Awareness of Sitting,* 2005. Stainless steel wires, 600cm. *Photograph by Wendy Tan.*

5 *The Stair, the Cloud, and the Sky (Sculpture 1)*, 2009. Stainless steel wire, 2.7m. *Photography by Jennisse Miyuki.*

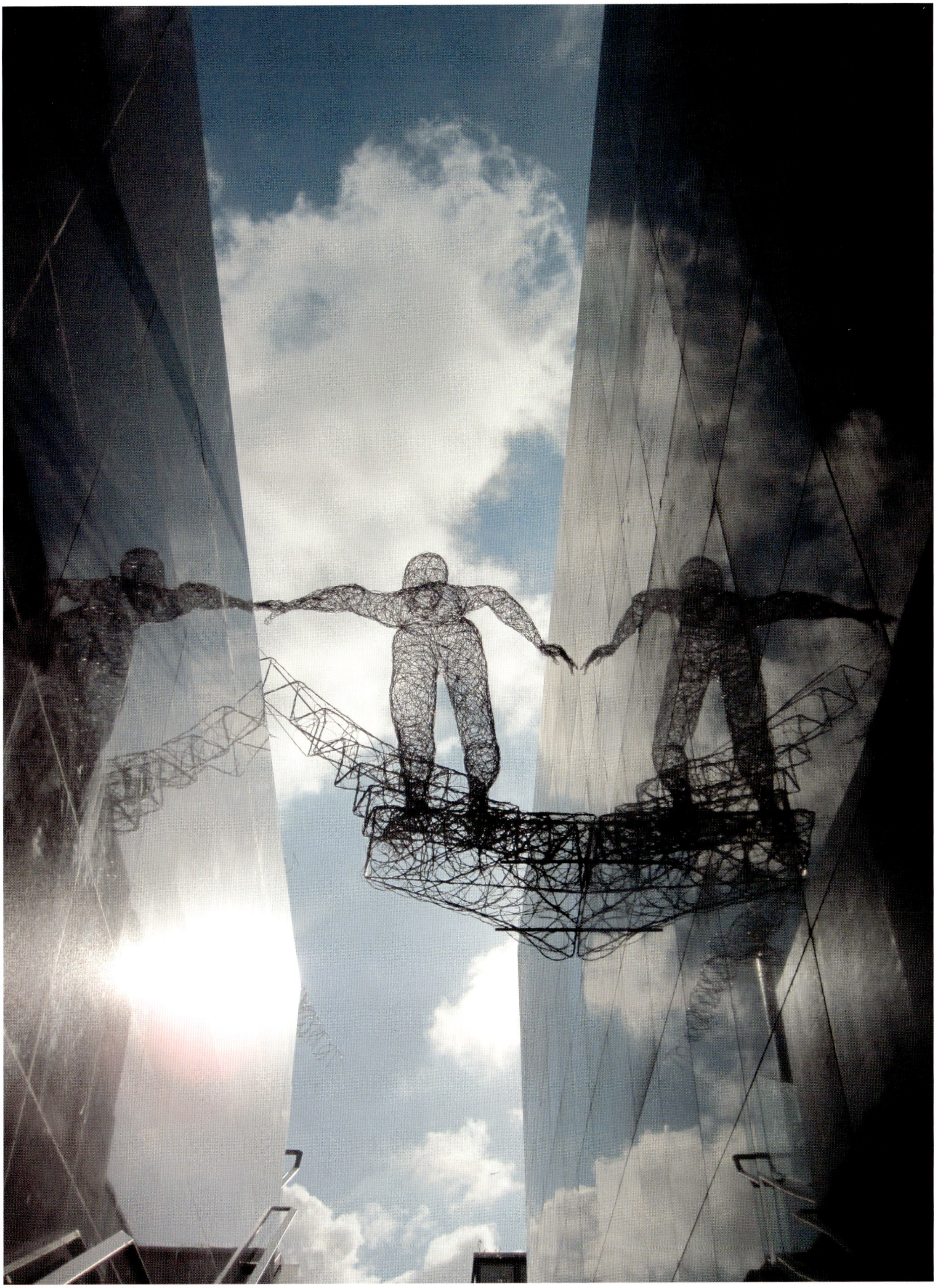

5

# Dan Townsend

Encinitas, California, USA
www.palmfish.com

Dan Townsend's Palm Fish idea came about because of his interest in the environment, about eighteen years ago. His fish are made from palm fronds and paper mâché, which makes them so unusual and fun. Dan grew up around the ocean and that, along with nature, became his inspiration that this was something that could be recycled and turned into art. His work has been seen in TV series, a multitude of restaurants, Sea World, and county fairs, and has been sold to many people around the world in gallery's and at many art shows.

*The thing that I would like to describe about myself and my artwork would be a constant curiosity I have about nature. Finding new discoveries and fusing them in art as a invention of the soul. I use recycled materials which can give a spark of creative nature and inspiration to me and everyone who sees this art. Hopefully, it will open our minds in the quest for creativity and permit us look at problems and see that anything is possible if you look hard enough. Besides, keeping it fun is always a key to keeping it interesting.*

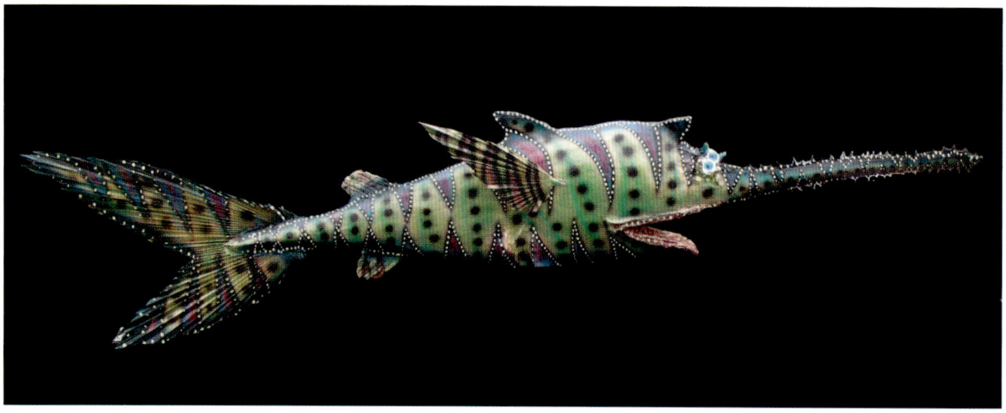

1

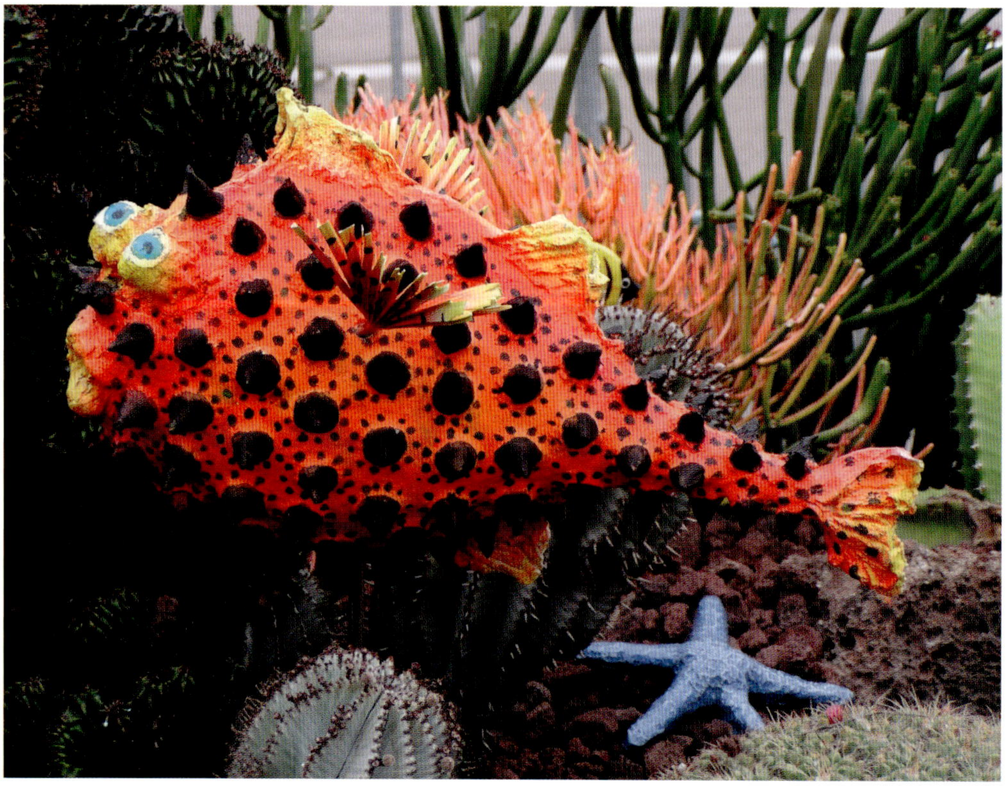

2

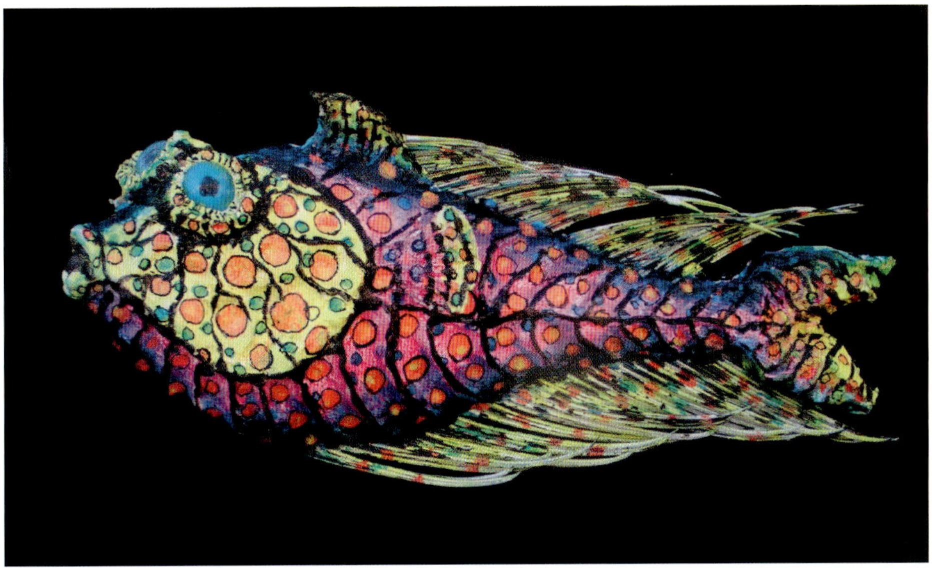

3

1 *Cecil the Saw Fish*, 2004. Mixed media, 64" x 14" x 6". *Photograph by Dan Townsend.*

2 *Pancho the Puffer,* 2003. Mixed media, 20" x 16" x 6". *Photograph by Dan Townsend.*

3 *Bernie the Bone Fish*, 2005. Mixed media, 14" x 7" x 3". *Photograph by Dan Townsend.*

4 *Randy the Rocket Fish,* 2003. Mixed media, 67" x 16" x 6". *Photograph by Dan Townsend.*

5 *Guitar Shark.* Mixed media, 60" x 30" x 6". *Photograph by Dan Townsend.*

6 *Bernie the Blowfish,* 2010. Mixed media, 18" x 15" x 6". *Photograph by Dan Townsend.*

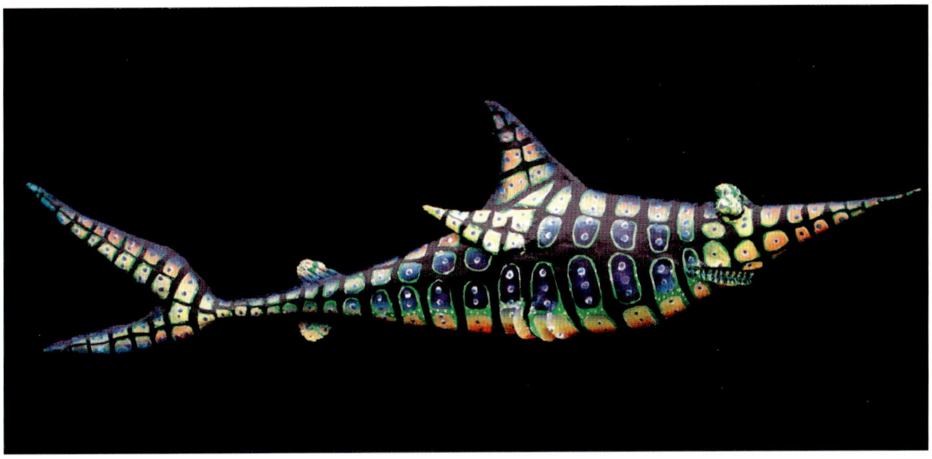

4

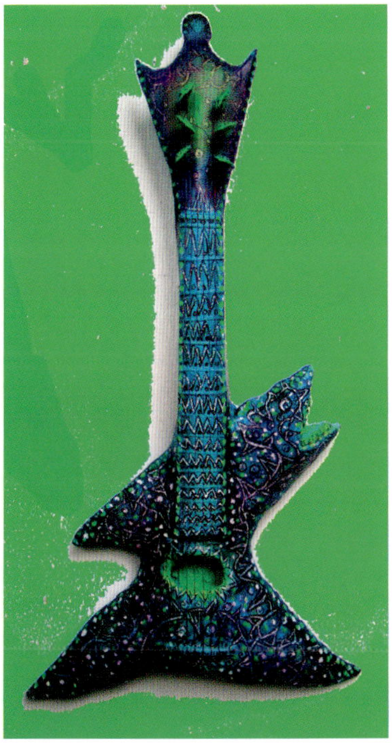

5

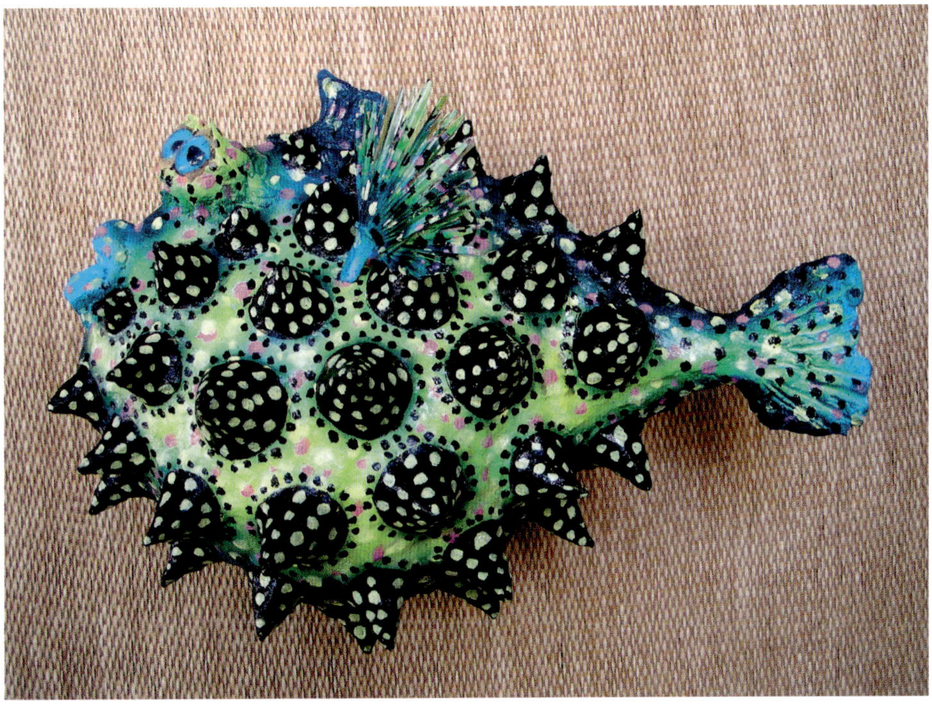

6

# James Tyler

Nyack, New York, USA
www.tylersculpture.com

James Tyler's sculptures can be seen in public parks and private sculpture gardens across the United States, including works in the Boston Subways, the Miami Design District, Davlan Park in Indianapolis, the Linden House Sculpture Park, and, most recently, the new Union Plaza in downtown Lincoln, Nebraska.

Currently residing in Nyack, New York, with his two children, Tyler is the Executive Director of the GAGA Arts Center, a not-for-profit visual and performing arts complex where he also maintains his studio.

*The brickhead sculptures were inspired by my enduring fascination with the great diversity of artistic constructs of humankind. The colossal stone heads of the Olmecs, the Temples of Angkor Wat, Michelangelo's David, or the spires of Manhattan; what is it that drives us to create so many beautifully improbable objects? I do not know the answer, but am content to follow behind and explore these well traveled paths for myself.*

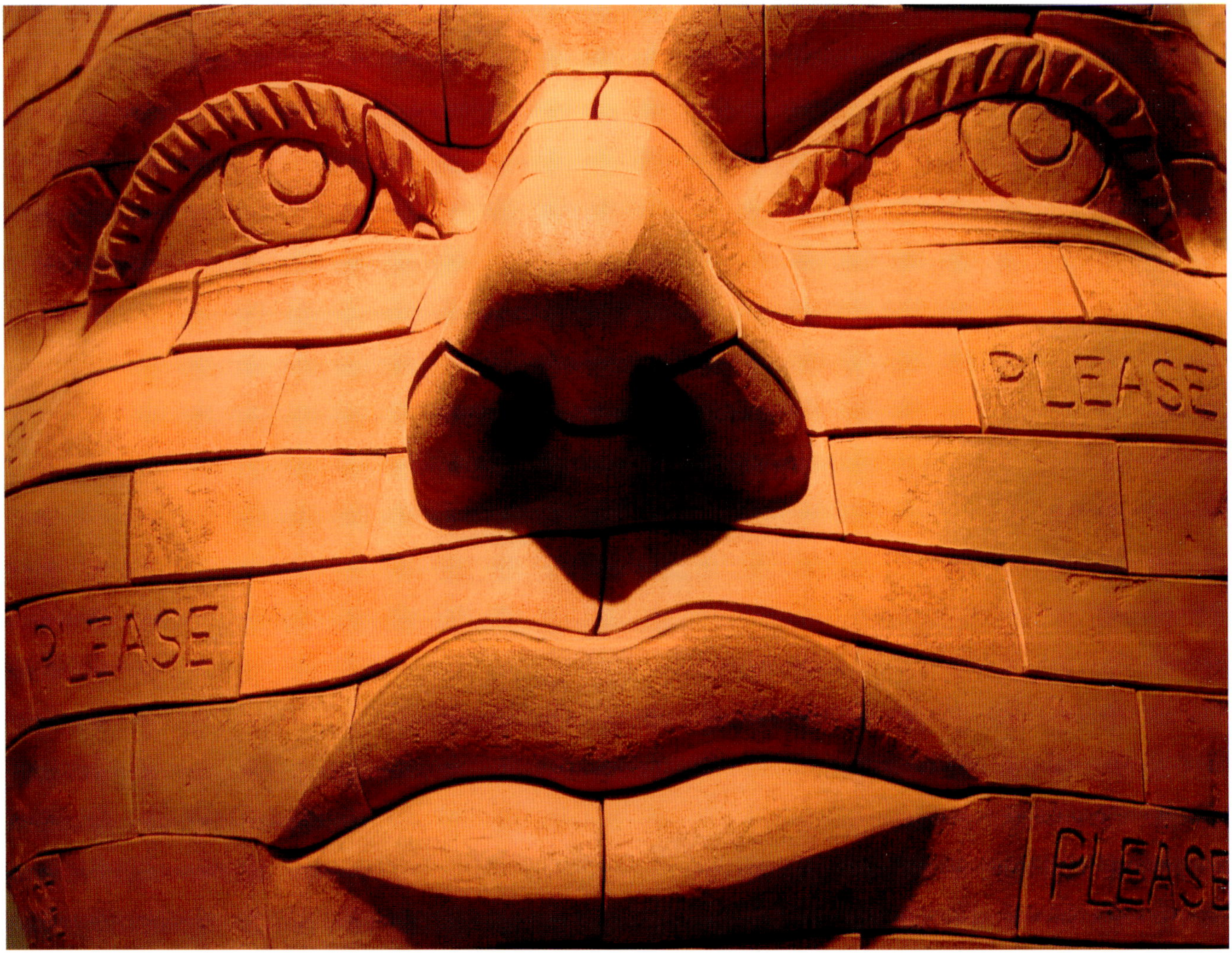


1

1 *Brickhead Please Stop* (detail), 2005. Ceramic brick, 68" x 46" x 50". *Photograph by James Tyler.*

2 *Brickhead Evolution*, 2004. Ceramic brick , sound elements, 60" x 50" x 50". *Photograph by James Tyler.*

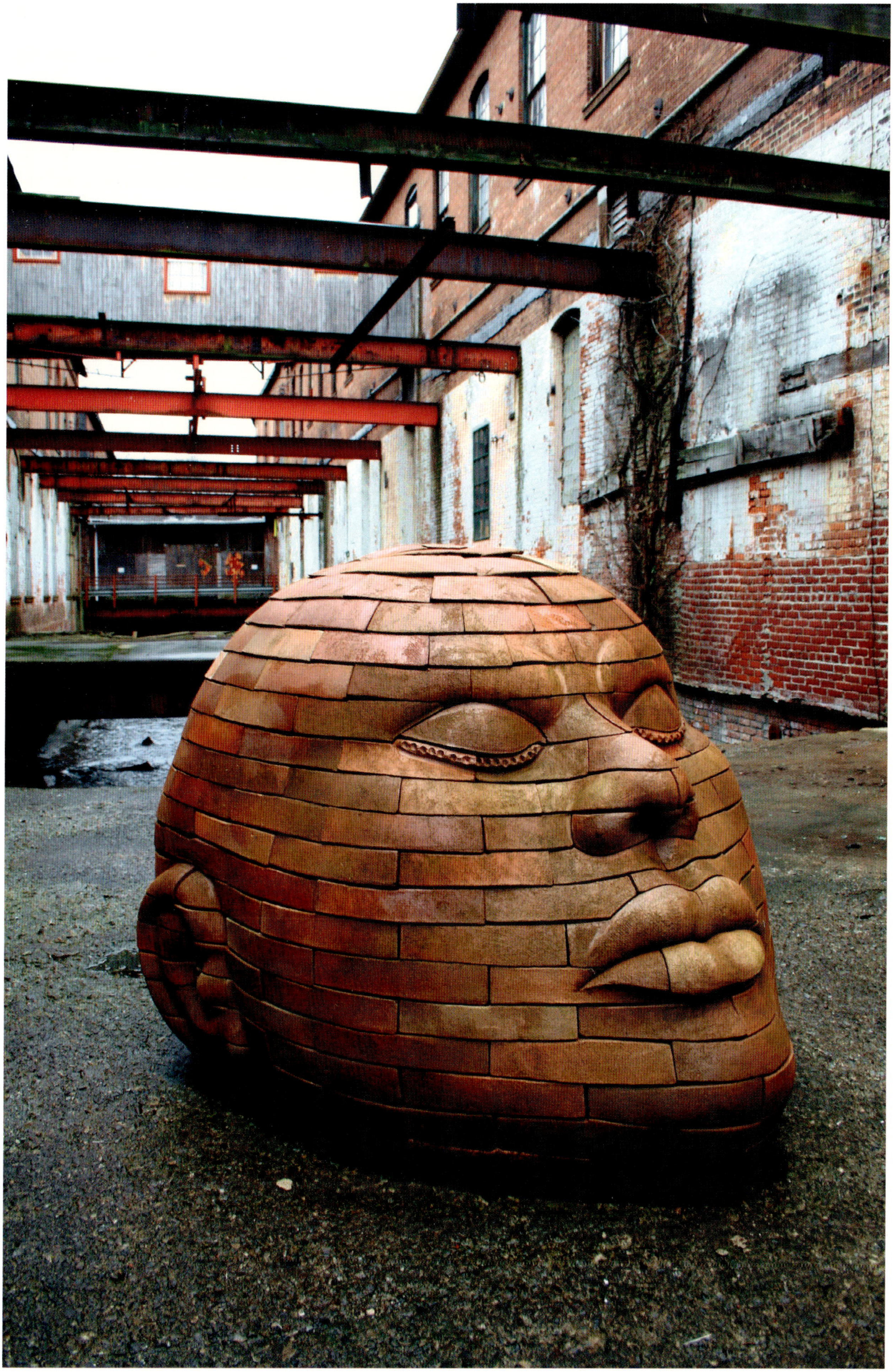

2

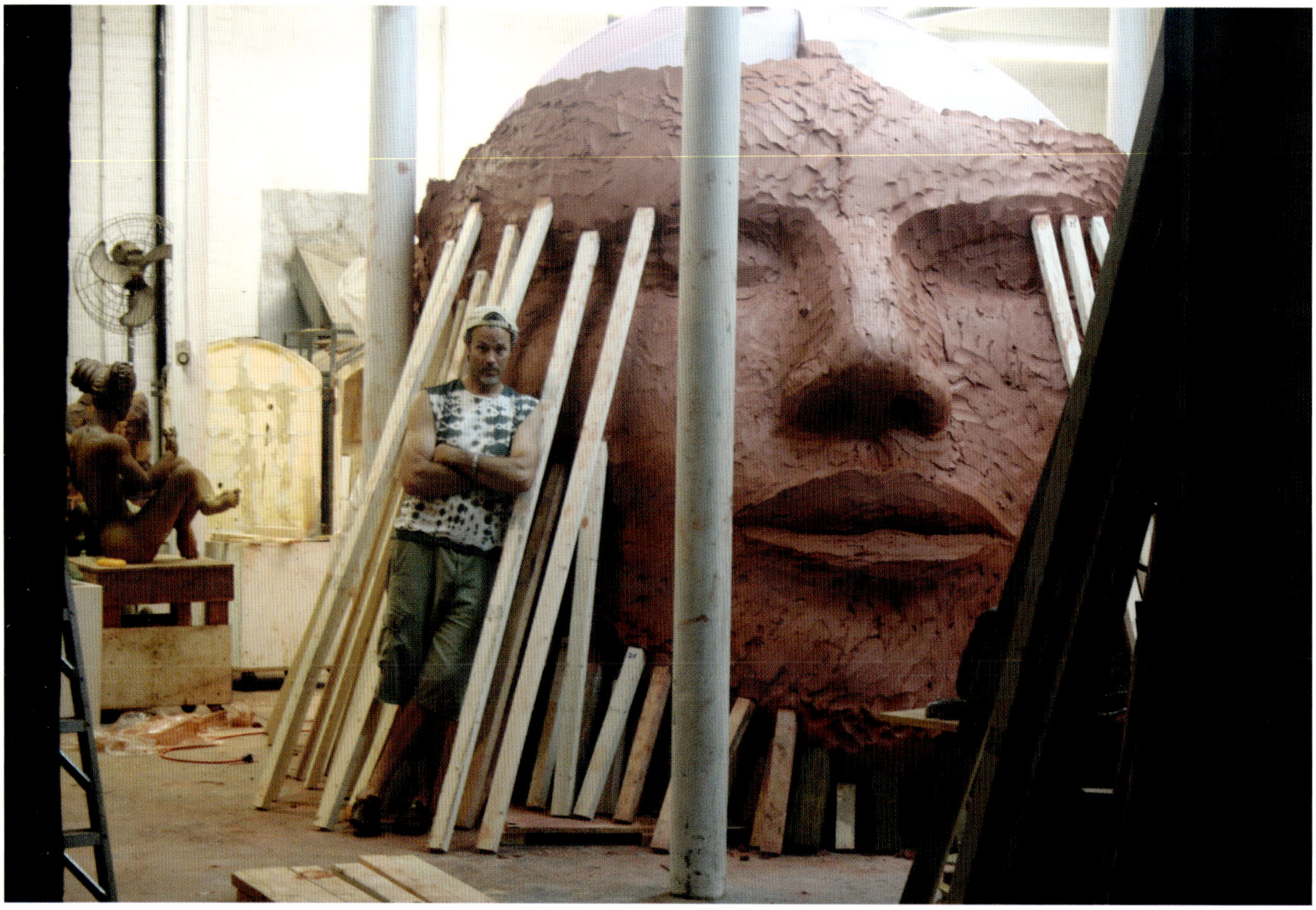

3

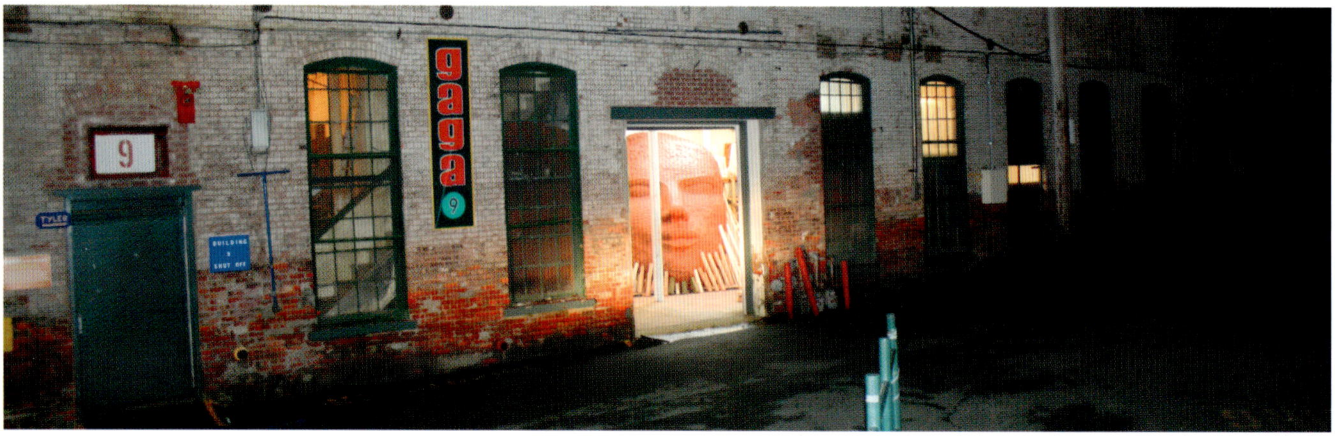


4

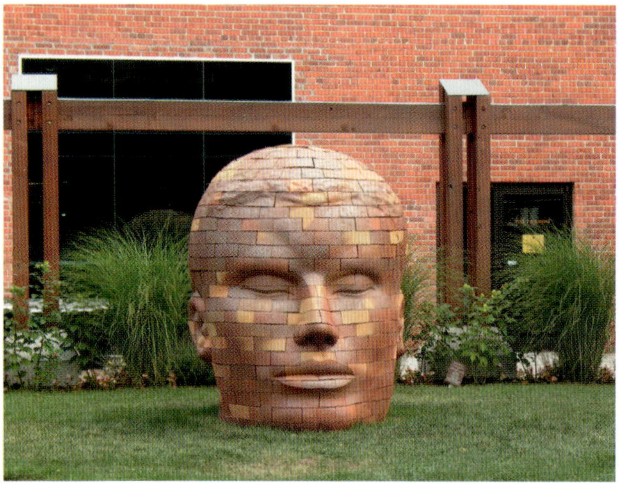

5

3 *Groundwater Colossus* [with artist, in progress], 2010. Ceramic brick, sound elements, 120" x 140" x 100". *Photograph by James Tyler.*

4 *Groundwater Colossus* [in studio–in progress], 2010. Ceramic brick, sound elements, 120" x 140" x 100". *Photograph by James Tyler.*

5 *Brickhead 3*, 2005. Ceramic brick, sound elements, 90" x 50" x 50". *Photograph by James Tyler.*

6 *Hudson Colossus* [in progress], 2011. Ceramic brick, sound elements, 130" x 96" x 100". *Photograph by James Tyler.*

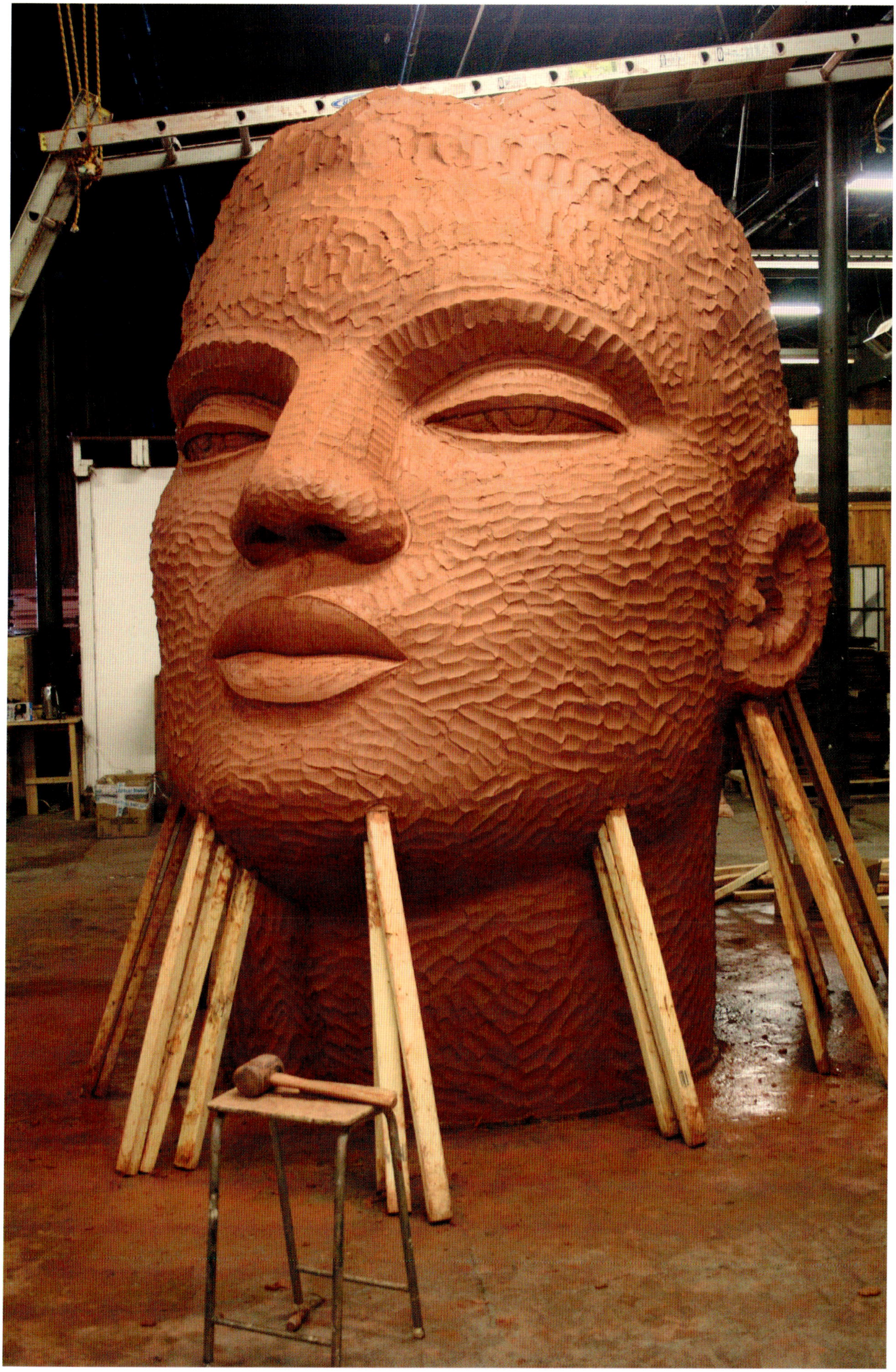

6

# Derek Uhlman

Norwalk, Connecticut, USA
www.uhlman.com

Derek Uhlman is an award-winning sculptor whose work comments on the relationship between modern man and nature. He is best known for his large-scale outdoor sculpture, having had several major corporate and private commissions and significant exhibitions. The artist began his career as a young apprentice to master sculptors Reuben Nakian and Ivan Biro. In 1982, Uhlman received his first solo commission for a 37,000 lb. marble sculpture, *Stone Flowers,* for General Foods Corporation. In 1989, he was invited by Kraft General Foods Foundation to design and fabricate the prestigious *World Food Prize* with Saul Bass. This international award is showcased annually at the Smithsonian Institution (Washington, DC).

Uhlman's sculptures are included in the collections of Rockefeller Center, New York, New York; General Electric Corporation Headquarters, Fairfield, Connecticut; Kraft General Foods Headquarters, Rye, New York; Daiwa Corporation Headquarters, Tokyo, Japan; as well as in private collections worldwide. He is a member of the International Sculpture Center, Hamilton, New Jersey, and Silvermine Guild of Artists, New Canaan, Connecticut. Exhibition venues include the National Academy of Design, New York, New York; Smithsonian Institution, Washington, DC; Hammond Museum, North Salem, New York; Kouros Sculpture Center, New York, New York; John Slade Ely House Center for Contemporary Art, New Haven, Connecticut; Stamford Museum, Stamford, Connecticut; Bruce Museum Sculpture Garden, Greenwich, Connecticut; Cortland Jessup Gallery, Provincetown, Massachusetts; Wohlfarth Gallery, Washington, DC, and Provincetown, Massachusetts; Silvermine Guild Galleries, New Canaan, Connecticut; Carriage Barn Arts Center, New Canaan, Connecticut; Greene Gallery, Guilford, Connecticut; and PMW Gallery, Stamford, Connecticut.

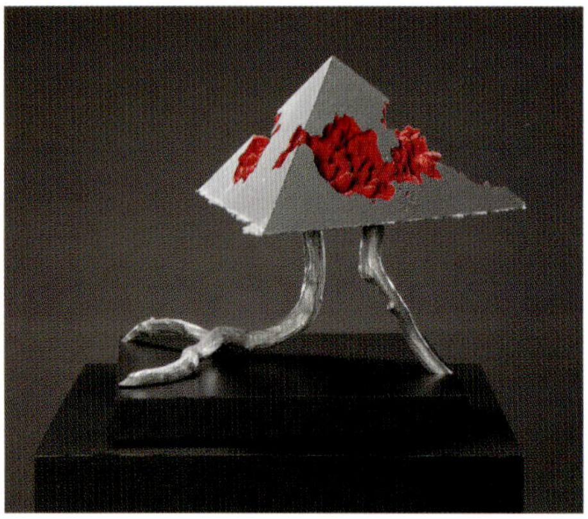

1

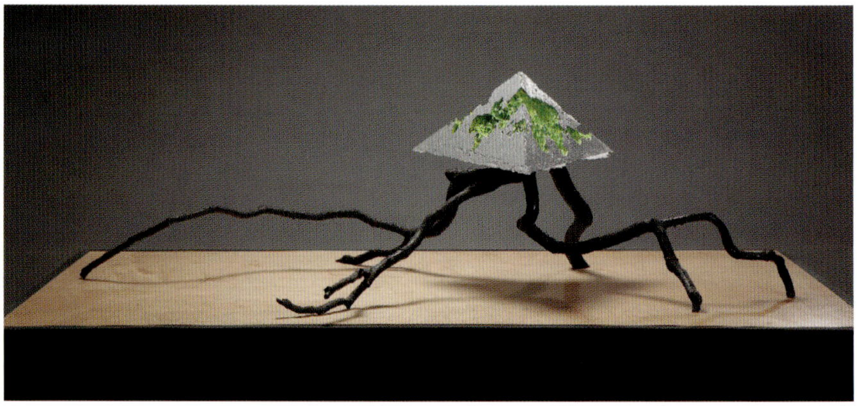

2

1 *Critter in Silver and Red*, 2008. Mixed media, 13" x 18" x 23". *Photograph by Bob Kieffer.*

2 *Critter in Silver and Green*, 2008. Mixed media, 20" x 66" x 36". *Photograph by Bob Kieffer.*

3 *Interlocking Duolith*, 1988. Marble, 50" x 50" x 12". *Photograph by Bob Kieffer.*

4 *Monolith 6*, 2009. Gypsum Cement, Foam, 35" x 15" x 13". *Photograph by Bob Kieffer.*

5 *Circular Duolith Group*, 2008. Mixed media, 36" x 64" x 64". *Photograph by Bob Kieffer.*

6 *Illusionary Duolith*, 2010. Rose Italian alabaster, 20" x 16" x 6". *Photograph by Bob Kieffer.*

7 *Stone of the Sun*, 1981. Bronze, 6" x 7." x 4". *Photograph by Bob Kieffer.*

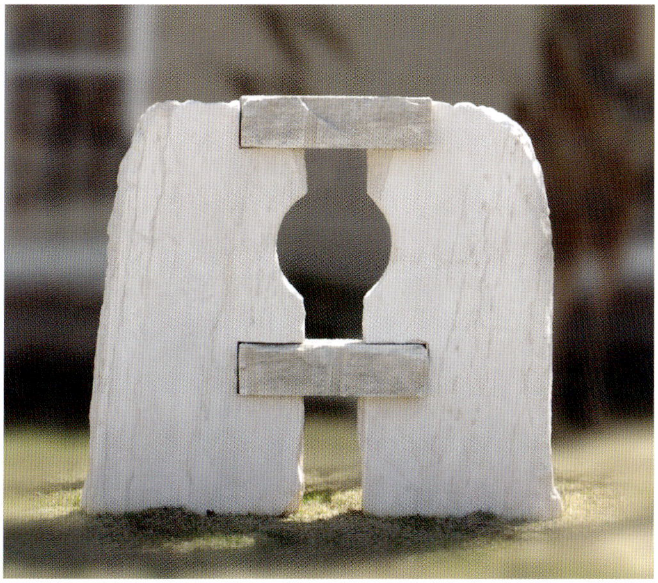

3

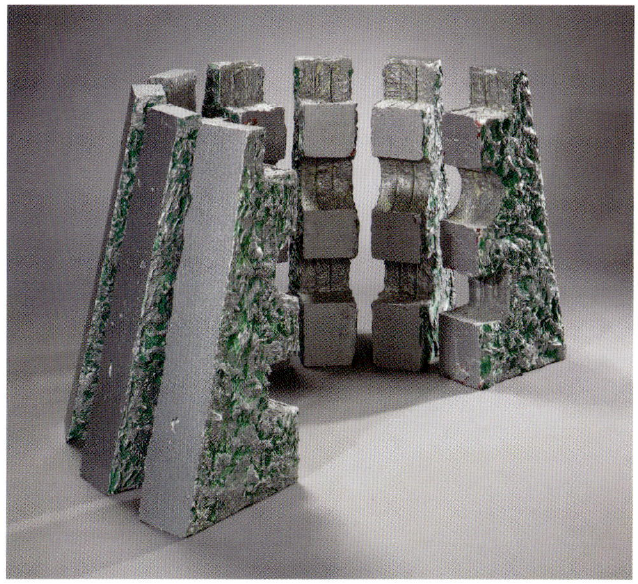

5

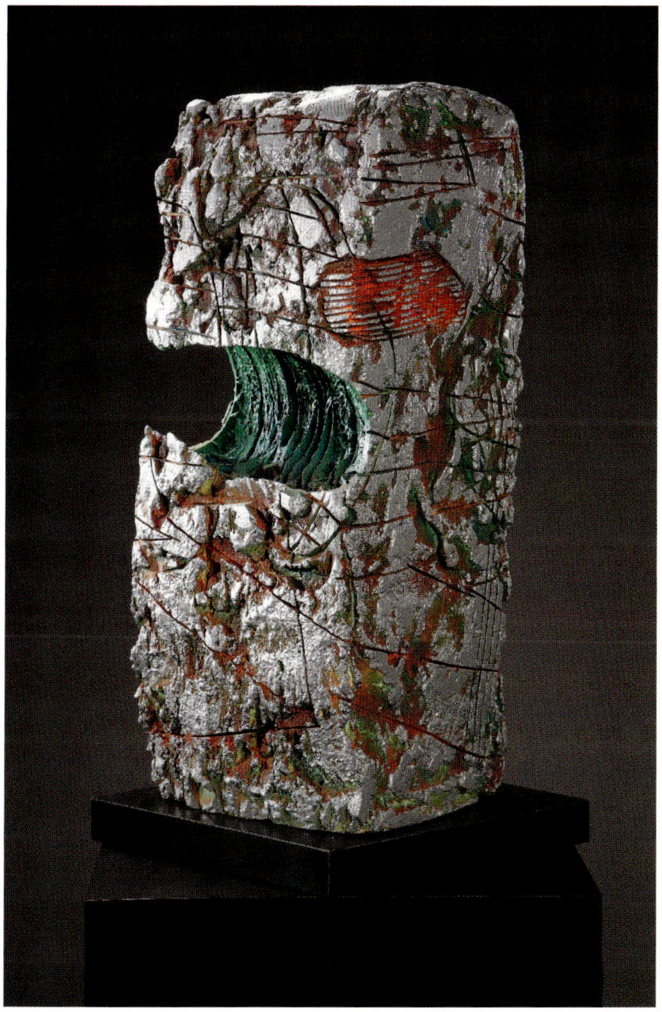

4

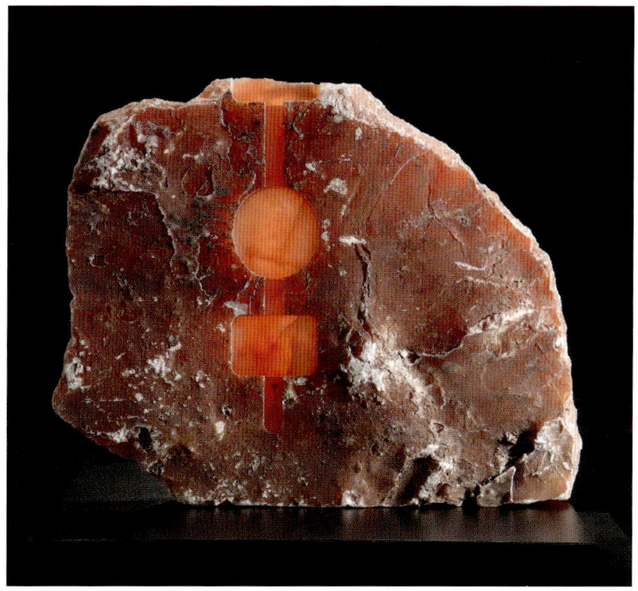

6

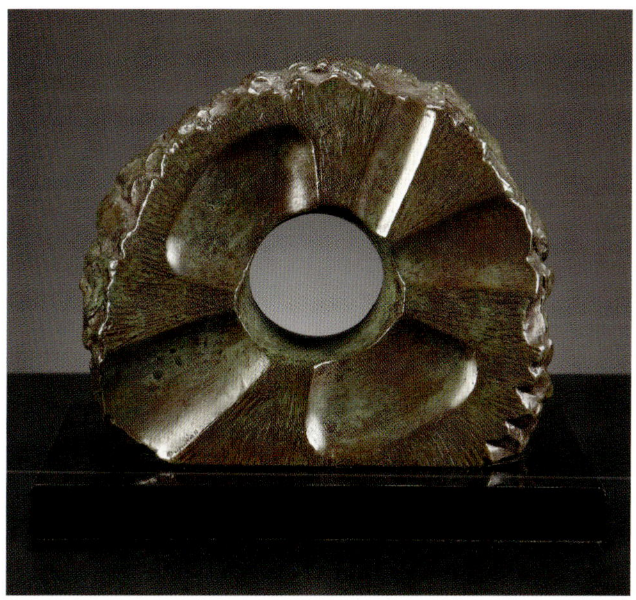

7

# David Vanorbeek

Sainte Colombe sur l'Hers, Aude, France
www.artdeev.com

*I am a professional artist. Every six seconds I think of my sculptures. For me, the great joy in my work comes from turning something considered worthless into the artwork it becomes. In this way I am showing my respect for the metal. The thread that runs like red wire through all my work is recycling. If I could, I would turn all the old metal and scrap iron into a museum of modern art.*

*People ask me, how do I get my ideas? I can only reply that I don't need ideas, I need metal.*

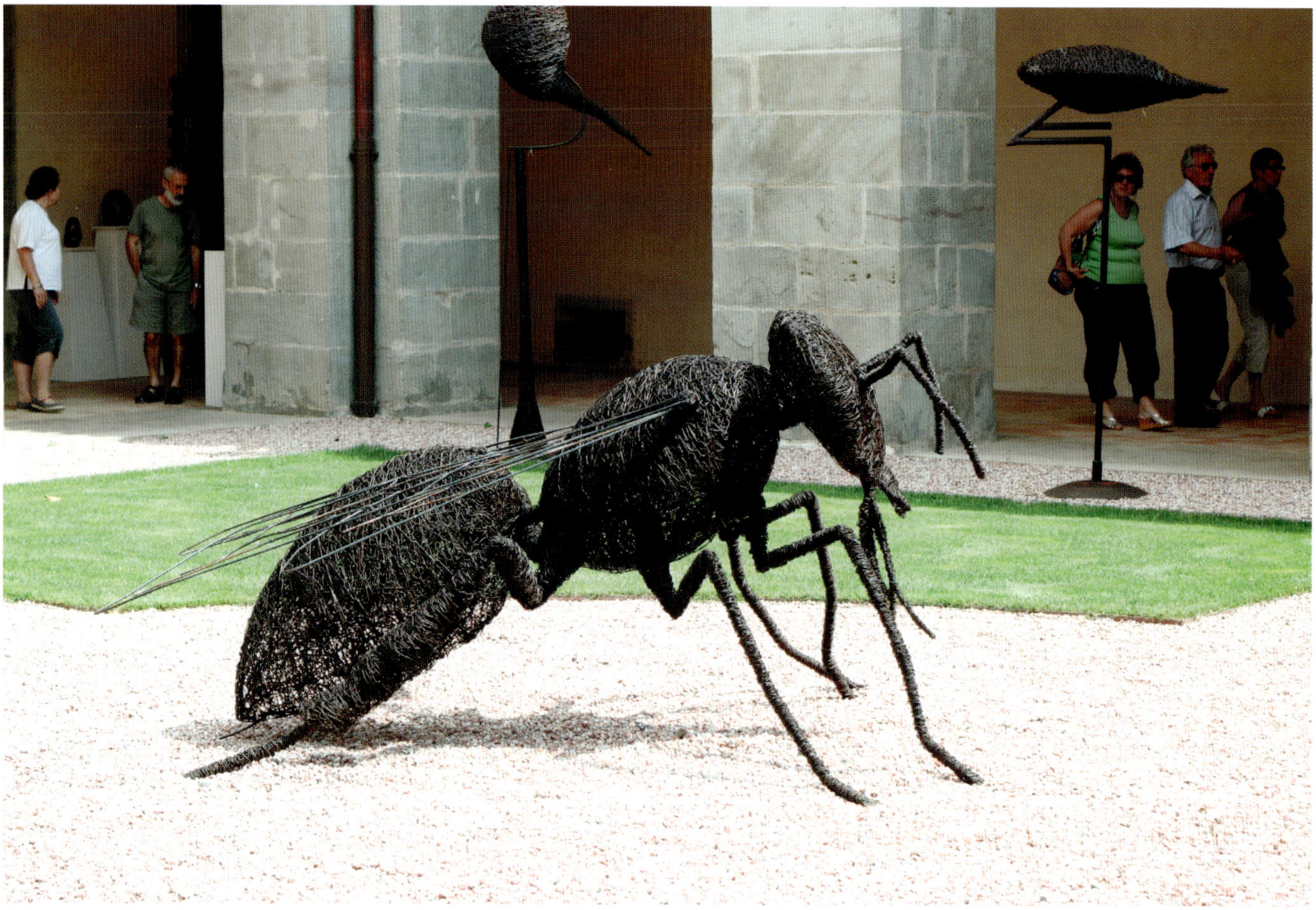

1

1 *Honeybee*, 2009. Iron wire, 240cm x 150cm x 140cm. *Photograph by David Vanorbeek.*

2 *La Crise*, 2009. Metal, stone, 300cm x 300cm x 50cm. *Photograph by David Vanorbeek.*

3 *Metal Wings*, 2009. Metal, 150cm x 110cm x 110cm. *Photograph by David Vanorbeek.*

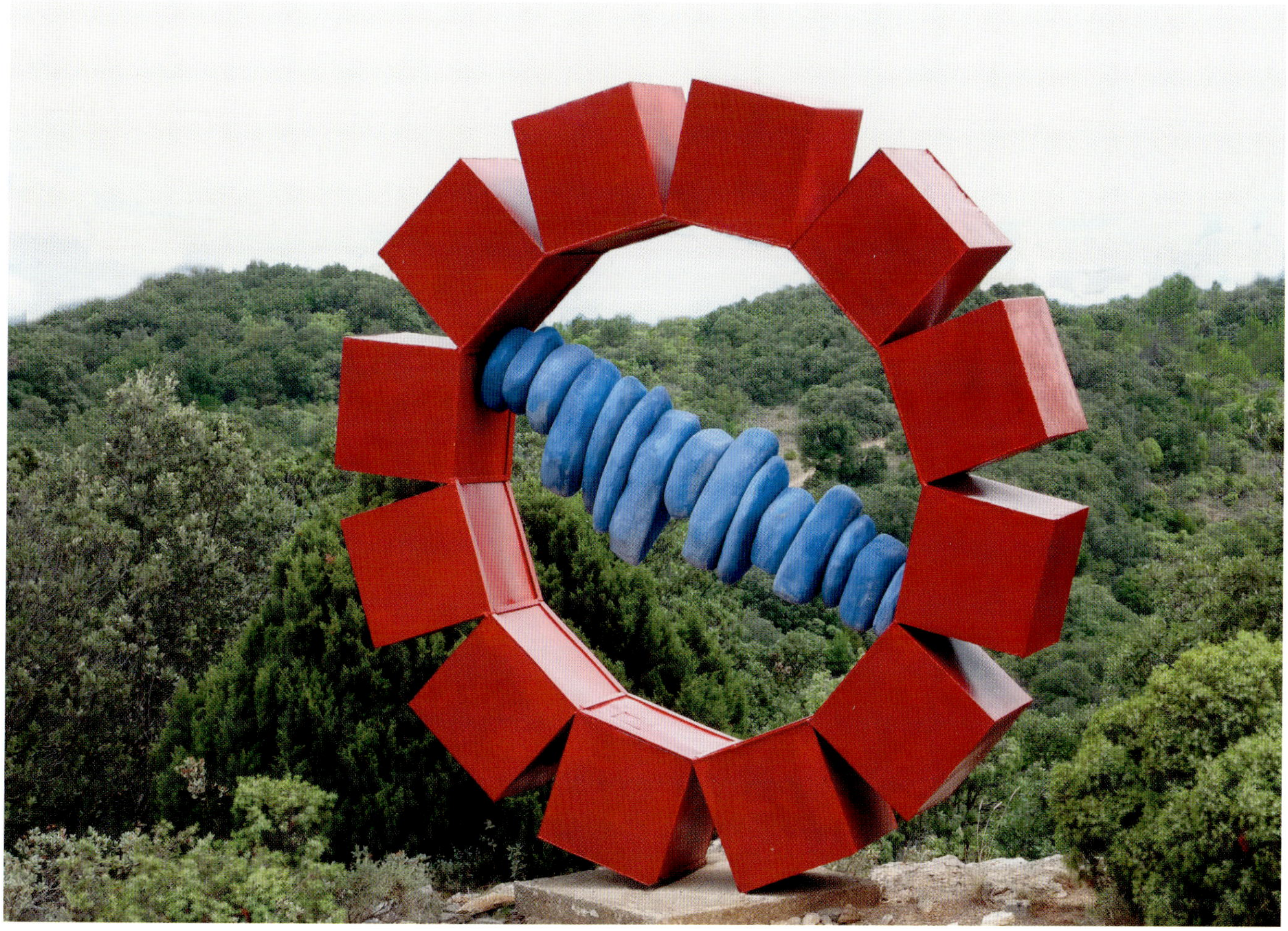

2

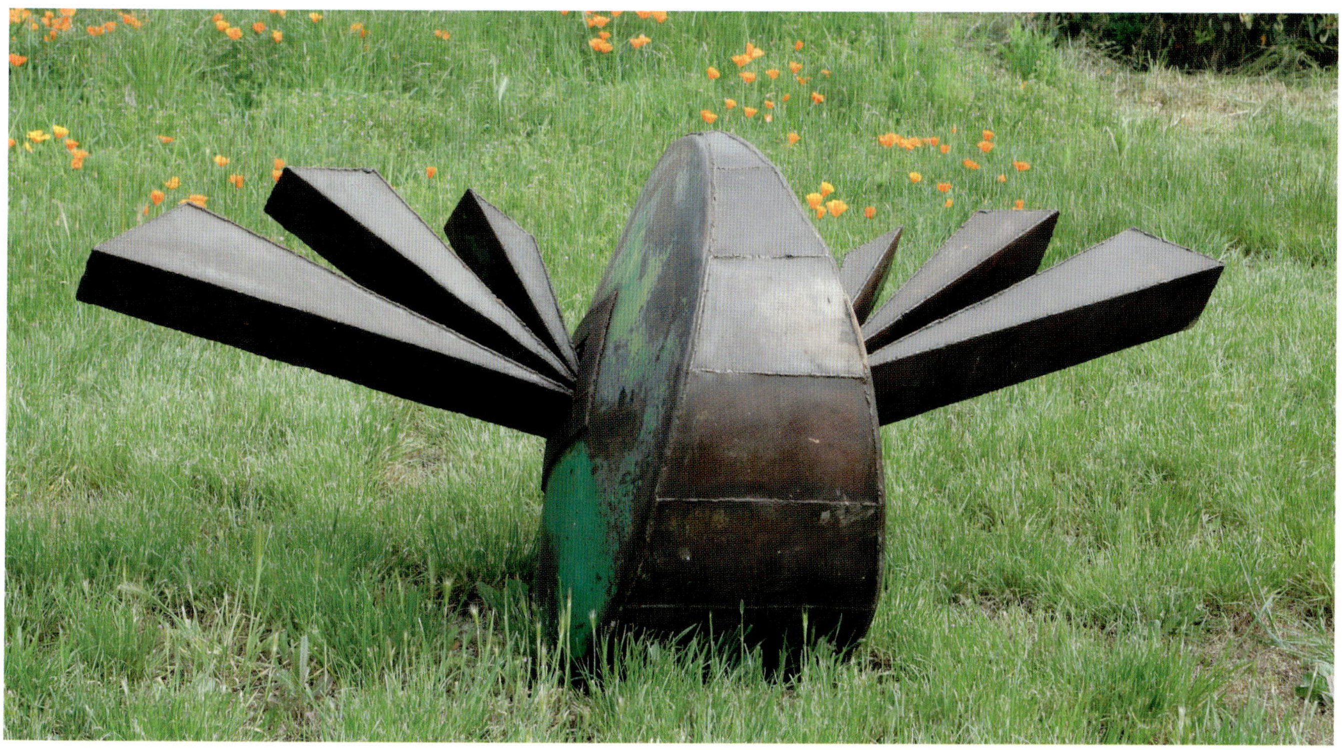

3

4

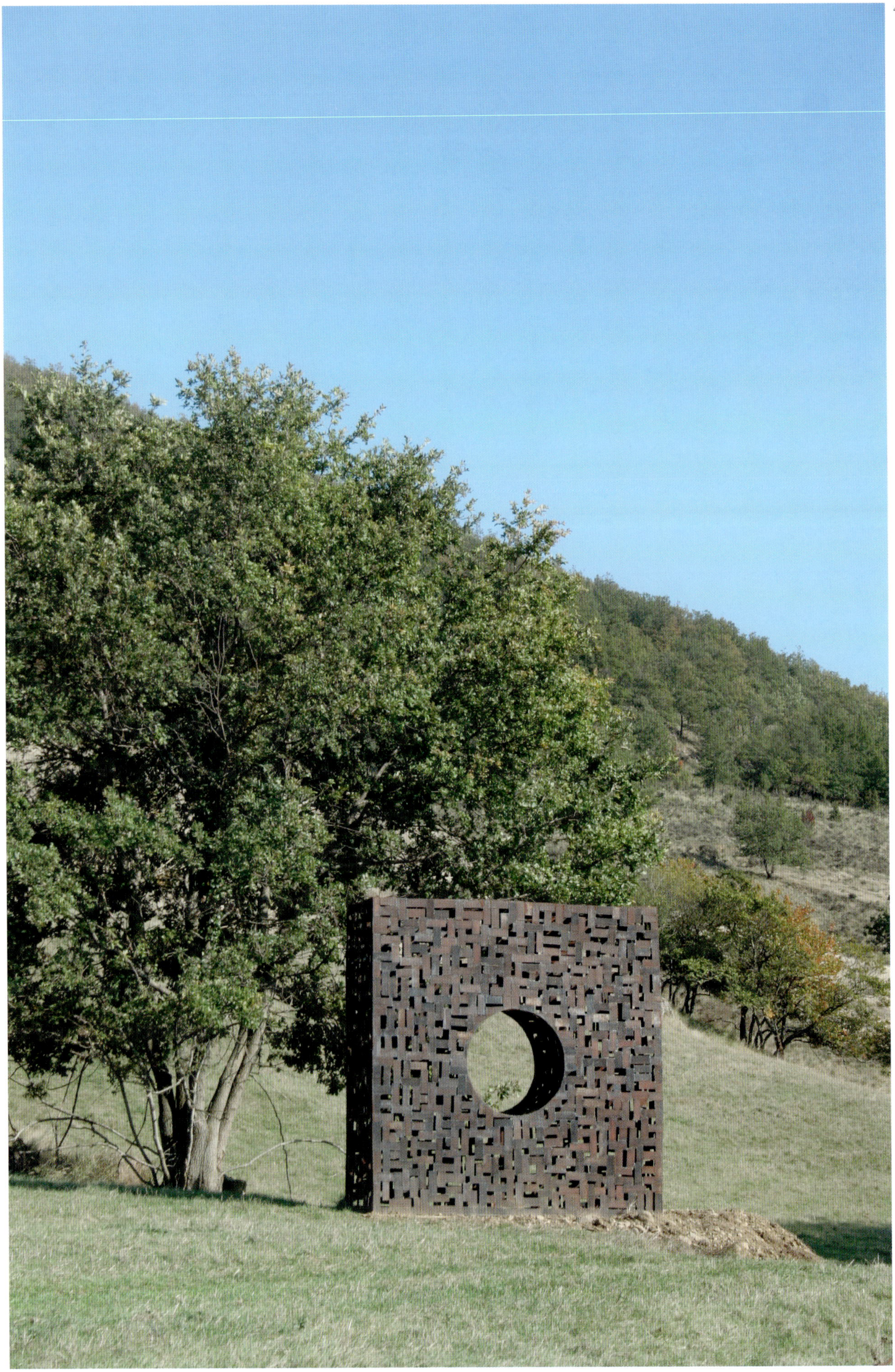

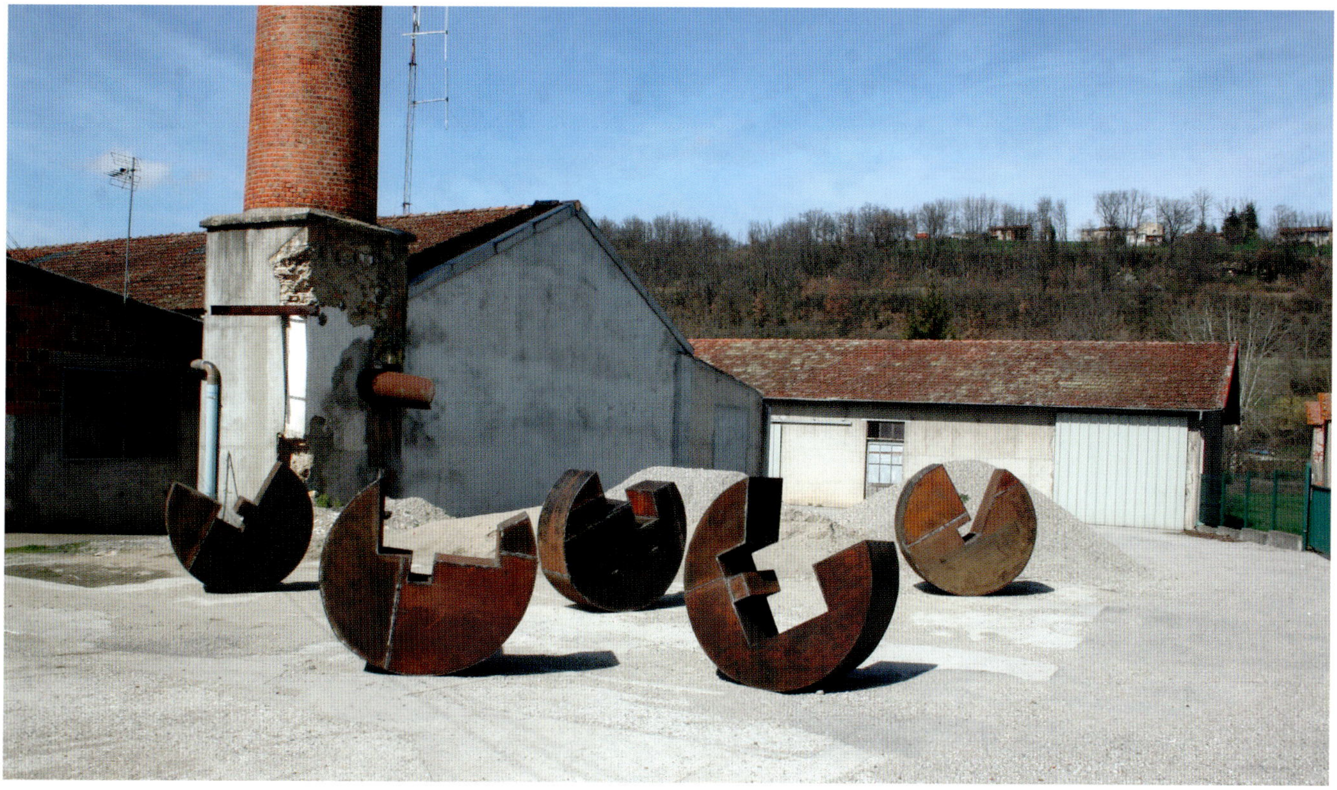

5

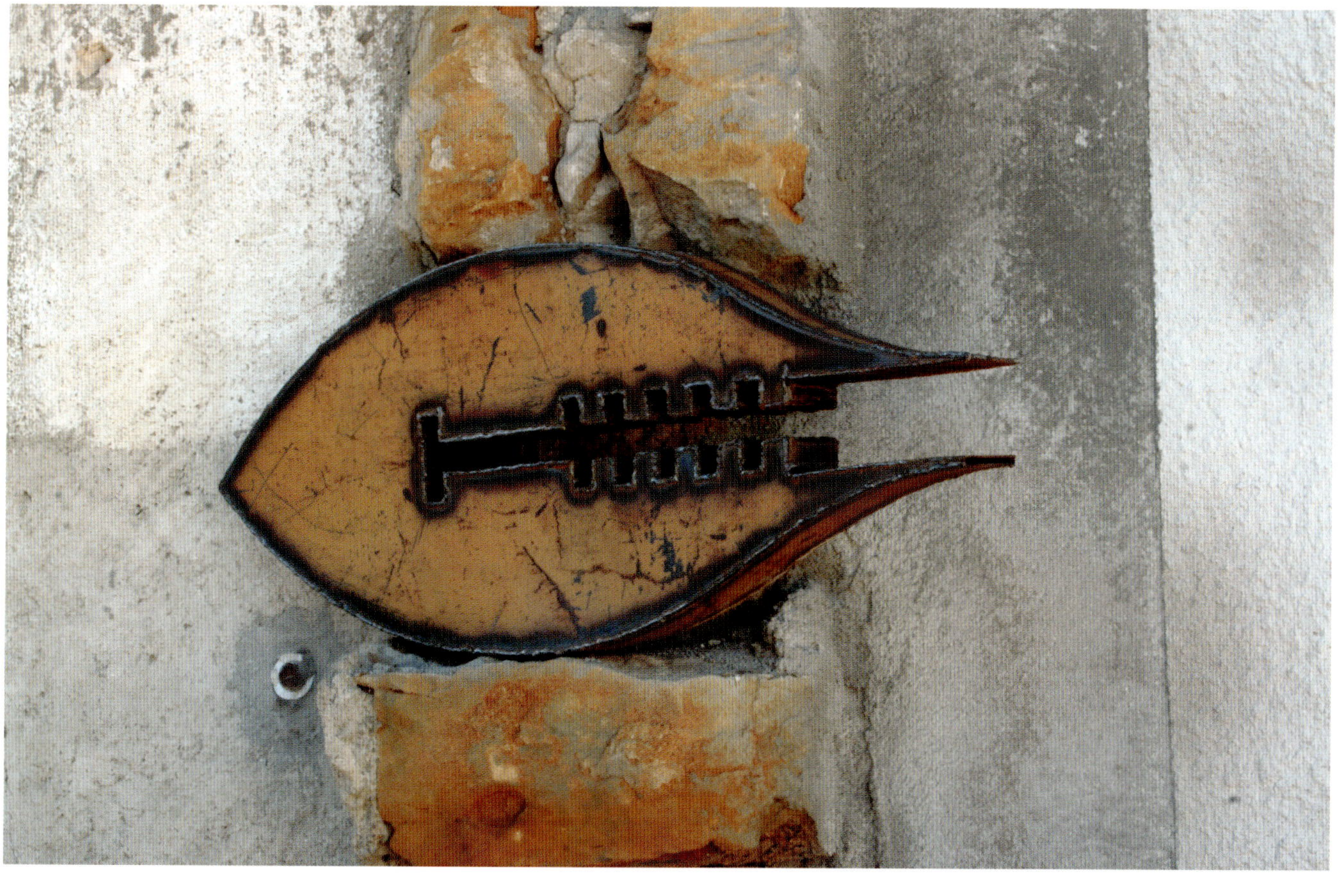

6

4 *Le Cercle Carré*, 2010. Metal, 280cm x 280cm x 100cm. *Photograph by David Vanorbeek.*

5 *The 5 3/4s – Less is More –*, 2011. 150cm x 150cm x 50 cm. *Photograph by David Vanorbeek.*

6 *Yellow Abstraction*, 2010. Metal, 100cm x 40cm x 10cm. *Photograph by David Vanorbeek.*

# Jim Victor

Conshohocken, Pennsylvania, USA
www.jimvictor.com

Born in Harrisburg, Pennsylvania, Jim Victor attended Bishop McDevitt High School, won a scholarship to York Academy of Art in1962, studied sculpture at Pennsylvania Academy of the Fine Arts (PAFA) in Philadelphia from 1963-1968, received a Cresson European Traveling Scholarship in 1967, and worked in the casting department of the University of Pennsylvania Museum from 1968-69. He began using sculpture as illustration in publications including the *New York Times* and the *Philadelphia Inquirer.* He taught sculpture and drawing at Rosemont College in 1974 and at PAFA from 1983-1993.

His first food sculpture was Mickey Rooney and Anne Miller in chocolate in about 1981 and his first butter sculpture was at the Pennsylvania Farm Show in 1995

*I'm a serious artist, but I really don't take myself that seriously. I'm still most interested in working with wood and stone, but, since we need to eat regularly, I have developed a food sculpture business.*

*Sometimes making art from food can be just as fulfilling and creative as anything I've done with more permanent media. Sometimes it is even better because of the natural fresh color of fruits and vegetables. Permanence does not concern me very much. I have made and will continue to make sculptures in bronze and permanence is relative.*

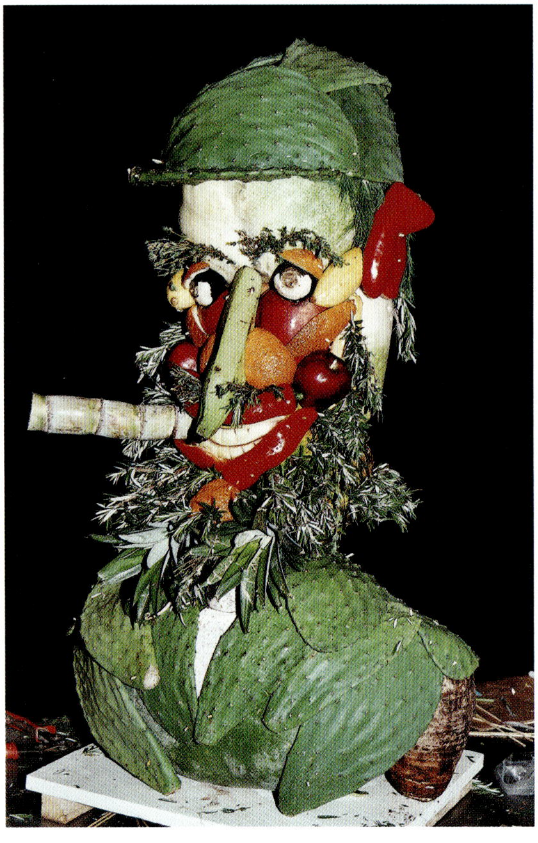

1

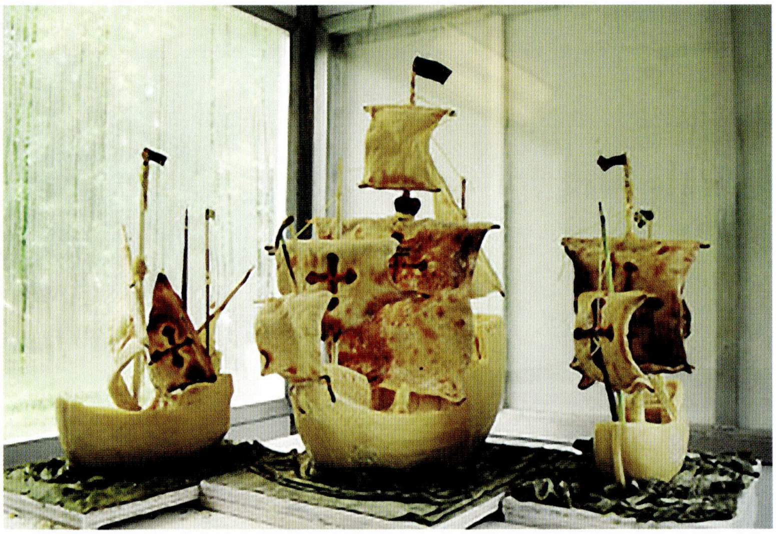

2

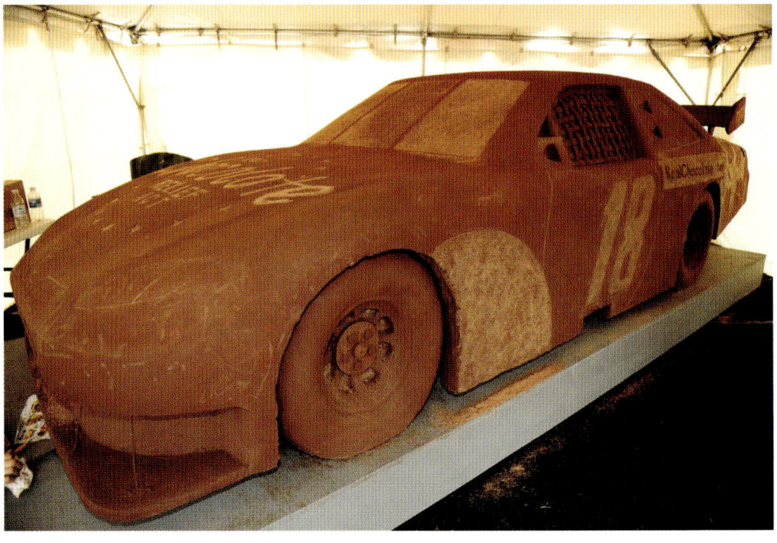


3

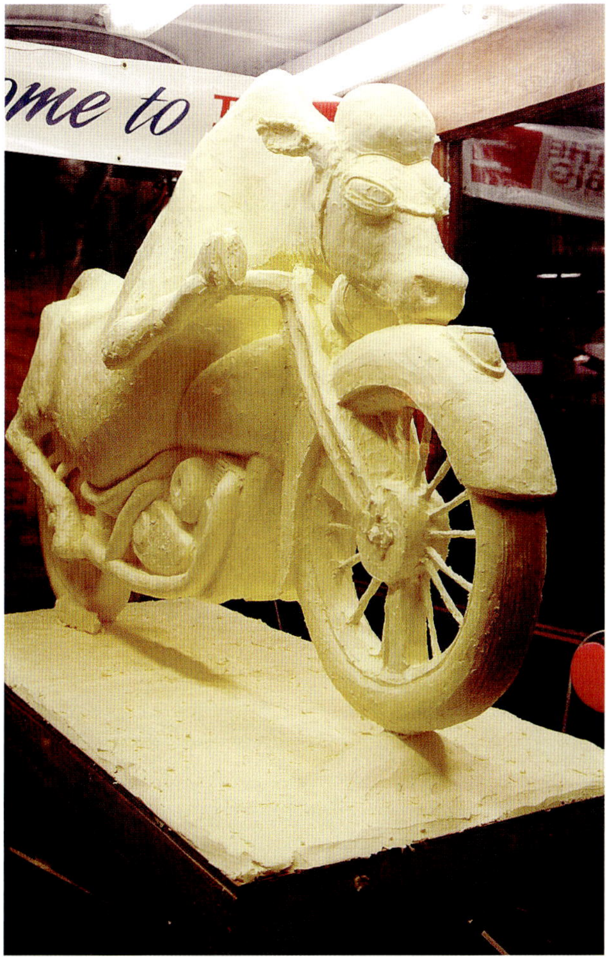

4

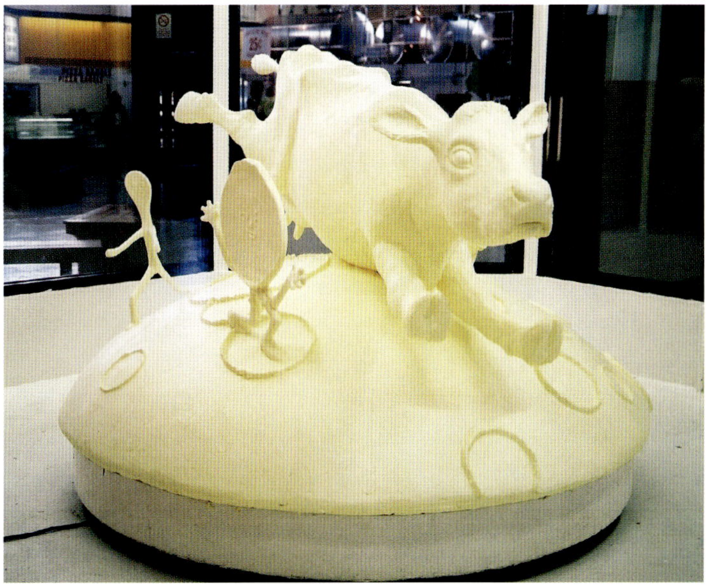

5

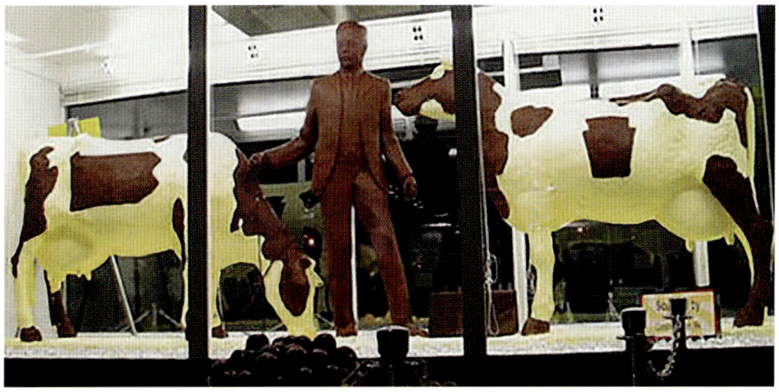

6

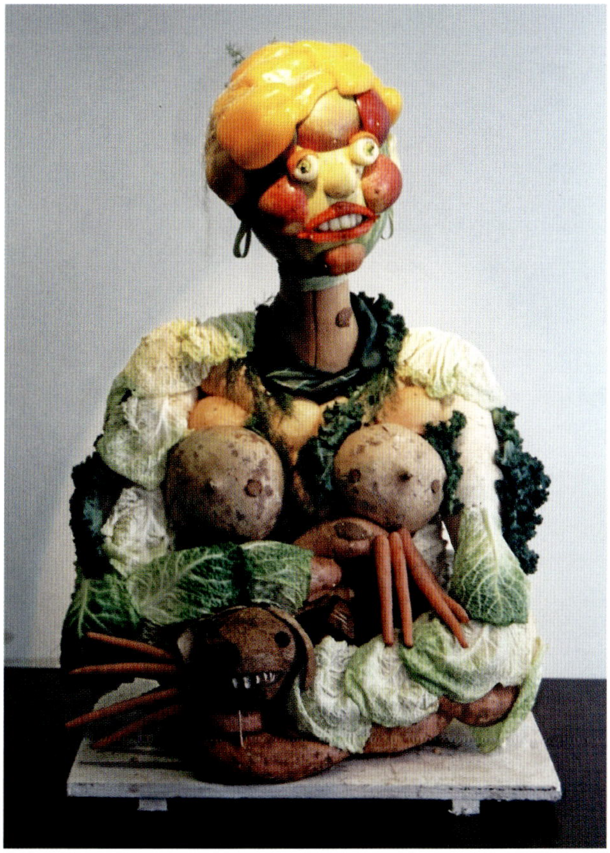

7

1 *Fidel Castro in Vegetables*, commission, 2008. 30" high.

2 *Nina, Pinta, and Santa Maria,* for Sorrento, Columbus day Parade, NYC, 2005. Ships made of Parmesan cheese, pizza dough for sails, roasted red peppers for the crosses, spaghetti for rigging, and spinach lasagna for the sea; approximagely 18" high.

3 *The Mars M&M Car* at Chicagoland Speedway, July 2009. Chocolate, lifesize.

4 *Riding with the Herd*, Eastern States Exposition, 2005, West Springfield, Massachusetts. Butter.

5 *The Cow Jumped Over the Moon*, New York State Fair, Syracuse, New York, 2008, Butter, approx 5' high x 8' long.

6 *Milton Hershey with Cows*, for Pennsylvania Farm Show, 2004. Butter and chocolate, lifesize.

7 *Mixed Vegetables*, birthday portrait commission, 2008. Approximately 3' tall.

# Vivian Visser

Chicago, Illinois, USA
www.vivianvisser.com

*I grew up among the trees of western Michigan, leaving to go to Detroit for art school. The lack of contact with nature left me with an undefinable sense of loss. I filled that void with sculpture made of natural materials, discovering the power of a reconnection with Nature.*

*I see the shelter form as embodying the souls desire to retreat into a comforting and protective environment. The human experience is explored through natural materials which bring the viewer away from the controlled, man made world, and into the raw and mysterious realm of nature where I believe we are vulnerable and the most real.*

*I have been creating sculptural works that explore our spiritual relationship with nature since the early 1990s. With works in national and international shows like Counter Currents Art Chicago, Sculpture Invasion, Koehnline Museum of Art, Fertile Ground–Honoring Nature in Art, Imlay Fine Art, Montclair, New Jersey, and Cool Globes–Hot Ideas for a Cooler Planet, the Climate Summit in Copenhagen, I have attempted to share my ideas about our need to create a better relationship with nature as a way to find peace within ourselves and each other. Most recently, I have been commissioned to create an interpretive public art work for the Openlands Lakeshore Preserve.*

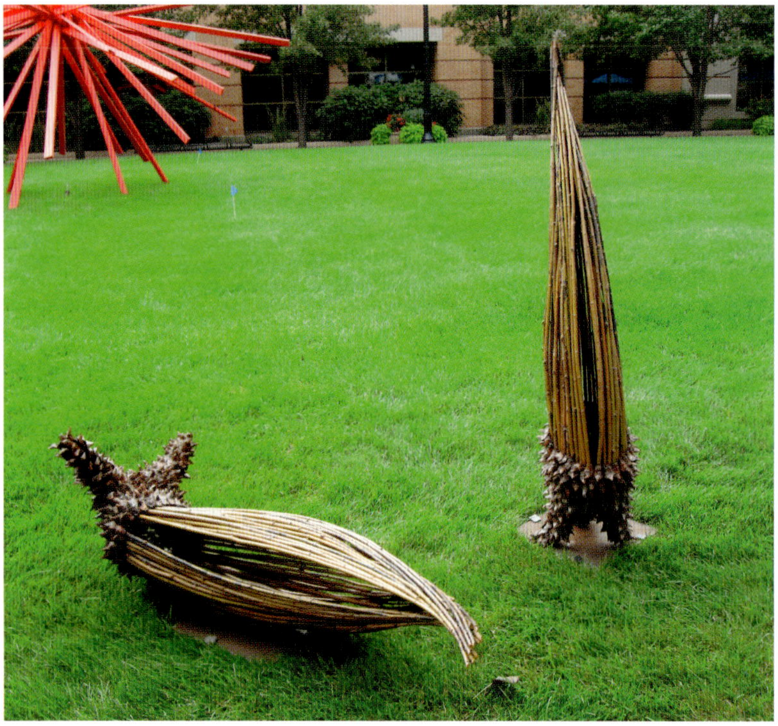

1

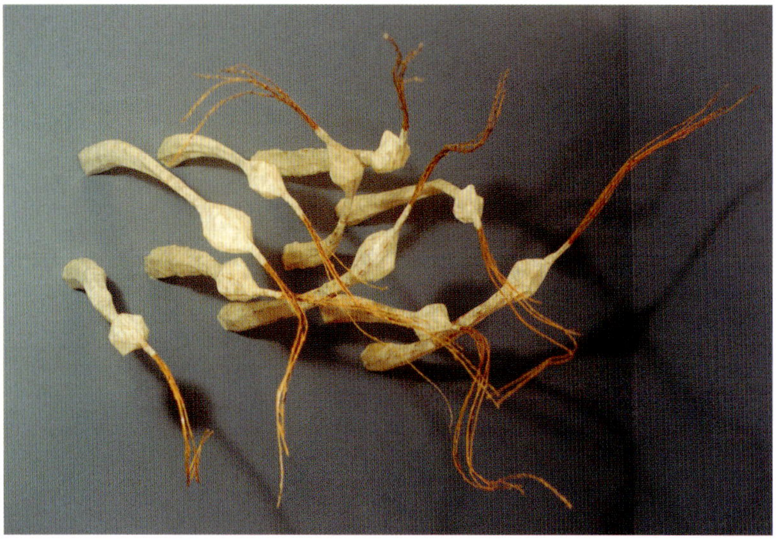

2

1 Untitled, 2010. 54" x 12" x 15" each. *Photograph by Vivian Visser.*

2 *Infect*, 2006. Willow, rice paper, 2" x 36" each of eleven segments. *Photograph by Vivian Visser.*

3 *Wiggle Root*, 2005. Willow, seed pods, 30" x 16" x 9". . *Photograph by Vivian Visser.*

4 *Coupling*, 2011. Hawthorn, horse hair, 6" x 6" x 6". *Photograph by Vivian Visser.*

5 *Small Pod #2*, 2011. Elm, Oriental arborvitae pods, 6" x 6" x 6". *Photograph by Vivian Visser.*

3

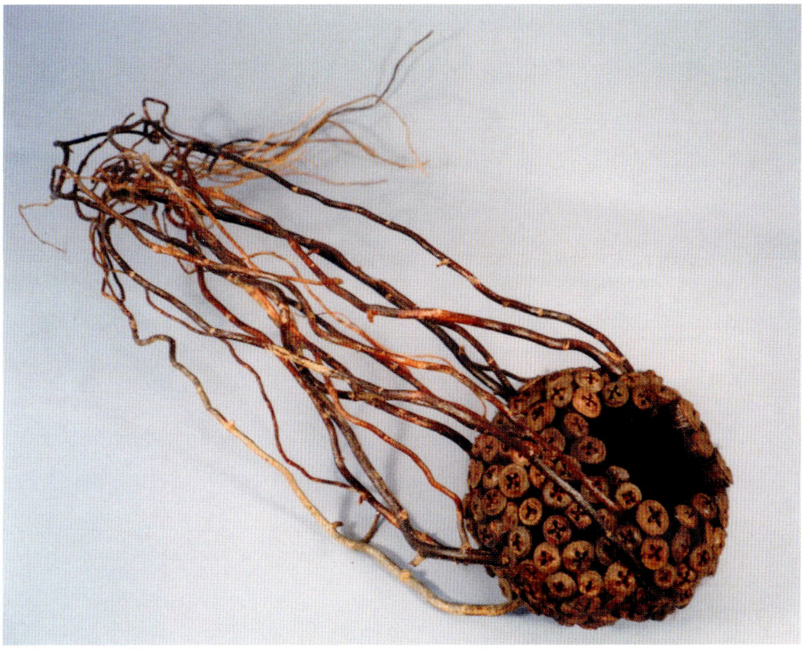

4

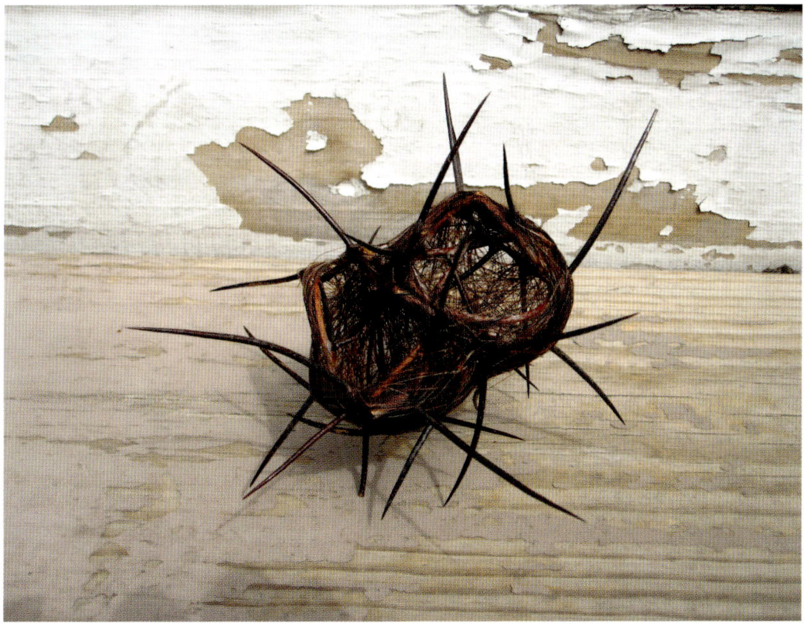

5

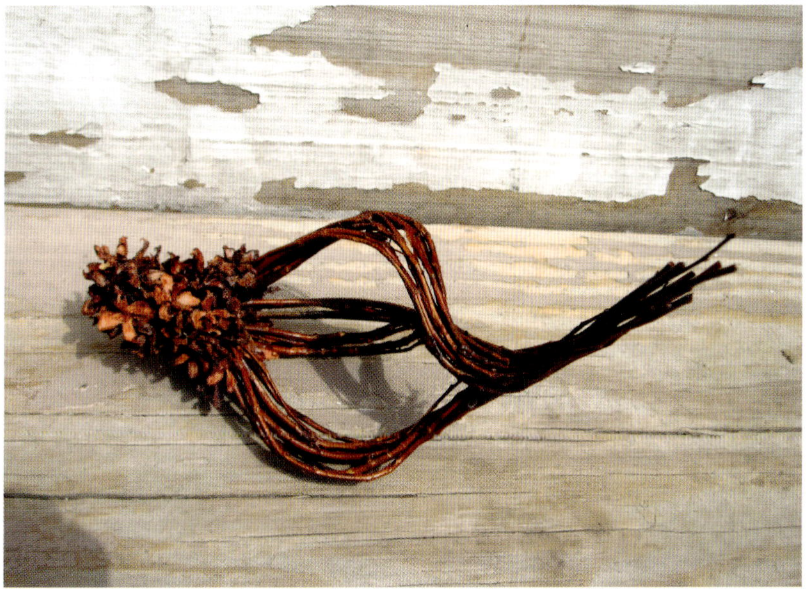

# Lynn Wartski

Hillsborough, North Carolina, USA
www.wartskisculpture.com

*I cannot remember a time when I have not created art. Primarily self-taught, design and sculpture studio studies accompanied my BS in biology and a secondary teaching credential. After teaching for several years, I followed my instincts into the studio. An early commission led me to work with copper and I discovered my medium. I live and work in North Carolina and am fortunate to have my work represented in several galleries, and to have received awards in juried shows. I have been an artist-in-residence in local schools, and teach classes and workshops in hand repoussé techniques.*

*An appreciation of nature and my biology background feed into my botanical themes, while the more whimsical pieces are light-hearted, and sometimes humorous. Recently, my sculpture has moved toward an increasingly "steampunk" style. I find myself intrigued by the marriage of the mechanical with the natural and the future with the past in these designs. I borrow from numerous metal working disciplines in my sculpting. Using hand tools to cut and shape metal, I employ both hot and mechanical joining methods. Texture and dimension are added to surfaces with repoussé, chasing, and patinas. Most of my work is left unsealed to naturally age with time. The materials used lend themselves to both outdoor and indoor settings, and my sculptures can find homes in both.*

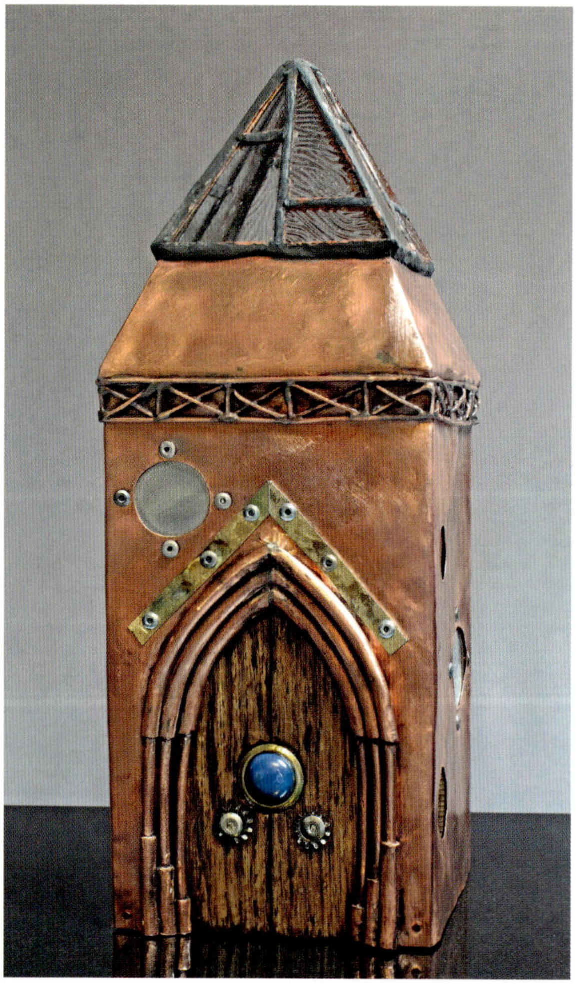

1

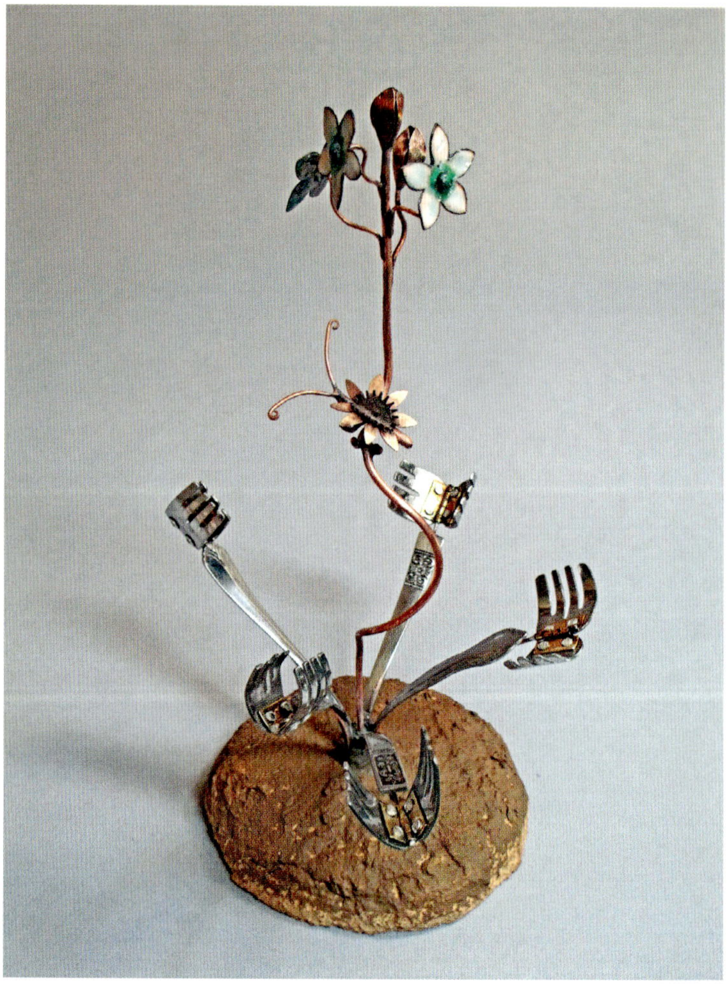

2

1 *Athena's Birdhouse*, 2010. Metal mixed media, 14" x 5" x 5". *Photograph by Lynn Wartski.*

2 *Carolina Carnivore*, 2011. Mixed metal, torch enamel, 14" x 9" x 11". *Photograph by Lynn Wartski.*

3 *Daisy Bee*, 2011. Metal mixed media, 14" x 16" x 16". *Photograph by Lynn Wartski.*

4 *Vintage Steam*, 2010. Metal mixed media, 41" x 19" x 9". *Photograph by Lynn Wartski.*

5 *Reclining Lily*, 2009. Copper, stone, 12" x 12" x 8". *Photograph by Lynn Wartski.*

6 *Joyous*, 2011. Mixed metal, 9" x 9" x 3". *Photograph by Lynn Wartski.*

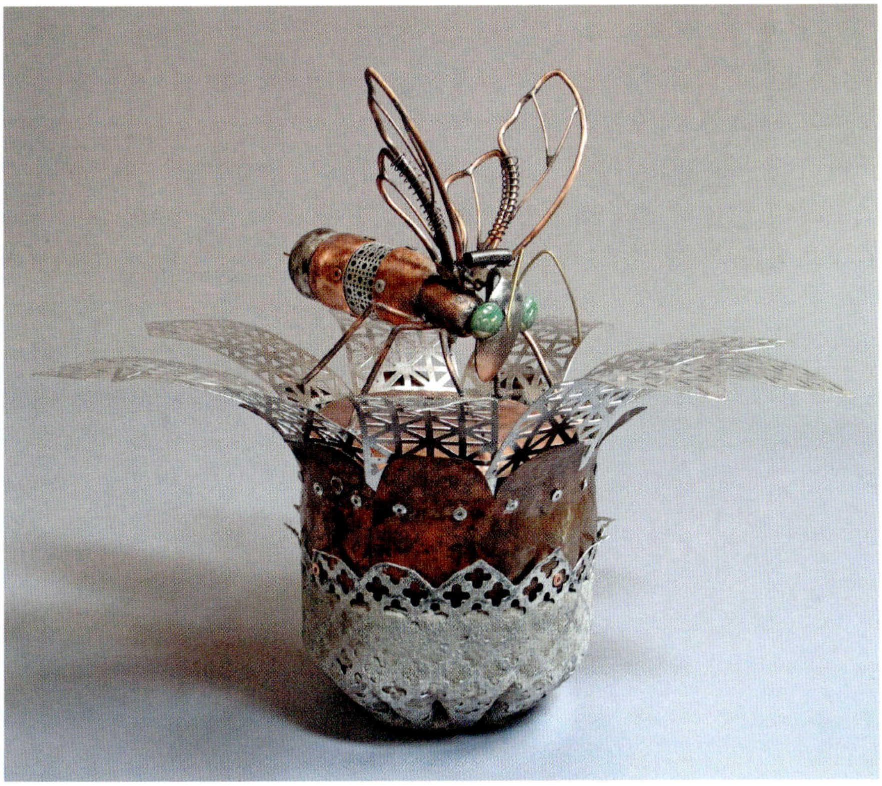
3

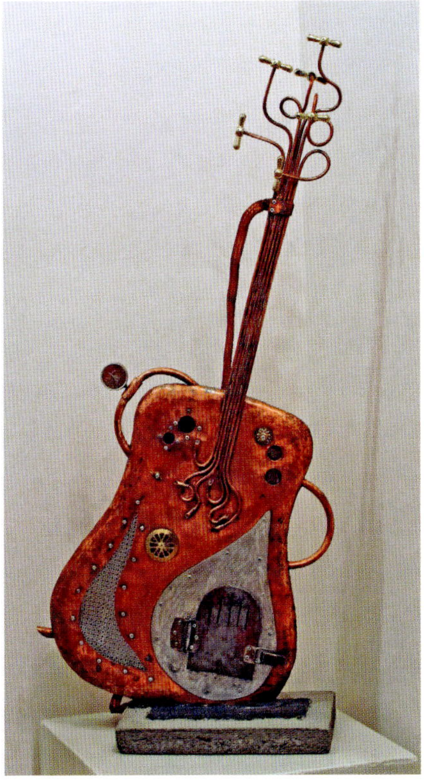
4

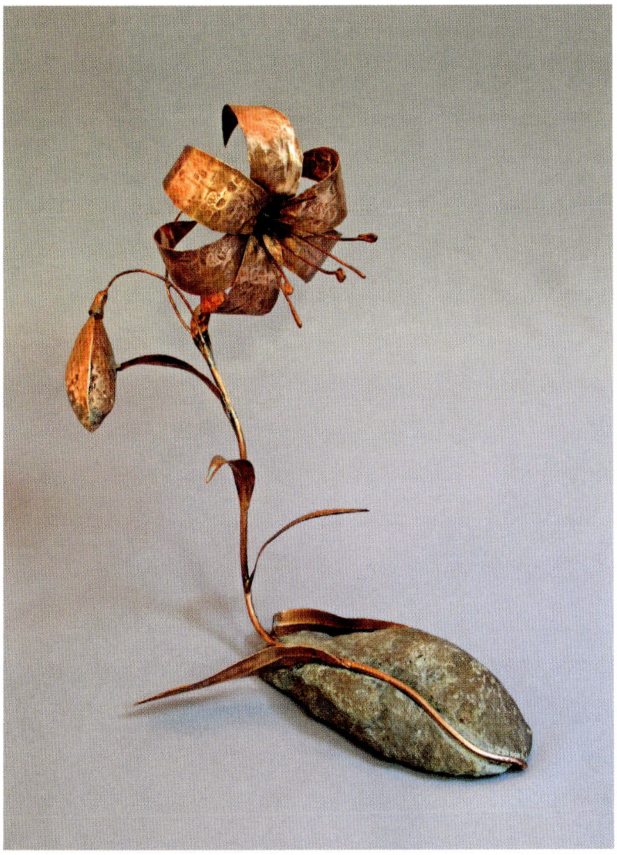
5

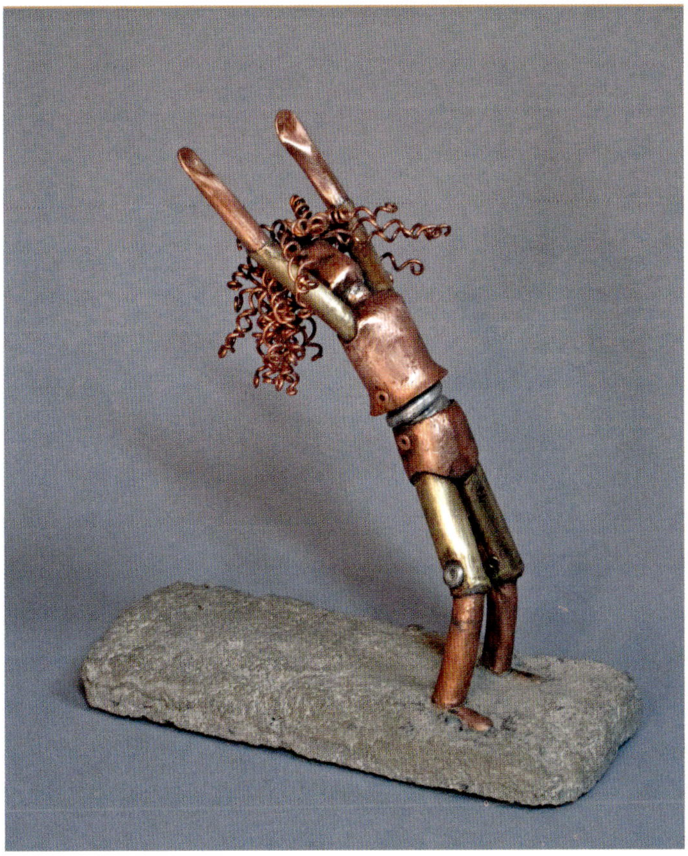
6

# Dan Woodard

Redwood City, California, USA
www.danwoodard.com

*Archetypes...myths...rituals. In my sculptures, both figurative and abstract, I employ my fascination with these concepts to evoke an emotional state within the viewer.*

*In my figurative work, my goal is to capture the ever changing state of the human condition through subtle changes in facial expression and body language. My abstract sculptures are divided into two series, "Artifacts From a Former World" and "Landscapes." The sculptures in both series are made of abstract forms covered with rich, textural surfaces. This combination results in a complex organic piece that evokes a sense of ancient artifacts, of ritualistic objects from an unknown culture, or of imagined landscapes.*

*However, be it figurative or abstract, my ultimate goal is to have the viewer feel both an emotional and a sensory familiarity with the work. I believe this feeling of déjà vu arises from both the collective unconscious and a mystical center we all share.*

*In 2006, after a successful career as a scriptwriter and director with over fifty national and international awards, I began actively pursuing a long held fascination with sculpture. In my first year of exhibiting, my work appeared in several shows including: "Made in California," "Art Outside the Box," and the "California Open Exhibition." Since then, my work has continued to appear in a variety of shows. I've also been honored as a Showcase Winner in the ARTslant International Competition and as a Featured Artist at utopicstudios.com.*

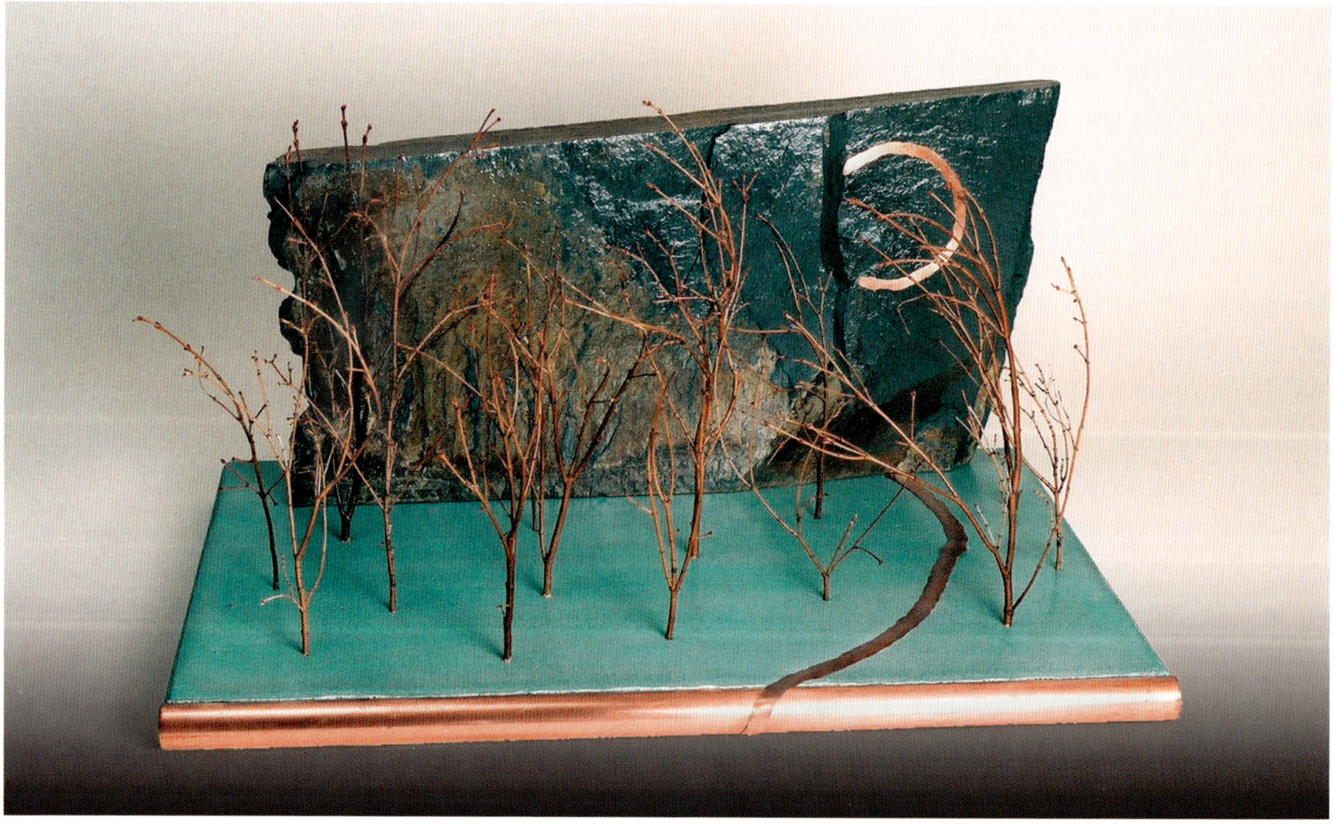

1

1 *Sunset,* 2009, Slate, wood, copper, 11" h. x 20" w. x 14" d. *Photograph by Dan Woodard.*

2 *One Sphere, Two Curves,* 2010. Cement, bronze leaf, patina, 19" h. x 61" w. x 17" d. *Photograph by Dan Woodard.*

3 *Burning Sun,* 2009. Mixed media, 12" h. x 12" w. x 5" d. *Photograph by Dan Woodard.*

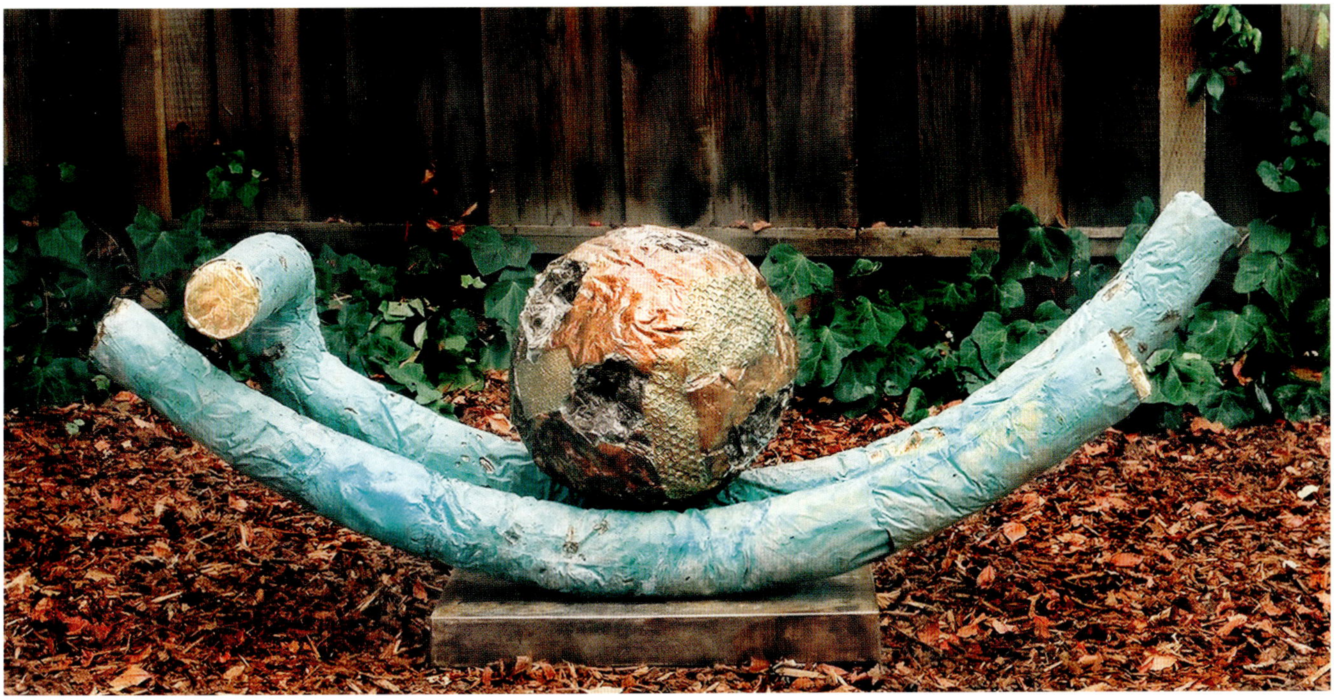

2

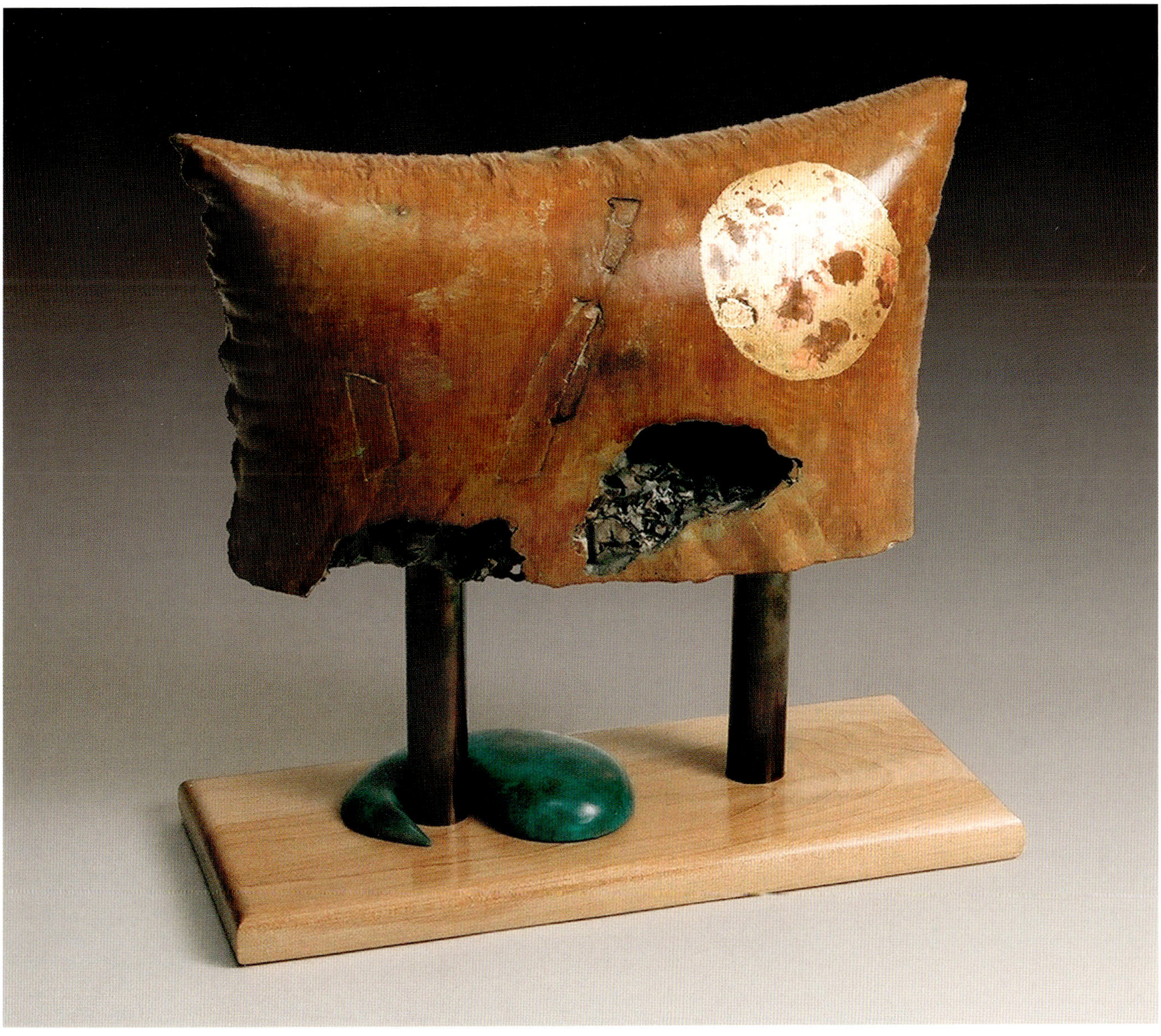

3

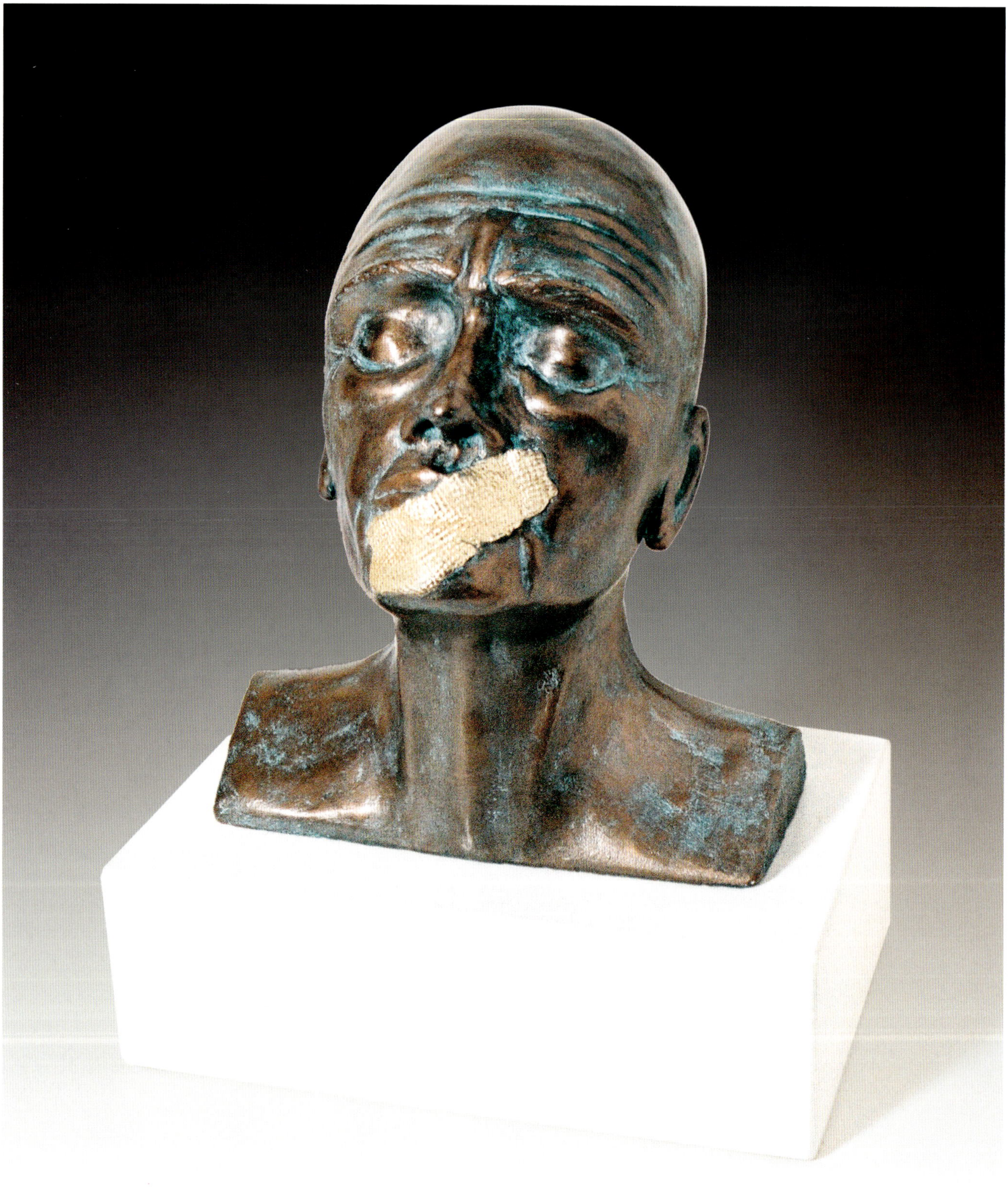

4

4 *Silence,* 2010. Cast stone, bronze coating, gold leaf, 13" h. x 10" w. x 8" d. *Photograph by Dan Woodard.*

5 *Ariadne*, 2010. Ceramic, bronze coating, patina, 24" h. x 11" w. x 10" d. *Photograph by Dan Woodard.*

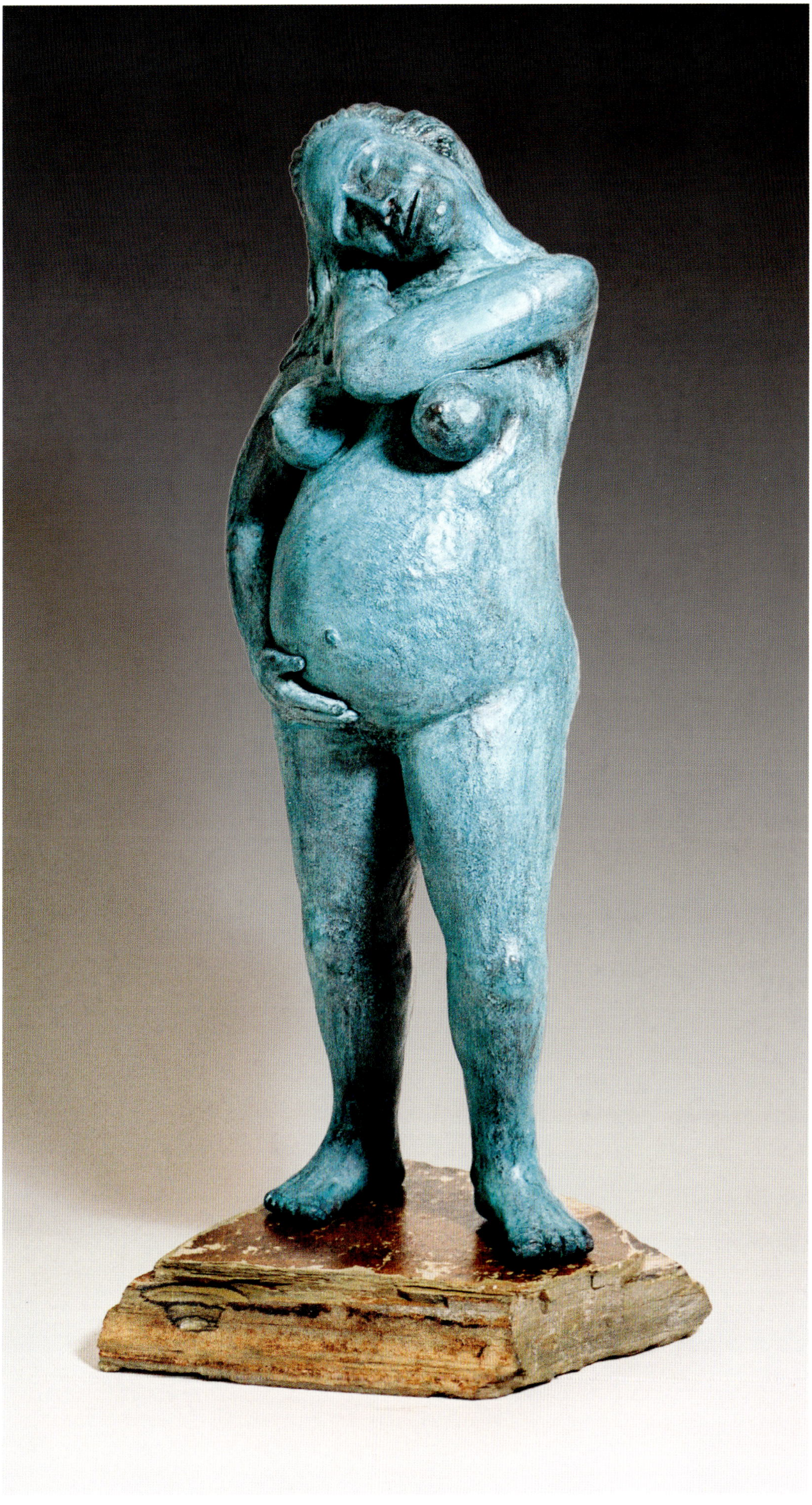

5

# Joni Younkins-Herzog

Sarasota, Florida, USA
www.joniyounkinsherzog.com

Joni Younkins-Herzog is a sculptor in Sarasota who grew up in the suburban sprawl outside of Atlanta, Georgia.

*My BFA in Ceramics is from the University of Georgia and MFA in Sculpture from Indiana University. I have taught courses at Ringling College of Art and Design; State College of Florida; Rogers State University in Claremore, Oklahoma; Indiana University, and in Medellin, Colombia S.A., where I received a partial Fulbirght Travel grant for my second residency through the Centro Colombo University.*

*A virtuoso in many mediums, I lure the viewer in with luscious colors and materials, to contemplate anxious content in close proximity. My works range widely in scale-from small wearable pieces to large sculptures and installation incorporating sound. My research and studio practice is dedicated to acquiring new technical skills in many materials, including re-purposed and recycled elements. Featured in exhibitions across the country and internationally, the sculptures combine beauty with absurdity, often blurring the lines between reality and fantasy.*

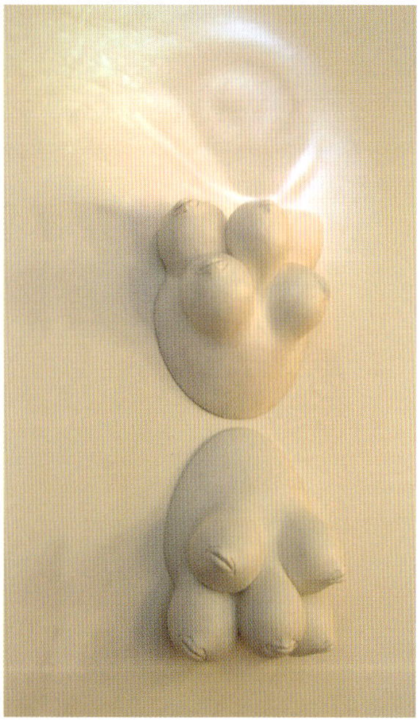

1

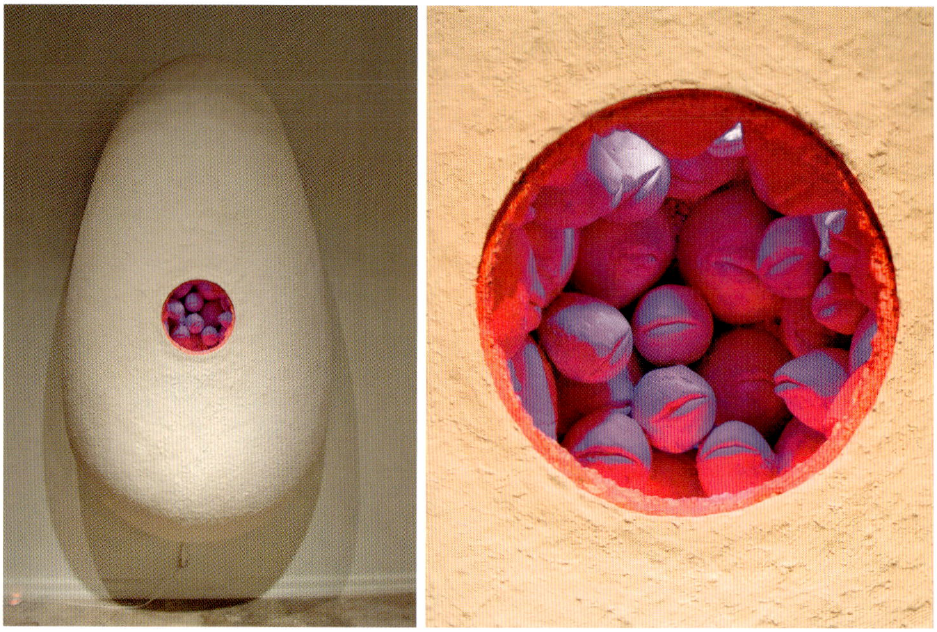

2

1 *Belly,* 2010. Plaster, video projection, 45" x 30" x 9". *Photograph by Joni Younkins-Herzog.*

2 *Spawn.* 2010. Re-purposed styrofoam, fiberglass, marine foam, polyester resin, steel, lace, light fixtures, paint, 77" x 42" x 22". *Photograph by Joni Younkins-Herzog.*

3 *Fecundity,* 2008. Fiberglass, forton, steel, fabric, lace, 168" x 120" x 96". *Photograph by Joni Younkins-Herzog.*

4 *Lust and Anxiety,* 2006. Cast hydrocal, 40" x 45" x 22" each. *Photograph by Joni Younkins-Herzog.*

5 *Basal Activation,* 2005. Hydrocal, fiberglass, steel, rubber, audio, 148" x 72" x 72". *Photograph by Joni Younkins-Herzog.*

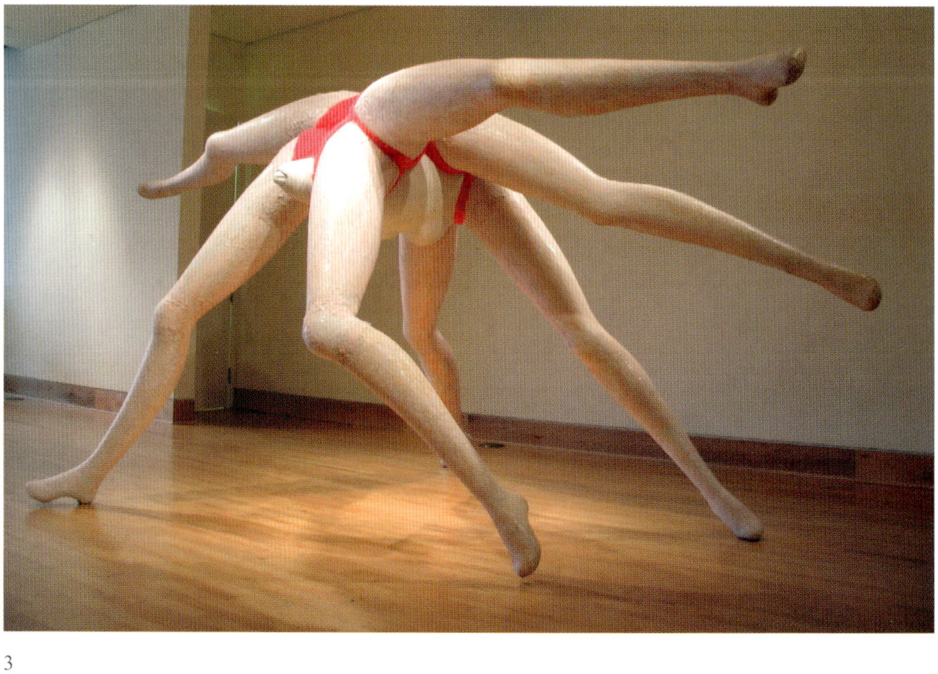

3

4
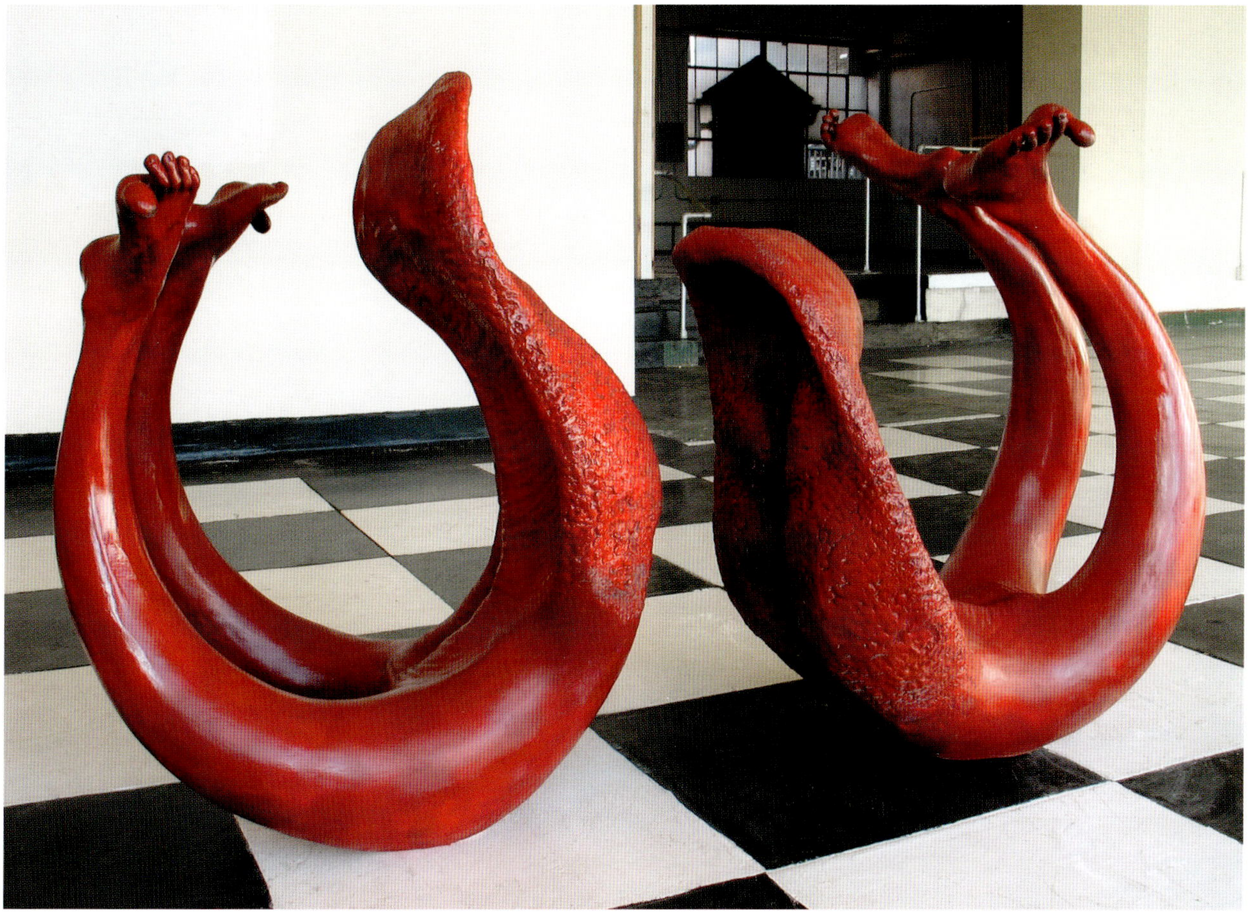

5
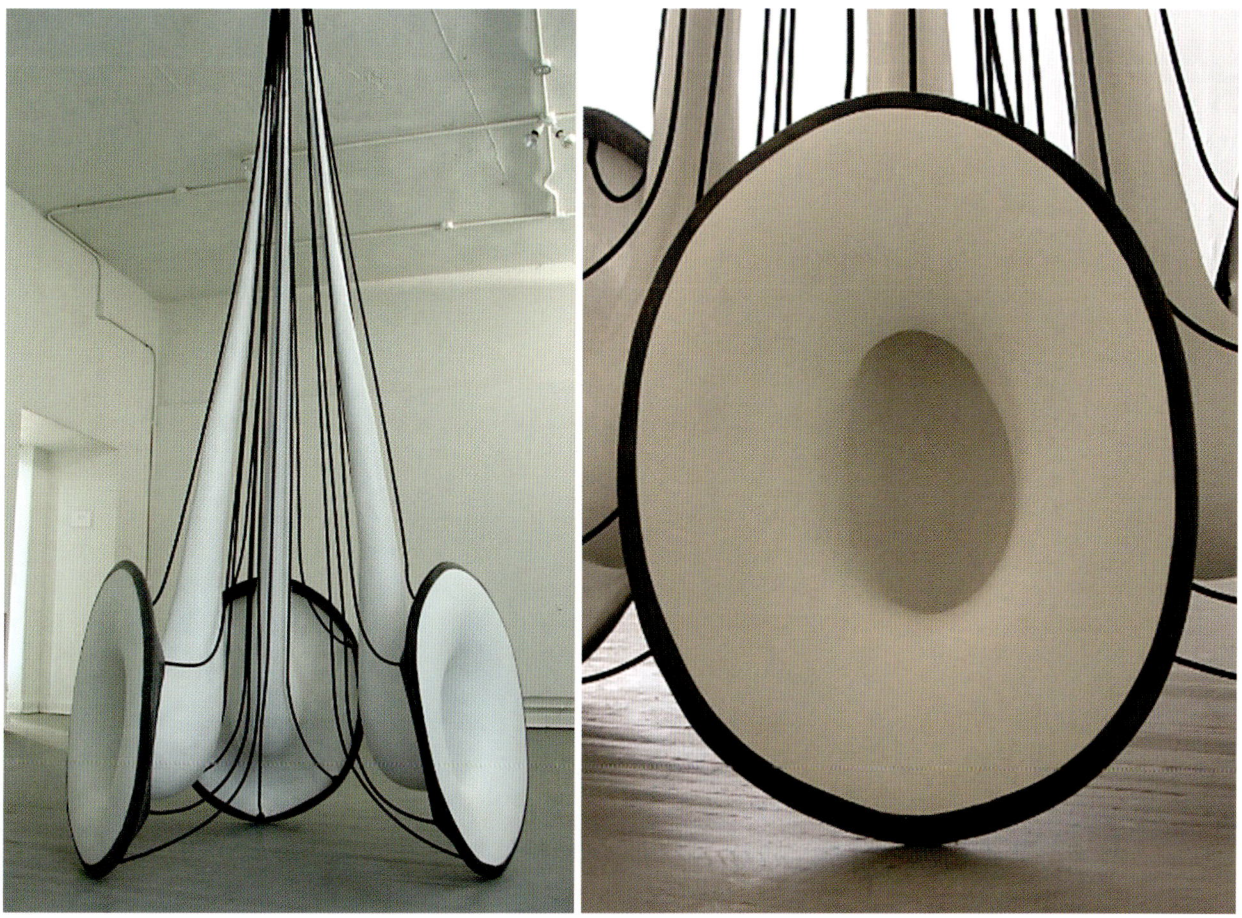

# Michael Zansky

West Nyack, New York, USA
www.michaelzansky.net

Michael Zansky has had numerous museum and gallery exhibitions throughout the U.S. and abroad. His installations are diverse, with themes that address everything from social and psychological issues to modern cosmology. Zansky's current gallery representation is with Nicholas Robinson Gallery in New York.

Thomas McEville wrote, "Zansky sees the uncertainty of it all as an element of humor, like a dog chasing its tail. In a sense, it is like the experience of Renaissance perspective when it was new, and the human came up against the cognitive uncertainty of experiencing space in a new way."

According to Edward Epstein, "Zansky's more contemplative work invites rather than invades – drawing us in to a series of miniature universes, like utopian spaces that mirror the real world..."

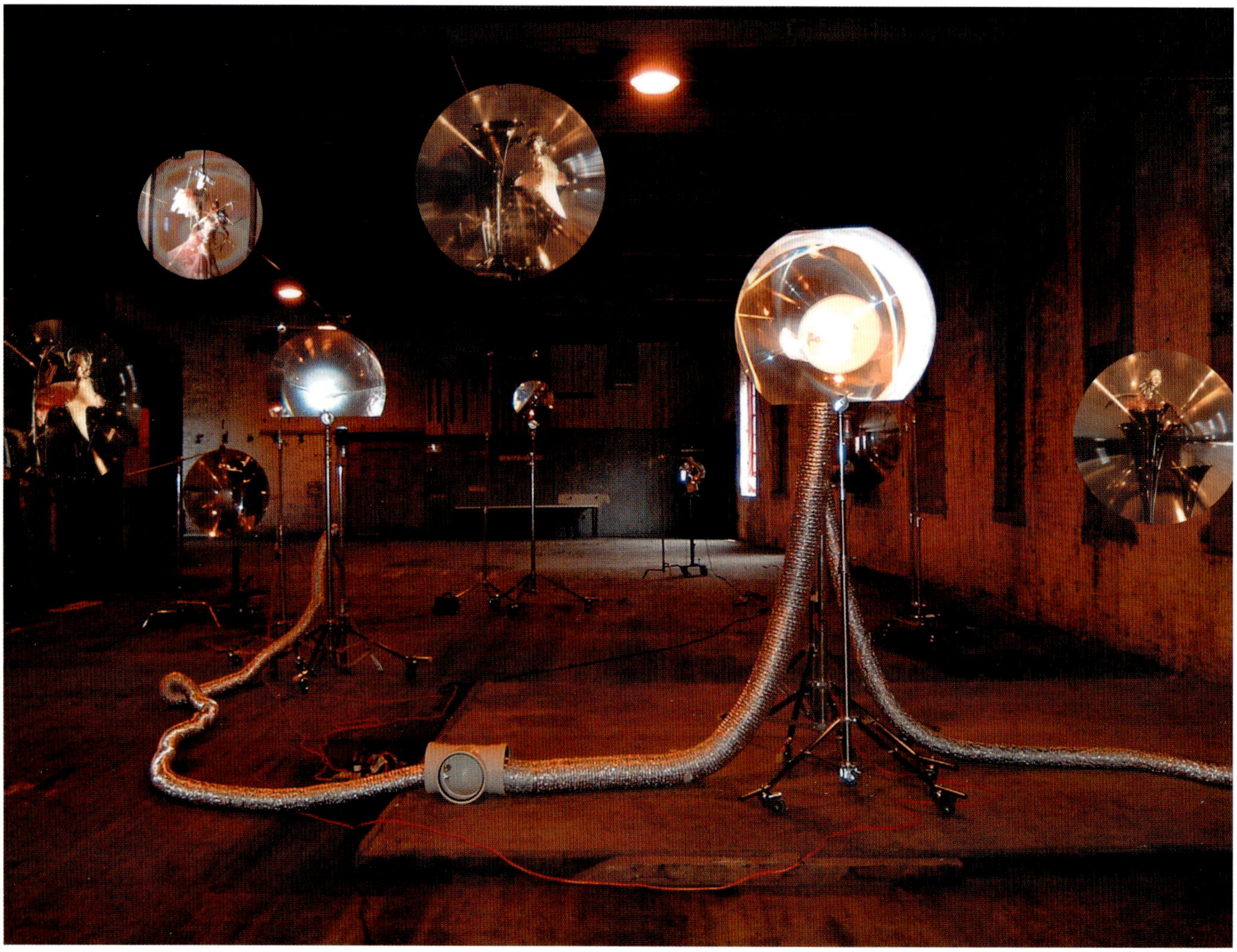

1

1 *American Panopticon*, 2011. Lenses, lights, motors, rotating discs and objects; size variable. *Photograph by Michael Zansky.*

2 *Tracer,* 2010. Lenses, lights, motors, rotating disc and objects; size variable. *Photograph by Michael Zansky.*

3 *Tracer* (detail), 2010. *Photograph by Michael Zansky*

4 *Western Lands 1*, 2009. Lenses, lights, motors, rotating discs and objects; size variable. *Photograph by Michael Zansky.*

5 *Western Lands 2*, 2009. Lenses, lights, motors, rotating discs and objects; size variable. *Photograph by Michael Zansky.*

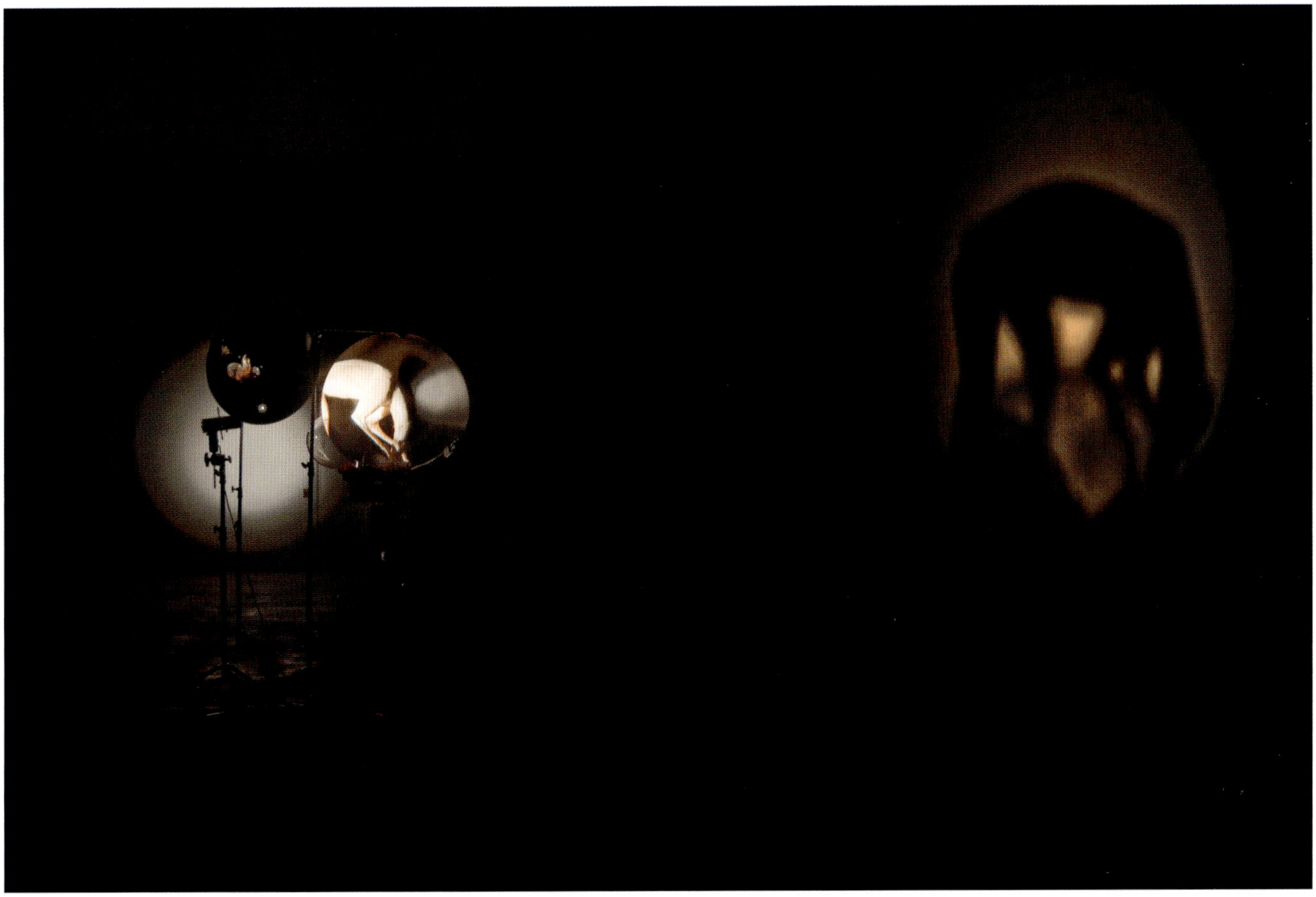

2

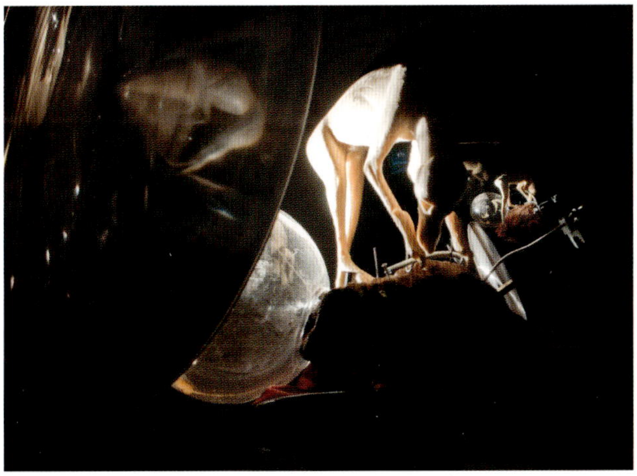

3

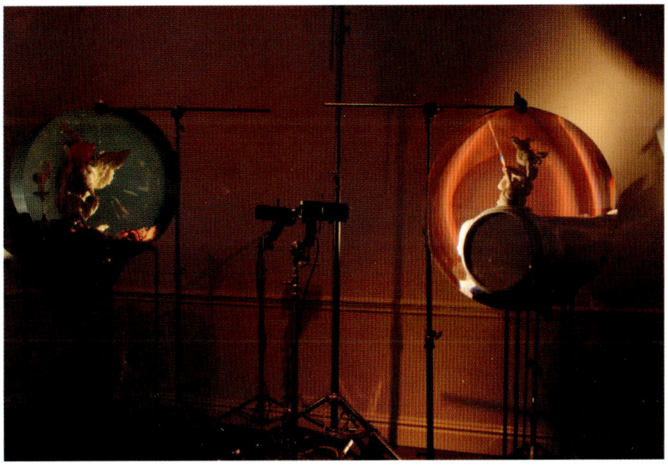

5

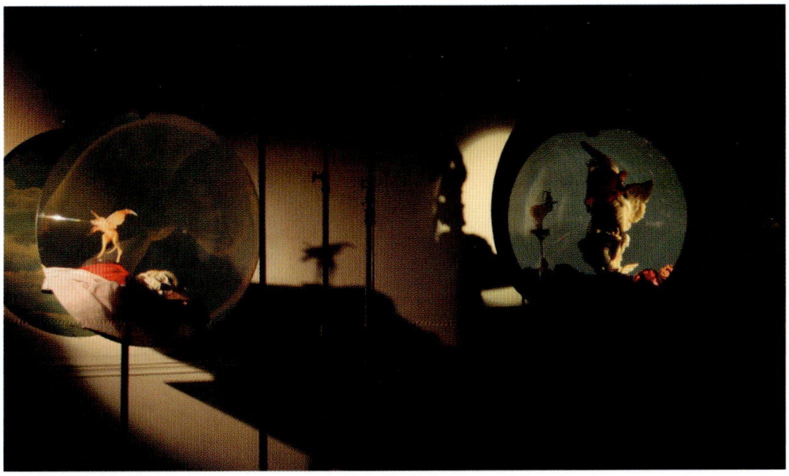

4

Schiffer Publishing Ltd. ——— 4880 Lower Valley Road ——— Atglen Pennsylvania 19310

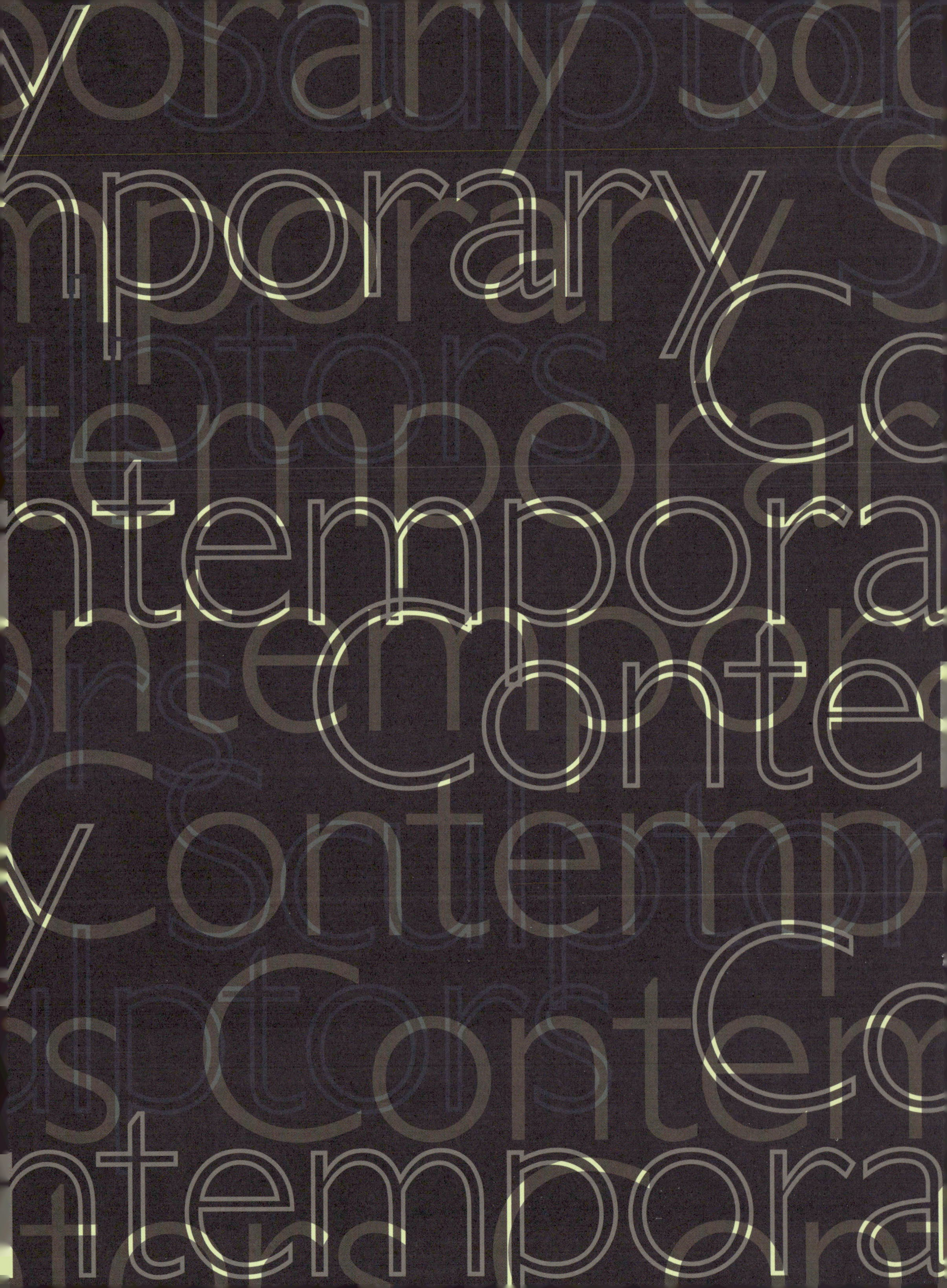